Correlation to Texas Essential Knowledge & Skills

Helping You Meet the Spelling TEKS —and More!

Spelling Connections and the Spelling TEKS

Spelling Connections has been carefully designed to teach, reinforce, and review every Texas Essential Knowledge and Skills standard for Spelling. Statements of Spelling TEKS appear throughout the Student and Teacher Editions.

Look for the map of Texas and the appropriate TEKS citation . . .

On every Planner spread in the Teacher Edition. The appropriate Spelling TEKS citations appear with the plan for every day of instruction to help you map your TEKS coverage throughout the week.

At the bottom of most Student Edition pages. Families will see the appropriate Spelling TEKS citation and be reassured that their child is receiving appropriate instruction and practice for success on Texas assessments.

At the bottom of most Teacher Edition pages. This point-of-use placement throughout the Teacher Edition gives you the confidence that the instructional techniques outlined in *Spelling Connections* will help you provide comprehensive spelling instruction.

Use the correlation that follows to identify the pages on which specific Spelling TEKS are met. In order to assure the vertical continuity of TEKS coverage across grades, this section also includes correlations to the Spelling TEKS for the surrounding grades.

Zaner-Bloser
The Language Arts and Reading Company

Spelling Grade 1   TEKS 1

Student Expectation	Breakout	Element	Subelement
(22) Oral and Written Conventions/Spelling. Students spell correctly. Students are expected to:			
(A) use phonological knowledge to match sounds to letters to construct known words;			
(B) use letter-sound patterns to spell:	**(1)** use letter-sound patterns to spell:	**(i)** consonant-vowel-consonant (CVC) words	
		(ii) consonant-vowel-consonant-silent e (CVCe) words	
		(iii) one-syllable words with consonant blends	

Historic red passenger car, Austin & Texas Central Railroad

Student Edition pages	Teacher Edition pages
17, 18, 19, 20, 21, 22, 23, 24, 25, 26, 27, 28, 29, 30, 31, 32, 33, 34, 35, 36, 37, 38, 39, 40, 41, 42, 44, 47, 48, 51, 52, 56, 58, 64, 67, 68, 72, 75, 76, 84, 92, 95, 96, 104, 108, 116, 123, 124, 127, 128, 130, 131, 132, 133, 135, 136, 144, 146, 148, 150, 152, 154, 155, 156, 158, 163, 164, 167, 170, 171, 172, 175, 176, 178, 183, 188, 190, 203, 204, 207, 209	T17, T18, T19, T20, T21, T22, T23, T24, T25, T26, T27, T28, T29, T30, T31, T32, T33, T34, T35, T36, T37, T38, T39, T40, T41, T42, T43, T44, T47, T48, T51, T52, T55, T56, T58, T64, T67, T68, T72, T75, T76, T84, T86, T87, T88, T90, T92, T94, T95, T96, T98, T104, T106, T108, T110, T114, T116, T118, T123, T124, T126, T127, T128, T130, T131, T132, T133, T135, T136, T138, T143, T144, T146, T147, T148, T150, T152, T154, T155, T156, T158, T163, T164, T166, T167, T168, T169, T170, T171, T172, T173, T174, T175, T176, T177, T178, T183, T187, T188, T189, T190, T191, T192, T193, T203, T204, T205, T206, T207, T208, T209, T210
48, 51, 63, 67, 68, 71, 72, 91, 92	T44, T47, T48, T51, T52, T55, T56, T63, T65, T67, T68, T71, T72, T75, T76, T83, T88, T91, T92, T184, T185, T187, T188, T189, T190
123, 124, 127, 128, 143, 144, 148, 152, 155	T123, T124, T127, T128, T143, T144, T145, T147, T148, T151, T152, T155, T199, T200
103, 104, 107, 108	T103, T104, T106, T107, T108, T109, T110, T195, T196, T202, T206, T208

Student Expectation	Breakout	Element	Subelement
(22) Oral and Written Conventions/Spelling. Students spell correctly. Students are expected to: *(continued)*			
(C) spell high-frequency words from a commonly used list;			
(D) spell base words with inflectional endings (e.g., adding "s" to make words plurals); and			
(E) use resources to find correct spellings			

Rock Window at Big Bend National Park

Student Edition pages	Teacher Edition pages
43, 44, 45, 46, 47, 48, 49, 50, 51, 52, 53, 54, 55, 56, 57, 58, 63, 64, 65, 66, 67, 68, 69, 70, 71, 72, 73, 74, 75, 76, 77, 78, 83, 84, 85, 86, 87, 88, 89, 90, 91, 92, 93, 94, 95, 96, 97, 98, 103, 104, 105, 106, 107, 108, 109, 110, 111, 112, 113, 114, 115, 116, 117, 118, 123, 125, 126, 127, 128, 129, 130, 131, 132, 133, 134, 135, 136, 137, 138, 143, 144, 145, 146, 147, 148, 149, 150, 151, 152, 153, 154, 155, 156, 157, 158, 163, 164, 165, 166, 167, 168, 169, 170, 171, 172, 173, 174, 175, 176, 177, 178, 183, 184, 185, 186, 187, 188, 189, 190, 191, 192, 193, 194, 195, 196, 197, 198, 199, 200, 201, 202, 203, 204, 205, 206, 207, 208, 209, 210	T43, T44, T45, T46, T47, T48, T49, T50, T51, T52, T53, T54, T55, T56, T57, T58, T63, T64, T65, T66, T67, T68, T69, T70, T71, T72, T73, T74, T75, T76, T77, T78, T83, T84, T85, T86, T87, T88, T89, T90, T91, T92, T93, T94, T95, T96, T97, T98, T103, T104, T105, T106, T107, T108, T109, T110, T111, T112, T113, T114, T115, T116, T117, T118, T123, T125, T126, T127, T128, T129, T130, T131, T132, T133, T134, T135, T136, T137, T138, T143, T144, T145, T146, T147, T148, T149, T150, T151, T152, T153, T154, T155, T156, T157, T158, T163, T164, T165, T166, T167, T168, T169, T170, T171, T172, T173, T174, T175, T176, T177, T178, T183, T184, T185, T186, T187, T188, T189, T190, T191, T192, T193, T194, T195, T196, T197, T198, T199, T200, T201, T202, T203, T204, T205, T206, T207, T208, T209, T210
111, 112, 115, 128, 148, 164, 168	T111, T112, T114, T115, T116, T117, T118, T128, T148, T164, T168, T197, T198
98, 118, 138, 153, 170, 173, 178	T98, T114, T118, T125, T126, T130, T134, T138, T146, T153, T158, T170, T173, T178

Student Expectation	Breakout	Element	Subelement	
(23) Oral and Written Conventions/Spelling. Students spell correctly. Students are expected to:				
(A) use phonological knowledge to match sounds to letters to construct unknown words				
(B) spell words with common orthographic patterns and rules:	**(i)** complex consonants (e.g., hard and soft c and g, ck)	**(1)** complex consonants		
	(ii) r-controlled vowels	**(1)** r-controlled vowels		
	(iii) long vowels (e.g., VCe-hope)	**(1)** long vowels		
	(iv) vowel digraphs (e.g., oo-book, fool, ee-feet), diphthongs (e.g., ou-out, ow-cow, oi-coil, oy-toy)	**(1)** vowel digraphs		
		(2) vowel diphthongs		

Student Edition pages	Teacher Edition pages
14, 15, 17, 18, 19, 20, 21, 23, 24, 25, 26, 27, 29, 31, 32, 33, 35, 36, 37, 38, 39, 41, 42, 43, 51, 52, 53, 55, 58, 59, 61, 64, 65, 67, 70, 71, 73, 74, 75, 76, 77, 79, 80, 81, 89, 90, 91, 93, 94, 95, 96, 97, 99, 100, 101, 102, 103, 105, 106, 107, 108, 109, 111, 113, 114, 115, 117, 119, 127, 128, 129, 131, 132, 134, 135, 137, 138, 139, 142, 143, 152, 153, 155, 156, 157, 165, 167, 169, 171, 172, 173, 175, 176, 177, 179, 181, 184, 185, 187, 188, 190, 191, 193, 194, 203, 204, 205, 207, 208, 210, 211, 213, 214, 216, 217, 219, 223, 225, 226, 229, 231, 232, 233, 241	T14, T15, T17, T18, T19, T20, T21, T23, T24, T25, T26, T27, T29, T31, T32, T33, T35, T36, T37, T38, T39, T41, T42, T43, T51, T52, T53, T55, T58, T59, T61, T64, T65, T67, T70, T71, T73, T74, T75, T76, T77, T79, T80, T81, T89, T90, T91, T93, T94, T95, T96, T97, T99, T100, T101, T102, T103, T105, T106, T107, T108, T109, T111, T113, T114, T115, T117, T119, T127, T128, T129, T131, T132, T134, T135, T137, T138, T139, T140, T142, T143, T150, T152, T153, T155, T156, T157, T165, T166, T167, T169, T171, T172, T173, T175, T176, T177, T179, T181, T184, T185, T187, T188, T190, T191, T193, T194, T203, T204, T205, T207, T208, T210, T211, T213, T214, T216, T217, T219, T223, T225, T226, T229, T231, T232, T233, T241
21, 24, 27, 30, 31, 36, 41, 53, 54, 55, 56, 57, 58, 59, 61, 62, 63, 64, 65, 66, 67, 68, 69, 114, 115, 117, 119, 128, 129, 131, 133, 150, 190, 191, 193, 194, 195, 210, 211, 212, 213, 215, 216, 217, 218, 219, 221, 229	T20, T21, T24, T25, T26, T27, T29, T30, T31, T32, T36, T41, T53, T54, T55, T56, T57, T58, T59, T61, T62, T63, T64, T65, T66, T67, T68, T69, T114, T115, T117, T119, T128, T129, T131, T133, T144, T150, T190, T191, T193, T194, T195, T210, T211, T212, T213, T215, T216, T217, T218, T219, T221, T229
184, 185, 186, 187, 188, 189, 204, 205, 206, 207, 208, 209, 222	T184, T185, T186, T187, T188, T189, T204, T205, T206, T207, T208, T209, T222
76, 77, 79, 80, 81, 90, 91, 92, 93, 94, 95, 96, 97, 99, 100, 101, 102, 103, 104, 105, 106, 107, 108, 109, 110, 111, 112, 113, 132, 179, 191, 194, 211, 217, 222, 223, 226, 229, 232, 233	T76, T77, T79, T80, T81, T90, T91, T92, T93, T94, T95, T96, T97, T98, T99, T100, T101, T102, T103, T104, T105, T106, T107, T108, T109, T110, T111, T112, T113, T132, T179, T191, T194, T211, T217, T222, T223, T226, T229, T232, T233
93, 94, 95, 96, 97, 98, 99, 100, 101, 108, 109, 111, 112, 113, 132, 135, 152, 153, 154, 155, 156, 220, 222, 223, 226, 229	T91, T93, T94, T95, T96, T97, T98, T99, T100, T101, T108, T109, T111, T112, T113, T132, T135, T144, T152, T153, T154, T155, T156, T220, T222, T223, T226, T229
134, 137, 138, 139, 157, 172, 173, 175, 176, 177, 222, 229, 232	T134, T137, T138, T139, T157, T172, T173, T175, T176, T177, T222, T229, T232

Student Expectation	Breakout	Element	Subelement	
(23) Oral and Written Conventions/Spelling. Students spell correctly. Students are expected to: *(continued)*				
(C) spell high-frequency words from a commonly used list				
(D) spell base words with inflectional endings (e.g., -ing and -ed)				
(E) spell simple contractions (e.g., isn't, aren't, can't)				
(F) use resources to find correct spellings				

Student Edition pages	Teacher Edition pages
14, 15, 16, 17, 18, 19, 20, 21, 22, 23, 24, 25, 26, 27, 28, 29, 30, 31, 32, 33, 34, 35, 36, 37, 38, 39, 40, 41, 42, 43, 52, 53, 54, 55, 56, 57, 58, 59, 60, 61, 62, 63, 64, 65, 66, 67, 68, 69, 70, 71, 72, 73, 74, 75, 76, 78, 79, 80, 81, 90, 91, 92, 93, 94, 95, 96, 97, 98, 99, 100, 101, 102, 103, 104, 105, 106, 107, 108, 109, 110, 111, 112, 113, 114, 115, 116, 117, 118, 119, 128, 129, 130, 131, 132, 133, 134, 135, 136, 137, 138, 139, 140, 141, 142, 143, 144, 145, 146, 147, 148, 149, 150, 151, 152, 153, 154, 155, 156, 157, 166, 167, 168, 169, 170, 171, 172, 173, 174, 175, 176, 177, 178, 179, 180, 181, 182, 183, 184, 185, 186, 187, 188, 189, 190, 191, 192, 193, 194, 195, 204, 205, 206, 207, 208, 209, 210, 211, 212, 213, 214, 215, 216, 217, 218, 219, 220, 221, 222, 223, 224, 225, 226, 227, 228, 229, 230, 231, 232, 233, 241	T14, T15, T16, T17, T18, T19, T20, T21, T22, T23, T24, T25, T26, T27, T28, T29, T30, T31, T32, T33, T34, T35, T36, T37, T38, T39, T40, T41, T42, T43, T52, T53, T54, T55, T56, T57, T58, T59, T60, T61, T62, T63, T64, T65, T66, T67, T68, T69, T70, T71, T72, T73, T74, T75, T76, T77, T78, T79, T80, T81, T90, T91, T92, T93, T94, T95, T96, T97, T98, T99, T100, T101, T102, T103, T104, T105, T106, T107, T108, T109, T110, T111, T112, T113, T114, T115, T116, T117, T118, T119, T128, T129, T130, T131, T132, T133, T134, T135, T136, T137, T138, T139, T140, T141, T142, T143, T144, T145, T146, T147, T148, T149, T150, T151, T152, T153, T154, T155, T156, T157, T166, T167, T168, T169, T170, T171, T172, T173, T174, T175, T176, T177, T178, T179, T180, T181, T182, T183, T184, T185, T186, T187, T188, T189, T190, T191, T192, T193, T194, T195, T204, T205, T206, T207, T208, T209, T210, T211, T212, T213, T214, T215, T216, T217, T218, T219, T220, T221, T222, T223, T224, T225, T226, T227, T228, T229, T230, T231, T232, T233, T241
62, 94, 100, 140, 141, 143, 144, 145, 146, 147, 148, 149, 150, 151, 194	T62, T68, T94, T100, T106, T138, T140, T141, T143, T144, T145, T146, T147, T148, T149, T150, T151, T194
178, 179, 180, 181, 182, 183	T178, T179, T180, T181, T182, T183
17, 23, 29, 35, 41, 51, 55, 67, 73, 77, 79, 89, 93, 99, 105, 111, 117, 127, 131, 137, 143, 149, 165, 169, 173, 175, 181, 182, 187, 203, 207, 219, 225	T17, T18, T23, T29, T33, T35, T41, T51, T55, T61, T67, T73, T77, T79, T89, T93, T99, T105, T111, T117, T127, T131, T137, T143, T149, T155, T165, T169, T173, T175, T181, T182, T187, T193, T203, T207, T219, T225

Student Expectation	Breakout	Element	Subelement	
(24) Oral and Written Conventions/Spelling. Students spell correctly. Students are expected to:				
(A) use knowledge of letter sounds, word parts, word segmentation, and syllabication to spell	**(1)** use knowledge of letter sounds to spell			
	(2) use knowledge of word parts to spell			
	(3) use knowledge of word segmentation to spell			
	(4) use knowledge of syllabication to spell			

Student Edition pages	Teacher Edition pages
14, 15, 17, 18, 19, 20, 21, 23, 24, 25, 26, 27, 29, 30, 31, 33, 35, 42, 51, 52, 53, 55, 56, 57, 58, 59, 61, 62, 63, 64, 69, 70, 71, 73, 74, 75, 76, 77, 79, 80, 81, 89, 90, 91, 93, 96, 97, 99, 101, 102, 105, 107, 108, 109, 111, 113, 115, 118, 127, 128, 129, 131, 132, 133, 134, 135, 137, 139, 140, 141, 143, 144, 145, 146, 147, 149, 151, 152, 153, 155, 156, 157, 165, 166, 167, 169, 171, 172, 173, 175, 177, 178, 179, 185, 191, 194, 203, 205, 217, 223, 227, 229	T14, T15, T17, T18, T19, T20, T21, T22, T23, T24, T25, T26, T27, T28, T29, T30, T31, T33, T35, T36, T42, T51, T52, T53, T55, T56, T57, T58, T59, T61, T62, T63, T64, T65, T67, T68, T69, T70, T71, T73, T74, T75, T76, T77, T79, T80, T81, T90, T91, T93, T94, T96, T97, T99, T100, T101, T102, T103, T105, T107, T108, T109, T111, T113, T114, T115, T118, T127, T128, T129, T131, T132, T133, T134, T135, T137, T139, T140, T141, T143, T144, T145, T146, T147, T149, T150, T151, T152, T153, T155, T156, T157, T165, T166, T167, T169, T171, T172, T173, T175, T177, T178, T179, T185, T191, T194, T203, T204, T205, T217, T223, T227, T229
24, 30, 56, 68, 74, 94, 100, 118, 150, 178, 181, 182, 183, 184, 187, 188, 189, 190, 191, 192, 193, 194, 195, 203, 204, 205, 207, 208, 209, 210, 211, 213, 214, 215, 216, 217, 218, 219, 220, 221, 222, 223, 225, 226, 228, 231, 232, 233, 241	T24, T30, T51, T56, T68, T74, T94, T100, T118, T150, T178, T181, T182, T183, T184, T187, T188, T189, T190, T191, T192, T193, T194, T195, T203, T204, T205, T207, T208, T209, T210, T211, T213, T214, T215, T216, T217, T218, T219, T220, T221, T222, T223, T225, T226, T228, T231, T232, T233, T241
14, 15, 17, 18, 19, 20, 21, 23, 24, 26, 27, 29, 30, 31, 32, 33, 35, 36, 37, 38, 39, 41, 42, 43, 52, 53, 56, 57, 58, 59, 61, 62, 63, 64, 65, 67, 68, 69, 70, 71, 73, 74, 75, 76, 77, 79, 80, 81, 89, 90, 91, 93, 94, 95, 96, 97, 99, 100, 101, 102, 103, 105, 106, 107, 108, 109, 111, 112, 113, 115, 117, 118, 127, 128, 129, 131, 132, 133, 134, 135, 137, 139, 140, 141, 143, 144, 145, 146, 147, 149, 150, 151, 153, 165, 170, 172, 175, 177, 179, 180, 185, 203, 204, 208, 223, 229	T14, T15, T17, T18, T20, T21, T23, T24, T26, T27, T29, T30, T31, T32, T33, T35, T36, T37, T38, T39, T41, T43, T51, T52, T53, T55, T56, T57, T58, T59, T61, T62, T63, T64, T65, T67, T68, T69, T70, T71, T73, T74, T75, T76, T77, T79, T80, T81, T90, T91, T93, T94, T95, T96, T97, T99, T100, T101, T102, T103, T105, T106, T107, T108, T109, T111, T112, T113, T115, T117, T118, T127, T128, T129, T131, T132, T133, T134, T135, T137, T139, T140, T141, T143, T144, T145, T146, T147, T149, T150, T151, T153, T165, T170, T172, T173, T175, T176, T177, T179, T180, T185, T203, T204, T208, T223, T229
19, 20, 24, 26, 31, 55, 56, 57, 59, 77, 80, 97, 109, 112, 114, 119, 127, 129, 132, 141, 166, 167, 169, 170, 171, 185, 188, 203, 205, 208, 211, 226, 229, 232, 233	T14, T20, T24, T26, T31, T42, T51, T52, T53, T55, T56, T57, T58, T59, T62, T69, T77, T80, T97, T106, T109, T112, T114, T119, T127, T129, T132, T138, T141, T150, T166, T167, T169, T170, T171, T185, T188, T203, T205, T208, T211, T226, T229, T232, T233

Student Expectation	Breakout	Element	Subelement	
(24) Oral and Written Conventions/Spelling. Students spell correctly. Students are expected to: *(continued)*				
(B) spell words with more advanced orthographic patterns and rules:	**(i)** consonant doubling when adding an ending			
	(ii) dropping final "e" when endings are added (e.g., -ing, -ed)			
	(iii) changing y to i before adding an ending			
	(iv) double consonants in middle of words			
	(v) complex consonants (e.g., scr-, -dge, -tch)			
	(vi) abstract vowels (e.g., ou as in could, touch, through, bought)			
(C) spell high-frequency and compound words from a commonly used list	**(1)** spell high-frequency words from a commonly used list			
	(2) spell compound words from a commonly used list			
(D) spell words with common syllable constructions (e.g., closed, open, final stable syllable)				
(E) spell single syllable homophones (e.g., bear/bare; week/weak; road/rode)				

Student Edition pages	Teacher Edition pages
24, 94, 138, 176, 184, 185, 187, 188, 189, 216, 217, 218, 219, 220, 221	T24, T94, T138, T176, T184, T185, T187, T188, T189, T216, T217, T218, T219, T220, T221
30, 68, 94, 100, 138, 178, 179, 181, 182, 183, 216, 217, 218, 219, 220, 221	T30, T68, T94, T100, T138, T178, T179, T181, T182, T183, T216, T217, T218, T219, T220, T221
74, 100, 138, 144, 176, 210, 211, 213, 214, 215, 226	T74, T100, T138, T144, T176, T210, T211, T213, T214, T215, T226
118, 166, 167, 169, 170, 171, 172, 173, 175, 176, 177	T118, T166, T167, T169, T170, T171, T172, T173, T175, T176, T177, T221
21, 24, 27, 36, 39, 42, 68, 90, 91, 93, 95, 96, 97, 99, 101, 102, 103, 105, 106, 107, 115, 147, 153, 185, 205, 223	T15, T18, T21, T24, T25, T27, T36, T39, T42, T53, T65, T68, T71, T80, T90, T91, T93, T95, T96, T97, T99, T100, T101, T102, T103, T105, T106, T107, T115, T147, T153, T185, T205
32, 33, 35, 36, 37, 38, 39, 41, 42, 43, 108, 109, 111, 112, 113, 115, 118, 128, 129, 131, 132, 133	T32, T33, T35, T36, T37, T38, T39, T41, T42, T43, T108, T109, T111, T112, T113, T115, T118, T128, T129, T131, T132, T133
14, 15, 16, 17, 18, 19, 20, 21, 22, 23, 24, 25, 26, 27, 28, 29, 30, 31, 32, 33, 34, 35, 36, 37, 38, 39, 40, 41, 42, 43, 52, 53, 54, 55, 56, 57, 58, 59, 60, 61, 62, 64, 65, 66, 67, 68, 69, 70, 71, 72, 73, 74, 75, 76, 77, 78, 79, 80, 81, 88, 90, 91, 92, 93, 94, 95, 96, 97, 98, 99, 100, 101, 102, 103, 104, 105, 106, 107, 108, 109, 110, 111, 112, 113, 114, 115, 116, 117, 118, 119, 126, 128, 129, 130, 131, 132, 133, 134, 135, 136, 137, 138, 139, 140, 141, 142, 143, 144, 145, 146, 147, 148, 149, 150, 151, 152, 153, 154, 155, 156, 157, 164, 166, 167, 168, 169, 170, 171, 172, 173, 174, 175, 176, 177, 178, 179, 180, 181, 182, 183, 184, 185, 186, 187, 188, 189, 190, 191, 192, 193, 194, 195, 202, 204, 205, 206, 207, 208, 209, 210, 211, 212, 213, 214, 215, 216, 217, 218, 219, 220, 221, 222, 223, 224, 225, 226, 227, 228, 229, 230, 231, 232, 233, 240	T14, T15, T16, T17, T18, T19, T20, T21, T22, T23, T24, T25, T26, T27, T28, T29, T30, T31, T32, T33, T34, T35, T36, T37, T38, T39, T40, T41, T42, T43, T52, T53, T54, T55, T56, T57, T58, T59, T60, T61, T62, T63, T64, T65, T66, T67, T68, T69, T70, T71, T72, T73, T74, T75, T76, T77, T78, T79, T80, T81, T88, T90, T91, T92, T93, T94, T95, T96, T97, T98, T99, T100, T101, T102, T103, T104, T105, T106, T107, T108, T109, T110, T111, T112, T113, T114, T115, T116, T117, T118, T119, T126, T128, T129, T130, T131, T132, T133, T134, T135, T136, T137, T138, T139, T140, T141, T142, T143, T144, T145, T146, T147, T148, T149, T150, T151, T152, T153, T154, T155, T156, T157, T164, T166, T167, T168, T169, T170, T171, T172, T173, T174, T175, T176, T177, T178, T179, T180, T181, T182, T183, T184, T185, T186, T187, T188, T189, T190, T191, T192, T193, T194, T195, T202, T204, T205, T206, T207, T208, T209, T210, T211, T212, T213, T214, T215, T216, T217, T218, T219, T220, T221, T222, T223, T224, T225, T226, T227, T228, T229, T230, T231, T232, T233, T240
56, 94, 106, 118, 150, 214, 228, 229, 230, 231, 232, 233	T56, T94, T106, T118, T150, T214, T228, T229, T230, T231, T232, T233
27, 52, 55, 56, 57, 59, 80, 97, 109, 112, 132, 138, 166, 169, 170, 171, 185, 188, 208, 211, 220, 226	T14, T18, T19, T20, T24, T25, T26, T27, T31, T52, T53, T55, T56, T57, T58, T59, T62, T77, T80, T97, T109, T112, T132, T138, T150, T166, T169, T170, T171, T185, T188, T208, T211, T216, T220, T226
42, 56, 62, 68, 74, 138, 144, 148, 150, 152, 153, 154, 155, 156, 157, 194	T42, T56, T62, T68, T74, T138, T144, T148, T149, T150, T152, T153, T154, T155, T156, T157, T194

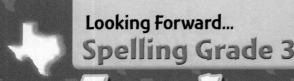

Student Expectation	Breakout	Element	Subelement	
(24) Oral and Written Conventions/Spelling. Students spell correctly. Students are expected to: *(continued)*				
(F) spell complex contractions (e.g., should've, won't)				
(G) use print and electronic resources to find and check correct spellings	**(1)** use print resources to find and check correct spellings			
	(2) use electronic resources to find and check correct spellings			

Skyline, Dallas, Texas

Student Edition pages	Teacher Edition pages
190, 191, 192, 193, 194, 195	T149, T190, T191, T192, T193, T194, T195
17, 23, 35, 41, 55, 61, 67, 73, 79, 89, 93, 99, 127, 131, 141, 143, 149, 153, 155, 165, 169, 173, 175, 179, 187, 191, 193, 203, 207, 213, 219, 225, 231, 241	T17, T23, T35, T41, T51, T55, T61, T67, T73, T79, T89, T93, T99, T127, T131, T141, T143, T149, T153, T155, T165, T169, T173, T175, T179, T187, T191, T193, T203, T207, T213, T219, T225, T231, T241
29, 51, 55, 89, 105, 117, 127, 137, 143, 165, 181, 203, 213, 241	T29, T35, T51, T55, T73, T89, T105, T111, T117, T127, T137, T143, T165, T181, T193, T203, T207, T213, T241

TEXAS Teacher Edition

Spelling Connections

J. Richard Gentry, Ph.D.

ZB Zaner-Bloser
The Language Arts and Reading Company

Opportunities Beyond Words

Proficient spelling is a key foundational skill critical to future academic and vocational success. With Spelling Connections, your students will become accomplished spellers and advance their writing, reading, and communication skills. Prepare your students with the only spelling program to provide opportunities beyond words!

Effective spelling instruction starts with the right words delivered at the right time. The word lists in **Spelling Connections** are the most carefully researched and crafted lists available. They are based on exhaustive research led by author J. Richard Gentry, Ph.D., a leading authority on spelling development and literacy instruction for over thirty years.

With **Spelling Connections ©2012,** our word lists have been expanded to provide differentiated instruction for all levels of students, including English Language Learners. Word lists are organized so students see the relationships among words, visually reinforcing valuable pattern and strategy instruction.

expand vocabulary

improve reading comprehension

accelerate writing skills

elevate test scores

Unlike integrated spelling instruction delivered through core reading programs, **Spelling Connections** provides complete, explicit instruction that

- utilizes a five-day plan with a page-per-day format—everything you need to deliver effective lessons without the need for extensive planning and prep work.

- delivers meaningful instruction and practice, including word sorting for all levels of students, to promote higher-level skill development in thinking, phonics, reading, and writing.

- provides diagnostic, formative, and summative assessments to monitor progress, including integrated standardized test practice for improved results on ✦ **Texas state assessments.**

- integrates technology tools for engaging, relevant spelling instruction and practice.

- contains embedded professional development that provides proven strategies for successful classroom instruction.

Prepare your students for spelling success that's beyond the test. With Spelling Connections, your students will retain, internalize, and transfer valuable spelling knowledge for improved results in all areas of literacy— in the classroom and beyond.

Spelling Connections

Welcome
From the Author

J. Richard Gentry, Ph.D.

It's no secret—the world is changing. With brain scan studies offering interesting new insights into how the brain operates during reading and writing, the importance of spelling and word knowledge is being recognized more now than at any other time in the history of education. Spelling is critical for twenty-first century literacy—from early phonemic awareness to assimilation of deep knowledge of word histories and the meaning gleaned from chunks of letters.

Spelling Connections builds the deep, word-specific knowledge base all students need for reading, writing, and overall communication success. With **Spelling Connections,** teachers will appreciate the explicit, research- and language-based differentiated instruction that supports the necessary role spelling plays in meaningful communication. Students will appreciate the new digital resources for interactive whiteboards, engaging word-sorting activities, and technology innovations found in **Spelling Connections Online** and **Digital Resources for Spelling Connections**. Our comprehensive, efficient approach to spelling instruction recognizes that spelling is important, brain-based, and validated through exhaustive research.

Give spelling the consideration it deserves and put effective spelling instruction back into your curriculum. With **Spelling Connections,** your students will be prepared for twenty-first century literacy success that translates beyond the classroom.

TEXAS
EDITION

Z3

Your Best Opportunity for Spelling Success

The new **Texas Spelling Connections** offers effective resources including an easy-to-follow Student Edition and a comprehensive Teacher Edition. Online games and activities, interactive materials, and a full array of optional resources are available to expand your instructional horizons beyond the classroom.

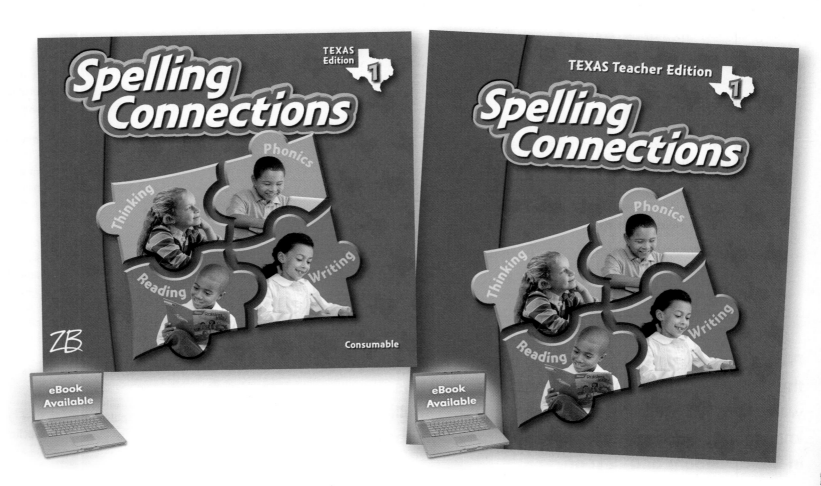

❧ **Texas Student Edition** and **Texas eStudent Edition** provide comprehensive daily spelling practice by connecting spelling to thinking, reading, writing, and phonics through engaging exercises and hands-on, minds-on activities.

❧ **Texas Teacher Edition** and **Texas eTeacher Edition** include step-by-step lesson plans with student objectives, English Language Learner support, and activities for daily differentiated instruction—everythin you need to develop successful spellers!

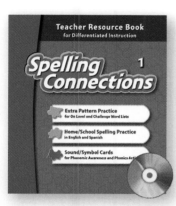

Teacher Resource Book for Differentiated Instruction provides convenient, reproducible materials for all students, and Home/School Spelling Practice letters in both English and Spanish. Also available on CD-ROM.

Texas Assessment Practice Book includes instructional unit tests and review unit tests in two standardized test formats for valuable testing practice. Also available on CD-ROM.

Spelling Support for English Language Learners offers targeted support masters for vocabulary practice to accelerate English Language Learners' language acquisition and spelling success. Also available on CD-ROM.

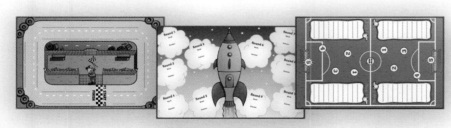

New! **Game Mats** provide fun, hands-on spelling practice, perfect for partner and center work.

Additional Digital Resources

Audio Conversations for English Language Learners contains spelling words used in a conversational setting to assist with the transfer of spelling knowledge into language acquisition.

New! **Audio Posttest Sentences** contains weekly posttest dictation sentences for the on level and challenge words in every unit. Use to support English Language Learners and for make-up spelling tests.

Word Sort CD-ROM contains printable word sort cards for each unit's spelling words within **Spelling Connections**, including challenge words.

New! **Spelling Connections Online** includes engaging interactive spelling games and activities, including word sorting, crossword puzzles, sentence completion, spelling bee, digital dictionary, and proofreading exercises.

New! **Classroom Management System for Spelling Connections Online** helps monitor and evaluate student progress. With this easy-to-use system you can set up class lists, control student preferences, develop reports, and generate school-to-home letters in English and Spanish.

New! **Digital Resources for Spelling Connections** offers engaging whole-class activities for use with interactive whiteboards and projection systems.

New! **Digital Dictionary** for each grade level (1–6) includes definitions and examples of usage for all words in **Spelling Connections**. Access through **Spelling Connections Online** and **Digital Resources for Spelling Connections**.

Propel Spelling Instruction Beyond Paper and Pencil

Connect students to successful spelling inside and outside the classroom. New technology resources provide appealing, action-packed instruction and practice that will advance your students' spelling ability beyond the weekly test.

Digital Resources for Spelling Connections offers activities for use with interactive whiteboards and classroom projectors. Includes interactive word sorting for modeling and student practice, proofreading exercises, a spelling bee for whole-class test preparation, and a variety of other activities to enhance the teaching and learning of spelling skills.

Digital Dictionary elevates students' understanding and use of digital and online reference materials as addressed by 🔺 **Texas state standards.** The dictionary contains all the words included in **Spelling Connections** for grades 1–6 for on, below, and above level. (Access via **Digital Resources for Spelling Connections** and **Spelling Connections Online**.)

Additional Technology Options

- Word Sort CD-ROM
- Audio Posttest Sentences CD
- Audio Conversations for English Language Learners CD

- Home/School Spelling Practice (available at www.zaner-bloser.com)
- 🔺 **Texas** Standardized Test Masters CD-ROM
- Spelling Support for English CD-ROM Language Learners

- Teacher Resource Book CD-ROM
- 🔺 **Texas** Student Edition eBook
- 🔺 **Texas** Teacher Edition eBook

Spelling Connections Online  amplifies the instruction in the
Texas Student Edition with fun, engaging, and interactive games including:

Word Sorting

Students sort spelling words to form a concrete understanding of the essential similarities and differences between words. This helps students develop into confident spellers.

Crossword Puzzle

Students expand vocabulary and phonics skills by completing challenging interactive puzzles.

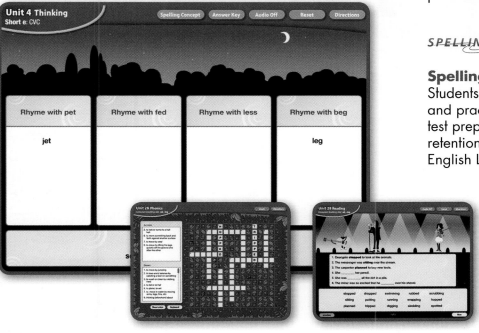

Sentence Completion

Students complete cloze sentence activities to enhance reading comprehension and vocabulary skills.

Proofreading

Students read engaging passages and use virtual proofreading symbols to correct spelling errors, punctuation, and capitalization. Provides valuable practice using skills tested on ➡ **Texas state assessments.**

SPELLING BEE

Spelling Bee

Students listen to spelling words in context sentences and practice spelling each one correctly. Perfect for test preparation, class competitions, and to reinforce retention of spelling words for all students, including English Language Learners.

Classroom Management System for Spelling Connections Online

Monitor and evaluate your students' daily progress as they use **Spelling Connections Online.** Everything you need to support their learning and practice at the touch of a button.

Use to
- set up class lists.
- control student access/preferences.
- develop reports.
- generate school-to-home letters.

Advance Every Student, Every Day

With the new **Spelling Connections**, all students advance their spelling skills every day with lessons tailored to meet their individual needs and level of spelling proficiency. Differentiated instruction is integrated into every unit through

- ready-made, research-based word lists for on and above level students.

- extended word sorts that include the on level words and weekly challenge words for above level students.

- assessments for on level and challenge words.

- interactive and engaging online games.

- literacy center activities.

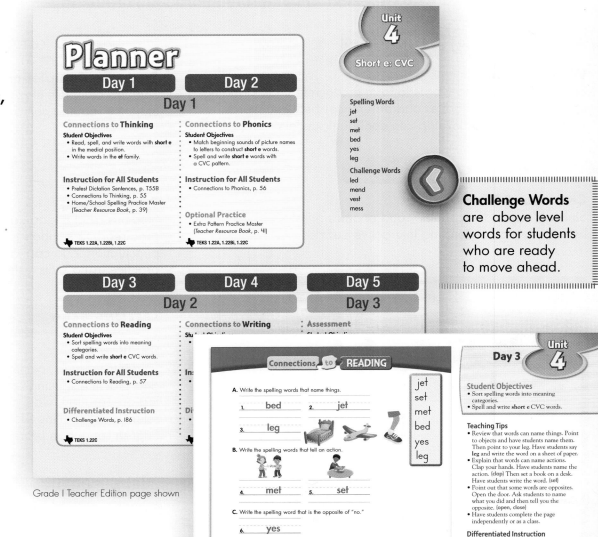

Challenge Words are above level words for students who are ready to move ahead.

Grade 1 Teacher Edition page shown

Make differentiated instruction fun for students with engaging interactive digital resources, online spelling activities, and Spelling Center activities.

Grade 1 Teacher Edition page shown

Provide Hands-On, Minds-On Opportunities

Word sorting is a valuable way to learn, practice, and internalize key spelling patterns. With **Spelling Connections,** your students will have a variety of opportunities to practice word sorting. Use the **Word Sort CD-ROM** to print word cards or provide engaging interactive virtual sorts using **Spelling Connections Digital Resources**.

Ready-made, printable word sort cards support **differentiated instruction**.

Digital Resources

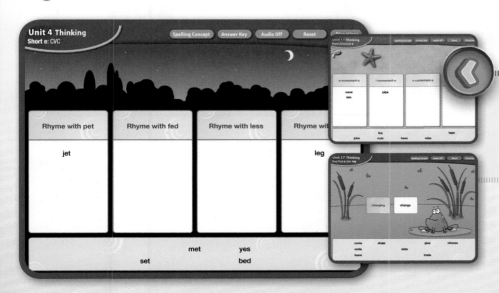

Interactive word sorts within **Digital Resources for Spelling Connections** and **Spelling Connections Online** are ideal for introducing new spelling principles to the whole class or small groups. Boost your students' interest with hands-on virtual word sorting.

Build Phonemic Awareness in Young Spellers

Spelling Connections builds phonemic awareness, a foundational skill important to spelling success. Developmentally appropriate and engaging exercises show young students how to notice, think about, and work with individual sounds in a given word. As students learn to distinguish and manipulate individual sounds, they become aware of new spelling patterns.

Phonemic Awareness

Identifying Initial Sounds

Say the name of this picture: .
Circle the pictures that start with the same sound.

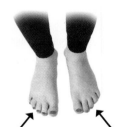

 Help your child name other words that start like **tent**.

13

Grade 1 Student Edition page shown

Phonemic Awareness lessons and activities are the first step in developing young students into good readers, writers, and spellers.

Texas Edition

Connect Sounds to Letters

Sounds and Letters activities develop sound-symbol awareness and teach students the relationship between spoken sounds and written letters.

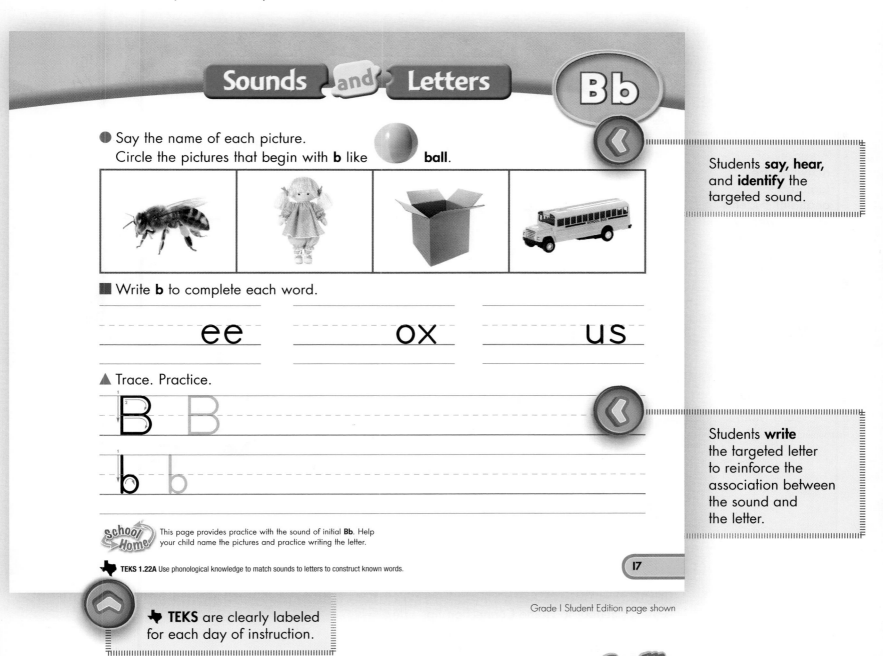

Sounds **and** Letters **Bb**

● Say the name of each picture.
Circle the pictures that begin with **b** like 🔵 **ball**.

Students **say, hear,** and **identify** the targeted sound.

■ Write **b** to complete each word.

_____ee   _____ox   _____us

▲ Trace. Practice.

B B

b b

Students **write** the targeted letter to reinforce the association between the sound and the letter.

School Home This page provides practice with the sound of initial **Bb**. Help your child name the pictures and practice writing the letter.

TEKS 1.22A Use phonological knowledge to match sounds to letters to construct known words.

17

Grade 1 Student Edition page shown

♦ **TEKS** are clearly labeled for each day of instruction.

Spelling Connections

Z11

A 5-Day Plan That Provides Opportunities Beyond Words!

Day 1
Connections to Thinking

Introduce your students to the weekly spelling principle with activities that present basic, concrete spelling strategies to help them visually identify spelling patterns and relate them to sound-letter relationships.

A variety of activities are featured to acquaint students with the weekly spelling principle including:

- Spelling Patterns
- Matching Words and Pictures
- Replace Letters
- Word Clues
- Word Math

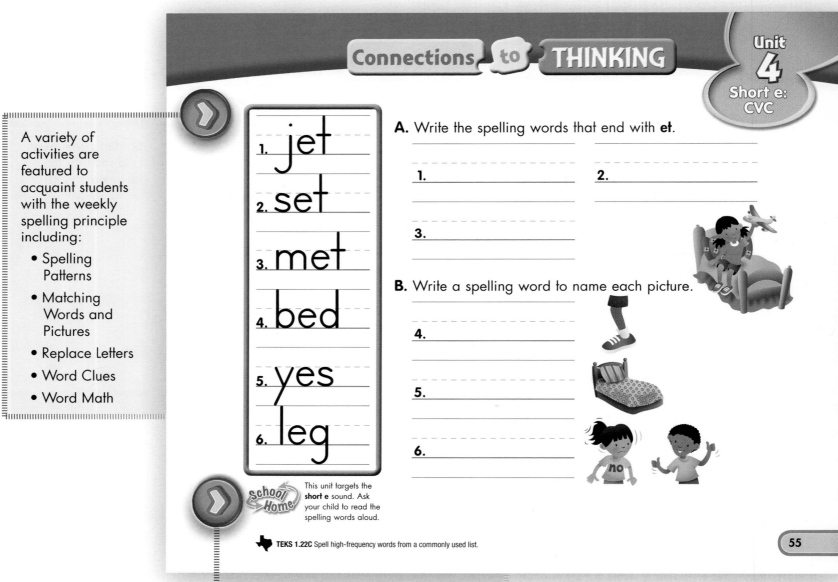

Connections to THINKING

Unit 4
Short e: CVC

1. jet
2. set
3. met
4. bed
5. yes
6. leg

A. Write the spelling words that end with **et**.

1. _____
2. _____
3. _____

B. Write a spelling word to name each picture.

4. _____
5. _____
6. _____

School Home This unit targets the **short e** sound. Ask your child to read the spelling words aloud.

TEKS 1.22C Spell high-frequency words from a commonly used list.

55

School-to-Home Connection tips offer suggestions on how to help students grow as spellers through practice at home.

Grade 1 Student Edition page shown

Texas Edition

Prepare young students for the next step in spelling as they build important sound-symbol awareness, phonics knowledge, and spelling skills with activities that invite them to see, say, hear, and write.

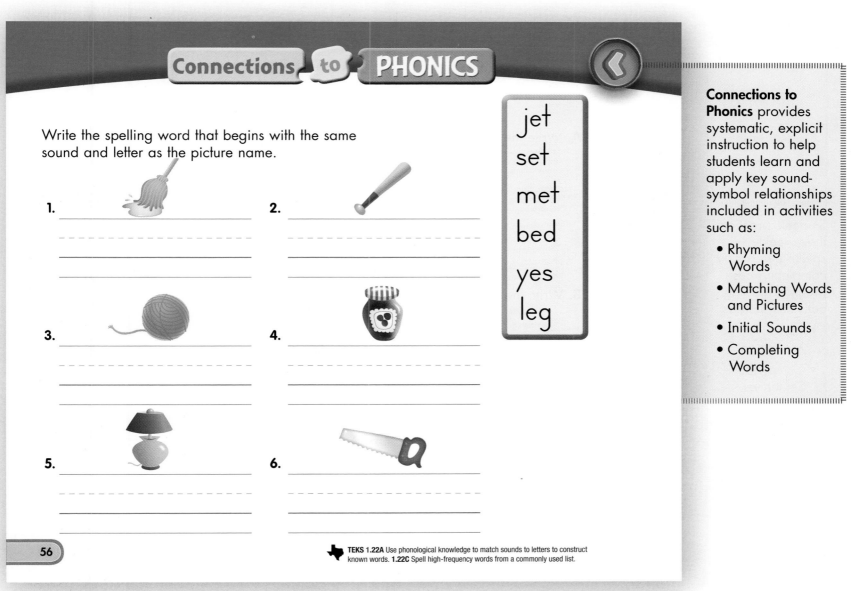

Connections **to** PHONICS

Write the spelling word that begins with the same sound and letter as the picture name.

jet
set
met
bed
yes
leg

1. _____

2. _____

3. _____

4. _____

5. _____

6. _____

56

TEKS **1.22A** Use phonological knowledge to match sounds to letters to construct known words. **1.22C** Spell high-frequency words from a commonly used list.

Connections to Phonics provides systematic, explicit instruction to help students learn and apply key sound-symbol relationships included in activities such as:

- Rhyming Words
- Matching Words and Pictures
- Initial Sounds
- Completing Words

Grade 1 Student Edition page shown

As students become familiar with the weekly word list, best-practice skill-building activities help them understand the meanings of words. Students develop comprehension skills through meaningful practice using spelling words in context.

Students practice their weekly spelling words by completing best-practice reading activities such as:

- Word Meanings
- Complete the Sentences
- Complete a Story
- Words With Opposite Meanings
- Complete the Spelling Words

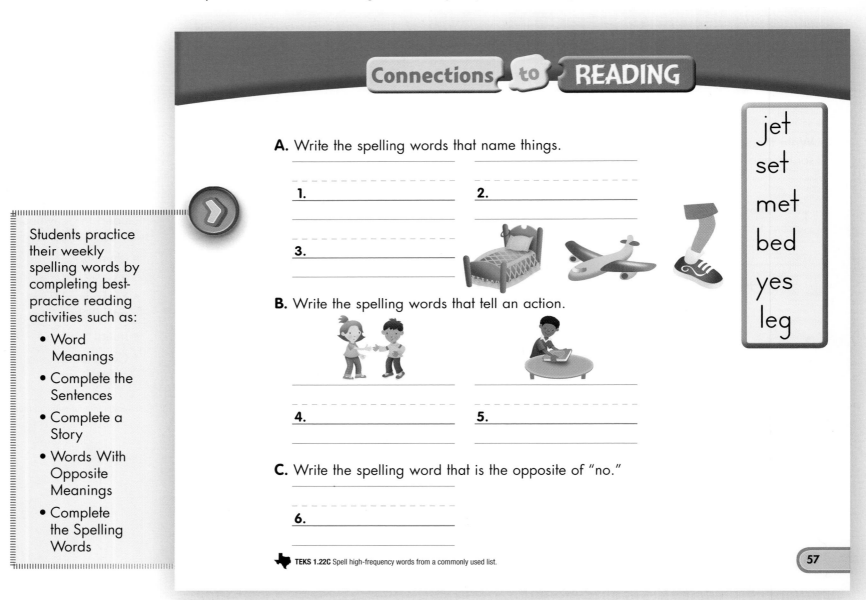

Connections to READING

jet
set
met
bed
yes
leg

A. Write the spelling words that name things.

1. _____   2. _____

3. _____

B. Write the spelling words that tell an action.

4. _____   5. _____

C. Write the spelling word that is the opposite of "no."

6. _____

TEKS 1.22C Spell high-frequency words from a commonly used list.

57

Grade 1 Student Edition page shown

On Day 4, students transfer the spelling skills they have learned during the week to their own writing through activities that prompt them to

- practice writing the weekly spelling words in context.
- proofread these words in the featured texts in Units 26–34.

Connections to WRITING

Write a spelling word to finish each tongue twister.

| jet |
| set |
| met |
| bed |
| yes |
| leg |

1. Sue _____ six shells in the shack.

2. Matt _____ merry mice in the mud.

3. Jack jumped on the jolly _____.

4. Lucky laid down on Lil's left _____.

5. _____, the yellow yak yelled, "Yippee!"

6. Bill's _____ has a blue blanket.

Promote students' transfer of spelling skills to writing with visual prompts included in activities such as:

- Completing Tongue Twisters
- Completing a Story
- Completing a Poem
- Completing a Letter
- Using the Spelling Words in Original Writing

58 TEKS 1.22A Use phonological knowledge to match sounds to letters to construct known words. 1.22C Spell high-frequency words from a commonly used list.

Grade 1 Student Edition page shown

Assess Each Student's Understanding

On Day 5, all students can prove mastery of the weekly spelling concept on the **weekly posttest**.

Day 5

Student Objectives
• Demonstrate mastery of the unit spelling words.

Posttest Assessment Options
Option 1: Administer the unit posttest using the dictation sentences at right.

Option 2: Assess students using the standardized test. See the *Standardized Test Master Book*, p. 8.

Note: Posttest sentences for the on level and challenge lists are available on the audio *Spelling Connections* Posttest CD.

Posttest Sentences
1. If you like bananas, write **yes**.
2. Will you **set** this on my desk?
3. Have you **met** my brother?
4. I can make my own **bed**.
5. My **leg** is asleep.
6. I watched the **jet** land.

Standardized Test Master Book, p. 8

★ As an option, you can use the reproducible test masters in the **Texas Standardized Test Master Book** to provide high-stakes testing practice for your students.

T58

★ TEKS 1.22A Use phonological knowledge to match sounds to letters to construct known words. **1.22C** Spell high-frequency words from a commonly used list.

Optional Practice and Assessment

Extra Challenge Practice Master, TRB, p. 42

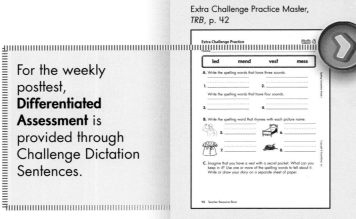

For the weekly posttest, **Differentiated Assessment** is provided through Challenge Dictation Sentences.

Challenge Dictation Sentences
1. Mark **led** the pony to the barn.
2. Will you **mend** my skirt?
3. Dad has a nice jacket and **vest**.
4. That room is a **mess**!

Note: Posttest sentences for the on level and challenge lists are available on the audio *Spelling Connections* Posttest CD.

T186

★ TEKS 1.22Bi Use letter-sound patterns to spell: consonant-vowel-consonant (CVC) words. **1.22C** Spell high-frequency words from a commonly used list.

Grade 1 Teacher Edition pages shown

Extend Spelling Practice

Because rote memorization is not enough, **Review Units** (every fifth unit in **Spelling Connections**) revisit the words featured during the previous four units to test how well students can apply the spelling concepts covered.

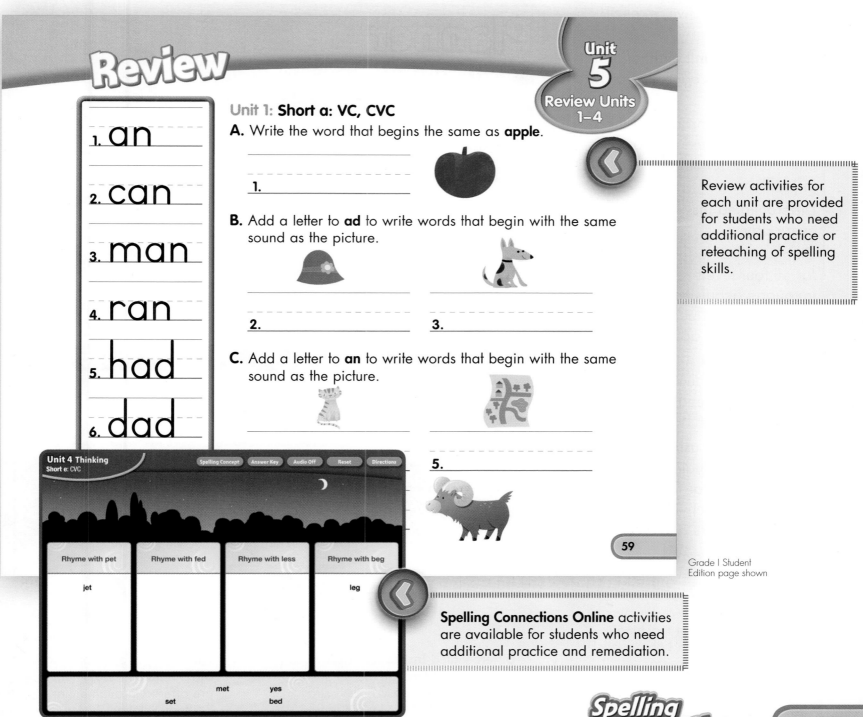

Review

Unit
5
Review Units
1–4

1. an
2. can
3. man
4. ran
5. had
6. dad

Unit 1: Short a: VC, CVC

A. Write the word that begins the same as **apple**.

1. _____

B. Add a letter to **ad** to write words that begin with the same sound as the picture.

2. _____   3. _____

C. Add a letter to **an** to write words that begin with the same sound as the picture.

5.

59

Review activities for each unit are provided for students who need additional practice or reteaching of spelling skills.

Unit 4 Thinking
Short e: CVC

Spelling Concept   Answer Key   Audio Off   Reset   Directions

Rhyme with pet	Rhyme with fed	Rhyme with less	Rhyme with beg
jet			leg

met   yes
set   bed

Spelling Connections Online activities are available for students who need additional practice and remediation.

Grade 1 Student Edition page shown

Spelling Connections

The Simplest Way to Teach Spelling

The **Spelling Connections** Texas Teacher Edition has everything you need to deliver effective, explicit spelling instruction:

- An expanded unit planner that clearly displays each day of instruction
- **TEKS** included throughout the unit at point of use and on the unit planner for streamlined instruction
- Differentiated Instruction every day
- Clear, explicit teaching tips for all four levels of English language acquisition—beginning, intermediate, advanced, and advanced-high
- Integrated daily word sorts, including individual sorts, buddy sorts, speed sorts, and teacher-led sorts
- Suggestions for using supporting technology and loads of ideas for fun games, practice, and activities—including centers and work stations

The **Unit Planner** includes a pacing guide with a flexible 3–5 day plan and provides a map for teaching students who are on and above level in their spelling skill progress.

Carefully crafted, research-based **word lists** are at the center of each unit and provide targeted instruction for all students regardless of their level of proficiency.

Grade I Teacher Edition page shown

Planner

Unit 4
Short e: CVC

Spelling Words
jet
set
met
bed
yes
leg

Challenge Words
led
mend
vest
mess

Day 1	Day 2

Day 1

Connections to **Thinking**
Student Objectives
- Read, spell, and write words with **short e** in the medial position.
- Write words in the **et** family.

Instruction for All Students
- Pretest Dictation Sentences, p. T55B
- Connections to Thinking, p. 55
- Home/School Spelling Practice Master (*Teacher Resource Book*, p. 39)

TEKS 1.22A, 1.22Bi, 1.22C

Connections to **Phonics**
Student Objectives
- Match beginning sounds of picture names to letters to construct **short e** words.
- Spell and write **short e** words with a CVC pattern.

Instruction for All Students
- Connections to Phonics, p. 56

Optional Practice
- Extra Pattern Practice Master (*Teacher Resource Book*, p. 41)

TEKS 1.22A, 1.22Bi, 1.22C

Day 3	Day 4	Day 5

Day 2 / Day 3

Connections to **Reading**
Student Objectives
- Sort spelling words into meaning categories.
- Spell and write **short e** CVC words.

Instruction for All Students
- Connections to Reading, p. 57

Differentiated Instruction
- Challenge Words, p. 186

TEKS 1.22C

Connections to **Writing**
Student Objectives
- Spell and write **short e** CVC words to complete alliterative sentences.

Instruction for All Students
- Connections to Writing, p. 58

Differentiated Instruction
- Extra Challenge Practice Master (*Teacher Resource Book*, p. 42)

TEKS 1.22A, 1.2

Assessment
Student Objectives
- Demonstrate mastery of the unit spelling words.

Assessment for All Students
- Posttest Dictation Sentences, p. T58, or
- *Standardized Test Master Book*, p. 8

Differentiated Assessment
- Challenge Dictation Sentences, p. TI86

T55A

Differentiated Instruction is provided for Days 2–4 through Extra Pattern Practice, Challenge Words, Extra Challenge Practice Masters, and **Spelling Connections Online**.

On Day 5, two options for **Differentiated Assessment** are offered through either Posttest Dictation Sentences or Standardized Test Masters.

Unit 4
Short e: CVC

Unit 4 Materials

Student Edition
pp. 55–58, 186

Teacher Edition
pp. T55A–T58, T186

 Teacher Resource Book
Unit 4 Practice Masters,
pp. 39–42, and
Sound/Symbol Cards

Standardized Test Master Book
Unit 4 Test Master, p. 8

Word Sort CD-ROM
Unit 4 Word Sort Cards for Teacher-
Led Sorts and Student Sorts

 **Digital Resources for
Spelling Connections**
Unit 4

 Spelling Connections Online
www.spellingconnectionsonline.com

**Spelling Support for
English Language Learners***
Unit 4 Practice Masters and
Audio Conversation

Spelling Center Activities*
Spelling Game Mats
Flip Folder, TRB, p. 155

*Spelling Support for English Language
Learners and Spelling Center Activities may
be used at any time during the week.

The week's **instructional materials** are clearly listed, including page references for convenient, easy preparation.

Assessment

Pretest Sentences (See procedures on p. Z30.)
1. The **jet** was flying low.
2. Please **set** the dish on the table.
3. I **met** a real clown!
4. May Karen sleep in my **bed**?
5. My mother said **yes**.
6. Can you hop on one **leg**?

The Science of Spelling

- When a single vowel appears in a closed syllable, it is usually short. Short vowel sounds rarely occur at the end of a word. Many CVC, CVCC, and CCVCC words have /ĕ/, as in **net**, **next**, and **shell**. There are relatively few high frequency words that begin with /ĕ/. (**echo, edge, edit, educate, effort, egg, elbow, elephant, elm, end, engine, exit,** and **extra**) Many students have trouble distinguishing the sounds of /ă/ and /ĕ/ (**man/men**) and /ĕ/ and /ĭ/ (**pen/ pin**), so they confuse the spellings.

The Science of Spelling focuses on the week's spelling principle and provides background information for teachers.

T55B

Weekly **pretest dictation sentences** are furnished to assess each individual student's spelling skill level. The pretest determines which students will also use the expanded word list, including the weekly challenge words.

Grade 1 Teacher
Edition page shown

Focus on Learning with These Easy-to-Follow Lessons!

Create an exciting learning environment for your students. Easy-to-follow, ready-made lessons provide everything you need for effective spelling instruction and reduced preparation time.

Daily **Student Objectives** are clearly labeled and presented at the point of use for easy reference.

Connections to **THINKING**

Unit **4** Short e: CVC

1. jet
2. set
3. met
4. bed
5. yes
6. leg

A. Write the spelling words that end with **et**.

1. jet   2. set
3. met

B. Write a spelling word to name each picture.

4. leg
5. bed
6. yes

This unit targets the **short e** sound. Ask your child to read the spelling words aloud.

TEKS 1.22C Spell high-frequency words from a commonly used list.

55

Day 1 Unit **4**

Student Objectives
- Read, spell, and write words with **short e** in the medial position.
- Write words in the **et** family.

Unit Pretest
- Administer the pretest on page T55B.

Teaching Tips
- Have students read the spelling words aloud, emphasizing and listening to /ĕ/.

WORD SORT CD-ROM
- Conduct a **Teacher-Led Sort** (see p. Z31) to reinforce the spelling pattern.
- Display or draw a picture of a jet. Have students name the picture. Write **jet** on the board. Have students name the vowel sound they hear and tell where it is in the word.
- Tell students that a spelling word rhymes with **jet** and begins with the letter **s**. Ask a volunteer to name the word and write it below **jet**. Do the same with **met**. Have students identify the rhyming sounds.
- Nod your head up and down and have students name the spelling word that tells what you are gesturing. (yes)
- Have students complete the page independently or as a class.

Home/School Word Lists TRB
- Have students take home the Home/School Spelling Practice Master.

Home/School Practice

Home/School Spelling Practice Master, *TRB*, p. 39

Home/School Spelling Practice Master, *TRB*, p. 40

English

Spanish

Home/School Spelling Practice pages provide a school-to-home word list and activity for each unit. Activities offer suggestions to involve families in students' learning. Available in both English and Spanish.

TEKS 1.22A Use phonological knowledge to match sounds to letters to construct known words. 1.22Bi Use letter-sound patterns to spell: consonant-vowel-consonant (CVC) words. 1.22C Spell high-frequency words from a commonly used list.

TEKS are included at point of use throughout the Teacher Edition for targeted instruction and easy planning.

T55

Grade 1 Teacher Edition page shown

Daily **Teaching Tips** offer valuable suggestions to make the most of your daily spelling instruction.

Unit 4 — Day 2

Student Objectives
• ...beginning sounds of picture names ...to construct **short e** words.
• ...write **short e** words with a CVC...

Teaching Tips
• Say the spelling words. Point out that all of the words have the **short e** sound spelled with one vowel between two consonants.
• Say **jet**, emphasizing the individual sounds /j/ /ĕ/ /t/. Have students say each spelling word slowly and listen for the beginning, middle, and ending sound.
• Display pictures of an egg, the numeral 10, and a jar. Ask students to identify the picture that begins with the same sound as **jet**. (jar) Continue with the medial and end sounds.
• Have students complete page 56 independently or as a class.

Extra Pattern Practice **TRB**
• Use the optional practice master below for extra practice with **short e**.

WORD SORT CD-ROM
• Provide time for students to use a **Buddy Sort** (see p. Z31) to practice their spelling words with a partner.

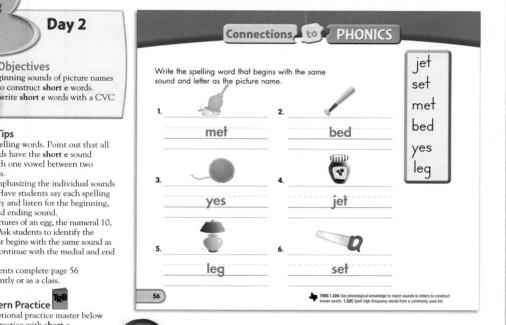

Connections to PHONICS

Write the spelling word that begins with the same sound and letter as the picture name.

1. met
2. bed
3. yes
4. jet
5. leg
6. set

jet
set
met
bed
yes
leg

56

TEKS 1.22A Use phonological knowledge to match sounds to letters to construct known words. 1.22C Spell high-frequency words from a commonly used list.

Suggestions for **word sorting** practice are included for each day of instruction.

Extra Pattern Practice

Extra Pattern Practice Master,
TRB, p. 41

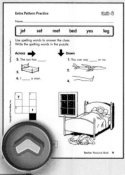

Pattern Practice Game: /ĕ/
Have a student write an **e** on a sheet of paper. A partner writes a consonant to the left and on the right of the **e** to construct a **short e** word. Then have partners switch. Have students continue until they have written several **short e** words.

Pattern Practice Games are a fun way for students to familiarize themselves with the unit spelling pattern.

T56

TEKS 1.22A Use phonological knowledge to match sounds to letters to construct known words. 1.22Bi Use letter-sound patterns to spell: consonant-vowel-consonant (CVC) words. 1.22C Spell high-frequency words from a commonly used list.

Extra practice targeting the weekly spelling principle is provided through optional **Extra Pattern Practice Masters**.

Grade 1 Teacher
Edition page shown

Meaningful Instruction for English Language Learners

Reinforce English language acquisition with meaningful differentiated instruction for English Language Learners at all levels—beginning, intermediate, advanced, and advanced-high.

Beginning-level activities provide multiple concrete strategies that enable students to illustrate or physically demonstrate the meaning of spelling words.

Intermediate-level activities promote the students' conversational English with activities such as storytelling, writing notes, letters, poetry, and short stories.

ELL Support

Unit 4

Choose from the activities below to reinforce English language acquisition.

Beginning

Word Meaning Write each spelling word on a flash card. Show each word and read it aloud. Use real objects, pictures, and pantomime to support meaning.

Beginning, Middle, End Say a spelling word. Have one student say the beginning sound, have a second student say the middle sound, and have a third student say the ending sound. Write the word on the board and have students copy it. Continue with the remaining spelling words.

Word Match Have students make flash cards for the spelling words or provide students with cards. Have students place the cards faceup. Read a spelling word aloud. Have students find the word and hold up the card.

What Am I? Have students work in pairs to complete the activities on page 9 of *Spelling Support for English Language Learners*.

Intermediate

Letter Substitution Write e on the board and say /ĕ/. Say each spelling word and have students repeat after you individually and in chorus. Then write et on the board. Have students say the word. Add **j** before **et** and have students say the word. Then erase **j** and add **s**. Continue with **m**. Invite students to suggest other beginning letters to make more words with **et**. (bet, get, let, net, pet, vet, wet, yet)

Nouns and Verbs Explain that nouns are words that name things, and verbs are words that name actions. Use **net** and **ran** as examples. Say and define each word. Then create a two-column chart with **net** and **ran** as column heads. Have students categorize other spelling words by writing them in the appropriate column. Add words to the chart each week.

What Am I? Have students work in pairs to complete the activities on page 9 of *Spelling Support for English Language Learners*.

Support for Spanish Speakers

Help students pronounce the **short e** sound. Have them notice that when they say /ĕ/ their mouth is open and their tongue is behind their bottom teeth. Say /ĕ/ and have students repeat. Contrast this with saying the name of the letter **e** when their lips are stretched wider as though smiling.

Play a "Simon Says" type of game to practice pronouncing and reading the **short a** and **short e** sounds. Have students make flash cards for **short a** and **short e** word pairs such as **pat** and **pet, bad** and **bed, pan** and **pen**. Start by having students put one pair of cards faceup on their desk. Say, *Simon says pat. Hold up the card that says pat*. Have students hold up their **pat** card and say the word. Gradually increase the number of words students choose from, using up to six cards (three pairs).

T55C

Grade 1 Teacher Edition page shown

Support for Spanish Speakers provides background information and suggestions for activities for teachers of Spanish-speaking students.

 Texas Edition

Unit 4

from the activities below to reinforce English language acquisition.

Advanced

Word Meaning List the spelling words on the board and read each word aloud as you point to it. Ask students to identify any words they do not know. Use real objects, pictures, and pantomime to support explanations of word meaning.

Finish the Sentence Write a question on the board that uses one or two spelling words, such as *Does a* **jet** *have a* **leg**? Ask a volunteer to read the sentence. Write a sentence that answers the question, but leave out the spelling words: *A _____ does not have a _____.* Ask students which spelling words are missing and write the words on the lines. (jet, leg) Ask a volunteer to read the answer. Continue the activity using the rest of the words.

True or False Use a spelling word in a statement that is true or false. For example, *Yes means the opposite of no. I rode the jet to school.* Have students say *true* if the sentence makes sense. If the sentence is false, ask students to explain why. Then have them use the spelling word in a true sentence.

What Am I? Have students work in pairs to complete the activities on page 9 of *Spelling Support for English Language Learners.*

Advanced High

Word Meaning List the spelling words on the board and read each word aloud as you point to it. Ask students to identify any words they do not know. Use real objects, pictures, and pantomime to support explanations of word meaning.

Story Words Encourage students to draw a picture that includes illustrations of spelling words. Then have students use the spelling words to tell a partner about their picture. The partner can write the spelling words heard in the story.

What Am I? Have students work in pairs to complete the activities on page 9 of *Spelling Support for English Language Learners.*

Spelling Support for English Language Learners

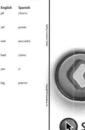

Practice Master, p. 9

Practice Master, p. 43

Audio Conversation available on CD

English/Spanish Word List, p. 58

Spelling Connections Online
Interactive online spelling activities provide additional ELL support.
www.spellingconnectionsonline.com

T55D

Grade I Teacher Edition page shown

The Role of Spelling and Word Knowledge in ELL Literacy

By Bertha Pérez, Ed.D. & Ellen Riojas Clark, Ph.D.

Within English literacy learning, what is the role of spelling and word knowledge for English language learners (ELLs)? Good spelling can help ELLs learn letter/sound correspondence and vocabulary, and develop automaticity in reading and writing words. Research points to a relationship between word knowledge and reading achievement (Blachowicz, et al. 2006). For ELLs, vocabulary appears to have a greater impact on reading than other components, including oral language (Proctor, et al., 2006).

Word knowledge, in particular academic vocabulary, is needed to be successful in reading, math, and other subjects, and schooling as a whole. Academic vocabulary is often decontextualized; it is the language of school, of academic discourse, and of texts. Academic vocabulary includes derivational word forms (e.g., adverbials), conditional/prepositional forms, and words that express relationships and give clues to syntax. The **Spelling Connections** activities suggested for ELLs build academic vocabulary.

> **The words learned by spelling patterns and relationships can assist ELLs in developing a rich vocabulary that supports reading and enhances writing.**

Spelling Connections incorporates research findings from studies of ELLs' English literacy development. These studies suggest that ELL reading success in grades K–1 can be predicted by phonological awareness (Geva & Yaghoub-Zadeh, 2006; Lafrance & Gottardo, 2005), development of the alphabetic principle (Manis, et al., 2004), and word knowledge (August, et al., 2005). In grades 2–6, ELL reading success can be predicted by fluency, the ability to read words with automaticity (Baker & Good, 1995), and by vocabulary, a major contributor to comprehension (August, et al., 2005; Lesaux, et al., 2006).

Through the systematic study of related words, students begin to see that English, like all other languages, is rule-governed. Words learned by spelling patterns and relationships can assist ELLs in developing a rich vocabulary that supports reading and enhances writing.

Pronunciation of Spelling Words and ELLs

Learning to spell words is important to vocabulary development, and proper pronunciation leads to better spelling: " … students need to see, hear, and say unfamiliar words whose meanings are being learned because this strengthens their memory for spellings, pronunciations, and meanings of the new words" (Rosenthal & Ehri, 2008, p. 189). Demanding proper pronunciation can be frustrating and stigmatizing for many ELLs. We offer a word of caution. Teachers must model good pronunciation and should frequently ask students to pronounce the word because this leads to better spelling. However, teachers should allow for approximations. For example, some Japanese-speakers may not pronounce the *l* or *r* and Spanish-speakers may sound an *e* before words beginning with *s*. Correct spelling can be attained with approximate pronunciations, and over time, children will assess mispronunciations and learn to compensate. Pronouncing words is about helping children spell and develop word knowledge, not about reducing their native accent.

Differentiated Instruction by ELL Levels

Spelling Connections provides differentiated instruction based on ELL levels. The ELL support is extensive, systematic, and sustained.

Beginning Level Second language acquisition research suggests that some ELLs may have a "quiet period" during which they are listening, rehearsing mentally, and not attempting to produce the new language. For some, this quiet period is a few weeks to a few months; for others, it can extend for many months. Children working with linguistic partners can support each other in understanding lesson expectations and word meanings. By encouraging children to use their native language to understand word meanings, they can focus on English pronunciation and spelling. Beginning-level activities provide multiple concrete strategies: the use of real objects and pictures, gestures, pantomime, and a variety of research-based ELL strategies, such as Total Physical Response (TPR). Students can illustrate or physically demonstrate, as in action verbs, the meaning of spelling words.

Bertha Pérez, Ed.D.   Ellen Riojas Clark, Ph.D.

Intermediate Level At the intermediate level, ELLs can use their conversational English to learn academic language and can be expected to produce approximate pronunciations. Students can work with partners to assist each other in interpreting meanings (using their native language when appropriate) and for pronunciation and oral language activities. The focus continues on activities that are concrete and contextualized. Activities also stress the use of the spelling words for different purposes, such as storytelling, and writing notes, letters, poetry, and short stories.

Advanced Level As ELLs demonstrate more understanding and speak conversational and academic English, more stress can be placed on identifying, contrasting, and categorizing specific phonemic elements of words and word meanings. Many popular second language activities, such as telephone use, riddles, and playing Simon Says are included to encourage language production and as fun ways for students to use the spelling words.

Advanced-High Level Activities at this level are more challenging. ELLs are asked to compare and contrast words, categorize words, and work with analogies and derivatives. More partner and independent activities are suggested to explore further spelling patterns and lesson elements, word associations, and meanings. Many activities also challenge students to incorporate spelling words in writing for different purposes such as science, social studies, or creative writing.

Support for Spanish Speakers

Support for Spanish speakers uniquely encompasses two components: comparing languages and cognates. In the comparing languages section, teachers gain knowledge about possible linguistic problems and transfers. This important teacher information helps avoid frustrating children over correct word pronunciations, especially at the beginning and intermediate levels.

The cognate section will assist Spanish speakers to develop deeper understanding of the English spelling words. By making associations with the Spanish cognate, the student examines root elements and origins to develop a nuanced understanding of words by comparing English and Spanish meanings. Also, by comparing the phonemic and morphological (prefixes, word endings, and so on) elements of the English and Spanish words, spelling abilities will be reinforced. The cognates selected have been carefully researched and although there are some whose meanings are variants (what some consider false cognates), the student is asked to identify differences and to investigate the changing meaning of words. The work with cognates is most important because it focuses on academic language. **This is groundbreaking work for a spelling program**.

Spelling is key for ELLs because of the ways in which it addresses letter/sound correspondence, vocabulary, and automatic word recognition—all integrated throughout **Spelling Connections**. ○

A complete list of references cited can be found at **www.zaner-bloser.com**.

Support for Spanish speakers uniquely encompasses two components: comparing languages and cognates.

Bertha Pérez, Ed.D.
Bertha Pérez began her career as a classroom teacher in San Antonio, Texas. Later she earned her doctorate from the University of Massachusetts at Amherst and served as professor of reading and biliteracy at San José State University, The University of Texas at El Paso, and The University of Texas at San Antonio. As a result of her literacy and biliteracy research, she has become an authority on biliteracy and on assisting English language learners to develop biliteracy.

Ellen Riojas Clark, Ph.D.
Ellen Riojas Clark holds a Ph.D. in Curriculum and Instruction from The University of Texas at Austin. She is a Professor of Bicultural Bilingual Studies at The University of Texas at San Antonio. Her research interests include the relationship between the constructs of self-concept, ethnic identity, self-efficacy, and good teaching; bilingual education teacher training; and the identification of gifted language-minority children.

Using Work Stations in Your Classroom

By Debbie Diller

What Is a Work Station?

A literacy work station is an area within the classroom where students work alone or interact with one another, using instructional materials to explore and expand their literacy. It is a place where a variety of activities reinforces and/or extends learning, often without the assistance of the classroom teacher. It is a time for children to practice reading, writing, speaking, listening, and working with letters and words.

Instructional Materials

Instructional materials already used in teaching go into the work stations. The idea is for the teacher to model how to use the materials first, using them with the students to be sure they understand how to use them, then moving these materials into the work stations for independent practice.

A Variety of Activities

Choice is an important feature in making literacy work stations successful. A station should include a variety of things for children to choose from, but there shouldn't be so many choices that the children feel overwhelmed. Aim for what I call "controlled choice." Provide several choices of activities within a work station. Any of the activities there should accomplish the practice the child needs, but allowing the child to choose the activity will enable him or her to learn more.

Time for Children to Practice

The emphasis at literacy work stations is on practice—meaningful, independent practice. It is a time for children to practice all that the teacher has been modeling. Thus, activities placed at the literacy work stations grow out of what the teacher has done during read aloud, shared reading, modeled writing, shared writing, small-group instruction and so on. Things aren't put into the work stations just to keep children busy.

The Spelling Work Station

Word sorts are great activities for a spelling work station. **Spelling Connections** provides a variety of differentiated word sort options—both on the interactive whiteboard and with Word Sort Cards— that students can do independently or with a partner. Students may also choose to practice their spelling words with such activities as one of the game mats or flip folder, or work with **Spelling Connections Online**. ○

Excerpted from *Literacy Work Stations: Making Centers Work* by Debbie Diller

Debbie Diller

Debbie Diller holds a master's degree in education from Temple University. In her experiences as a classroom teacher, Title I reading specialist, migrant education teacher, literacy coach, national consultant, and author, she has acquired a deep understanding of child development and literacy development. She uses her knowledge to address the differentiated needs of students. In addition to Literacy Workstations, *Diller is the author of* Spaces & Places: Designing Classrooms for Literacy, Making the Most of Small Groups, *and* Practice with Purpose.

Current Research: A Conversation

By J. Richard Gentry, Ph.D.

Dr. Gentry, a nationally acclaimed expert in literacy with particular research focus in spelling and beginning reading development, began his career as a classroom teacher. He earned his Ph.D. in reading education from the University of Virginia and served as professor of elementary education and reading at Western Carolina University. Dr. Gentry's research, writing, and extensive work with students and teachers for over thirty years have had a powerful impact for promoting literacy.

In addition to writing popular books such as The Science of Spelling, Spel…Is a Four-Letter Word, Teaching Kids to Spell, My Kid Can't Spell!, *and* Breakthrough in Beginning Reading and Writing, *Dr. Gentry conducts workshops that have helped thousands of school districts adopt better practices for spelling instruction.*

Spelling Connections *provides the curriculum and resources you need to deliver effective, explicit, research-based instruction in spelling. More than 30 years of spelling research and research synthesis have contributed to the success and effectiveness of* **Spelling Connections***. No other program offers the extensive research perspective outlined below.*

What does the latest research say about teaching spelling in the 21st century?

Technology, such as in brain scanning studies, and advancements in educational research have shown that spelling is critical for proficiency in both reading and writing. After decades of receiving instructional short shrift—and disastrous results from its neglect—the importance of teaching spelling is being rediscovered, revitalized in schools that are succeeding, and reasserted by the research community (Joshi, Treiman, Carreker, & Moats, 2009).

The twenty-first century view is that English spelling is complex and requires a specialized memory system that draws from deep levels of language-based knowledge rather than a reliance on memorizing words. We've learned that teaching spelling is a brain-building boon for effective reading and writing, creating a "dictionary in the brain" for every reader and writer (Gentry, 2004; Paulesu, 2001).

What specific new research developments are reflected in the new **Spelling Connections**?

There is a new "overlapping wave" perspective that disputes the claim that spelling can be taught with one strategy such as memorizing high-use words or word sorting—two popular single-strategy approaches (Sharp, Sinatra, & Reynolds, 2008). **Spelling Connections** recognizes the complexity of spelling and teaches from a multistrategic perspective. Teachers who use **Spelling Connections** actually teach spelling—they don't just assign it. We incorporate enough word sorting so that key words and patterns are committed to memory.

Automatically knowing a word's correct spelling and activating that knowledge becomes a strategy that replaces less accurate strategies such as sounding the word out or guessing. Children are adaptive and will move to more effective strategies if we teach those strategies. Knowing how to spell a word because of gained understanding of the structure of English spelling is a great strategy!

What new trends should be avoided?

Replacing research-based, stand-alone spelling books with the inferior spelling component of a reading program is neither research-based nor effective. Spelling components of reading programs were developed to sell reading programs, not to teach spelling. They greatly reduce the spelling curriculum. Their most egregious flaw is that they pull words from reading stories and do not necessarily follow the research-based principle of focusing on words and patterns that children need for writing. They ignore the basic research finding that it's harder to spell a word correctly than it is to read a word correctly (Bosman & Van Orden, 1997).

Substituting a reading program's weak spelling component for a strong, research-based, spelling curriculum is shortchanging students. Stories selected for a reading program should not drive the spelling curriculum; rather, a good spelling curriculum is organized around the words and patterns children at a particular grade level need for their writing (Gentry, 2004; Graham, 1983).

By J. Richard Gentry, Ph.D.

I have analyzed many spelling components of reading programs and found a multiplicity of problems ranging from arbitrary memorize-and-test word lists to worksheets that waste time and do not teach spelling concepts.

A recent development in some reading programs is that the spelling component attempts to "look like" research-based spelling programs by including patterns. However, these programs may tend to collapse too many patterns into too few lessons resulting in a truncated and confusing curriculum. In many of these spelling components, there is no explanation for how words were chosen and no evidence of a spiraling curriculum in which lessons build upon what students know.

What's the difference between "teaching spelling" and "assigning spelling"?

Spelling Connections gives teachers the resources and options they need to teach spelling. Teachers who simply give students the spelling pages from the reading program or give out a word list and test on Friday aren't teaching; they are assigning.

Good spelling teachers use pretest results to determine how much focus particular students need and which connections need to be addressed. Good spelling teachers make instructional decisions regarding how to present material with options for focus, intensity, and differentiation.

For example, if most students show weakness on a particular pretest, the teacher might plan a whole-class teacher-led word sort to help students grasp the unit concept followed by an interactive word sort or buddy sort. If only a small

group showed difficulty with the pattern, the teacher might pull those students for a teacher-led sort.

How does this comprehensive, research-based program differ from other methods of teaching spelling?

Comprehensive is the key word. **Spelling Connections** is based on a comprehensive synthesis of research underscoring the fact that learning to spell is complex. Other methods often focus on a single research-based principle, or a gimmick that is not research-based. The deep research base for **Spelling Connections** covers a spectrum of spelling issues and practices. It reflects the complexity of spelling and the important connection of spelling to reading and writing (Gentry, 2004). Research clearly documents that knowledge of spelling is connected to reading, writing, and vocabulary development because they all depend upon the same underlying language abilities (Snow, Griffin, & Burns, 2005).

Is it necessary to teach spelling explicitly or is there a more effective way for children to learn word-specific knowledge?

There are two theories regarding instructional approaches for spelling acquisition (Allal, 1997). The first calls for specific instruction in spelling, and **Spelling Connections** fits into this category. The other calls for integrating spelling into writing and reading instruction. There is little or no empirical research base for the latter theory (Allal, 1997). While the aim of that approach might seem desirable, research has not come forth to

- support abandoning explicit, stand-alone spelling instruction.
- integrate spelling into reading instruction.
- support abandoning a research-based curriculum for an inquiry-based word sorting program.
- validate nonsystematic spelling instruction in the context of "writer's workshop" or writing lessons (Joshi et al., 2009; Allal, 1997).

Spelling Connections recognizes the functional, social, and contextual advantages to CONNECTING spelling to writing and reading and helps teachers make these powerful connections to reading and writing in every unit.

Can't I just pull a grade-level word list from the Internet or use the one from my reading program?

Spelling researcher Linda Allal writes, "Study of word lists is very widespread in elementary schools, but many teachers do not apply the principles that assure instructional effectiveness" (1997, p. 136).

Practices that lead to problems include no individualization, badly designed exercises, developmentally inappropriate words, words irrelevant to writing, too many worksheets, and testing words without teaching spelling. We follow the research-based practice of anchoring our program with a unit pretest/posttest word list, which is very different from assigning a list to be memorized and giving a test on Friday.

For example, **Spelling Connections** provides options for differentiating instruction via the word list. Our word list is thoroughly researched, and all words were carefully selected with the developmental appropriateness of the type and timing of instruction in mind.

We provide research-based study strategies and activities and have carefully designed relevant exercises that connect to writing and reading to insure that the skills learned will be reinvested in reading and writing situations.

We have made sure you avoid the pitfalls of bad practice and given you the tools to teach spelling, not just assign it.

How were words chosen for the word lists?

The spelling words and their organization for study are vital to a good spelling program. Research demonstrates that a spelling program must teach the words that students use in writing (E. Horn, 1960; Hollingsworth, 1965; T.D. Horn, 1969; Graves, 1981; Smith & Ingersoll, 1984). A good spelling program will identify these words by using both studies of children's writings (Rinsland, 1945; Smith & Ingersoll, 1984) and studies that note how often particular words appear in print (Thorndike & Lorge, 1944; Kucera & Francis, 1967; Carroll et al., 1971; Fry et al., 1985).

Other considerations should include the word's degree of difficulty, universality, permanence, and application to other areas of the curriculum.

We conducted the most thorough word analysis ever accomplished to develop the word lists in **Spelling Connections**. In all, 22 published word lists and vocabulary studies were analyzed.

The result was a list of more than 7,800 words organized in these word categories: On Level, Above Level, Below Level, Review, and Assessment. Word selection criteria include words most frequently used at specific grade levels for writing

(writing level), words most frequently used for reading (reading level), difficulty level for students at particular grade levels (proficiency level), and other criteria such as frequently misspelled words in each grade.

How can I be sure words are presented at the appropriate grade level?

Research provides clear evidence that spelling should be taught systematically (T.D. Horn, 1969; Joshi et al., 2009). The right words and patterns must be presented at the right time. Because spelling growth is a developmental process, the organization of words and their placement make a difference in how easily students learn to spell them. New information is built upon previous lessons and what children already know (Bear et al., 2000; Ganske, 2000).

The **Spelling Connections** word list is organized according to principles set forth by linguistic, cognitive, and developmental theory research. We have incorporated the massive research evidence for teaching letter recognition, the alphabetic principle, and phonics (Adams, 1990; National Reading Council, 1998; National Reading Panel, 2000).

Our curriculum is informed by phase observation and developmental research on the development of sound, pattern, and meaning (Ehri, 1997; Gentry, 1982, 2007; Templeton & Morris, 2000). It includes morphological development for prefixes and suffixes, Greek and Latin bases or roots, and word histories or origins (Venezky, 1999).

Which works best—the pretest/posttest word list, word sorting, teaching spelling rules, or other exercises?

Spelling Connections includes all of the above with correct balance. In a comprehensive review of spelling research, Steve Graham (1983) validated the use of the language-based, stand-alone program with the pretest/posttest word lists (Graham, 1983, p. 563, reported in Allal, 1997, p. 135). Graham outlined five research-based principles in his synthesis:

1. Use word lists but not arbitrary lists. Construct lists to reflect words and patterns likely to be used by writers at developmentally appropriate grade levels and teach a few key rules.

2. Pretest and have students self-correct.

3. Teach students to use a research-based word study technique. Our look-say-see-write-check technique is directly based on a method Ernest Horn validated (Horn, 1954).

4. Use the "test-study-test" cycle.

5. Use spelling games and other alternative activities to increase motivation and to take advantage of the social context of learning.

Each of these research-based strategies has been built into **Spelling Connections**.

Spelling Connections enables students to build a deep and wide word-specific knowledge base to support the reading, writing, and communication skills needed for language proficiency. ○

Complete research, word studies consulted for compiling word lists, and bibliography can be found at **www.zaner-bloser.com**.

Professional Development

Assessment

Spelling assessment often utilizes a general screening inventory and specific feature inventories. **Spelling Connections** provides both, including two general screening inventories at each grade level (Start-of-Year and End-of-Year) and unit pretests each week.

Start-of-Year and End-of-Year Tests

Two survey tests (Form A and Form B) are included at the back of this Teacher Edition. The words on these tests were chosen from the on level word lists in each **Spelling Connections** Student Edition. A dictation sentence for each word is also provided. Administer either Form A or Form B at the beginning of the year and the other form at the end of the year. A comparison of these scores will help measure each student's annual spelling progress.

Instructional Units

Weekly Pretest The pretest is a valuable part of spelling instruction and helps students target spelling words they do not know. To administer the pretest each week, use the **Pretest Sentences** in the Teacher Edition. Follow this procedure for each word:

1. Say the spelling word.
2. Read the context sentence aloud.
3. Say the word again.
4. Remind students to write the word to the best of their ability.

It is important that each student self-check his or her pretest. Page 12 in the Student Edition details the steps for taking and checking a pretest. Use this page as the basis for a minilesson. You might also introduce students to the Circle/Dot self-correction technique at right.

Weekly Posttest Two posttest options provide differentiated assessment each week.

Option 1: Administer the unit posttest using the dictation sentences provided on Day 5 of the Teacher Edition. Challenge dictation sentences are located in the Challenge section in the back of the Teacher Edition. Administer this option in the same way as the pretest. All posttest sentences are available on the **Audio Posttest Sentences CD**.

Option 2: Assess students using the reproducible standardized tests (see **Standardized Test Master Book**). This option tests students' ability to identify correct or incorrect spellings within a standardized test format.

Review Units

Developmental Spelling Checks You can learn a great deal about a student's progress toward correct spelling by asking him or her to attempt to spell specifically selected words, such as **eagle,** that are not on a Grade 1 spelling list. For example, when a young student produces **EGL** for **eagle,** he or she is demonstrating a great deal of knowledge. This knowledge includes

- full phonemic awareness. This writer has realized that **eagle** is composed of three sounds: /e/—/g/—/l/.

- an understanding of sound-symbol relationships. This writer realizes that /e/ is often represented by **e,** /g/ by **g,** and /l/ by **l.**

To help you measure this progress, **Spelling Connections** author J. Richard Gentry has included a Developmental Spelling Check in the planner pages of each Review Unit (every fifth unit) in the Teacher Edition. Each Developmental Spelling Check includes a list of words specifically chosen by Dr. Gentry to measure spelling growth throughout the first grade year. Dr. Gentry has also included the kinds of spellings students who are progressing normally in their spelling growth might generate for each word. Unlike a weekly spelling test, these checks should not be corrected by the student. They are a tool for you to use in assessing overall literacy growth.

Circle/Dot Self-Correction Technique

Self-correction on a pretest or study test is a research-validated technique that leads to improved learning. Use these steps for the Circle/Dot self-correction technique.

- Spell the word aloud, one letter at a time. Tell students to listen as you call out each letter. Remind them to place a dot below each correct letter, circle each incorrect letter, and draw a circle for a missing letter.

- Tell students to use the circles to see the part of the word that gave them trouble.

- Have students rewrite the word correctly.

The Science of Word Sorting

Word sorting, one of the core instructional strategies in **Spelling Connections,** is a research-based method to develop automatic control of spelling patterns. The activity is based on the fact that the brain learns to do tasks automatically by firing neurons over and over. Sorting words in particular patterns through various sorting options—teacher-led sorts, individual sorts, buddy sorts, speed sorts, and so on—is an effective technique for focusing students' attention on the spelling patterns and on variations among those patterns within the English spelling system. Understanding the similarities and differences between and among words will help students inspect words successfully, internalize the spelling system, and develop into independent spellers.

Types of Word Sorts

Teacher-Led Sorts A teacher-led sort, often following the pretest, is an opportunity for you to teach the pattern, show how the pattern might contrast with another pattern, and model how the word sort is done. Once you point out the patterns highlighted in the unit lesson explicitly, students share in sorting the words under your direction so that they recognize and understand the important pattern elements.

Individual Sorts Students sort words independently for individual practice. Once students have mastered the sort, they should write the sorted words in columns. This aids in learning the pattern and serves as a record of which word sorts a student has mastered.

Buddy Sorts Buddy sorts take advantage of the social context of learning and allow for repetition and practice under highly motivational circumstances. For example, below level spellers might work with above level spellers and benefit from recognizing the pattern and reading the words sorted, even though they may not be able to spell the challenging words. Buddy sorts greatly increase the number of times students engage with the unit pattern.

Speed Sorts Speed sorting leads to automatic recognition and production of the targeted spelling patterns. Students may speed sort individually, trying to improve upon the number of seconds it takes to sort a stack of word cards representing the targeted patterns. They may also compete with buddies or in teams to see who can complete a sort in the shortest time and with the greatest accuracy.

Blind Sorts For a blind word sort, a student reads a word card to a partner, asking the partner to identify in which of the defined spelling pattern categories the word fits. If the partner identifies the correct category, he or she then places the word card in that category.

Open Word Sorts In an open word sort, individuals secretly decide on the criteria for the word sort and then sort the words according to those criteria. The other students attempt to define the criteria after examining the completed word sort.

Multi-Unit Word Sorts Combine word sort cards from two or more units to contrast various patterns. Multi-unit word sorts are useful in the review units.

Word Sorting Three Ways

Word Sort Cards

Hands-On Manipulatives

Students sort individual word cards according to spelling patterns as an individual study activity or in classroom spelling work stations or centers. Large word sort cards are available for Teacher-Led Sorts. Available on CD-ROM.

Interactive Word Sorts

Digital Resources for Spelling Connections

Virtual hands-on word sorts for the whole class. Use to introduce, review, or practice unit spelling patterns.

Spelling Connections Online

Online word sorting games provide fun pattern practice at home or at school.

Spelling Connections Technology

Spelling Connections technology is carefully designed to help you teach important spelling concepts while engaging students in fun, active learning experiences.

Digital Resources for Spelling Connections

Created to be used on any interactive whiteboard or basic computer projection system, **Digital Resources for Spelling Connections** provides integrated support for every unit. These whole-group activities allow you to introduce the spelling concept and invite students to the interactive whiteboard to participate in exciting learning activities.

Choose from games and activities that offer daily support and connect spelling instruction to reading, writing, thinking, and phonics. Students will engage in a variety of game-like interactive word sorts, interactive crossword puzzles, proofreading and sentence completion activities, and spelling bees.

Spelling Connections Online

The same engaging games provided in the digital resources package can also be accessed online by individual students, from school or home. With **Spelling Connections Online,** students log in to play a range of exciting games that develop skills and provide practice for every spelling list, every week. The integrated content management system allows you to log in to view or print reports detailing student progress.

Sound-Symbol Awareness

Two types of cards in Grade 1 **Spelling Connections** help students develop sound-symbol awareness.

Sound/Symbol Cards

A set of 124 **Sound/Symbol Cards** is included in the **Teacher Resource Book.** Duplicate these so that each student has a set of cards. Suggestions for using the Sound/Symbol Cards appear throughout this Teacher Edition.

Alphabet and Picture Cards

The Student Edition includes a set of 26 perforated **Alphabet and Picture Cards** (picture on one side, letter on the reverse). Use these cards with these activities:

Consonants and Vowels Sort Invite students to sort the cards into two piles, consonants and vowels.

What's the Letter? Ask each student to spread the cards letter side up. Say a word and ask students to hold up the card with the letter they hear at the beginning of the word. For example, if you say **hat,** students would hold up **H.** Also use this activity to practice final or medial sounds.

Picture and Sound Match Pair each student with a partner. Ask one student to spread the cards picture side up. Ask the other student to spread his or her cards letter side up. Have students take turns matching a letter to the picture whose name begins with that sound.

Alphabet Recap Ask each student to put the cards in alphabetical order. (Students may use the number in the lower left corner of each card if they need help.) Prompt students to sing "The Alphabet Song" as they look at each letter. Ask each student to randomly pick a card from the pile and identify the letter. For a greater challenge, ask the student to name a word that begins with that letter.

Letters and Names Ask students to spread their cards letter side up. Ask each student, in turn, to stand up and say his or her first name out loud. Invite the class to hold up the card showing the letter that begins the student's name. Ask the "name student" to decide whether the class's response is correct.

Letters and Shapes Ask each student to spread the cards letter side up. Describe a letter's shape. For example, to describe **O** you might say, "I am thinking of a letter that looks like a big circle. What's the letter?" Ask students to hold up the letter. **Note:** Because this activity requires students to picture letters in their minds, it may be challenging.

Word Families Pair each student with a partner. Write common word families (e.g., **-at, -an, -ap, -in, -op,** etc.) on cards. Give one card to each pair of students. Ask students to take turns putting a letter in front of this card and reading the newly formed word out loud. Partners should decide whether the combination they have created is a real word. Have students write a list of the words they create.

Long and Short Vowels Ask each student to spread the cards picture side up and then sort them into three groups:
- picture names with a short vowel sound
- picture names with a long vowel sound
- picture names whose vowel sound is neither clearly long nor short

Can You Spell It? Organize partners. Ask one student to spread the cards picture side up and the other student to display the cards letter side up. Tell students to take turns choosing a picture and using letters from the other pile to spell the picture name. **Note:** The only items that repeat letters within a word are **ball, egg, Jeep, queen, umbrella,** and **zipper.**

Spelling Connections

TEXAS Edition 1

J. Richard Gentry, Ph.D.

ZB **Zaner-Bloser**
The Language Arts and Reading Company

Author

J. Richard Gentry, Ph. D.

Reviewers

Paula Boales, Killeen ISD, Killeen, TX
Sherry Durham, Ed. D., Lufkin ISD, Lufkin, TX
Karyn L. Huskisson, Klein Instructional Center, Spring, TX
Carmen Ramos, San Benito CISD, San Benito, TX
Susan Shogan, Round Rock ISD, Round Rock, TX
Linda Stout, Crawford ISD, Crawford, TX

ELL and Spanish Consultants

Ellen Riojas Clark, Ph.D., Professor, College of Education and Human
 Development, Division of Bicultural-Bilingual Studies, The University of
 Texas at San Antonio, TX
Bertha Pérez, Ed.D., Professor Emeritus of Literacy, College of Education
 and Human Development, The University of Texas at San Antonio, TX
Rocio Reyes-Moore, Spanish Language Productions, Alexandria, OH

ISBN 978-0-7367-6866-5

Copyright © 2012 Zaner-Bloser, Inc.

Zaner-Bloser, Inc., P.O. Box 16764, Columbus, Ohio 43216-6764
1-800-421-3018
www.zaner-bloser.com
Printed in the United States of America   10 11 12 13 14 997 5 4 3 2 1

Certified Chain of Custody
Promoting Sustainable
Forest Management
www.sfiprogram.org

This SFI label applies to the text paper.

Table of Contents

3

4

6

Bonus Pages:
My Spelling Dictionary
My Spelling Dictionary Front Cover
High Frequency Writing Words/
    Manuscript Alphabet Back Cover
Alphabet and Picture Cards

9

Word Sorting

A word sort helps you see how words are the same. The words **hat, sat,** and **mat** go together in a word sort. They all have the letters **at**. Word sorting can help you remember how to spell words.

There are different kinds of word sorts you can use with your spelling words.

- **Individual Sort**—Sort your words by yourself.
- **Buddy Sort**—Sort with a partner.
- **Speed Sorts on Your Own**—Time yourself as you sort your words. Then start over and try to get faster!
- **Speed Sorts With a Team**—See which team can sort the fastest and with the most right answers.

Buddy Sort using the word sort cards

Word sort on an interactive whiteboard

10

Spell Check

When you write on a computer, spell check can help you find spelling mistakes.

If you type **yuo** when you meant to type **you,** then spell check will let you know you made a mistake. It will even ask if you meant to type **you**.

But if you type **sick** and you meant to type **sock,** spell check cannot help. Why? Because **sick** and **sock** are both words, and spell check doesn't know you typed the wrong word.

Spell check helps find misspelled words.

1. **Get** ready for the test. Have your paper and pencil ready.

2. **Listen** to your teacher say the word and use it in a sentence.

3. **Write** the word. Use your best handwriting.

4. **Check** your words with your teacher. Listen to your teacher say the word. Say the word aloud.

5. **Listen** to your teacher spell the word.

6. **Put** a check above each correct letter. Circle a letter that is not correct.

7. **Write** each misspelled word correctly. Say the word. Say each letter out loud.

Planner

Identifying Initial Sounds

Student Objectives
- Compare and contrast initial sounds in words.
- Identify pictures that begin with the initial sound of /t/.

Instruction for All Students
- Identifying Initial Sounds, p. 13

Recognizing Rhyme

Student Objectives
- Listen for word endings that sound the same.
- Identify pictures whose names rhyme.

Instruction for All Students
- Recognizing Rhyme, p. 14

Counting Sounds in Words

Student Objectives
- Segment and identify picture names with two phonemes.

Instruction for All Students
- Counting Sounds in Words, p. 15

Counting Sounds in Words

Student Objectives
- Segment and identify picture names with three phonemes.

Instruction for All Students
- Counting Sounds in Words, p. 16

Unit Materials

Student Edition
pp. 13–16

Teacher Edition
pp. T13A–T16

 Teacher Resource Book
Elkonin Box Practice Master, p. 154
Sound/Symbol Cards

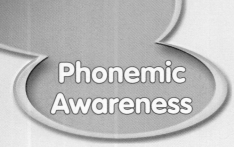

Phonemic Awareness

A Word from the Author on...

SPELLING AND PHONEMIC AWARENESS

J. Richard Gentry, Ph.D.

To become a good speller, a student must learn to segment the sounds in words. For example, he or she must eventually learn that a word like **pig** has three sounds: the sound of /**p**/, the sound of /ĭ/, and the sound of /**g**/. The ability to segment these sounds is called **phonemic awareness**. Phonemic awareness is not only useful in learning how to spell; it is necessary, though not sufficient, for learning how to read. The critical understandings about sounds in words that come with phonemic awareness will help your students become proficient readers and writers.

The first four lessons in Grade 1 *Spelling Connections* focus on the basic elements of phonemic awareness.

- The first lesson (p. 13) asks students to discriminate the initial sound in words.
- The second lesson (p. 14) features recognition of rhyming words, identifying similar ending sounds.
- The third and fourth lessons (pp. 15–16) highlight segmenting, or distinguishing, the sounds in words. (In the word **pig,** for example, phonemic awareness includes the ability to distinguish the /**p**/, /ĭ/, and /**g**/ sounds.)

Students who cannot negotiate these lessons need further work in building phonemic awareness.

Elkonin Boxes
One very effective technique for building phonemic awareness is using Elkonin Boxes. (A reproducible blackline for this purpose is included in the Appendix of the *Teacher Resource Book*.) Elkonin Boxes help students make the auditory discrimination necessary to hear and count the number of sounds in words. Directions for using Elkonin Boxes are included in this Teacher Edition (p. T15).

A Word About Spelling Development
There are five phases in the developmental process of learning to spell: precommunicative, semiphonetic, phonetic, transitional, and conventional (correct). Each student passes through these five developmental phases. As students move through the semiphonetic and phonetic phases, they must develop a robust phonemic awareness. Attention to spelling instruction helps take phonemic awareness one step further to matching those sounds with letters. The **Sounds and Letters** lessons that follow the **Phonemic Awareness** lessons are constructed so that you can facilitate learning and easily monitor this essential connection.

The Science of Spelling ◀ • •

- Developing phonemic awareness is critical to literacy. It is part of a continuum that includes learning letters, matching letters to sounds, and learning phonics—all parts of the process of unlocking the alphabetic principle. The beginning reader/writer will note the sounds in words and think in terms of using one letter for each sound. Eventually, the reader/writer will understand that groups of letters can make one sound. This leads to automatic chunking of spelling patterns and frees the brain to concentrate more on critical thinking and problem-solving.

ELL Support

Choose from the activities below to reinforce English language acquisition.

Beginning

Develop Phonemic Awareness Tell students that you will slowly read a list of words. They should raise their hands when they hear a word with a different initial sound from the previous words. Read three or four words with the same initial sound before switching sounds. For example: **goat, game, get, moon.**

Rhyming Words Say pairs of rhyming words. Have students listen to and repeat the words. Then tell students you will say more pairs of words. Some will rhyme and some will not. Have students say *yes* when they hear a rhyming pair of words and *no* when they hear a pair of words that do not rhyme.

Clapping Game Say the word **lake**. Then say the word again, segmenting the sounds, /l/ /ā/ /k/. Segment the sounds again and have students clap the sounds you say. Ask students how many claps they made. (three) Continue with additional words with two, three, and four sounds. Have students clap each phoneme in a word as you say them. Then have students repeat the sounds and clap again.

Words and Pictures Display Sound/Symbol Cards for **can, cat,** and **rat.** Have students identify the pictures. Hold up the cards again, one at a time, and have students say the names. Ask them to listen to the first sound in each picture name. Have them tell you which picture name does not have the same initial sound as the other two picture names. (rat)

Intermediate

1, 2, 3... Provide each student with a sheet of paper on which are printed the numbers 1, 2, 3, or have students write the numbers 1, 2, 3 on paper. Tell students you will say a sound. Then you will say three words. One of the words will start with the sound. Students will circle the number that corresponds to the word that starts with the sound. For example, say /b/. Have students repeat. Then say **cat, bed, pan.** Repeat the words and then have students say them. Ask students if the first word starts with /b/. (no) Ask if the second word starts with /b/. (yes) Have students circle the number 2 on their papers. Continue with additional sounds and words.

Rhyming Words Review with students that rhyming words have the same ending sounds. Give an example, such as **cat/hat.** Tell students you will say three words. They will listen for the ending sounds and tell you which words rhyme. Say the following groups of words: **ran, can, bat; sand, band, dump; nest, nap, best; take, lane, mane; hop, hit, stop.**

Count the Sounds Say the word **go.** Ask students to tell how many sounds there are in **go.** (two) Then say the word again, this time segmenting and clearly pronouncing each sound. Have students count aloud the sounds they hear. (two) Say additional words for students to guess. For example: **nut** (three), **yolk** (three), **by** (two), **ape** (two), **frame** (four).

Support for Spanish Speakers

Comparing Languages Phonemes in English words may be difficult for Spanish-speaking students, since Spanish has 18 consonant phonemes while English has 26. Both languages have these five vowels: **a, e, i, o, u.** However, English uses an additional eight vowel spellings. In addition, Spanish does not contain the English sounds for **dg, j, sh, th,** and **z.** Provide students with frequent practice listening for and pronouncing these phonemes.

Choose from the activities below to reinforce English language acquisition.

Advanced

Sounds Yes or No Provide each student with two index cards: one printed "yes" and the other "no." Tell students that you will say a word. They are to listen to the beginning sound. Then you will say another word. If the second word has the same beginning sound as the first word, students should hold up the "yes" card. If the second word does not have the same beginning sound, students should hold up the "no" card. Example word pairs: **dig/dog, bed/tent.**

Picture Rhymes Display the Sound/Symbol Card for **hive.** Name the picture and have students repeat it. Say the word again and tell students to listen to the ending sound. Then, one at a time, display the following Sound/Symbol Cards. Have students raise their hands when you show a picture whose name rhymes with **hive.** Display the following cards: **tub, net, dive.** Continue with other cards and words. Suggestions include **house/mouse, fish/dish, box/fox, dog/frog, mop/hop.**

How Many Sounds? Tell students you will say two words. Have them listen carefully to the number of sounds in each word and then tell you which word has the greatest number of sounds. For example, pronounce each sound as you say **can** and **do.** Students should identify **can** (3) as having more sounds than **do** (2). Continue with additional words. As students improve, do less segmentation when you pronounce the words.

Advanced High

Sound Sort Provide pairs of students with the Sound/Symbol Cards for **fox, fish, jet, jacket, mop, mouse, nail, net, web, window, bed, bird, dog, dish, goat, goose, leg,** and **lock.** Have students mix the cards. Then have partners work together to sort and pair pictures whose names start with the same sound. Provide assistance as necessary to identify a picture.

Listen Quick Give students a sound, such as /**m**/. Tell students you will read a list of words. For each word they hear that begins with the /**m**/ sound, have them make a mark on their paper. At a moderate pace, say **rose, skate, mop, yarn, zoo, bear, box, mom, mitten, toast, man, cub, fish, dog, apple, cat, mail, moon, move, sheep, bee, pie.** Students should have seven marks on their papers when you finish reading the list. Continue with other target sounds and lists.

Short and Long Words Display the Sound/Symbol Cards for **zero, six, wagon,** and **egg.** Point to and say the name of each picture. Call on a volunteer to put the pictures in order according to the number of sounds in the word. (**egg, six, zero, wagon**) Segment the sounds in the words to check the order. Continue with additional sets of cards.

Phonemic Awareness

Identifying Initial Sounds

Say the name of this picture: .
Circle the pictures that start with the same sound.

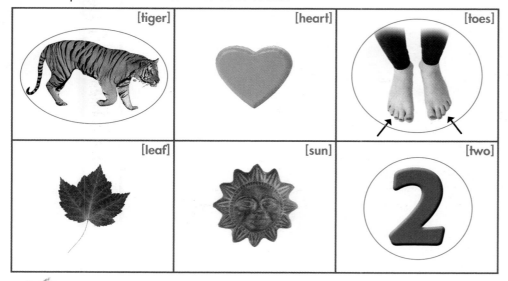

[tiger] [heart] [toes]

[leaf] [sun] [two]

School Home Help your child name other words that start like **tent**.

13

Student Objectives
- Compare and contrast initial sounds in words.
- Identify pictures that begin with the initial sound of /t/.

Teaching Tips
- Display the Sound/Symbol Card for **mop**. Have students identify the picture.
- Ask students to say the word **mop** and listen for the beginning sound. Have students say the /**m**/ sound separately.
- Display the Sound/Symbol Card for **mouse**. Have students identify the picture. Ask if the word **mouse** begins with the same sound as **mop**. (yes) Have students say both words, emphasizing the initial sound.
- Display the Sound/Symbol Card for **pie**. Follow the same procedure, asking if the word **pie** begins with the same sound as **mop** and **mouse**. (no) Have students say all three words, emphasizing the initial sound in each word.
- Repeat with the Sound/Symbol Cards for **top, ten,** and **bat**.
- Work with students to complete page 13. Say the word **tent** and ask if the word **tiger** has the same beginning sound. Follow the same procedure throughout the page. If a student hears the same sound at the end of the word **heart,** point out that the /**t**/ sound can be heard at the beginning and end of words.

Matching Words

Play a game of Duck, Duck, Goose with students. Explain that you will say three words. Students should listen for the word that does not match. Say, *duck, duck, goose*. Have students tell you which word does not match. (goose) Then have students sit in a circle. Demonstrate how to play the game. Pat each student on the shoulder in turn and say **duck**. For one student, say **goose**. Have that student stand and try to tag you before you can walk around the circle and sit in the student's place. Change the activity by using additional animal names, such as **dog, dog, cat** and **fish, fish, bear**.

Student Objectives
- Listen for word endings that sound the same.
- Identify pictures whose names rhyme.

Teaching Tips
- Display the Sound/Symbol Card for **cat**. Have students identify the picture.
- Say **cat,** segmenting the initial sound from the rest of the word, **/k/ /ă/ /t/.** Have students repeat. Then say **at** and have students listen to the sound.
- Tell students that words rhyme when they have the same ending sound. Say **cat** again. Then say **sat.** Explain that **cat** and **sat** have the same ending sound, **at.**
- Work with students to complete page 14. Say **cat.** Then point to the picture of the car. Have students identify the picture. Ask if **cat** and **car** rhyme or have the same ending sound. **(no)** Do the same with **bat.** **(yes)** Model circling the picture of the bat to show that the picture name rhymes with **cat.**
- Continue with the remaining pictures.

Recognizing Rhyme

Say the name of this picture: .

Say the name of each picture below. Circle the pictures that rhyme with **cat**.

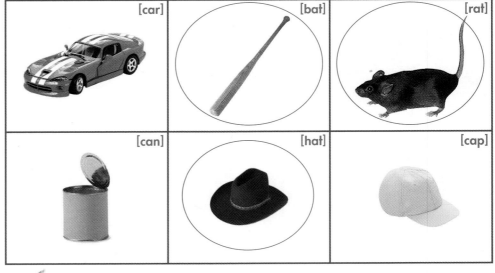

[car] [bat] [rat]

[can] [hat] [cap]

School Home Help your child name other words that rhyme with **cat**.

14

Rhyming Words
Have students work in groups of three. Give each group a set of five Sound/Symbol Cards. Possibilities for sets include **six, sled, zipper, quarter, bed; zoo, yarn, frog, quilt, dog; bird, acorn, dish, fish, rose; apple, kangaroo, lock, frame, game;** and **shave, dig, house, cave, hammer.** Help students identify the pictures as needed. Have each group find the two picture names that rhyme in each set of cards. **(sled, bed; frog, dog; dish, fish; frame, game; shave, cave)** Then ask students to trade their set of cards with another group and then find the rhyming words in the new set of cards. Have students continue trading until they have worked with all the sets of cards.

Phonemic Awareness

Counting Sounds in Words

Say the name of this picture: 🐝 . **Bee** has two sounds.

Say the first sound in **bee**. Say the second sound in **bee**.

Say the name of this picture: 🫘 . **Bean** has three sounds.

Circle the picture in each pair that has two sounds.

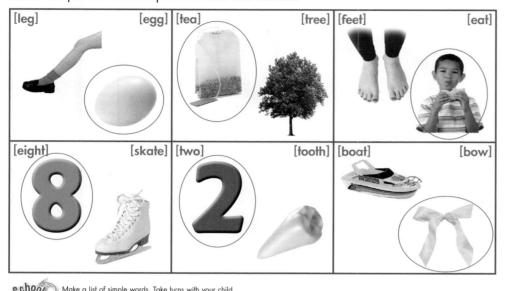

Make a list of simple words. Take turns with your child. One of you says a word, and one of you tells the number of sounds in the word.

15

Student Objectives
• Segment and identify picture names with two phonemes.

Teaching Tips
• Say and segment the word **bee** into individual sounds, /b/ /ē/. Then say /b/ again and have students repeat. Do the same with /ē/. Ask students how many sounds they hear in **bee**. (two)
• Follow the same procedure with the word **bean**. Have students say and identify the three sounds in **bean**.
• Model completing the first item. Have students name the first picture. Say and segment **leg**, /l/ /ĕ/ /g/, and have students repeat. Ask how many sounds they heard. (three) Have students name the second picture. Say and segment **egg**, /ĕ/ /g/, and have students repeat. Ask how many sounds they heard. (two) Demonstrate circling the egg picture.
• Identify the remaining pictures, and have students circle the picture in each pair that has two sounds.

Elkonin Box Practice Master

TRB, p. 154

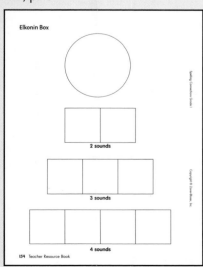

Using Elkonin Boxes

Give each student a copy of the Elkonin Box Practice Master and three markers, such as buttons. Point to the first picture on page 15. Ask students to listen as you say the word **leg**. Slowly say /l/ /ĕ/ /g/. Explain that **leg** has three sounds. Then say, *How many sounds do you hear in the word feet?* /f/ /ē/ /t/ (three) *That's right. Three sounds.* Have students find the row of three squares on their paper. Direct them to put a marker in the box that shows where they hear /f/ in **feet**. Do the same with /ē/ and /t/. Have students practice by saying the names of other pictures on page 15 and using markers to show how many sounds they hear in each word.

Student Objectives
• Segment and identify picture names with three phonemes.

Teaching Tips
• Review with students the procedure they used to identify the number of sounds in a word. Say **bag**. Then segment **bag**, /b/ /ă/ /g/. Have students repeat. Ask them how many sounds they heard. **(three)**
• Model the first item on page 16. Ask students to identify the picture. **(cake)** Then segment the word **cake**, /k/ /ā/ /k/. Have students repeat. Ask them how many sounds they heard. **(three)** Demonstrate how to circle the picture to show that the picture name **cake** has three sounds.
• Work through the third item. Explain to students that they will not circle the picture of the nest because the word **nest** has four sounds.
• Identify the remaining pictures as needed. Provide copies of the Elkonin Box Practice Master and markers to help students count sounds.

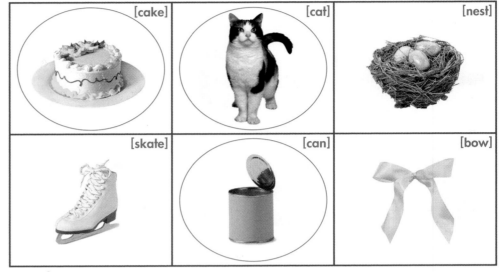

Phonemic Awareness

Counting Sounds in Words

Say: ▯ **bag**. Say the first sound in **bag**. Say the second sound in **bag**. Say the third sound in **bag**. **Bag** has three sounds. Say the name of each picture. Circle the pictures with names that have three sounds.

[cake] [cat] [nest]

[skate] [can] [bow]

School Home Play a game with your child. Take turns. One of you says a word with only two or three sounds, and the other tells the number of sounds in the word.

16

Practice Counting Sounds
Hold up the following Sound/Symbol Cards one at a time: **up, pie, mop, nut, wood, yo-yo,** and **last**. For each card, have students say the word that names the picture. Then have students say the individual sounds they hear in the picture name. Help them to isolate the sounds one by one and in order. Then work with students to count the number of sounds they hear in each word. If needed, draw Elkonin Boxes on the board and place a mark in or shade each box as students identify each sound.

Recognizing Consonant Sounds

Student Objectives
- Identify pictures whose names begin with a given consonant sound.
- Identify pictures whose names end with the consonant sound **x /ks/**.
- Write the consonant that represents the initial sound to complete words.
- Write the upper- and lowercase forms of consonant letters **b, c, d, f, g, h, j, k, l, m, n, p, q, r, s, t, v, w,** and **y.**

Instruction for All Students
- Recognizing Consonant Sounds, pp. 17–37

 TEKS 1.22A

Recognizing Initial Vowel Sounds

Student Objectives
- Identify pictures whose names begin with a given short vowel sound.
- Write the vowel that represents the initial sound to complete words.
- Write the upper- and lowercase forms of vowel letters **a, e, i, o, u.**

Instruction for All Students
- Recognizing Initial Vowel Sounds, pp. 38–42

 TEKS 1.22A

Unit Materials

Student Edition
pp. 17–42

Teacher Edition
pp. T17A–T42

 Teacher Resource Book
Sound/Symbol Cards

 Word Sort CD-ROM
Grade 1

 Digital Resources for Spelling Connections
Sounds and Letters

 Spelling Connections Online
www.spellingconnectionsonline.com

Learning Styles

Visual Learners
Divide the class into two teams. Use three sets of Alphabet and Picture Cards from the back of the Student Edition. Give a letter to each student on Team A and the same letters to the students on Team B. Keep a set of the same letters for yourself. Hold up a letter and ask students who have the same letter to stand beside you. As an alternative, have students hold up their letters when they see the one you display. The team who responds the quickest scores a point.

Auditory Learners
Write the targeted letter on the board. Say its sound in an exaggerated way, such as /**bbbbbbbb**/. Ask students to repeat the sound. Then say three sounds, drawing whenever possible from sounds that have already been taught. Have students clap when they hear the sound named by the letter written on the board.

Kinesthetic Learners
As you introduce each letter, model it on the board, writing both uppercase and lowercase forms. Have students "trace" both forms in the air. Then write both forms of the targeted letter in several more places on the board. Invite students to take turns coming up and tracing the letters with their fingers.

Providing More Help

Help students begin each page (17–42) by identifying the first picture with them. For example, on page 17, help students identify the picture of the bee. As you do so, exaggerate the initial targeted sound in the picture name. Ask students to repeat it. Invite students to identify the next picture and say the sound they hear at the beginning of its name. Ask students whether it is the same sound as in the first picture. As needed, identify the sound, exaggerate it, and have students repeat it. Ask students to draw a line from each picture to its name after they have written the initial letter to complete the spelling.

When students get to page 42, explain that the sound they will listen for, /**ks**/, is not at the beginning of each word, but at the end.

Language and Cultural Differences

Some sounds may present difficulties for students who do not easily hear or pronounce them because of regional speech differences or first-language backgrounds that do not include this sound. For example, some regional dialects make no distinction between the **short e** and **short i** sounds. In general, English language learners may need extra practice with consonant blends, such as **st** in **nest**.

Provide ample time for students to practice unfamiliar sounds in a friendly environment. Students might do this in small groups or one-on-one with you or a classroom assistant. If possible, help students learn jokes, riddles, or songs that contain the targeted sounds.

Some pictures, and the concepts they name, may be unrecognizable to students. These may include the bicycle horn on page 22, which may be something some students do not have; the quilt on page 29, which may be referred to by a different name in their own homes; or the bottle of ink on page 40, which may not be part of their experience with ink. Help students identify these picture names and make links between what they already know and the new concept presented on the page.

ELL Support

Choose from the activities below to reinforce English language acquisition.

Beginning

Marking Pages Make sure that students have the vocabulary to understand the directions that tell them how to mark the pages. Demonstrate each marking method on the board or on an overhead projector. Say each direction as you show the action. Markings to demonstrate include circle, color, underline, and draw a box. Have students copy your actions on paper.

Pick a Letter Provide students with writing paper and a set of letters written on index cards. Have students mix the cards and then select one. Direct them to write both uppercase and lowercase forms on their paper. Have students continue until they have written several letters. Suggest they save the cards they have not looked at so they can continue their writing practice at a later time.

I Am Letters Give each student a strip of card stock and have them print their first name on it. Remind them to write the first letter as an uppercase or capital letter. Then ask students to spell their names and say the whole name.

Label Objects Brainstorm with students the names of classroom objects that do not begin with blends or digraphs. Possibilities include **pen, book, desk, computer, window, door**. Say each name, emphasizing the beginning sound. Have students write the letter that makes the beginning sound on a sticky note and label the object with the letter.

Intermediate

What's the Letter? Provide students with writing paper. Say a letter and have students write it on their papers. Continue saying letters at random. After students have written several letters, slowly say the letters again so that students can check their papers. As an alternative, have students write both the uppercase and lowercase forms of each letter.

Sound to Letter Say a word (no beginning blends or digraphs), emphasizing the beginning sound. For example, say **mop** as **mmmop**. Have students repeat. Then have them write the lowercase letter that makes the beginning sound. Ask students to say the sound of the letter they wrote. Continue with several words and letters.

Letter Bingo Prepare 4 x 4 Bingo cards with lowercase letters placed at random in the spaces on each card. Provide students with card stock markers to cover the spaces. Say a letter. If students have that letter on their card, they cover it with a marker. The first students to cover all the letters in a straight line — vertically, horizontally, or diagonally — yells *Bingo*. As students become more proficient, prepare cards that have both lowercase and uppercase letters. When you call out a letter, say *big* or *little* before naming the letter.

Support for Spanish Speakers

Comparing Languages Both English and Spanish use the same alphabet. However, some students may need help associating an unfamiliar sound to letters they already know. For example, **h** is silent in Spanish and **v** is pronounced like **b**.

Students also may have difficulty pronouncing words that contain **w** since this letter is not used in Spanish words. These students may also have difficulty with the /**sh**/ and /**th**/ sounds.

Choose from the activities below to reinforce English language acquisition.

Advanced

Begin With a Letter Have students punch out the Alphabet Picture Cards in the back of their books. Invite them to find a partner. Have students select a picture and show it to their partner without revealing the letters on the back. The partner names the picture and writes the letter that makes the initial sound of the picture name. The card is then turned over for the partner to check the letter. Encourage students to continue until they have written several letters. Assist with photo identification if needed.

Big or Little Have students work with a partner to alternately call out letters at random for their partner to write. As they call out a letter, have students also say *big* or *little* to tell whether to write an uppercase or lowercase letter.

Concentration Write each letter on two index cards. Start with both cards for a group of consonants. Arrange the cards facedown in an array. Have partners alternate turning over two cards. If the cards show the same letters, the student keeps the cards. If they do not, the cards are turned back over. Provide students with another set of letters when they finish matching the first set. As students become more proficient at identifying matches, add more letters to the array. As an alternate activity, print the two index cards with a lowercase letter on one card and an uppercase letter on the second card.

Advanced High

At the End In the Sounds and Letters unit, **x** is the only final sound. Provide practice in discriminating this sound and matching the sound to the letter. Give each student an index card and have them write a large **X** on it. Model writing the letter on the board if needed. Then say the following sets of words: **web, cat, fox; pot, mix, sock; tax, kite, bed; car, sun, six**. Have students listen to the final sound in each word and hold up their cards when they hear the /**ks**/ sound. Then write **fox, mix, tax,** and **six** on the board, leaving off the final **x**. Call on volunteers to write **x** at the end of the words.

Teacher Says Check that students can follow directions by preparing a grid of pictures and giving each student a copy. Call out directions for marking the pictures. For example, say, *Draw an X on the car, circle the leaf, underline the rake, and draw a box around the apple.* Note any students who have difficulty understanding any of the vocabulary. Model for them the different actions as you say the directions again.

The First Sound and Letter To help students discriminate initial vowel sounds and match the sounds to letters, say a word such as **ant**. Have students repeat. Then say, /ă/, /ă/, /ă/, /ă/, **ant** and have students repeat. Then say, *Write the letter that spells /ă/ in ant.* Continue with the remaining vowels and the words **elf, ink, off,** and **up**.

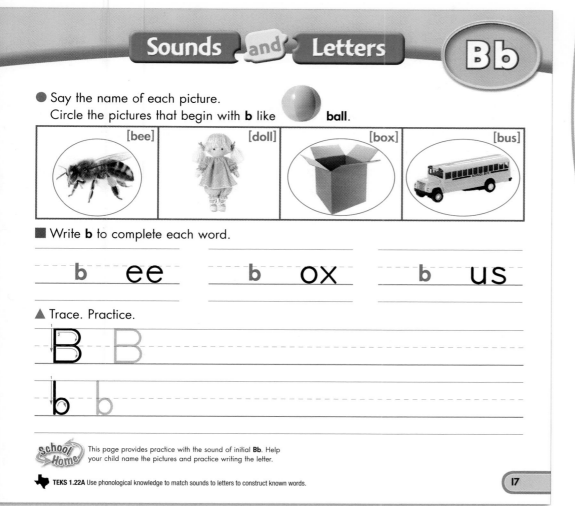

- Say the name of each picture.
  Circle the pictures that begin with **b** like **ball**.

| [bee] | [doll] | [box] | [bus] |

■ Write **b** to complete each word.

b ee   b ox   b us

▲ Trace. Practice.

B B

b b

School Home
This page provides practice with the sound of initial **Bb**. Help your child name the pictures and practice writing the letter.

TEKS 1.22A Use phonological knowledge to match sounds to letters to construct known words.

17

Sounds and Letters Bb

Student Objectives
- Identify the /b/ sound spelled **b**.
- Write initial **b** to spell words.
- Practice writing uppercase **B** and lowercase **b**.

Teaching Tips
- Model sorting for /b/ with the Sound/ Symbol Cards for **bag, open, bird,** and **bed**. As you hold up each card, slowly say the word that names the picture. Then say /b/. Ask students if any of the words you just named begin with the /b/ sound.
- Slowly repeat **bag, bird,** and **bed**. Emphasize the /b/ sound. Ask students to repeat /b/ and the word.
- Write **B** on the board. Tell students that this is a capital **B**. Explain that the letter **B** makes the /b/ sound. Do the same with lowercase **b**.
- Write **at** on the board. Then write **b** to the left of **at**. Explain that **b-a-t** spells **bat**. Say the word, emphasizing /b/. Have students repeat.
- Have students complete page 17.

Optional Letter Chant

Teach students the following chants to say as they practice writing the letters **B** and **b**. Model writing the letters as you say the chant.

Uppercase B
Pull down straight. Lift. Slide right.
Curve forward right, then slide left.
Don't stop now, there's more to do yet.
Slide right. Curve right. Now slide left.
When you look back,
B seems easy, I'll bet!

Lowercase b
Pull down straight.
Push up without a sound.
Now circle right.
Go all the way around.
Keep that bottom
Very close to the ground.

TEKS 1.22A Use phonological knowledge to match sounds to letters to construct known words.

T17

 **Sounds and Letters**

Student Objectives
- Identify the /k/ sound spelled **c**.
- Write initial **c** to spell words.
- Practice writing uppercase **C** and lowercase **c**.

Teaching Tips
- Display the Sound/Symbol Cards for **cab, fox, echo, calf, sun, stream,** and **cub**. Help students identify each picture.
- Hold up the cards again one by one. Ask students to clap or raise their hand when they see something that begins with /k/. When students are correct, say the word, such as **calf,** and then say the initial sound, /k/.
- Say **cab,** /k/. Have students say the word and the initial sound. Write **c** on the board. Tell students that **c** makes the /k/ sound at the beginning of **cab**. Explain that the letter is a lowercase or small **c**.
- Write **C** on the board. Tell students that this is a capital or big **C**. Explain that the capital **C** also makes the /k/ sound.
- Help students do the first item on page 18. Then have them complete the page.

Optional Letter Chant

Teach students the following chants to say as they practice writing the letters **C** and **c**. Model writing the letters as you say the chant.

Uppercase C and Lowercase c
Circle back left,
That's all you do
To write uppercase **C**
And lowercase **c**, too.

Find the C
Display an alphabet chart. Say **cup, cub, car**. Ask a volunteer to point to the letter on the chart that stands for the initial sound of **cup, cub,** and **car**.

Sounds and Letters  Dd

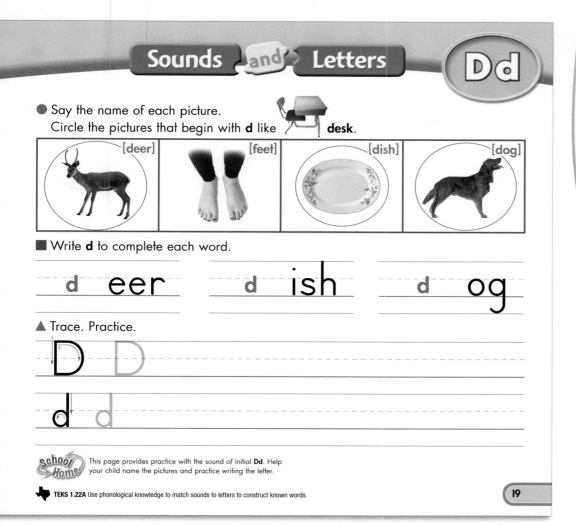

● Say the name of each picture.
Circle the pictures that begin with **d** like 🪑 **desk**.

| [deer] | [feet] | [dish] | [dog] |

■ Write **d** to complete each word.

d eer   **d** ish   **d** og

▲ Trace. Practice.

D D D

d d

School Home This page provides practice with the sound of initial **Dd**. Help your child name the pictures and practice writing the letter.

TEKS 1.22A Use phonological knowledge to match sounds to letters to construct known words.

19

Sounds and Letters Dd

Student Objectives
- Identify the /d/ sound spelled **d**.
- Write initial **d** to spell words.
- Practice writing uppercase **D** and lowercase **d**.

Teaching Tips
- Display the Sound/Symbol Cards for **bag, box, cave, dog, dive,** and **dish.** Help students identify and say the name of each picture as needed. Then have students sort the cards into two groups: pictures with names that begin with the /d/ sound and pictures with names that don't.
- Say **dog,** /d/. Have students repeat the word and the initial sound. Write **d** on the board. Tell students that **d** makes the /d/ sound at the beginning of **dog.**
- Write **D** next to **d** on the board. Point to each letter and identify it as lowercase or small **d,** or capital or big **d.** Explain that both letters make the /d/ sound. If any students' names begin with **D,** write the name on the board and underline the capital **D.**
- Help students do the first item on page 19. Then have them complete the page.

Optional Letter Chant
Teach students the following chants to say as they practice writing the letters **D** and **d.** Model writing the letters as you say the chant.

Uppercase D
Pull down straight.
Then lift, and off we go.
Slide right. Curve right. Slide left.
For uppercase **D**
That's all you need to know!

Lowercase d
Circle back left, all the way around.
Keep that bottom close to the ground.
Push up straight. Pull down straight, too.
No one writes lowercase **d**
Better than you!

TEKS 1.22A Use phonological knowledge to match sounds to letters to construct known words.

T19

Ff Sounds and Letters

Student Objectives
- Identify the /f/ sound spelled f.
- Write initial f to spell words.
- Practice writing uppercase F and lowercase f.

Teaching Tips
- Arrange the following Sound/Symbol Cards in the shape of a fan: **kite, fall, jet, tooth, food, fish, tire,** and **fox.** Ask volunteers to choose a card, name the picture, and say whether the picture name begins with the /f/ sound. Display the cards for **fall, food, fish,** and **fox.** Have students say the picture names aloud, emphasizing initial /f/.
- Write **f** on the board. Tell students that this letter makes the /f/ sound they heard at the beginning of the words **fall, food, fish,** and **fox.**
- Write **F** next to **f.** Identify each letter as lowercase or uppercase. Explain that both letters make the /f/ sound.
- Write **fish** on the board. Ask a volunteer to circle **f.** Have students say **fish.**
- Help students do the first item on page 20. Then have them complete the page.

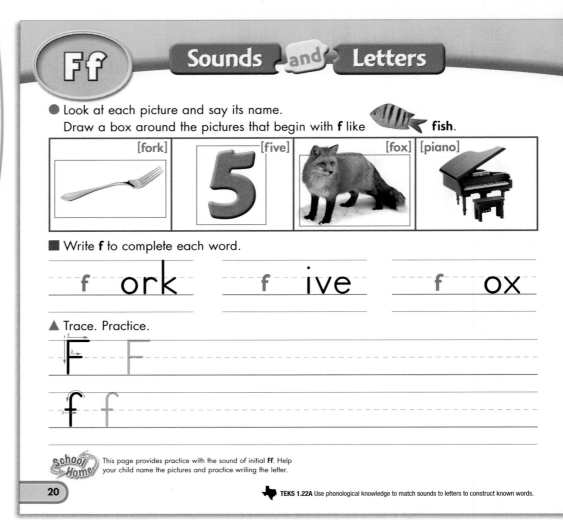

Optional Letter Chant
Teach students the following chants to say as they practice writing the letters F and f. Model writing the letters as you say the chant.

Uppercase F
Pull down straight—that's how to begin.
Lift. Slide right. Lift and slide right again.
Write uppercase **F** in green, blue, or red.
Now write friendly letters to Franny and Fred.

Lowercase f
Curve back left;
Pull down straight.
Left and slide right;
Your **f** should be great!

Picture F
Brainstorm with students things that start with the /f/ sound. Examples may be **fox, five, fork, fish, face, family, frog, flower,** and **flag.** Give students flags cut from construction paper. Have them draw a picture of something that starts with /f/ on their flags. Then have them write **Ff** under the picture.

 TEKS 1.22A Use phonological knowledge to match sounds to letters to construct known words.

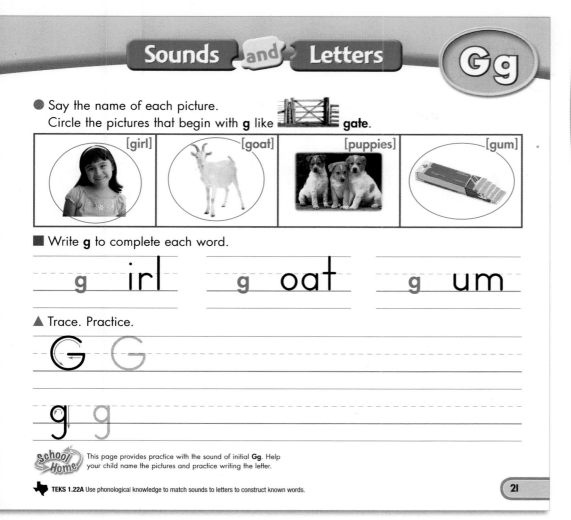

Sounds and Letters

● Say the name of each picture.
  Circle the pictures that begin with **g** like [gate image] **gate**.

| [girl] | [goat] | [puppies] | [gum] |

■ Write **g** to complete each word.

g irl   g oat   g um

▲ Trace. Practice.

G G

g g

School Home This page provides practice with the sound of initial **Gg**. Help your child name the pictures and practice writing the letter.

TEKS 1.22A Use phonological knowledge to match sounds to letters to construct known words.

21

Student Objectives
- Identify the /g/ sound spelled **g**.
- Write initial **g** to spell words.
- Practice writing uppercase **G** and lowercase **g**.

Teaching Tips
- Write **g** on the board. Say the word **gate** and repeat the initial /g/ sound as you point to the letter. Then write **d** on the board. Review the /d/ sound with students.
- Display the Sound/Symbol Cards for **goat, dive, golf, goose, game, dog, dish,** and **dig**. Hold up each card and help students name the picture. Then tell students to listen for the beginning sound of each picture name as you say the words. Call on volunteers to place the cards on the board under the correct letter.
- Write **G** next to **g** on the board. Identify each letter as lowercase or uppercase. Explain that both letters make the /g/ sound.
- Help students do the first item on page 21. Then have them complete the page.

Optional Letter Chant
Teach students the following chants to say as they practice writing the letters **G** and **g**. Model writing the letters as you say the chant.

Uppercase G
Circle back left.
Slide left. Can you see?
Now you can make
Uppercase **G**.

Lowercase g
Circle back left, all the way around.
Keep that bottom down to the ground.
Push up straight. Pull down the same.
Curve back left. Keep your strokes loose.
With this little **g** you can write **goose**.

TEKS 1.22A Use phonological knowledge to match sounds to letters to construct known words.

T21

Student Objectives
- Identify the /h/ sound spelled **h**.
- Write initial **h** to spell words.
- Practice writing uppercase **H** and lowercase **h**.

Teaching Tips
- Have four students hold the following Sound/Symbol Cards in front of the class: **hop, hammer, stick,** and **hive.** Help students name each picture. Tell them to listen for words that begin with the **/h/** sound as you say the words again. Ask them which student has a picture whose name does not begin with the **/h/** sound. Have that student sit down.
- Give a new group of students these cards: **house, Jeep, last,** and **nest.** Repeat the same process. Only the student with the **house** should be left standing.
- Write **H** and **h** on the board. Identify the letters and tell students that both letters make the **/h/** sound. Demonstrate how to write each letter.
- Help students do the first item on page 22. Then have them complete the page.

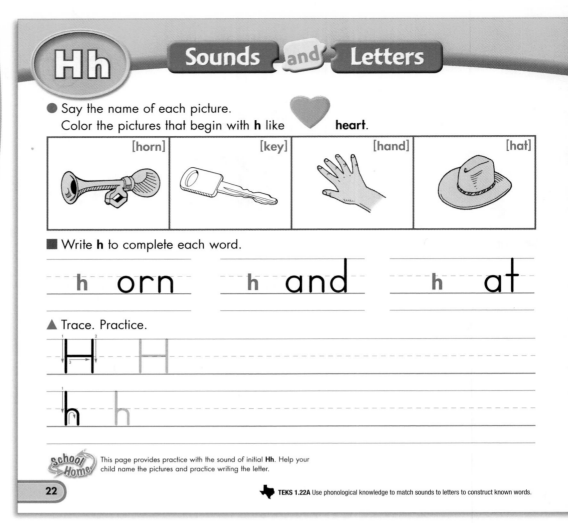

Optional Letter Chant
Teach students the following chants to say as they practice writing the letters **H** and **h**. Model writing the letters as you say the chant.

Uppercase H
Pull down straight
Not once but twice.
Slide in the middle
And **H** will look nice.

Lowercase h
Pull down straight.
Push up, and hold steady.
Curve right. Pull down straight,
And your **h** will be ready.

Hey, It's H
Have students sit in a circle. Give one student a pocket mirror. Have the student hold the mirror in front of his or her mouth and say, "Hey!" Point out how the mirror fogs briefly when the **/h/** sound is pronounced correctly. Pass the mirror around the circle and have each student say "Hey!" at the mirror. Then pass the mirror again. This time have students say another word that begins with **/h/**.

 TEKS 1.22A Use phonological knowledge to match sounds to letters to construct known words.

Sounds and Letters — Jj

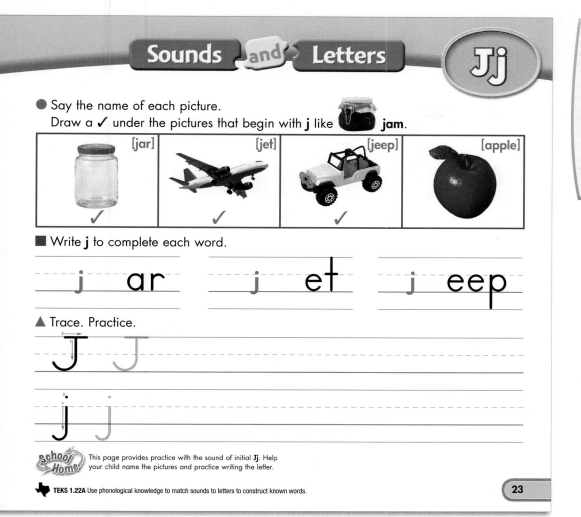

● Say the name of each picture.
Draw a ✓ under the pictures that begin with **j** like **jam**.

[jar]	[jet]	[jeep]	[apple]
✓	✓	✓	

■ Write **j** to complete each word.

j ar   j et   j eep

▲ Trace. Practice.

J J

j j

School Home
This page provides practice with the sound of initial **Jj**. Help your child name the pictures and practice writing the letter.

TEKS 1.22A Use phonological knowledge to match sounds to letters to construct known words.

23

Sounds and Letters — Jj

Student Objectives
- Identify the /j/ sound spelled **j**.
- Write initial **j** to spell words.
- Practice writing uppercase **J** and lowercase **j**.

Teaching Tips
- Ask the class to stand up. Show students these Sound/Symbol Cards: **open, ape, jacket, jar, spider, jet, unicorn,** and **Jeep**. Say the word that names each picture. Then hold up one card at a time and ask students to jump up when they see a picture whose name begins with the /j/ sound. After each correct identification, write **j** on the board.
- Write **J** next to **j** on the board. Name the letters and tell students that both letters make the /j/ sound they hear at the beginning of **jar**. Demonstrate how to write each letter.
- Help students do the first item on page 23. Then have them complete the page.
- Note that **Jeep** begins with a capital letter because it is a proper noun. The answer **jeep** should also be acceptable.

Optional Letter Chant

Teach students the following chants to say as they practice writing the letters **J** and **j**. Model writing the letters as you say the chant.

Uppercase J
Pull down straight.
Then left curve back.
Do you know the rhyme
About young Jack?
Lift. Slide right.
He went up a hill
To fetch some water
With his friend Jill.

Lowercase j
Pull down straight.
Curve back left.
Lift but don't quit.
Your **j**'s not done yet.
Finished it's not
Because you've still got
To put on a dot
Like a jaguar's spot.

TEKS 1.22A Use phonological knowledge to match sounds to letters to construct known words.

Kk Sounds and Letters

Student Objectives
- Identify the /k/ sound spelled **k**.
- Write initial **k** to spell words.
- Practice writing uppercase **K** and lowercase **k**.

Teaching Tips
- Say the word **kitten,** emphasizing the initial /k/ sound. Then display the following Sound/Symbol Cards: **kite, ax, kiss, eagle, kangaroo, kick,** and **mop.** Ask students to name each picture. Assist where necessary. Call on volunteers to take down the pictures that do not begin with the /k/ sound. Then have students say the names again of the cards that are left.
- Write **K** and **k** on the board. Point out that **K** is the capital or big letter and **k** is the lowercase or small letter. Tell students that both letters make the /k/ sound they hear at the beginning of **kitten.** Demonstrate how to write each letter.
- Help students do the first item on page 24. Then have them complete the page.

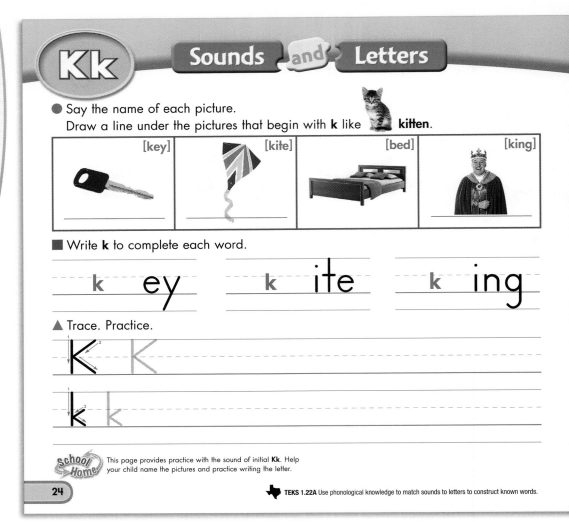

Optional Letter Chant
Teach students the following chants to say as they practice writing the letters **K** and **k.** Model writing the letters as you say the chant.

Uppercase K
Pull down straight.
Lift. Let's go!
Slant left. Slant right.
It's big **K**, you know.

Lowercase k
Follow those steps
To make small **k**, too.
Soon you'll write words
Like **king** and **kangaroo.**

K Hunt
Invite students to go on a **K** hunt. Before students come to class, place pictures of objects around the room. You can use the Sound/Symbol Cards for **kangaroo, kick, kiss,** and **kite.** Also place pictures whose names do not begin with the /k/ sound. Tell students that when you say *go,* they should hunt for **K** pictures in the room. Students who successfully bring a **K** picture to the front of the room and name the picture will score a point.

 TEKS 1.22A Use phonological knowledge to match sounds to letters to construct known words.

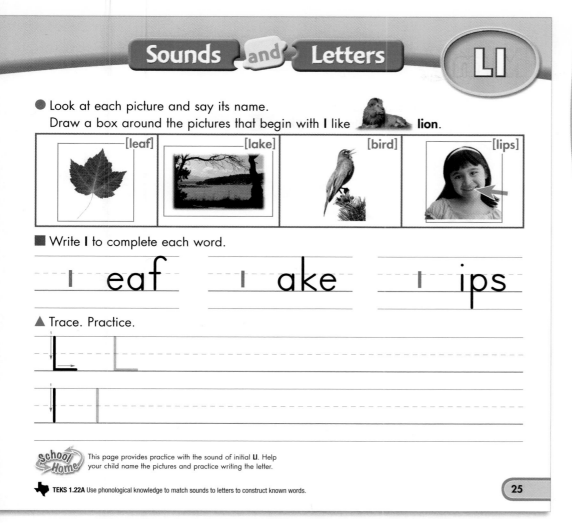

- Look at each picture and say its name.
Draw a box around the pictures that begin with **l** like 🦁 **lion**.

[leaf]   [lake]   [bird]   [lips]

■ Write **l** to complete each word.

l eaf   l ake   l ips

▲ Trace. Practice.

School Home This page provides practice with the sound of initial **Ll**. Help your child name the pictures and practice writing the letter.

TEKS 1.22A Use phonological knowledge to match sounds to letters to construct known words.

25

Student Objectives
- Identify the /l/ sound spelled l.
- Write initial l to spell words.
- Practice writing uppercase **L** and lowercase l.

Teaching Tips
- Give pairs of students the following Sound/Symbol Cards: **ostrich, path, lock, leg, moth, laugh, goat,** and **last.** Ask partners to work together to identify the word that names each picture. If necessary, guide students to the correct word. Then have pairs identify on the four cards with pictures whose names begin with the /l/ sound.
- Write **L** and l on the board. Have student pairs use their cards to make the shape of an uppercase **L** and then a lowercase l.
- Point out that **L** is the capital or big letter, and l is the small letter. Tell students that both letters make the /l/ sound they hear at the beginning of **late.** Demonstrate how to write each letter.
- Help students do the first item on page 25. Then have them complete the page.

Optional Letter Chant
Teach students the following chants to say as they practice writing the letters **L** and l. Model writing the letters as you say the chant.

Uppercase L
Pull down straight.
Slide right well.
That's how you write
Uppercase L!

Lowercase l
Pull down straight,
Like a rope down a well.
That's all it takes
To write lowercase l.

L and Not L
Write **Ll** on two index cards. Draw a red line through one of the cards and explain to students that this means "not L." Tape each index card to a box. Have students draw pictures or write words, including people's names that begin with **L** and with letters they have learned so far. Have them place their pictures and words in the appropriate box. Some examples of L pictures are **lion, ladder, leaf, lollipop, lamp, lake,** and **leg.** Review the pictures/words in each box with the class.

TEKS 1.22A Use phonological knowledge to match sounds to letters to construct known words.

T25

Mm Sounds and Letters

Student Objectives
- Identify the /m/ sound spelled **m**.
- Write initial **m** to spell words.
- Practice writing uppercase **M** and lowercase **m**.

Teaching Tips
- Display the following Sound/Symbol Cards: **mitten, old, paint, rash, moth, mouse,** and **hive**. Help students name each picture. Then say **moon, mmmmmm**. Ask volunteers to come forward and point to a picture whose name begins with the /**m**/ sound. Each time a student is correct, say, *Marvelous!* or *¡Muy bien!*
- Model writing **M** and **m** on the board. Point to and identify each letter. Tell students that both letters make the /**m**/ sound they hear at the beginning of **moon**. If any students' names begin with **M**, invite them to write their name on the board.
- Help students do the first item on page 26. Then have them complete the page.

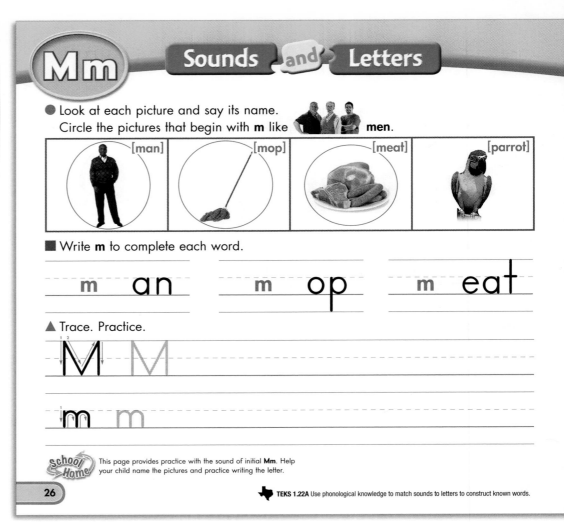

Optional Letter Chant
Teach students the following chants to say as they practice writing the letters **M** and **m**. Model writing the letters as you say the chant.

Uppercase M
Pull down straight. Lift. Slant right.
Slant up, and pull down.
If you write your ups and downs
Smooth and light,
Then uppercase **M**
Is sure to be right!

Lowercase m
Pull down straight. Push up. Curve right.
Pull down straight. Push up. Curve right.
Pull down straight.
You've reached the end
Of the steps it takes to make lowercase **m**.

M Animals
Provide large paper plates for making masks. Say animal names that start with **m**. Show pictures if available. Have students choose an animal to draw on their plate. Cut eyeholes and attach string or yarn to tie the masks. Then have an animal march. Have each student say his or her animal name. Possible **m** animals are mallard, muskrat, mole, mammoth, mackerel, mink, marlin, meerkat, moth, mountain goat, mastiff, macaw, mustang, mouse, moth, monkey, moose, mule. As an alternative, allow students to make monster masks.

 TEKS 1.22A Use phonological knowledge to match sounds to letters to construct known words.

● Look at each picture and say its name.
Draw a line under the pictures that begin with **n** like **9** **nine**.

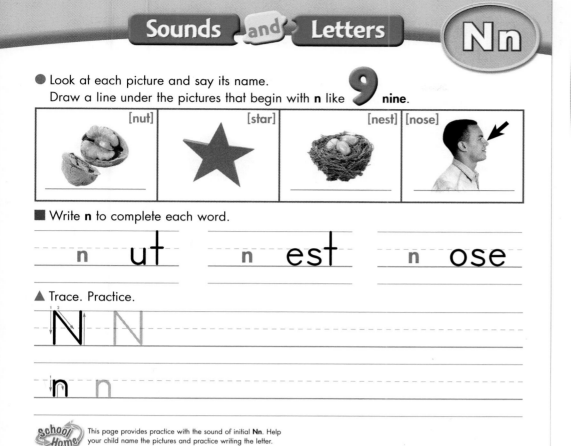

[nut] [star] [nest] [nose]

■ Write **n** to complete each word.

_n_ ut   _n_ est   _n_ ose

▲ Trace. Practice.

N N

n n

School Home This page provides practice with the sound of initial **Nn**. Help your child name the pictures and practice writing the letter.

TEKS 1.22A Use phonological knowledge to match sounds to letters to construct known words.

27

Sounds and Letters Nn

Student Objectives
- Identify the /**n**/ sound spelled **n**.
- Write initial **n** to spell words.
- Practice writing uppercase **N** and lowercase **n**.

Teaching Tips
- Model the /**n**/ sound by saying **nice** and emphasizing the initial sound.
- Give groups of students the following Sound/Symbol Cards: **rash, zigzag, net, old, nut, cub, nail, vacuum,** and **nest**. Help students identify picture names if necessary. Model making a winning tic-tac-toe pattern out of these nine cards by arranging them so that three cards whose picture names begin with **n** appear in a row. Then ask students to arrange the cards in a different winning tic-tac-toe pattern of words with the /**n**/ sound.
- Write **N** and **n** on the board. Point to and identify each letter. Tell students that both letters make the /**n**/ sound they hear at the beginning of **nice**.
- Help students do the first item on page 27. Then have them complete the page.

Optional Letter Chant
Teach students the following chants to say as they practice writing the letters **N** and **n**. Model writing the letters as you say the chant.

Uppercase N
Pull down straight.
Lift. Slant right.
Push up straight.
Uppercase **N** is in sight!

Lowercase n
Pull down straight.
Push up. Curve right.
Pull down straight
To write **no** and **night**.

TEKS 1.22A Use phonological knowledge to match sounds to letters to construct known words.

T27

Student Objectives

- Identify the /p/ sound spelled **p**.
- Write initial **p** to spell words.
- Practice writing uppercase **P** and lowercase **p**.

Teaching Tips

- Display the following Sound/Symbol Cards: **nut, paint, pie, net, dog, pour, dish, hammer, path, cub, plug,** and **planet**. Help students name each picture. Say each name again, emphasizing the initial sound. Have students repeat.
- Place the cards facedown on a table and invite students to play Sound Concentration. The first student turns over two cards, names both pictures, and identifies the initial sound in each. If both picture names start with /p/, the student removes the cards and takes another turn. If either picture name begins with a sound other than /p/, the student turns the cards facedown again and the next student takes a turn. Continue until the six cards with initial /p/ picture names have been matched and removed.
- Write **P** and **p** on the board. Point to and name each letter. Tell students that both letters make the /p/ sound they hear at the beginning of **pie**.
- Help students do the first item on page 28. Then have them complete the page.

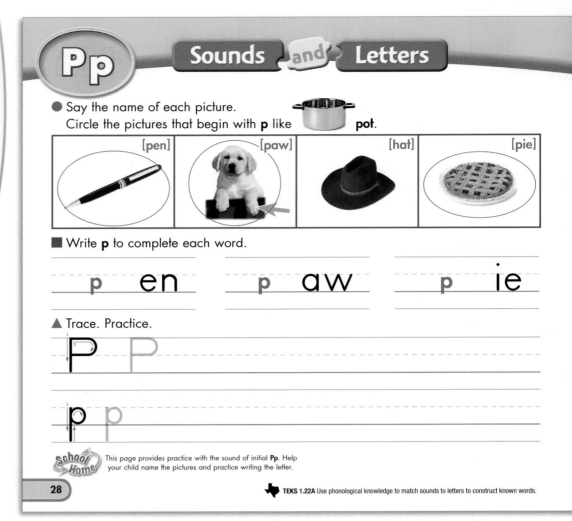

TEKS 1.22A Use phonological knowledge to match sounds to letters to construct known words.

Optional Letter Chant

Teach students the following chants to say as they practice writing the letters **P** and **p**. Model writing the letters as you say the chant.

Uppercase P
Pull down straight.
Lift and slide.
Curve, slide left.
Write **P** with pride.

Lowercase p
Pull down straight.
Then push up.
Circle right all the way,
Like a sideways cup.

P for Pie
Have students draw a pie and write a capital **P** in the middle. As an alternative, give each student two paper plates for the top and bottom of a pie they can color and decorate. Talk about all the **P** words that name things that could go in a pie. Start with possible pies such as peach, pumpkin, peanut butter, pear, plum, pudding, papaya, pizza, and potato. Then start naming silly pies such as paper, pearl, parrot, pencil, pig, pin, pillow, plastic, poodle, popcorn, and panda. Then ask each student what kind of pie he or she has made. Accept all **P** words.

TEKS 1.22A Use phonological knowledge to match sounds to letters to construct known words.

Sounds and Letters — Qq

● Say the name of each picture.
Draw a box around the pictures that begin with **q** like **quarter**.

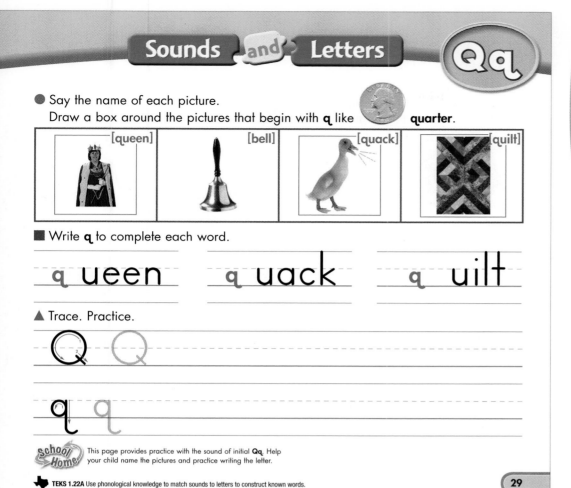

[queen] [bell] [quack] [quilt]

■ Write **q** to complete each word.

q ueen   q uack   q uilt

▲ Trace. Practice.

Q Q

q q

This page provides practice with the sound of initial **Qq**. Help your child name the pictures and practice writing the letter.

TEKS 1.22A Use phonological knowledge to match sounds to letters to construct known words.

29

Sounds and Letters — Qq

Student Objectives
• Identify the /kw/ sound spelled q.
• Write initial **q** to spell words.
• Practice writing uppercase Q and lowercase q.

Teaching Tips
• Demonstrate the /**kw**/ sound using **quick** and **quiet**. Say **quick** and have students repeat it and listen for the beginning sound. Then have students say **quiet**, /**kw**/. Do the same with **quick**.
• Place the following Sound/Symbol Cards in a bag: **quail, nail, house, quarter, fox, queen,** and **quilt**. Call on a volunteer to draw one card. Say the picture name. Ask if the word begins with the /**kw**/ sound. If it does, students should be quiet. If it doesn't, they say, *No*.
• Each time students are quiet, write Q and q on the board. Point to and name uppercase Q and lowercase q.
• Help students do the first item on page 29. Then have them complete the page.

Optional Letter Chant

Teach students the following chants to say as they practice writing the letters Q and q. Model writing the letters as you say the chant.

Uppercase Q
Circle back left,
All the way around.
Lift. Slant right.
Take that tail to the ground.

Lowercase q
Circle back left,
All the way around.
Keep little **q**
Quite close to the ground.
Push up straight.
Pull down straight, too.
Curve forward right.
That's lowercase **q**.

TEKS 1.22A Use phonological knowledge to match sounds to letters to construct known words.

T29

Student Objectives
- Identify the /r/ sound spelled **r**.
- Write initial **r** to spell words.
- Practice writing uppercase **R** and lowercase **r**.

Teaching Tips
- Say the /r/ sound. Ask students to repeat, and say, *Right!*
- Hold up the following Sound/Symbol Cards one by one and say each picture name: **rash, jet, lock, rose, rain, fall, roof,** and **upset.** Have students signal thumbs-up when they hear the /r/ sound and thumbs-down when they do not. When they are correct, say, *Right,* emphasizing the /r/ sound.
- Demonstrate how to write uppercase **R** and lowercase **r**. Name the letters and tell students that both letters make the /r/ sound. If any students' names begin with **R,** call on them to write their name on the board.
- Answer any questions about the items on page 30. Then have students complete the page.

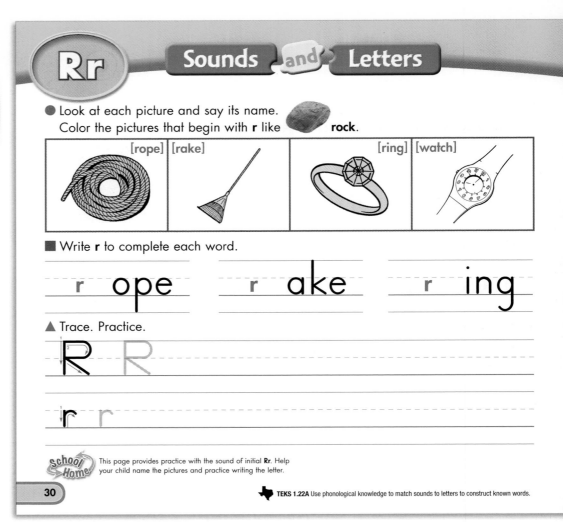

Rr — Sounds and Letters

● Look at each picture and say its name. Color the pictures that begin with **r** like **rock**.

[rope] [rake] [ring] [watch]

■ Write **r** to complete each word.

r ope   r ake   r ing

▲ Trace. Practice.

R R

r r

30

TEKS 1.22A Use phonological knowledge to match sounds to letters to construct known words.

Optional Letter Chant
Teach students the following chants to say as they practice writing the letters **R** and **r**. Model writing the letters as you say the chant.

Uppercase R
Pull down and lift.
Then slide right.
There are three more steps.
Don't hold your pencil too tight!
Curve forward right. Slide left. Slant right.
For uppercase **R,**
These steps are just right!

Lowercase R
First thing you do
Is pull down straight.
Then push up and curve right.
Lowercase **r** is great!

Radio R
Ask students if they have listened to a radio, particularly radio news broadcasts. Work with students to create radio headlines with words that begin with the /r/ sound. For example, say, *The news today on Radio **R** is that it's **raining***. Suggest other words for students to use, such as **rabbit, rug, ring, robot, rake, rumble,** and **race**.

TEKS 1.22A Use phonological knowledge to match sounds to letters to construct known words.

Sounds and Letters — Ss

Look at each picture and say its name.
Draw a line under the pictures that begin with **s** like **6 six**.

| [sail] | [sock] | [sun] | [toad] |

Write s to complete each word.

s ail   s ock   s un

▲ Trace. Practice.

S S

s s

School Home This page provides practice with the sound of initial **Ss**. Help your child name the pictures and practice writing the letter.

TEKS 1.22A Use phonological knowledge to match sounds to letters to construct known words.

31

Student Objectives
- Identify the /s/ sound spelled **s**.
- Write initial **s** to spell words.
- Practice writing uppercase **S** and lowercase **s**.

Teaching Tips
- Demonstrate the /s/ sound by saying **see** and emphasizing the initial sound. Have students repeat.
- Display the Sound/Symbol Cards for **safe, roof, mop, six, jar,** and **sock**. Ask students to identify the pictures that begin with the /s/ sound. Help identify pictures if needed. Then display the cards for **thimble, sun, yo-yo,** and **box**. Ask a volunteer to find the picture whose name begins with the /s/ sound.
- Write **S** and **s**. Name the letters and tell students that both make the /s/ sound. Call on volunteers to write the letters on the board.
- Answer any questions about the items on page 31. Then have students complete the page.

Optional Letter Chant
Teach students the following chants to say as they practice writing the letters **S** and **s**. Model writing the letters as you say the chant.

Uppercase S
Curve back left.
Curve forward right.
That's how uppercase **S**
Is made just right.

Lowercase s
Curve back left.
Curve forward right.
Write lowercase **s**,
But not too tight!

Sorry
Clear a space in the classroom. Then designate a start and a finish line and have students line up in two groups at the start. Tell students you will say a word. If the word begins with the /s/ sound, the first student in each group will take a step. If the word does not begin with the /s/ sound, students should stay in place. If a student makes a misstep, he or she has to take a step back. Then both students go to the end of their lines. The next students in line start where the previous student was standing. Play until each group makes it across the finish line.

TEKS 1.22A Use phonological knowledge to match sounds to letters to construct known words.

T31

Tt Sounds and Letters

Student Objectives
- Identify the /t/ sound spelled **t**.
- Write initial **t** to spell words.
- Practice writing uppercase **T** and lowercase **t**.

Teaching Tips
- Say the words **ten** and **tune**, emphasizing the initial sound. Tell students that both words begin with the /t/ sound.
- Give partners these Sound/Symbol Cards: **tooth, rose, queen, tub, toast, tire, plug,** and **frog**. Ask students to find the four pictures whose names begin with the /t/ sound. Have partners arrange these cards to form the shape of an uppercase **T** and then a lowercase **t**.
- Write **T** and **t**. Name the letters and tell students that both make the /t/ sound. Call on volunteers to write the letters on the board.
- Answer any questions about the items on page 32. Then have students complete the page.

TEKS 1.22A Use phonological knowledge to match sounds to letters to construct known words.

Optional Letter Chant
Teach students the following chants to say as they practice writing the letters **T** and **t**. Model writing the letters as you say the chant.

Uppercase T
Pull down straight.
Lift. Then go to the top.
Slide left to right,
Not too far. Now stop!

Lowercase t
Pull down straight.
Lift up to the middle.
That's how to write
A **t** that is little.

Tell Me
Place objects or pictures of objects with names that begin with /t/ in several lunch bags. Examples include tea bag, tiger, toy, numeral 10, table, tape, telephone, tennis ball, tie, tire, tissue, tomato, toothpick, toothpaste, turtle, towel, tub, and television. Invite partners to select a bag and name the picture or object inside. Ask if the name begins with /t/ and then write it on the board. Review the list with students at the end of the activity.

 TEKS 1.22A Use phonological knowledge to match sounds to letters to construct known words.

Sounds and Letters · Vv

● Say the name of each picture.
Draw a ✓ under the pictures that begin with **v** like **vest**.

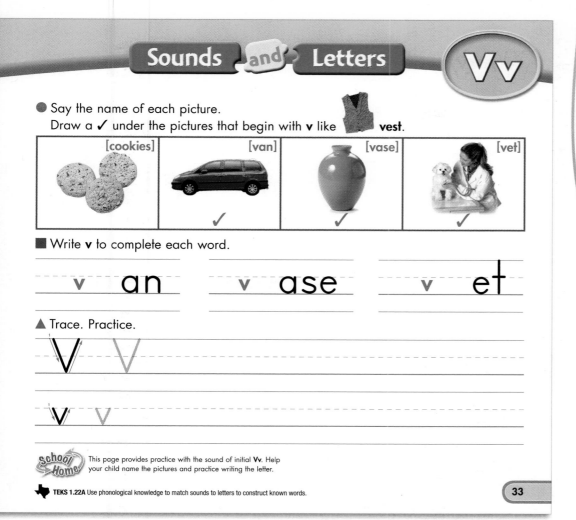

[cookies]	[van]	[vase]	[vet]
	✓	✓	✓

■ Write **v** to complete each word.

v an   v ase   v et

▲ Trace. Practice.

V V

v v

School Home This page provides practice with the sound of initial **Vv**. Help your child name the pictures and practice writing the letter.

TEKS 1.22A Use phonological knowledge to match sounds to letters to construct known words.

33

Sounds and Letters · Vv

Student Objectives
- Identify the /v/ sound spelled **v**.
- Write initial **v** to spell words.
- Practice writing uppercase **V** and lowercase **v**.

Teaching Tips
- Say **vacuum, vase, vine,** and **violin,** emphasizing the initial sound. Tell students that each word begins with the /**v**/ sound.
- Place the following Sound/Symbol Cards on the chalk tray: **tub, rain, six, vase, vine, cave, bird, paint, vacuum,** and **violin.** Have volunteers pick up each picture, name it, and say the initial sound. If the name begins with the /**v**/ sound, ask the student to place the cards on a separate part of the chalk tray. Say the names and have students repeat.
- Write **V** and **v** on the board. Name the letters and tell students that both make the /**v**/ sound they hear at the beginning of **van.** Call on volunteers to write the letters on the board.
- Answer any questions about page 33. Then have students complete the page.

Optional Letter Chant
Teach students the following chants to say as they practice writing the letters **V** and **v**. Model writing the letters as you say the chant.

Uppercase V
Slant right and slant up
For uppercase **V**.
It's really quite easy,
Don't you agree?

Lowercase v
Slant right and slant up
For lowercase **v**.
It's just half as tall
As uppercase **V**.

TEKS 1.22A Use phonological knowledge to match sounds to letters to construct known words.

T33

Ww Sounds and Letters

Student Objectives
- Identify the /w/ sound spelled **w**.
- Write initial **w** to spell words.
- Practice writing uppercase **W** and lowercase **w**.

Teaching Tips
- Place the following Sound/Symbol Cards in one area of the chalk tray: **tooth, sock, wood,** and **bag.** Place these cards on another area: **web, dig, fall,** and **goose.** Have students name all the pictures and then identify the two pictures with names that begin with the same sound. Say the names, emphasizing the initial sound, and have students repeat. Tell them that each word (**wood, web**) begins with the /w/ sound.
- Hold up the following cards: **window, rose, nut,** and **wagon.** Have students identify the picture names that begin with the /w/ sound.
- Write **W** and **w** on the board. Tell students that both letters make the /w/ sound they hear at the beginning of **web.** Call on volunteers to write the letters.
- Answer any questions about page 34. Then have students complete the page.

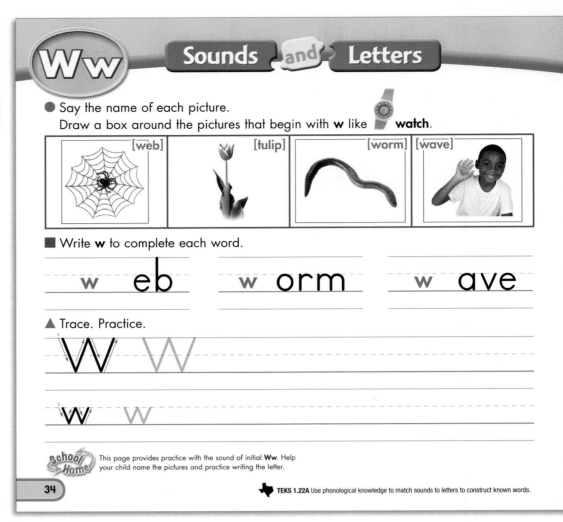

Optional Letter Chant

Teach students the following chants to say as they practice writing the letters **W** and **w.** Model writing the letters as you say the chant.

Uppercase W
Slant down right
And slant up, too.
Now make these strokes again
To write a **W.**

Lowercase w
Slant down right
And then slant up,
Do this twice,
And your **w** will be nice!

Window Watch
Ask students to look out the window and describe you what they see. Then ask them to close their eyes and imagine they are looking through a different window. Say, *Outside there are all kinds of things with names that start with /w/. I see a woodchuck walking on a windy winter day. What do you see?* Help students brainstorm words that begin with /w/. Possibilities include **ocean waves, windmill, weasel, watchdog, wishing well, wildcat, woodchuck,** and **walrus.** Accept words that begin with /wh/, such as **whale** and **wheel.** Provide paper and markers and encourage students to draw the scene they imagined.

 TEKS 1.22A Use phonological knowledge to match sounds to letters to construct known words.

● Say the name of each picture.
Color the pictures that end with **x** like **box**.

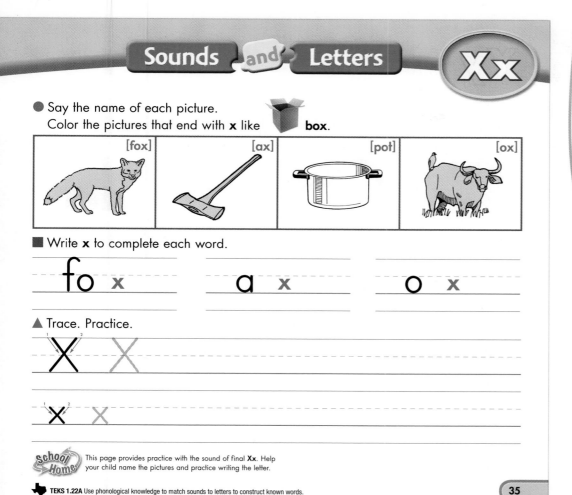

[fox]   [ax]   [pot]   [ox]

■ Write **x** to complete each word.

fo x   a x   o x

▲ Trace. Practice.

X X

x x

 TEKS 1.22A Use phonological knowledge to match sounds to letters to construct known words.

35

Sounds and Letters Xx

Student Objectives
• Identify the **/ks/** sound spelled **x**.
• Write final **x** to spell words.
• Practice writing uppercase **X** and lowercase **x**.

Teaching Tips
• Say **box** and ask students to listen for the **/ks/** sound at the end of the word. Emphasize the final sound and have students repeat.
• Hold up the following Sound/Symbol Cards and say the name of each picture, emphasizing the final **/ks/** sound: **ax, box, fox,** and **six**. Then mix the cards with the cards for **dish, kiss, jar,** and **hop**. Hold up the cards one by one. Ask students to raise their hand when they see a picture whose name ends with the **/ks/** sound.
• Write **X** and **x** on the board. Tell students that both letters make the **/ks/** sound they hear at the end of **box**. Write **box** and circle **x** at the end. Then call on volunteers to write the letters.
• Answer any questions about page 35. Then have students complete the page.

Optional Letter Chant
Teach students the following chants to say as they practice writing the letters **X** and **x**. Model writing the letters as you say the chant.

Uppercase X and Lowercase X
Slant right. Lift.
Now quick like a fox,
Slant left, and
Write **x** to finish **ox**.

X Marks the Spot
Mark a large X on the floor with masking tape. Call on volunteers to stand on the X. Say three words, one of which ends with the **/ks/** sound. For example, say **car, box, lot**. Ask the student to say the word that ends with **/ks/**. Continue until all volunteers have had a turn. Possible final **x** words include **fix, ax, six, tax, ox, fox, mix, box, relax, index, wax, hex, fax, vex**.

TEKS 1.22A Use phonological knowledge to match sounds to letters to construct known words.

T35

Yy **Sounds and Letters**

Student Objectives
- Identify the /y/ sound spelled **y**.
- Write initial **y** to spell words.
- Practice writing uppercase **Y** and lowercase **y**.

Teaching Tips
- Tell students that the word **yes** begins with the /y/ sound. Have students say **yes** and then the beginning /y/ sound.
- Display the following Sound/Symbol Cards: **yo-yo, ape, nest, yarn, yolk, jacket, thumb,** and **yell**. Ask students to take turns coming up and pointing out a picture whose name begins with the /y/ sound. When a student is correct, ask the rest of the class to say *Yes!*
- Write **Y** and **y** on the board. Tell students that both letters make the /y/ sound they hear at the beginning of **yes**. Write **yes** and underline **y**. Then call on volunteers to write the letters.
- Answer any questions about page 36. Then have students complete the page.

Optional Letter Chant

Teach students the following chants to say as they practice writing the letters **Y** and **y**. Model writing the letters as you say the chant.

Uppercase Y
Slant right. Lift. Slant left.
Then pull straight down.
Write to Yasmin, Yelena, and Yoko
to invite them to town.

Lowercase y
Slant right. Lift.
You're not done yet.
To finish small **y**,
You've got to slant left.

TEKS 1.22A Use phonological knowledge to match sounds to letters to construct known words.

Sounds and Letters

● Look at each picture and say its name.
Draw a box around the pictures that begin with **z** like **zipper**.

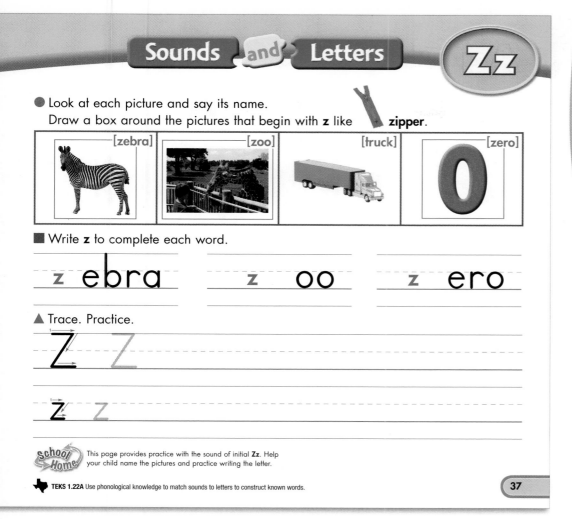

[zebra]   [zoo]   [truck]   [zero]

■ Write **z** to complete each word.

z ebra   z oo   z ero

▲ Trace. Practice.

Z Z

z z

This page provides practice with the sound of initial **Zz**. Help your child name the pictures and practice writing the letter.

School Home

TEKS 1.22A Use phonological knowledge to match sounds to letters to construct known words.

37

Sounds and Letters

Student Objectives
• Identify the /z/ sound spelled z.
• Write initial z to spell words.
• Practice writing uppercase Z and lowercase z.

Teaching Tips
• Say **zipper**, emphasizing the initial /z/ sound. Then have students say **zipper**, /z/. Explain that /z/ is the beginning sound of **zipper**.
• Place the following Sound/Symbol Cards facedown on a desk: **mitten, nail, path, zero, zigzag, vine, sun, zipper, calf, zoo,** and **mouse.** Have students take turns turning over a card and naming the picture. Tell students to place the card to the right if the name begins with the same sound as **zipper**. All other cards go on the left.
• Write **Z** and **z** on the board. Have students repeat the picture names beginning with the /z/ sound as you point to the letters. Ask volunteers to write **Z** and **z** on the board.
• Answer any questions about page 37. Then have students complete the page.

Optional Letter Chant
Teach students the following chants to say as they practice writing the letters **Z** and **z**. Model writing the letters as you say the chant.

Uppercase Z
Begin **Z** with a slide—
Make sure you slide right!
Slant left to the baseline;
Then end with one more slide right.

Lowercase z
Slide right.
Slant down left and then slide right.
Both **z**'s are the same—
Except for the height.

Consonant Capers
Name each consonant letter students have learned so far. Then assign a letter to each student. Say the letter and have the student who has that letter perform the following action: **/b/ b** bow, **/k/ c** shiver with cold, **/d/ d** dip down, **/f/ f** show five fingers, **/g/ g** gobble like a turkey, **/h/ h** hop on one foot, **/j/ j** jump up, **/k/ k** blow a kiss, **/l/ l** raise the left hand, **/m/ m** moo like a cow, **/n/ n** shake the head "no," **/p/ p** pat the head, **/kw/ q** quack like a duck, **/r/ r** raise the right hand, **/s/ s** hiss like a snake, **/t/ t** pretend to talk on the phone, **/w/ w** wave both hands, **/ks/ x** draw a six in the air, **/y/ y** yawn.

TEKS 1.22A Use phonological knowledge to match sounds to letters to construct known words.

Aa Sounds and Letters

Student Objectives
- Identify the /ă/ sound spelled **a**.
- Write initial **a** to spell words.
- Practice writing uppercase **A** and lowercase **a**.

Teaching Tips
- Say **apple**. Then say the /ă/ sound. Have students repeat /ă/, **apple.**
- Display the following Sound/Symbol Cards: **bird, kick, apple, ax, nest,** and **pie.** Have students identify the picture names. Then call on a volunteer to sort the cards into two groups—cards whose picture names begin with the **short a** sound and cards whose picture names do not.
- Write **A** and **a** on the board. Have students repeat the picture names beginning with the /ă/ sound as you point to the letters. Explain that **A** and **a** make the /ă/ sound students hear at the beginning of **apple.** Ask volunteers to write **A** and **a** on the board.
- Answer any questions about page 38. Then have students complete the page.

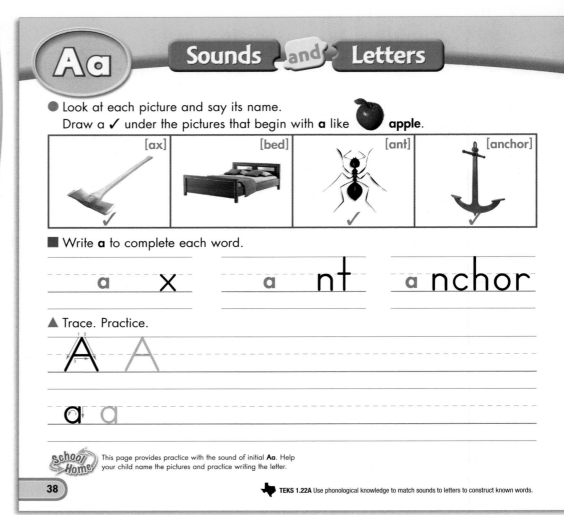

Optional Letter Chant

Teach students the following chants to say as they practice writing the letters **A** and **a**. Model writing the letters as you say the chant.

Uppercase A	Lowercase a
Slant left. Slant right.	Circle back.
You've come partway.	Go around all the way.
Now lift and slide	Push up, pull down
To write uppercase **A**.	To write lowercase **a**.

TEKS 1.22A Use phonological knowledge to match sounds to letters to construct known words.

Sounds and Letters **Ee**

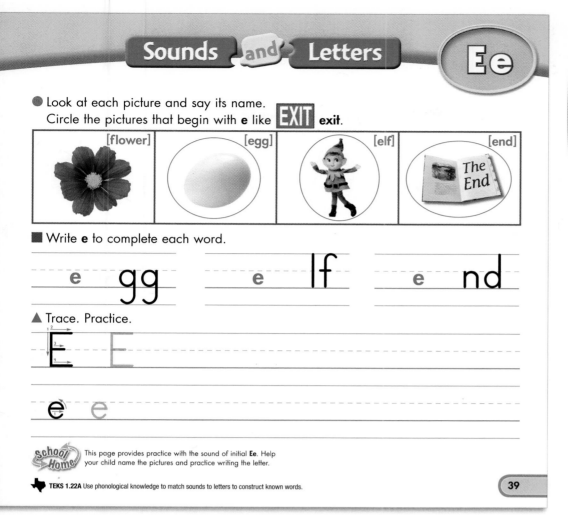

● Look at each picture and say its name.
Circle the pictures that begin with **e** like **EXIT** exit.

[flower] [egg] [elf] [end]

■ Write **e** to complete each word.

e gg   e lf   e nd

▲ Trace. Practice.

E E

e e

School Home
This page provides practice with the sound of initial **Ee**. Help your child name the pictures and practice writing the letter.

TEKS 1.22A Use phonological knowledge to match sounds to letters to construct known words.

39

Student Objectives
- Identify the /ĕ/ sound spelled **e**.
- Write initial **e** to spell words.
- Practice writing uppercase **E** and lowercase **e**.

Teaching Tips
- Say **elephant** and have students repeat it. Tell students to listen as you say the word again. Explain that the /ĕ/ sound is the beginning sound of **elephant**.
- Hold up the following Sound/Symbol Cards: **yarn, zoo, egg,** and **echo**. Help students name each picture. Tell them to raise their hand when they hear a picture name that begins with the **short e** sound.
- Write **E** and **e** on the board. Have students repeat the picture names beginning with the /ĕ/ sound as you point to the letters. Explain that **E** and **e** make the /ĕ/ sound students hear at the beginning of **egg**. If any students have names that begin with **E**, invite them to write their name on the board.
- Answer any questions about page 39. Then have students complete the page.

Optional Letter Chant
Teach students the following chants to say as they practice writing the letters **E** and **e**. Model writing the letters as you say the chant

Uppercase E
Pull down straight.
Lift and slide right.
Lift again and then slide
right in the middle.
One more lift and other slide right—
There's an uppercase **E**
that's fit as a fiddle.

Lowercase e
Slide right, straight across;
To the left circle back.
Your pencil should glide
Like a train on its track.

Pass the Egg
Bring in a plastic or wooden egg. Have students sit in a circle. Tell them that you will start passing the egg around the circle. Then you will say a list of words. If a word begins with the **short e** sound, the student with the egg should hold onto it and not pass it. If the word begins with another sound, the student should pass the egg as quickly as possible. Possible **short e** words to intersperse in the list include **enter, exit, elf, end, ever, elephant, elk, edit, energy, exam,** and **excuse**.

TEKS 1.22A Use phonological knowledge to match sounds to letters to construct known words.

T39

Ii Sounds and Letters

Student Objectives
- Identify the /ĭ/ sound spelled **i**.
- Write initial **i** to spell words.
- Practice writing uppercase **I** and lowercase **i**.

Teaching Tips
- Say **inch,** emphasizing the /ĭ/ sound. Help students discriminate the **short i** sound from the **short e** sound by saying **inch/egg.** Ask students to listen carefully and then repeat the words.
- Hold up the following Sound/Symbol Cards: **igloo, tub, iguana, zipper,** and **nail.** Help students name each picture. Then say the picture names again. Tell students to point to the ceiling with an index finger when they hear a picture name that begins with the same sound as **inch.**
- Write **I** and **i** on the board. Have students repeat the two picture names that begin with the /ĭ/ sound as you point to the letters. Explain that **I** and **i** make the /ĭ/ sound students hear at the beginning of **inch.** Call on volunteers to write the letters on the board.
- Answer any questions about page 40. Then have students complete the page.

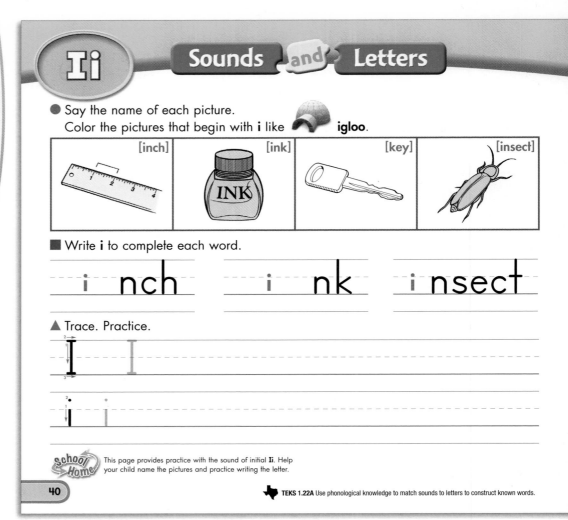

Ii Sounds and Letters

● Say the name of each picture.
Color the pictures that begin with **i** like igloo.

[inch]	[ink]	[key]	[insect]

■ Write **i** to complete each word.

i nch   i nk   i nsect

▲ Trace. Practice.

I

i

School Home This page provides practice with the sound of initial **Ii**. Help your child name the pictures and practice writing the letter.

40

TEKS 1.22A Use phonological knowledge to match sounds to letters to construct known words.

Optional Letter Chant

Teach students the following chants to say as they practice writing the letters **I** and **i.** Model writing the letters as you say the chant.

Uppercase I
Pull down straight. Lift.
Slide right. Lift. Slide right.
I's are so easy,
I could make them all night.

Lowercase i
Pull down straight.
Lift, then dot.
Lowercase i
Is what you've got!

TEKS 1.22A Use phonological knowledge to match sounds to letters to construct known words.

Sounds and Letters

● Say the name of each picture.
Circle the pictures that begin with **o** like ostrich.

[olive] [ox] [off] [parrot]

■ Write **o** to complete each word.

o live   o x   o ff

▲ Trace. Practice.

School Home This page provides practice with the sound of initial **Oo**. Help your child name the pictures and practice writing the letter.

TEKS 1.22A Use phonological knowledge to match sounds to letters to construct known words.

41

Student Objectives
- Identify the /ŏ/ sound spelled **o**.
- Write initial **o** to spell words.
- Practice writing uppercase **O** and lowercase **o**.

Teaching Tips
- Say **ox**, emphasizing the /ŏ/ sound. Explain to students that the **short o** sound is the sound they hear at the beginning of the word **ox**.
- Display the following Sounds/Symbol Cards: **wagon, ostrich, octagon,** and **vacuum**. Ask students to raise their hand when they see a picture whose name begins with the **short o** sound. Help with picture identification as needed.
- Write **O** and **o** on the board. Identify which letter is the capital letter and which is the lowercase letter. Point out that the letters are the same shape, but the capital **O** is bigger. Have students write **O** and **o** in the air with a finger. Explain that **o** is the letter that begins the word **ox**.
- Answer any questions about page 41. Then have students complete the page.

Optional Letter Chant
Teach students the following chants to say as they practice writing the letters **O** and **o**. Model writing the letters as you say the chant.

Uppercase O and Lowercase o
Circle back left.
Go all the way.
O and o are easy.
We can go all day!

That's Odd
Say **odd**. Ask students what sound begins the word **odd**. (short o or /ŏ/) Explain that **odd** means "different or strange." Then tell students you will name some animals. They should ask you, *What's odd about the [name of animal]?* Name the following animals and give students one odd fact about each: **octopus** (has eight legs), **ocelot** (a cat that likes to swim), **otter** (eats floating on its back and uses its stomach as a table), **ostrich** (a bird that cannot fly). Say the animal names and have students say the sound that begins each word.

TEKS 1.22A Use phonological knowledge to match sounds to letters to construct known words.

T41

Uu — Sounds and Letters

Student Objectives
- Identify the /ŭ/ sound spelled **u**.
- Write initial **u** to spell words.
- Practice writing uppercase **U** and lowercase **u**.

Teaching Tips
- Say **umbrella**, emphasizing the initial /ŭ/ sound. Have students say the word and then say /ŭ/. Explain that **short u** is the sound they hear at the beginning of **umbrella**.
- Hold up the following Sound/Symbol Cards one by one: **igloo**, **upset**, **wagon**, **kangaroo**, **iguana**, **jet**, **bed**, and **up**. Have students say the name of each picture. Help identify pictures as needed. Then say the names again and have students stand up when they hear the /ŭ/ sound at the beginning of the picture name.
- Write **U** and **u** on the board. Identify which is the capital letter and which is the lowercase letter. Explain that these letters make the /ŭ/ sound students hear at the beginning of **umbrella**.
- Answer any questions about page 42. Then have students complete the page.

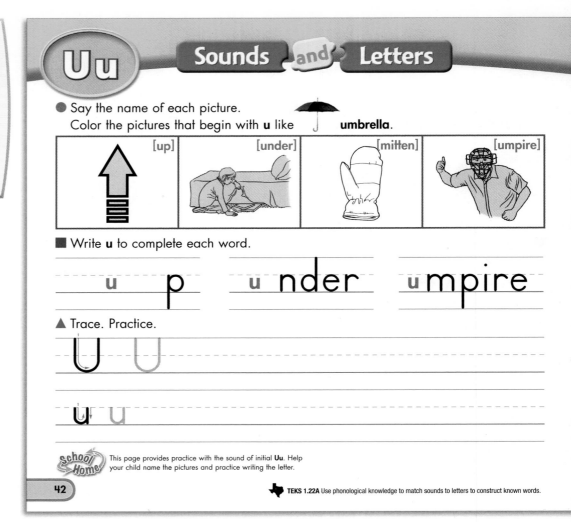

Optional Letter Chant
Teach students the following chants to say as they practice writing the letters **U** and **u**. Model writing the letters as you say the chant.

Uppercase U
Pull down straight.
Curve right. Push up.
An uppercase **U**
Looks like a big cup.

Lowercase u
Pull down straight.
Get ready to curve.
Curve right. Push up.
Pull down. Don't swerve!
If lowercase **u** keeps its head below the line,
Then your **ups** and **umbrellas** will look just fine.

TEKS 1.22A Use phonological knowledge to match sounds to letters to construct known words.

Planner

Day 1 | Day 2

Day 1

Connections to **Thinking**

Student Objectives
- Read, spell, and write words with **short a** in the initial and medial position.

Instruction for All Students
- Pretest Dictation Sentences, p. T43B
- Connections to Thinking, p. 43
- Home/School Spelling Practice Master (*Teacher Resource Book*, p. 27)

TEKS 1.22A, 1.22C

Connections to **Phonics**

Student Objectives
- Match the initial sounds in picture names and spelling words.
- Blend the initial sounds of picture names to spell and write **short a** VC and CVC words.

Instruction for All Students
- Connections to Phonics, p. 44

Optional Practice
- Extra Pattern Practice Master (*Teacher Resource Book*, p. 29)

TEKS 1.22A, 1.22Bi, 1.22C

Spelling Words
an
can
man
ran
had
dad

Challenge Words
ant
tag
lap
pants

Day 3 | Day 4 | Day 5

Day 2

Connections to **Reading**

Student Objectives
- Spell and write **short a** VC and CVC words to complete sentences.

Instruction for All Students
- Connections to Reading, p. 45

Differentiated Instruction
- Challenge Words, p. 183

TEKS 1.22C

Connections to **Writing**

Student Objectives
- Spell and write **short a** VC and CVC words to complete a story.

Instruction for All Students
- Connections to Writing, p. 46

Differentiated Instruction
- Extra Challenge Practice Master (*Teacher Resource Book*, p. 30)

TEKS 1.22C

Day 3

Assessment

Student Objectives
- Demonstrate mastery of the unit spelling words.

Assessment for All Students
- Posttest Dictation Sentences, p. T46, or
- *Standardized Test Master Book*, p. 5

Differentiated Assessment
- Challenge Dictation Sentences, p. T183

Unit 1 Materials

Student Edition
pp. 43–46, 183

Teacher Edition
pp. T43A–T46, T183

 Teacher Resource Book
Unit 1 Practice Masters,
pp. 27–30, and
Sound/Symbol Cards

Standardized Test Master Book
Unit 1 Test Master, p. 5

 Word Sort CD-ROM
Unit 1 Word Sort Cards for Teacher-
Led Sorts and Student Sorts

 Digital Resources for Spelling Connections
Unit 1

Spelling Connections Online
www.spellingconnectionsonline.com

Spelling Support for English Language Learners*
Unit 1 Practice Masters and
Audio Conversation

Spelling Center Activities*
Spelling Game Mats
Flip Folder, *TRB*, p. 155

*Spelling Support for English Language
Learners *and* Spelling Center Activities *may
be used at any time during the week.*

Assessment

Pretest Sentences (See procedures on p. Z30.)

1. Would you like **an** apple?
2. We **can** go to the party.
3. That **man** helped me.
4. Mary **ran** in the race.
5. We **had** fun at the park.
6. Is your **dad** at home?

The Science of Spelling

- Short vowel spellings are highly consistent and dependable. The **short a** sound is spelled **a** 97% of the time in the initial (**an**) and medial (**man**) positions.
- Short vowels are usually found singly or in syllables in which the vowel is immediately preceded and followed by a consonant (CVC: **can**), consonant blend (CVCC: **cast**), or consonant digraph (CVCC: **cash**). Each of these patterns functions the same way.

 # ELL Support

Unit 1

Choose from the activities below to reinforce English language acquisition.

Beginning

Letter Identification If students cannot yet identify or write all letters of the English alphabet, have them work with alphabet flash cards. Students can take turns with a partner, drawing a card, pronouncing the letter name, and writing the letter on a sheet of paper.

Word Sort Write each spelling word on a card. Demonstrate the **short a** sound in isolation. Have students repeat it several times. Say each word and have students repeat it. Next, segment each word into its component sounds, and then blend the sounds to say the word. Have students sort the words into word families (an, ad). Point to each group of cards and ask, *Which letters are the same in these words?* Students can point to or say **an** or **ad**. Say each word and have students repeat.

Word Meaning Make flash cards for the spelling words. Hold up each card and say the word. Introduce the words **man, can, ran,** and **dad** with picture support. Display all the flash cards and pictures and have students match them. Encourage students to practice saying all the words.

Making Words List the spelling words on the board. Then write each word on a card and cut the letters apart. Mix the letters. Have students select letters to reconstruct the words. As they build each word, have students say the sound of each letter and then blend the sounds to say the word.

Intermediate

Letter Substitution Write **a** and say /ă/. Say each spelling word and have students repeat after you, individually and in chorus. Then write **an** on the board. Have students say the word. Add **c** and have students say **can**. Erase **c** and add **m**, and then erase **m** and add **r**. Invite students to suggest other beginning letters.

Picture Sentences On the board, write several sentences that include spelling words. Prompt students to help you create these. Read each sentence aloud and have students repeat. Then have students choose a sentence and illustrate it. Encourage students to make up their own sentences and illustrate them.

Rhyming Words Say a few words that rhyme with a spelling word. For example, say **man** and then **can, van,** and **ran**. Write a spelling word from each word family on a piece of paper and have students write rhyming words under it. Display the lists where students can add to them at any time. Have partners find the rhyming word that completes each sentence on page 6 in *Spelling Support for English Language Learners.*

Support for Spanish Speakers

Comparing Languages Some Spanish speakers may have difficulty hearing and pronouncing the /ă/ sound. In Spanish, the letter **a** stands for a sound that is similar to **short o** in English.

Because **h** is silent in Spanish, some Spanish speakers may have trouble pronouncing the /h/ sound. For example, they may say **ad** instead of **had**. Provide many opportunities for students to practice listening to and pronouncing words that include the /h/ sound.

Pronunciation Practice Beginning students may need brief, ongoing practice sessions to learn to pronounce **short a** words. To help students practice /ă/, model pronunciation of the spelling words and have students repeat them. Segment the sounds with emphasis on /ă/. Teach students to segment the sounds in **short a** CVC words and then blend them. Have students brainstorm other words with /ă/, using word families such as **at, an, and, ack,** and **ag**. Learning to produce the sounds of a new language is challenging. Encourage students by praising effort and approximations as they learn first to hear and then to produce new sounds.

Choose from the activities below to reinforce English language acquisition.

Advanced

Word Meaning List the spelling words on the board. Then ask questions that can be answered with the words. For example, *Which word means "one"?* (an) *Which word says you moved fast?* (ran) *Which word names a male parent?* (dad)

Making Sentences Write a sentence using a spelling word, such as *I can sing*. Work with students to create other sentences with **can**. Then have partners work together to write sentences that correctly use each spelling word. Explain that the word **can** has two meanings: "to know how or be able to" and "a metal container." Have students choose a picture in a book and describe it in two or three sentences. Write or have students write sentences and underline the spelling words they used.

Rhyming Words Have students create a list of words that rhyme with each spelling word. Students can add to the lists at any time and refer to them for writing assignments. Have students work with a partner to find the rhyming word that completes each sentence on page 6 in *Spelling Support for English Language Learners*.

Advanced High

Words and Sentences Provide large index cards. Have partners take turns writing a spelling word on one side of a card and a sentence using the word on the reverse side. Then have students read their words and sentences together.

Story Pictures Have students draw pictures that illustrate three spelling words and that tell a story in sequence. Then have them write a sentence for each picture. Ask students to read their stories aloud.

Making Sentences Have students write as many three-letter **short a** words as they can. Then have them use as many of the words as possible in a story. Partners can take turns saying a sentence while the other partner writes it on paper.

Riddles Encourage students to think of riddles using the spelling words. Partners can share riddles and challenge each other to figure out the words. For example, *I begin with **c**. You can find me in a store. I am made of metal.* (can)

Spelling Support for English Language Learners

Practice Master, p. 6

Practice Master, p. 42

 Audio Conversation available on CD

English/Spanish Word List, p. 57

Spelling Connections Online
Interactive online spelling activities provide additional ELL support.
www.spellingconnectionsonline.com

1. an
2. can
3. man
4. ran
5. had
6. dad

School Home!
This unit targets the **short a** sound. Ask your child to read the spelling words to you.

A. Write the spelling words that end with **ad.**

1. had
2. dad

B. Write the spelling words that end with **an.**

3. an
4. can
5. man
6. ran

43

Day 1

Unit
1

Student Objectives
• Read, spell, and write words with **short a** in the initial and medial position.

Unit Pretest
• Administer the pretest on page T43B.

Teaching Tips
• Have students read each spelling word aloud, emphasizing and listening to /ă/.

• Conduct a **Teacher-Led Sort** (see p. Z31) to introduce the **an** and **ad** word families.
• Show the Sound/Symbol Card for **bag.** Have students say **bag** and tell the vowel sound they hear. Write **bag** on the board and circle the **a.**
• Show the cards for **ax, cab, calf, last, path,** and **rash.** Have students name each picture, emphasizing the **short a** sound. Write the picture names. Ask a volunteer to circle **a** in each word. Explain that when a word has only one vowel, the vowel sound is usually short.
• Write **an** and read it aloud. Add **c** and **m** and have volunteers read the new words. (can, man) Do the same with **h, d,** and **ad.** (had, dad)
• Have students complete page 43 as a class.

Home/School Word Lists **TRB**
• Have students take home the Home/School Spelling Practice Master.

Home/School Practice

Home/School Spelling
Practice Master, *TRB*, p. 27

Home/School Spelling Practice	Unit 1
Name_____	

1. an
2. can
3. man
4. ran
5. had
6. dad

1.
2.
3.
4.
5.
6.

Spelling Practice Activity

Dear Family:
Ask your child to write the spelling words correctly on the blank lines.

Your support, encouragement, and involvement are vital to your child's education. Therefore, your help in reinforcing the skills taught in school will

greatly enhance your child's success in spelling. Throughout the school year you will receive lists of the words your child will be learning, as well as some suggestions for spelling and writing activities that you and your child can do together.

Teacher Resource Book **27**

English

Home/School Spelling
Practice Master, *TRB*, p. 28

Práctica de ortografía para el hogar o la escuela	Unit 1
Nombre_____	

1. an   un, una
2. can   puede
3. man   hombre
4. ran   corrió
5. had   tuvo
6. dad   papá

1.
2.
3.
4.
5.
6.

Actividad de ortografía

Querida familia:
Pida a su hijo(a) que escriba correctamente las palabras de ortografía en los renglones en blanco.

Su apoyo, entusiasmo y cooperación son vitales para la educación de su hijo(a). Por lo tanto, su participación en el reforzamiento de las

destrezas que su hijo(a) aprenda en la escuela, contribuirá grandemente a que él o ella mejore su ortografía. A lo largo del año escolar, usted recibirá unas listas con las palabras que su hijo(a) ha ido aprendiendo, así como actividades de escritura y ortografía que sugerimos para que las realice junto con su hijo(a).

28 Teacher Resource Book

Spanish

T43

Unit 1 Day 2

Student Objectives
- Match the initial sounds in picture names and spelling words.
- Blend the initial sounds of picture names to spell and write **short a** VC and CVC words.

Teaching Tips
- Write the spelling words on the board. Have students read each word aloud and identify the letter that spells /ă/. Circle the **a** in each word.
- Display pictures of a cat, an apple, and a net. Have students say the beginning sound of each picture name. Write the corresponding letter for each sound. Then blend the sounds to say **can**.
- Ask, *Is the /ă/ spelling at the beginning, middle, or end of the word?* **(middle)** Have students note that it comes between two consonants. Tell them this is a common spelling pattern for short vowel sounds.
- Have students complete page 44 independently or as a class.

Extra Pattern Practice **TRB**
- Use the optional practice master below for extra practice with **short a**.

WORD SORT CD-ROM
- Provide time for students to use a **Buddy Sort** to practice their spelling words with a partner (see p. Z31).

Connections to PHONICS

A. Draw a line to match each spelling word with the picture name that begins with the same sound.

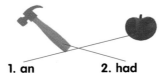

1. **an**   2. **had**   3. **man**   4. **ran**

B. Name each picture. Write the first letter of each picture name to make a spelling word.

5. _____ **dad**   6. _____ **had**

7. _____ **ran**   8. _____ **man**

9. _____ **an**   10. _____ **can**

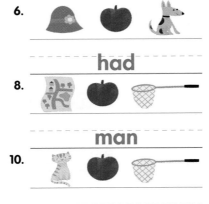

an
can
man
ran
had
dad

44

> TEKS **1.22A** Use phonological knowledge to match sounds to letters to construct known words. **1.22C** Spell high-frequency words from a commonly used list.

Extra Pattern Practice

Extra Pattern Practice Master,
TRB, p. 29

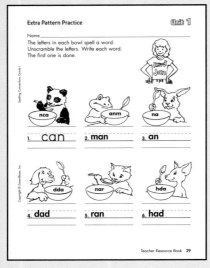

Pattern Practice Game: /ă/

To reinforce the **short a** spelling pattern, remind students that /ă/ is the **short a** sound they hear in **dad**. Display letter cards **b, c, d, f, h, l, m, p, r, s,** and **t**. Write **an** and **ad** on the board. Have students select a letter card and place it next to **an** or **ad** to make a word. Ask students to pronounce the word they make. Possible words are **ban, can, fan, man, pan, ran, tan, bad, dad, fad, had, lad, mad, pad,** and **sad**. List students' words on the board. Ask what short vowel spelling pattern they see in all the words. **(one vowel between two consonants)**

T44

> TEKS **1.22A** Use phonological knowledge to match sounds to letters to construct known words. **1.22Bi** Use letter-sound patterns to spell: consonant-vowel-consonant (CVC) words. **1.22C** Spell high-frequency words from a commonly used list.

Connections to READING

Write a spelling word to complete each sentence.

an	can	dad

an
can
man
ran
had
dad

1. My __**dad**__ is a teacher.

2. I have __**an**__ apple.

3. You __**can**__ paint with me.

had	man	ran

4. We __**ran**__ to your house.

5. A __**man**__ is on the swing.

6. The worm __**had**__ a hat.

 TEKS 1.22C Spell high-frequency words from a commonly used list.

45

Student Objectives
• Spell and write **short a** VC and CVC words to complete sentences.

Teaching Tips
• Read the spelling words and identify /ă/ in each word.
• Read the directions and explain that each spelling word has meaning. Students are to select the word that makes sense in each sentence.
• Complete the first item together. Model how to read the sentence three times with each different word in the blank and decide which word makes sense (**dad**). Have students write the word.
• Remind students that we use **a** before naming words that begin with a consonant sound and **an** before words that begin with a vowel sound.
• Have students complete page 45 independently or continue to do the activity as a class.

Differentiated Instruction
• Use the **Challenge Words** activity on page 183 with students who are ready to transfer their knowledge of **short a** to new words.
• An Extra Challenge Practice Master is available on page 30 in the *TRB*.
• Dictation sentences for the challenge words are available on page T183.

More Fun With Spelling for Differentiation

Digital Resources for Spelling Connections

Interactive digital resources include word sorts, pattern practice, and proofreading activities for individual and whole-group instruction. (Interactive whiteboard compatible; see p. Z32.)

Spelling Connections Online

Interactive online spelling activities include word sorts, crossword puzzles, sentence completion, proofreading practice, and spelling bees with words from each unit (see p. Z32). www.spellingconnectionsonline.com

Spelling Center Activities

Spelling Game Mats
Place one of the spelling games in a learning center to provide a fun way for students to practice their spelling words (see p. Z26).

Flip Folder
Students can use a Flip Folder to practice spelling words independently (see p. Z32).

Word Sort CD-ROM
Printable, unit-specific word cards for spelling and challenge words can be used for Teacher-Led, Individual, Buddy, and Speed Sorts (see p. Z31).

 TEKS 1.22C Spell high-frequency words from a commonly used list.

T45

Unit 1 — Day 4

Student Objectives
- Spell and write **short a** VC and CVC words to complete a story.

Teaching Tips
- Read the directions with students.
- Point out that a story has a beginning, a middle, and an end. Have students identify the three parts of a familiar story.
- Have students complete the story independently or as a class. After they finish, read all the sentences aloud. Help students identify the story's beginning, middle, and end.

WORD SORT CD-ROM
- Invite students to practice for the weekly test by doing an **Individual Sort** or a **Speed Sort** (see p. Z31).

Connections to WRITING

Look at the picture. Use your spelling words to complete a story about the picture.

an
can
man
ran
had
dad

1. The _____ **man** _____ was on the bike.

2. He _____ **had** _____ a bag of apples.

3. He waved to my _____ **dad** _____.

4. Then _____ **an** _____ apple fell.

5. My dad _____ **ran** _____.

6. My dad _____ **can** _____ help.

46

TEKS 1.22C Spell high-frequency words from a commonly used list.

1-Minute Handwriting Hint

The backward circle in the lowercase **a** begins below the midline. Be sure that the vertical stroke touches the circle.

a ← TOUCH

Day 5

Student Objectives
- Demonstrate mastery of the unit spelling words.

Posttest Assessment Options
Option 1: Administer the unit posttest using the dictation sentences at right.

Option 2: Assess students using the standardized test. See the *Standardized Test Master Book,* p. 5.

Note: Posttest sentences for the on level and challenge lists are available on the audio *Spelling Connections* Posttest CD.

Posttest Sentences
1. Did that **man** make the toys?
2. I had **an** egg for breakfast.
3. Your **dad** is tall.
4. Judy **can** help you.
5. Tuffy **ran** up a tree!
6. Have you **had** a good day?

Standardized Test Master Book, p. 5

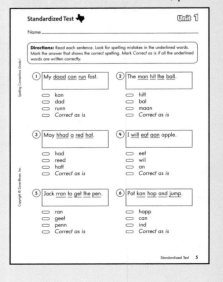

T46

TEKS 1.22C Spell high-frequency words from a commonly used list.

Planner

Day 1

Day 2

Day 1

Connections to **Thinking**

Student Objectives
- Read, spell, and write words with **short a** in the initial and medial position.

Instruction for All Students
- Pretest Dictation Sentences, p. T47B
- Connections to Thinking, p. 47
- Home/School Spelling Practice Master (*Teacher Resource Book*, p. 31)

TEKS 1.22A, 1.22Bi, 1.22C

Connections to **Phonics**

Student Objectives
- Segment sounds to determine the number of sounds in words.
- Spell and write **short a** words with a VC and CVC pattern.
- Track letters in a-b-c order.

Instruction for All Students
- Connections to Phonics, p. 48

Optional Practice
- Extra Pattern Practice Master (*Teacher Resource Book*, p. 33)

TEKS 1.22A, 1.22Bi, 1.22C

Spelling Words
am
at
cat
hat
has
and

Challenge Words
bag
mat
pan
lamp

Day 3

Day 4

Day 5

Day 2

Day 3

Connections to **Reading**

Student Objectives
- Spell and write **short a** VC and CVC words to complete sentences.

Instruction for All Students
- Connections to Reading, p. 49

Differentiated Instruction
- Challenge Words, p. 184

TEKS 1.22C

Connections to **Writing**

Student Objectives
- Spell and write **short a** VC and CVC words to complete a poem.

Instruction for All Students
- Connections to Writing, p. 50

Differentiated Instruction
- Extra Challenge Practice Master (*Teacher Resource Book*, p. 34)

TEKS 1.22C

Assessment

Student Objectives
- Demonstrate mastery of the unit spelling words.

Assessment for All Students
- Posttest Dictation Sentences, p. T50, or
- *Standardized Test Master Book*, p. 6

Differentiated Assessment
- Challenge Dictation Sentences, p. T184

Unit 2 Materials

Student Edition
pp. 47–50, 184

Teacher Edition
pp. T47A–T50, T184

 Teacher Resource Book
Unit 2 Practice Masters,
pp. 31–34, and
Sound/Symbol Cards

 Standardized Test Master Book
Unit 2 Test Master, p. 6

 Word Sort CD-ROM
Unit 2 Word Sort Cards for Teacher-
Led Sorts and Student Sorts

 Digital Resources for Spelling Connections
Unit 2

Spelling Connections Online
www.spellingconnectionsonline.com

Spelling Support for English Language Learners*
Unit 2 Practice Masters and
Audio Conversation

Spelling Center Activities*
Spelling Game Mats
Flip Folder, *TRB*, p. 155

*Spelling Support for English Language
Learners *and Spelling Center Activities may
be used at any time during the week.*

Assessment

Pretest Sentences (See procedures on p. Z30.)

1. I **am** happy to see you.
2. Look **at** my picture.
3. Did your **cat** have kittens?
4. Is this your **hat**?
5. Jason **has** a new book.
6. Red **and** yellow make orange.

The Science of Spelling ◄••

- Ninety-seven percent of the time, /ă/ is spelled **a**. Only a few words (**have, plaid,** and **laugh**) have /ă/ spelled in any other way. These variant spellings are generally a result of pronunciation changes over time. Because of this consistent pattern, /ă/ is a good sound to start both reading and spelling instruction.

ELL Support

Choose from the activities below to reinforce English language acquisition.

Beginning

Letter/Sound Identification Write each spelling word on a flash card. Show each card, say the word, and have students repeat it. Ask, *What sound is the same in all the words?* (/ă/) Display all the cards. Ask, *What letter is the same in all the words?* (a) Have students read the words aloud. Guide them to see the connection between the letter **a** and the **short a** sound.

Making Words List the spelling words on the board. Then write each word on a card and cut the letters apart. Mix the letters. Have students select letters to reconstruct the words. As they put each word together, have students say the sound of each letter and then blend the sounds to say the word. As an extension, spell a word by saying the sound each letter makes. Students select a letter for each sound to construct the word. Have them say the word.

Intermediate

Letter Substitution Write **a** on the board and say /ă/. Say each spelling word, emphasizing /ă/, and have students repeat. Then write **at** on the board. Have students say the word. Add **c** before **at** and have students say the word. Erase **c** and add **h**. Invite students to suggest other beginning letters.

Picture Sentences On the board, write several sentences that include spelling words. Prompt students to help you create these. Read each sentence aloud and have students repeat. Then have students choose a sentence and illustrate it. Encourage students to make up their own sentences and illustrate them.

Rhyming Words On newsprint, have students create a list of words that rhyme with the spelling words. Write a spelling word and have students write rhyming words under it. Students can add to the list at any time. Encourage them to make up a poem using the words on the list.

Support for Spanish Speakers

The /ă/ and /h/ sounds may be difficult for Spanish speakers to hear or pronounce. Provide students with brief daily opportunities to practice /ă/ and /h/ by repeating spelling words, segmenting the phonemes, and blending the words.

To ensure that students know the meanings of the spelling words, write each word on the board. Say each word clearly and have students repeat it. Ask a volunteer to use a word in a sentence or to tell something about the meaning of the word, and then have students write the word.

To help students discriminate the **short a** sound, have them take turns drawing a box around the letter **a** in each word on the board. Ask students whether the **short a** sound is in the beginning or in the middle of the word.

Choose from the activities below to reinforce English language acquisition.

Advanced

Word Meaning List the spelling words on the board and read each word aloud as you point to it. Ask students to identify any words they do not know. Use real objects, pictures, and pantomime to support explanations of word meaning. Then ask questions that can be answered using spelling words. For example, *Which word names a kind of pet?* (cat) *Which word names something you wear on your head?* (hat) *Which word helps you tell what someone owns?* (has) *Which word do you use to say you have two things?* (and)

Word Match Write each spelling word on two index cards. Turn the cards facedown in random order. Have pairs alternate turning over two cards. If the cards match in some way (end in **at,** begin with **a,** or begin with **h**), the cards are removed. If they do not match, they are turned over and left on the table. As students become more proficient, add words and change the matching rules.

Say It, Write It Have partners take turns saying a sentence using a spelling word. The partner writes the spelling word used in the sentence.

Finish the Sentence Have students complete the activities on page 7 of *Spelling Support for English Language Learners.*

Advanced High

Word Meaning List the spelling words on the board. Read each word aloud as you point to it. Ask students to identify any words they do not know. Use real objects, pictures, and pantomime to support explanations of word meaning. Provide large index cards. Have partners work together to write a question about a spelling word on one side of a card and the answer on the reverse. Partners meet with another pair to ask their questions.

Rhyming Words Have students select one or more spelling words and write as many rhyming words as they can think of. Partners can then work together to write pairs of sentences with end words that rhyme.

Riddles Encourage students to think of riddles using the spelling words. They can share riddles with a partner and see if they can guess the words. For example, *I begin with* **c.** *I am a pet. I say meow.* (cat)

Finish the Sentence Have students complete the activities on page 7 of *Spelling Support for English Language Learners.*

Spelling Support for English Language Learners

Practice Master, p. 7

Practice Master, p. 42

 Audio Conversation available on CD

English/Spanish Word List, p. 57

 **Spelling Connections Online**
Interactive online spelling activities provide additional ELL support.
www.spellingconnectionsonline.com

Connections to THINKING

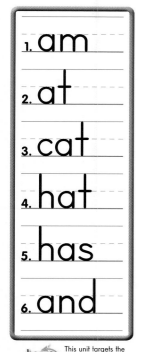

1. am
2. at
3. cat
4. hat
5. has
6. and

A. Write the spelling words that begin like **apple**.

1. _am_

2. _at_

3. _and_

B. Write the spelling words that have **short a** in the middle, like **bat**.

4. _cat_

5. _hat_

6. _has_

 School Home

This unit targets the **short a** sound. Ask your child to read the spelling words aloud.

47

Student Objectives
• Read, spell, and write words with **short a** in the initial and medial position.

Unit Pretest
• Administer the pretest on page T47B.

Teaching Tips
• Have students read the spelling words aloud, emphasizing and listening to /ă/.

WORD SORT CD-ROM

• Conduct a **Teacher-Led Sort** (see p. Z31) to reinforce the spelling pattern.
• Use these Sound/Symbol Cards to review **short a: apple, ax, bag, cab, calf, last,** and **rash**.
• Write **at** on the board. Ask a volunteer to name the beginning sound. Remind students that when a word has only one vowel, the vowel sound is usually short. Ask a volunteer to read the word.
• Introduce remaining spelling words in the same way. Ask which spelling words rhyme. (**at, hat, cat**)
• Then ask which words have **short a** spelled with **a** between two consonants. (**hat, cat**) Have students generate a list of other words that rhyme.
• Have students complete the page.

Home/School Word Lists TRB
• Have students take home the Home/ School Spelling Practice Master.

Home/School Practice

Home/School Spelling
Practice Master, *TRB*, p. 31

Home/School Spelling
Practice Master, *TRB*, p. 32

English

Spanish

Student Objectives

- Segment sounds to determine the number of sounds in words.
- Spell and write **short a** words with a VC and CVC pattern.
- Track letters in a-b-c order.

Teaching Tips

- Write **cat** on the board and read it aloud. Have students say the word, stretching each sound and holding up a finger each time they hear a different sound. Ask, *How many fingers are you holding up? How many sounds do you hear in* **cat**? (three) Continue by asking such questions as, *Is the first sound you hear a vowel or a consonant sound? What vowel sound do you hear? Where is the vowel sound?* Repeat with other words.
- Have students complete Parts A and B independently or as a class.
- Review a-b-c order by singing the ABC song or reciting the alphabet with the class.
- Have students complete part C with a partner.

Extra Pattern Practice TRB

- Use the optional practice master below for extra practice with **short a**.

WORD SORT CD-ROM

- Provide time for students to use a **Buddy Sort** to practice their spelling words with a partner (see p. Z31).

Connections to PHONICS

A. Write the words that have two sounds.

1. am
2. at

B. Write the words that have three sounds.

3. cat
4. hat
5. has
6. and

am
at
cat
hat
has
and

C. Use your pencil to track the letters in a-b-c order. The first two are tracked for you.

```
f  a  g  b  w  r  c  l  s  d  v  e  f
a  b  g  t  h  d  q  i  n  j  h  k  l
m  z  c  n  d  o  i  x  p  d  q  r  w
s  g  t  o  m  u  b  s  v  w  h  x  l
y  v  z
```

48

TEKS 1.22A Use phonological knowledge to match sounds to letters to construct known words. 1.22Bi Use letter-sound patterns to spell: consonant-vowel-consonant (CVC) words. 1.22C Spell high-frequency words from a commonly used list.

Extra Pattern Practice

Extra Pattern Practice Master,
TRB, p. 33

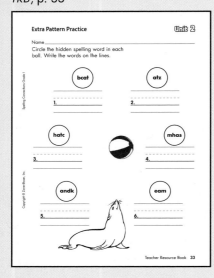

Pattern Practice Game: /ă/

To reinforce /ă/ spellings, generate a list of words that rhyme with **cat**. Then write **at** on the board. Display the letter cards **b, c, f, h, m, p, r,** and **s**. Have students select a letter card and place it next to **at** to make a word. Have the class pronounce each new word. Then have students create a poem using as many of these words as they can. Write their poem on the board and then read it aloud.

TEKS 1.22A Use phonological knowledge to match sounds to letters to construct known words. 1.22Bi Use letter-sound patterns to spell: consonant-vowel-consonant (CVC) words. 1.22C Spell high-frequency words from a commonly used list.

Write the correct word in each sentence.

has   cat

am
at
cat
hat
has
and

1. The _____cat_____ ran up a tree.

2. The man _____has_____ a hammer.

am   and

3. I _____am_____ happy.

4. I can run _____and_____ jump.

at   hat

5. The monkey had on a tan _____hat_____.

6. Jan is _____at_____ school.

TEKS 1.22C Spell high-frequency words from a commonly used list.

49

Student Objectives
• Spell and write **short a** VC and CVC words to complete sentences.

Teaching Tips
• Ask students to choose a spelling word from the list and use it in a sentence.
• Write students' sentences on the board, or type the sentences and provide each student with a copy. Leave a blank for each spelling word.
• Have students write the spelling word to complete each sentence. Then have them read the sentences.
• Have students complete page 49 individually or as a class. Ask volunteers to read the completed sentences aloud.
• Challenge students to look for the spelling words when they read.

Differentiated Instruction
• Use the **Challenge Words** activity on page 184 with students who are ready to transfer their knowledge of **short a** to new words.
• An Extra Challenge Practice Master is available on page 34 in the *TRB*.
• Dictation sentences for the challenge words are available on page T184.

More Fun With Spelling for Differentiation

▶ Digital Resources for Spelling Connections
Interactive digital resources include word sorts, pattern practice, and proofreading activities for individual and whole-group instruction. (Interactive whiteboard compatible; see p. Z32.)

▶ Spelling Connections Online
Interactive online spelling activities include word sorts, crossword puzzles, sentence completion, proofreading practice, and spelling bees with words from each unit (see p. Z32). www.spellingconnectionsonline.com

Spelling Center Activities

Spelling Game Mats
Place one of the spelling games in a learning center to provide a fun way for students to practice their spelling words (see p. Z26).

Flip Folder
Students can use a Flip Folder to practice spelling words independently (see p. Z32).

Word Sort CD-ROM
Printable, unit-specific word cards for spelling and challenge words can be used for Teacher-Led, Individual, Buddy, and Speed Sorts (see p. Z31).

TEKS 1.22C Spell high-frequency words from a commonly used list.

T49

Student Objectives
- Spell and write **short a** VC and CVC words to complete a poem.

Teaching Tips
- Read the poem on page 50. Have students identify the rhyming words. (**fat, sat, hat, splat, that**)
- Read and explain the directions.
- Have students complete the page independently or do the activity as a class. Read the completed poem aloud.
- Explain that sensory details tell what you see, hear, feel, taste, or smell. Ask students to pick out words in the poem that provide sensory details. (**not fat, big, flat**) Have them suggest other sensory details they could add.

🔵 WORD SORT CD-ROM
- Invite students to practice for the weekly test by doing an **Individual Sort** or a **Speed Sort** (see p. Z31).

Connections to WRITING

Cat-astrophe

Cat is fat.   Hat went splat.
When he sat   That was that!
On my hat,   — Kevin O'Hara

Write another poem about the cat. Use spelling words.

I _____ **am** _____ not fat.

I am just a big _____ **cat** _____.

I sat on that _____ **hat** _____,

_____ **and** _____ I made it flat

to get _____ **at** _____ the rat

he _____ **has** _____ under his hat.

am
at
cat
hat
has
and

50

🟫 **TEKS 1.22C** Spell high-frequency words from a commonly used list.

1-Minute Handwriting Hint
The lowercase **t** begins at the headline.
The letter is crossed at the midline.

CROSS

Day 5

Student Objectives
- Demonstrate mastery of the unit spelling words.

Posttest Assessment Options
Option 1: Administer the unit posttest using the dictation sentences at right.
Option 2: Assess students using the standardized test. See the *Standardized Test Master Book*, p. 6.

Note: Posttest sentences for the on level and challenge lists are available on the audio *Spelling Connections* Posttest CD.

Posttest Sentences
1. Corey is **at** school.
2. Write your first **and** last names.
3. The wind blew my **hat** off.
4. I **am** making this for you.
5. Why is the **cat** purring?
6. Tim **has** a cold.

Standardized Test Master Book, p. 6

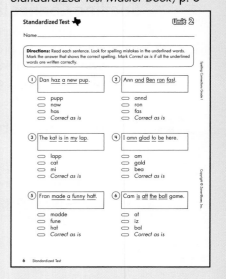

Standardized Test   Unit 2

Name _____

Directions: Read each sentence. Look for spelling mistakes in the underlined words. Mark the answer that shows the correct spelling. Mark *Correct as is* if all the underlined words are written correctly.

① Dan haz a new pup.
- pupp
- naw
- has
- Correct as is

② Ann and Ben ran fast.
- annd
- ron
- fas
- Correct as is

③ The kat is in my lap.
- lapp
- cat
- mi
- Correct as is

④ I amn glad to be here.
- am
- gald
- bea
- Correct as is

⑤ Fran made a funny hatt.
- madde
- fune
- hat
- Correct as is

⑥ Cam is att the ball game.
- at
- iz
- bal
- Correct as is

6   Standardized Test

 TEKS 1.22C Spell high-frequency words from a commonly used list.

Planner

Day 1

Day 2

Day 1

Connections to **Thinking**

Student Objectives
- Read, spell, and write words with **short e** in the medial position.
- Write rhyming words with /ĕ/.

Instruction for All Students
- Pretest Dictation Sentences, p. T5lB
- Connections to Thinking, p. 5l
- Home/School Spelling Practice Master (*Teacher Resource Book,* p. 35)

TEKS 1.22A, 1.22Bi, 1.22C

Connections to **Phonics**

Student Objectives
- Match sounds to letters to construct **short e** words.
- Spell and write **short e** words with a CVC pattern.

Instruction for All Students
- Connections to Phonics, p. 52

Optional Practice
- Extra Pattern Practice Master (*Teacher Resource Book,* p. 37)

TEKS 1.22A, 1.22Bi, 1.22C

Spelling Words
let
get
net
pet
pen
men

Challenge Words
hen
wet
den
fed

Day 3

Day 4

Day 5

Day 2

Day 3

Connections to **Reading**

Student Objectives
- Spell and write **short e** CVC words to complete sentences.

Instruction for All Students
- Connections to Reading, p. 53

Differentiated Instruction
- Challenge Words, p. 185

TEKS 1.22C

Connections to **Writing**

Student Objectives
- Spell and write **short e** CVC words to complete a story.

Instruction for All Students
- Connections to Writing, p. 54

Differentiated Instruction
- Extra Challenge Practice Master (*Teacher Resource Book,* p. 38)

TEKS 1.22C

Assessment

Student Objectives
- Demonstrate mastery of the unit spelling words.

Assessment for All Students
- Posttest Dictation Sentences, p. T54, or
- *Standardized Test Master Book,* p. 7

Differentiated Assessment
- Challenge Dictation Sentences, p. Tl85

Unit 3

Short e: CVC

Unit 3 Materials

Student Edition
pp. 51–54, 185

Teacher Edition
pp. T51A–T54, T185

 Teacher Resource Book
Unit 3 Practice Masters,
pp. 35–38, and
Sound/Symbol Cards

Standardized Test Master Book
Unit 3 Test Master, p. 7

 Word Sort CD-ROM
Unit 3 Word Sort Cards for Teacher-
Led Sorts and Student Sorts

 **Digital Resources for
Spelling Connections**
Unit 3

Spelling Connections Online
www.spellingconnectionsonline.com

**Spelling Support for
English Language Learners***
Unit 3 Practice Masters and
Audio Conversation

Spelling Center Activities*
Spelling Game Mats
Flip Folder, *TRB*, p. 155

*Spelling Support for English Language
Learners *and Spelling Center Activities* may
be used at any time during the week.*

Assessment

Pretest Sentences (See procedures on p. Z30.)

1. Please **let** me try that.
2. Did you **get** a balloon?
3. Carlos has a fish in his **net**.
4. Are you going to the **pet** show?
5. Susan writes letters with a funny **pen**!
6. The **men** are singing a song.

The Science of Spelling ◄ • •

Spelling /ĕ/ is very consistent. It is spelled **e** 93% of the time. The vowel digraph **ea** accounts for 4% of /ĕ/ spellings, such as in **bread, health,** and **threat**. The other spellings of /ĕ/ are rare. For example, **ai** in **again** and **said, ay** in **says, ie** in **friend,** and **u** in **bury**. These spellings are usually the result of changes in pronunciation over time.

ELL Support

Choose from the activities below to reinforce English language acquisition.

Beginning

Word Meaning Write each spelling word on a flash card. Show each word and read it aloud. Use real objects, pictures, and pantomime to support meaning.

Letter/Sound Identification Write each spelling word on a flash card. Show each card, say the word, and have students repeat it. Ask, *What sound is the same in all the words? (/ĕ/)* Display all the cards. Ask, *What letter is the same in all the words? (e)* Have students read the words aloud. Guide them to see the connection between the letter **e** and the **short e** sound.

Word Match Have students make flash cards for the spelling words or provide students with cards. Have students place the cards faceup. Read a spelling word aloud. Have students find the word and hold up the card.

Word/Picture Match Have students cut out the word and picture cards on page 8 of *Spelling Support for English Language Learners*. Read the instructions for playing the game, and have students play with a partner.

Intermediate

Word Meaning Write the spelling words on the board. Say each word aloud and have students repeat it. Use real objects, pictures, and pantomime to support the meaning of unfamiliar words. Ask a volunteer to choose a word and use it in a sentence or tell something about its meaning. If necessary, clarify and expand the definition. Then have students write the word on a piece of paper. Students may look at the word on the board to be sure they have spelled it correctly.

What Is It? Give each student two 3 x 5 cards. Have students write *Yes* on one card and *No* on the other. Hold up a flash card from Unit 3, such as **pen**. Ask, *Is it something you eat?* Have students respond by showing the correct answer card. **(no)** Then ask, *Can you write with it?* After students show the *Yes* card, have them read the word. Ask a volunteer to use the word in a sentence. Continue with the remaining words.

Word/Picture Match Have students cut out the word and picture cards on page 8 of *Spelling Support for English Language Learners*. Read the instructions for playing the game and have students play with a partner.

Support for Spanish Speakers

The **short e** sound may be difficult for some Spanish speakers to reproduce. The **short e** sound may be difficult for some students to hear or pronounce because of regional speech differences or first-language backgrounds that do not include this sound.

To help students discriminate the **short e** sound, write these words on the board.

man, **men**	mat, **met**	pat, **pet**
sat, **set**	bad, **bed**	

Give each student an **e** cut from construction paper. Say each pair of words on the board and ask students to listen for the different vowel sound in each word. Define the two words in each pair. Then say the words again and ask students to hold up their letters when they hear the **short e** sound.

Unit 3

Choose from the activities below to reinforce English language acquisition.

Advanced

Word Meaning List the spelling words. Have students identify any unfamiliar words. Use real objects, pictures, and pantomime to support meaning as you explain words. Then ask questions that can be answered using spelling words. For example, *Which word means more than one man?* (men) *Which word names something you can use to catch a fish?* (net) *Which word names something you can write with?* (pen) *Which word can you use to tell about a dog or a cat that lives with you?* (pet)

Making Sentences Have a student choose two spelling words. A partner writes a sentence using the words, such as *The pet is in the pen.* Encourage students to illustrate their sentences.

Word/Picture Match Have students cut out the word and picture cards on page 8 of *Spelling Support for English Language Learners.* Read the instructions for playing the game and have students play with a partner. Then have students complete the other activities on the page.

Advanced High

Word Meaning List the spelling words. Have students identify any unfamiliar words. Use real objects, pictures, and pantomime to support meaning as you explain words. Provide pairs with large index cards. Have partners work together to write a question about a spelling word on one side of a card and the answer on the reverse. Partners meet with another pair to ask their questions.

Word Sort Have students sort spelling words into two groups: action and things. Point out that **pet** can be used in both groups. Ask students to write a sentence to illustrate each meaning, such as *I pet the dog. My pet is a cat.*

Story Words Encourage students to draw a scene that includes illustrations of spelling words. Then have students use the spelling words to tell a partner about their picture. The partner can write the spelling words heard in the story.

Word/Picture Match Have students cut out the word and picture cards on page 8 of *Spelling Support for English Language Learners.* Read the instructions for playing the game and have students play with a partner. Then have students complete the other activities on the page.

Spelling Support for English Language Learners

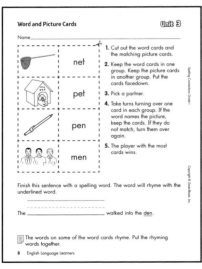

Practice Master, p. 8

Practice Master, p. 43

Audio Conversation available on CD

English/Spanish
Word List, p. 58

Spelling Connections Online
Interactive online spelling activities
provide additional ELL support.
www.spellingconnectionsonline.com

Connections to THINKING

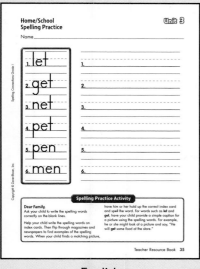

1. let
2. get
3. net
4. pet
5. pen
6. men

 School Home
This unit teaches **short e**. Ask your child to find the rhyming words on the spelling list.

A. Write the spelling words that end with **en**.

1. pen
2. men

B. Write the spelling words that end with **et**.

3. let
4. get
5. net
6. pet

TEKS 1.22Bi Use letter-sound patterns to spell: consonant-vowel-consonant (CVC) words. **1.22C** Spell high-frequency words from a commonly used list.

51

Day 1 — Unit 3

Student Objectives
- Read, spell, and write words with **short e** in the medial position.
- Write rhyming words with /ĕ/.

Unit Pretest
- Administer the pretest on page T51B.

Teaching Tips
- Have students read the spelling words aloud, emphasizing and listening to /ĕ/.

 **WORD SORT CD-ROM**

- Conduct a **Teacher-Led Sort** (see p. Z31) to introduce the spelling pattern.
- Show the Sound/Symbol Cards for **bed, jet, leg, nest, net, shell, sled, stem, yell,** and **web.** Have students name each picture, emphasizing the **short e** sound. Write the picture names. Ask a volunteer to circle **e** in each word. Remind students that when a word has one vowel between two consonants, the vowel sound is usually short.
- Write **et** on the board. Guide students in reading it aloud. Write **l** in front of **et.** Ask a volunteer to read the word and use it in a sentence. Do the same with **get, pet,** and **net.**

Home/School Word Lists **TRB**
- Have students take home the Home/School Spelling Practice Master.

Home/School Practice

Home/School Spelling
Practice Master, *TRB*, p. 35

Home/School Spelling
Practice Master, *TRB*, p. 36

Home/School Spelling Practice — Unit 3
Name _____

1. let
2. get
3. net
4. pet
5. pen
6. men

Spelling Practice Activity

Dear Family,
Ask your child to write the spelling words correctly on the blank lines.

Help your child write the spelling words on index cards. Then flip through magazines and newspapers to find examples of the spelling words. When your child finds a matching picture,

have him or her hold up the correct index card and spell the word. For words such as **let** and **get,** have your child provide a simple caption for a picture using the spelling words. For example, he or she might look at a picture and say, "We will **get** some food at the store."

Teacher Resource Book 35

Práctica de ortografía para el hogar o la escuela — Unit 3
Nombre _____

1. let — permitir; dar; dejar
2. get — obtener
3. net — red
4. pet — animalito; mascota
5. pen — pluma; corral
6. men — hombres

Actividad de ortografía

Querida familia:
Pida a su hijo(a) que escriba correctamente las palabras de ortografía en los renglones en blanco.

Ayude a su hijo(a) a escribir correctamente en tarjetas las palabras de ortografía que debe aprender. Luego, busquen en revistas y periódicos ejemplos de estas palabras.

Cuando su hijo(a) encuentre una ilustración que corresponda a alguna de las tarjetas, pídale que levante la tarjeta con la palabra correspondiente y que la deletree. Para palabras como **let** (permitir) o **get** (obtener, conseguir), muéstrele una ilustración o pídale que imagine y diga una leyenda que incluya estas palabras. Por ejemplo, en una ilustración puede decir: "Él va a conseguir comida en la tienda".

36 Teacher Resource Book

English

Spanish

TEKS 1.22A Use phonological knowledge to match sounds to letters to construct known words. **1.22Bi** Use letter-sound patterns to spell: consonant-vowel-consonant (CVC) words. **1.22C** Spell high-frequency words from a commonly used list.

T51

Student Objectives

- Match sounds to letters to construct **short e** words.
- Spell and write **short e** words with a CVC pattern.

Teaching Tips

- Say the spelling words, emphasizing the **short e** sound.
- Say each of the word pairs below. Have students raise their hand when they hear a word with /ĕ/.

man/men	pen/pan
pat/pet	not/net
get/got	let/lit
pet/pit	lot/let
net/nut	pen/pin

- Write **pet** on the board. Challenge students to change one letter to make another spelling word. Write the words as students suggest them.
- Have students complete page 52 independently or as a class.

Extra Pattern Practice ![TRB]

- Use the optional practice master below for extra practice with **short e**.

![WORD SORT] CD-ROM

- Provide time for students to use a **Buddy Sort** (see p. Z31) to practice their spelling words with a partner.

Connections to PHONICS

A. Four spelling words rhyme. Write the words.
Circle the letters that are the same in all the words.

1. l(et)
2. g(et)
3. n(et)
4. p(et)

B. Write the word that rhymes and tells about the picture.

5. ten ___?___   **men**
6. hen ___?___   **pen**
7. wet ___?___   **pet**
8. get ___?___   **net**

Word bank:
let
get
net
pet
pen
men

52

TEKS 1.22A Use phonological knowledge to match sounds to letters to construct known words. 1.22C Spell high-frequency words from a commonly used list.

Extra Pattern Practice

Extra Pattern Practice Master,
TRB, p. 37

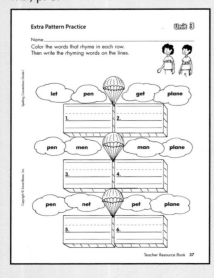

Pattern Practice Game: /ĕ/

Display letter cards **b, g, j, l, m, n, p, s, v, w,** and **y.** Write **et** on the board. Have students select a letter card and place it next to **et** to make a word. Ask students to pronounce the words they make. Possible words are **bet, get, jet, let, met, net, pet, set, vet, wet,** and **yet.** List students' words on the board. Ask what short vowel spelling pattern they see in all the words. **(one vowel between two consonants)**

TEKS 1.22A Use phonological knowledge to match sounds to letters to construct known words. **1.22Bi** Use letter-sound patterns to spell: consonant-vowel-consonant (CVC) words. **1.22C** Spell high-frequency words from a commonly used list.

Connections to READING

Write a spelling word to complete each sentence.

men	pen

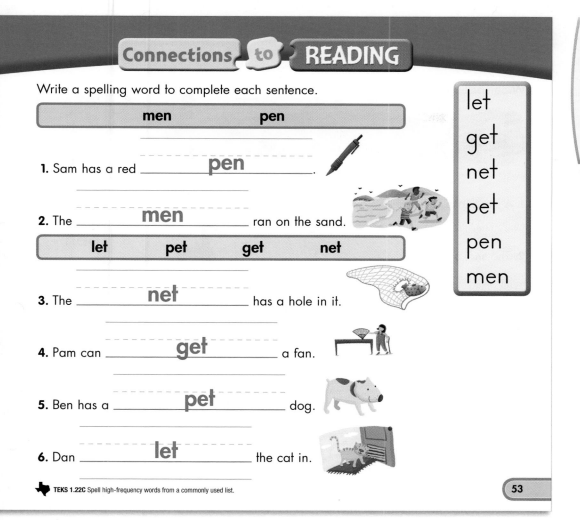

1. Sam has a red ____pen____ .

2. The ____men____ ran on the sand.

let	pet	get	net

3. The ____net____ has a hole in it.

4. Pam can ____get____ a fan.

5. Ben has a ____pet____ dog.

6. Dan ____let____ the cat in.

let
get
net
pet
pen
men

 TEKS 1.22C Spell high-frequency words from a commonly used list.

53

Student Objectives
- Spell and write **short e** CVC words to complete sentences.

Teaching Tips
- Write a sentence using a spelling word, leaving a blank for the spelling word. For example, *I can _____ the book.*
- Read the sentence aloud, pausing for the blank. Then say the sentence twice more, inserting **let** and then **get** in the blank.
- Ask students which spelling word correctly completes the sentence. (get) Call on a volunteer to write the word in the sentence.
- Have students complete the page independently or as a class.

Differentiated Instruction
- Use the **Challenge Words** activity on page 185 with students who are ready to transfer their knowledge of **short e** to new words.
- An Extra Challenge Practice Master is available on page 38 in the *TRB*.
- Dictation sentences for the challenge words are available on page T185.

More Fun With Spelling for Differentiation

Digital Resources for Spelling Connections

Interactive digital resources include word sorts, pattern practice, and proofreading activities for individual and whole-group instruction. (Interactive whiteboard compatible; see p. Z32.)

Spelling Connections Online

Interactive online spelling activities include word sorts, crossword puzzles, sentence completion, proofreading practice, and spelling bees with words from each unit (see p. Z32). www.spellingconnectionsonline.com

Spelling Center Activities

Spelling Game Mats
Place one of the spelling games in a learning center to provide a fun way for students to practice their spelling words (see p. Z26).

Flip Folder
Students can use a Flip Folder to practice spelling words independently (see p. Z32).

Word Sort CD-ROM
Printable, unit-specific word cards for spelling and challenge words can be used for Teacher-Led, Individual, Buddy, and Speed Sorts (see p. Z31).

TEKS 1.22C Spell high-frequency words from a commonly used list.

T53

Student Objectives
- Spell and write **short e** CVC words to complete a story.

Teaching Tips
- Remind students that a story has a beginning, a middle, and an end. Recall the beginning, middle, and end of a familiar story.
- Discuss a story students might tell about the picture on page 54.
- Read and explain the directions.
- Have students complete the page independently or as a class.
- Read the completed story. Have students identify the beginning, middle, and end.

WORD SORT CD-ROM
- Invite students to practice for the weekly test by doing an **Individual Sort** or a **Speed Sort** (see p. Z31).

Connections to WRITING

Write spelling words to complete the story.

let
get
net
pet
pen
men

1. A big snake is in the __**pen**__.

2. The snake is a big __**pet**__.

3. The girl __**let**__ the snake out.

4. The __**men**__ see the snake.

5. One man tried to __**get**__ the snake.

6. At last he used a __**net**__.

54

TEKS 1.22C Spell high-frequency words from a commonly used list.

1-Minute Handwriting Hint

The lowercase **e** begins with a slide right stroke. The circle back stroke touches the beginning stroke.

BEGIN HERE → e

Day 5

Student Objectives
- Demonstrate mastery of the unit spelling words.

Posttest Assessment Options
Option 1: Administer the unit posttest using the dictation sentences at right.

Option 2: Assess students using the standardized test. See the *Standardized Test Master Book*, p. 7.

Note: Posttest sentences for the on level and challenge lists are available on the audio *Spelling Connections* Posttest CD.

Posttest Sentences
1. Does your father **let** you help him?
2. I will **get** Mom a birthday card.
3. We can hit the ball over the **net**.
4. Is a cat a good **pet**?
5. Write your name with a **pen**.
6. These **men** are waiting for the bus.

Standardized Test Master Book, p. 7

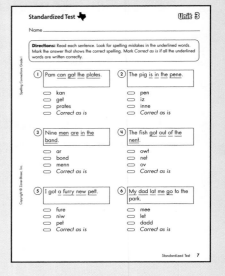

T54

 TEKS 1.22C Spell high-frequency words from a commonly used list.

Planner

Day 1 | Day 2

Day 1

Connections to **Thinking**

Student Objectives
- Read, spell, and write words with **short e** in the medial position.
- Write words in the **et** family.

Instruction for All Students
- Pretest Dictation Sentences, p. T55B
- Connections to Thinking, p. 55
- Home/School Spelling Practice Master (*Teacher Resource Book*, p. 39)

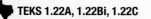 **TEKS 1.22A, 1.22Bi, 1.22C**

Connections to **Phonics**

Student Objectives
- Match beginning sounds of picture names to letters to construct **short e** words.
- Spell and write **short e** words with a CVC pattern.

Instruction for All Students
- Connections to Phonics, p. 56

Optional Practice
- Extra Pattern Practice Master (*Teacher Resource Book*, p. 41)

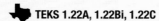 **TEKS 1.22A, 1.22Bi, 1.22C**

Spelling Words
jet
set
met
bed
yes
leg

Challenge Words
led
mend
vest
mess

Day 3 | Day 4 | Day 5

Day 2 | | Day 3

Connections to **Reading**

Student Objectives
- Sort spelling words into meaning categories.
- Spell and write **short e** CVC words.

Instruction for All Students
- Connections to Reading, p. 57

Differentiated Instruction
- Challenge Words, p. 186

TEKS 1.22C

Connections to **Writing**

Student Objectives
- Spell and write **short e** CVC words to complete alliterative sentences.

Instruction for All Students
- Connections to Writing, p. 58

Differentiated Instruction
- Extra Challenge Practice Master (*Teacher Resource Book*, p. 42)

TEKS 1.22A, 1.22C

Assessment

Student Objectives
- Demonstrate mastery of the unit spelling words.

Assessment for All Students
- Posttest Dictation Sentences, p. T58, or
- *Standardized Test Master Book*, p. 8

Differentiated Assessment
- Challenge Dictation Sentences, p. T186

Unit 4

Short e: CVC

Unit 4 Materials

Student Edition
pp. 55–58, 186

Teacher Edition
pp. T55A–T58, T186

 Teacher Resource Book
Unit 4 Practice Masters,
pp. 39–42, and
Sound/Symbol Cards

 Standardized Test Master Book
Unit 4 Test Master, p. 8

 Word Sort CD-ROM
Unit 4 Word Sort Cards for Teacher-
Led Sorts and Student Sorts

 **Digital Resources for
Spelling Connections**
Unit 4

 Spelling Connections Online
www.spellingconnectionsonline.com

**Spelling Support for
English Language Learners***
Unit 4 Practice Masters and
Audio Conversation

Spelling Center Activities*
Spelling Game Mats
Flip Folder, *TRB*, p. 155

*Spelling Support for English Language
Learners *and* Spelling Center Activities *may
be used at any time during the week.*

Assessment

Pretest Sentences (See procedures on p. Z30.)

1. The **jet** was flying low.
2. Please **set** the dish on the table.
3. I **met** a real clown!
4. May Karen sleep in my **bed**?
5. My mother said **yes**.
6. Can you hop on one **leg**?

The Science of Spelling

When a single vowel appears in a closed syllable, it is usually short. Short vowel sounds rarely occur at the end of a word. Many CVC, CVCC, and CCVCC words have /ĕ/, as in **net, next,** and **shell**. There are relatively few high frequency words that begin with /ĕ/. (**echo, edge, edit, educate, effort, egg, elbow, elephant, elm, end, engine, exit,** and **extra**) Many students have trouble distinguishing the sounds of /ă/ and /ĕ/ (**man/men**) and /ĕ/ and /ĭ/ (**pen/pin**), so they confuse the spellings.

ELL Support

Choose from the activities below to reinforce English language acquisition.

Beginning

Word Meaning Write each spelling word on a flash card. Show each word and read it aloud. Use real objects, pictures, and pantomime to support meaning.

Beginning, Middle, End Say a spelling word. Have one student say the beginning sound, have a second student say the middle sound, and have a third student say the ending sound. Write the word on the board and have students copy it. Continue with the remaining spelling words.

Word Match Have students make flash cards for the spelling words or provide students with cards. Have students place the cards faceup. Read a spelling word aloud. Have students find the word and hold up the card.

What Am I? Have students work in pairs to complete the activities on page 9 of *Spelling Support for English Language Learners*.

Intermediate

Letter Substitution Write **e** on the board and say /ĕ/. Say each spelling word and have students repeat after you individually and in chorus. Then write **et** on the board. Have students say the word. Add **j** before **et** and have students say the word. Then erase **j** and add **s**. Continue with **m**. Invite students to suggest other beginning letters to make more words with **et**. (bet, get, let, net, pet, vet, wet, yet)

Nouns and Verbs Explain that nouns are words that name things, and verbs are words that name actions. Use **net** and **ran** as examples. Say and define each word. Then create a two-column chart with **net** and **ran** as column heads. Have students categorize other spelling words by writing them in the appropriate column. Add words to the chart each week.

What Am I? Have students work in pairs to complete the activities on page 9 of *Spelling Support for English Language Learners*.

Support for Spanish Speakers

Help students pronounce the **short e** sound. Have them notice that when they say /ĕ/ their mouth is open and their tongue is behind their bottom teeth. Say /ĕ/ and have students repeat. Contrast this with saying the name of the letter **e** when their lips are stretched wider as though smiling.

Play a "Simon Says" type of game to practice pronouncing and reading the **short a** and **short e** sounds. Have students make flash cards for **short a** and **short e** word pairs such as **pat** and **pet, bad** and **bed, pan** and **pen**. Start by having students put one pair of cards faceup on their desk. Say, *Simon says pat. Hold up the card that says pat.* Have students hold up their **pat** card and say the word. Gradually increase the number of words students choose from, using up to six cards (three pairs).

Choose from the activities below to reinforce English language acquisition.

Advanced

Word Meaning List the spelling words on the board and read each word aloud as you point to it. Ask students to identify any words they do not know. Use real objects, pictures, and pantomime to support explanations of word meaning.

Finish the Sentence Write a question on the board that uses one or two spelling words, such as *Does a **jet** have a **leg**?* Ask a volunteer to read the sentence. Write a sentence that answers the question, but leave out the spelling words: *A _____ does not have a _____.* Ask students which spelling words are missing and write the words on the lines. (jet, leg) Ask a volunteer to read the answer. Continue the activity using the rest of the words.

True or False Use a spelling word in a statement that is true or false. For example, *Yes means the opposite of no. I rode the jet to school.* Have students say *true* if the sentence makes sense. If the sentence is false, ask students to explain why. Then have them use the spelling word in a true sentence.

What Am I? Have students work in pairs to complete the activities on page 9 of *Spelling Support for English Language Learners.*

Advanced High

Word Meaning List the spelling words on the board and read each word aloud as you point to it. Ask students to identify any words they do not know. Use real objects, pictures, and pantomime to support explanations of word meaning.

Story Words Encourage students to draw a picture that includes illustrations of spelling words. Then have students use the spelling words to tell a partner about their picture. The partner can write the spelling words heard in the story.

What Am I? Have students work in pairs to complete the activities on page 9 of *Spelling Support for English Language Learners.*

Spelling Support for English Language Learners

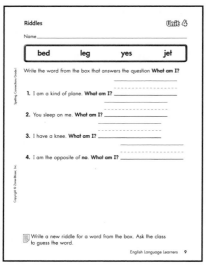

Practice Master, p. 9

Practice Master, p. 43

 Audio Conversation available on CD

English/Spanish Word List, p. 58

 **Spelling Connections Online**
Interactive online spelling activities provide additional ELL support.
www.spellingconnectionsonline.com

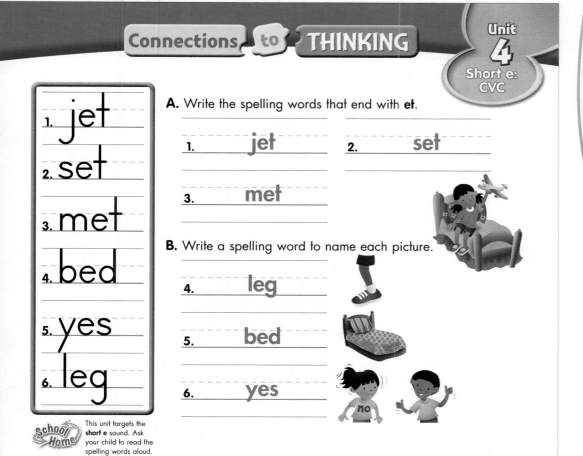

A. Write the spelling words that end with **et**.

1. ___jet___   2. ___set___

3. ___met___

B. Write a spelling word to name each picture.

4. ___leg___

5. ___bed___

6. ___yes___

1. jet
2. set
3. met
4. bed
5. yes
6. leg

This unit targets the **short e** sound. Ask your child to read the spelling words aloud.

TEKS 1.22C Spell high-frequency words from a commonly used list.

55

Student Objectives
- Read, spell, and write words with **short e** in the medial position.
- Write words in the **et** family.

Unit Pretest
- Administer the pretest on page T55B.

Teaching Tips
- Have students read the spelling words aloud, emphasizing and listening to /ĕ/.

 **WORD SORT CD-ROM**

- Conduct a **Teacher-Led Sort** (see p. Z31) to reinforce the spelling pattern.
- Display or draw a picture of a jet. Have students name the picture. Write **jet** on the board. Have students name the vowel sound they hear and tell where it is in the word.
- Tell students that a spelling word rhymes with **jet** and begins with the letter **s**. Ask a volunteer to name the word and write it below **jet**. Do the same with **met**. Have students identify the rhyming sounds.
- Nod your head up and down and have students name the spelling word that tells what you are gesturing. (yes)
- Have students complete the page independently or as a class.

Home/School Word Lists **TRB**
- Have students take home the Home/School Spelling Practice Master.

Home/School Practice

Home/School Spelling
Practice Master, *TRB*, p. 39

Home/School Spelling
Practice Master, *TRB*, p. 40

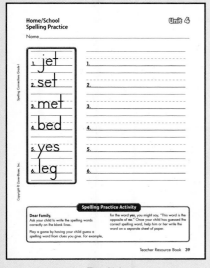

English

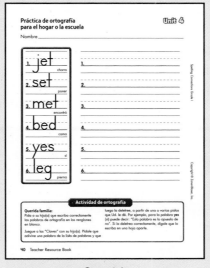

Spanish

 TEKS **1.22A** Use phonological knowledge to match sounds to letters to construct known words. **1.22Bi** Use letter-sound patterns to spell: consonant-vowel-consonant (CVC) words. **1.22C** Spell high-frequency words from a commonly used list.

Student Objectives
- Match beginning sounds of picture names to letters to construct **short e** words.
- Spell and write **short e** words with a CVC pattern.

Teaching Tips
- Say the spelling words. Point out that all of the words have the **short e** sound spelled with one vowel between two consonants.
- Say **jet**, emphasizing the individual sounds /j/ /ĕ/ /t/. Have students say each spelling word slowly and listen for the beginning, middle, and ending sound.
- Display pictures of an egg, the numeral 10, and a jar. Ask students to identify the picture that begins with the same sound as **jet**. (**jar**) Continue with the medial and end sounds.
- Have students complete page 56 independently or as a class.

Extra Pattern Practice **TRB**
- Use the optional practice master below for extra practice with **short e**.

WORD SORT CD-ROM
- Provide time for students to use a **Buddy Sort** (see p. Z31) to practice their spelling words with a partner.

Connections to PHONICS

Write the spelling word that begins with the same sound and letter as the picture name.

jet
set
met
bed
yes
leg

1. met

2. bed

3. yes

4. jet

5. leg

6. set

TEKS 1.22A Use phonological knowledge to match sounds to letters to construct known words. **1.22C** Spell high-frequency words from a commonly used list.

Extra Pattern Practice

Extra Pattern Practice Master,
TRB, p. 41

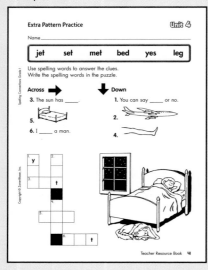

Pattern Practice Game: /ĕ/

Have a student write an **e** on a sheet of paper. A partner writes a consonant on the left and on the right of the **e** to construct a **short e** word. Then have partners switch. Have students continue until they have written several **short e** words.

TEKS 1.22A Use phonological knowledge to match sounds to letters to construct known words. **1.22Bi** Use letter-sound patterns to spell: consonant-vowel-consonant (CVC) words. **1.22C** Spell high-frequency words from a commonly used list.

A. Write the spelling words that name things.

1. bed

2. jet

3. leg

B. Write the spelling words that tell an action.

4. met

5. set

C. Write the spelling word that is the opposite of "no."

6. yes

jet
set
met
bed
yes
leg

TEKS 1.22C Spell high-frequency words from a commonly used list.

57

Student Objectives
- Sort spelling words into meaning categories.
- Spell and write **short e** CVC words.

Teaching Tips
- Review that words can name things. Point to objects and have students name them. Then point to your leg. Have students say **leg** and write the word on a sheet of paper.
- Explain that words can name actions. Clap your hands. Have students name the action. **(clap)** Then set a book on a desk. Have students write the word. **(set)**
- Point out that some words are opposites. Open the door. Ask students to name what you did and then tell you the opposite. **(open, close)**
- Have students complete the page independently or as a class.

Differentiated Instruction
- Use the **Challenge Words** activity on page 186 with students who are ready to transfer their knowledge of **short e** to new words.
- An Extra Challenge Practice Master is available on page 42 in the *TRB*.
- Dictation sentences for the challenge words are available on page T186.

More Fun With Spelling for Differentiation

Digital Resources for Spelling Connections

Interactive digital resources include word sorts, pattern practice, and proofreading activities for individual and whole-group instruction. (Interactive whiteboard compatible; see p. Z32.)

Spelling Connections Online

Interactive online spelling activities include word sorts, crossword puzzles, sentence completion, proofreading practice, and spelling bees with words from each unit (see p. Z32). www.spellingconnectionsonline.com

Spelling Center Activities

Spelling Game Mats
Place one of the spelling games in a learning center to provide a fun way for students to practice their spelling words (see p. Z26).

Flip Folder
Students can use a Flip Folder to practice spelling words independently (see p. Z32).

Word Sort CD-ROM
Printable, unit-specific word cards for spelling and challenge words can be used for Teacher-Led, Individual, Buddy, and Speed Sorts (see p. Z31).

TEKS 1.22C Spell high-frequency words from a commonly used list.

Student Objectives
- Spell and write **short e** CVC words to complete alliterative sentences.

Teaching Tips
- To introduce alliteration, repeat a familiar tongue twister like *Rubber baby buggy bumpers.* Have students identify the sound that is repeated. Explain that poets often use repeated sound in their poems.
- Have students complete the page independently or as a class. Have students read the sentences as fast as they can and then identify the sound that is repeated in each.
- Guide students' attention to item 5. Ask, *What kind of letter do we write at the beginning of every sentence?* (**a capital or an uppercase letter**) *How should we write the word that starts this sentence?* (**start with a capital or uppercase Y**)

WORD SORT CD-ROM
- Invite students to practice for the weekly test by doing an **Individual Sort** or a **Speed Sort** (see p. Z31).

Connections to WRITING

Write a spelling word to finish each tongue twister.

jet
set
met
bed
yes
leg

1. Sue _____ **set** _____ six shells in the shack.

2. Matt _____ **met** _____ merry mice in the mud.

3. Jack jumped on the jolly _____ **jet** _____.

4. Lucky laid down on Lil's left _____ **leg** _____.

5. _____ **Yes** _____, the yellow yak yelled, "Yippee!"

6. Bill's _____ **bed** _____ has a blue blanket.

58

1-Minute Handwriting Hint
The **j** consists of a vertical stroke and a curve-left stroke. The curve stroke is part of a circle motion.

j ← CURVE LEFT

Day 5

Student Objectives
- Demonstrate mastery of the unit spelling words.

Posttest Assessment Options
Option 1: Administer the unit posttest using the dictation sentences at right.
Option 2: Assess students using the standardized test. See the *Standardized Test Master Book*, p. 8.

Note: Posttest sentences for the on level and challenge lists are available on the audio *Spelling Connections* Posttest CD.

Posttest Sentences
1. If you like bananas, write **yes**.
2. Will you **set** this on my desk?
3. Have you **met** my brother?
4. I can make my own **bed**.
5. My **leg** is asleep.
6. I watched the **jet** land.

Standardized Test Master Book, p. 8

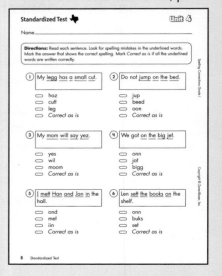

Standardized Test — Unit 4

Name _____

Directions: Read each sentence. Look for spelling mistakes in the underlined words. Mark the answer that shows the correct spelling. Mark *Correct as is* if all the underlined words are written correctly.

1. My <u>legg</u> has a small cut.
- haz
- cutt
- leg
- Correct as is

2. Do not jump on the <u>bed</u>.
- jup
- beed
- oon
- Correct as is

3. My mom will say <u>yez</u>.
- yes
- wil
- moom
- Correct as is

4. We got on the big <u>jet</u>.
- onn
- jat
- bigg
- Correct as is

5. I <u>mett</u> Han and Jan in the hall.
- ond
- met
- iin
- Correct as is

6. Len <u>sett</u> the books on the shelf.
- onn
- buks
- set
- Correct as is

8 Standardized Test

Planner

Day 1

Day 1

Unit 1: Short a: VC, CVC

Student Objectives
- Review the spelling pattern and words from Unit I.

Instruction for All Students
- Unit I Review, p. 59
- Home/School Spelling Practice Master (*Teacher Resource Book*, p. 43)

Day 2

Unit 2: Short a: VC, CVC

Student Objectives
- Review the spelling pattern and words from Unit 2.

Instruction for All Students
- Unit 2 Review, p. 60

Unit 1
Short a: VC, CVC

an	ran
can	had
man	dad

Unit 2
Short a: VC, CVC

am	hat
at	has
cat	and

Unit 3
Short e: CVC

let	pet
get	pen
net	men

Unit 4
Short e: CVC

jet	bed
set	yes
met	leg

Day 3

Day 2

Unit 3: Short e: CVC

Student Objectives
- Review the spelling pattern and words from Unit 3.

Instruction for All Students
- Unit 3 Review, p. 6I

Day 4

Day 2

Unit 4: Short e: CVC

Student Objectives
- Review the spelling pattern and words from Unit 4.

Instruction for All Students
- Unit 4 Review, p. 62

Day 5

Day 3

Assessment

Student Objectives
- Demonstrate mastery of the review unit spelling words.

Assessment for All Students
- Posttest Assessment Options
  - ✦ Posttest Dictation Sentences, p. T62, or
  - ✦ *Standardized Test Master Book*, p. 9

Unit 5 Materials

Student Edition
pp. 59–62
Alphabet and Picture Cards

Teacher Edition
pp. T59A–T62

 Teacher Resource Book
Unit 5 Practice Masters,
pp. 43–44

 Standardized Test Master Book
Unit 5 Test Master, p. 9

 Word Sort CD-ROM
Unit 5 Word Sort Cards for Teacher-
Led Sorts and Student Sorts

 **Digital Resources for
Spelling Connections**
Unit 5

 Spelling Connections Online
www.spellingconnectionsonline.com

Spelling Center Activities*
Spelling Game Mats
Flip Folder, *TRB,* p. 155

**Spelling Center Activities may be used at
any time during the week.*

Developmental Spelling Check

Administer the following **Developmental Spelling Check** to evaluate spelling growth. Remind students that this is not a test for a grade; students are not expected to spell these words conventionally. Author J. Richard Gentry has provided (in parentheses) typical Phase 3 Phonetic Spellings for each word. Students who produce these or similar spellings are demonstrating full phonemic awareness since each letter corresponds to a sound in the word. These spellings are a middle first-grade benchmark.

To administer, say each word aloud, read the sentence, and then say the word again.

Animal Words and Sample Phonetic Spellings

camel	A **camel** lives in the desert.	(KAML, CAML)
elephant	The **elephant** has a trunk.	(LEFANT, LEFUNT, LEFENT)
tiger	A **tiger** has lots of stripes.	(TIGR)
monkey	That **monkey** is funny!	(MUKE, MNGKE)
giraffe	A **giraffe** has a long neck.	(JRAF, GRAF)

ELL Support

Choose from the activities below to reinforce English language acquisition.

Beginning

Short Vowel Sounds Write **a** and **e** on the board. Pronounce each spelling word and have students repeat after you. Point to the corresponding vowel on the board and repeat the vowel sound. Have students repeat it and say the word again. Have students hang the flash cards from Units 1–4 under the correct vowel.

Word Match Have students make flash cards for the spelling words or provide students with cards. Have students place the cards faceup. Read a spelling word aloud. Have students find the word and hold up the card.

Intermediate

Word Meaning Make flash cards for the spelling words. Introduce each word by showing the flash card, saying the word, and using real objects, pictures, and pantomime to support word meaning. For example, show a photograph of a child playing with a dog. Point to the dog and say, *This dog is a pet. You can play with a pet. Do you have a pet?*

Short Vowel Sounds Write **a** and **e** on the board. To teach or review the sounds, hold up a flash card, say the sound, and have students repeat. Model pronunciation of spelling words with that sound. Make **a** and **e** flash cards for each student. Say each spelling word. Have students hold up the corresponding short vowel card and repeat the word.

Support for Spanish Speakers

The **short a** and **short e** sounds may be difficult for some students to hear or pronounce because of regional speech differences or first-language backgrounds that do not include these sounds. Provide brief pronunciation practice regularly as needed. Remember that correct spelling can be achieved even when pronunciation is different.

To ensure that students know the meanings of the spelling words, write each word on the board. Say each word clearly and have students repeat it. Ask a volunteer to use the word in a sentence or to tell something about its meaning. If necessary, review the word in context, using a picture or pantomime. Ask students to check their word with the word on the board to be sure they spelled it correctly.

Unit 5

Choose from the activities below to reinforce English language acquisition.

Advanced

Word Meaning List the spelling words on the board. Then ask questions that can be answered using the words. For example, ask *Which word names something you can sleep in?* (bed) *Which word names something you can fly in?* (jet) *Which word names an animal that says meow?* (cat) *Which word names one male person?* (man)

Word Matching Make two sets of spelling word flash cards for each review unit. Shuffle the cards from two units; then spread them out facedown. Have students take turns turning over two cards. If the cards do not match, they are replaced in their original positions. Students who find matching words keep those cards. Repeat the game, using cards from different units.

Making Sentences Have a student choose two spelling words. A partner writes a sentence using the words, such as *The hat is on the cat.* Encourage students to illustrate their sentences.

Advanced High

Riddles Encourage students to think of riddles using the spelling words. They can share riddles with a partner and see if they can guess the words. For example, *I begin with n. You can use me to catch a fish.* (net)

Words and Sentences Model for students how to write a sentence that demonstrates an understanding of word meaning. For example, *I have a pet cat.* Work with students to generate two more examples. Then have students work in pairs to write a sentence for each spelling word to demonstrate their understanding of the word's meaning.

 Spelling Connections Online
Interactive online spelling activities provide additional ELL support.
www.spellingconnectionsonline.com

T59D

Review

Review

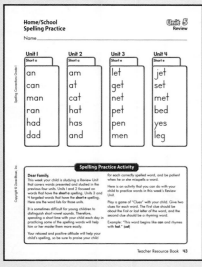

1. an
2. can
3. man
4. ran
5. had
6. dad

This unit reviews **short a** and **short e**. Ask your child to read the spelling list on each page aloud.

Unit 1: Short a: VC, CVC

A. Write the word that begins the same as **apple**.

1. an

B. Add a letter to **ad** to write words that begin with the same sound as the picture.

2. had   3. dad

C. Add a letter to **an** to write words that begin with the same sound as the picture.

4. can   5. man

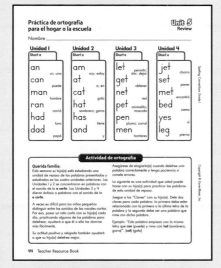

6. ran

59

Day 1 — Unit 5

Student Objectives
- Review the spelling patterns and words from Unit 1.

Reteaching the Skill
- Write **an** and **ad** on the board. Ask students where the letter **a** is in **an** and **ad**. (at the beginning) Underline the letter **a**.
- Add the letter **c** to **an** on the board. Ask students to pronounce **can** and tell where the vowel **a** is. (in the middle) Underline the letter **a** in **can**. Remind students that if there is one vowel between two consonants, it usually has a short sound (/ă/).
- Repeat the activity with **man, ran, had,** and **dad**. Have volunteers underline the letter **a** in each word.
- Tell students to complete page 59 independently.

Letters and Sounds Review
- Throughout the unit, use the **Alphabet and Picture Cards** to review letters and sounds. See page Z32 for activity suggestions.

Review Word List

Unit 5 Home/School Spelling Practice Master, TRB, p. 43

Unit 5 Home/School Spelling Practice Master, TRB, p. 44

English   Spanish

T59

Student Objectives
• Review the spelling patterns and words from Unit 2.

Reteaching the Skill
• Ask students to draw a picture of themselves playing with a cat. Then tell them to draw a hat on either themselves or the cat.
• Next, ask students to use the spelling words and write sentences that tell about their pictures.
• Encourage students to share their sentences with the class.
• Tell students to complete page 60 independently.

Review

1. am
2. at
3. cat
4. hat
5. has
6. and

Unit 2: Short a: VC, CVC

A. Write the spelling words that end with **at**.

1. at
2. cat
3. hat

B. Write a spelling word to fill each blank.

4. Jack _____ and _____ Jill went up the hill.

5. I _____ am _____ so smart.

6. Our cat _____ has _____ three kittens.

60

Extra Pattern Practice

Divide the following Sound/Symbol Cards among pairs of students: **apple, ax, bag, bed, cab, calf, echo, egg, grasshopper, hammer, jacket, kangaroo, jet, last, leg, nest, net, path, rash, shell, sled, stem, upset, wagon, web, yell,** and **zigzag.** Have partners sort their cards into groups: Words with the **short e** sound and Words with the **short a** sound. Then ask partners to choose pairs of words and use them in sentences. The first sentence should include two **short a** words. The second sentence should include two **short e** words. The third sentence should include one **short a** word and one **short e** word. Partners can create their sentences orally. Invite them to share with the class. Challenge them to write their sentences as well.

Review

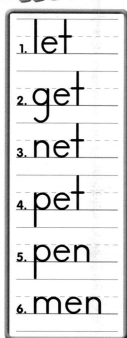

1. let
2. get
3. net
4. pet
5. pen
6. men

Unit 3: **Short e: CVC**

A. Write the spelling word that names the picture.

1. net

2. pet

3. pen

4. men

B. Write the words that rhyme with **net** and **pet**. Put a line under the word family **et**.

5. <u>let</u>

6. <u>get</u>

61

Day 3

Unit 5

Student Objectives

- Review the spelling pattern and words from Unit 3.

Reteaching the Skill

- Write **let, get, net, pet, pen,** and **men** on the board and say each word. Ask students where the letter **e** is in each word. (in the middle, between two consonants)
- Have students draw a large circle on a piece of paper and write an **e** in the center. Ask them to write the letter **p** before the **e** and the letter **n** after the **e** to make **pen**. Tell them that **e** is now between two consonants, so it has the /ĕ/ sound.
- Have students draw another circle and write the letter **e** in the center. Tell them to add an initial and final consonant to make another spelling word. Continue until all the spelling words are placed in their "pens."
- Tell students to complete page 61 independently.

More Fun With Spelling for Differentiation

 ### Digital Resources for Spelling Connections

Interactive digital resources include word sorts, pattern practice, and proofreading activities for individual and whole-group instruction. (Interactive whiteboard compatible; see p. Z32.)

 ### Spelling Connections Online

Interactive online spelling activities include word sorts, crossword puzzles, sentence completion, proofreading practice, and spelling bees with words from each unit (see p. Z32). www.spellingconnectionsonline.com

 ### Spelling Center Activities

Spelling Game Mats

Place one of the spelling games in a learning center to provide a fun way for students to practice their spelling words (see p. Z26).

Flip Folder

Students can use a Flip Folder to practice spelling words independently (see p. Z32).

Word Sort CD-ROM

Printable, unit-specific word cards for spelling and challenge words can be used for Teacher-Led, Individual, Buddy, and Speed Sorts (see p. Z31).

T61

Unit 5

Day 4

Student Objectives
- Review the spelling pattern and words from Unit 4.

Reteaching the Skill
- Write **jet, set, met, bed, yes,** and **leg** on the board.
- Ask each student to write his or her name and one spelling word on a sheet of paper. Then have students exchange papers.
- Have students write a sentence using the name and the word on the paper they receive. For example, *Lee is in bed.*
- Then have each student write his or her name and another spelling word under the sentence. Encourage students to exchange papers with someone who has a spelling word they have not used. Continue until students have used all of the spelling words.
- Tell students to complete page 62 independently or as a class.

Review

1. jet
2. set
3. met
4. bed
5. yes
6. leg

Unit 4: Short e: CVC

A. Write the spelling word to fill in each blank.

1. You sit in a chair. You sleep on a __?__ .

2. Your hand is on your arm.
   Your foot is on your __?__ .

1. bed   2. leg

B. Name each picture. Write the first letter of each picture name to make a spelling word.

3. jet   4. met

5. set   6. yes

62

Day 5

Assessment
Student Objectives
- Demonstrate mastery of the review unit spelling words.

Posttest Assessment Options
Option 1: Administer the posttest using the dictation sentences at right.

Option 2: Assess students using the standardized test. See the *Standardized Test Master Book,* p. 9.

Note: Posttest sentences for the on level and challenge lists are available on the audio *Spelling Connections* Posttest CD.

Posttest Sentences
1. Your **dad** is tall.
2. Tuffy **ran** up a tree!
3. The wind blew my **hat** off.
4. I **am** making this for you.
5. I will **get** Mom a birthday card.
6. These **men** are waiting for the bus.
7. Have you **met** my brother?
8. I can make my own **bed.**

Standardized Test Master Book, p. 9

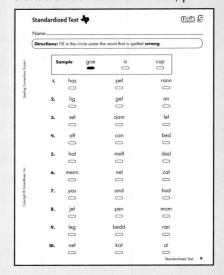

Planner

Day 1

Day 2

Day 1

Connections to **Thinking**

Student Objectives
- Read, spell, and write words with **short i** in the initial and medial position.

Instruction for All Students
- Pretest Dictation Sentences, p. T63B
- Connections to Thinking, p. 63
- Home/School Spelling Practice Master (*Teacher Resource Book*, pp. 45–46)

 TEKS 1.22Bi, 1.22C

Connections to **Phonics**

Student Objectives
- Match sounds to letters to construct words with **short i**.
- Blend the initial sounds of picture names to spell and write **short i** VC and CVC words.

Instruction for All Students
- Connections to Phonics, p. 64

Optional Practice
- Extra Pattern Practice Master (*Teacher Resource Book*, p. 47)

 TEKS 1.22A, 1.22C

Spelling Words

it
bit
sit
is
his
in

Challenge Words

sip
tip
lid
wig

Day 3

Day 4

Day 5

Day 2

Day 3

Connections to **Reading**

Student Objectives
- Spell and write **short i** VC and CVC words to complete sentences.

Instruction for All Students
- Connections to Reading, p. 65

Differentiated Instruction
- Challenge Words, p. 187

 TEKS 1.22Bi, 1.22C

Connections to **Writing**

Student Objectives
- Spell and write **short i** VC and CVC words to complete sentences in a story.

Instruction for All Students
- Connections to Writing, p. 66

Differentiated Instruction
- Extra Challenge Practice Master (*Teacher Resource Book*, p. 48)

 TEKS 1.22C

Assessment

Student Objectives
- Demonstrate mastery of the unit spelling words.

Assessment for All Students
- Posttest Dictation Sentences, p. T66, or
- *Standardized Test Master Book*, p. 10

Differentiated Assessment
- Challenge Dictation Sentences, p. T187

Unit 6 Materials

Student Edition
pp. 63–66, 187

Teacher Edition
pp. T63A–T66, T187

 Teacher Resource Book
Unit 6 Practice Masters,
pp. 45–48, and
Sound/Symbol Cards, pp. 7–26

 Standardized Test Master Book
Unit 6 Test Master, p. 10

 Word Sort CD-ROM
Unit 6 Word Sort Cards for Teacher-
Led Sorts and Student Sorts

 **Digital Resources for
Spelling Connections**
Unit 6

 Spelling Connections Online
www.spellingconnectionsonline.com

**Spelling Support for
English Language Learners***
Unit 6 Practice Masters
and Audio Conversation

Spelling Center Activities*
Spelling Game Mats
Flip Folder, *TRB*, p. 155

*Spelling Support for English Language
Learners *and Spelling Center Activities may
be used at any time during the week.*

Assessment

Pretest Sentences (See procedures on p. Z30.)

1. The key was lost, but now John has **it**.

2. My dog **bit** its own tail!

3. May I **sit** by you?

4. Rita **is** not here.

5. I have a coat like **his**.

6. Would you like to come **in**?

The Science of Spelling ◄ • •

- Spelling /ĭ/ with the single letter **i** is consistent almost 94% of the time. The other common spelling for /ĭ/ is **y** as in **gym**. Like other short vowels, /ĭ/ occurs at the beginning of a word or as a single vowel between two consonants in a syllable. Some people confuse /ĭ/ and /ĕ/ because the sounds are similar. This confusion can cause some spelling problems.

ELL Support

Choose from the activities below to reinforce English language acquisition.

Beginning

Word Meanings Write the spelling words on the board. Say each word and have students repeat. Then use a combination of gestures, pictures, real objects, and pantomime to provide context and support word meaning. For example, sit in a chair to demonstrate the meaning of **sit**. Say, *I sit in a chair.* Show an apple with a bite out of it to demonstrate **bit** and say, *I bit the apple.* Students can listen to the Unit 6 spelling words on the audio recording.

Segmenting and Blending Say a spelling word. Say the word again, this time segmenting sounds, as in **/b/ /ĭ/ /t/.** Have students say each sound individually, and then have them blend the sounds. Write the word on the board and have students copy it. Follow the same process for the rest of the words.

Rhyming Say the words **it, bit,** and **sit.** Explain that these words rhyme because they end with the same sounds, **/ĭ/ /t/.** Say the words again and have students repeat them. Then say **it, bit, dog,** and **sit.** Ask students which word does not rhyme with the others. **(dog)** Point out that **dog** does not rhyme because it does not have the **/ĭ/ /t/** sounds at the end. Repeat with the words **it, man, kit,** and **lit.** Write the words **it, bit,** and **sit** on the board. Show students that each word ends with **it.** Call on volunteers to suggest other words that rhyme with **it,** such as **fit, hit,** and **lit.**

Intermediate

Word Meanings Write the spelling words on the board. Say each word clearly and have students repeat. Say a sentence using a spelling word to demonstrate the meaning. Then ask a volunteer to say another sentence using the same word. For example, *It **is** time to read. It **is** time to play.*

Word Families Write **it** on the board. Have students say the word. Tell students that there are many words in the **it** family. Provide letter cards for **b, f, h, k, l, p, s,** and **w,** or have students make cards on card stock. Call on volunteers to choose a letter card, hold it to the left of **it,** and read the new word. List the new words on the board. (Possible words: **bit, fit, hit, kit, lit, pit, sit, wit**)

Segmenting and Blending Create a deck of spelling word cards. Have partners take turns drawing a card, sounding out the word, and then blending the sounds to pronounce the word smoothly. Students keep each card they sound out and read aloud. Students can listen to the Unit 6 words on the audio recording.

Support for Spanish Speakers

Comparing Languages English vowels are a challenging learning task for most Spanish speakers. The Spanish language has fewer vowel sounds and fewer variations in how those sounds are pronounced and spelled. The English **short i** sound may be difficult for Spanish speakers to hear or pronounce. The letter **i** in Spanish represents a sound that is similar to **long e** in English. Spelling words provide an excellent opportunity for Spanish speakers to listen to clear pronunciation of single words, to practice approximating the sounds of English, and to develop English sound-symbol correspondence.

Unit 6

Choose from the activities below to reinforce English language acquisition.

Advanced

Discriminating Sounds Write the words **sit** and **his** on the board. Sound out the words, pointing to each letter, and have students repeat. Ask students which letters they see in both words. Ask what is different about the sound letter **s** makes in each word. (It has a different sound.) Point out that the **s** in **sit** makes the /**s**/ sound and the **s** in **his** makes the /**z**/ sound.

Telling True or False Use a spelling word in a statement that is true or false. For example, *In means the opposite of out. Our school is on the moon.* Have students say *true* if the sentence is true. If the sentence is false, ask students to explain what makes it false. Then have them use the spelling word in a true sentence. Have students complete the activities on page 10 in *Spelling Support for English Language Learners*.

Advanced High

Drawing Word Characters Have students use what they know about the meaning of a spelling word to create a character whose name is that word. Ask students to describe their character based on what they know about the spelling word. For example, *Sit* could be lazy and never want to move. **His** would think that all toys belong to him. Encourage students to introduce and describe their character.

Writing Sentences Encourage students to select two spelling words to use in a written sentence. For example, *His book is in the bag.* Have students trade sentences with a partner. The partner reads the sentence aloud and points out the spelling words. Then the partner writes a sentence using the same words for the first student to read. Students can hear the spelling words used in conversation on the audio recording. The conversation for Unit 6 is in print form on page 44 of *Spelling Support for English Language Learners*.

Spelling Support for English Language Learners

Practice Master, p. 10

Practice Master, p. 44

Audio Conversation
available on CD

English/Spanish
Word List, p. 59

Spelling Connections Online
Interactive online spelling activities
provide additional ELL support.
www.spellingconnectionsonline.com

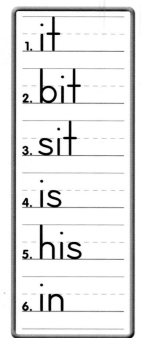

1. it
2. bit
3. sit
4. is
5. his
6. in

A. Write the spelling words that end with **is**.

1.   is
2.   his

B. Write the spelling words that end with **it**.

3.   it
4.   bit
5.   sit

C. Write the spelling word that ends with **n**.

6.   in

School Home This unit teaches **short i**. Ask your child to name words that rhyme with **bit**.

 TEKS **1.22Bi** Use letter-sound patterns to spell: consonant-vowel-consonant (CVC) words. **1.22C** Spell high-frequency words from a commonly used list.

63

Day 1   Unit 6

Student Objectives
• Read, spell, and write words with **short i** in the initial and medial position.

Unit Pretest
• Administer the pretest on page T63B.

Teaching Tips
• Read the spelling words aloud, emphasizing the **short i** sound. Then have students read the words with you.

 WORD SORT CD-ROM

• Conduct a **Teacher-Led Sort** (see p. Z31) to introduce the spelling pattern.
• Use the following Sound/Symbol Cards to introduce the **short i** sound: **dig, dish, fish, igloo, kiss, six, spill, stick, thick, thimble, zigzag, zipper.**
• Write **it** on the board. Have a volunteer read the word and use it in a sentence. Introduce the rest of the spelling words in the same way.
• Point out the VC and CVC spelling patterns in the words. Explain that these patterns signal a short vowel sound.
• Have students complete the page independently or as a class.

Home/School Word Lists
• Have students take home the Home/School Spelling Practice Master.

Home/School Practice

Home/School Spelling
Practice Master, *TRB*, p. 45

Home/School Spelling
Practice Master, *TRB*, p. 46

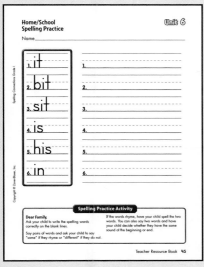

English   Spanish

TEKS **1.22Bi** Use letter-sound patterns to spell: consonant-vowel-consonant (CVC) words. **1.22C** Spell high-frequency words from a commonly used list.

T63

Unit 6 — Day 2

Student Objectives
- Match sounds to letters to construct words with **short i**.
- Blend the initial sounds of picture names to spell and write **short i** VC and CVC words.

Teaching Tips
- Say **it**, emphasizing the individual sounds /ĭ/ /t/. Ask students how many sounds they hear. Write **it** on the board. Have students say the two sounds with you.
- Complete the first item in Part B as a class. Guide students in naming the three pictures: bee, inchworm, tree. Ask, *What is the first sound in* **bee**? (/b/) *What is the first sound in* **inchworm**? (/ĭ/) *What is the first sound in* **tree**? (/t/) *Blend the three sounds to say a spelling word. What is the word?* (**bit**) Have students write **bit** on the line.
- Have students complete page 64 with a partner.

Extra Pattern Practice
- Use the optional practice master below for extra practice with **short i**.

WORD SORT CD-ROM
- Provide time for students to use a **Buddy Sort** to practice their spelling words with a partner (see p. Z31).

A. Write the spelling words that begin with the same sound.

1. **it**   2. **in**

3. **is**

Circle the number of sounds in each word above.

1   (2)   3

B. Blend the first sound in each picture name to say a spelling word. Write the word.

4. **bit**   5. **sit**

6. **his**

it
bit
sit
is
his
in

TEKS 1.22A Use phonological knowledge to match sounds to letters to construct known words.
1.22C Spell high-frequency words from a commonly used list.

Extra Pattern Practice

Extra Pattern Practice Master,
TRB, p. 47

Pattern Practice Game: /ĭ/

Provide partners with letter cards for **b, f, k, p,** and **w**. Write **it** on a sheet of paper. The first partner places a letter in front of **it** to make a word. The second partner reads the word and writes it on another sheet of paper. Then have partners switch. Have students do the same with **in**.

TEKS 1.22A Use phonological knowledge to match sounds to letters to construct known words. **1.22C** Spell high-frequency words from a commonly used list.

Connections to READING

Write a spelling word to complete each sentence.

it
bit
sit
is
his
in

1. Marcus **bit** the apple.

2. Sam's hat **is** big.

3. Han has a new cat. He likes **it**.

4. Will you **sit** in this chair?

5. Dad can sit **in** the sun.

6. Li has a book in **his** bag.

TEKS 1.22C Spell high-frequency words from a commonly used list.

65

Student Objectives
• Spell and write **short i** VC and CVC words to complete sentences.

Teaching Tips
• Write the spelling words on the board. Say the words and review that each word has the **short i** sound. Ask students to insert the spelling pattern (VC or CVC) in each word.
• Read the directions. Explain to students that they will write a spelling word to complete each sentence.
• Read the first sentence aloud, pausing at the blank. Read the sentence again, this time with **it** in the blank. Ask students if the sentence makes sense. (no) Ask, *Which word should we try next?* Read the sentence with the word students suggest. Ask if the sentence makes sense. Continue this way until you have the correct word. (bit)
• Have students complete the page independently or as a class.

Differentiated Instruction
• Use the **Challenge Words** activity on page 187 with students who are ready to transfer their knowledge of **short i** to new words.
• An Extra Challenge Practice Master is available on page 48 in the *TRB*.
• Dictation sentences for the challenge words are available on page T187.

More Fun With Spelling for Differentiation

▶ Digital Resources for Spelling Connections
Interactive digital resources include word sorts, pattern practice, and proofreading activities for individual and whole-group instruction. (Interactive whiteboard compatible; see p. Z32.)

▶ Spelling Connections Online
Interactive online spelling activities include word sorts, crossword puzzles, sentence completion, proofreading practice, and spelling bees with words from each unit (see p. Z32). www.spellingconnectionsonline.com

Spelling Center Activities

Spelling Game Mats
Place one of the spelling games in a learning center to provide a fun way for students to practice their spelling words (see p. Z26).

Flip Folder
Students can use a Flip Folder to practice spelling words independently (see p. Z32).

Word Sort CD-ROM
Printable, unit-specific word cards for spelling and challenge words can be used for Teacher-Led, Individual, Buddy, and Speed Sorts (see p. Z31).

TEKS 1.22Bi Use letter-sound patterns to spell: consonant-vowel-consonant (CVC) words.
1.22C Spell high-frequency words from a commonly used list.

Student Objectives

- Spell and write **short i** VC and CVC words to complete sentences in a story.

Teaching Tips

- Tell students that the pictures tell a story.
- Read and explain the directions.
- Have students complete the page independently or do the activity as a class.
- Read the completed sentences. Have students identify the beginning, middle, and end of the story.

WORD SORT CD-ROM

- Invite students to practice for the weekly test by doing an **Individual Sort** or a **Speed Sort** (see p. Z31).

Connections to WRITING

Look at the pictures. Write the spelling words to finish the story.

The Dog and His Bone

it
bit
sit
is
his
in

1. The dog _____ **bit** _____ the bone.

2. See the dog _____ **sit** _____ in front of the window.

3. He sees a dog that wants _____ **his** _____ bone.

4. He drops his bone _____ **in** _____ the street.

5. The dog _____ **is** _____ sad.

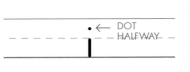

6. The dog wishes he did not drop _____ **it** _____.

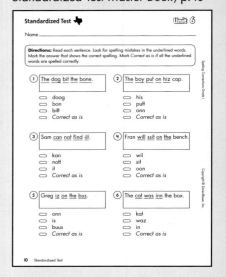

66

TEKS 1.22C Spell high-frequency words from a commonly used list.

1-Minute Handwriting Hint

The lowercase **i** begins at the midline with a pulldown straight stroke. The **i** is dotted halfway between the headline and the midline.

• ← DOT HALFWAY

Day 5

Student Objectives

- Demonstrate mastery of the unit spelling words.

Posttest Assessment Options

Option 1: Administer the unit posttest using the dictation sentences at right.

Option 2: Assess students using the standardized test. See the *Standardized Test Master Book*, p. 10.

Note: Posttest sentences for the on level and challenge lists are available on the audio *Spelling Connections* Posttest CD.

Posttest Sentences

1. Would you like to try **it**?
2. Put your papers **in** the bag.
3. Toby is with **his** uncle.
4. Jan **bit** into the apple.
5. I will **sit** over there.
6. Today **is** my birthday.

Standardized Test Master Book, p. 10

Standardized Test   Unit 6

Name _____

Directions: Read each sentence. Look for spelling mistakes in the underlined words. Mark the answer that shows the correct spelling. Mark Correct as is if all the underlined words are spelled correctly.

① The dog <u>bit</u> the bone.
- ⊙ doog
- ⊙ bon
- ⊙ bitt
- ⊙ Correct as is

② The boy put on <u>hiz</u> cap.
- ⊙ his
- ⊙ putt
- ⊙ onn
- ⊙ Correct as is

③ Sam <u>can</u> <u>not</u> find <u>iit</u>.
- ⊙ kan
- ⊙ nott
- ⊙ it
- ⊙ Correct as is

④ Fran <u>will</u> <u>ssit</u> on the bench.
- ⊙ wil
- ⊙ sit
- ⊙ oon
- ⊙ Correct as is

⑤ Greg <u>iz</u> <u>on</u> the bus.
- ⊙ onn
- ⊙ is
- ⊙ buus
- ⊙ Correct as is

⑥ The <u>cat</u> was <u>inn</u> the box.
- ⊙ kat
- ⊙ waz
- ⊙ in
- ⊙ Correct as is

10 Standardized Test

TEKS 1.22C Spell high-frequency words from a commonly used list.

Planner

Day 1 | Day 2

Day 1

Connections to **Thinking**

Student Objectives
- Read, spell, and write words with **short i** in the initial and medial position.

Instruction for All Students
- Pretest Dictation Sentences, p. T67B
- Connections to Thinking, p. 67
- Home/School Spelling Practice Master (*Teacher Resource Book*, pp. 49–50)

TEKS 1.22A, 1.22Bi, 1.22C

Connections to **Phonics**

Student Objectives
- Spell and write rhyming words with **short i**.

Instruction for All Students
- Connections to Phonics, p. 68

Optional Practice
- Extra Pattern Practice Master (*Teacher Resource Book*, p. 51)

TEKS 1.22A, 1.22Bi, 1.22C

Day 3 | Day 4 | Day 5

Day 2 | Day 3

Connections to **Reading**

Student Objectives
- Spell and write **short i** VC and CVC words to complete a story.

Instruction for All Students
- Connections to Reading, p. 69

Differentiated Instruction
- Challenge Words, p. 188

TEKS 1.22C

Connections to **Writing**

Student Objectives
- Spell and write **short i** VC and CVC words to complete a story.

Instruction for All Students
- Connections to Writing, p. 70

Differentiated Instruction
- Extra Challenge Practice Master (*Teacher Resource Book*, p. 52)

TEKS 1.22C

Assessment

Student Objectives
- Demonstrate mastery of the unit spelling words.

Assessment for All Students
- Posttest Dictation Sentences, p. T70, or
- *Standardized Test Master Book*, p. II

Differentiated Assessment
- Challenge Dictation Sentences, p. T188

Spelling Words
if
big
dig
pig
did
him

Challenge Words
bib
pin
rip
zip

Unit 7 Materials

Student Edition
pp. 67–70, 188

Teacher Edition
pp. T67A–T70, T188

 Teacher Resource Book
Unit 7 Practice Masters,
pp. 49–52, and
Sound/Symbol Cards, pp. 7–26

 Standardized Test Master Book
Unit 7 Test Master, p. 11

 Word Sort CD-ROM
Unit 7 Word Sort Cards for Teacher-
Led Sorts and Student Sorts

 **Digital Resources for
Spelling Connections**
Unit 7

 Spelling Connections Online
www.spellingconnectionsonline.com

**Spelling Support for
English Language Learners***
Unit 7 Practice Masters
and Audio Conversation

Spelling Center Activities*
Spelling Game Mats
Flip Folder, *TRB*, p. 155

*Spelling Support for English Language
Learners *and Spelling Center Activities* may
be used at any time during the week.

Assessment

Pretest Sentences (See procedures on p. Z30.)

1. Do you know **if** she is coming?
2. That boat is really **big**!
3. I helped **dig** that hole.
4. My aunt has a **pig**.
5. What **did** you do?
6. I gave **him** a ball.

The Science of Spelling ◄ • •

- **Short i** is spelled **i** 94% of the time. There are a few other minor spellings of the sound (for example, **busy, build, women, pretty**). These spellings are mainly a result of pronunciation changes over time. These isolated spellings can be taught and learned as needed. Only words of foreign origin end in the letter **i** (for example, **fungi, spaghetti, taxi**). The letter **i** at the end of a word makes a long vowel sound—/ī/ or /ē/.

ELL Support

Choose from the activities below to reinforce English language acquisition.

Beginning

Alphabetizing Use an alphabet chart to review alphabetical order. Have students sing or say the alphabet with you. Then write three spelling words on the board. Call on a volunteer to underline the initial letter in each word. Have students name the letter. Then ask students to find each letter on the alphabet chart. Ask which letter comes first, second, and third. Call on a volunteer to write the three spelling words in alphabetical order.

Word Meanings Act out or use hand gestures and facial expressions to provide context and demonstrate spelling words. For example, pantomime digging a hole. Ask students to identify the spelling word. (dig) Write the word on the board, read it aloud, and have students repeat it.

Discriminating Sounds Say the words **big, pig,** and **dig.** Ask students how the words are alike. Say the words again and have students repeat. Then say **cat.** Ask students if this word ends with the same sound as **big, pig,** and **dig.** (no) Call on a volunteer to explain. (The word ends in /t/, not /g/.) Repeat with the words **rig, tan, wig,** and **fig.** Then write the words **big, pig,** and **dig** on the board. Ask students to underline **ig** in each word.

Intermediate

Word Meanings Write the spelling words on index cards. Have a student select a card at random and say the word. Then ask another student to use the word in a sentence. Use real objects, pictures, and pantomime to provide context and support meaning of unfamiliar words. Write the sentence on the board and have a volunteer underline the spelling word.

Segmenting and Blending Create a deck of spelling word cards. Have partners take turns drawing a card, sounding out the word, and then blending the sounds to pronounce the word smoothly. Students place the cards they have read at the bottom of the pile. Encourage students to continue drawing cards until each partner has had an opportunity to read every word.

Word Families Write **i** and say /ĭ/. Say each spelling word and have students repeat. Then write **big** on the board. Have students say the word. Call on a volunteer to erase **b** and add **p.** (pig) Ask another student to erase **p** and add **d.** (dig) Then have a student erase the final **g** and add **d.** (did) Write **ig** and **id** on the board. Invite students to write beginning letters to make **short i** words. (Possible words: big, dig, fig, gig, jig, pig, rig, wig; bid, did, hid, kid, lid, rid)

Support for Spanish Speakers

Comparing Languages Spanish speakers may have difficulty hearing and pronouncing some English consonants. A few consonant sounds are quite different in the two languages. For example, the consonant sound /d/ is much softer in Spanish and somewhat similar to the unvoiced /th/ in English. Give students opportunities to practice pronouncing spelling words one-on-one with a native English-speaking adult. Brief sessions every day or several times a week can be especially helpful. It is important to praise the students' efforts and to accept gradual improvements in English pronunciation.

Choose from the activities below to reinforce English language acquisition.

Advanced

Word Meanings List the spelling words on the board. Ask questions that provide clues to a word, such as *What is an animal that says oink?* (pig) *Which word means the same as large?* (big) Invite students to think of their own questions for a partner to answer.

Writing Sentences Write this sentence on the board: *The **big** **pig** will **dig** under the fence.* Ask students to read the sentence aloud with you. Then call on volunteers to underline the **short i** words. Read these words aloud with students. Encourage students to make up their own sentences using as many spelling words as possible. Have partners work together to complete the activities on page II of *Spelling Support for English Language Learners*.

Advanced High

Writing a Story Provide this story starter: *If I saw a big pig dig, I would _____.* Have students write what they would think and do, using as many spelling words as possible.

Synonyms and Antonyms Encourage students to keep a list of synonyms and antonyms for spelling words. For example, **big—large; pig—hog; big—small**. Have them add to their list as they learn new words.

Writing Sentences Encourage students to use two or more spelling words in a written sentence. For example, ***Did** you **dig** this hole?* Have students trade sentences with a partner. The partner reads the sentence aloud and circles all the spelling words. Partners can extend the activity by incorporating previously learned spelling words into their sentences. Students can hear the spelling words for Unit 7 used in a brief conversation on the audio recording. The conversation is reproduced in print on page 44 of *Spelling Support for English Language Learners*.

Spelling Support for English Language Learners

Practice Master, p. II

Practice Master, p. 44

Audio Conversation
available on CD

English/Spanish
Word List, p. 59

Spelling Connections Online
Interactive online spelling activities
provide additional ELL support.
www.spellingconnectionsonline.com

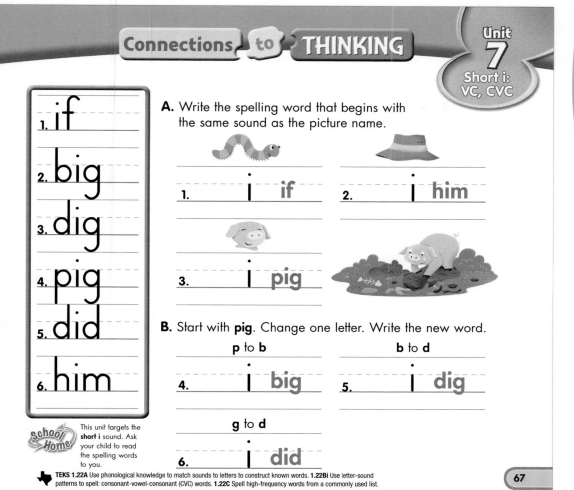

A. Write the spelling word that begins with the same sound as the picture name.

1. i **if**
2. i **him**
3. i **pig**

B. Start with **pig**. Change one letter. Write the new word.

p to b
4. i **big**

b to d
5. i **dig**

g to d
6. i **did**

Spelling Word List
1. if
2. big
3. dig
4. pig
5. did
6. him

School Home! This unit targets the **short i** sound. Ask your child to read the spelling words to you.

TEKS 1.22A Use phonological knowledge to match sounds to letters to construct known words. **1.22Bi** Use letter-sound patterns to spell: consonant-vowel-consonant (CVC) words. **1.22C** Spell high-frequency words from a commonly used list.

67

Day 1

Unit 7

Student Objectives
• Read, spell, and write words with **short i** in the initial and medial position.

Unit Pretest
• Administer the pretest on page T67B.

Teaching Tips
• Read the spelling words aloud, emphasizing the **short i** sound. Then have students read the words with you.

WORD SORT CD-ROM

• Conduct a **Teacher-Led Sort** (see p. Z31) to introduce or reinforce the spelling pattern.
• Write **pig** on the board. Have students read the word aloud. Then erase the **p** and add **d**. Have students read the new word. (**dig**) Erase the **d** and add **b**. Have students read the word. (**big**)
• Use the Sound/Symbol cards for **dig, dish, fish, igloo,** and **kick** to further review the **short i** sound. Remind students that when **i** is the only vowel in a word, it will usually have a short sound.
• Have students complete the page independently or as a class.

Home/School Word Lists **TRB**
• Have students take home the Home/School Spelling Practice Master.

Home/School Practice

Home/School Spelling
Practice Master, *TRB*, p. 49

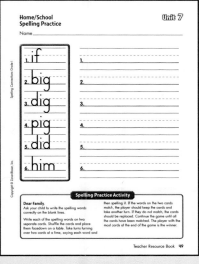

English

Home/School Spelling
Practice Master, *TRB*, p. 50

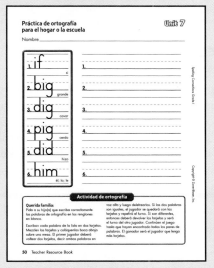

Spanish

TEKS 1.22A Use phonological knowledge to match sounds to letters to construct known words. **1.22Bi** Use letter-sound patterns to spell: consonant-vowel-consonant (CVC) words. **1.22C** Spell high-frequency words from a commonly used list.

T67

Unit 7 · Day 2

Student Objectives

- Spell and write rhyming words with **short i**.

Teaching Tips

- Give each student a cutout of an inchworm. Tell students to raise their inchworm when they hear the **short i** sound. Say: **if, big, dig, pig, did, pet, him, hat, and, it, bit, sit, men, wet, is, his, has, pit, hid, had**. Write the words with **short i** on the board. Have students point out the VC or CVC pattern in each word. Prompt them to tell you that the vowel in these patterns is short. Ask volunteers to circle **i** in each word.
- Explain that words rhyme when they have the same ending sounds. Provide examples such as **lip/sip/dip**. Have students identify the sounds that are the same. (/i//p/)
- Write **did** on the board. Challenge students to name as many rhyming words as they can. (**Possible answers: bid, hid, kid, lid, rid**)

Extra Pattern Practice

- Use the optional practice master below for extra practice with **short i**.

WORD SORT CD-ROM

- Provide time for students to use a **Buddy Sort** to practice their spelling words with a partner (see p. Z31).

Connections to PHONICS

Write the word that rhymes with the underlined word and goes with the picture.

if
big
dig
pig
did
him

1. Bev has a dig.

pig

2. Dad's hand is pig.

big

3. I hid get a pet.

did

4. The cat ran to dim.

him

5. The men will big a hole.

dig

6. Get the hat stiff you can.

if

68

Extra Pattern Practice

Extra Pattern Practice Master,
TRB, p. 5l

Pattern Practice Game: /ĭ/

Write the following phonograms on large index cards: **it, ig, in, ip**. Have partners take turns selecting a card and adding a consonant to the beginning of the phonogram to construct words. Encourage them to write the words. (**Possible words: bit, fit, hit, kit, lit, pit, sit, wit; big, dig, fig, jig, pig, rig, wig; bin, din, fin, kin, pin, tin, win; dip, hip, lip, nip, rip, sip, tip, yip**) Have students read the words aloud. Ask how they know that the vowel is short in all the words. (**All the words have the CVC spelling pattern.**)

Connections to READING

Write each spelling word once to complete the story.

Once there was a pink **1.** named Squeak.
He loved to **2.** in his pen.
Squeak saw a garden full of vegetables.
Squeak said, "I want to eat those vegetables.
Maybe **3.** I dig a **4.** hole I will get to the garden."
And he **5.** ! Squeak ate and ate.
"Get **6.** !" shouted the farmer. "Get him out of my garden!"
Squeak ran to his pen and hid. He never tried to dig out of the
pen again!

> if
> big
> dig
> pig
> did
> him

1. **pig**
2. **dig**
3. **if**
4. **big**
5. **did**
6. **him**

TEKS 1.22C Spell high-frequency words from a commonly used list.

69

Student Objectives
• Spell and write **short i** VC and CVC words to complete a story.

Teaching Tips
• Remind students that a story has a beginning, a middle, and an end. Recall the beginning, middle, and end of a familiar story.
• Discuss a story students might tell about the picture on page 69.
• Read and explain the directions.
• Have students complete the page independently or as a class.
• Read the completed story. Have students identify the beginning, middle, and end.

Differentiated Instruction
• Use the **Challenge Words** activity on page 188 with students who are ready to transfer their knowledge of **short i** to new words.
• An Extra Challenge Practice Master is available on page 52 in the *TRB*.
• Dictation sentences for the challenge words are available on page T188.

More Fun With Spelling for Differentiation

▶ Digital Resources for Spelling Connections
Interactive digital resources include word sorts, pattern practice, and proofreading activities for individual and whole-group instruction. (Interactive whiteboard compatible; see p. Z32.)

▶ Spelling Connections Online
Interactive online spelling activities include word sorts, crossword puzzles, sentence completion, proofreading practice, and spelling bees with words from each unit (see p. Z32). www.spellingconnectionsonline.com

Spelling Center Activities

Spelling Game Mats
Place one of the spelling games in a learning center to provide a fun way for students to practice their spelling words (see p. Z26).

Flip Folder
Students can use a Flip Folder to practice spelling words independently (see p. Z32).

Word Sort CD-ROM
Printable, unit-specific word cards for spelling and challenge words can be used for Teacher-Led, Individual, Buddy, and Speed Sorts (see p. Z31).

 TEKS 1.22C Spell high-frequency words from a commonly used list.

T69

Student Objectives
- Spell and write **short i** VC and CVC words to complete a story.

Teaching Tips
- Read the directions. Explain to students that they will write a spelling word in each sentence to complete the beginning and middle of the story.
- Have students complete the page independently or as a class. Then discuss their ideas for the story ending. Write a sentence on the board for each suggestion and then choose the class favorite.

WORD SORT CD-ROM
- Invite students to practice for the weekly test by doing an **Individual Sort** or a **Speed Sort** (see p. Z31).

Connections to WRITING

Write the spelling words to finish the story.

1. The _____**big**_____ wolf yelled.

2. "Little _____**pig**_____, let me in!"

3. "I will break down your door _____**if**_____ you do not let me in," the wolf said.

4. "I will not let you in!" said the pig to _____**him**_____.

5. The wolf _____**did**_____ break the door.

6. The pig said, "I will run and _____**dig**_____ a hole."

Tell what happens to the wolf.

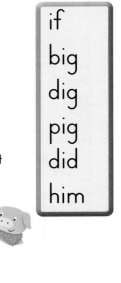

if
big
dig
pig
did
him

70

1-Minute Handwriting Hint

Be sure to close the backward circle in the lowercase **g**. The tail of the lowercase **g** fills the entire space below the baseline.

g ← FILL SPACE

Day 5

Student Objectives
- Demonstrate mastery of the unit spelling words.

Posttest Assessment Options

Option 1: Administer the unit posttest using the dictation sentences at right.

Option 2: Assess students using the standardized test. See the *Standardized Test Master Book*, p. 11.

Note: Posttest sentences for the on level and challenge lists are available on the audio *Spelling Connections* Posttest CD.

Posttest Sentences
1. What **did** you say?
2. Will you help me **dig** the hole?
3. See **if** anyone is here.
4. I took my **pig** to the fair.
5. Show **him** where to go.
6. I have never seen such a **big** tree!

Standardized Test Master Book, p. 11

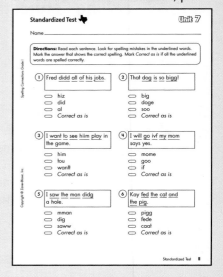

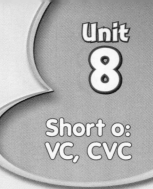

Planner

Day 1

Day 2

Day 1

Connections to **Thinking**

Student Objectives
- Read, spell, and write words with **short o** in the medial position.

Instruction for All Students
- Pretest Dictation Sentences, p. T7IB
- Connections to Thinking, p. 7I
- Home/School Spelling Practice Master (*Teacher Resource Book,* pp. 53–54)

 **TEKS 1.22Bi, 1.22C**

Connections to **Phonics**

Student Objectives
- Segment phonemes in **short o** words.
- Match sounds to letters to construct **short o** CVC words.

Instruction for All Students
- Connections to Phonics, p. 72

Optional Practice
- Extra Pattern Practice Master (*Teacher Resource Book,* p. 55)

 **TEKS 1.22A, 1.22Bi, 1.22C**

Spelling Words
not
hot
pot
got
box
fox

Challenge Words
ox
jog
cod
trot

Day 3

Day 4

Day 5

Day 2

Day 3

Connections to **Reading**

Student Objectives
- Spell and write **short o** CVC words.
- Identify opposites.
- Sort words into conceptual categories.

Instruction for All Students
- Connections to Reading, p. 73

Differentiated Instruction
- Challenge Words, p. 189

 TEKS 1.22C

Connections to **Writing**

Student Objectives
- Spell and write **short o** CVC words to complete a fable.

Instruction for All Students
- Connections to Writing, p. 74

Differentiated Instruction
- Extra Challenge Practice Master (*Teacher Resource Book,* p. 56)

 TEKS 1.22C

Assessment

Student Objectives
- Demonstrate mastery of the unit spelling words.

Assessment for All Students
- Posttest Dictation Sentences, p. T74, or
- *Standardized Test Master Book,* p. I2

Differentiated Assessment
- Challenge Dictation Sentences, p. T189

Unit 8 Materials

Student Edition
pp. 71–74, 189

Teacher Edition
pp. T71A–T74, T189

 Teacher Resource Book
Unit 8 Practice Masters,
pp. 53–56, and
Sound/Symbol Cards, pp. 7–26

 Standardized Test Master Book
Unit 8 Test Master, p. 12

Word Sort CD-ROM
Unit 8 Word Sort Cards for Teacher-
Led Sorts and Student Sorts

 Digital Resources for Spelling Connections
Unit 8

 Spelling Connections Online
www.spellingconnectionsonline.com

Spelling Support for English Language Learners*
Unit 8 Practice Masters
and Audio Conversation

Spelling Center Activities*
Spelling Game Mats
Flip Folder, *TRB*, p. 155

*Spelling Support for English Language Learners *and Spelling Center Activities *may be used at any time during the week.*

Assessment

Pretest Sentences (See procedures on p. Z30.)

1. Cam does **not** have a chair.

2. Is the water **hot**?

3. That **pot** is too big.

4. I **got** two books from the library.

5. I need a **box** for my toys.

6. I saw a **fox** at the zoo.

The Science of Spelling

- The spelling of **o** for /ŏ/ is not as dependable as other short vowel spellings. **Short o** is spelled **o** 79% of the time. It is also spelled **a** as in **father** almost 10% of the time and **au** as in **autumn** and **aw** as in **crawl** on a regular basis.

- The letter **o** also spells /ŭ/ in many words, such as **son, mother, front, done, some, none,** and **oven.** For this reason, the spelling for /ŏ/ and /ŭ/ are often confused.

ELL Support

Choose from the activities below to reinforce English language acquisition.

Beginning

Word Meanings Use real objects and pantomime to act out a spelling word and then describe your action. For example, set a big pot on your desk and pretend it is on a stove. Lift the pot as if it were filled and heavy and say, *I **got** the **pot**.* Then pantomime touching the pot and blowing on your finger. Say, *The **pot** is **hot**.* Have students perform each action and repeat what you say. Write each spelling word on the board, read it aloud, and have students repeat.

Matching Sound to Print Make flash cards of spelling words and place them faceup on a table. Read a spelling word aloud. Call on a volunteer to find the corresponding card and hold it up. Then have students say the word. Students can hear the spelling words pronounced singly on the audio recording.

Rhyming Words Write the words **hot, pot,** and **got** on the board. Help students read the words and ask what they notice about them. (They sound the same, or rhyme.) Explain that these words rhyme because they end with the same sounds, /ŏ/ /t/. Then write **sat**. Have students read the word and explain why it does not rhyme with the other words. (It has a short a sound instead of a short o sound.) Repeat with the words **box, fox,** and **mix**.

Rebus Sentences On the board, create rebus sentences using spelling words. Use stick-figure drawings or clip art and blank lines in place of the spelling words. Call on volunteers to write the missing words in the blanks. Students then say the spelling words chorally.

Intermediate

Word Meaning Ask a volunteer to choose a spelling word and write it on the board. Call on a second volunteer to read the word and a third volunteer to say a sentence using the word. Students can hear the spelling words for Unit 8 pronounced singly and in context on the audio recording.

Matching Words and Pictures Have students cut apart the cards on page 12 of *Spelling Support for English Language Learners.* Then have partners mix their cards and play the game. When they finish, encourage them to work together to complete the remaining activities on page 12.

Word Families Write **o** and say /ŏ/. Say each spelling word and have students repeat. Then write **ot** on the board. Have students come to the board and make a spelling word by writing the consonant **n, h, p,** or **g** in front of **ot**. Have students read the words they write. Invite students to suggest another beginning letter to make **short o** words with **ot**. (Possible words: cot, dot, jot, lot, rot, tot)

Support for Spanish Speakers

Comparing Languages English has many more final consonant sounds than Spanish, so some native speakers of Spanish may need practice pronouncing final consonants. Invite students to play word games by changing the final consonant of CVC words. For example, ask, *May I have a **hat** sandwich?* And then say, *Oops! I mean a **ham** sandwich!* Ask students which letter sound is different in **hat/ham**. Other word pairs to play with include **bed/bell; log/lot; hot/hop; job/jog; mom/mop; can/cat; hit/his; sit/sip; fin/fit;** and **not/nod**.

Choose from the activities below to reinforce English language acquisition.

Advanced

Word Meanings Use flash cards to present the spelling words. Give a meaning for each word. Use real objects, pictures, and gestures to provide context and support word meaning. Then ask questions that students can answer with a spelling word, such as *What is an animal with red fur and a bushy tail?* (fox) *What is something you can cook food in on the stove?* (pot) *What is a container you can put things in?* (box)

Word Sort Provide several picture cards of animals and objects whose names include short vowels, such as **fox, pot, cat, box, pig, man, jet, bed, pin,** and **dot**. Have students sort the cards according to the short vowel sound. Then have them write the **short o** words.

Read Aloud Write these sentences on the board: *A fox got in a box. The pot is not hot.* Have volunteers take turns reading the sentences. Ask students to write a new sentence using at least one spelling word. Record students reading their sentences. Then play the recording for the class. Students can hear the Unit 8 spelling words used in a brief conversation on the audio recording. The conversation is in print form on page 45 of *Spelling Support for English Language Learners.* Have students follow along with the print version and then read the conversation with a partner.

Advanced High

Spelling Short o Words Print an **o** in the middle of a sheet of paper. Have students print a beginning and an ending letter on sticky notes and attach them to the paper. Ask students to say the words they make and use them in sentences.

Storytelling Encourage students to use two spelling words in a written sentence to start a story. For example, *The **pot** is too **hot**.* Have students trade sentences with a partner. The partner reads the sentence aloud and points out the spelling words. Then the partner adds a sentence that continues the story. Students can hear the Unit 8 spelling words on the audio recording.

Describing Pictures Have students draw pictures to illustrate sentences using current and previously learned spelling words. For example, students can draw a **fox** in a **box**. Have students describe their picture to a partner without showing the picture. Explain that the description can be true or false. For example, if they drew a picture of a fox next to a box, they could describe their picture as a fox in a box. The partner then looks at the picture. If the description is true, the partner repeats it. If the description is not true, the partner corrects it. For example, the partner might say, *The fox is not in the box* or *The fox is next to the box.*

Spelling Support for English Language Learners

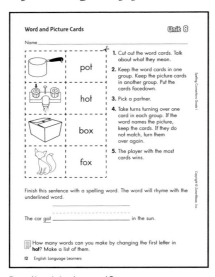

Practice Master, p. 12

Practice Master, p. 45

Audio Conversation available on CD

English/Spanish Word List, p. 60

 Spelling Connections Online
Interactive online spelling activities provide additional ELL support.
www.spellingconnectionsonline.com

Connections to THINKING

1. not
2. hot
3. pot
4. got
5. box
6. fox

A. Write the spelling words that end in **ox**.

1. box
2. fox

B. Write the spelling words that end in **ot**.

3. not
4. hot
5. pot
6. got

This unit is about **short o**. Ask your child to name other words that rhyme with **hot**.

TEKS 1.22C Spell high-frequency words from a commonly used list.

71

Student Objectives
• Read, spell, and write words with **short o** in the medial position.

Unit Pretest
• Administer the pretest on page T71B.

Teaching Tips
• Read the spelling words aloud, emphasizing the **short o** sound. Then have students read the words with you.

 **CD-ROM**

• Conduct a **Teacher-Led Sort** (see p. Z31) to introduce or reinforce the spelling pattern.
• Say **box**. Point out that the sound in the middle of **box** is the **short o** sound.
• Write **not** on the board. Ask students how many vowels are in the word. Have them name the vowel. (**o**) Remind students that when a word has only one vowel, the vowel sound is usually short. Point out the CVC pattern and remind students that this spelling pattern also signals a short vowel sound.
• Introduce the remaining words.
• Have students complete the page independently or as a class.

Home/School Word Lists
• Have students take home the Home/School Spelling Practice Master.

Home/School Practice

Home/School Spelling
Practice Master, *TRB*, p. 53

Home/School Spelling
Practice Master, *TRB*, p. 54

English	Spanish

Home/School
Spelling Practice
Unit 8
Name

1. not
2. hot
3. pot
4. got
5. box
6. fox

1.
2.
3.
4.
5.
6.

Spelling Practice Activity

Dear Family,
Ask your child to write the spelling words correctly on the blank lines.

Play a new game of "Clues" with your child. Give two clues for each word. The first clue should be about the first or last letter of the word, and the second clue should be a rhyming word.

Example: "This word begins like **boy** and rhymes with **fox**. What is it?" **(box)**

Once your child has said the correct word, have him or her spell it.

Teacher Resource Book 53

Práctica de ortografía
para el hogar o la escuela
Unit 8
Nombre

1. not — no
2. hot — caliente
3. pot — olla
4. got — tuvo; obtuvo
5. box — caja
6. fox — zorro; zorra

1.
2.
3.
4.
5.
6.

Actividad de ortografía

Querida familia:
Pida a su hijo(a) que escriba correctamente las palabras de ortografía en los renglones en blanco.

Juegue a las "Claves" con su hijo(a). Dele dos claves para cada palabra: la primera debe estar relacionada con la primera o la última letra de la palabra y la segunda debe ser una palabra que rime con dicha palabra.

Ejemplo: "Esta palabra empieza con la misma letra que **boy** (muchacho) y rima con **fox** (zorro)". **(box)** (caja)

Si su hijo(a) dice la palabra correcta, pídale que la deletree.

54 Teacher Resource Book

 TEKS 1.22Bi Use letter-sound patterns to spell: consonant-vowel-consonant (CVC) words. **1.22C** Spell high-frequency words from a commonly used list.

Student Objectives
- Segment phonemes in **short o** words.
- Match sounds to letters to construct **short o** CVC words.

Teaching Tips
- Say **hot, pot,** and **got**. Pronounce each sound, /h//ŏ//t/, and have students repeat as you point to the corresponding letter.
- Ask students to name another letter sound that could be added before /ŏ//t/ to make a word. (/n/ for **not**) Next say **ox** and ask, *What letter sounds could we add before /ŏ//x/ to make new words?* (/b/ for **box**; /f/ for **fox**)
- Write the spelling words on the board and point to the letter that spells the /ŏ/ sound in each word.
- Have students complete page 72 independently or as a class.
- Have students point out the CVC pattern in each word. Prompt them to tell you that the vowel in this pattern is short.

Extra Pattern Practice
- Use the optional practice master below for extra practice with **short o**.

WORD SORT CD-ROM
- Provide time for students to use a **Buddy Sort** to practice their spelling words with a partner (see p. Z31).

Connections to PHONICS

A. Name the picture. Match the sound you hear at the beginning of the picture to write the first letter of a spelling word. Write **ox** to finish each word.

1.

   box

2.

   fox

B. Name each picture. Match the sound you hear at the beginning of each picture to write the first and last letters of each spelling word.

3.   o   pot

4.   o   got

5.   o   hot

6.   o   not

not
hot
pot
got
box
fox

72

TEKS **1.22A** Use phonological knowledge to match sounds to letters to construct known words. **1.22Bi** Use letter-sound patterns to spell: consonant-vowel-consonant (CVC) words. **1.22C** Spell high-frequency words from a commonly used list.

Extra Pattern Practice

Extra Pattern Practice Master,
TRB, p. 55

Pattern Practice Game: /ŏ/

Have students write **ot** on a sheet of paper. Provide letter cards for **c, d, g, h, j, l, n, p, r,** and **t**. Have partners take turns placing a letter card in front of **ot** to make words. Encourage students to write the words they make. Then have them choose one or more words and use them in sentences.

TEKS **1.22A** Use phonological knowledge to match sounds to letters to construct known words. **1.22Bi** Use letter-sound patterns to spell: consonant-vowel-consonant (CVC) words. **1.22C** Spell high-frequency words from a commonly used list.

Connections to READING

A. Write the spelling word that means the opposite.

1. cold ___hot___

B. Write the spelling word that goes with each pair of words.

2. bird, deer, ___fox___

3. pan, dish, ___pot___

4. get, gave, ___got___

5. no, never, ___not___

6. bag, sack, ___box___

not
hot
pot
got
box
fox

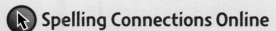

TEKS 1.22C Spell high-frequency words from a commonly used list.

73

Student Objectives
- Spell and write **short o** CVC words.
- Identify opposites.
- Sort words into conceptual categories.

Teaching Tips
- Say, *Up is the opposite of **down**. What is the opposite of **on**?* (**off**) Challenge students to name other pairs of opposites.
- Remind students that we can group things that are similar. Provide an example. Write **shirt** and **shoes** on the board and read them aloud. Say, *These are things that people wear. What are some other things that belong in this group?* (**Possible answers: pants, skirt, dress, shorts, hat, socks**)
- Explain that we can put words into groups. Say, *Yes, Okay. All right. Do these words make a group?* (**yes**) *How are they alike?* (**They mean almost the same thing.**)
- Have students complete the page independently or as a class.

Differentiated Instruction
- Use the **Challenge Words** activity on page 189 with students who are ready to transfer their knowledge of **short o** to new words.
- An Extra Challenge Practice Master is available on page 56 in the *TRB*.
- Dictation sentences for the challenge words are available on page T189.

More Fun With Spelling for Differentiation

Digital Resources for Spelling Connections
Interactive digital resources include word sorts, pattern practice, and proofreading activities for individual and whole-group instruction. (Interactive whiteboard compatible; see p. Z32.)

Spelling Connections Online
Interactive online spelling activities include word sorts, crossword puzzles, sentence completion, proofreading practice, and spelling bees with words from each unit (see p. Z32). www.spellingconnectionsonline.com

Spelling Center Activities

Spelling Game Mats
Place one of the spelling games in a learning center to provide a fun way for students to practice their spelling words (see p. Z26).

Flip Folder
Students can use a Flip Folder to practice spelling words independently (see p. Z32).

Word Sort CD-ROM
Printable, unit-specific word cards for spelling and challenge words can be used for Teacher-Led, Individual, Buddy, and Speed Sorts (see p. Z31).

TEKS 1.22C Spell high-frequency words from a commonly used list.

Student Objectives
- Spell and write **short o** CVC words to complete a fable.

Teaching Tips
- Discuss that a fable is a story that has a useful truth. Relate different fables, such as "The Tortoise and the Hare." Tell students that the pictures on this page tell the beginning and end of a fable.
- Read the directions. Have students complete the beginning and middle of the fox and crow fable. Then discuss their ideas for the story ending.
- Discuss the useful truth of this fable. Have students tell about a time when they tricked someone or someone tricked them.

WORD SORT CD-ROM
- Invite students to practice for the weekly test by doing an **Individual Sort** or a **Speed Sort** (see p. Z31).

Connections to WRITING

Write a spelling word to complete each sentence. Then tell what will happen next.

not
hot
pot
got
box
fox

1. The crow has cheese. The _____ **fox** _____ wants it. _____

2. The crow will _____ **not** _____ give the cheese to the fox.

3. "I will make cheese soup for us in a big _____ **pot** _____," the fox said. _____

4. "Will the soup be good and _____ **hot** _____?" asked the crow. _____

5. "Yes," the fox said. "Put the cheese in this _____ **box** _____." _____

6. The fox _____ **got** _____ the cheese in the box.

74

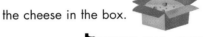
TEKS 1.22C Spell high-frequency words from a commonly used list.

1-Minute Handwriting Hint

The two slant strokes in the lowercase **x** cross midway.

CROSS MIDWAY — X

Day 5

Student Objectives
- Demonstrate mastery of the unit spelling words.

Posttest Assessment Options
Option 1: Administer the unit posttest using the dictation sentences at right.
Option 2: Assess students using the standardized test. See the *Standardized Test Master Book*, p. 12.

Note: Posttest sentences for the on level and challenge lists are available on the audio *Spelling Connections* Posttest CD.

Posttest Sentences
1. My soup is too **hot**.
2. I **got** a dish for Dad.
3. Please do **not** shut the door.
4. May I have this **box**?
5. Pour the milk into this **pot**.
6. A baby **fox** is called a kit.

Standardized Test Master Book, p. 12

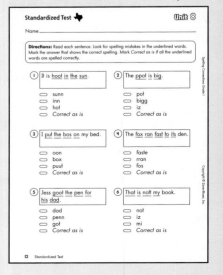

T74

TEKS 1.22C Spell high-frequency words from a commonly used list.

Planner

Day 1

Day 2

Day 1

Connections to **Thinking**

Student Objectives
- Read, spell, and write words with **short o** in the initial and medial position.

Instruction for All Students
- Pretest Dictation Sentences, p. T75B
- Connections to Thinking, p. 75
- Home/School Spelling Practice Master (*Teacher Resource Book,* pp. 57–58)

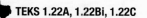 **TEKS 1.22A, 1.22Bi, 1.22C**

Connections to **Phonics**

Student Objectives
- Blend phonemes in **short o** words.
- Match sounds to letters to construct **short o** CVC words.

Instruction for All Students
- Connections to Phonics, p. 76

Optional Practice
- Extra Pattern Practice Master (*Teacher Resource Book,* p. 59)

TEKS 1.22A, 1.22Bi, 1.22C

Spelling Words
on
mom
job
hop
top
mop

Challenge Words
rod
hog
body
jot

Day 3

Day 4

Day 5

Day 2

Day 3

Connections to **Reading**

Student Objectives
- Spell and write **short o** CVC words.
- Identify opposites.
- Identify and write action words.

Instruction for All Students
- Connections to Reading, p. 77

Differentiated Instruction
- Challenge Words, p. 190

TEKS 1.22C

Connections to **Writing**

Student Objectives
- Spell and write **short o** CVC words to complete a story.

Instruction for All Students
- Connections to Writing, p. 78

Differentiated Instruction
- Extra Challenge Practice Master (*Teacher Resource Book,* p. 60)

TEKS 1.22C

Assessment

Student Objectives
- Demonstrate mastery of the unit spelling words.

Assessment for All Students
- Posttest Dictation Sentences, p. T78, or
- *Standardized Test Master Book,* p. 13

Differentiated Assessment
- Challenge Dictation Sentences, p. T190

Unit 9 Materials

Student Edition
pp. 75–78, 190

Teacher Edition
pp. T75A–T78, T190

 Teacher Resource Book
Unit 9 Practice Masters,
pp. 57–60, and
Sound/Symbol Cards, pp. 7–26

Standardized Test Master Book
Unit 9 Test Master, p. 13

 Word Sort CD-ROM
Unit 9 Word Sort Cards for Teacher-
Led Sorts and Student Sorts

 **Digital Resources for
Spelling Connections**
Unit 9

 Spelling Connections Online
www.spellingconnectionsonline.com

**Spelling Support for
English Language Learners***
Unit 9 Practice Masters
and Audio Conversation

Spelling Center Activities*
Spelling Game Mats
Flip Folder, *TRB*, p. 155

*Spelling Support for English Language
Learners *and* Spelling Center Activities *may
be used at any time during the week.*

Assessment

Pretest Sentences (See procedures on p. Z30.)

1. Your pencil is **on** the floor.
2. My **mom** works in an office.
3. I am done with my **job**.
4. I can **hop** over that puddle!
5. What is on **top** of the table?
6. Do you have to **mop** the floor?

The Science of Spelling ◄···

- As students gain spelling fluency, they will encounter spelling exceptions.
- **Short o** is spelled **o** only 79% of the time.
- It is also spelled **oa** (**broad**), **ou** (**cough**), and **ow** (**knowledge**). Once the **o** spelling is secure and students know that **o** is a reliable spelling, the exceptions can be introduced.

ELL Support

Choose from the activities below to reinforce English language acquisition.

Beginning

Word Meanings Act out spelling words. For example, place a book **on** a table, pantomime using a **mop,** or **hop** on one foot. Ask students to identify the spelling word. Write the word on the board, read it aloud, and have students repeat. Invite volunteers to select spelling words to act out.

Rolling Vowels Cover a number cube with tape. Write a vowel—**a, e, i, o**—on four of the sides. Leave two sides blank. Provide consonant letter cards. Have students roll the cube to select a medial vowel. A student who rolls a blank can choose any vowel. Have the student write the vowel on paper and then select two consonant letter cards to place on either side of it to build a word. Help students build words. Then have students say the words.

Blending Words Say /ŏ/ and have students repeat. Write *10* on the board and have students read it. Ask what sound is at the beginning of **ten**. (/t/) Show a picture of an octopus. Name the picture and have students repeat. Ask what sound is at the beginning of **octopus**. (/ŏ/) Then display a pen and have students name it. Ask what sound is at the beginning of **pen**. (/p/) Have students say the beginning sounds of **ten, octopus,** and **pen,** and then blend the sounds to say a spelling word. (top) Continue with other spelling words.

Intermediate

Picture Dictionary Have students create a picture dictionary for spelling words by writing each word and drawing a picture that illustrates its meaning.

Writing Words Write **o** and say /ŏ/. Say each spelling word and have students repeat. Then write **hop** on the board. Have students say the word. Erase **h** and add **t**. Have students say the word. (top) Call on a volunteer to erase **t** and add **m**. (mop) Invite students to suggest other beginning letters to add to **op**. (Possible words: bop, cop, lop, pop)

Writing a Story Have partners use four to six spelling words in an oral story. When students are satisfied with their story, help them write it. Encourage partners to illustrate each sentence and create a storyboard by pasting their pictures on a strip of newsprint.

Support for Spanish Speakers

As language users, we usually learn to speak before we learn to read and write a language. (In this case, "speaking" includes not only vocal speech, but also sign language and other forms of nonvocal, verbal speech.) The ability to read depends on a student's knowledge of language and expectations of sentence structure and meaning. That is why it is so important to encourage spoken communication in English as often as possible. The topic of the conversation is relatively unimportant. If you have students who are reluctant to speak before the class, arrange small groupings or pairs for speech opportunities.

Choose from the activities below to reinforce English language acquisition.

Advanced

Word Meanings List the spelling words on the board. Ask a question that includes the meaning of a word and have students answer with the correct word. For example: *What is something you use to clean the floor?* (mop) *What is a word for a female parent?* (mom) *What is another word for work?* (job) Then have partners work together to complete the sentences on page 13 of *Spelling Support for English Language Learners*.

Writing Spelling Words Provide a set of spelling word flash cards or have students make their own. Place the cards facedown. Ask a student to draw the top card, read the word, spell and write it while looking at the card, use it in a sentence, and then spell or write it (and the sentence) from memory. Students can hear the Unit 9 spelling words on the audio recording.

Correcting Spelling Have students write a sentence using one or more spelling words. Have them spell one of the spelling words incorrectly. For example, a student may write *The **foxx** can **hop on** the **box**.* Have students trade sentences with a partner and correct each other's errors.

Advanced High

Synonyms and Antonyms Encourage students to keep lists of synonyms and antonyms for spelling words. For example, antonyms: *on—off;* synonyms: *hop—jump; job—work.* Have students add to their lists as they find new words. Invite volunteers to demonstrate their word pairs physically, with gestures, or in illustrations.

Writing Sentences Encourage students to use two or more spelling words in a written sentence. For example, *Mom has the mop.* Have students trade sentences with a partner. The partner reads the sentence aloud and identifies the spelling words. The partner then writes a sentence using the same two words, leaving blanks for the words. The first student writes the words in the correct spaces and reads the new sentence aloud. Students can hear the Unit 9 spelling words used in conversation on the audio recording. The conversation is in print on page 45 of *Spelling Support for English Language Learners*. Have students follow along with the recording and then read the conversation with a partner.

Spelling Support for English Language Learners

Practice Master, p. 13

Practice Master, p. 45

Audio Conversation available on CD

English/Spanish Word List, p. 60

Spelling Connections Online
Interactive online spelling activities provide additional ELL support.
www.spellingconnectionsonline.com

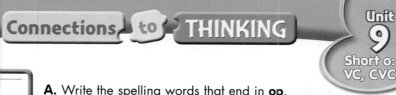
Connections to THINKING

1. on
2. mom
3. job
4. hop
5. top
6. mop

A. Write the spelling words that end in **op**.

1. hop
2. top
3. mop

B. Write the spelling word that has the same first and last letter.

4. mom

C. Write the word that has two letters.

5. on

D. Write the word that begins with the same sound as **jet**.

6. job

School Home This unit teaches **short o**. Help your child read the words in the spelling list aloud.

 TEKS 1.22A Use phonological knowledge to match sounds to letters to construct known words. **1.22C** Spell high-frequency words from a commonly used list.

75

Student Objectives

- Read, spell, and write words with **short o** in the initial and medial position.

Unit Pretest

- Administer the pretest on page T75B.

Teaching Tips

- Read the spelling words aloud. Have students listen for the **short o** sound. Then have students read the words.

 **WORD SORT CD-ROM** ▶

- Conduct a **Teacher-Led Sort** (see p. Z31) to reinforce the spelling pattern.
- Review **short o** by saying the word **mom**. Remind students that the sound in the middle of **mom** is the **short o** sound. Use the Sound/Symbol Cards for **box, fox,** and **ostrich** to further review **short o**.
- Show the Sound/Symbol Card for **hop**. Have a volunteer write **hop** on the board. Do the same to introduce **mop**.
- Say the remaining spelling words and ask volunteers to write them on the board.
- Have students point out the VC or CVC pattern in each word. Prompt them to tell you that the vowel in these patterns is short.

Home/School Word Lists **TRB**

- Have students take home the Home/School Spelling Practice Master.

Home/School Practice

Home/School Spelling
Practice Master, *TRB*, p. 57

Home/School Spelling
Practice Master, *TRB*, p. 58

English

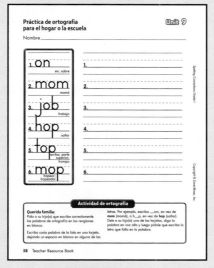

Spanish

TEKS 1.22A Use phonological knowledge to match sounds to letters to construct known words. **1.22Bi** Use letter-sound patterns to spell: consonant-vowel-consonant (CVC) words. **1.22C** Spell high-frequency words from a commonly used list.

T75

Student Objectives
- Blend phonemes in **short o** words.
- Match sounds to letters to construct **short o** CVC words.

Teaching Tips
- Display pictures of a hat, an octopus, and a pig. Ask students to name each picture and listen for the beginning sounds. Then have them say just the beginning sound of each picture name. Pronounce each sound, **/h//ŏ//p/**, and have students repeat. Write the word and have students read it.
- Write the remaining spelling words on the board. Point to the letter that makes the **/ŏ/** sound in each word.
- Have students point out the VC or CVC pattern in each word. Prompt them to tell you that the vowel in these patterns is short.
- Have students complete page 76 independently or as a class.

Extra Pattern Practice
- Use the optional practice master below for extra practice with **short o**.

WORD SORT CD-ROM
- Provide time for students to use a **Buddy Sort** to practice their spelling words with a partner (see p. Z31).

Connections to PHONICS

Name each picture. Then say the beginning sound of each picture name. Write the word you say.

on	
mom	
job	
hop	
top	
mop	

1. _____ job

2. _____ top

3. _____ on

4. _____ mom

5. _____ hop

6. _____ mop

TEKS 1.22A Use phonological knowledge to match sounds to letters to construct known words. **1.22C** Spell high-frequency words from a commonly used list.

Extra Pattern Practice

Extra Pattern Practice Master,
TRB, p. 59

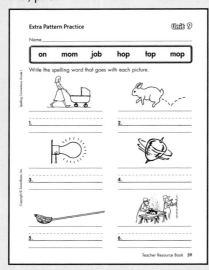

Rhyming: /ŏ/
In a Think/Pair/Share activity, ask students to select two rhyming words from the word list. Have each student write the first line of a rhyme using one of the words. Have students trade papers and write the second line of the rhyme using the other spelling word. For example, *Take the mop. Now we hop.* Tell students that the meaning of the spelling words should make sense in their rhymes. Have partners read their rhymes to the class.

TEKS 1.22A Use phonological knowledge to match sounds to letters to construct known words. **1.22Bi** Use letter-sound patterns to spell: consonant-vowel-consonant (CVC) words. **1.22C** Spell high-frequency words from a commonly used list.

Connections to READING

A. Write the spelling word that is the opposite.

1. off **on**

2. bottom **top**

B. Write the word that tells what someone is doing.

3. **hop**

4. **mop**

5–6. My **mom** has a big **job** .

on
mom
job
hop
top
mop

TEKS 1.22C Spell high-frequency words from a commonly used list.

77

Student Objectives
- Spell and write **short o** CVC words.
- Identify opposites.
- Identify and write action words.

Teaching Tips
- Take a book off a desk. Say, *I take the book off* the desk. Then put the book back on the desk. Ask students to describe what you do. **(You put the book on the desk.)** Remind students that **off** and **on** are opposites. Review other opposites, such as up/down and in/out.
- Point out that some of the spelling words tell what someone is doing. Hop on one foot. Ask, *What did I do?* **(hop)** Write **hop** on the board and have students read it aloud.
- Read the directions and have students complete the page independently or as a class.

Differentiated Instruction
- Use the **Challenge Words** activity on page 190 with students who are ready to transfer their knowledge of **short o** to new words.
- An Extra Challenge Practice Master is available on page 60 in the *TRB*.
- Dictation sentences for the challenge words are available on page T190.

More Fun With Spelling for Differentiation

▶ Digital Resources for Spelling Connections
Interactive digital resources include word sorts, pattern practice, and proofreading activities for individual and whole-group instruction. (Interactive whiteboard compatible; see p. Z32.)

▶ Spelling Connections Online
Interactive online spelling activities include word sorts, crossword puzzles, sentence completion, proofreading practice, and spelling bees with words from each unit (see p. Z32). www.spellingconnectionsonline.com

Spelling Center Activities

Spelling Game Mats
Place one of the spelling games in a learning center to provide a fun way for students to practice their spelling words (see p. Z26).

Flip Folder
Students can use a Flip Folder to practice spelling words independently (see p. Z32).

Word Sort CD-ROM
Printable, unit-specific word cards for spelling and challenge words can be used for Teacher-Led, Individual, Buddy, and Speed Sorts (see p. Z31).

Student Objectives
• Spell and write **short o** CVC words to complete a story.

Teaching Tips
• Read the directions. Explain to students that they will write a spelling word in each sentence to tell the beginning, middle, and end of the story.
• Have students complete the page independently or as a class. Ask volunteers to read the sentences aloud. Discuss students' answers to the two questions.

WORD SORT CD-ROM
• Invite students to practice for the weekly test by doing an **Individual Sort** or a **Speed Sort** (see p. Z31).

Connections to WRITING

Write spelling words to finish the story.

on	
mom	
job	
hop	
top	
mop	

1. I get __**on**__ the stool.

2. I want the drink on __**top**__ of the table.

3. I __**hop**__ down off the stool.

4. My __**mom**__ sees me drop the drink.

5. She has a __**job**__ for me.

6. I get to __**mop**__ the floor.

Circle **yes** or **no**.
Has this happened to you?   yes   no
Did you help mop the floor?   yes   no

78

🢩 TEKS 1.22C Spell high-frequency words from a commonly used list.

1-Minute Handwriting Hint
The tail of the lowercase **p** fills the entire space below the baseline. The forward circle begins halfway between the midline and the baseline.

CIRCLE BEGINS HERE → p ← FILL SPACE

Day 5

Student Objectives
• Demonstrate mastery of the unit spelling words.

Posttest Assessment Options
Option 1: Administer the unit posttest using the dictation sentences at right.
Option 2: Assess students using the standardized test. See the *Standardized Test Master Book*, p. 13.

Note: Posttest sentences for the on level and challenge lists are available on the audio *Spelling Connections* Posttest CD.

Posttest Sentences
1. Did my **mom** call?
2. We have a **job** to do.
3. Our house is on the **top** of the hill.
4. Are your feet **on** the floor?
5. I will clean the floor with this **mop**.
6. Can you **hop** like a bunny?

Standardized Test Master Book, p. 13

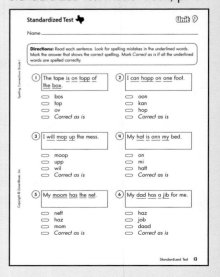

 TEKS 1.22C Spell high-frequency words from a commonly used list.

Planner

Day 1

Day 1

Unit 6: Short i: VC, CVC

Student Objectives
- Review the spelling patterns and words from Unit 6.

Instruction for All Students
- Unit 6 Review, p. 79
- Home/School Spelling Practice Masters (*Teacher Resource Book*, pp. 61–62)

Day 2

Unit 7: Short i: VC, CVC

Student Objectives
- Review the spelling patterns and words from Unit 7.

Instruction for All Students
- Unit 7 Review, p. 80

Unit 6
Short i: VC, CVC

it	is
bit	his
sit	in

Unit 7
Short i: VC, CVC

if	pig
big	did
dig	him

Unit 8
Short o: VC, CVC

not	got
hot	box
pot	fox

Unit 9
Short o: VC, CVC

on	hop
mom	top
job	mop

Day 3

Day 2

Unit 8: Short o: VC, CVC

Student Objectives
- Review the spelling pattern and words from Unit 8.

Instruction for All Students
- Unit 8 Review, p. 81

Day 4

Day 2

Unit 9: Short o: VC, CVC

Student Objectives
- Review the spelling patterns and words from Unit 9.

Instruction for All Students
- Unit 9 Review, p. 82

Day 5

Day 3

Assessment

Student Objectives
- Demonstrate mastery of the review unit spelling words.

Assessment for All Students
- Posttest Assessment Options
  - ✦ Posttest Dictation Sentences, p. T82, or
  - ✦ *Standardized Test Master Book*, p. 14

Unit 10

Unit 10 Materials

Student Edition
pp. 79–82
Alphabet and Picture Cards
(See page Z32 for
suggested activities.)

Teacher Edition
pp. T79A–T82

 Teacher Resource Book
Unit 10 Practice Masters,
pp. 61–62

 Standardized Test Master Book
Unit 10 Test Master,
p. 14

 Word Sort CD-ROM
Unit 10 Word Sort Cards for Teacher-
Led Sorts and Student Sorts

 **Digital Resources for
Spelling Connections**
Unit 10

Spelling Connections Online
www.spellingconnectionsonline.com

Spelling Center Activities*
Spelling Game Mats
Flip Folder, *TRB*, p. 155

**Spelling Center Activities may be used at
any time during the week.*

Developmental Spelling Check

Administer the following **Developmental Spelling Check** to evaluate spelling growth. Remind students that this is not a test for a grade; students are not expected to spell these words conventionally. Author J. Richard Gentry has provided (in parentheses) typical Phase 3 Phonetic Spellings for each word. Students who produce these or similar spellings are demonstrating full phonemic awareness since each letter corresponds to a sound. These spellings are a middle first-grade benchmark.

To administer, say each word aloud, read the sentence, and then say the word again.

Bird Words and Sample Phonetic Spellings

eagle	The **eagle** has big wings	(EGL)
blackbird	Where is the **blackbird**?	(BLAKBRD)
red bird	The **red bird** has a yellow beak.	(RAD BRD)
bluebird	The **bluebird** flew away.	(BLUBRD)
owl	The wise **owl** said, "Who!"	(AL)
turkey	We will eat **turkey** on Thanksgiving.	(TRKE, CHRKE)
chicken	I love to eat fried **chicken**.	(TREKN, CHEKN)

ELL Support

Choose from the activities below to reinforce English language acquisition.

Beginning

Word Meanings Write the four lists of spelling words on the board. Call on volunteers to choose a word and demonstrate its meaning in some way, such as through gestures, pantomime, total physical response, or illustration. Have other students identify the word. Point to the word on the board, read it aloud, and have students repeat it.

Solving Puzzles Create box puzzles on large-box grid paper to review short vowels **a, e, i,** and **o**. Mark off a 3 x 3 block. Leave the center square blank. Write consonants above and below and to the left and right of the center square. Have students write the correct vowel in the center. For example:

	n	
p	o	t
	t	

Intermediate

Word Meanings Write the spelling words on the board. Say each word clearly and have students repeat. Ask a volunteer to choose a word and use it in a sentence or tell something about its meaning. If necessary, clarify and expand the definition. Use real objects, pictures, and pantomime to provide context and support meaning. Then have students write the word on a piece of paper. Students may look at the word on the board to be sure they have spelled it correctly.

Word Families Write each phonogram on a paper lunch bag: **an, ad, at, et, en, it, ig, ot, ox, op**. Have students select one bag and find the spelling words that end with that phonogram. Have them write each word on an index card or slip of paper and put it in the bag. Have students count the words in each bag to determine which family is the largest.

Categories Explain that nouns are words that name things, verbs are words that name actions, and adjectives tell more about nouns. Use **box, dig,** and **hot** as examples. Create a three-column chart on the board. Have students categorize as many spelling words as possible, writing the words or taping word cards in the appropriate column.

Support for Spanish Speakers

Short Vowel Practice Because most of the English short vowel sounds are not used in Spanish, Spanish speakers may need extra practice to learn short vowel sounds and spellings. Write CVC words, leaving out the medial vowel. Have students fill in different vowels to make words. For example, write **n_t, l_g,** w_g, t_p, h_t, g_t, b_d, s_t. Students can construct **net, not, lag, leg, log, wag, wig, top, tip, tap, hit, hat, hot, get, got, bad, bed, bid,** and **sit, sat, set.** Have students pronounce the words and listen for the vowel sounds. Invite students to choose five words to illustrate.

Unit 10

Choose from the activities below to reinforce English language acquisition.

Advanced

Word Meanings List the spelling words on the board. Have students think of questions to ask about the words. For example: *Which word names something you cook in?* (pot) *Which word tells what you do in a chair?* (sit) *Which word tells what you use to clean the floor?* (mop) *What do you do when you make a hole in the ground?* (dig) Have students share their questions for other students to answer.

Concentration Write each review spelling word on an index card. Shuffle the cards and place them facedown in a grid. Invite partners to take turns turning over two cards. If the words on the cards have the same vowel sound, the student keeps the cards. If the words do not have the same vowel sound, the cards are turned over again. Partners play until all of the cards have been matched.

Writing Sentences Have a student choose a spelling word. A partner uses the word in a sentence, such as *The **pig** runs.* The first student illustrates the partner's sentence. Encourage students to write their sentences on their pictures.

Advanced High

Guess the Word Give partners spelling word flash cards. Have each partner select a word without showing it. Students then try to guess their partner's word by asking ten questions. For example, *Does the word have a **short a** sound?* The partner answers *yes* or *no.* The partner shows the card if a word is not identified after ten questions.

Writing Words Encourage students to draw a picture that includes illustrations of spelling words. Then have students use the spelling words to tell a partner about their picture. The partner can write the spelling words heard in the story.

Riddles Encourage students to create riddles for the spelling words and share them with a partner. For example, *My name begins with **p**. I say oink.* (pig)

Writing Sentences Have students write sentences, leaving a blank space for each spelling word. Students trade papers with a partner and complete each other's sentences. As an alternative, students can select one to three review spelling words and challenge a partner to write a sentence using all the words.

 Spelling Connections Online
Interactive online spelling activities
provide additional ELL support.
www.spellingconnectionsonline.com

Review

1. it
2. bit
3. sit
4. is
5. his
6. in

School Home
This unit reviews **short i** and **short o**. Ask your child to read the spelling words on each page aloud.

Unit 6: Short i: VC, CVC

Write two spelling words to finish each sentence.

1–2. This book _____ is _____ his _____.

3–4. I will _____ sit _____ in _____ this chair.

5–6. Ow! _____ It _____ bit _____ me!

79

Student Objectives
- Review the spelling patterns and words from Unit 6.

Reteaching the Skill
- Write **it, bit, sit, is, his,** and **in** on the board. Ask students which vowel is in each word. Remind them that when a word has only one vowel followed by a consonant, the vowel sound is usually short. Pronounce the words and ask students to repeat them.
- Ask students which words end with the same two letters. (it, bit, sit; is, his) Remind them that words that end in the same sounds are rhyming words.
- Ask volunteers to write the rhyming words in two columns on the board. Have other volunteers circle the letters that are the same in the words in each column.
- Tell students to complete page 79 independently.

Letters and Sounds Review
- Throughout the unit, use the **Alphabet and Picture Cards** to review letters and sounds. See page Z32 for activity suggestions.

Review Word List

Home/School Spelling
Practice Master, *TRB*, p. 61

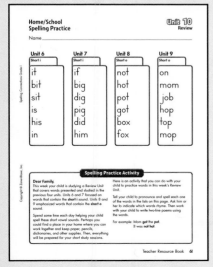

English

Home/School Spelling
Practice Master, *TRB*, p. 62

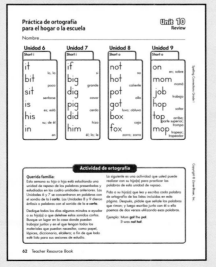

Spanish

Student Objectives
• Review the spelling patterns and words from Unit 7.

Reteaching the Skill
• Divide the class into groups of three. Tell students they will work together to spell the spelling words.
• Tell students that when you say a spelling word, one member of the group will write the first letter of the word on a sheet of paper and then pass the paper to the second group member. The second member will write the middle letter and pass the paper to the third member who will write the final letter.
• Then all three group members should look at the word and say it aloud. For the word **if,** two members write and the third member says the word.
• Tell students to take turns writing the first, middle, and final letters.
• Tell students to complete page 80 independently.

Review

1. if
2. big
3. dig
4. pig
5. did
6. him

Unit 7: Short i: VC, CVC

A. Write the spelling words that end with **ig**.

1.   big   2.   dig

3.   pig

B. Write the word that has the same first and last letter.

4.   did

C. Write the word that has two letters.

5.   if

D. Write the word that starts with the same sound as  .

6.   him

80

Extra Pattern Practice

Mixed-Up Sentences
Write the following sentences on the board. Have students read each sentence aloud and tell what is wrong. Ask volunteers to rewrite the sentences correctly on the board.

I. Matt has a pig big. (Matt has a big pig.)

2. I get did him. (I did get him.)

3. Ask Ted if can dig. (Ask if Ted can dig.)

Invite students to write their own mixed-up sentences using the spelling words. Have them exchange papers with a partner and rewrite the sentences.

Review

1. not
2. hot
3. pot
4. got
5. box
6. fox

Unit 8: Short o: VC, CVC

A. Add a letter to **ox** to make two words.

1.   box

2.   fox

B. Add a letter to **ot** to make four words.

3.   not

4.   hot

5.   pot

6.   got

81

Student Objectives

- Review the spelling pattern and words from Unit 8.

Reteaching the Skill

- Write the unit spelling words on the board. Read the words aloud and ask students to repeat them.
- Note that all the spelling words follow the consonant-vowel-consonant (CVC) pattern. Remind students that the vowel in this pattern usually has the short sound.
- Write **net, hit, pet, get,** and **fix** on the board. Ask students to change the vowel in each word to make a spelling word. (not, hot, pot, got, fox)
- Tell students to complete page 81 independently.

More Fun With Spelling for Differentiation

 Digital Resources for Spelling Connections

Interactive digital resources include word sorts, pattern practice, and proofreading activities for individual and whole-group instruction. (Interactive whiteboard compatible; see p. Z32.)

 Spelling Connections Online

Interactive online spelling activities include word sorts, crossword puzzles, sentence completion, proofreading practice, and spelling bees with words from each unit (see p. Z32). www.spellingconnectionsonline.com

 Spelling Center Activities

Spelling Game Mats
Place one of the spelling games in a learning center to provide a fun way for students to practice their spelling words (see p. Z26).

Flip Folder
Students can use a Flip Folder to practice spelling words independently (see p. Z32).

Word Sort CD-ROM
Printable, unit-specific word cards for spelling and challenge words can be used for Teacher-Led, Individual, Buddy, and Speed Sorts (see p. Z31).

Unit 10 — Day 4

Student Objectives
- Review the spelling patterns and words from Unit 9.

Reteaching the Skill
- Ask students to look around their classroom. Then ask them what **jobs** they can do to help keep it neat and clean. Ask, *What **job** can you do? Can you clean off the **top** of your desks? Can you **mop** the floor? Can you put the library books **on** the shelf? Can you ask your **mom** to help?*
- On the board, write the spelling words you used.
- Tell students to think about these questions as they write about jobs they can do to help keep their classroom neat and clean. Encourage them to use spelling words. Then have students illustrate their sentences.
- Tell students to complete page 82 independently or as a class.

Review

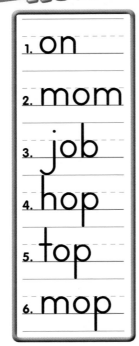

1. on
2. mom
3. job
4. hop
5. top
6. mop

Unit 9: Short o: VC, CVC

A. Write the words that end with **op**.

1. hop
2. top
3. mop

B. Write a spelling word to answer each question.

4. Which word is the same backward and forward? **mom**

5. Which word is **no** spelled backward? **on**

6. Which word starts with the same sound as ✈ ? **job**

82

Day 5

Assessment
Student Objectives
- Demonstrate mastery of the review unit spelling words.

Posttest Assessment Options
Option 1: Administer the posttest using the dictation sentences at right.

Option 2: Assess students using the standardized test. See the *Standardized Test Master Book*, p. 14.

Note: Posttest sentences for the on level and challenge lists are available on the audio *Spelling Connections* Posttest CD.

Posttest Sentences
1. Put your papers **in** the bag.
2. I will **sit** over there.
3. What **did** you say?
4. I took my **pig** to the fair.
5. My soup is too **hot**.
6. May I have this **box**?
7. We have a **job** to do.
8. Our house is on the **top** of the hill.

Standardized Test Master Book, p. 14

	Sample	at	net	yas
		○	○	●
1.	fox	sitt	dig
2.	his	gott	hot
3.	bitt	it	job
4.	pigg	did	hop
5.	momm	on	sit
6.	got	did	iz
7.	boks	if	not
8.	itt	pot	in
9.	ife	big	mop
10.	top	fox	himm

Standardized Test — Unit 10

Directions: Fill in the circle under the word that is spelled **wrong**.

Planner

Day 1
Day 2

Day 1

Connections to **Thinking**

Student Objectives
- Read, spell, and write words with **short u** in the initial and medial position.

Instruction for All Students
- Pretest Dictation Sentences, p. T83B
- Connections to Thinking, p. 83
- Home/School Spelling Practice Master (*Teacher Resource Book*, pp. 63–64)

TEKS 1.22Bi, 1.22C

Connections to **Phonics**

Student Objectives
- Match sounds to letters to construct CVC words with **short u**.

Instruction for All Students
- Connections to Phonics, p. 84

Optional Practice
- Extra Pattern Practice Master (*Teacher Resource Book,* p. 65)

TEKS 1.22A, 1.22C

Spelling Words
up
us
bus
cut
but
nut

Challenge Words
snug
dug
bump
hum

Day 3
Day 4
Day 5

Day 2
Day 3

Connections to **Reading**

Student Objectives
- Spell and write **short u** CVC words.
- Understand and identify opposites.

Instruction for All Students
- Connections to Reading, p. 85

Differentiated Instruction
- Challenge Words, p. 191

TEKS 1.22C

Connections to **Writing**

Student Objectives
- Spell and write **short u** CVC words to complete sentences in a paragraph.

Instruction for All Students
- Connections to Writing, p. 86

Differentiated Instruction
- Extra Challenge Practice Master (*Teacher Resource Book,* p. 66)

TEKS 1.22A, 1.22C

Assessment

Student Objectives
- Demonstrate mastery of the unit spelling words.

Assessment for All Students
- Posttest Dictation Sentences, p. T86, or
- *Standardized Test Master Book*, p. 15

Differentiated Assessment
- Challenge Dictation Sentences, p. T191

Unit 11 Materials

Student Edition
pp. 83–86, 191

Teacher Edition
pp. T83A–T86, T191

 Teacher Resource Book
Unit 11 Practice Masters,
pp. 63–66, and
Sound/Symbol Cards

 Standardized Test Master Book
Unit 11 Test Master, p. 15

 Word Sort CD-ROM
Unit 11 Word Sort Cards for Teacher-
Led Sorts and Student Sorts

 **Digital Resources for
Spelling Connections**
Unit 11

Spelling Connections Online
www.spellingconnectionsonline.com

**Spelling Support for
English Language Learners***
Unit 11 Practice Masters and
Audio Conversation

Spelling Center Activities*
Spelling Game Mats
Flip Folder, *TRB*, p. 155

*Spelling Support for English Language
Learners *and* Spelling Center Activities may
be used at any time during the week.

Assessment

Pretest Sentences (See procedures on p. Z30.)

1. My balloon is going **up**!
2. Can Eric come with **us**?
3. I rode the **bus** to town.
4. Will you please **cut** this string?
5. I don't have a pet, **but** I would like one.
6. A **nut** just fell from that tree.

The Science of Spelling ◄ • •

- The **short u** sound is spelled **u** 78% of the time. The only other common **short u** spelling (17% of the time) is **o** as in **among**.

ELL Support

Choose from the activities below to reinforce English language acquisition.

Beginning

Word Meaning Write the spelling words on the board. Read each word aloud and have students repeat. Use pictures, gestures, and pantomime to provide context and support word meaning. For example, point **up,** pantomime **cut**ting bread, and spread your arms wide to demonstrate **us**. Students can hear the Unit II spelling words pronounced singly and in context sentences on the audio recording.

Illustrate Words Give each student a large index card. Write **bus** on the board. Say the word and have students repeat. Then have students write **bus** on one side of their index card and draw a picture of a bus on the other side. Continue with additional spelling words that can be illustrated.

Rolling Vowels Review the short vowels. Cover a number cube with tape. Write one vowel on each of five sides of the cube. Leave one side blank. Provide consonant letter cards. Have students roll the cube to select a medial vowel. If the blank side is rolled, students can choose a vowel. Have them write the vowel on a sheet of paper. Then have them select two consonant cards and place them on either side of the vowel to make a CVC word. Write the word on the board and have students read it aloud.

Intermediate

Word Meaning Write the spelling words on the board. Say each word and have students repeat. Ask a volunteer to choose a word and use it in a sentence or tell something about the meaning of the word. If necessary, clarify and expand the definition. Use real objects, pictures, and pantomime to provide context and support meaning of unfamiliar words. Then have students write the words on a sheet of paper. Students may refer to the words on the board to check their spelling.

Storytelling Write each spelling word on an index card. Stack the cards facedown on a table. Have students work in pairs. One student draws a card and uses the word in an oral sentence to begin a story. The partner draws a card and uses that word in a sentence to continue the story. Have partners continue until they have used all the spelling words.

Support for Spanish Speakers

Comparing Languages English vowels may be a challenging learning task for Spanish speakers. The Spanish language has fewer vowels sounds and fewer variations in how those sounds are spelled. Short vowel phonemes that do not exist in Spanish include **-ub, -ug, -um,** and **-un**.

Choose from the activities below to reinforce English language acquisition.

Advanced

Word Meanings Tell students that you are thinking of a spelling word. Provide a clue that will help students determine which word. For example, *This is something you might ride to school.* (bus) *This is what you do when you take a whole apple and make pieces.* (cut) *This a word that names our whole group.* (us) *This is the opposite of down.* (up)

Word Sort Display several picture cards whose names have short vowels, such as **mop, hop, cut, leg, dig, pen, hat, can, pig, pin, bus,** and **nut**. Ask students to sort the cards according to short vowel sound. Then have them write the **short u** words. Extend the activity by having students think of other ways to sort the words, such as by action words and naming words.

Complete Sentences Write a sentence on the board with a blank for a spelling word, such as *I ride a _____ to school.* Read the sentence and pause at the blank. Ask students which spelling word completes the sentence. (bus) Have a volunteer write **bus** in the blank. Then have partners work together to complete the activities on page 14 of *Spelling Support for English Language Learners.*

Advanced High

Word Characters Have students use what they know about the meaning of a spelling word to create a character whose name is that word. Ask students to describe their character based on what they know about the spelling word. For example, **Up** could be looking up. **Bus** could be a bus. Encourage students to introduce and describe themselves as their character.

Conversation Have students listen to the conversation on the audio recording. Then have partners read the print form of the conversation on page 46 of *Spelling Support for English Language Learners.* As an extension, encourage students to continue the conversation, using as many spelling words as possible.

True or False Use a spelling word in a statement that is true or false. For example, **Up** *means the opposite of* **down.** *A* **bus** *takes us to the lunchroom.* Have students say "true" if the sentence is true. If the sentence is false, ask students to explain what makes it false. Then have them use the spelling word in a true sentence. Have students complete the activities on page 14 in *Spelling Support for English Language Learners.*

Spelling Support for English Language Learners

Practice Master, *TRB*, p. 14

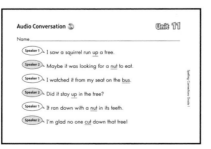

Practice Master, p. 46

 Audio Conversation
available on CD

English/Spanish
Word List, p. 61

Spelling Connections Online
Interactive online spelling activities
provide additional ELL support.
www.spellingconnectionsonline.com

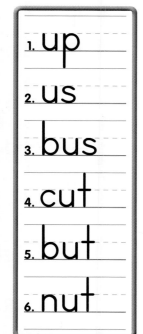

1. up
2. us
3. bus
4. cut
5. but
6. nut

A. Write the spelling words that end in **us**.

1. _____ us _____
2. _____ bus _____

B. Write the spelling words that end in **ut**.

3. _____ cut _____
4. _____ but _____

5. _____ nut _____

C. Write the spelling word that ends in **up**.

6. _____ up _____

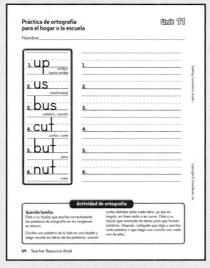

 School Home
This unit teaches **short u**. Ask your child to name other words that start with **short u** as in **up**.

TEKS 1.22C Spell high-frequency words from a commonly used list.

83

Day 1

Unit **11**

Student Objectives
• Read, spell, and write words with **short u** in the initial and medial position.

Unit Pretest
• Administer the pretest on page T83B.

Teaching Tips
• Have students read the spelling words aloud, listening for and overemphasizing /ŭ/ in each word.

 WORD SORT CD-ROM
• Conduct a **Teacher-Led Sort** (see p. Z31).
• Write the words on the board. Point to the letter that makes the **short u** sound. Remind students that when a word has only one vowel between two consonants, the vowel sound is usually short.
• Ask students to sit in a circle. Give one student a cutout of a large nut. Ask the student to say a word with the same **short u** sound as in **nut,** and then pass the cutout to someone else. Continue until everyone has had a turn.
• Have students complete the page independently or as a class.

Home/School Word Lists TRB
• Have students take home the Home/School Spelling Practice Master.

Home/School Practice

Home/School Spelling
Practice Master, *TRB*, p. 63

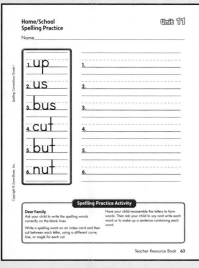

English

Home/School Spelling
Practice Master, *TRB*, p. 64

Spanish

TEKS 1.22Bi Use letter-sound patterns to spell: consonant-vowel-consonant (CVC) words.
1.22C Spell high-frequency words from a commonly used list.

T83

Unit 11 — Day 2

Student Objectives
- Match sounds to letters to construct CVC words with **short u**.

Teaching Tips
- Display the Sound/Symbol Card for **up** and have students name the picture. Ask a volunteer to write the word on the board. Do the same with **nut**.
- Play "I Am Thinking of a Word…" with the remaining words. Give clues such as *I am thinking of a word that begins with /ŭ/ and ends with /s/.* Have volunteers write the corresponding letters on the board. Then have students read the word aloud.
- Ask students to name the first picture on page 84. (cub) Ask, *What is the first sound in* **cub**? (/k/) *Which spelling word begins with the same sound?* (cut) If necessary, ask students to read each word aloud and tell you whether the initial sound matches the initial sound in **cub**.
- Have students complete page 84 independently or as a class.

Extra Pattern Practice **TRB**
- Use the optional practice master below for extra practice with **short u**.

WORD SORT CD-ROM
- Provide time for students to use a **Buddy Sort** (see p. Z31) to practice their spelling words with a partner.

Write the spelling words that begin with the same sound as the picture names.

| up |
| us |
| bus |
| cut |
| but |
| nut |

1. cut

2. nut

3. up

5. bus

4. us

6. but

84

TEKS 1.22A Use phonological knowledge to match sounds to letters to construct known words.
1.22C Spell high-frequency words from a commonly used list.

Extra Pattern Practice

Extra Pattern Practice Master,
TRB, p. 65

Sentence Puzzles: /ŭ/
Ask students to write each of the spelling words in a sentence. Collect the sentences, check them for clarity, and return them to students. Ask students to work in pairs to cut each sentence into separate words and then take turns putting it back together. If time allows, students may change partners and put the new partners' sentences together.

TEKS 1.22A Use phonological knowledge to match sounds to letters to construct known words.
1.22C Spell high-frequency words from a commonly used list.

Connections to READING

Write a spelling word to finish each sentence.
Circle **yes** if the sentence tells about the picture.
Circle **no** if it does not tell about the picture.

up	
us	
bus	
cut	
but	
nut	

1. The bird is __**up**__ in the sky. yes (no)

2. Jan gets on the __**bus**__ . (yes) no

3. The __**nut**__ is in the box. (yes) no

4. My dog runs to __**us**__ . yes (no)

5. Mom will __**cut**__ the big apple. (yes) no

6. The day was cold, __**but**__ now it is hot. (yes) no

 TEKS 1.22C Spell high-frequency words from a commonly used list.

85

Student Objective
- Spell and write **short u** CVC words.
- Understand and identify opposites.

Teaching Tips
- Explain that opposites are things that are completely different. Ask a student to stand and then sit. Ask another to turn the light off and then on. Ask another to open a book and then close it. Point out the opposites in each situation and have the class repeat. For example, **Off** *is the opposite of* **on**. Challenge students to name and/or demonstrate other pairs of opposites.
- Read the directions on page 85. Explain to students that they will write a spelling word to complete each sentence. Then they will decide if the sentence tells about the picture and circle **yes** or **no**. If needed, model the first item.
- When students have finished, read each sentence as a class. Ask students to tell if they circled **yes** or **no** and explain why.

Differentiated Instruction
- Use the **Challenge Words** activity on page 191 with students who are ready to transfer their knowledge of **short u** to new words.
- An Extra Challenge Practice Master is available on page 66 in the *TRB*.
- Dictation sentences for the challenge words are available on page T191.

More Fun With Spelling for Differentiation

Digital Resources for Spelling Connections
Interactive digital resources include word sorts, pattern practice, and proofreading activities for individual and whole-group instruction. (Interactive whiteboard compatible; see p. Z32.)

Spelling Connections Online
Interactive online spelling activities include word sorts, crossword puzzles, sentence completion, proofreading practice, and spelling bees with words from each unit (see p. Z32). www.spellingconnectionsonline.com

Spelling Center Activities

Spelling Game Mats
Place one of the spelling games in a learning center to provide a fun way for students to practice their spelling words (see p. Z26).

Flip Folder
Students can use a Flip Folder to practice spelling words independently (see p. Z32).

Word Sort CD-ROM
Printable, unit-specific word cards for spelling and challenge words can be used for Teacher-Led, Individual, Buddy, and Speed Sorts (see p. Z31).

TEKS 1.22C Spell high-frequency words from a commonly used list.

Student Objectives
• Spell and write **short u** CVC words to complete sentences in a paragraph.

Teaching Tips
• Read the directions. Explain to students that they will write a spelling word to complete each sentence in a paragraph.
• Have students complete Part A as a class or independently. Read the paragraph aloud. Then discuss what students will write about their own bus trip.
• Give students practice with alphabetizing words. Have them say the alphabet. Write **us, bus,** and **cut** on the board. Have volunteers underline the first letter in each word. Model how to alphabetize the words using those letters. Then write **up, but,** and **nut** on the board. Have students tell how to alphabetize these words.

WORD SORT CD-ROM
• Invite students to practice for the weekly test by doing an **Individual Sort** or a **Speed Sort** (see p. Z31).

Connections to WRITING

A. Write a spelling word to complete each sentence.

A __1.__ trip is fun. You go __2.__ the steps. You find a good seat. Take a snack with you. You can __3.__ an apple and a carrot. Put in a __4.__ or two. Eat on the bus, __5.__ save some for __6.__ .

1. bus   2. up

3. cut   4. nut

5. but   6. us

up
us
bus
cut
but
nut

B. Write about a bus trip. Tell what you want to see. Use spelling words.

I want to see _____

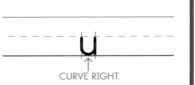

86

TEKS 1.22C Spell high-frequency words from a commonly used list.

1-Minute Handwriting Hint

The lowercase **u** contains two pull down straight strokes. The curve forward stroke is part of the circle motion.

u
CURVE RIGHT

Day 5

Student Objectives
• Demonstrate mastery of the unit spelling words.

Posttest Assessment Options
Option 1: Administer the unit posttest using the dictation sentences at right.
Option 2: Assess students using the standardized test. See the *Standardized Test Master Book,* p. 15.

Note: Posttest sentences for the on level and challenge lists are available on the audio *Spelling Connections* Posttest CD.

Posttest Sentences
1. Will this **nut** grow into a tree?
2. Please help **us** clean the room.
3. The elevator is going **up**.
4. You may come, **but** you must be very quiet.
5. Is the **bus** late?
6. Jeff will **cut** the paper with scissors.

Standardized Test Master Book, p. 15

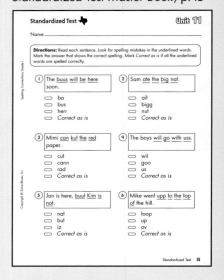

 TEKS 1.22A Use phonological knowledge to match sounds to letters to construct known words. **1.22C** Spell high-frequency words from a commonly used list.

Planner

Day 1 | Day 2

Day 1

Connections to **Thinking**

Student Objectives
- Read, spell, and write words with **short u** in the medial position.

Instruction for All Students
- Pretest Dictation Sentences, p. T87B
- Connections to Thinking, p. 87
- Home/School Spelling Practice Master (*Teacher Resource Book*, pp. 67–68)

🚩 **TEKS 1.22A, 1.22C**

Connections to **Phonics**

Student Objectives
- Replace medial vowels to construct **short u** CVC words.

Instruction for All Students
- Connections to Phonics, p. 88

Optional Practice
- Extra Pattern Practice Master (*Teacher Resource Book*, p. 69)

🚩 **TEKS 1.22A, 1.22Bi, 1.22C**

Spelling Words
fun
run
sun
tug
bug
rug

Challenge Words
hut
pup
bud
cub

Day 3 | Day 4 | Day 5

Day 2 | Day 3

Connections to **Reading**

Student Objectives
- Spell and write **short u** CVC words to match meanings.

Instruction for All Students
- Connections to Reading, p. 89

Differentiated Instruction
- Challenge Words, p. 192

🚩 **TEKS 1.22C**

Connections to **Writing**

Student Objectives
- Spell and write **short u** CVC words to complete sentences in a paragraph.

Instruction for All Students
- Connections to Writing, p. 90

Differentiated Instruction
- Extra Challenge Practice Master (*Teacher Resource Book*, p. 70)

🚩 **TEKS 1.22A, 1.22C**

Assessment

Student Objectives
- Demonstrate mastery of the unit spelling words.

Assessment for All Students
- Posttest Dictation Sentences, p. T90, or
- *Standardized Test Master Book*, p. 16

Differentiated Assessment
- Challenge Dictation Sentences, p. T192

Unit 12 Materials

Student Edition
pp. 87–90, 192

Teacher Edition
pp. T87A–T90, T192

 Teacher Resource Book
Unit 12 Practice Masters,
pp. 67–70, and
Sound/Symbol Cards

 Standardized Test Master Book
Unit 12 Test Master, p. 16

 Word Sort CD-ROM
Unit 12 Word Sort Cards for Teacher-
Led Sorts and Student Sorts

 **Digital Resources for
Spelling Connections**
Unit 12

 Spelling Connections Online
www.spellingconnectionsonline.com

**Spelling Support for
English Language Learners***
Unit 12 Practice Masters and
Audio Conversation

Spelling Center Activities*
Spelling Game Mats
Flip Folder, *TRB*, p. 155

*Spelling Support for English Language
Learners *and *Spelling Center Activities may
be used at any time during the week.*

Assessment

Pretest Sentences (See procedures on p. Z30.)

1. Did you have **fun** at the zoo?

2. I can **run** to the tree.

3. The **sun** is going down.

4. My dog likes to **tug** at my socks.

5. Is there a **bug** on me?

6. Jane has a blue **rug**.

The Science of Spelling ◀ • •

Short u, like other short vowels, is found in closed CVC (**cut**), CCVC (**shut**), and CVCC (**hush**) syllables or at the beginning of VC words (**us**). Replacing short vowels in one-syllable words (**bag/ big/beg/bug**) or creating series of rhyming words (**bug/tug/rug/dug**) reinforces the short vowel patterns, which are useful in both reading and spelling.

Choose from the activities below to reinforce English language acquisition.

Beginning

Word Meaning Write the spelling words on the board. Then use gestures, pantomime, and pictures to demonstrate or show the meaning of each word. For example, draw a picture of the **sun** or a **bug,** or pantomime **tug**ging on a rope. Call on students to come to the board and point to the corresponding word.

Making Words Provide or make letter cards for **b, f, r, s,** and **t.** List the spelling words on the board. Have students select a letter card and find the spelling word that begins with that letter. Ask students to read the word aloud. Students can hear Unit 12 spelling words pronounced singly on the audio recording.

Draw Pictures Demonstrate drawing a picture to illustrate a spelling word. For example, draw a **bug**. Ask students to identify the spelling word. Write the word on the board, read it aloud, and have students repeat. Encourage students to draw pictures to illustrate each spelling word.

Flash Cards Provide a set of word cards for this unit. Spread the cards faceup on a table. Read a spelling word aloud and have students hold up the corresponding card.

Identify the Vowel Write **a, e, i, o,** and **u** on the board. Then say a spelling word from Unit 12 or a previous unit. Have a student come up and point to the vowel that spells the short vowel sound in the word. Continue until everyone has a turn.

Intermediate

Picture Dictionary Have students add the Unit 12 spelling words to their picture dictionary by writing each word and drawing a picture to illustrate its meaning.

Word-Picture Match Have students cut out the cards on page 15 of *Spelling Support for English Language Learners*. Have partners combine word cards and picture cards to play the game. Then have partners work together to do the remaining activities.

Create New Words Write **u** on the board and say /ŭ/. Say each spelling word and have students repeat. Then write a spelling word on the board. Ask students how they can change a letter to make another spelling word. Call on a volunteer to erase one letter and write a different one to make a spelling word. Invite students to suggest other beginning letters to make **short u** words with **-un** and **-ug. (Possible words: bun, dun, gun; dug, hug, jug, lug, mug)**

Support for Spanish Speakers

Comparing Languages English vowels may be a challenging learning task for Spanish speakers. The Spanish language has fewer vowel sounds and fewer variations in how those sounds are spelled. Spanish-speaking students may have the same problem with **short u** as they do with **short a,** pronouncing it like **o** in **hot** or **a** in **father**.

Sound Discrimination To help students discriminate the **short u** sound, display pictures of objects with names that have a medial **short u,** such as **cup**. Say the picture name and ask students to say the middle sound. Write **u** and explain that this letter spells /ŭ/. Write **cop** and **cup**. Point to and say each word distinctly. Then say **cub**. Ask students to say the written word that has the same middle sound as **cub. (cup)**

Choose from the activities below to reinforce English language acquisition.

Advanced

Word Meaning List the spelling words on the board. Say a sentence with **it** in place of a spelling word. For example, *It goes on the floor.* Have students repeat the sentence and replace **it** with a spelling word. (The rug goes on the floor.) Point out that students may need to use the word **the** or **a** before the spelling word so that the sentence makes sense.

Add a Vowel Write an incomplete word on the board. Ask volunteers to write different vowels to make as many words as they can. For example, write **n_t**. Students can write **net, not, nut**. Other words to use include **l_g, t_p, h_t, b_t, f_n,** and **b_g**. (Possible words: lag, leg, log, lug; tap, tip, top; hat, hit, hot, hut; bat, bet, bit, but; fan, fin, fun; bag, big, beg, bog, bug)

Create a Poem Create three-line poems in which a rhyming spelling word ends each line. Write the poem on the board. Invite students to help you finish it by telling you which spelling word should be written at the end of each line. Then have students read the finished poem with you. For example:

> We have so much _____ (fun)
> When we jump and _____, (run)
> And when we play in the _____. (sun)

Invite students to write their own poems using rhyming words from Unit 12 and from previous units.

Advanced High

Character Words Ask students to think what they would be like if their name were a spelling word. Then play "Who Are You?" Call on volunteers to describe themselves without giving their names. Have other students guess who they are. Before each volunteer speaks, ask, *Who are you?*

Writing Sentences Have students write a sentence that uses a spelling word and then give the sentence to a partner. The partner reads the sentence aloud and identifies the spelling word. Then the partner writes a sentence using a different spelling word. Have partners pass sentences back and forth until they have used all of the spelling words.

Find Words Have students find spelling words in other books in the classroom. Ask students to copy sentences in which they find a spelling word. Then have them read their sentences to a partner.

Conversation Students can hear the Unit 12 spelling words used in an oral conversation on the audio recording. The conversation can be found in print on page 46 of *Spelling Support for English Language Learners*. Have students follow along with the recording and then read the conversation with a partner.

Spelling Support for English Language Learners

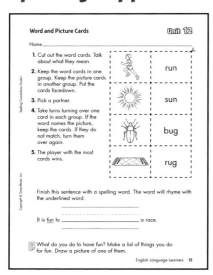

Practice Master, *TRB*, p. 15

Practice Master, p. 46

 Audio Conversation available on CD

English/Spanish Word List, p. 61

Spelling Connections Online
Interactive online spelling activities provide additional ELL support.
www.spellingconnectionsonline.com

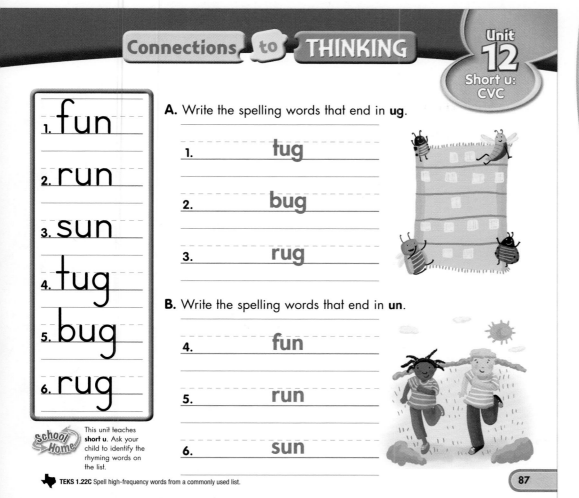

1. fun
2. run
3. sun
4. tug
5. bug
6. rug

A. Write the spelling words that end in **ug**.

1. tug
2. bug
3. rug

B. Write the spelling words that end in **un**.

4. fun
5. run
6. sun

TEKS 1.22C Spell high-frequency words from a commonly used list.

87

Day 1

Unit 12

Student Objectives
• Read, spell, and write words with **short u** in the medial position.

Unit Pretest
• Administer the pretest on page T87B.

Teaching Tips
• Have students read the spelling words aloud, listening for and emphasizing /ŭ/ in each word.

WORD SORT CD-ROM

• Conduct a **Teacher-Led Sort** (see p. Z31) to introduce or reinforce the spelling pattern.
• Show the Sound/Symbol Card for **sun**. Have students name the picture. Ask a volunteer to write **sun** on the board.
• Say the following sentences and ask students to name the **short u** word in each: *I had fun. I can run. I see a bug. You can sit on the rug.* Write **fun, run, bug,** and **rug** on the board. Ask students which words end in the same way. (**fun, run; bug, rug**)
• Have students complete the page independently or as a class.

Home/School Word Lists **TRB**
• Have students take home the Home/School Spelling Practice Master.

Home/School Practice

Home/School Spelling Practice Master, *TRB*, p. 67

Home/School Spelling Practice Master, *TRB*, p. 68

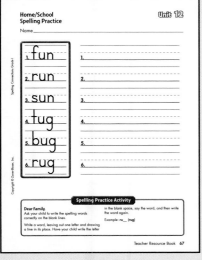

English

Spanish

TEKS 1.22A Use phonological knowledge to match sounds to letters to construct known words. **1.22C** Spell high-frequency words from a commonly used list.

Student Objectives
- Replace medial vowels to construct **short u** CVC words.

Teaching Tips
- Write the word **bag** on the board and have students read it aloud. Identify the middle sound as **short a**. Then erase the **a** and write **u**. Read the new word and have students repeat it. Point to **u** and review that it makes the /ŭ/ sound.
- Write **fan** on the board. Have students read it aloud. Then ask a volunteer to erase the **a** and write **u** in its place. Ask students to read the new word.
- Have students complete page 88 independently or as a class.
- When students have finished, ask them to read each pair of words and identify the middle, or vowel, sound in each word. Challenge them to try other vowels to make more words.

Extra Pattern Practice **TRB**
- Use the optional practice master below for extra practice with **short u**.

WORD SORT CD-ROM
- Provide time for students to use a **Buddy Sort** (see p. Z31) to practice their spelling words with a partner.

Connections to PHONICS

Replace the middle letter in each word to write a spelling word.

big	fan
1. **bug**	2. **fun**
rag	ran
3. **rug**	4. **run**
son	tag
5. **sun**	6. **tug**

fun
run
sun
tug
bug
rug

88

TEKS 1.22C Spell high-frequency words from a commonly used list.

Extra Pattern Practice

Extra Pattern Practice Master,
TRB, p. 69

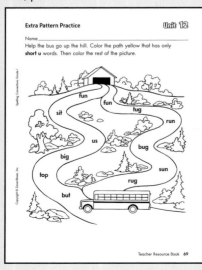

Pattern Practice Game: /ŭ/

Cut out large letters **f, r, s, t,** and **b**. On three sheets of paper, print **un**. On three more sheets, print **ug**. Say the spelling words aloud. Then say the sounds /ŭ/ /n/. Tell students that **un** is not a word. Explain that the /f/ sound added to **un** makes the word **fun**. Give a student the cutout letter **f**. Give another student a paper with **un** on it. Have the students stand next to each other to make the word **fun**. Repeat with **r** and **s**. Next say /ŭ/ /g/. Do the same activity with the **t, b,** and **r** cutouts and the **ug** papers.

TEKS 1.22A Use phonological knowledge to match sounds to letters to construct known words.
1.22Bi Use letter-sound patterns to spell: consonant-vowel-consonant (CVC) words.
1.22C Spell high-frequency words from a commonly used list.

Connections to READING

Write the spelling word that matches each meaning.

fun
run
sun
tug
bug
rug

1. This word means "a good time."

fun

2. It is another name for an insect.

bug

3. This is a covering for a floor.

rug

4. You do this when you pull on something.

tug

5. It gives us heat and light.

sun

6. This means "to move very fast on foot."

run

TEKS 1.22C Spell high-frequency words from a commonly used list.

89

Student Objectives
• Spell and write **short u** CVC words to match meanings.

Teaching Tips
• Write the spelling words on the board.
• Pantomime pulling on the door. Ask, *Which word tells what I do?* (**tug**) Have a volunteer point to and read aloud the word **tug**.
• Ask, *Which word names something that gives light?* (**sun**) Have a volunteer point to and read **sun**.
• Ask students to help you write simple sentences using the spelling words, such as *We **run**. The **bug** crawls.* For each sentence, ask a volunteer to circle the naming word. Have another volunteer draw a line under the doing word.
• Have students complete page 89.

Differentiated Instruction
• Use the **Challenge Words** activity on page 192 with students who are ready to transfer their knowledge of **short u** to new words.
• An Extra Challenge Practice Master is available on page 70 in the *TRB*.
• Dictation sentences for the challenge words are available on page T192.

More Fun With Spelling for Differentiation

Digital Resources for Spelling Connections

Interactive digital resources include word sorts, pattern practice, and proofreading activities for individual and whole-group instruction. (Interactive whiteboard compatible; see p. Z32.)

Spelling Connections Online

Interactive online spelling activities include word sorts, crossword puzzles, sentence completion, proofreading practice, and spelling bees with words from each unit (see p. Z32). www.spellingconnectionsonline.com

Spelling Center Activities

Spelling Game Mats
Place one of the spelling games in a learning center to provide a fun way for students to practice their spelling words (see p. Z26).

Flip Folder
Students can use a Flip Folder to practice spelling words independently (see p. Z32).

Word Sort CD-ROM
Printable, unit-specific word cards for spelling and challenge words can be used for Teacher-Led, Individual, Buddy, and Speed Sorts (see p. Z31).

TEKS 1.22C Spell high-frequency words from a commonly used list.

T89

Student Objectives
- Spell and write **short u** CVC words to complete sentences in a paragraph.

Teaching Tips
- Have students look at the picture on page 90 and talk about what they see. Read the directions. Tell students that the sentences tell about the picture.
- Explain to students that they will write a spelling word to complete each sentence in the paragraph.
- Model how to use a dictionary to find the meaning of unfamiliar words. As students complete the writing activity, have them look up unfamiliar words.
- Have students complete Part A as a class or independently. Read the paragraph aloud. Then discuss what students will write about a summer day.

WORD SORT CD-ROM
- Invite students to practice for the weekly test by doing an **Individual Sort** or a **Speed Sort** (see p. Z31).

Day 5

Student Objectives
- Demonstrate mastery of the unit spelling words.

Posttest Assessment Options
Option 1: Administer the unit posttest using the dictation sentences at right.

Option 2: Assess students using the standardized test. See the *Standardized Test Master Book*, p. 16.

Note: Posttest sentences for the on level and challenge lists are available on the audio *Spelling Connections* Posttest CD.

Connections to WRITING

A. Write a spelling word to complete each sentence.

We play in the warm __1.__ on a summer day. We __2.__ a race. We pull and __3.__ on a rope. We see a yellow __4.__ on a leaf. We sit on a __5.__ to eat. We laugh and have lots of __6.__ !

1. sun
2. run
3. tug
4. bug
5. rug
6. fun

B. Write about a summer day. Tell what you do. Use spelling words.

On a summer day I _____

90

TEKS 1.22C Spell high-frequency words from a commonly used list.

fun
run
sun
tug
bug
rug

1-Minute Handwriting Hint
The lowercase **n** contains two pull down straight strokes. Be sure that both strokes are parallel. The curve forward stroke in the letter is part of the circle motion.

PARALLEL

n

Posttest Sentences
1. Did you have **fun** at the party?
2. There is a **bug** on the leaf.
3. The **sun** is shining in my eyes.
4. Give a quick **tug** on the rope.
5. It is dangerous to **run** down the stairs.
6. The walls match the **rug**.

Standardized Test Master Book, p. 16

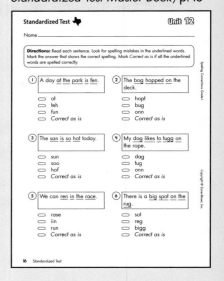

 TEKS 1.22A Use phonological knowledge to match sounds to letters to construct known words. **1.22C** Spell high-frequency words from a commonly used list.

Planner

Day 1
Day 2

Day 1

Connections to **Thinking**

Student Objectives
- Read, spell, and write words with a short vowel in the medial position.

Instruction for All Students
- Pretest Dictation Sentences, p. T91B
- Connections to Thinking, p. 91
- Home/School Spelling Practice Master (*Teacher Resource Book*, pp. 71–72)

 TEKS 1.22Bi, 1.22C

Connections to **Phonics**

Student Objectives
- Spell and write CVC words to reinforce short vowel spellings.
- Blend initial, medial, and final sounds of picture names to write CVC words with short vowels.

Instruction for All Students
- Connections to Phonics, p. 92

Optional Practice
- Extra Pattern Practice Master (*Teacher Resource Book*, p. 73)

TEKS 1.22A, 1.22Bi, 1.22C

Spelling Words
bad
yet
fix
dot
hug
tub

Challenge Words
wag
pop
mix
bend

Day 3
Day 4
Day 5

Day 2
Day 3

Connections to **Reading**

Student Objectives
- Spell and write words with short vowels in context.

Instruction for All Students
- Connections to Reading, p. 93

Differentiated Instruction
- Challenge Words, p. 193

 TEKS 1.22C

Connections to **Writing**

Student Objectives
- Spell and write CVC words with short vowels to complete a friendly letter.
- Write a friendly letter using CVC words with short vowels.

Instruction for All Students
- Connections to Writing, p. 94

Differentiated Instruction
- Extra Challenge Practice Master (*Teacher Resource Book*, p. 74)

TEKS 1.22A, 1.22C

Assessment

Student Objectives
- Demonstrate mastery of the unit spelling words.

Assessment for All Students
- Posttest Dictation Sentences, p. T94, or
- *Standardized Test Master Book*, p. 17

Differentiated Assessment
- Challenge Dictation Sentences, p. T193

Unit 13 Materials

Student Edition
pp. 91–94, 193

Teacher Edition
pp. T91A–T94, T193

 Teacher Resource Book
Unit 13 Practice Masters,
pp. 71–74, and
Sound/Symbol Cards

 Standardized Test Master Book
Unit 13 Test Master, p. 17

 Word Sort CD-ROM
Unit 13 Word Sort Cards for Teacher-
Led Sorts and Student Sorts

 **Digital Resources for
Spelling Connections**
Unit 13

 Spelling Connections Online
www.spellingconnectionsonline.com

**Spelling Support for
English Language Learners***
Unit 13 Practice Masters and
Audio Conversation

Spelling Center Activities*
Spelling Game Mats
Flip Folder, *TRB*, p. 155

*Spelling Support for English Language
Learners *and* Spelling Center Activities *may
be used at any time during the week.*

Assessment

Pretest Sentences (See procedures on p. Z30.)

1. The garbage has a **bad** smell.
2. Did Juan come home **yet**?
3. Will you **fix** my bike?
4. Put a **dot** over the **i**.
5. I gave Dad a big **hug**!
6. The water in the **tub** is cold.

The Science of Spelling ◄· ·

- Often at the beginning of Phase 3, students will spell short vowel sounds incorrectly because they are matching the short vowel sound with the sound of the vowel name. For example, the letter name for **a** is very close in sound to /ĕ/. The similarity sometimes leads a beginner to spell /ĕ/ with an **a** (**pat** for **pet**). Likewise, beginners might spell /ĭ/ with an **e** (**pet** for **pit**) and /ŭ/ with an **o** (**cot** for **cut**). This is one reason why teaching short vowels and their spellings is critically important for beginners.

Choose from the activities below to reinforce English language acquisition.

Beginning

Word Meaning Write the spelling words on the board. Introduce each word by pointing to it and reading it aloud. Then use a real object, a picture, or pantomime to illustrate meaning and provide context. Say the word again. For example, draw a dot on the board. Point to the dot and say **dot**. Have students repeat.

Make Words Write the spelling words on the board, leaving out the vowels. Read the first word, clearly pronouncing the vowel as well as the beginning and ending consonants. Ask students which short vowel sound they hear. Then call on a volunteer to come up and write the vowel to complete the word. Continue with other words.

Concentration Write each spelling word on two index cards. Mix the cards and place them facedown in a grid. Have partners take turns turning over two cards at a time. If the words match, the student says the word aloud and keeps the cards. If the words do not match, the student turns the cards back over.

Onsets and Rimes Write each spelling word on a large index card. Cut the initial consonant off each word. Mix the consonant cards and stack them facedown on a table. Arrange the other cards faceup on the table. Have students take turns drawing a consonant card and placing it with one of the word endings to make a spelling word. Have students read the word they make.

Intermediate

Word Meaning Write the spelling words on the board. Say each word clearly and have students repeat it. Say a sentence that illustrates the meaning of a word, such as *I will try to* **fix** *the broken dish*. Have students tell you which spelling word they heard in the sentence. Then call on a volunteer to use the spelling word in another sentence. Continue with the remaining words.

Rhyming Words List the spelling words horizontally on the board. Have students write rhyming words under each spelling word. (Possible words: bad—dad, fad, had, lad, mad, pad, sad; yet—bet, get, jet, let, met, net, pet, set, wet; fix—mix, six; dot—cot, got, hot, jot, lot, not, pot, rot, tot; hug—bug, dug, jug, lug, mug, rug, tug; tub—cub, hub, rub)

Segmenting and Blending Create a deck of spelling word cards. Have partners take turns drawing a card, sounding out the word, and then blending the sounds to pronounce the word. Students keep each card they sound out and read aloud. Students can listen to the Unit 12 words on the audio recording.

Support for Spanish Speakers

Comparing Languages English vowels are a challenging learning task for most Spanish speakers. The Spanish language has fewer vowel sounds and fewer variations in how those sounds are spelled. The English **short i** sound may be difficult for Spanish speakers to hear or pronounce. The letter **i** in Spanish represents a sound that is similar to **long e** in English. Spelling words provide an excellent opportunity for Spanish speakers to listen to clear pronunciation of single words, to practice approximating the sounds of English, and to develop English sound-symbol correspondence.

Choose from the activities below to reinforce English language acquisition.

Advanced

Word Meaning List the spelling words on the board. Ask a question that students can answer with a spelling word, such as *What do you do when you repair something?* (fix) Have the student who answers the question ask another question that can be answered with a spelling word. Continue until everyone has had a turn.

Riddles Have partners work together to answer the "What am I?" questions on page 16 of *Spelling Support for English Language Learners*. Then have them do the second activity. Encourage hem to continue to change the first letter in each word to write new words.

Emotional Words Have partners choose a spelling word and practice saying it in different tones of voice, such as happy, sad, angry, excited, scared, and bored. Then have them choose one word and one emotion and decide why a character in a story would say the word that way.

Categorize Create a five-column chart with the column headings **a, e, i, o,** and **u.** Have volunteers write each spelling word in the appropriate column. Then have them add spelling words from earlier units to each column. Encourage students to continue to add to the lists as they learn more words with short vowel sounds.

Advanced High

Create a Storyboard Have students draw three pictures to show the sequence of events in a story about a dot. Encourage students to write a sentence about each picture and then read the sentences in order as they point to each picture. If available, read *The Dot and the Line* by Norton Juster.

Sentence Blanks Have students write a sentence using two spelling words, leaving blanks for the words. Encourage students to trade sentences with a partner. The partner reads the sentence aloud and writes the missing spelling words.

Tic-Tac-Toe Ask students if they know how to play tic-tac-toe. Explain the game if needed. Prepare grids that are large enough for students to write a short vowel word in each space. Each partner chooses a vowel for the game and begins by writing a word with that vowel in a space. The winner writes three words with the same short vowel diagonally, horizontally, or vertically.

Write Stories Have students review and list the short vowel spelling words they have learned so far. Then have them work with a partner to write a story using as many of the words as possible. Encourage students to illustrate their stories.

Spelling Support for English Language Learners

Practice Master, *TRB*, p. 16

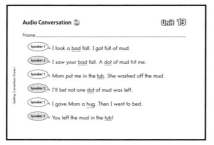

Practice Master, p. 47

 Audio Conversation available on CD

English/Spanish
Word List, p. 62

Spelling Connections Online
Interactive online spelling activities provide additional ELL support.
www.spellingconnectionsonline.com

Connections to THINKING

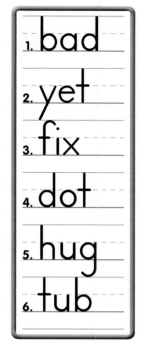

1. bad
2. yet
3. fix
4. dot
5. hug
6. tub

A. Write letters to finish each spelling word.

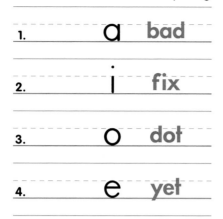

1. a bad
2. i fix
3. o dot
4. e yet

B. Write a **u** to finish each spelling word.

5. h __ g hug
6. t __ b tub

School Home
This unit reviews the **short vowel sounds**. Ask your child to name a word that rhymes with each spelling word.

 TEKS 1.22Bi Use letter-sound patterns to spell: consonant-vowel-consonant (CVC) words. **1.22C** Spell high-frequency words from a commonly used list.

91

Day 1 — Unit 13

Student Objectives
- Read, spell, and write words with a short vowel in the medial position.

Unit Pretest
- Administer the pretest on page T91B.

Teaching Tips
- Have students read the spelling words aloud, listening for and emphasizing the short vowel sound in each word.

 **WORD SORT CD-ROM**
- Conduct a **Teacher-Led Sort** (see p. Z31) to reinforce the spelling patterns.
- Use the Sound/Symbol Cards for **bag, bed, box, dig,** and **tub** to review the short vowel sounds. Remind students that when a word has only one vowel between two consonants, the vowel sound is usually short.
- Write **bad** on the board. Ask a volunteer to read the word and identify the short vowel. Then have the student use the word in a sentence.
- Continue in the same way with the remaining spelling words.
- Have students complete the page independently or as a class.

Home/School Word Lists TRB
- Have students take home the Home/School Spelling Practice Master.

Home/School Practice

Home/School Spelling
Practice Master, *TRB*, p. 71

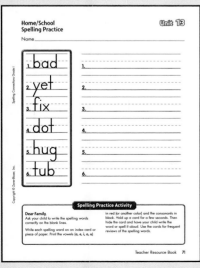

English

Home/School Spelling
Practice Master, *TRB*, p. 72

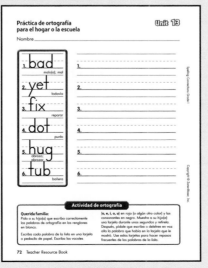

Spanish

TEKS 1.22Bi Use letter-sound patterns to spell: consonant-vowel-consonant (CVC) words.
1.22C Spell high-frequency words from a commonly used list.

T91

Student Objectives
- Spell and write CVC words to reinforce short vowel spellings.
- Blend initial, medial, and final sounds of picture names to write CVC words with short vowels.

Teaching Tips
- Display the Sound/Symbol Cards for **bed**, **cup**, and **bag**. Have students say the name of each picture.
- Say **bed**. Ask students to identify the beginning sound and the letter that makes the sound. (/b/, b) Write **b** on the board. Say **cup**. Have students identify the sound in the middle of **cup** and the letter that makes the sound. (/ŭ/, u) Write **u**. Then say **bag**. Ask students to identify the sound at the end of **bag** and the letter that makes the sound. (/g/, g) Write **g**.
- Have students read the word on the board. (**bug**)
- Have students complete page 92 independently or as a class.

Extra Pattern Practice
- Use the optional practice master below for extra practice with short vowels.

WORD SORT CD-ROM
- Provide time for students to use a **Buddy Sort** (see p. Z31) to practice their spelling words with a partner.

Connections to PHONICS

Name each picture. Match the sound you hear at the beginning, middle, and end of the picture names to write a spelling word.

1. _bad_
2. _dot_
3. _fix_
4. _hug_
5. _tub_
6. _yet_

bad
yet
fix
dot
hug
tub

92

TEKS **1.22A** Use phonological knowledge to match sounds to letters to construct known words. **1.22Bi** Use letter-sound patterns to spell: consonant-vowel-consonant (CVC) words. **1.22C** Spell high-frequency words from a commonly used list.

Extra Pattern Practice

Extra Pattern Practice Master,
TRB, p. 73

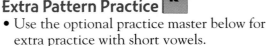

Short Vowel Practice
Say the spelling words, emphasizing the short vowel sound in each. Organize the class into five groups and assign a vowel sound to each group. Tell each group to stand and then sit down when it hears its vowel sound. Say each spelling word. Then say the following: **mix, wag, pop, it, bend, can, let, not, up, bus, big, box, him, pen, fed, his, lap, cut, nut, men, dad, man, pet, hum**.

TEKS **1.22A** Use phonological knowledge to match sounds to letters to construct known words.
1.22Bi Use letter-sound patterns to spell: consonant-vowel-consonant (CVC) words.
1.22C Spell high-frequency words from a commonly used list.

Connections to READING

Write the spelling word that completes each sentence.

bad
yet
fix
dot
hug
tub

1. Can I __?__ the net?

   fix

2. Is the __?__ red?

   dot

3. The cat was __?__ .

   bad

4. You can __?__ Mom.

   hug

5. Can pup get in the __?__ ?

   tub

6. Can you see the sun rise __?__ ?

   yet

TEKS 1.22C Spell high-frequency words from a commonly used list.

93

Student Objectives
- Spell and write words with short vowels in context.

Teaching Tips
- Write the spelling words on the board. Read them aloud and have students repeat them.
- Tell students to raise their hand when they hear a spelling word. Say, *I can fix my bike.* Have students say the spelling word they heard. **(fix)**
- Write on the board: *Are we there _____?* Read the sentence and pause at the blank. Ask students which spelling word will finish the sentence. **(yet)** Call on a volunteer to write the word in the blank.
- Have students complete page 93.

Differentiated Instruction
- Use the **Challenge Words** activity on page 193 with students who are ready to transfer their knowledge of short vowels to new words.
- An Extra Challenge Practice Master is available on page 74 in the *TRB*.
- Dictation sentences for the challenge words are available on page T193.

More Fun With Spelling for Differentiation

▶ Digital Resources for Spelling Connections
Interactive digital resources include word sorts, pattern practice, and proofreading activities for individual and whole-group instruction. (Interactive whiteboard compatible; see p. Z32.)

▶ Spelling Connections Online
Interactive online spelling activities include word sorts, crossword puzzles, sentence completion, proofreading practice, and spelling bees with words from each unit (see p. Z32. www.spellingconnectionsonline.com

Spelling Center Activities

Spelling Game Mats
Place one of the spelling games in a learning center to provide a fun way for students to practice their spelling words (see p. Z26).

Flip Folder
Students can use a Flip Folder to practice spelling words independently (see p. Z32).

Word Sort CD-ROM
Printable, unit-specific word cards for spelling and challenge words can be used for Teacher-Led, Individual, Buddy, and Speed Sorts (see p. Z31).

TEKS 1.22C Spell high-frequency words from a commonly used list.

T93

Student Objectives
- Spell and write CVC words with short vowels to complete a friendly letter.
- Write a friendly letter using CVC words with short vowels.

Teaching Tips
- Ask students what kind of writing is in the first activity. (a letter) Then ask how they know it is a letter. (It says Dear Grandma. It's signed Love, Fran.)
- Talk about the parts of a letter.
- Read the directions and have students complete Part A independently or as a class. Ask them to read the completed letter aloud.
- Read the prompt for Part B and have students complete it independently. Tell students to write things in the order that they happened. Ask volunteers to read their letter aloud. Prompt them to point out the parts of their letter. Have other students identify spelling words in the letters.

WORD SORT CD-ROM
- Invite students to practice for the weekly test by doing an **Individual Sort** or a **Speed Sort** (see p. Z31).

Day 5

Student Objectives
- Demonstrate mastery of the unit spelling words.

Posttest Assessment Options
Option 1: Administer the unit posttest using the dictation sentences at right.

Option 2: Assess students using the standardized test. See the *Standardized Test Master Book*, p. 17.

Note: Posttest sentences for the on level and challenge lists are available on the audio *Spelling Connections* Posttest CD.

Connections to WRITING

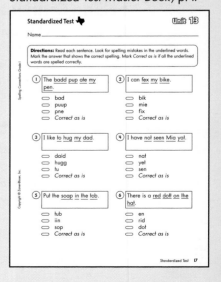

A. Write spelling words to finish the letter.

Dear Grandma,

My new pup has a black __1.__ on his head. He was __2.__ today. He ran in the mud. I had to wash him in the __3.__. We had to __4.__ the fence, too. He does not know how to sit __5.__. He does like to __6.__ me.

Love, Fran

1. dot	2. bad
3. tub	4. fix
5. yet	6. hug

Word box: bad, yet, fix, dot, hug, tub

B. Write a letter on a sheet of paper. Tell about your day. Use spelling words.

94

TEKS 1.22C Spell high-frequency words from a commonly used list.

1-Minute Handwriting Hint
Be sure that the pull down straight stroke in the lowercase **b** is straight. The forward circle begins halfway between the midline and the baseline.

CIRCLE BEGINS HERE → **b** ← STRAIGHT

Posttest Sentences
1. I filled the **tub** for your bath.
2. I forgot to put a **dot** above the **j**.
3. Has it stopped raining **yet**?
4. I can **fix** it myself.
5. Don't go out if the weather is **bad**.
6. I like to **hug** my dog.

Standardized Test Master Book, p. 17

Standardized Test — Unit 13

Name

Directions: Read each sentence. Look for spelling mistakes in the underlined words. Mark the answer that shows the correct spelling. Mark *Correct as is* if all the underlined words are spelled correctly.

1. The badd pup ate my pen.
   - ☐ bad
   - ☐ puup
   - ☐ pne
   - ☐ Correct as is

2. I can fex my bike.
   - ☐ bik
   - ☐ mie
   - ☐ fix
   - ☐ Correct as is

3. I like to hug my dad.
   - ☐ daid
   - ☐ hugg
   - ☐ tu
   - ☐ Correct as is

4. I have not seen Mia yat.
   - ☐ nat
   - ☐ yet
   - ☐ sen
   - ☐ Correct as is

5. Put the soap in the tob.
   - ☐ tub
   - ☐ iin
   - ☐ sop
   - ☐ Correct as is

6. There is a red dott on the hat.
   - ☐ en
   - ☐ rid
   - ☐ dot
   - ☐ Correct as is

Standardized Test 17

 TEKS 1.22A Use phonological knowledge to match sounds to letters to construct known words. **1.22C** Spell high-frequency words from a commonly used list.

Planner

Day 1

Day 1

Connections to **Thinking**

Student Objectives
- Read, spell, and write high-frequency words.

Instruction for All Students
- Pretest Dictation Sentences, p. T95B
- Connections to Thinking, p. 95
- Home/School Spelling Practice Master (*Teacher Resource Book*, pp. 75–76)

🔶 TEKS 1.22A, 1.22C

Day 2

Connections to **Phonics**

Student Objectives
- Use phonetic clues to write high-frequency words.

Instruction for All Students
- Connections to Phonics, p. 96

Optional Practice
- Extra Pattern Practice Master (*Teacher Resource Book*, p. 77)

🔶 TEKS 1.22A, 1.22C

Spelling Words
a
I
to
of
the
was
are

Challenge Words
ago
goes
easy
only

Day 3

Day 2

Connections to **Reading**

Student Objectives
- Write high-frequency words in context.

Instruction for All Students
- Connections to Reading, p. 97

Differentiated Instruction
- Challenge Words, p. 194

🔶 TEKS 1.22C

Day 4

Day 2

Connections to **Writing**

Student Objectives
- Write high-frequency words to complete a poem.
- Write a poem using high-frequency words.

Instruction for All Students
- Connections to Writing, p. 98

Differentiated Instruction
- Extra Challenge Practice Master (*Teacher Resource Book*, p. 78)

🔶 TEKS 1.22A, 1.22C, 1.22E

Day 5

Day 3

Assessment

Student Objectives
- Demonstrate mastery of the unit spelling words.

Assessment for All Students
- Posttest Dictation Sentences, p. T98, or
- *Standardized Test Master Book*, p. 18

Differentiated Assessment
- Challenge Dictation Sentences, p. T194

Unit 14 Materials

Student Edition
pp. 95–98, 194

Teacher Edition
pp. T95A–T98, T194

 Teacher Resource Book
Unit 14 Practice Masters,
pp. 75–78, and
Sound/Symbol Cards

 Standardized Test Master Book
Unit 14 Test Master, p. 18

 Word Sort CD-ROM
Unit 14 Word Sort Cards for Teacher-Led Sorts and Student Sorts

 Digital Resources for Spelling Connections
Unit 14

 Spelling Connections Online
www.spellingconnectionsonline.com

Spelling Support for English Language Learners*
Unit 14 Practice Masters and Audio Conversation

Spelling Center Activities*
Spelling Game Mats
Flip Folder, *TRB*, p. 155

*Spelling Support for English Language Learners *and Spelling Center Activities *may be used at any time during the week.*

Assessment

Pretest Sentences (See procedures on p. Z30.)
1. Do you want to play **a** game?
2. **I** like to swim.
3. Is Alan going **to** the store?
4. One **of** those birds sings sweetly.
5. Is **the** door locked?
6. When **was** your birthday?
7. Those colors **are** bright.

The Science of Spelling ◄· ·

- High-frequency words are words that appear most often in print. Ten percent of all words in printed English are **I, and,** and **the**. Many high-frequency words are considered sight words because one or more phonemes do not match the common sounds the letters make. Therefore, they are difficult to decode and must be memorized so they can be identified by sight. For example, in the word **of,** the **o** makes a **short u** sound while the **f** makes a **v** sound. Learning to recognize these words is important in developing fluency.

Choose from the activities below to reinforce English language acquisition.

Beginning

Word Meaning Explain that some English words are used often in writing and speech. Demonstrate by walking to the door. Say, *I walked to the door.* Write the sentence on the board. Read it aloud, underlining the words **I, to,** and **the**. Gesture to yourself and the door as you repeat the action. Continue with the remaining spelling words. Then ask students to repeat your actions and sentences.

Segment Words Write the spelling words on the board. Segment each word into phonemes and compare the number of sounds to the number of letters. For example, **the** and **are** each have three letters and two phonemes. Identify letter combinations that make one sound, such as **th** in **the,** and silent letters, such as the **e** in **are**. Also point out the different sounds for letters such as

f/v/, s/z/, o/oo/, and o/ŭ/. Say each word aloud, enunciating each sound. Have students repeat. Then blend the sounds to pronounce the word and have students repeat. Finally, point to and have students chorally read each spelling word. Students can hear the Unit 14 spelling words pronounced singly on the audio recording.

Rebus Sentences On the board, create sentences using spelling words, rebus pictures, and short vowel words that students already know. For example, *The* (photo of a dog) *was big.* Then erase the spelling words, leaving blanks. Help students recreate the sentences by writing the spelling words. Then have students read the sentences with you. Students can hear the Unit 14 spelling words in context sentences on the audio recording.

Intermediate

Word Meaning Say each spelling word clearly and have students repeat it. Ask a volunteer to come to the board and write the word. Then have another volunteer use the word in a sentence or tell something about the meaning of it. If necessary, clarify and expand the definition, using objects, pictures, and pantomime.

Listen to and Use Spelling Words Provide support with pronunciations by having students listen to and interact with the audio recording. Students can practice the conversations and elaborate on them to improve pronunciations while gaining a better understanding of word meanings. The conversation for Unit 14 is in print form on page 47 of *Spelling Support for English Language Learners.*

Crossword Puzzle Create a crossword puzzle using as many spelling words as possible. Fill in some letters to get students started. Then have partners work together to complete the puzzle. Show students how you created the puzzle and invite students to create their own puzzles. For example:

		t	o
w		h	
a	r	e	
s			

Support for Spanish Speakers

Comparing Languages Spanish speakers may have difficulty hearing and pronouncing some English consonants. Some consonant sounds are quite different in the two languages. For example, the consonant sound /d/ is much softer in Spanish and somewhat similar to the unvoiced /th/ in English. Give students

opportunities to practice pronouncing spelling words one-on-one with a native English-speaking adult. Brief sessions every day or several times a week can be especially helpful. It is important to praise the students' efforts and to accept gradual improvements in English pronunciation.

Choose from the activities below to reinforce English language acquisition.

Advanced

Identify and Write Words Tell students that they will be using the spelling words in this unit in everything they write. Select a book to read aloud to students. Read a few pages slowly. Have students raise their hand when they hear a spelling word. Then have them write the word. Encourage students to write their own sentences using the spelling words.

Complete Sentences Have partners work together to complete the sentences on page 17 of *Spelling Support for English Language Learners*. Then have them do the second activity on page 17. Encourage them to trade pictures with their partner and read the sentence aloud.

Telephone Organize students into groups of three or four. Have one student in each group create a sentence using a spelling word and whisper it to another group member, who whispers it to another, and so on. The final student writes the sentence. Students then compare the written sentence with what they said.

True or False Use spelling words in statements that students identify as true or false. For example, say, *I am your teacher.* Students can say **yes** or **no** to identify the statement as true or false. If the sentence is false, ask students to explain what makes it false. Then have them use the spelling word in a true sentence. Invite students to make their own statements for a partner to identify as true or false.

Advanced High

Write a Letter Have students write a letter to a friend or family member telling what they did in school that day. Have students read their letter and point out the spelling words they used.

Sentence Mix-ups Write simple sentences using the spelling words. Cut each sentence into individual words and place the words in an envelope. Have students put the sentence back together. Encourage students to write and cut apart their own sentences for a partner to reconstruct. Then have partners complete the sentences on page 17 of *Spelling Support for English Language Learners*.

Conversation Have students listen to the Unit 14 oral conversation on the audio recording. Then have partners read the print version of the conversation on page 47 of *Spelling Support for English Language Learners*. Encourage partners to continue the conversation and write the sentences they say.

Spelling Support for English Language Learners

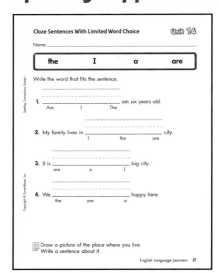

Practice Master, *TRB*, p. 17

Practice Master, p. 47

Audio Conversation
available on CD

English/Spanish
Word List, p. 62

Spelling Connections Online
Interactive online spelling activities
provide additional ELL support.
www.spellingconnectionsonline.com

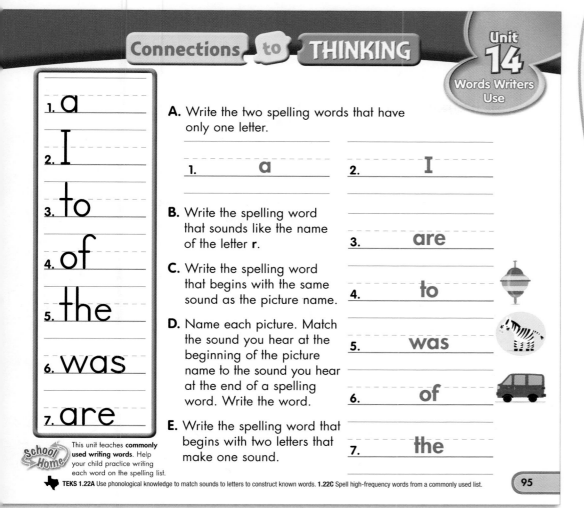

Connections to THINKING

Unit 14
Words Writers Use

1. a
2. I
3. to
4. of
5. the
6. was
7. are

A. Write the two spelling words that have only one letter.

1. _____ a
2. _____ I

B. Write the spelling word that sounds like the name of the letter **r**.

3. _____ are

C. Write the spelling word that begins with the same sound as the picture name.

4. _____ to

D. Name each picture. Match the sound you hear at the beginning of the picture name to the sound you hear at the end of a spelling word. Write the word.

5. _____ was

6. _____ of

E. Write the spelling word that begins with two letters that make one sound.

7. _____ the

School Home This unit teaches **commonly used writing words.** Help your child practice writing each word on the spelling list.

TEKS 1.22A Use phonological knowledge to match sounds to letters to construct known words. 1.22C Spell high-frequency words from a commonly used list.

95

Day 1

Unit 14

Student Objectives
• Read, spell, and write high-frequency words.

Unit Pretest
• Administer the pretest on page T95B.

Teaching Tips
• Have students read the spelling words aloud and talk about the different sounds they hear and the letters that make them.

 **CD-ROM**

• Conduct a **Teacher-Led Sort** (see p. Z31).
• Explain that some letters do not always make the same sound.
• Tell students that the word **a** does not usually sound like the name of the letter that spells it. As an example, say, *You have a happy face.* Emphasize the schwa sound of **a**.
• Note the word **I** sounds exactly like the name of the letter that spells it. As an example say, *I can hear you.*
• Point out that the word **of** ends with the letter **f** but has a /v/ sound. The word **was** ends with **s** but has a /z/ sound.
• Have students complete the page independently or as a class.

Home/School Word Lists 🅣🅡🅑
• Have students take home the Home/School Spelling Practice Master.

Home/School Practice

Home/School Spelling
Practice Master, *TRB*, p. 75

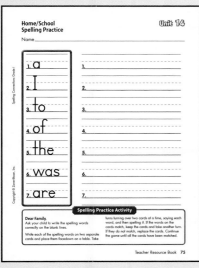

English

Home/School Spelling
Practice Master, *TRB*, p. 76

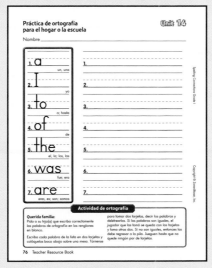

Spanish

 TEKS 1.22A Use phonological knowledge to match sounds to letters to construct known words.
1.22C Spell high-frequency words from a commonly used list.

T95

Unit 14 — Day 2

Student Objectives
- Use phonetic clues to write high-frequency words.

Teaching Tips
- Write the spelling words on the board. Say, *I am thinking of a word. It has two letters. It ends with a /v/ sound.* (**of**) Ask a volunteer to point to the word **of**.
- Write **are** on the board and ask students to read it aloud. Say, *This word is **are**, as in We **are** learning to spell important words.* Point out that an **e** at the end of a word is often silent. Compare the spellings of **are** and **the** and the sound of **e** in each.
- Write **the** on the board and ask students to read it aloud. Ask which letter makes the /**th**/ sound. Say, *Sometimes letters work together to make a new sound. **T** and **h** work together that way.* Circle **th** and have students practice making the /**th**/ sound.
- Have students complete page 96.

Extra Pattern Practice TRB
- Use the optional practice master below for extra practice with high-frequency words.

WORD SORT CD-ROM
- Provide time for students to use a **Buddy Sort** (see p. Z31) to practice their spelling words with a partner.

Connections to PHONICS

Use the clues to find the spelling words. Write the words.

Word bank: a I to of the was are

1. ● one letter ■ a capital letter ▲ sounds like its name

I

2. ● three letters ■ two sounds ▲ the **e** makes no sound

are

3. ● three letters ■ two sounds ▲ the **e** makes a sound

the

4. ● three letters ■ three sounds ▲ starts like **win**

was

5. ● one letter ■ one sound ▲ sometimes sounds like its letter name

a

6. ● two letters ■ two sounds ▲ starts like **tug**

to

7. ● two letters ■ two sounds ▲ ends with the **v** sound

of

96

TEKS 1.22A Use phonological knowledge to match sounds to letters to construct known words. **1.22C** Spell high-frequency words from a commonly used list.

Extra Pattern Practice

Extra Pattern Practice Master,
TRB, p. 77

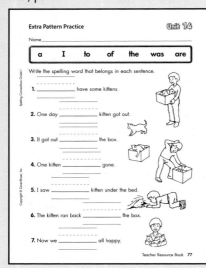

Spelling Practice
Say sentences using the spelling words. Have students raise their hand when they hear a spelling word. Say, **I** like **to** sing. One **of** those pencils is mine. Can you hear **the** dog bark? Books **are** good gifts. My cat **was** here. Would you like a pen? Call on volunteers to come to the board and write the words.

TEKS 1.22A Use phonological knowledge to match sounds to letters to construct known words. **1.22C** Spell high-frequency words from a commonly used list.

Connections to READING

A. Write the spelling words that go before words that name things.

1. ____a____   2. ____the____

B. Write the spelling word you use to tell about you.

3. ____I____

C. Write a spelling word to finish each sentence.

to	was	are	of

4. The men ____are____ wet.

5. Pam ____was____ on a jet.

6. Jim ran ____to____ the bed.

7. Ed has one ____of____ the pens.

a
I
to
of
the
was
are

TEKS 1.22C Spell high-frequency words from a commonly used list.

97

Student Objectives
• Write high-frequency words in context.

Teaching Tips
• Tell students that two of the spelling words can help them name things. Write **dog** and **cat** on the board. Ask students to use a spelling word in front of one of the words. (the, a) Then ask which spelling word they would use when they talk about themselves. (I)
• Write on the board: *Walk _____ the door.* Read the sentence and pause at the blank. Ask students which spelling word will finish the sentence. (to) Call on a volunteer to write the word in the blank.
• Have students complete page 97.

Differentiated Instruction
• Use the **Challenge Words** activity on page 194 with students who are ready to add to their knowledge of high-frequency words.
• An Extra Challenge Practice Master is available on page 78 in the *TRB*.
• Dictation sentences for the challenge words are available on page T194.

More Fun With Spelling for Differentiation

Digital Resources for Spelling Connections
Interactive digital resources include word sorts, pattern practice, and proofreading activities for individual and whole-group instruction. (Interactive whiteboard compatible; see p. Z32.)

Spelling Connections Online
Interactive online spelling activities include word sorts, crossword puzzles, sentence completion, proofreading practice, and spelling bees with words from each unit (see p. Z32). www.spellingconnectionsonline.com

Spelling Center Activities

Spelling Game Mats
Place one of the spelling games in a learning center to provide a fun way for students to practice their spelling words (see p. Z26).

Flip Folder
Students can use a Flip Folder to practice spelling words independently (see p. Z32).

Word Sort CD-ROM
Printable, unit-specific word cards for spelling and challenge words can be used for Teacher-Led, Individual, Buddy, and Speed Sorts (see p. Z31).

TEKS 1.22C Spell high-frequency words from a commonly used list.

T97

Student Objectives
- Write high-frequency words to complete a poem.
- Write a poem using high-frequency words.

Teaching Tips
- Read the directions for Part A.
- Have students complete Part A as a class or independently. When students have finished, ask them to read the completed poem aloud.
- Read the directions for Part B. Give students a few minutes to brainstorm ideas. Remind them that poems often use sensory words, or words that tell how things look, feel, sound, and smell. Have students brainstorm sensory words about an object in the classroom. Tell students to write their poem on a separate sheet of paper. Encourage them to use sensory words.
- Invite volunteers to read their poems aloud. Discuss any sensory words. Have the class identify the spelling words used.

WORD SORT CD-ROM
- Invite students to practice for the weekly test by doing an **Individual Sort** or a **Speed Sort** (see p. Z31).

Day 5

Student Objectives
- Demonstrate mastery of the unit spelling words.

Posttest Assessment Options
Option 1: Administer the unit posttest using the dictation sentences at right.
Option 2: Assess students using the standardized test. See the *Standardized Test Master Book*, p. 18.

Note: Posttest sentences for the on level and challenge lists are available on the audio *Spelling Connections* Posttest CD.

Connections to WRITING

A. Write a spelling word to finish each line of the poem.

Last night _____ **I** _____ dreamed I _____ **was** _____ a star,

And I was shining where you _____ **are** _____.

Full _____ **of** _____ blinking, twinkling light,

I could brighten up _____ **the** _____ night.

I sent _____ **a** _____ happy light _____ **to** _____ you

So you could dream some sweet dreams, too.

B. Write a poem about something you would like to be. Use spelling words. Review your work. Use a dictionary to check your spelling.

| a |
| I |
| to |
| of |
| the |
| was |
| are |

98

TEKS **1.22C** Spell high-frequency words from a commonly used list. **1.22E** Use resources to find correct spellings.

1-Minute Handwriting Hint

The uppercase **I** begins at the headline with a pulldown straight stroke. The two slide right strokes should be the same length.

SAME LENGTH

Posttest Sentences
1. Which **of** these books is yours?
2. My mother **was** going to come.
3. Where **are** your crayons?
4. **I** have to go now.
5. Have you ever seen **a** spider?
6. You may give this **to** Dale.
7. Stand on **the** black line.

Standardized Test Master Book, p. 18

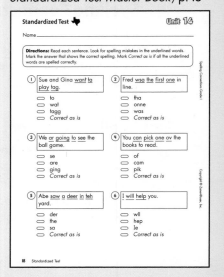

Standardized Test   Unit 14

Name _____

Directions: Read each sentence. Look for spelling mistakes in the underlined words. Mark the answer that shows the correct spelling. Mark *Correct as is* if all the underlined words are spelled correctly.

1. Sue and Gina <u>want ta</u> play tag.
  - ○ to
  - ○ wat
  - ○ tagg
  - ○ Correct as is

2. Fred <u>wsa</u> <u>the</u> first one in line.
  - ○ tha
  - ○ onne
  - ○ was
  - ○ Correct as is

3. <u>We ar</u> going to see the ball game.
  - ○ se
  - ○ are
  - ○ ging
  - ○ Correct as is

4. You <u>can</u> pick one <u>ov</u> the books to read.
  - ○ of
  - ○ cam
  - ○ pik
  - ○ Correct as is

5. Abe <u>saw a deer in teh</u> yard.
  - ○ der
  - ○ the
  - ○ sa
  - ○ Correct as is

6. <u>I will help you.</u>
  - ○ wll
  - ○ hep
  - ○ Ie
  - ○ Correct as is

18 Standardized Test

 TEKS **1.22A** Use phonological knowledge to match sounds to letters to construct known words.
1.22C Spell high-frequency words from a commonly used list. **1.22E** Use resources to find correct spellings.

Planner

Day 1

Day 1

Unit 11: Short u: VC, CVC

Student Objectives
- Review the spelling patterns and words from Unit 11.

Instruction for All Students
- Unit 11 Review, p. 99
- Home/School Spelling Practice Master (*Teacher Resource Book*, pp. 79–80)

Day 2

Unit 12: Short u: CVC

Student Objectives
- Review the spelling pattern and words from Unit 12.

Instruction for All Students
- Unit 12 Review, p. 100

Unit 11
Short u: VC, CVC

up	cut
us	but
bus	nut

Unit 12
Short u: CVC

fun	tug
run	bug
sun	rug

Unit 13
Short Vowel Review: CVC

bad	dot
yet	hug
fix	tub

Unit 14
Words Writers Use

a	of	are
I	the	
to	was	

Day 3

Day 2

Unit 13: Short Vowel Review

Student Objectives
- Review the spelling pattern and words from Unit 13.

Instruction for All Students
- Unit 13 Review, p. 101

Day 4

Unit 14: Words Writers Use

Student Objectives
- Review the spelling words from Unit 14.

Instruction for All Students
- Unit 14 Review, p. 102

Day 5

Day 3

Assessment

Student Objectives
- Demonstrate mastery of the review unit spelling words.

Assessment for All Students
- Posttest Assessment Options
  - ✦ Posttest Dictation Sentences, p. T102, or
  - ✦ *Standardized Test Master Book*, p. 19

Unit 15 Materials

Student Edition
pp. 99–102
Alphabet and Picture Cards
(See page Z32 for
suggested activities.)

Teacher Edition
pp. T99A–T102

 Teacher Resource Book
Unit 15 Practice Masters,
pp. 79–80

 Standardized Test Master Book
Unit 15 Test Master, p. 19

 Word Sort CD-ROM
Unit 15 Word Sort Cards for Teacher-
Led Sorts and Student Sorts

 **Digital Resources for
Spelling Connections**
Unit 15

Spelling Connections Online
www.spellingconnectionsonline.com

Spelling Center Activities*
Spelling Game Mats
Flip Folder, *TRB*, p. 155

   **Spelling Center Activities may be used
   at any time during the week.*

Developmental Spelling Check

Administer the following **Developmental Spelling Check** to evaluate spelling growth. Remind students that this is not a test for a grade; students are not expected to spell these words conventionally. Author J. Richard Gentry has provided (in parentheses) typical Phase 3 Phonetic Spellings for each word. Students who produce these or similar spellings are demonstrating full phonemic awareness since each letter corresponds to a sound in the word. These spellings are a middle first-grade benchmark.

To administer, say each word aloud, read the sentence, and then say the word again.

Coin Words and Sample Phonetic Spellings

penny	Did Mom give you a **penny**?	(PENE)
dime	Ten pennies make one **dime**.	(DIM)
nickel	That new **nickel** is very shiny.	(NEKL)
quarter	One **quarter** equals 25 cents.	(QWRTR)
silver dollar	A **silver dollar** is heavy.	(SELVR DALR)

ELL Support

Choose from the activities below to reinforce English language acquisition.

Beginning

Word Meaning Write the spelling words on the board and read them aloud with students. Use realia, pictures, and pantomime to review meanings. For example, show a picture of a bus. Point to the bus and say **bus**. Have students repeat.

Blend Sounds List the spelling words on the board. Then write each word on a card and cut the letters apart. Mix the letters. Have partners choose a word and find the letter cards needed to reconstruct it. As they arrange the letters to spell the word, have them say the sound of each letter and then blend the sounds to say the word. Students can hear the words for Units 11–14 pronounced singly on the audio recording.

Complete Sentences Write the review words on the board. Then write several sentences, leaving blanks that could be completed with the words. For example, write *I felt a _____ on the rope.* Read the sentence aloud and have students tell which word makes sense in the sentence. (tug) Continue, reading each sentence and having students complete it.

Intermediate

Word Meaning Write the review spelling words on the board. Say each word and have students repeat it. Tell students you are thinking of one of the words. Provide meaning and phonics clues for students to guess the word. For example, say, *I am thinking of a word that tells about something on the floor. The word ends with /g/.* (rug)

Categorize Words Create a three-column chart on the board with the headings *Naming Words, Doing Words,* and *Describing Words.* Review each kind of word. Provide examples by saying **bus, run,** and **bad.** Have students tell which category each word belongs in. Then have students categorize as many review spelling words as possible and write each one in the appropriate column.

Word Families Write **u** and say /ŭ/. Say each **short u** spelling word and have students repeat chorally. Then write **ut** on the board and have students read it aloud. Invite a volunteer to come up and write an initial consonant to spell a word. Ask another volunteer to erase that consonant and write another one to spell a different word. Continue with **un** and **ug**. After students have written all of the spelling words with **-ut, -un,** and **-ug,** invite them to suggest other beginning letters to make **short u** words.

Support for Spanish Speakers

Comparing Languages The **r** sound is rolled in Spanish, so Spanish-speaking students may find it difficult to pronounce **r-controlled vowels**. Some students may also have difficulty pronouncing the letter **w**. Additionally, /**th**/ is not a part of the Spanish language. Students will need to practice hearing and producing these sounds.

Pronouncing Words Review short vowels with students by focusing on letter-sound correlations and building CVC pattern words with short vowels. Write a CVC word, such as **hat,** on the board. Have students name the vowel and say the short sound. Then have them name two additional words with the same short vowel sound.

Unit 15

Choose from the activities below to reinforce English language acquisition.

Advanced

Word Meaning Write each review spelling word on an index card. Then ask questions that can be answered using the words. For example, *Which word do you use to talk about yourself?* (I) *Which word names a floor covering?* (rug) *Which word says you put something back together?* (fix) *What do some students ride to school?* (bus) Have volunteers select the card that answer each question and read the word aloud.

Write Words Have partners take turns. One says a sentence using at least one spelling word. The other writes the spelling word or words used in the sentence. Partners can continue until they use all the review words.

Spell and Write Provide a set of flash cards of the spelling words or have students make their own. Place the cards facedown on a table. Ask a student to select the top card, read the word, spell and write it while looking at the card, use it in a sentence, and then write it from memory.

Compare and Contrast Ask partners to select two spelling review words. Have one partner tell how the words are alike and the other tell how the words are different. For example, both **tub** and **tug** have three letters, begin with **t,** and have **u** in the middle. The words end with different letters. **Tub** names a thing and **tug** names an action.

Advanced High

Synonyms and Antonyms List the review spelling words on the board. Ask students to pick a word and then say or write a word that means the opposite or one that has similar meaning. For example, for **fix** students may say **break**. For **bus** they may say **train**. Talk about why the words are similar or different.

Spelling Word Pictures Encourage students to draw a picture that illustrates several spelling words. Then have students trade pictures with a partner. The partner tries to identify the spelling words used and writes them on a sheet of paper.

Write Sentences Have students write fill-in-the-blank sentences, using blanks for spelling words. Then have partners complete each other's sentences. As an alternative, students can randomly select one to three spelling words and challenge a partner to write a sentence using all of the words.

Mystery Words Encourage students to think of riddles using the spelling words. They can share riddles with a partner and see if they can guess the words. For example, *I have a hard shell. I begin with **n**.* (nut)

 Spelling Connections Online
Interactive online spelling activities
provide additional ELL support.
www.spellingconnectionsonline.com

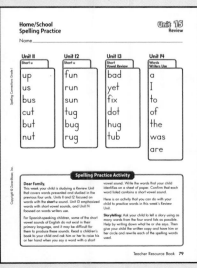

1. up
2. us
3. bus
4. cut
5. but
6. nut

School Home
This unit reviews **short u**, short vowels, and commonly used words. Ask your child to read the spelling words on each page aloud.

Unit 11: Short u: VC, CVC

A. Change the vowel in the middle to write a spelling word.

cat	net
1. cut	2. nut

bit	
3. but	

B. Write the spelling word that rhymes.

fuss	cup
4. bus	5. up

C. Change the first letter to write a spelling word.

is	
6. us	

99

Student Objectives
• Review the spelling patterns and words from Unit 11.

Reteaching the Skill
• Write **up, us, bus, cut, but,** and **nut** on the board. Ask if the **u** comes at the end of the word. (no) Ask what kind of letter follows the **u**. (consonant) Remind students that when there is only one vowel in a word and it is followed by a consonant, it usually makes the short vowel sound.
• Have students read each spelling word, emphasizing the **short u** sound.
• Write **cot, bat,** and **not** on the board. Call on volunteers to erase the vowel in each word and replace it with **u**. (cut, but, nut) Have students read the words.
• Have students complete page 99 independently.

Letters and Sounds Review
• Throughout the unit, use the **Alphabet and Picture Cards** to review letters and sounds. See page Z32 for activity suggestions.

Review Word List

Home/School Spelling
Practice Master, *TRB*, p. 79

Home/School Spelling
Practice Master, *TRB*, p. 80

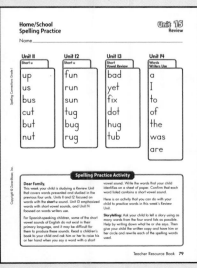

English

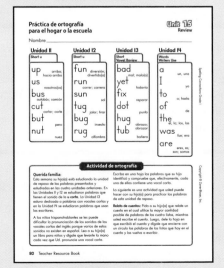

Spanish

Unit 15 — Day 2

Student Objectives
- Review the spelling pattern and words from Unit 12.

Reteaching the Skill
- Display pictures of the numeral ten, a tub, and a pig. Help students name the pictures.
- Say **ten**. Ask students what sound they hear at the beginning of **ten**. (/t/) Then say **tub**. Ask what sound they hear in the middle of **tub**. (/ŭ/) Say **pig**. Ask what sound they hear at the end of **pig**. (/g/) Ask students to say all three sounds together, /t/ /ŭ/ /g/, to make a spelling word. (**tug**)
- Have students complete page 100 independently.

Review

1. fun
2. run
3. sun
4. tug
5. bug
6. rug

100

Unit 12: Short u: CVC
Name each picture. Match the sound you hear at the beginning, middle, and end of each picture name to write a spelling word.

1. fun
2. bug
3. run
4. tug
5. rug
6. sun

Extra Pattern Practice

Words and Sentences
Write the words **fun, run, sun, tug, bug,** and **rug** on index cards. Spread the cards facedown on a table. Ask a volunteer to draw a card, read the word, spell it, and use it in a sentence. Have the class repeat the word, spell it, and repeat the student's sentence. Continue the activity until all students have had a turn.

1. bad
2. yet
3. fix
4. dot
5. hug
6. tub

Unit 13: Short Vowel Review: CVC

Write the spelling word that begins with the same sound as each picture name.

1. d**o**t

2. h**u**g

3. f**i**x

4. y**e**t

5. b**a**d

6. t**u**b

101

Student Objectives
- Review the spelling pattern and words from Unit 13.

Reteaching the Skill
- Write **bad, yet, fix, dot, hug,** and **tub** on the board. Remind students that since there is one vowel followed by a consonant in each word, the vowel makes a short vowel sound. Tell students to listen as you say each word, emphasizing the short vowel sound.
- Write **lad, set, mix, not, mug,** and **cub** on the board. Remind students that words that end with the same sounds rhyme. Call on volunteers to say the spelling word that rhymes with each word and write it next to the word on the board. (lad, bad; set, yet; mix, fix; not, dot; mug, hug; cub, tub)
- Have students complete page 101 independently.

More Fun With Spelling for Differentiation

Digital Resources for Spelling Connections

Interactive digital resources include word sorts, pattern practice, and proofreading activities for individual and whole-group instruction. (Interactive whiteboard compatible; see p. Z32.)

Spelling Connections Online

Interactive online spelling activities include word sorts, crossword puzzles, sentence completion, proofreading practice, and spelling bees with words from each unit (see p. Z32). www.spellingconnectionsonline.com

Spelling Center Activities

Spelling Game Mats
Place one of the spelling games in a learning center to provide a fun way for students to practice their spelling words (see p. Z26).

Flip Folder
Students can use a Flip Folder to practice spelling words independently (see p. Z32).

Word Sort CD-ROM
Printable, unit-specific word cards for spelling and challenge words can be used for Teacher-Led, Individual, Buddy, and Speed Sorts (see p. Z31).

Student Objectives
• Review the spelling words from Unit 14.

Reteaching the Skill
• Remind students that they often use the words **a**, **I**, **to**, **of**, **the**, **was**, and **are** when they write.
• Note that when **a** and **the** are pronounced, the vowels **a** and **e** often have the schwa (/ə/) sound. Illustrate the sound by saying **a** in a sample sentence, such as *There is a bird in the tree*. Also pronounce **the**, isolating the /ə/ sound.
• Point out that the word **I** is always capitalized. Remind students that the **f** in **of** makes a /v/ sound, the **s** in **was** makes a /z/ sound, the **o** in **to** makes an /o͞o/ sound, and the **e** in **are** is silent.
• Have students complete page 102 independently or as a class.

Review

1. a
2. I
3. to
4. of
5. the
6. was
7. are

Unit 14: Words Writers Use
Use the clues to write each spelling word.

1. ends with **f** that sounds like a **v**

   of

2. starts with two letters that make one sound

   the

3. ends with **s** that sounds like a **z**

   was

4. has an **e** that makes no sound

   are

5. a capital letter that sounds like its name

   I

6. one letter and sometimes sounds like its name

   a

7. starts with the same sound as **top**

   to

102

Day 5

Assessment
Student Objectives
• Demonstrate mastery of the review unit spelling words.

Posttest Assessment Options
Option 1: Administer the posttest using the dictation sentences at right.

Option 2: Assess students using the standardized test. See the *Standardized Test Master Book*, p. 19.

Note: Posttest sentences for the on level and challenge lists are available on the audio *Spelling Connections* Posttest CD.

Posttest Sentences
1. I can **fix** my bike.
2. We had fun, **but** now it is bedtime.
3. One **of** those books is mine.
4. Can I open the present **yet**?
5. Ben **was** on the bus.
6. Would you like **to** go with me?
7. The boys will **run** in the race.
8. The bird ate a **nut**.
9. Let us sit on the **rug**.
10. Will you go with **us** to the park?

Standardized Test Master Book, p. 19

Planner

Day 1   Day 2

Day 1

Connections to **Thinking**

Student Objectives
- Read, spell, and write words with initial consonant blends.

Instruction for All Students
- Pretest Dictation Sentences, p. TI03B
- Connections to Thinking, p. 103
- Home/School Spelling Practice Masters (*Teacher Resource Book*, pp. 81–82)

🔶 TEKS 1.22Biii, 1.22C

Connections to **Phonics**

Student Objectives
- Match sounds to symbols to spell words with initial consonant blends.

Instruction for All Students
- Connections to Phonics, p. 104

Optional Practice
- Extra Pattern Practice Master (*Teacher Resource Book*, p. 83)

🔶 TEKS 1.22A, 1.22Biii, 1.22C

Spelling Words
grin
spin
skip
frog
plum
slam

Challenge Words
snap
grab
plug
slip

Day 3   Day 4   Day 5

Day 2   Day 3

Connections to **Reading**

Student Objectives
- Use letter clues to spell words with initial consonant blends.
- Write words with initial consonant blends to complete sentences.

Instruction for All Students
- Connections to Reading, p. 105

Differentiated Instruction
- Challenge Words, p. 195

🔶 TEKS 1.22C

Connections to **Writing**

Student Objectives
- Write words with initial consonant blends to complete a story.
- Write a response to literature.

Instruction for All Students
- Connections to Writing, p. 106

Differentiated Instruction
- Extra Challenge Practice Master (*Teacher Resource Book*, p. 84)

🔶 TEKS 1.22A, 1.22Biii, 1.22C

Assessment

Student Objectives
- Demonstrate mastery of the unit spelling words.

Assessment for All Students
- Posttest Dictation Sentences, p. TI06, or
- *Standardized Test Master Book*, p. 20

Differentiated Assessment
- Challenge Dictation Sentences, p. TI95

Unit 16 Materials

 Student Edition
pp. 103–106, 195

Teacher Edition
pp. T103A–T106, T195

 Teacher Resource Book
Unit 16 Practice Masters,
pp. 81–84, and
Sound/Symbol Cards

 Standardized Test Master Book
Unit 16 Test Master, p. 20

Word Sort CD-ROM
Unit 16 Word Sort Cards for Teacher-
Led Sorts and Student Sorts

 Digital Resources for Spelling Connections
Unit 16

 Spelling Connections Online
www.spellingconnectionsonline.com

Spelling Support for English Language Learners*
Unit 16 Practice Masters and
Audio Conversation

Spelling Center Activities*
Spelling Game Mats
Flip Folder, *TRB*, p. 155

*Spelling Support for English Language Learners *and Spelling Center Activities may be used at any time during the week.*

Assessment

Pretest Sentences (See procedures on p. Z30)
1. Many people **grin** when they are happy.
2. You will get dizzy if you **spin** around.
3. Can you **skip** down the street?
4. Our pond has a **frog** in it.
5. Would you like a juicy **plum**?
6. Please do not **slam** the door.

The Science of Spelling ◄··

- A consonant blend, also called a consonant cluster, is a group of consonants that appear together with no vowel between them. For example, **st** in **stop** and **gr** in **green**. In a blend, each consonant is sounded. Blends are distinguished from consonant digraphs, which are groups of consonants that make one sound (**church**), silent letters that make no sound (**sign**), and double consonants (**bell**) that make one sound.

ELL Support

Choose from the activities below to reinforce English language acquisition.

Beginning

Understanding Word Meanings Write the spelling words on the board. Say each word and use gestures, pictures, and pantomime to support word meaning. For example, point to your face and grin. Point to the word **grin**. Have students repeat.

Segmenting and Blending Write the spelling words on the board. Call on volunteers to identify the vowel and the consonants in each word. Slide your hand under the first two letters of a word and explain that the sounds of these letters slide together when the word is pronounced. Demonstrate by first segmenting a word into phonemes and then blend the sounds to pronounce the word. Have students repeat by first segmenting and then blending the sounds.

Flash Cards Provide each student with flash cards for the spelling words or have students make their own cards. Tell students to arrange their cards faceup on the table. Read a spelling word aloud. Have students identify and hold up the corresponding word card. Students can hear the Unit 16 spelling words pronounced singly on the audio recording.

Rebus Sentences On the board, create sentences using spelling words, rebus pictures, and words that students already know. For example, *A frog hops on the box.* Then erase the spelling words, leaving blanks. Help students recreate the sentences by writing the spelling words. Then have students read the sentences with you. Students can hear the spelling words in context sentences on the audio recording.

Intermediate

Understanding Word Meanings Write the spelling words on the board. Say each word clearly and have students repeat. Ask a volunteer to choose a word and use it in a sentence or tell something about the meaning of the word. If necessary, clarify and expand the definition. Then have students write the word on a piece of paper. Students may look at the word on the board to be sure they have spelled it correctly.

Matching Word Parts Print each spelling word on a large index card. Then cut each word apart between the initial consonant blend and the end part. Have students select a consonant blend and an end part to create a spelling word. Then have students write the words they create.

Making Conversation Provide support with pronunciations by having students listen to and interact with the audio recording. Students can practice the conversations and elaborate on them to improve pronunciations while gaining a better understanding of the word meanings. Partners can read the print form of the audio dialogue on page 48 of *Spelling Support for English Language Learners*.

Matching Pictures and Words Provide students with copies of page 18 of *Spelling Support for English Language Learners*. Encourage pairs to cut out and combine their cards to make a stack of pictures and a stack of words. Have them play the game described on page 18 and then complete the remaining activities.

Support for Spanish Speakers

Comparing Languages Spanish speakers may have difficulty hearing and pronouncing some English consonants blends. For example, in Spanish the consonant blend **sl** is always preceded by the vowel **e** or **i**. Some Spanish-speaking students may therefore tend to say /ĕ/ before **sl** words. The **pl** blend, on the other hand, is spelled and pronounced in essentially the same way in both Spanish and English. With the exception of the /**r**/ sound, the **gr** and **fr** blends are also pronounced similarly in both languages. Students can find Spanish translations of the English spelling words on page 63 of *Spelling Support for English Language Learners*.

Choose from the activities below to reinforce English language acquisition.

Advanced

Understanding Word Meanings Provide students with a set of flash cards for the spelling words, or have students make their own. Place the cards facedown. Ask a student to select the top card, read the word, spell and write it while looking at the card, use it in a sentence, and then spell or write the word (and the sentence) from memory.

Questions Write the spelling words on the board. Then ask questions that can be answered with the spelling words. For example, *What is an animal that lives in a pond and hops?* (frog) *What do you do when you close a door hard?* (slam)

Word Hunt Provide a student dictionary. Show students how to find words that begin with the same consonant blends as the spelling words. Have students copy any four-letter words they find. For example, students may find **free, fret, from, grab, grid, grim, plan, plot, plug, skid, skim, skin, slab, sled, slim, span, spit, spot**. Create a comprehensive list. Ask students to select words to talk about with a partner or a small group.

Word Sort Have students sort the spelling words into two categories: naming words and doing words. Then have them select a word from each category to write or say a sentence. For example, *The plum can spin.*

Advanced High

Word Questions Have students work with a partner to write a question about a spelling word on one side of an index card. They write the answer on the reverse side. Partners can team with another pair to ask their questions.

Word Guess Have partners give each other spelling and meaning clues for a word they are thinking of. For example, *The word begins with /s/. The word ends in /m/. It can make a loud noise.* (slam)

Sentence Mix-ups Write simple sentences using the spelling words. Cut each sentence into individual words and place the words in an envelope. Have students put the sentence back together. Encourage students to write and cut apart their own sentences for a partner to reconstruct.

Finding Words Have students find spelling words in other books in the classroom. Ask students to read the sentence in which they find a spelling word.

Character Names Have students create characters whose names are spelling words. Ask students to describe their characters based on what they know about the spelling words. For example, **Grin** could always be smiling, **Spin** could be constantly turning, and **Frog** could have a croaky voice.

Complete Sentences Have students select a spelling word for a partner to use in a written sentence. Encourage students to continue writing until each partner has written a sentence for every word.

Spelling Support for English Language Learners

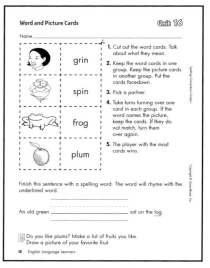

Practice Master, *TRB*, p. 18

Practice Master, p. 48

Audio Conversation available on CD

English/Spanish
Word List, p. 63

Spelling Connections Online
Interactive online spelling activities provide additional ELL support.
www.spellingconnectionsonline.com

Connections to THINKING

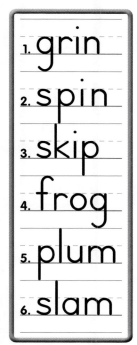

1. grin
2. spin
3. skip
4. frog
5. plum
6. slam

A. Write the spelling words that begin with a consonant and **r**.

1. _____ frog
2. _____ grin

B. Write the spelling words that begin with a consonant and **l**.

3. _____ slam
4. _____ plum

C. Write the spelling words that begin with **sp** and **sk**.

5. _____ spin
6. _____ skip

This unit teaches consonant blends, such as **gr** in **grin**. Help your child name other words that start with these blends.

 TEKS 1.22Biii Use letter-sound patterns to spell: one-syllable words with consonant blends. 1.22C Spell high-frequency words from a commonly used list.

103

Student Objectives
• Read, spell, and write words with initial consonant blends.

Unit Pretest
• Administer the pretest on page T103B.

Teaching Tips

WORD SORT CD-ROM

• Conduct a **Teacher-Led Sort** (see p. Z31) to introduce or reinforce the spelling pattern.
• Write **pin** on the board and have students read it aloud. Add **s** to write **spin** and have students read it aloud. Circle **sp** and explain that these letters are a consonant blend. Point out that even though the sounds of **s** and **p** slide together, you can still hear each one.
• Have students read the spelling words aloud, listening for the sound of each letter.
• Use Sound/Symbol Cards to introduce and reinforce consonant blends: **grapes, grasshopper (gr); spider, spill (sp); skate, skunk (sk); frame, frog (fr); planet, plug (pl); sled, slide (sl)**.
• Have students complete the page independently or as a class.

Home/School Word Lists TRB
• Have students take home the Home/School Spelling Practice Master.

Home/School Practice

Home/School Spelling
Practice Master, *TRB*, p. 81

Home/School Spelling
Practice Master, *TRB*, p. 82

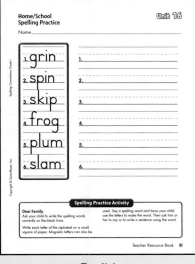

English

Spanish

TEKS 1.22Biii Use letter-sound patterns to spell: one-syllable words with consonant blends.
1.22C Spell high-frequency words from a commonly used list.

T103

Student Objectives
- Match sounds to symbols to spell words with initial consonant blends.

Teaching Tips
- Explain that sometimes two letters work together to make sounds. Say **grin**, emphasizing **gr**. Tell students that the /g/ and /r/ are working together. Then say the sounds of **sp, sk, fr, pl,** and **sl**.
- Ask students to look at the first item on page 104. Have them name the pictures and identify the initial sound of each name. Ask what letters make those sounds. **(p, l)** Write **pl** on the board. Remind students that **pl** is a consonant blend. Prompt them to scan the word list and find the word that begins with **pl**. Ask a volunteer to write the word on the board. Have the class read the word aloud.
- Have students complete page 104 independently or as a class.

Extra Pattern Practice **TRB**
- Use the optional practice master below for extra practice with consonant blends.

WORD SORT CD-ROM
- Provide time for students to use a **Buddy Sort** (see p. Z31) to practice their spelling words with a partner.

Connections to PHONICS

Name each picture. Match the sound you hear at the beginning of each picture name to the two letters that begin a spelling word. Write the word.

1. plum
2. frog
3. grin
4. slam
5. spin
6. skip

grin
spin
skip
frog
plum
slam

TEKS 1.22A Use phonological knowledge to match sounds to letters to construct known words. **1.22Biii** Use letter-sound patterns to spell: one-syllable words with consonant blends. **1.22C** Spell high-frequency words from a commonly used list.

Extra Pattern Practice

Extra Pattern Practice Master,
TRB, p. 83

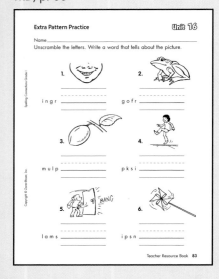

Pattern Practice: CCVC

Have students listen for the consonant blend at the beginning of each of the following words: **grin, spin, skip, frog, plum, slam, grab, slip, snap, plug.** Then write the spelling words on the board. Ask volunteers to circle the beginning consonant blends.

TEKS 1.22A Use phonological knowledge to match sounds to letters to construct known words. **1.22Biii** Use letter-sound patterns to spell: one-syllable words with consonant blends. **1.22C** Spell high-frequency words from a commonly used list.

Connections to READING

Write a spelling word to finish each sentence.

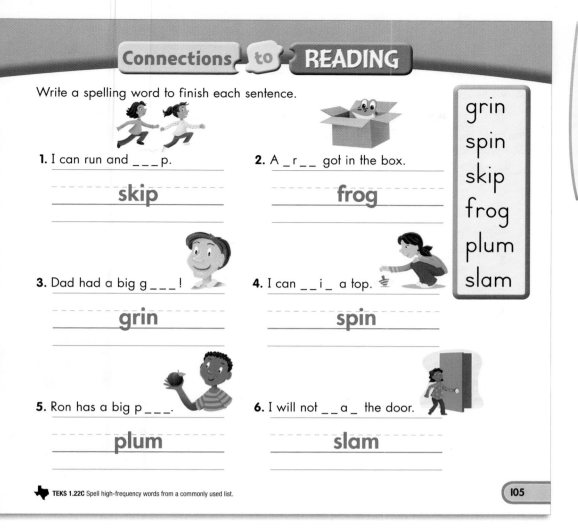

grin
spin
skip
frog
plum
slam

1. I can run and ___ p.

skip

2. A _ r _ _ got in the box.

frog

3. Dad had a big g ___ !

grin

4. I can __ i _ a top.

spin

5. Ron has a big p ___ .

plum

6. I will not __ a _ the door.

slam

 TEKS 1.22C Spell high-frequency words from a commonly used list.

105

Student Objectives
- Use letter clues to spell words with initial consonant blends.
- Write words with initial consonant blends to complete sentences.

Teaching Tips
- Write the spelling words on the board. Then write *A _ r _ _ is on the rug.* Ask students how many letters are in the missing word. (4) Ask what the second letter is. (r) Have students identify the spelling word that completes the sentence. (frog)
- Point out that the number of letters in the missing word, the given second letter, and the information in the sentence are clues that help identify the missing word.
- Have students complete page 105 independently or as a class.

Differentiated Instruction
- Use the **Challenge Words** activity on page 195 with students who are ready to transfer their knowledge of initial consonant blends to new words.
- An Extra Challenge Practice Master is available on page 84 in the *TRB*.
- Dictation sentences for the challenge words are available on page T195.

More Fun With Spelling for Differentiation

Digital Resources for Spelling Connections

Interactive digital resources include word sorts, pattern practice, and proofreading activities for individual and whole-group instruction. (Interactive whiteboard compatible; see p. Z32.)

Spelling Connections Online

Interactive online spelling activities include word sorts, crossword puzzles, sentence completion, proofreading practice, and spelling bees with words from each unit (see p. Z32). www.spellingconnectionsonline.com

Spelling Center Activities

Spelling Game Mats
Place one of the spelling games in a learning center to provide a fun way for students to practice their spelling words (see p. Z26).

Flip Folder
Students can use a Flip Folder to practice spelling words independently (see p. Z32).

Word Sort CD-ROM
Printable, unit-specific word cards for spelling and challenge words can be used for Teacher-Led, Individual, Buddy, and Speed Sorts (see p. Z31).

 TEKS 1.22C Spell high-frequency words from a commonly used list.

Unit 16 — Day 4

Student Objectives
- Write words with initial consonant blends to complete a story.
- Write a response to literature.

Teaching Tips
- Have students look at the illustration on page 106 and talk about what they see. Ask questions such as, *What is the frog looking at? What is the frog wishing?*
- Read the directions for Part A. Explain to students that they will write a spelling word in each sentence to finish the story.
- Have students complete Part A as a class. Read each sentence aloud and guide students to choose the best word to complete it. Read the completed story aloud.
- Read the directions for Part B. Ask, *Do you think the frog will get the plum?* Have students write their answer and then write to explain it. Invite volunteers to share their answers. Encourage discussion.

WORD SORT CD-ROM
- Invite students to practice for the weekly test by doing an **Individual Sort** or a **Speed Sort** (see p. Z31).

Day 5

Student Objectives
- Demonstrate mastery of the unit spelling words.

Posttest Assessment Options
Option 1: Administer the unit posttest using the dictation sentences at right.

Option 2: Assess students using the standardized test. See the *Standardized Test Master Book,* p. 20.

Note: Posttest sentences for the on level and challenge lists are available on the audio *Spelling Connections* Posttest CD.

Connections to WRITING

A. Write spelling words to finish the story.

The __1.__ looks up. He sees a big __2.__ . The frog goes up the tree. He tries to __3.__ the plum to snap the stem. Oh, no! The plum falls. It will __4.__ on the ground. It will bounce and __5.__ into the pond. The frog is not sad. He has a big __6.__ .

grin
spin
skip
frog
plum
slam

1. frog
2. plum
3. spin
4. slam
5. skip
6. grin

B. Write about the story.

Do you think the frog will get the plum? _____ yes

Why?

possible answer: The frog can swim.

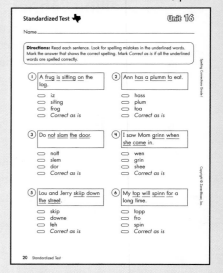

106

TEKS 1.22C Spell high-frequency words from a commonly used list.

1-Minute Handwriting Hint

The lowercase **r** begins at the midline with a pulldown straight stroke. There is a pause at the bottom of the first stroke.

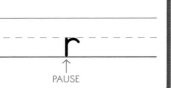
r
↑
PAUSE

Posttest Sentences
1. He has a funny **grin** on his face.
2. I keep my **frog** in an aquarium.
3. Can you **skip** quickly?
4. You will get dizzy if you **spin** around.
5. Have you ever eaten a **plum**?
6. You must **slam** that door hard.

Standardized Test Master Book, p. 20

Standardized Test — **Unit 16**

Name _____

Directions: Read each sentence. Look for spelling mistakes in the underlined words. Mark the answer that shows the correct spelling. Mark *Correct as is* if all the underlined words are spelled correctly.

1. A frug is sitting on the log.
   - iz
   - sitting
   - frog
   - Correct as is

2. Ann has a plumm to eat.
   - hass
   - plum
   - toa
   - Correct as is

3. Do not slam the door.
   - nott
   - slem
   - dor
   - Correct as is

4. I saw Mom grinn when she came in.
   - wen
   - grin
   - shee
   - Correct as is

5. Lou and Jerry skiip down the street.
   - skip
   - downe
   - teh
   - Correct as is

6. My top will spinn for a long time.
   - topp
   - fro
   - spin
   - Correct as is

20 Standardized Test

 TEKS 1.22A Use phonological knowledge to match sounds to letters to construct known words. **1.22Biii** Use letter-sound patterns to spell: one-syllable words with consonant blends. **1.22C** Spell high-frequency words from a commonly used list.

Day 1

Day 2

Day 1

Connections to **Thinking**

Student Objectives
- Read, spell, and write words with initial and final consonant blend **st**.

Instruction for All Students
- Pretest Dictation Sentences, p. T107B
- Connections to Thinking, p. 107
- Home/School Spelling Practice Masters (*Teacher Resource Book*, pp. 85–86)

🖐 TEKS 1.22Biii, 1.22C

Connections to **Phonics**

Student Objectives
- Blend and spell words with initial and final consonant blend **st**.

Instruction for All Students
- Connections to Phonics, p. 108

Optional Practice
- Extra Pattern Practice Master (*Teacher Resource Book*, p. 87)

🖐 TEKS 1.22A, 1.22Biii, 1.22C

Spelling Words
best
rest
fast
must
step
still

Challenge Words
stir
stiff
rust
post

Day 3

Day 4

Day 5

Day 2

Day 3

Connections to **Reading**

Student Objectives
- Write words with consonant blend **st** to complete a story.

Instruction for All Students
- Connections to Reading, p. 109

Differentiated Instruction
- Challenge Words, p. 196

🖐 TEKS 1.22C

Connections to **Writing**

Student Objectives
- Write words with consonant blend **st** to complete a paragraph.
- Write a response to literature.

Instruction for All Students
- Connections to Writing, p. 110

Differentiated Instruction
- Extra Challenge Practice Master (*Teacher Resource Book*, p. 88)

🖐 TEKS 1.22A, 1.22Biii, 1.22C

Assessment

Student Objectives
- Demonstrate mastery of the unit spelling words.

Assessment for All Students
- Posttest Dictation Sentences, p. T110, or
- *Standardized Test Master Book*, p. 21

Differentiated Assessment
- Challenge Dictation Sentences, p. T196

Unit 17 Materials

Student Edition
pp. 107–110, 196

Teacher Edition
pp. T107A–T110, T196

 Teacher Resource Book
Unit 17 Practice Masters,
pp. 85–88, and
Sound/Symbol Cards

 Standardized Test Master Book
Unit 17 Test Master, p. 21

Word Sort CD-ROM
Unit 17 Word Sort Cards for Teacher-
Led Sorts and Student Sorts

 **Digital Resources for
Spelling Connections**
Unit 17

 Spelling Connections Online
www.spellingconnectionsonline.com

**Spelling Support for
English Language Learners***
Unit 17 Practice Masters and
Audio Conversation

Spelling Center Activities*
Spelling Game Mats
Flip Folder, *TRB*, p. 155

*Spelling Support for English Language
Learners *and Spelling Center Activities may
be used at any time during the week.*

Assessment

Pretest Sentences (See procedures on p. Z30)

1. Marie is the **best** jumper.
2. If you are tired, take a **rest**.
3. That train is going **fast**.
4. You **must** wear a coat if it is cold.
5. Can you **step** over that log?
6. Is it **still** raining?

The Science of Spelling ◀··

- A consonant blend, also called a
  consonant cluster, is a group of
  consonants that appear together with no
  vowel between them. Blends can appear
  at the beginning (**play**) or end (**halt**) of a
  word. In English the longest initial blend
  is three letters (**split**) and the longest final
  blend is four letters (**twelfth**).

ELL Support

Choose from the activities below to reinforce English language acquisition.

Beginning

Understanding Word Meanings Write the spelling words on the board. Say each word and use gestures, pictures, and pantomime to support word meaning. For example, pantomime taking a step. Point to the word **step** and have students repeat.

Making Words List the spelling words on the board. Then write each word on a card. Cut out the letters and scramble them. Have students select letters to reconstruct the words. As they build each word, have students say the sound of each letter and then blend the sounds to say the word. As an extension, spell a word by saying the sound each letter makes. Have the students select a letter for each sound to construct the word.

Flash Cards Provide each student with flash cards for the spelling words or have students make their own cards. Tell students to arrange their cards faceup on the table. Read a spelling word aloud. Have students identify and hold up the corresponding word card. Students can hear the Unit 17 spelling words pronounced singly on the audio recording.

Making Sentences Provide students with spelling word cards. Say a word and have students hold up the correct word card. Invite students to use each spelling word in an oral sentence. Write each sentence, leaving out the spelling word. Read the sentence, pausing at the blank. Have students say the missing word or write the word in the blank. Then read the completed sentence.

Intermediate

Matching Word Parts Print each spelling word on a large index card. Then cut each word apart between the consonant blend and the rest of the word. Mix the parts together. Have students select a consonant blend and another word part to create spelling words. Then have students write the words they create.

Conversation Provide support with pronunciations by having students listen to and interact with the audio recording. Students can practice the conversations and elaborate on them to improve pronunciations while gaining a better understanding of word meanings. Partners can read the print form of the audio dialogue on page 48 of *Spelling Support for English Language Learners*.

Rhyming Words Write **est** on the board. Have volunteers come up and write initial letters to spell two spelling words. (best, rest) Point out that these words rhyme because they end with the same sounds. Ask students to suggest other words that rhyme with **best** and **rest**. (jest, nest, pest, test, west, zest) Call on volunteers to write these words on the board. Do the same with **fast**. (cast, last, mast, past) Talk about the meanings of these words. Then post the list as a word bank for students to use when writing poetry.

Support for Spanish Speakers

Comparing Languages Spanish speakers may have difficulty hearing and pronouncing some English consonant blends. The **l** and **r** blends are the same in Spanish and English. The **s** blends and blends formed with three letters are not found in Spanish. In Spanish words that include **str,** the **s** and **tr** are separate syllables. Students can find Spanish translations of the English spelling words on page 63 of *Spelling Support for English Language Learners*.

Practice Consonant Blends Introduce the initial **st** blend by writing the words **till, tab, tag, tall,** and **tub** on the board. Say the words aloud and have students repeat. Then write an **s** in front of each word. Segment the initial /s/, /t/ and then say each word. Have students repeat the words chorally.

Choose from the activities below to reinforce English language acquisition.

Advanced

Understanding Word Meanings Write the spelling words on the board. Then ask questions that can be answered with the words. For example, *What word says that something is better than anything else?* (best) *What do you do when you are tired?* (rest) *What is another word for* quick *or* rapid? (fast)

Write Spelling Words Provide students with flash cards for the spelling words, or have students make their own. Place the cards facedown. Ask a student to select the top card, read the word, spell and write it while looking at the card, use it in a sentence, and then spell or write the word (and the sentence) from memory. Students can hear the Unit 17 spelling words pronounced singly and in context sentences on the audio recording.

Complete Sentences Provide partners with a copy of page 19 in *Spelling Support for English Language Learners.* Have students work together to complete the sentences and then list other words that begin or end with **st**. Provide pairs with a student dictionary to help them with ideas.

Correct Spelling Have students use two or more spelling words in a written sentence and spell one of the words incorrectly. For example: *You* **musst** *run* **fast** *to win the race.* Have students exchange sentences with a partner and correct each others' errors.

Advanced High

Word Questions Have students work with a partner to write a question about a spelling word on one side of an index card. They write the answer on the reverse side. Partners can team with another pair to ask their questions.

Word Guess Have partners give each other spelling and meaning clues for a word they are thinking of. For example, *The word begins with* **st**. *It is something you do on stairs.* (step)

Sentence Mix-ups Write simple sentences using the spelling words. Cut each sentence into words and place the words in an envelope. Have students put the sentence back together. Encourage students to write and cut apart their own sentences for a partner to reconstruct.

Finding Words Have students find spelling words in other books in the classroom. Ask students to read the sentence in which they find a spelling word.

Complete Sentences Have students select a spelling word for a partner to use in a written sentence. Encourage students to continue writing until each partner has a written sentence for all of the words.

Conversation Have partners listen to the spelling words in conversation on the audio recording. Then have them read the print version of the conversation on page 48 of *Spelling Support for English Language Learners.* Encourage students to extend the conversation using additional spelling words.

Spelling Support for English Language Learners

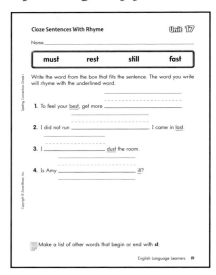

Practice Master, *TRB*, p. 19

Practice Master, p. 48

 Audio Conversation available on CD

English/Spanish Word List, p. 63

 Spelling Connections Online
Interactive online spelling activities provide additional ELL support.
www.spellingconnectionsonline.com

1. best
2. rest
3. fast
4. must
5. step
6. still

This unit teaches the consonant blend **st**. Help your child name other words that start with **st**.

A. Write the spelling words that begin with **st**.

1. step
2. still

B. Write the spelling words that end in **st**.

3. best
4. rest
5. fast
6. must

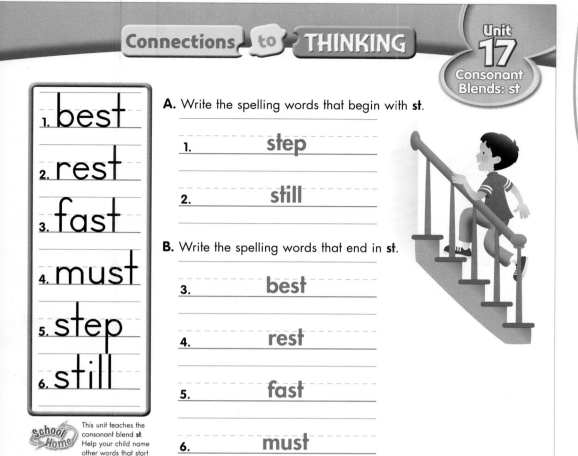

TEKS 1.22Biii Use letter-sound patterns to spell: one-syllable words with consonant blends. **1.22C** Spell high-frequency words from a commonly used list.

I07

Student Objectives
- Read, spell, and write words with initial and final consonant blend **st**.

Unit Pretest
- Administer the pretest on page T107B.

Teaching Tips
- Say each spelling word and have students repeat. Ask, *Is the /st/ sound at the beginning or at the end of this word?* Have students read the list of spelling words aloud.

WORD SORT CD-ROM
- Conduct a **Teacher-Led Sort** (see p. Z31) to introduce or reinforce the spelling pattern.
- Use the Sound/Symbol Cards for **steam, stem, stick,** and **stove** to provide more practice with /**st**/. Review that, although the sounds in a consonant blend slide together, both sounds can be heard. Also remind students that when a word has only one vowel, the vowel sound is usually short.
- Have students complete the page independently or as a class.

Home/School Word Lists
- Have students take home the Home/School Spelling Practice Master.

Home/School Practice

Home/School Spelling
Practice Master, *TRB*, p. 85

English

Home/School Spelling
Practice Master, *TRB*, p. 86

Spanish

TEKS 1.22Biii Use letter-sound patterns to spell: one-syllable words with consonant blends.
1.22C Spell high-frequency words from a commonly used list.

T107

Student Objectives
- Blend and spell words with initial and final consonant blend **st**.

Teaching Tips
- Explain that /s/ and /t/ work together to make the sound at the beginning of **step** and at the end of **best**.
- Write **st** on a sheet of paper. Show the Sound/Symbol Card for **bag**. Ask students to name the picture. Ask, *What is the first sound you hear in the word bag?* (**/b/**) Ask a volunteer to write **b** on a sheet of paper. Repeat the process with the Sound/Symbol Card for **egg**.
- Hold up the paper with **st**. Invite the volunteers who wrote **b** and **e** to stand with you and hold up their papers to make a spelling word. Have the class read the word aloud.
- Use other Sound/Symbol Cards and repeat the activity to build other spelling words.
- Have students complete page 108 independently or as a class.

Extra Pattern Practice **TRB**
- Use the optional practice master below for extra practice with initial and final consonant blend **st**.

WORD SORT CD-ROM
- Provide time for students to use a **Buddy Sort** (see p. Z31) to practice their spelling words with a partner.

A. Name each picure. Match the beginning sound of each picture name. Add **st** to write a spelling word.

1. 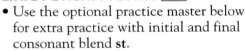 + st = __fast__

2. + st = __must__

B. Write the spelling words that rhyme.

3. __best__   4. __rest__

C. Put **st** in place of the first letter in each word. Write the spelling word.

dill   pep

5. __still__   6. __step__

best
rest
fast
must
step
still

108

TEKS **1.22A** Use phonological knowledge to match sounds to letters to construct known words. **1.22Biii** Use letter-sound patterns to spell: one-syllable words with consonant blends. **1.22C** Spell high-frequency words from a commonly used list.

Extra Pattern Practice

Extra Pattern Practice Master,
TRB, p. 87

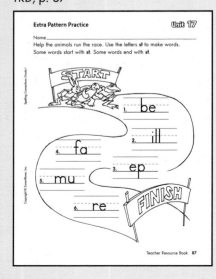

Pattern Practice: CCVC and CVCC
Give each student a red paper and a green paper. Say, *I will say a list of words. If you hear /st/ at the beginning of the word, raise your green flag. If you hear /st/ at the end of the word, raise your red flag. Say these words aloud, emphasizing /st/:* **best, rest, fast, must, step, still, post, stir, rust, stiff, stop, mist, bust.**

TEKS **1.22A** Use phonological knowledge to match sounds to letters to construct known words.
1.22Biii Use letter-sound patterns to spell: one-syllable words with consonant blends.
1.22C Spell high-frequency words from a commonly used list.

Complete the spelling words to finish the story.

Jen is in a _____ race. Without taking one

__**s**tep_____, she can __**s**till_____

have fun. Jen can go __**f**ast_____!

Jen __**m**ust_____ not __**r**est_____

until the _____ race is over. The __**b**est_____

racer will win a gold cup.

best
rest
fast
must
step
still

TEKS 1.22C Spell high-frequency words from a commonly used list.

109

Student Objectives
• Write words with consonant blend **st** to complete a story.

Teaching Tips
• List the spelling words on the board. Review with students that the consonant blend **st** can appear at the beginning or end of a word.
• Write the following questions on the board. Read each one aloud and have students write the missing word.
  1. Is the cat _____ outside? (**still**)
  2. Will we win if we run _____? (**fast**)
  3. Who left the toy on the _____? (**step**)
  4. Why _____ we hurry? (**must**)
  5. May I drink the _____ of the milk? (**rest**)
  6. Did you do your _____ work? (**best**)
• Have students complete page 109 independently or as a class.

Differentiated Instruction
• Use the **Challenge Words** activity on page 196 with students who are ready to transfer their knowledge of consonant blend **st** to new words.
• An Extra Challenge Practice Master is available on page 88 in the *TRB*.
• Dictation sentences for the challenge words are available on page T196.

More Fun With Spelling for Differentiation

Digital Resources for Spelling Connections
Interactive digital resources include word sorts, pattern practice, and proofreading activities for individual and whole-group instruction. (Interactive whiteboard compatible; see p. Z32.)

Spelling Connections Online
Interactive online spelling activities include word sorts, crossword puzzles, sentence completion, proofreading practice, and spelling bees with words from each unit (see p. Z32). www.spellingconnectionsonline.com

Spelling Center Activities
Spelling Game Mats
Place one of the spelling games in a learning center to provide a fun way for students to practice their spelling words (see p. Z26).

Flip Folder
Students can use a Flip Folder to practice spelling words independently (see p. Z32).

Word Sort CD-ROM
Printable, unit-specific word cards for spelling and challenge words can be used for Teacher-Led, Individual, Buddy, and Speed Sorts (see p. Z31).

TEKS 1.22C Spell high-frequency words from a commonly used list.

T109

Unit 17 — Day 4

Student Objectives
- Write words with consonant blend **st** to complete a paragraph.
- Write a response to literature.

Teaching Tips
- Have students look at the illustration on page 110 and talk about what they see. Talk about the Pony Express. Point out the saddle bag on the horse and explain that this bag held the mail.
- Read the directions for Part A. Explain to students that they will write a spelling word in each sentence to complete the paragraph.
- Have students complete Part A as a class. Guide students to choose the best word to complete each sentence. Read the completed story aloud.
- Read the directions for Part B. Ask, *How do we send mail today?* Then ask, *Do you think the Pony Express would be a good way to send mail today?* Have students write their answer and then write to explain it. Invite volunteers to share their answers. Encourage discussion.

WORD SORT CD-ROM
- Invite students to practice for the weekly test by doing an **Individual Sort** or a **Speed Sort** (see p. Z31).

Day 5

Student Objectives
- Demonstrate mastery of the unit spelling words.

Posttest Assessment Options
Option 1: Administer the unit posttest using the dictation sentences at right.
Option 2: Assess students using the standardized test. See the *Standardized Test Master Book,* p. 21.

Note: Posttest sentences for the on level and challenge lists are available on the audio *Spelling Connections* Posttest CD.

Connections to WRITING

A. Write spelling words to finish the story.

Once, the Pony Express was the __1.__ way to get mail to the West. A rider on a __2.__ horse took mail bags many miles. He did not __3.__ until he got the mail to another horse and rider. The new horse and rider did not miss a __4.__ . The rider knew he __5.__ hurry. He could __6.__ ride fast after many hours.

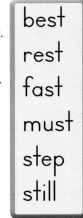

1. **best**
2. **fast**
3. **rest**
4. **step**
5. **must**
6. **still**

B. Would this be a good way to send mail today? Why or why not? Write what you think.

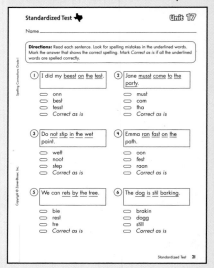

Possible answer: No. It is not fast today.

 TEKS 1.22C Spell high-frequency words from a commonly used list.

1-Minute Handwriting Hint

There is less space between two circle letters than there is between circle and straight-line letters or between two straight-line letters.

LEAST AMOUNT OF SPACE → MORE OPEN

Posttest Sentences
1. Which story did you like **best**?
2. Try to **step** over the puddle.
3. It's time to take a **rest**.
4. Some students are **still** painting.
5. You **must** come straight home.
6. Do you want to see me run **fast**?

Standardized Test Master Book, p. 21

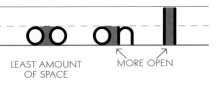

 **TEKS 1.22A** Use phonological knowledge to match sounds to letters to construct known words.
1.22Biii Use letter-sound patterns to spell: one-syllable words with consonant blends.
1.22C Spell high-frequency words from a commonly used list.

Planner

Day 1 ## Day 2

Day 1

Connections to **Thinking**

Student Objectives
- Read, spell, and write one-syllable words and add **-s** to form plurals.
- Read, spell, and write one-syllable words and add **-s** to form singular present tense.

Instruction for All Students
- Pretest Dictation Sentences, p. T111B
- Connections to Thinking, p. 111
- Home/School Spelling Practice Masters (*Teacher Resource Book*, pp. 89–90)

TEKS 1.22C, 1.22D

Connections to **Phonics**

Student Objectives
- Substitute vowels to write spelling words.
- Identify and practice alternative sounds for the letter **s**.

Instruction for All Students
- Connections to Phonics, p. 112

Optional Practice
- Extra Pattern Practice Master (*Teacher Resource Book*, p. 91)

TEKS 1.22C, 1.22D

Spelling Words
bugs
cats
pigs
sits
runs
gets

Challenge Words
pumps
chips
cards
twins

Day 3 ## Day 4 ## Day 5

Day 2

Connections to **Reading**

Student Objectives
- Write words with inflectional endings to complete a paragraph and describe a picture.

Instruction for All Students
- Connections to Reading, p. 113

Differentiated Instruction
- Challenge Words, p. 197

TEKS 1.22C

Connections to **Writing**

Student Objectives
- Write words with inflectional endings to complete a paragraph and describe a picture.
- Write a response to literature.
- Use a dictionary to find correct spellings.

Instruction for All Students
- Connections to Writing, p. 114

Differentiated Instruction
- Extra Challenge Practice Master (*Teacher Resource Book*, p. 92)

TEKS 1.22A, 1.22C, 1.22D, 1.22E

Day 3

Assessment

Student Objectives
- Demonstrate mastery of the unit spelling words.

Assessment for All Students
- Posttest Dictation Sentences, p. T114, or
- *Standardized Test Master Book*, p. 22

Differentiated Assessment
- Challenge Dictation Sentences, p. T197

Unit 18 Materials

Student Edition
pp. 111–114, 197

Teacher Edition
pp. T111A–T114, T197

 Teacher Resource Book
Unit 18 Practice Masters,
pp. 89–92, and
Sound/Symbol Cards

Standardized Test Master Book
Unit 18 Test Master, p. 22

 Word Sort CD-ROM
Unit 18 Word Sort Cards for Teacher-
Led Sorts and Student Sorts

 **Digital Resources for
Spelling Connections**
Unit 18

Spelling Connections Online
www.spellingconnectionsonline.com

**Spelling Support for
English Language Learners***
Unit 18 Practice Masters and
Audio Conversation

Spelling Center Activities*
Spelling Game Mats
Flip Folder, *TRB*, p. 155

*Spelling Support for English Language
Learners *and Spelling Center Activities* may
be used at any time during the week.

Assessment

Pretest Sentences (See procedures on p. Z30)

1. In the summer you see lots of **bugs**.
2. Megan has two white **cats**.
3. Did you know that **pigs** eat corn?
4. Jason **sits** with David on the floor.
5. Jennifer **runs** around the bases.
6. The bird **gets** worms for its babies.

The Science of Spelling

- In English, inflectional endings are used to indicate plurals (**cats, bushes**), verb tense (**rests, rested, resting**), and comparisons (**smarter, smartest**). Adding the letter **s** makes most singular nouns plural (**cat/cats**). Adding **-s** to a verb forms the singular present tense (**sit/sits**).

  Inflectional endings are distinguished from prefixes and suffixes, which change the meaning of a word.

ELL Support

Choose from the activities below to reinforce English language acquisition.

Beginning

Understanding Word Meanings Write the spelling words on the board. Say each word and use pictures and pantomime to support word meaning. For example, show a picture of two cats. Point to each cat. Say, *One cat plus one cat equals two cats*. Then point to the word **cats**. Say the word and have students repeat.

Making Words List the spelling words. Then write each base word on a card. Write a letter **s** on another card. Have students select a card and read the word. Then have the student place the **s** next to the end of the word. Have the student read the new word. Students can hear the Unit 18 spelling words pronounced singly on the audio recording.

Word Sort Have students make word cards for the spelling words or provide students with cards. Have students sort the words into naming words and doing words. Then have students select a word to illustrate. Prompt them to write their word on their picture.

Making Sentences Provide students with spelling word cards. Say a word and have students hold up the corresponding word card. Invite students to use each spelling word in an oral sentence. Write each sentence, leaving out the spelling word. Read the sentence, pausing at the blank. Have students say the missing word or write the word in the blank. Then read the completed sentence.

Intermediate

Understanding Word Meanings Write the spelling words on the board. Say each word clearly and have students repeat. Ask a volunteer to choose a word and use it in a sentence or tell something about the meaning of the word. If necessary, clarify and expand the definition. Then have students write the word on a piece of paper. Students may look at the word on the board to be sure they have spelled it correctly.

More Than One Explain the concept of plurals by writing the word **girl** on the board. Help students read the word. Then ask one girl to stand beside you. Say, *There is one girl standing beside me.* Point to the word **girl** on the board. Then invite another girl to stand beside you and the first girl. Say, *Now there are two girls standing beside me.* Add **-s** to the word **girl**.

Picture and Word Match Provide students with copies of page 20 of *Spelling Support for English Language Learners*. Encourage pairs to cut out and combine their cards to make a stack of pictures and a stack of words. Have them play the game described on page 20 and then complete the remaining activities.

Support for Spanish Speakers

Comparing Languages Spanish-speaking students will understand adding **-s** to a noun to show more than one, since **-s** is added to many words in Spanish to form plurals. Adding **-s** to verbs to form the singular present tense may be confusing to students, as the conjugation of Spanish verbs is different from that of English even though the rules are similar. For example, *I speak* is *yo hablo* in Spanish while *he speaks* is *el habla*. Students can find Spanish translations of the English spelling words on page 64 of *Spelling Support for English Language Learners*.

Choose from the activities below to reinforce English language acquisition.

Advanced

Understanding Word Meanings Provide students with a set of flash cards for the spelling words or have students make their own. Place the cards facedown on a table. Ask a student to select the top card, read the word, spell and write it while looking at the card, use it in a sentence, and then write the word (and the sentence) from memory.

More Than One Create two columns on the board. Label the first column *One* and the second column *More Than One*. Have students list naming words in the first column, such as **pig, cat, hen, bat, bug, plum, frog, pot, jet, nut, rug, pet,** and **hat**. Then have them add **-s** to each word and write the plural in the second column. Encourage students to select words and create oral sentences. Students can hear the Unit 18 spelling words used in context on the audio recording.

Writing Sentences Encourage students to use two spelling words in a compound sentence. For example, *The dog sits, and the cats meow.* Have students trade sentences with a partner. The partner reads the sentence aloud and points out the spelling words. Students can hear the Unit 18 spelling words read in context sentences on the audio recording.

Conversation Provide support with pronunciations by having students listen to and interact with the audio recording. Students can practice the conversations and elaborate on them to improve pronunciations while gaining a better understanding of the word meanings. Partners can read the print form of the audio dialogue on page 49 of *Spelling Support for English Language Learners*.

Advanced High

Word Guess Have partners give each other spelling and meaning clues for a word they are thinking of. For example, *This word tells what a person does in a chair. It has a **short i** sound.* (sits)

Nouns and Verbs Write simple sentences using the spelling words, such as *The **cats run**. The **cat runs**.* Point out that when the naming word names just one, the doing word has an **s** on the end. When the naming word names two or more, the doing word has no **s** on the end. Have students write a sentence with a singular subject and a verb that ends in **s**. Have them trade sentences with a partner who rewrites the sentence with a plural subject and a verb that does not end in **s**.

Write Words Encourage students to draw a picture that includes illustrations of spelling words. Then have students use the spelling words to tell a partner about their picture. The partner can write the spelling words heard in the story. As an extension, have partners write the oral story on the back of the picture.

Complete Sentences Have students select a spelling word for a partner to use in a written sentence. Encourage students to continue writing until each partner has written sentences for all of the words.

Spelling Support for English Language Learners

Practice Master, *TRB*, p. 20

Practice Master, p. 49

 Audio Conversation available on CD

English/Spanish Word List, p. 64

 **Spelling Connections Online**
Interactive online spelling activities provide additional ELL support.
www.spellingconnectionsonline.com

1. bugs
2. cats
3. pigs
4. sits
5. runs
6. gets

School Home This unit targets the **-s** ending. Ask your child to read the spelling words aloud.

A. Add and write.

1. 1 🐱 + 1 🐱 = 2 _____ cats

2. 1 🐞 + 1 🐞 = 2 _____ bugs

3. 1 🐷 + 1 🐷 = 2 _____ pigs

B. Add s to each word. Write the spelling word.

4. get _____ gets

5. run _____ runs

6. sit _____ sits

TEKS 1.22C Spell high-frequency words from a commonly used list. **1.22D** Spell base words with inflectional endings.

Student Objectives
- Read, spell, and write one-syllable words and add **-s** to form plurals.
- Read, spell, and write one-syllable words and add **-s** to form singular present tense.

Unit Pretest
- Administer the pretest on page T111B.

Teaching Tips
WORD SORT CD-ROM 🖱

- Conduct a **Teacher-Led Sort** (see p. Z31) to introduce or reinforce the spelling pattern.
- Have students read the spelling words aloud, listening for the sound the letter **s** makes. Explain that **s** can make /s/ or /z/.
- Write **cats** on the board. Ask, *What letter makes this word mean more than one?* Explain that **s** is added to many naming words to make them mean more than one.
- Write **sit** on the board. Ask a volunteer to come forward. Say, *[Student] will sit on the chair.* After the student sits, say, *[Student] sits on the chair.*
- Write **sits**. Explain that **s** added to an action word shows that one person besides *I* or *you* is doing something right now.
- Have students complete the page.

Home/School Word Lists **TRB**
- Have students take home the Home/ School Spelling Practice Master.

Home/School Practice

Home/School Spelling
Practice Master, *TRB*, p. 89

Home/School Spelling
Practice Master, *TRB*, p. 90

Home/School Spelling Practice — Unit 18

Name _____

1. bugs   1. _____
2. cats   2. _____
3. pigs   3. _____
4. sits   4. _____
5. runs   5. _____
6. gets   6. _____

Spelling Practice Activity

Dear Family,
Ask your child to write the spelling words correctly on the blank lines.

Write each spelling word on a card. On another set of cards write each word without the final **s**. Give your child two pairs of words, for example,

"bugs, bug" and "cats, cat." Say one of the words and have your child hold up the card for that word. If he or she chooses the correct card, have him or her keep that card. Continue this game until your child has "won" all of the cards.

Teacher Resource Book **89**

English

Práctica de ortografía para el hogar o la escuela — Unit 18

Nombre _____

1. bugs (insectos)   1. _____
2. cats (gatos)   2. _____
3. pigs (cerdos)   3. _____
4. sits (se sienta)   4. _____
5. runs (corre)   5. _____
6. gets (obtiene)   6. _____

Actividad de ortografía

Querida familia:
Pida a su hijo(a) que escriba correctamente las palabras de ortografía en los renglones en blanco.

Escriba cada palabra de la lista en una tarjeta. Ahora, escriba cada palabra de la lista en otra tarjeta, pero sin incluir la **s** final de la

palabra. Después, dé a su hijo(a) dos pares de palabras; por ejemplo: bug, bugs y cat, cats. A continuación, diga una de las palabras y pida a su hijo(a) que levante la tarjeta con esa palabra. Si levanta la tarjeta correcta, dígale que se quede con ella. Continúen el juego hasta que hayan acabado todas las tarjetas.

90 Teacher Resource Book

Spanish

TEKS 1.22C Spell high-frequency words from a commonly used list.
1.22D Spell base words with inflectional endings.

TIII

Student Objectives
- Substitute vowels to write spelling words.
- Identify and practice alternative sounds for the letter **s**.

Teaching Tips
- Review short vowel sounds with students. Show Sound/Symbol Cards for **bag, leg, dig, hop,** and **nut**. Have students name each picture and identify the short vowel sound.
- Challenge students to change the vowel sound in each word to say a new word.
- Ask students to sort the cards into groups: naming words and action words. Write the words in two columns on the board.
- Review with students that **s** can be added to naming words to show more than one and to action words to show that one person is doing something right now.
- Invite volunteers to add **-s** to each word on the board. Ask the class to read the words aloud. Ask, *In which words does **s** make the /z/ sound?* (**bags, legs, digs**)
- Have students complete the page.

Extra Pattern Practice **TRB**
- Use the optional practice master below for extra practice with adding **-s**.

WORD SORT CD-ROM
- Provide time for students to use a **Buddy Sort** (see p. Z31) to practice their spelling words with a partner.

Connections to PHONICS

A. Change each vowel sound to say a spelling word. Write the word.

1. cots   **cats**
2. sets   **sits**
3. bags   **bugs**
4. pegs   **pigs**

Word box: bugs, cats, pigs, sits, runs, gets

B. Sometimes when you add **s**, it makes the sound of **s**. Sometimes it makes the sound of **z**.

5. Write the word that ends with the sound of **z**.   **runs**

6. Write the word that ends with the sound of **s**.   **gets**

TEKS 1.22C Spell high-frequency words from a commonly used list. **1.22D** Spell base words with inflectional endings.

Extra Pattern Practice

Extra Pattern Practice Master,
TRB, p. 91

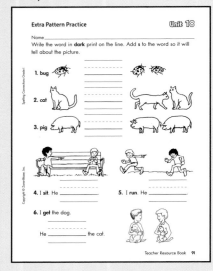

Making More Than One

Before class, make a decorated cutout letter **s**. Say the spelling words aloud, emphasizing the /s/ or /z/ sound at the end of each word and holding up the letters. Have the class say the words. Read the following story:
- "I want someone to chase cats with me," said a dog.
- "I wish I had a friend to share my lunch," said a hen.
- "I can help!" said Special **S,** turning **dog** into **dogs** and **hen** into **hens**.

Write **dog** and **hen** on the board. Have volunteers hold the **s** next to each word and say the new words.

 TEKS 1.22C Spell high-frequency words from a commonly used list.
1.22D Spell base words with inflectional endings.

Connections to READING

Look at the picture. Write spelling words to complete the sentences.

bugs
cats
pigs
sits
runs
gets

A frog _____**sits**_____ on a log.

It _____**gets**_____ the _____**bugs**_____ .

The _____**pigs**_____ dig in the mud. The _____**cats**_____

rest in the sun. A lamb _____**runs**_____ in the grass.

 TEKS 1.22C Spell high-frequency words from a commonly used list.

113

Student Objectives
• Write words with inflectional endings to complete a paragraph and describe a picture.

Teaching Tips
• Write the following sentences on the board and help students read them. Ask students to change each sentence so that it uses a spelling word.
  1. I see a **bug**. (I see some bugs.)
  2. My **cat** likes milk. (My cats like milk.)
  3. Did you feed the **pig**? (Did you feed the pigs?)
  4. Pat will **sit** by Ann. (Pat sits by Ann.)
  5. Ray will **run** home. (Ray runs home.)
  6. Will Dara **get** a chance to play? (Dara gets a chance to play.)
• Have students look at the illustration on page 113 and describe what they see.
• Read the directions. Explain to students that the sentences tell about the picture.
• Have students complete page 113. Read the completed story aloud.

Differentiated Instruction
• Use the **Challenge Words** activity on page 197 with students who are ready to transfer their knowledge of adding **-s** to new words.
• An Extra Challenge Practice Master is available on page 92 in the *TRB*.
• Dictation sentences for the challenge words are available on page T197.

More Fun With Spelling for Differentiation

 ### Digital Resources for Spelling Connections
Interactive digital resources include word sorts, pattern practice, and proofreading activities for individual and whole-group instruction. (Interactive whiteboard compatible; see p. Z32.)

 ### Spelling Connections Online
Interactive online spelling activities include word sorts, crossword puzzles, sentence completion, proofreading practice, and spelling bees with words from each unit (see p. Z32). www.spellingconnectionsonline.com

Spelling Center Activities
Spelling Game Mats
Place one of the spelling games in a learning center to provide a fun way for students to practice their spelling words (see p. Z26).

Flip Folder
Students can use a Flip Folder to practice spelling words independently (see p. Z32).

Word Sort CD-ROM
Printable, unit-specific word cards for spelling and challenge words can be used for Teacher-Led, Individual, Buddy, and Speed Sorts (see p. Z31).

TEKS 1.22C Spell high-frequency words from a commonly used list.

T113

Unit 18 — Day 4

Student Objectives
- Write words with inflectional endings to complete a paragraph and describe a picture.
- Write a response to literature.
- Use a dictionary to find correct spellings.

Teaching Tips
- Have students look at the illustration on page 114 and describe what they see.
- Read the directions for Part A. Explain to students that they will write a spelling word in each sentence to tell about the picture.
- Read the first two sentences aloud. Guide students to refer to the picture. Ask, *Which animals are eating? Do you think Ben fed the pigs?* Guide students to write **pigs**.
- Complete Part A as a class. Read the completed paragraph.
- Tell students to write their answer to the question in Part B. Ask them to review their answer and circle two words they are not sure about. Have them check the spelling of each word in a picture dictionary.
- Invite volunteers to share their answers.

WORD SORT CD-ROM
- Invite students to practice for the weekly test by doing an **Individual Sort** or a **Speed Sort** (see p. Z31).

Day 5

Student Objectives
- Demonstrate mastery of the unit spelling words.

Posttest Assessment Options
Option 1: Administer the unit posttest using the dictation sentences at right.

Option 2: Assess students using the standardized test. See the *Standardized Test Master Book*, p. 22.

Note: Posttest sentences for the on level and challenge lists are available on the audio *Spelling Connections* Posttest CD.

Connections to WRITING

A. Write spelling words to finish the story.

Ben lives on a farm. He feeds the __1.__ . He __2.__ eggs from the hens. He pets his two __3.__ . He __4.__ to catch the cow. Then he __5.__ on the hay to rest. He sees some __6.__ .

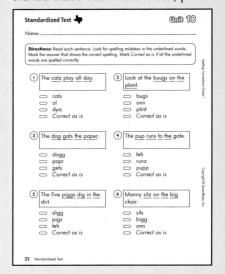

1.	pigs	2.	gets
3.	cats	4.	runs
5.	sits	6.	bugs

Word box: bugs · cats · pigs · sits · runs · gets

B. What would you like to do on a farm?

Possible answer: I would like to feed the hens.

114

TEKS 1.22C Spell high-frequency words from a commonly used list.

1-Minute Handwriting Hint
The top and bottom of the lowercase **s** should be even.

s EVEN

Posttest Sentences
1. My mother **runs** in marathons.
2. How many **cats** are in the basket?
3. Those baby **pigs** are cute!
4. We will go outside when it **gets** warmer.
5. Tanya **sits** in her rocking chair.
6. Spiders catch **bugs** in their webs.

Standardized Test Master Book, p. 22

Standardized Test — Unit 18

Name _____

Directions: Read each sentence. Look for spelling mistakes in the underlined words. Mark the answer that shows the correct spelling. Mark Correct as is if all the underlined words are spelled correctly.

1. The catz play all day.
   - cats
   - al
   - dya
   - Correct as is

2. Look at the buugs on the plant.
   - bugs
   - onn
   - plint
   - Correct as is

3. The dog gats the paper.
   - dogg
   - papr
   - gets
   - Correct as is

4. The pup runz to the gate.
   - teh
   - runz
   - pupp
   - Correct as is

5. The five piggs dig in the dirt.
   - digg
   - pigs
   - teh
   - Correct as is

6. Manny sitz on the big chair.
   - sits
   - bigg
   - onn
   - Correct as is

22 Standardized Test

 TEKS 1.22A Use phonological knowledge to match sounds to letters to construct known words. **1.22C** Spell high-frequency words from a commonly used list. **1.22D** Spell base words with inflectional endings. **1.22E** Use resources to find correct spellings.

Planner

Day 1

Day 2

Day 1

Connections to **Thinking**

Student Objectives
- Read, spell, and write one-syllable words and add **-ing** to form present participles.

Instruction for All Students
- Pretest Dictation Sentences, p. T115B
- Connections to Thinking, p. 115
- Home/School Spelling Practice Master (*Teacher Resource Book*, pp. 93–94)

 TEKS 1.22C, 1.22D

Connections to **Phonics**

Student Objectives
- Identify and write words with given vowel sounds.

Instruction for All Students
- Connections to Phonics, p. 116

Optional Practice
- Extra Pattern Practice Master (*Teacher Resource Book*, p. 95)

 TEKS 1.22A, 1.22C, 1.22D

Spelling Words
doing
going
seeing
feeding
feeling
keeping

Challenge Words
mowing
picking
packing
bending

Day 3

Day 4

Day 5

Day 2

Day 3

Connections to **Reading**

Student Objectives
- Write words with inflectional endings to complete sentences and tell about a picture.

Instruction for All Students
- Connections to Reading, p. 117

Differentiated Instruction
- Challenge Words, p. 198

 TEKS 1.22C, 1.22D

Connections to **Writing**

Student Objectives
- Write words with inflectional endings to complete a poem.
- Write a poem.
- Use a dictionary to find correct spellings.

Instruction for All Students
- Connections to Writing, p. 118

Differentiated Instruction
- Extra Challenge Practice Master (*Teacher Resource Book*, p. 96)

 TEKS 1.22A, 1.22C, 1.22D, 1.22E

Assessment

Student Objectives
- Demonstrate mastery of the unit spelling words.

Assessment for All Students
- Posttest Dictation Sentences, p. T118, or
- *Standardized Test Master Book*, p. 23

Differentiated Assessment
- Challenge Dictation Sentences, p. T198

Unit 19 Materials

Student Edition
pp. 115–118, 198

Teacher Edition
pp. T115A–T118, T198

 Teacher Resource Book
Unit 19 Practice Masters,
pp. 93–96, and
Sound/Symbol Cards

Standardized Test Master Book
Unit 19 Test Master, p. 23

 Word Sort CD-ROM
Unit 19 Word Sort Cards for Teacher-Led Sorts and Student Sorts

 Digital Resources for Spelling Connections
Unit 19

 Spelling Connections Online
www.spellingconnectionsonline.com

Spelling Support for English Language Learners*
Unit 19 Practice Masters and
Audio Conversation

Spelling Center Activities*
Spelling Game Mats
Flip Folder, *TRB*, p. 155

*Spelling Support for English Language Learners *and* Spelling Center Activities *may be used at any time during the week.*

Assessment

Pretest Sentences (See procedures on p. Z30)

1. Do you know what she is **doing**?
2. We are **going** on vacation.
3. I hope we will be **seeing** each other soon.
4. We are **feeding** the chickens.
5. The baby is **feeling** happy.
6. Is Chris **keeping** the kitten inside today?

The Science of Spelling ◄···

- The inflectional ending **-ing** is used to indicate verb tenses. Present participles are formed with **-ing** and are used with **is** and **are**.

  Rules apply when adding **-ing**.

  - Most words add **-ing** (**playing**).
  - When a verb ends with **e**, drop the **e** before adding **-ing** (**make/making**).
  - When a verb ends with **ie**, drop the **ie**, replace it with **y**, and add **-ing** (**die/dying**).
  - When a verb ends with a letter sequence of **consonant-vowel-consonant**, double the final consonant (**put/putting**).

ELL Support

Choose from the activities below to reinforce English language acquisition.

Beginning

Understanding Word Meanings Write the spelling words on the board. Say each word and use objects, pictures, gestures, and pantomime to provide context and support word meaning. Then describe what you are doing. For example, pantomime feeding a pet and say, *I am **feeding** my dog.* Then point to the word **feeding**. Say the word and have students repeat.

Hear and Say Have students write each spelling word on an index card. Say a word and have students hold up the corresponding word card. Then say a sentence using each word. Have students hold up the card for the spelling word they hear in the sentence. Call on volunteers to create their own sentences using the spelling words. Students can heard the spelling words for Unit 19 used in context on the audio recording.

Alphabetical Order Use an alphabet chart to review alphabetical order. Have students say the alphabet with you. Then write three spelling words on the board. Call on a volunteer to underline the initial letter in each word. Have students name the letter. Then ask students to find each letter on the alphabet chart. Ask which letter comes first, second, and third. Call on a volunteer to write the three spelling words in alphabetical order.

Intermediate

What Are You Doing Right Now? List the spelling words on the board. Say each word clearly and have students repeat it. Ask a volunteer, *What are you doing right now?* Have the student answer with a sentence that uses a spelling word, such as *I am going to the playground.* Write students' sentences on the board. Have students read them chorally with you. Students can hear the spelling words used in context on the audio recording.

Picture Sentences Have students illustrate sentences you create with spelling words, such as *We are going to the park.* Write each sentence and have students copy it onto their paper. Read each sentence aloud and have students repeat it. Encourage students to make up and illustrate their own sentences using spelling words.

Complete Sentences Provide students with copies of page 21 of *Spelling Support for English Language Learners.* Encourage pairs to work together to write spelling words to complete the sentences. Then have them do the activity at the bottom of the page.

Support for Spanish Speakers

Comparing Languages In English, present participles are formed by adding **-ing** to verbs. In Spanish, how present participles are formed depends on how the verb ends. For a verb ending in *ar,* the *ar* is dropped and *ando* added. For a verb ending in *er* or *ir,* the *er* or *ir* is dropped and *iendo* added.

For example, *cantar* (sing) becomes *cantando* (singing); *comer* (eat) becomes *comiendo.* Spanish does not use present participles as nouns. Students can find Spanish translations of the English spelling words on page 64 of *Spelling Support for English Language Learners.*

Choose from the activities below to reinforce English language acquisition.

Advanced

More -ing Words Ask students to say as many action words as they can think of, such as **jump, look,** and **bang.** List the words or call on volunteers to write them on the board. Choose words to which **-ing** can be added without doubling the final letter or changing the spelling. Point to and read the word, and ask a volunteer to write the word on the board and add **-ing.** Have the student read the new word.

Correct Spelling Have students write a sentence using a spelling word that is spelled incorrectly. For example, a student may write *I am feling sad.* Have students trade sentences with a partner and correct each other's errors.

Write Sentences Encourage students to use two spelling words in a written sentence. For example, *I am going to see how Jan is feeling.* Have students trade sentences with a partner. The partner reads the sentence aloud and points out the spelling words. Students can hear the Unit 19 spelling words read in context sentences on the audio recording.

Conversation Provide support with pronunciations by having students listen to and interact with the audio recording. Students can practice the conversations and elaborate on them to improve pronunciation while gaining a better understanding of word meanings. Partners can read the print form of the audio dialog on page 49 of *Spelling Support for English Language Learners.*

Advanced High

Word Guess Have partners give each other spelling and meaning clues for a word they are thinking of. For example, *The word is like* looking. *It has a long* **e** *sound.* (**seeing**)

What Happened? Have partners take turns asking each other, *What happened?* The partner answers with a sentence that starts with *I was _____* and uses one of the spelling words, such as *I was feeling sad.* The partner continues the story and tells what happened next. For example: *I was feeling sad. So I told my mom. She read me a funny story. Then I was feeling happy.*

Write Sentences List sentence topics that use spelling words, such as *doing dishes, going to the park, feeding a cat.* Have students select a topic and write two or three sentences about it. Encourage students to share their sentences with a partner.

Missing Words Have students select a spelling word and write a sentence in which the spelling word is missing. Have partners trade papers and complete each other's sentences by writing the missing spelling word in the blank.

Spelling Support for English Language Learners

Home/Spelling Practice Master
TRB, p. 21

Practice Master, p. 49

 Audio Conversation
available on CD

English/Spanish
Word List, p. 64

	English	Spanish
1.	doing	haciendo
2.	going	yendo
3.	seeing	viendo
4.	feeding	dando de comer; alimentando
5.	feeling	sintiendo
6.	keeping	guardando

Spelling Connections Online
Interactive online spelling activities provide additional ELL support.
www.spellingconnectionsonline.com

Add **ing** to each word in the box.
Write the spelling word.

do	see	keep	feel	go	feed

1. doing
2. going
3. seeing
4. feeding
5. feeling
6. keeping

1. **doing**
2. **seeing**
3. **keeping**
4. **feeling**
5. **going**
6. **feeding**

This unit focuses on the **-ing** ending. Take turns with your child, saying the spelling words with and without this ending.

TEKS 1.22C Spell high-frequency words from a commonly used list. **1.22D** Spell base words with inflectional endings.

II5

Day 1

Unit
19

Student Objectives
• Read, spell, and write one-syllable words and add **-ing** to form present participles.

Unit Pretest
• Administer the pretest on page T115B.

Teaching Tips
• Read each word aloud and have students listen for /ing/. Then have students read the words aloud. Many students will not hear the /**n**/ and may spell phonetically (**keepig**). Sounding out the words and identifying /**ng**/ is very important.

WORD SORT **CD-ROM**

• Conduct a **Teacher-Led Sort** (see p. Z31) to introduce or reinforce the spelling pattern.
• Write **do** on the board. Explain that **-ing** can be added to an action word to mean that someone is doing the action right now. Give an example, such as *I am* **doing** *this now.*
• Write the base words for the remaining spelling words on the board. After students have read a word, add **-ing**. Ask students to read the new word and use it in a sentence.
• Have students complete the page independently or as a class.

Home/School Word Lists TRB
• Have students take home the Home/School Spelling Practice Master.

Home/School Practice

Home/School Spelling
Practice Master, *TRB*, p. 93

Home/School Spelling
Practice Master, *TRB*, p. 94

Home/School Spelling Practice	Unit 19
Name_____	

1. doing   1._____
2. going   2._____
3. seeing   3._____
4. feeding   4._____
5. feeling   5._____
6. keeping   6._____

Spelling Practice Activity

Dear Family,
Ask your child to write the spelling words correctly on the blank lines.

Play a game by asking your child to name and spell a word from clues you give. Possible clues

would be definitions or words with similar or opposite meanings.

Example: For the word **feeding:** *This is what you see people doing for the birds in the winter.*

Teacher Resource Book 93

English

Práctica de ortografía para el hogar o la escuela	Unit 19
Nombre_____	

1. doing haciendo   1._____
2. going yendo   2._____
3. seeing viendo   3._____
4. feeding dando de comer; alimentando   4._____
5. feeling sintiendo 5._____
6. keeping guardando 6._____

Actividad de ortografía

Querida familia,
Pida a su hijo(a) que escriba correctamente las palabras de ortografía en los renglones en blanco.

Juegue con su hijo(a) y pídale que adivine y deletree una palabra a partir de las pistas que

Ud. le dé. Las pistas pueden ser definiciones; o palabras con el mismo significado o significado opuesto.

Por ejemplo, para la palabra **feeding** (**alimentando**) una pista puede ser: *Es algo que la gente hace por las aves durante el invierno.*

94 Teacher Resource Book

Spanish

TEKS 1.22C Spell high-frequency words from a commonly used list.
1.22D Spell base words with inflectional endings.

TII5

Student Objectives
- Identify and write words with given vowel sounds.

Teaching Tips
- Review long vowel sounds with students. Show Sound/Symbol Cards for **paint, eat, slide, open,** and **vacuum.** Have students name each picture and identify the long vowel sound.
- Have students add **-ing** to each word and say the new word. Challenge students to provide other action words with long vowel sounds. Have them add **-ing** to these words and use each one in a sentence.
- Write **do** on the board and ask students to read it aloud. Ask what sound the **o** makes. (/oo/)
- Have students complete page 116 independently or as a class.

Extra Pattern Practice TRB
- Use the optional practice master below for extra practice with adding **-ing.**

WORD SORT CD-ROM
- Provide time for students to use a **Buddy Sort** (see p. Z31) to practice their spelling words with a partner.

Connections to PHONICS

doing
going
seeing
feeding
feeling
keeping

A. Write the words that have the **long e** sound.

1. seeing
2. feeding
3. feeling
4. keeping

B. Write the word that has the **long o** sound.

5. going

C. Write the word that has an **o** that makes a sound like **oo.**

6. doing

116

TEKS 1.22A Use phonological knowledge to match sounds to letters to construct known words.
1.22C Spell high-frequency words from a commonly used list.

Extra Pattern Practice

Extra Pattern Practice Master,
TRB, p. 95

Adding -ing

Say the words **do, go, see, feed, feel,** and **keep.** Then say **doing, going, seeing, feeding, feeling,** and **keeping.** Call on volunteers to write the base words. Then have other students come up and add **-ing** to each word. Read the following sentences. Have students raise their hand when they hear /ing/:
- We are **doing** our work.
- She is **going** to school.
- They are **seeing** the movie.
- He is **feeding** the baby.
- Her sister is **feeling** sick.
- I am **keeping** my promise.

 TEKS **1.22A** Use phonological knowledge to match sounds to letters to construct known words.
1.22C Spell high-frequency words from a commonly used list. **1.22D** Spell base words with inflectional endings.

Connections to READING

Write a spelling word to complete each sentence.

1. What is she _____ **doing** _____ ?

2. She is _____ **feeling** _____ the horse's leg.

3. She is _____ **seeing** _____ if it is hurt.

4. She is _____ **going** _____ to fix the leg.

5. Matt is _____ **keeping** _____ the horse still.

6. He is _____ **feeding** _____ it grass.

doing
going
seeing
feeding
feeling
keeping

 TEKS 1.22C Spell high-frequency words from a commonly used list.

117

Student Objectives
- Write words with inflectional endings to complete sentences and tell about a picture.

Teaching Tips
- Write these sentences on the board. Call on volunteers to add **-ing** to the incomplete words. Read the sentences aloud.
  1. You are **do**____ this job for me. (doing)
  2. I am **go**____ for a walk. (going)
  3. Dad is **see**____ who it is. (seeing)
  4. Rachel is **keep**____ the book. (keeping)
  5. Are you **feel**____ well? (feeling)
  6. Li is **feed**____ her dogs. (feeding)
- Have students look at the illustration on page 117 and describe what they see.
- Read the directions. Explain that these sentences tell about the picture.
- Have students complete the page.
- Challenge students to think of other **-ing** words they could use in sentences about the picture. For example, *The girl is petting the horse.*

Differentiated Instruction
- Use the **Challenge Words** activity on page 198 with students who are ready to transfer their knowledge of adding **-ing** to new words.
- An Extra Challenge Practice Master is available on page 96 in the *TRB*.
- Dictation sentences for the challenge words are available on page T198.

More Fun With Spelling for Differentiation

Digital Resources for Spelling Connections
Interactive digital resources include word sorts, pattern practice, and proofreading activities for individual and whole-group instruction. (Interactive whiteboard compatible; see p. Z32.)

Spelling Connections Online
Interactive online spelling activities include word sorts, crossword puzzles, sentence completion, proofreading practice, and spelling bees with words from each unit (see p. Z32). www.spellingconnectionsonline.com

Spelling Center Activities

Spelling Game Mats
Place one of the spelling games in a learning center to provide a fun way for students to practice their spelling words (see p. Z26).

Flip Folder
Students can use a Flip Folder to practice spelling words independently (see p. Z32).

Word Sort CD-ROM
Printable, unit-specific word cards for spelling and challenge words can be used for Teacher-Led, Individual, Buddy, and Speed Sorts (see p. Z31).

TEKS 1.22C Spell high-frequency words from a commonly used list.
1.22D Spell base words with inflectional endings.

T117

Unit 19 — Day 4

Student Objectives
- Write words with inflectional endings to complete a poem.
- Write a poem.
- Use a dictionary to find correct spellings.

Teaching Tips
- Read the directions. Explain to students that they will write a spelling word in each line to finish the poem.
- Have students complete Part A as a class or independently. Read the completed poem aloud with students.
- Have students write their own summer poem on a separate sheet of paper. Ask them to review their poem and circle two words they are not sure about. Have them check the spelling of each word in a picture dictionary.
- Invite volunteers to read their poem aloud.

 **CD-ROM**
- Invite students to practice for the weekly test by doing an **Individual Sort** or a **Speed Sort** (see p. Z31).

Day 5

Student Objectives
- Demonstrate mastery of the unit spelling words.

Posttest Assessment Options
Option 1: Administer the unit posttest using the dictation sentences at right.

Option 2: Assess students using the standardized test. See the *Standardized Test Master Book*, p. 23.

Note: Posttest sentences for the on level and challenge lists are available on the audio *Spelling Connections* Posttest CD.

Connections to WRITING

A. Write spelling words to finish the poem.

My eyes are for ___**1.**___ .
My fingers are for ___**2.**___ .
My body is for ___**3.**___ .
My legs are for ___**4.**___ .
My mouth is for ___**5.**___ .
My heart is for ___**6.**___ .

1. seeing	2. feeling
3. doing	4. going
5. feeding	6. keeping

Word box:
doing
going
seeing
feeding
feeling
keeping

B. Write a short poem that tells what you see outside in the summer. Tell how you feel. Circle two words you are not sure about. Check the spelling in your dictionary.

118

 TEKS **1.22C** Spell high-frequency words from a commonly used list. **1.22E** Use resources to find correct spellings.

1-Minute Handwriting Hint
The slide right stroke in the lowercase **f** must be correct or the spacing between the **f** and the letter that follows will be incorrect.

Posttest Sentences
1. Walter is **keeping** track of the score.
2. Is your mother **feeling** better?
3. Are you **going** to the pet show?
4. You will be **seeing** many dinosaur bones.
5. You are **doing** a fine job.
6. That robin is **feeding** its babies.

Standardized Test Master Book, p. 23

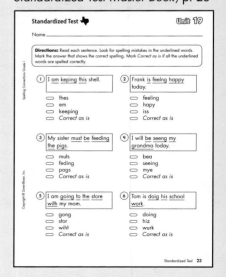

TEKS **1.22A** Use phonological knowledge to match sounds to letters to construct known words. **1.22C** Spell high-frequency words from a commonly used list. **1.22D** Spell base words with inflectional endings. **1.22E** Use resources to find correct spellings.

Planner

Day 1

Day 2

Day 1

Unit 16: Initial Consonant Blends

Student Objectives
- Review the spelling patterns and words from Unit 16.

Instruction for All Students
- Unit 16 Review, p. 119
- Home/School Spelling Practice Master (*Teacher Resource Book*, pp. 97–98)

Unit 17: Consonant Blends: st

Student Objectives
- Review the spelling pattern and words from Unit 17.

Instruction for All Students
- Unit 17 Review, p. 120

Unit 16
Initial Consonant Blends

grin	frog
spin	plum
skip	slam

Unit 17
Consonant Blends: st

best	must
rest	step
fast	still

Unit 18
Inflectional Endings: -s

bugs	sits
cats	runs
pigs	gets

Unit 19
Inflectional Endings: -ing

doing	feeding
going	feeling
seeing	keeping

Day 3

Day 4

Day 5

Day 2

Day 3

Unit 18: Inflectional Endings: -s

Student Objectives
- Review the spelling rule and words from Unit 18.

Instruction for All Students
- Unit 18 Review, p. 121

Unit 19: Inflectional Endings: -ing

Student Objectives
- Review the spelling rule and words from Unit 19.

Instruction for All Students
- Unit 19 Review, p. 122

Assessment

Student Objectives
- Demonstrate mastery of the review unit spelling words.

Assessment for All Students
- Posttest Assessment Options
  - ✦ Posttest Dictation Sentences, p. T122, or
  - ✦ *Standardized Test Master Book*, p. 24

Unit 20 Materials

Student Edition
pp. 119–122
Alphabet and Picture Cards
(See pages Z32 for
suggested activities.)

Teacher Edition
pp. T119A–T122

 Teacher Resource Book
Unit 20 Practice Masters,
pp. 97–98

 Standardized Test Master Book
Unit 20 Test Master, p. 24

 Word Sort CD-ROM
Unit 20 Word Sort Cards for Teacher-
Led Sorts and Student Sorts

 **Digital Resources for
Spelling Connections**
Unit 20

 Spelling Connections Online
www.spellingconnectionsonline.com

Spelling Center Activities*
Spelling Game Mats
Flip Folder, *TRB*, p. 155

*Spelling Center Activities may be used
at any time during the week.*

Developmental Spelling Check

Administer the following **Developmental Spelling Check** to evaluate spelling growth. Remind students that this is not a test for a grade; students are not expected to spell these words conventionally. Author J. Richard Gentry has provided (in parentheses) typical Phase 3 Phonetic Spellings for each word. Students who produce these or similar spellings are demonstrating full phonemic awareness, since each letter corresponds to a sound in the word. These spellings are a middle first-grade benchmark.

Tell students you would like them to try writing these clothing words. To administer, say each word aloud, read the sentence, and then say the word again.

Clothing and Sample Phonetic Spellings

hat	Dad bought a new **hat** for winter.	(HET)
shoes	I like my red **shoes**.	(SHUS)
socks	You need two **socks** to make a pair.	(SAKS)
shirt	My **shirt** lost a button.	(SHRT)
jeans	There is a hole in your **jeans**.	(GNS)
dress	That yellow **dress** is pretty.	(DRAS, JRAS)
jacket	Please button your **jacket**.	(JAKT, GAKT)
coat	Where is your **coat**?	(KOT, COT)

ELL Support

Choose from the activities below to reinforce English language acquisition.

Beginning

Understanding Word Meanings List the review spelling words on the board. Point to a word along with a real object, picture, or pantomime to provide context and support meaning as you pronounce the word. For example, show a picture of a **frog**. Point to the frog and say **frog**. Have students repeat. Invite volunteers to choose a spelling word and demonstrate the meaning in some way.

Make Words List the spelling words on the board. Then write each word on a card. Cut the words apart between the consonant blend or the inflectional ending and the rest of the word. Have students select parts to reconstruct the words. Have students say the words. Students can hear the words for Units 16–19 pronounced singly on the audio recording.

Flash Cards Provide pairs with flash cards for the review words. Have students take turns showing each other cards and reading the words. Encourage them to set aside words they have trouble with and bring those cards to you for help.

Complete Sentences Invite students to use each spelling word in an oral sentence. Write each sentence, leaving out the spelling word. Read the sentence, pausing at the blank. Have students say the missing word or write the word in the blank. Then read the completed sentence.

Intermediate

Word Grab Bag Place spelling word flash cards in a paper bag. Invite a volunteer to select a card and read the word. Then have the student pass the card to another student who says a sentence using the word. Students can hear the words from Units 16–19 in context sentences on the audio recording.

Illustrate Words List the review spelling words on the board. Have students select words to illustrate in a picture. For example, students may draw cats that run fast after bugs. On the picture, have students write the words they illustrated.

Categorize Words Review with students that some words name things, some words name actions, and other words are used to describe. Say **bugs, slam,** and **fast** as examples. Create a three-column chart on the board. Have students categorize as many review spelling words as possible by writing the words or taping word cards in the appropriate column.

Picture Dictionary Have students look at their Picture Dictionary and add any review spelling words they had not previously listed. Encourage them to create sentences using as many review words as they can.

Support for Spanish Speakers

Comparing Languages Spanish speakers may have difficulty hearing and pronouncing some English consonant blends. The **l** and **r** blends are the same in Spanish and English. The **s** blends are not found in Spanish.

Spanish-speaking students will understand adding **-s** to a noun to show more than one, as **-s** is added to many words in Spanish to form plurals. Adding **-s** to verbs to form the singular present tense may be confusing to students, as the conjugation of Spanish verbs is different from that of English even though the rules are similar. In English, present participles are formed by adding **-ing** to verbs. In Spanish, the way that present participles are formed depends on the ending of the verb.

Unit 20

Choose from the activities below to reinforce English language acquisition.

Advanced

Telephone Organize students into groups of three or four. Have one student in each group write a sentence using a spelling word. Without showing the card, the student whispers the sentence to someone else in the group. That person whispers it to someone else, and so on. The final student writes the sentence. The first and last students then read their written sentences for the group to compare.

Spell and Write Write the following review spelling words on the board: **grin, spin, skip, frog, plum, slam, step,** and **rest**. Have students add **-s** to a word and write a sentence using the new word.

Word Grid Have partners draw lines to divide a sheet of paper into quarters. Partner 1 writes a review spelling word in one of the squares. Partner 2 writes a different spelling word—but one that is related to the first word in some way—in another square. Partner 1 then writes another related word in the third square, and Partner 2 completes the grid with another word in the fourth square. For example, if the first word is **gets,** the second word could be **going** because they both start with **g**. The third word could be **skip** because it is an action word like the first two words, and the fourth word could be **step** because it ends with **p,** like **skip** and is also an action word. Have students talk about how their words are related.

Advanced High

Charades Have students pick a card with a review spelling word and dramatize the word in some way, using gestures, pantomime, sounds, or sketches to provide context and support word meaning. After other students guess the word, another student draws a card, and play continues until all the review words have been covered.

Job Descriptions Have students select two or three review spelling words. Have them write sentences or draw a picture to describe a job that utilizes these words. For example, the words **cats, feeding,** and **fast** could describe a job feeding fast cats.

Riddles Encourage students to think of riddles using the spelling words. They can share riddles with a partner and see if they can guess the words. For example, *I end with a consonant blend. I am another word for* quick. (fast) Collect the riddles in a classroom book titled *Our Spelling Word Riddles.*

Write Sentences Have students select two or three review spelling words to write sentences in which the spelling words are missing. Have partners trade papers and write the missing words to complete each other's sentences. As an alternative, students can randomly select one to three of the review spelling words and challenge a partner to write a sentence using all of the words.

 Spelling Connections Online
Interactive online spelling activities provide additional ELL support.
www.spellingconnectionsonline.com

Review

Unit 16: Initial Consonant Blends

1. grin
2. spin
3. skip
4. frog
5. plum
6. slam

A. Write the spelling words that begin with an **r** blend.

1. grin
2. frog

B. Write the spelling words that begin with an **l** blend.

3. plum
4. slam

C. Write the spelling word that rhymes with each word.

hip	tin
5. skip	6. spin

This unit reviews consonant blends and the word endings **-s** and **-ing**. Ask your child to read the spelling words on each page aloud.

119

Day 1

Unit **20**

Student Objectives
- Review the spelling patterns and words from Unit 16.

Reteaching the Skill
- Write **grin, spin, skip, frog, plum,** and **slam** on the board. Remind students that each word begins with a consonant blend—**gr, sp, sk, fr, pl,** or **sl.**
- Ask students to look at each spelling word and listen to the beginning sounds of the consonant blend as you point to it and pronounce the word.
- Ask students to say each word aloud, emphasizing the consonant blend sounds at the beginning of the word, as a volunteer underlines the letters in the blend.
- Tell students to complete page 119 independently. Remind them that they will use each word one time.

Letters and Sounds Review
- Throughout the unit, use the **Alphabet and Picture Cards** to review letters and sounds. See page Z32 for activity suggestions.

Review Word List

Home/School Spelling
Practice Master, *TRB*, p. 97

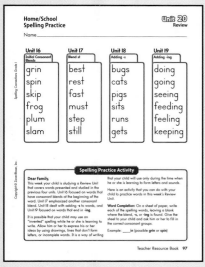

English

Home/School Spelling
Practice Master, *TRB*, p. 98

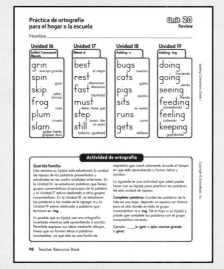

Spanish

Student Objectives
- Review the spelling pattern and words from Unit 17.

Reteaching the Skill
- Write **best, rest, fast, must, step,** and **still** on the board. Remind students that the **s** and **t** slide together to make the /st/ sound at the beginning or end of each word.
- Pronounce each word and ask students to listen for /st/. Have volunteers circle the **st** blend in each word on the board. Have students note whether the blend is at the beginning or end of the word.
- Tell students to write the words on their own papers and to circle the **st** blend in each word. Have students take turns using the spelling words in sentences.
- Tell students to complete page 120 independently.

Review

1. best
2. rest
3. fast
4. must
5. step
6. still

Unit 17: Consonant Blends: st

A. Complete each spelling word.

1. rest st
2. fast st
3. best st
4. st step

B. Write the spelling word that rhymes with each word.

dust	hill
5. must	6. still

120

Extra Pattern Practice

Ask a Question
Write the following statements on the board. Have students change the order of the words to ask questions. Then have volunteers write the questions next to the sentences.

1. Ned **must** sit on the **step**. (Must Ned sit on the step?)
2. Bess is **still** in bed. (Is Bess still in bed?)
3. It is his **best** pen. (Is it his best pen?)
4. A jet is **fast**. (Is a jet fast?)
5. Rob can get the **rest** of the nuts. (Can Rob get the rest of the nuts?)

Review

1. bugs
2. cats
3. pigs
4. sits
5. runs
6. gets

Unit 18: Inflectional Endings: -s

A. Add **s** to the word to show more than one.

bug

cat

1. **bugs**
2. **cats**

pig

3. **pigs**

B. Write a spelling word to finish each sentence.

4. One bug _____**sits**_____ on a leaf.

5. One cat _____**runs**_____ in the house.

6. One pig _____**gets**_____ lunch.

121

Student Objectives

- Review the spelling rule and words from Unit 18.

Reteaching the Skill

- Hold up a hat and say **hat**. Write **hat** on the board. Hold up two hats and say **hats**. Add **-s** to **hat**. Remind students that **-s** is often added to a naming word to make it mean more than one.
- Write **bug, cat,** and **pig** on the board. Ask volunteers to make each word mean more than one. (**bugs, cats, pigs**)
- Remind students that the letter **s** may be added to a word to show an action done by one person except *you* or *I*. Provide an example: *I* **sit**. *You* **sit**. *He* **sits**.
- Write the following sentences on the board and ask students to finish the last sentence in each group:
  I run. You run. He _____. (**runs**)
  I get it. You get it. She _____ it. (**gets**)
- Tell students to complete page 121 independently.

More Fun With Spelling for Differentiation

▶ Digital Resources for Spelling Connections

Interactive digital resources include word sorts, pattern practice, and proofreading activities for individual and whole-group instruction. (Interactive whiteboard compatible; see p. Z32.)

▶ Spelling Connections Online

Interactive online spelling activities include word sorts, crossword puzzles, sentence completion, proofreading practice, and spelling bees with words from each unit (see p. Z32). www.spellingconnectionsonline.com

Spelling Center Activities

Spelling Game Mats
Place one of the spelling games in a learning center to provide a fun way for students to practice their spelling words (see p. Z26).

Flip Folder
Students can use a Flip Folder to practice spelling words independently (see p. Z32).

Word Sort CD-ROM
Printable, unit-specific word cards for spelling and challenge words can be used for Teacher-Led, Individual, Buddy, and Speed Sorts (see p. Z31).

Student Objectives
• Review the spelling rule and words from Unit 19.

Reteaching the Skill
• Write **seeing** on the board. Circle **see** and underline **ing**. Say, *I am seeing you right now* to illustrate the meaning.
• Write the other base words on the board: **do, go, feed, feel, keep**.
• Organize the class into pairs. Ask one student in each pair to choose a word from the board and write it on a sheet of paper. The partner adds **-ing** to the word. The partner then chooses a word, writes it, and gives it to the first student to add **-ing**. Continue until partners have spelled all the words.
• Tell students to complete page 122 independently or as a class.

Review

1. doing
2. going
3. seeing
4. feeding
5. feeling
6. keeping

122

Unit 19: **Inflectional Endings: -ing**
A. Add **ing** to each word to write a spelling word.

1. feel   feeling
2. keep   keeping
3. go   going
4. do   doing

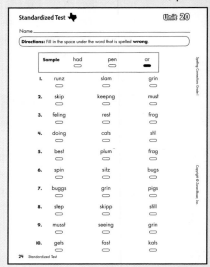

B. Write the spelling word that goes with each picture.

5.   seeing   6.   feeding

Day 5

Assessment
Student Objectives
• Demonstrate mastery of the review unit spelling words.

Posttest Assessment Options
Option 1: Administer the posttest using the dictation sentences at right.
Option 2: Assess students using the standardized test. See the *Standardized Test Master Book*, p. 24.

Note: Posttest sentences for the on level and challenge lists are available on the audio *Spelling Connections* Posttest CD.

Posttest Sentences
1. The dog **runs** down the hall.
2. I am **keeping** the book in my desk.
3. Are you **still** going to the party?
4. What are you **doing**?
5. The **frog** sat on the rock.
6. The boy **sits** down.
7. There are two **bugs** on the leaf.
8. I can **skip** to the fence.
9. Ken **must** watch out for the ball.
10. Four **cats** sleep on the bed.

Standardized Test Master Book, p. 24

Standardized Test		Unit 20
Name		

Directions: Fill in the space under the word that is spelled **wrong**.

Sample	had	pen	ar
1.	runz	slam	grin
2.	skip	keepng	must
3.	feling	rest	frog
4.	doing	cats	stil
5.	best	plum	frog
6.	spin	sitz	bugs
7.	buggs	grin	pigs
8.	step	skipp	still
9.	musst	seeing	grin
10.	gets	fast	kats

24 Standardized Test

Planner

Day 1 | Day 2

Day 1

Connections to Thinking

Student Objectives
- Read, spell, and write consonant-vowel-consonant-silent e (CVCe) words.
- Distinguish **short a** and **long a** sounds.

Instruction for All Students
- Pretest Dictation Sentences, p. T123B
- Connections to Thinking, p. 123
- Home/School Spelling Practice Masters (*Teacher Resource Book*, pp. 99–100)

 TEKS 1.22A, 1.22Bii, 1.22C

Connections to Phonics

Student Objectives
- Distinguish **short a** and **long a** sounds.
- Write rhyming words.

Instruction for All Students
- Connections to Phonics, p. 124

Optional Practice
- Extra Pattern Practice Master (*Teacher Resource Book*, p. 101)

TEKS 1.22A, 1.22Bii, 1.22C

Spelling Words

came
name
same
game
gate
gave

Challenge Words

wake
ape
mane
tame

Day 3 | Day 4 | Day 5

Day 2

Connections to Reading

Student Objectives
- Write spelling words to complete sentences.
- Use a dictionary to check spelling.

Instruction for All Students
- Connections to Reading, p. 125

Differentiated Instruction
- Challenge Words, p. 199

TEKS 1.22C, 1.22E

Connections to Writing

Student Objectives
- Identify spelling words in a story.
- Identify rhyming words.
- Use spelling words to write sentences.
- Use a dictionary to check spelling.

Instruction for All Students
- Connections to Writing, p. 126

Differentiated Instruction
- Extra Challenge Practice Master (*Teacher Resource Book*, p. 102)

TEKS 1.22A, 1.22C, 1.22E

Day 3

Assessment

Student Objectives
- Demonstrate mastery of the unit spelling words.

Assessment for All Students
- Posttest Dictation Sentences, p. T126, or
- *Standardized Test Master Book*, p. 25

Differentiated Assessment
- Challenge Dictation Sentences, p. T199

Unit 21 Materials

Student Edition
pp. 123–126, 199

Teacher Edition
pp. T123A–T126, T199

 Teacher Resource Book
Unit 21 Practice Masters,
pp. 99–102, and
Sound/Symbol Cards

 Standardized Test Master Book
Unit 21 Test Master, p. 25

Word Sort CD-ROM
Unit 21 Word Sort Cards for Teacher-
Led Sorts and Student Sorts

 **Digital Resources for
Spelling Connections**
Unit 21

 Spelling Connections Online
www.spellingconnectionsonline.com

**Spelling Support for
English Language Learners***
Unit 21 Practice Masters and
Audio Conversation

Spelling Center Activities*
Spelling Game Mats
Flip Folder, *TRB*, p. 155

*Spelling Support for English Language
Learners *and Spelling Center Activities may
be used at any time during the week.*

Assessment

Pretest Sentences (See procedures on p. Z30.)

1. Tanya **came** to my house.
2. What is your **name**?
3. Your shoes are the **same** as mine.
4. Would you like to play a **game**?
5. The **gate** is open.
6. My father **gave** Mom a present.

The Science of Spelling

- The consonant-vowel-consonant-silent **e** (CVCe) pattern is one of the first patterns that beginning readers and spellers learn. The presence of the **silent e** in a one-syllable word usually marks the preceding vowel as a long sound if there is only one consonant between the vowel and **e**. If there is more than one consonant, the vowel sound is usually short, as in **fence** and **bronze**. The exceptions are most words that end in **ange,** as in **range**, and **aste,** as in **taste**.

ELL Support

Choose from the activities below to reinforce English language acquisition.

Beginning

Word Meanings Write the spelling words on the board. Say each word and use real objects, pictures, and pantomime to provide context and support word meaning. For example, point to yourself and say, *My name is _____.* Point to a student and say, *Your name is _____.* Then point to and read the word **name** on the board. Have students repeat. Students can hear the Unit 21 spelling words pronounced singly on the audio recording.

Making Words Have students work with a partner. Provide the frame __a__e to each pair. Designate partners as Number 1 and Number 2. Provide letter cards for **c, n, s, g** to each Number 1 partner and **m, t,** and **v** to each Number 2. Say, *Number 1 Partners, put a letter on the first blank line.* Demonstrate if necessary. Then say, *Number 2 Partners, put a letter on the second blank line.* Give partners time to blend the letter sounds and agree on the word. Call on partners to read their word out loud. Partners can continue the activity until they have made each spelling word. Encourage them to read the words aloud.

Intermediate

Word Meanings Write the spelling words on the board. Say each word clearly and have students repeat it. Ask a volunteer to choose a word and use it in a sentence or tell something about its meaning. If necessary, clarify and expand the definition. Use real objects, pictures, and pantomime to provide context and support meaning of unfamiliar words. Have students write the words on a piece of paper. Students may look at the words on the board to be sure they have spelled them correctly.

Picture Sentences Have students illustrate sentences you create with spelling words, such as *We go in the gate.* Write each sentence and have students copy it onto their pictures. Read each sentence aloud and have students repeat it. Encourage students to make up and illustrate their own sentences using spelling words.

Riddles Provide students with copies of Page 22 of *Spelling Support for English Language Learners.* Encourage pairs to work together to write spelling words to answer the riddles and complete the activity at the bottom of the page.

Support for Spanish Speakers

Comparing Languages English vowels are challenging for most Spanish speakers as the Spanish language has fewer vowel sounds and fewer variations in how those sounds are spelled. Some English long vowel sounds are similar to the sounds represented by different vowels in Spanish. For example, the **long a** sound is similar to the sound represented by the letter **e** and the diphthong **ei** in Spanish, as in *sé* (I know) and *reina* (queen).

Spelling words provide an excellent opportunity for Spanish speakers to listen to clear pronunciation of single words, to practice approximating the sounds of English, and to develop English sound-symbol correspondence.

Spanish translations of the English spelling words are on page 65 of *Spelling Support for English Language Learners.*

Choose from the activities below to reinforce English language acquisition.

Advanced

Word Meanings List the spelling words on the board. Point to each word as you say it and have students repeat. Then ask questions that can be answered using spelling words. For example, *What word tells what people call you?* (name) *What word tells that two things are alike?* (same) *What word tells about something you play?* (game)

Spelling Words That Rhyme Write **came, name, same,** and **game** on the board. Ask students which letters are the same in all the words. (ame) Ask a volunteer to underline those letters in each word. Point to the underlined letters and say, *These are the same.* Extend the activity by providing words that rhyme with **gate** (late, date, rate, state) and **gave** (cave, pave, rave, save, wave).

Making Sentences Encourage students to use two spelling words in a written sentence. For example, *Sam and I have the same name.* Have students trade sentences with a partner. The partner reads the sentence aloud and underlines the spelling words.

Conversation Provide support with listening comprehension by having students listen to and interact with the audio recording. Students can listen to and practice the recorded conversations. The audio recording offers students opportunities to improve pronunciation while gaining a better understanding of spelling word usage. Partners can read the print form of the audio dialogue on page 50 of *Spelling Support for English Language Learners.*

Advanced High

Mystery Words With a partner, have students provide spelling and meaning clues for a word they are thinking of. For example, *The word begins with* **g**. *It names something you can open. It rhymes with* **late**. (gate)

Storytelling Have students use three spelling words in a story. One word should be in the story's beginning, one in the middle, and one in the end. Have students write their story and then illustrate the three sentences that contain spelling words. Invite students to share their stories with the group.

Word Characters Have students create characters whose names are spelling words. Ask students to describe their characters based on what they know about the spelling word. For example, **Gate** might always ask someone for a password before letting the person go by.

Comparing and Contrasting Words Provide students with spelling word flash cards. Have partners select two words. Then have them use a Venn diagram to compare and contrast features of the words. Students can examine shared letters, number of letters, rhyme, spelling patterns, word meaning, and parts of speech.

Spelling Support for English Language Learners

Practice Master, p. 22

Practice Master, p. 50

Audio Conversation available on CD

English/Spanish Word List, p. 65

Spelling Connections Online
Interactive online spelling activities provide additional ELL support.
www.spellingconnectionsonline.com

Use the letter clues to write the spelling words.

1. came
2. name
3. same
4. game
5. gate
6. gave

1. n _ m _

name

2. s _ m _

same

3. g _ m _

game

4. c _ m _

came

5. g _ t _

gate

6. g _ v _

gave

 School Home

This unit targets the **long a** sound spelled **a-consonant-e**. Ask your child to name rhyming words in the spelling list.

TEKS 1.22A Use phonological knowledge to match sounds to letters to construct known words. **1.22Bii** Use letter-sound patterns to spell: consonant-vowel-consonant-silent e (CVCe) words. **1.22C** Spell high-frequency words from a commonly used list.

123

Student Objectives
- Read, spell, and write consonant-vowel-consonant-silent **e** (CVCe) words.
- Distinguish **short a** and **long a** sounds.

Unit Pretest
- Administer the pretest on page T123B.

Teaching Tips
- Have students read the spelling words aloud, emphasizing and listening to /ā/.

 WORD SORT CD-ROM

- Conduct a **Teacher-Led Sort** (see p. Z31) to introduce the spelling pattern.
- Write **cap** on the board and ask a student to read it aloud. Write **e** at the end of **cap** and read the new word. Point out that the **e** in **cape** is silent, but that it changes the **short a** sound to a **long a** sound. Explain that **long a** sounds like its name. Say **cap** and **cape** and ask students to listen for the different vowel sounds.
- Write **c__m__**. Ask a volunteer to write **a** between **c** and **m**. Call on another volunteer to write **e** after **m**. Help students read the new word. Introduce each spelling word in this way.
- Have students complete the page independently or as a class.

Home/School Word Lists TRB
- Have students take home the Home/School Spelling Practice Master.

Home/School Practice

Home/School Spelling
Practice Master, *TRB*, p. 99

Home/School Spelling
Practice Master, *TRB*, p. 100

English

Spanish

TEKS 1.22A Use phonological knowledge to match sounds to letters to construct known words. **1.22Bii** Use letter-sound patterns to spell: consonant-vowel-consonant-silent e (CVCe) words. **1.22C** Spell high-frequency words from a commonly used list.

T123

Unit 21 — Day 2

Student Objectives
- Distinguish **short a** and **long a** sounds.
- Write rhyming words.

Teaching Tips
- Write **cape** on the board. Read the word aloud and have students repeat it. Underline **a** and **e** as you review with students that when they see **a-consonant-e** in a word, the **a** makes the **long a** sound.
- Write **pan** and **pane** on the board. Before students read the words, ask them which word has the **long a** sound. (the word with a-consonant-e) Then have students read the words. Call on a volunteer to circle the **long a** word.
- Have students complete page 124 independently or as a class.

Extra Pattern Practice
- Use the optional practice master below for extra practice with **long a**.

WORD SORT CD-ROM
- Provide time for students to use a **Buddy Sort** (see p. Z31) to practice their spelling words with a partner.

Connections to PHONICS

came
name
same
game
gate
gave

A. Circle the word that has the **long a** sound. Then write the word you circled.

1. (came) cat

came

2. bad (game)

game

3. (same) man

same

4. (name) nap

name

B. Write a spelling word that rhymes with each word.

5. cave

gave

6. late

gate

124

TEKS 1.22A Use phonological knowledge to match sounds to letters to construct known words.
1.22Bii Use letter-sound patterns to spell: consonant-vowel-consonant-silent e (CVCe) words.
1.22C Spell high-frequency words from a commonly used list.

Extra Pattern Practice

Extra Pattern Practice Master,
TRB, p. 101

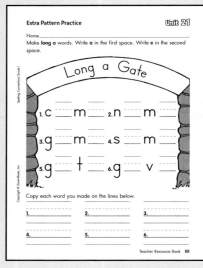

Pattern Practice
Draw two house shapes on the board. Label one *Short a* and the other *Long a*. In the **short a** house, write **rat, can, man, pan, fat, fad,** and **cam**. Tell students that all of the **short a** words want to move to the **long a** house. Ask volunteers to write a **short a** word in the **long a** house and add an **e**. Help students read the new words. (rate, cane, mane, pane, fate, fade, came)

T124

TEKS **1.22A** Use phonological knowledge to match sounds to letters to construct known words.
1.22Bii Use letter-sound patterns to spell: consonant-vowel-consonant-silent e (CVCe) words.
1.22C Spell high-frequency words from a commonly used list.

Write a spelling word to complete each sentence.

came
name
same
game
gate
gave

1. I ___**gave**___ Kate a big plum.

2. Dave and I have the ___**same**___ shirt.

3. Kay has a new ___**game**___ to play.

4. My dad ___**came**___ to get me.

5. Jack ran to open the ___**gate**___.

6. What is your ___**name**___?

TEKS 1.22C Spell high-frequency words from a commonly used list.

125

Student Objectives
- Write spelling words to complete sentences.
- Use a dictionary to check spelling.

Teaching Tips
- List the spelling words on the board. Then write *Jane ____ me a pen.* Read the sentence with different spelling words in the blank. Ask students which word makes the most sense. **(gave)** Call on a volunteer to write **gave** in the blank.
- On the board, add an **n** to the end of **pen**. Show students how they can check the correct spelling. Remind students that a dictionary is arranged in a-b-c or alphabetical order. Have students find the "p section" in their dictionary as you model the same. Prompt students to find **pen**. Ask, *Does **pen** have one **n** or two?* **(one)** Ask a volunteer to correct the word on the board.
- Have students complete page 125 independently or as a class.

Differentiated Instruction
- Use the **Challenge Words** activity on page 199 with students who are ready to transfer their knowledge of **long a** to new words.
- An Extra Challenge Practice Master is available on page 102 in the *TRB*.
- Dictation sentences for the challenge words are available on page T199.

More Fun With Spelling for Differentiation

Digital Resources for Spelling Connections
Interactive digital resources include word sorts, pattern practice, and proofreading activities for individual and whole-group instruction. (Interactive whiteboard compatible; see p. Z32.)

Spelling Connections Online
Interactive online spelling activities include word sorts, crossword puzzles, sentence completion, proofreading practice, and spelling bees with words from each unit (see p. Z32). www.spellingconnectionsonline.com

Spelling Center Activities

Spelling Game Mats
Place one of the spelling games in a learning center to provide a fun way for students to practice their spelling words (see p. Z26).

Flip Folder
Students can use a Flip Folder to practice spelling words independently (see p. Z32).

Word Sort CD-ROM
Printable, unit-specific word cards for spelling and challenge words can be used for Teacher-Led, Individual, Buddy, and Speed Sorts (see p. Z31).

TEKS 1.22C Spell high-frequency words from a commonly used list.
1.22E Use resources to find correct spellings.

T125

Student Objectives
- Identify spelling words in a story.
- Identify rhyming words.
- Use spelling words to write sentences.
- Use a dictionary to check spelling.

Teaching Tips
- Have students read the spelling words aloud.
- Read the first sentence of the paragraph aloud. Ask, *Which words in this sentence are spelling words?* (gave, same, name) Have students underline the words in their book.
- Complete Part A as a class.
- Have students complete Part B independently. Ask volunteers to identify the words that rhyme.
- Read the directions for Part C aloud. Have students complete this section independently. Remind them to write complete sentences. Have students circle at least one word they are not sure about. Have them check the spelling in a dictionary.
- Invite volunteers to read their work aloud.

WORD SORT CD-ROM
- Invite students to practice for the weekly test by doing an **Individual Sort** or a **Speed Sort** (see p. Z31).

Day 5

Student Objectives
- Demonstrate mastery of the unit spelling words.

Posttest Assessment Options
Option 1: Administer the unit posttest using the dictation sentences at right.
Option 2: Assess students using the standardized test. See the *Standardized Test Master Book*, p. 25.

Note: Posttest sentences for the on level and challenge lists are available on the audio *Spelling Connections* Posttest CD.

Connections to WRITING

A. Underline the spelling words you read in the paragraph.

Mom and Dad <u>gave</u> their first baby the <u>same</u> <u>name</u> as Gramps. His is Raymond. I am Raylene. Gramps wrote Ray on the front <u>gate</u>. When I <u>came</u> in, Gramps asked, "Who is Ray?" I said, "I am Ray." He said, "No, I am Ray." Then we said, "We are Ray!" That was a fun <u>game</u>.

B. Write each spelling word. Circle the words that rhyme.

1. gave
2. (same)
3. (name)
4. gate
5. (came)
6. (game)

C. Use spelling words to write about your name on a separate sheet of paper.

came
name
same
game
gate
gave

TEKS 1.22C Spell high-frequency words from a commonly used list.

1-Minute Handwriting Hint

The lowercase **m** contains three pulldown straight strokes. Be sure that the spaces between the vertical strokes are even.

m — EVEN SPACES

Posttest Sentences
1. What should I **name** the kitten?
2. We put a new latch on the **gate**.
3. Will you play a **game** with me?
4. Gail **came** home yesterday.
5. You and I like the **same** things.
6. Shawn **gave** me this truck.

Standardized Test Master Book, p. 25

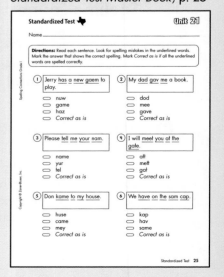

TEKS 1.22A Use phonological knowledge to match sounds to letters to construct known words. **1.22C** Spell high-frequency words from a commonly used list. **1.22E** Use resources to find correct spellings.

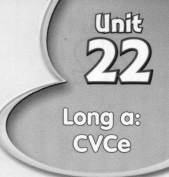

Planner

Day 1

Day 2

Day 1

Connections to **Thinking**

Student Objectives
- Read, spell, and write consonant-vowel-consonant-silent **e** (CVCe) words.
- Identify the **long a** sound.

Instruction for All Students
- Pretest Dictation Sentences, p. T127B
- Connections to Thinking, p. 127
- Home/School Spelling Practice Masters (*Teacher Resource Book*, pp. 103–104)

TEKS 1.22A, 1.22Bii, 1.22C

Connections to **Phonics**

Student Objectives
- Distinguish **short a** and **long a** sounds.
- Match CVCe words with the long vowel sound.
- Add **-s** to spelling words to make plurals.

Instruction for All Students
- Connections to Phonics, p. 128

Optional Practice
- Extra Pattern Practice Master (*Teacher Resource Book*, p. 105)

TEKS 1.22A, 1.22Bii, 1.22C, 1.22D

Spelling Words
lake
rake
bake
make
take
made

Challenge Words
lace
lane
vase
date

Day 3

Day 4

Day 5

Day 2

Day 3

Connections to **Reading**

Student Objectives
- Write spelling words in which **a**-consonant-silent **e** makes the **long a** sound.
- Group spelling words with similar meanings.

Instruction for All Students
- Connections to Reading, p. 129

Differentiated Instruction
- Challenge Words, p. 200

TEKS 1.22C

Connections to **Writing**

Student Objectives
- Identify spelling words in a story.
- Identify rhyming words.
- Use spelling words to write sentences.
- Use a dictionary to check spelling.

Instruction for All Students
- Connections to Writing, p. 130

Differentiated Instruction
- Extra Challenge Practice Master (*Teacher Resource Book*, p. 106)

TEKS 1.22A, 1.22C, 1.22E

Assessment

Student Objectives
- Demonstrate mastery of the unit spelling words.

Assessment for All Students
- Posttest Dictation Sentences, p. T130, or
- *Standardized Test Master Book*, p. 26

Differentiated Assessment
- Challenge Dictation Sentences, p. T200

Unit 22 Materials

Student Edition
pp. 127–130, 200

Teacher Edition
pp. T127A–T130, T200

 Teacher Resource Book
Unit 22 Practice Masters,
pp. 103–106, and
Sound/Symbol Cards

 Standardized Test Master Book
Unit 22 Test Master, p. 26

 Word Sort CD-ROM
Unit 22 Word Sort Cards for Teacher-
Led Sorts and Student Sorts

 **Digital Resources for
Spelling Connections**
Unit 22

 Spelling Connections Online
www.spellingconnectionsonline.com

**Spelling Support for
English Language Learners***
Unit 22 Practice Masters and
Audio Conversation

Spelling Center Activities*
Spelling Game Mats
Flip Folder, *TRB*, p. 155

*Spelling Support for English Language
Learners *and* Spelling Center Activities *may
be used at any time during the week.*

Assessment

Pretest Sentences (See procedures on p. Z30.)

1. There are fish in the **lake**.
2. I like to **rake** leaves.
3. Will you **bake** these potatoes?
4. We will **make** a card for Grandma.
5. May we **take** Poochie with us?
6. Jason **made** a present for you.

The Science of Spelling ◄ • •

The **long a** sound can be spelled many different ways. These spelling variations represent differences in pronunciation that have converged into the same sound. Spellings of the once different sounds have been retained. Some are more frequent than others. **Long a** is spelled **a_e** 75% of the time, **ai** 14% of the time, and **ay** 7% of the time. Less frequent spellings are **ei,** as in **veil,** and **ey,** as in **prey**.

ELL Support

Choose from the activities below to reinforce English language acquisition.

Beginning

Word Meanings Write the spelling words on the board. Say each word and use real objects, pictures, and pantomime to provide context and support word meaning. For example, show a picture of a rake, say **rake,** then pantomime using a rake. Say, *I am using a rake.*

Complete Sentences Write the spelling words on the board. Then write several sentences, leaving blanks that could be completed with the words. For example, write *I saw a boat on the* _____. Read the sentence aloud and have students tell which word makes sense in the sentence. (lake) Continue, reading each sentence and having students complete it.

Word Families Write **a** and say /ā/. Say each spelling word and have students repeat after you individually and in chorus. Then write **ake** on the board. Say /āk/ and have students repeat. Tell students you are going to say a beginning consonant sound and they will blend it with /āk/ to make a spelling word. Demonstrate with /l/ to make **lake.** Guide students to say /l/ /āk/ and then blend the sounds to say **lake.** Write **l** on the board to complete the word. Write **ake** again under the word **lake** and repeat the steps with /r/, /b/, /m/, and /t/. Begin a new column on the board with **ade.** Repeat the steps with the initial sound /m/. Review Unit 21 words **came, name, same, game, gate,** and **gave** and follow the same procedure with **ame, ate,** and **ave.** Explain that **ake, ade, ame, ate,** and **ave** are **long a** word families. Invite students to suggest other beginning sounds to make long **a** words with **ake, ade, ame, ate,** and **ave.** (fake, cake, wake, fade, wade, fame, lame, tame, late, state, Dave, brave)

Intermediate

Word Meanings Make flash cards for the spelling words. Display a flash card, say the word, and have students repeat it. Show photographs or illustrations for **lake, rake,** and **bake.** Pick up a book and say, *I take my book.* Pick up a sheet of paper and say, *I can make a fan.* Fold the paper into a fan and then say, *I made a fan.* After presenting a word, hang it on the board. Ask a volunteer to choose a word and use it in a sentence or tell something about its meaning. If necessary, clarify and expand the definition. Then have students write the words on a piece of paper. Students may look at the words on the board to be sure they have spelled them correctly.

Illustrate Words Have students draw and label pictures that illustrate the spelling words. Have them write **make** and **made** to label the same picture and complete the sentence frames *Today I make* _____ and *Yesterday I made* _____. Encourage students to make up and illustrate sentences using spelling words, too.

Support for Spanish Speakers

Comparing Languages Although Spanish does have an initial silent **h,** as in the words *hambre* (hunger) and *honor* (honor), Spanish does not have a final **silent e.** Final **e** is always pronounced in Spanish.

The Spanish word for **make** (*hacer*) is also irregular. **Made** translates into the following simple past tense forms: *hice* (I made), *hiciste* (you made), *hizo* (he/she made), *hicimos* (we made), *hicisteis* (you made), *hicieron* (they made). Point out to Spanish speakers that there are many word endings for **made** in Spanish but in English, **make** changes to **made.**

Long a Have students note that when they say the **long a** sound, their mouth is open and the tongue is in the middle of the mouth. As they complete the sound, have students note that the jaw and the tongue move up a bit.

Unit 22

Choose from the activities below to reinforce English language acquisition.

Advanced

Word Sort Explain that nouns are words that name things and verbs are words that name actions. Use **lake** and **make** as examples. Create a two-column chart on the board with the headings *Nouns* and *Verbs*. Have students categorize the spelling words by writing the words or taping word cards in the appropriate column. Add words to the chart each week.

Words and Pictures Provide copies of page 23 of *Spelling Support for English Language Learners*. Have pairs cut out the word and picture cards and place them facedown in two stacks. Then have them play the game as described. Encourage pairs to complete the activities at the bottom of the page. Students can hear the spelling words pronounced singly and used in context on the audio recording.

Ask and Answer Questions Write a question on the board that uses one or two spelling words, such as *Can you **take** a **rake**?* Ask a volunteer to read the sentence. Write a sentence frame that answers the question: *Yes, you can _____ a _____.* Ask students which spelling words are missing (take, rake) and write the words on the lines. Ask a volunteer to read the answer. Continue the activity using the rest of the words. Students can hear the spelling words in context sentences on the audio recording.

Conversation Provide support with pronunciations by having students listen to and interact with the audio recording. Students can practice the conversations and elaborate on them to improve pronunciations while gaining a better understanding of the word meanings. Partners can read the print form of the audio dialogue on page 50 of *Spelling Support for English Language Learners*.

Advanced High

Word Meanings Have students write questions using definitions of the spelling words. For example, *What is the opposite of **give**?* (take) *What is a **lake** made of?* (water) *What can help you gather leaves?* (rake)

Writing Sentences Have students write a sentence that uses a spelling word and then give the sentence to a partner. The partner reads the sentence aloud and identifies the spelling word. Then the partner writes a sentence using a different spelling word. Have partners pass sentences back and forth until they have used all of the spelling words.

Spelling Support for English Language Learners

Practice Master, p. 23

Practice Master, p. 50

 Audio Conversation available on CD

Word List	Unit 22
English	**Spanish**
1. lake	lago
2. rake	rastrillar; rastrillo
3. bake	hornear
4. make	hacer
5. take	tomar
6. made	hecho; hizo

English/Spanish Word List, p. 65

 Spelling Connections Online
Interactive online spelling activities provide additional ELL support.
www.spellingconnectionsonline.com

Use the letter clues to write the spelling words.

1. lake
2. rake
3. bake
4. make
5. take
6. made

1. b _ k _

bake

2. l _ k _

lake

3. t _ k _

take

4. m _ d _

made

5. r _ k _

rake

6. m _ k _

make

TEKS 1.22A Use phonological knowledge to match sounds to letters to construct known words. **1.22Bii** Use letter-sound patterns to spell: consonant-vowel-consonant-silent e (CVCe) words. **1.22C** Spell high-frequency words from a commonly used list.

127

Day 1 Unit 22

Student Objectives
- Read, spell, and write consonant-vowel-consonant-silent **e** (CVCe) words.
- Identify the **long a** sound.

Unit Pretest
- Administer the pretest on page T127B.

Teaching Tips
- Have students read the spelling words aloud, emphasizing and listening to /ā/.

WORD SORT CD-ROM
- Conduct a **Teacher-Led Sort** (see p. Z31) to reinforce the spelling pattern.
- Review with students that a vowel preceding a consonant and a **silent e** usually makes a long sound.
- Use the Sound/Symbol Cards for **ape, cave, frame, game,** and **safe** to review and reinforce the **long a** sound.
- Play "I Am Thinking of a Word… ." Use clues such as *I am thinking of a word that rhymes with Jake and begins with l* **(lake)** to introduce each word. After students identify a word, have a volunteer write it on the board.
- Have students complete the page independently or as a class.

Home/School Word Lists
- Have students take home the Home/School Spelling Practice Master.

Home/School Practice

Home/School Spelling
Practice Master, *TRB*, p. 103

Home/School Spelling
Practice Master, *TRB*, p. 104

English

Spanish

TEKS 1.22A Use phonological knowledge to match sounds to letters to construct known words. **1.22Bii** Use letter-sound patterns to spell: consonant-vowel-consonant-silent e (CVCe) words. **1.22C** Spell high-frequency words from a commonly used list.

T127

Student Objectives
- Distinguish **short a** and **long a** sounds.
- Match CVCe words with the long vowel sound.
- Add **-s** to spelling words to make plurals.

Teaching Tips
- Write **mad** on the board and have students read it aloud. Ask what vowel sound they hear in **mad**. (short a) Then write **e** at the end of **mad**. Have students read the word. Ask what vowel sound they hear in **made**. (long a)
- Review with students that adding **-s** to the end of a naming word will show that the word means more than one. Write **name** on the board. Ask a volunteer to write **-s** at the end. Have students read the word. Then say, *I know all of your names.*
- Have students complete page 128 independently or as a class.

Extra Pattern Practice
- Use the optional practice master below for extra practice with **long a**.

WORD SORT CD-ROM
- Provide time for students to use a **Buddy Sort** (see p. Z31) to practice their spelling words with a partner.

Connections to PHONICS

A. Circle the **long a** words. Then write them.

1. ran (take) man — take
2. (bake) tack map — bake
3. rat tap (made) — made
4. ham (make) mat — make

lake rake bake make take made

B. Write the spelling word that names the picture. Add **s** to the end.

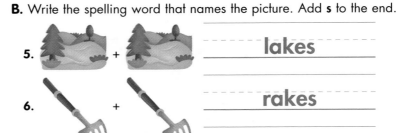

5. lakes
6. rakes

TEKS 1.22A Use phonological knowledge to match sounds to letters to construct known words. 1.22Bii Use letter-sound patterns to spell: consonant-vowel-consonant-silent e (CVCe) words. 1.22C Spell high-frequency words from a commonly used list. 1.22D Spell base words with inflectional endings.

128

Extra Pattern Practice

Extra Pattern Practice Master, TRB, p. 105

Pattern Practice Game: /a/

Cut out five large letters: **l, r, b, m,** and **t**. Say the words **lake, rake, bake, make,** and **take**. Explain that all these words have the ending sounds /ā/ /k/. Ask students to repeat the words. Explain that adding the /l/ sound before /ā/ /k/ makes the word **lake**. Write the letters **ake** on the board. Have students say **lake** aloud while a volunteer holds up the **l** before **ake**. Continue to make other words by using the remaining letters.

T128

TEKS 1.22A Use phonological knowledge to match sounds to letters to construct known words. 1.22Bii Use letter-sound patterns to spell: consonant-vowel-consonant-silent e (CVCe) words. 1.22C Spell high-frequency words from a commonly used list. 1.22D Spell base words with inflectional endings.

Connections to READING

A. Write the spelling word that goes with each group.

pond   stream

fry   boil

shovel   hoe

1. **lake**

2. **bake**

3. **rake**

lake
rake
bake
make
take
made

B. Write the missing spelling words.

4. I will **make** a cake in the oven.

5. I will **take** it to a party.

6. I will say, "I **made** a cake."

 TEKS 1.22C Spell high-frequency words from a commonly used list.   I29

Student Objectives
- Write spelling words in which **a**-consonant-silent **e** makes the **long a** sound.
- Group spelling words with similar meanings.

Teaching Tips
- Review that we can put words with similar meanings into groups. Write **door** on the board. Point to the classroom door and say **door**. Then write **gate**. Explain that **gate** and **door** can go together because both are things you can open and walk through. Then write **cook**. Ask which spelling word could go with **cook**. (**bake**)
- Write the sentence *She will ____ you home.* Ask students which spelling word makes the most sense in the sentence. (**take**) Call on a volunteer to write **take** in the blank.
- Have students complete page 129 independently or as a class. Tell them they will use each spelling word only one time.

Differentiated Instruction
- Use the **Challenge Words** activity on page 200 with students who are ready to transfer their knowledge of **long a** to new words.
- An Extra Challenge Practice Master is available on page 106 in the *TRB*.
- Dictation sentences for the challenge words are available on page T200.

More Fun With Spelling for Differentiation

Digital Resources for Spelling Connections
Interactive digital resources include word sorts, pattern practice, and proofreading activities for individual and whole-group instruction. (Interactive whiteboard compatible; see p. Z32.)

Spelling Connections Online
Interactive online spelling activities include word sorts, crossword puzzles, sentence completion, proofreading practice, and spelling bees with words from each unit (see p. Z32). www.spellingconnectionsonline.com

Spelling Center Activities

Spelling Game Mats
Place one of the spelling games in a learning center to provide a fun way for students to practice their spelling words (see p. Z26).

Flip Folder
Students can use a Flip Folder to practice spelling words independently (see p. Z32).

Word Sort CD-ROM
Printable, unit-specific word cards for spelling and challenge words can be used for Teacher-Led, Individual, Buddy, and Speed Sorts (see p. Z31).

Student Objectives
- Identify spelling words in a story.
- Identify rhyming words.
- Use spelling words to write sentences.
- Use a dictionary to check spelling.

Teaching Tips
- Have partners take turns reading the sentences in Part A to each other. The listener should identify any spelling words. Both partners should underline them.
- Have students complete Part B independently. Have students read the rhyming words aloud. Ask, *How do you know these words are rhyming words?* (They end with the same sounds.)
- Have students complete Part C independently. Remind them to write complete sentences. Tell students to review their work to make sure they have spelled all the spelling words correctly. Have students circle at least one word they are not sure about. Have them check the spelling in a dictionary.
- Invite volunteers to read their work aloud.

WORD SORT CD-ROM
- Invite students to practice for the weekly test by doing an **Individual Sort** or a **Speed Sort** (see p. Z31).

Day 5

Student Objectives
- Demonstrate mastery of the unit spelling words.

Posttest Assessment Options
Option 1: Administer the unit posttest using the dictation sentences at right.

Option 2: Assess students using the standardized test. See the *Standardized Test Master Book*, p. 26.

Note: Posttest sentences for the on level and challenge lists are available on the audio *Spelling Connections* Posttest CD.

Connections to WRITING

A. Underline the spelling words in the paragraph below.

I like to go to a camp by a <u>lake</u>. I learn lots of fun things. I <u>bake</u> cookies. I <u>make</u> mobiles. I <u>take</u> swimming lessons. Last year, I <u>made</u> a campfire. We had to <u>rake</u> the ground first. Then we put sticks in a pile for the fire.

| lake |
| rake |
| bake |
| make |
| take |
| made |

B. Write each spelling word. Circle the words that rhyme.

1. (lake)
2. (bake)
3. (make)
4. (take)
5. made
6. (rake)

C. On a separate sheet of paper, use the spelling words to write about something you would like to do at a camp.

I30

TEKS 1.22A Use phonological knowledge to match sounds to letters to construct known words. **1.22C** Spell high-frequency words from a commonly used list.

1-Minute Handwriting Hint

The second stroke of the lowercase **k** begins at the midline and slants left to halfway between the midline and the baseline. The letter ends with a slant right stroke. Be sure that the right side of the letter is even.

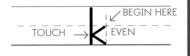

Posttest Sentences
1. We are going to the **lake** for a picnic.
2. May I help you **rake** the leaves?
3. Would you like to **make** a necklace?
4. It will not **take** long to get home.
5. We will **bake** apples for dessert.
6. I **made** my lunch all by myself.

Standardized Test Master Book, p. 26

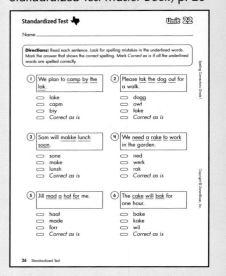

 TEKS 1.22A Use phonological knowledge to match sounds to letters to construct known words. **1.22C** Spell high-frequency words from a commonly used list. **1.22E** Use resources to find correct spellings.

Planner

Day 1   ## Day 2

Day 1

Connections to **Thinking**

Student Objectives
- Read, spell, and write words with the **long e** sound.
- Identify the **long e** sound.

Instruction for All Students
- Pretest Dictation Sentences, p. T131B
- Connections to Thinking, p. 131
- Home/School Spelling Practice Master (*Teacher Resource Book,* pp. 107–108)

TEKS 1.22A, 1.22C

Connections to **Phonics**

Student Objectives
- Use phonological knowledge to identify and write spelling words with the **long e** sound.

Instruction for All Students
- Connections to Phonics, p. 132

Optional Practice
- Extra Pattern Practice Master (*Teacher Resource Book,* p. 109)

TEKS 1.22A, 1.22C

Unit 23

Long e: e, ee

Spelling Words
he
me
we
she
be
see

Challenge Words
peek
deed
beet
peel

Day 3   ## Day 4   ## Day 5

Day 2 (Day 3 / Day 4)   ### Day 3 (Day 5)

Connections to **Reading**

Student Objectives
- Write spelling words with the **long e** sound to complete a poem.

Instruction for All Students
- Connections to Reading, p. 133

Differentiated Instruction
- Challenge Words, p. 201

TEKS 1.22A, 1.22C

Connections to **Writing**

Student Objectives
- Identify spelling words in a story.
- Use spelling words to write a story.
- Use a dictionary to check spelling.

Instruction for All Students
- Connections to Writing, p. 134

Differentiated Instruction
- Extra Challenge Practice Master (*Teacher Resource Book,* p. 110)

TEKS 1.22A, 1.22C, 1.22E

Assessment

Student Objectives
- Demonstrate mastery of the unit spelling words.

Assessment for All Students
- Posttest Dictation Sentences, p. T134, or
- *Standardized Test Master Book,* p. 27

Differentiated Assessment
- Challenge Dictation Sentences, p. T201

T131A

Unit 23 Materials

Student Edition
pp. 131–134, 201

Teacher Edition
pp. T131A–T134, T201

 Teacher Resource Book
Unit 23 Practice Masters,
pp. 107–110, and
Sound/Symbol Cards

 Standardized Test Master Book
Unit 23 Test Master, p. 27

 Word Sort CD-ROM
Unit 23 Word Sort Cards for Teacher-
Led Sorts and Student Sorts

 **Digital Resources for
Spelling Connections**
Unit 23

 Spelling Connections Online
www.spellingconnectionsonline.com

**Spelling Support for
English Language Learners***
Unit 23 Practice Masters and
Audio Conversation

Spelling Center Activities*
Spelling Game Mats
Flip Folder, *TRB*, p. 155

*Spelling Support for English Language
Learners *and* Spelling Center Activities *may
be used at any time during the week.*

Assessment

Pretest Sentences (See procedures on p. Z30.)

1. I think **he** is sleeping.
2. Watch **me** skip.
3. May **we** play with you?
4. Is **she** your sister?
5. When will we **be** there?
6. I **see** a rainbow.

The Science of Spelling ◀ · ·

- **Long e** is the most common long vowel sound in English. There are nearly twice as many words with **long e** as there are with **long a**. There are also several spellings. The most frequent spelling (44%) is **y**, as in **many**. **Long e** is spelled **e_e** 16% of the time and **i**, as in **machine**, 15% of the time.

ELL Support

Choose from the activities below to reinforce English language acquisition.

Beginning

Word Meanings Write the spelling words on the board. Say each word and use gestures and pantomime to provide context and support word meaning. For example, point to your eyes and then to the class and say, *I see you.* Put your index finger to your lips and whisper, *Shh! I can be quiet.* Point to students and ask, *Can you be quiet? Be quiet!*

Making Words Distribute letter cards for **b, h, m, w,** and **s.** Write a large **e** on the board. Encourage students to come up and hold a letter card to the left of **e** to make a two-letter spelling word. Then invite the students holding **s** and **h** to come up and make a three-letter word. Write a second **e** next to the first **e** and have the student

holding **s** come up and make another three-letter word. Have students say each word as it is made. Students can hear the spelling words pronounced singly on the audio recording.

Writing a Story Have partners use four to six of the spelling words to create an oral story. When students are satisfied with their story, help them write it in a few sentences. Encourage partners to illustrate their story and copy the sentences below or on the back of the picture. As an alternative, students can create an illustration for each sentence and create a storyboard by pasting their pictures on a longer strip of paper.

Intermediate

Word Meanings Write the spelling words on the board. Say each word clearly and have students repeat it. Play "Simon Says." Tell students when Simon says **he** everyone points to a boy, and when Simon says **she** everyone points to a girl. All point to themselves for **me** and make a circling motion to indicate **we.** To act out **be,** have students stand with hands on hips. For **see,** have them shade their eyes and look out. Then have students write the words on a piece of paper. Students may look at the words on the board to be sure they have spelled them correctly.

Pronoun Practice Distribute **he, she,** and two **we** word cards to four students. Make sure that a boy gets **he** and a girl gets **she.** Distribute **me** and **we** cards to all students. Tell students you will call out one of the words. The student or students with that card should stand up and hold their card high. Everyone else should point to that person or persons. Tell students when you call out **me** everyone stands up and points to him or herself. When you call out **we** everyone stands and points to everyone including themselves. Call out each pronoun. When students have learned what to do, redistribute the **he** and **she** cards and call out the words at a fast pace.

Support for Spanish Speakers

Comparing Languages Some English long vowel sounds are similar to the sounds represented by different letters in Spanish. For example, the **long e** sound is similar to the sound of **i** in Spanish, as in *sí* (yes) and *mí* (me).

Students can find Spanish translations of the English spelling words on page 66 of *Spelling Support for English Language Learners.*

Choose from the activities below to reinforce English language acquisition.

Advanced

Word Meanings Write the spelling words on the board. Read each word aloud and have students repeat. Ask volunteers to use each word in a sentence. If students have trouble using **be,** provide examples such as, *It is important to be nice to each other,* and *Be very quiet and listen carefully!*

Dramatic Play Have students work with a partner to develop a simple dialogue between siblings using the spelling words. Have partners perform their dialogues for the group. Have students listen to the conversation on the audio recording. Partners can read the print form of the audio dialogue on page 51 of *Spelling Support for English Language Learners*.

Word Recognition Review the spelling words. Ask students what kind of book might have these words. (a fiction story or biography) Have partners choose a book from the classroom library. Have them read the story and locate the spelling words. Ask students to read aloud sentences and phrases that contain spelling words.

Advanced High

Word Meanings List the spelling words on the board. Read each word aloud as you point to it. Ask students to identify any words they do not know. Have students offer statements using the spelling words. Write the sentences on the board and have students underline the spelling words.

Questions Provide large index cards. Have partners work together to write a question about a spelling word on one side of a card and the answer on the reverse. Partners meet with another pair to ask their questions.

Words and Sentences Provide students with copies of page 24 of *Spelling Support for English Language Learners*. Have partners work together to complete the sentences. Then have them do the activity at the bottom of the page. Students can hear the spelling words pronounced singly and used in context on the audio recording.

Writing Poems Have students use the spelling words to write short rhyming poems. For example: *I wish that he/could come with me. I know that we/have lots to see.* Encourage students to read their poems aloud to a partner.

Spelling Support for English Language Learners

Practice Master, p. 24

Practice Master, p. 51

Audio Conversation available on CD

English/Spanish Word List, p. 66

Spelling Connections Online
Interactive online spelling activities provide additional ELL support.
www.spellingconnectionsonline.com

Connections to THINKING

Unit 23
Long e: e, ee

Use the letter clues to write the spelling words.

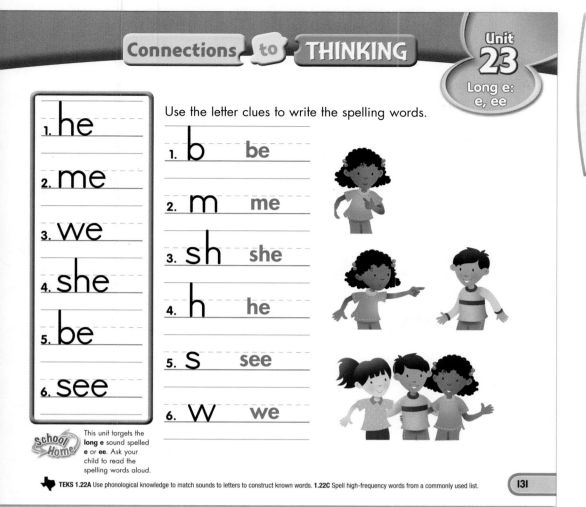

1. he
2. me
3. we
4. she
5. be
6. see

1. b__ be
2. m__ me
3. sh__ she
4. h__ he
5. s__ see
6. w__ we

School Home This unit targets the **long e** sound spelled **e** or **ee**. Ask your child to read the spelling words aloud.

 TEKS 1.22A Use phonological knowledge to match sounds to letters to construct known words. **1.22C** Spell high-frequency words from a commonly used list.

131

Student Objectives
- Read, spell, and write words with the **long e** sound.
- Identify the **long e** sound.

Unit Pretest
- Administer the pretest on page T131B.

Teaching Tips
- Have students read the spelling words aloud, emphasizing and listening to /ē/.

 **WORD SORT CD-ROM**
- Conduct a **Teacher-Led Sort** (see p. Z31) to introduce the spelling pattern.
- Introduce the **long e** sound by asking students to listen for it in **me**. Point out that the **long e** sound is the letter name.
- Play charades to introduce the rest of the spelling words. Ask the student who guesses a word how many e's the word contains. Then have him or her write the word on the board.
- Point out that the two consonants at the beginning of **she** work together to make one sound that is different from the individual letter sounds.
- Have students complete the page independently or as a class.

Home/School Word Lists
- Have students take home the Home/School Spelling Practice Master.

Home/School Practice

Home/School Spelling
Practice Master, *TRB*, p. 107

Home/School Spelling
Practice Master, *TRB*, p. 108

Home/School Spelling Practice Unit 23
Name _____

1. he
2. me
3. we
4. she
5. be
6. see

1. _____
2. _____
3. _____
4. _____
5. _____
6. _____

Spelling Practice Activity

Dear Family,
Ask your child to write the spelling words correctly on the blank lines.

Write the spelling words on index cards and lay them facedown on the table. Have your child pick

on index card and read the word aloud. Then have him or her spell the word on a separate sheet of paper. Continue the activity until all the words have been used.

Teacher Resource Book 107

English

Práctica de ortografía para el hogar o la escuela Unit 23
Nombre _____

1. he — él
2. me — me; mí
3. we — nosotros
4. she — ella
5. be — ser; estar
6. see — ver; ve; vea

1. _____
2. _____
3. _____
4. _____
5. _____
6. _____

Actividad de ortografía

Querida familia:
Pida a su hijo(a) que escriba correctamente las palabras de ortografía en los renglones en blanco.

Escriba cada palabra en una tarjeta y coloque todas las tarjetas boca abajo sobre una mesa.

Primero, pida a su hijo(a) que tome una de las tarjetas y lea la palabra en voz alta. Luego, pídale que las escriba en una hoja de papel. Continúen esta actividad hasta que hayan utilizado todas las tarjetas.

108 Teacher Resource Book

Spanish

 TEKS 1.22A Use phonological knowledge to match sounds to letters to construct known words. **1.22C** Spell high-frequency words from a commonly used list.

T131

Student Objectives

- Use phonological knowledge to identify and write spelling words with the **long e** sound.

Teaching Tips

- Write the spelling words on the board and read them aloud. Ask students what vowel sound they hear. **(long e)** Review that the **long e** sound can be spelled with one or two e's.
- Show the Sound/Symbol Card for **ball**. Ask students to name the picture. Ask, *What sound do you hear at the beginning of* **ball**? *(/b/) What letter spells that sound?* **(b)** Write **b** on the board. Then ask, *What sound do you hear at the end of* **bee**? *(/ē/) What letter spells /ē/?* **(e)** Write **e** after **b**. *What spelling word is this?* **(be)**
- Have students complete page 132 independently or as a class.

Extra Pattern Practice TRB

- Use the optional practice master below for extra practice with **long e**.

WORD SORT CD-ROM

- Provide time for students to use a **Buddy Sort** (see p. Z31) to practice their spelling words with a partner.

Connections to PHONICS

A. Use the clue to write the word.

sounds like

has two vowels, has one vowel sound

1. _____ **be**   2. _____ **see**

begins with two letters that make one sound

3. _____ **she**

B. Name the picture. Use the first sound in the picture name and the ending sound in  to make a spelling word. Write the word.

4. _____ **he**   5. _____ **me**

6. _____ **we**

he
me
we
she
be
see

132

TEKS 1.22A Use phonological knowledge to match sounds to letters to construct known words.
1.22C Spell high-frequency words from a commonly used list.

Extra Pattern Practice

Extra Pattern Practice Master,
TRB, p. 109

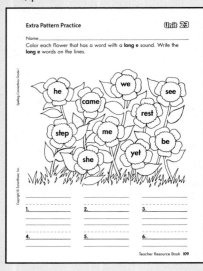

Long e Practice

Say the words **he, me, we, she, be,** and **see,** emphasizing the **long e** sound. Ask students to repeat each word. Then have students sit in a circle. Put on a pair of sunglasses. Say, *These glasses help me see on a sunny day.* Have a student put on the glasses and say a word with the **long e** sound. Continue until each student has had a turn. Then write the words on the board and have volunteers circle the letters that spell the **long e** sound.

TEKS 1.22A Use phonological knowledge to match sounds to letters to construct known words. **1.22C** Spell high-frequency words from a commonly used list.

Write spelling words to finish the rhyme.

Instead of Ann, you can just say __1.__ .
And Ben is sometimes known as __2.__ .
A word for you and me is __3.__ .
Together we're silly as can __4.__ !
When my friends need help they ask __5.__ .
We like each other, as you can __6.__ .

he
me
we
she
be
see

1. she
2. he
3. we
4. be
5. me
6. see

TEKS 1.22A Use phonological knowledge to match sounds to letters to construct known words. **1.22C** Spell high-frequency words from a commonly used list.

I33

Student Objectives
• Write spelling words with the **long e** sound to complete a poem.

Teaching Tips
• Review with students that words rhyme when they end with the same sounds. Provide an example, such as **lake/take**.
• Write the spelling words on the board and have students read them. Ask which words rhyme. **(all of them)**
• Say, *When I'm alone, I say me. When I'm with you, I say _____.* Pause and ask students which spelling word best completes the rhyme. **(we)** Write the sentences on the board and have a volunteer write **we** to finish the rhyme.
• Have students complete page 133 independently or as a class.

Differentiated Instruction
• Use the **Challenge Words** activity on page 201 with students who are ready to transfer their knowledge of **long e** to new words.
• An Extra Challenge Practice Master is available on page 110 in the *TRB*.
• Dictation sentences for the challenge words are available on page T201.

More Fun With Spelling for Differentiation

Digital Resources for Spelling Connections
Interactive digital resources include word sorts, pattern practice, and proofreading activities for individual and whole-group instruction. (Interactive whiteboard compatible; see p. Z32.)

Spelling Connections Online
Interactive online spelling activities include word sorts, crossword puzzles, sentence completion, proofreading practice, and spelling bees with words from each unit (see p. Z32). www.spellingconnectionsonline.com

Spelling Center Activities
Spelling Game Mats
Place one of the spelling games in a learning center to provide a fun way for students to practice their spelling words (see p. Z26).

Flip Folder
Students can use a Flip Folder to practice spelling words independently (see p. Z32).

Word Sort CD-ROM
Printable, unit-specific word cards for spelling and challenge words can be used for Teacher-Led, Individual, Buddy, and Speed Sorts (see p. Z31).

 TEKS 1.22A Use phonological knowledge to match sounds to letters to construct known words. **1.22C** Spell high-frequency words from a commonly used list.

Student Objectives
- Identify spelling words in a story.
- Use spelling words to write a story.
- Use a dictionary to check spelling.

Teaching Tips
- Have partners take turns reading the sentences in Part A to each other. The listener should identify any spelling words. Both partners should underline the words.
- Have students complete Part B independently.
- Remind students that a story has a beginning, a middle, and an end. Read the directions for Part C aloud. Have students complete this section independently. Tell students to review their work to make sure they have spelled all spelling words correctly. Have students circle one word they are not sure about and check the spelling in a dictionary.
- Invite volunteers to read their story ending aloud. Encourage discussion.

WORD SORT CD-ROM
- Invite students to practice for the weekly test by doing an **Individual Sort** or a **Speed Sort** (see p. Z31).

Day 5

Student Objectives
- Demonstrate mastery of the unit spelling words.

Posttest Assessment Options
Option 1: Administer the unit posttest using the dictation sentences below.
Option 2: Assess students using the optional standardized test. See the *Standardized Test Master Book,* p. 27.

Note: Posttest sentences for the on level and challenge lists are available on the audio *Spelling Connections* Posttest CD.

Connections to WRITING

A. Underline the spelling words in the paragraph.

The fox can <u>see</u> the bunny. Then <u>he</u> says, "You can not hide from <u>me</u>."
The bunny is ready to run. Then <u>she</u> says, "Can <u>we</u> <u>be</u> friends? I have a gift for you. You have to close your eyes."
The fox wants the gift. The fox shuts his eyes.

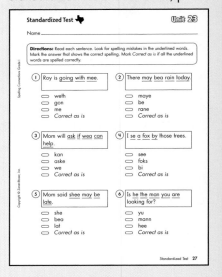

he
me
we
she
be
see

B. Write the spelling words.

1. see
2. he
3. me
4. she
5. we
6. be

C. Use the spelling words to write the rest of the story on a separate sheet of paper. How can the bunny get away from the fox?

134

TEKS 1.22C Spell high-frequency words from a commonly used list.

1-Minute Handwriting Hint
Line quality refers to the smoothness or evenness of the writing line. If students are applying too much pressure to the pencil, the line quality may be too heavy. If the line quality is too light, the student may be using a pencil with very hard lead or may not be applying enough pressure.

Posttest Sentences
1. I hope **she** will be here today.
2. If you stand up, you can **see** better.
3. Do you think **he** is angry?
4. I will **be** ready at two o'clock.
5. Can **we** go to the zoo?
6. Follow **me** and do what I do.

Standardized Test Master Book, p. 27

Standardized Test ⬆ Unit 23
Name _____

Directions: Read each sentence. Look for spelling mistakes in the underlined words. Mark the answer that shows the correct spelling. Mark Correct as is if all the underlined words are spelled correctly.

① Roy is going with <u>mee</u>.
- weth
- gon
- me
- Correct as is

② There may <u>bea</u> rain today.
- maye
- be
- rane
- Correct as is

③ Mom will <u>ask</u> <u>if</u> <u>wea</u> can help.
- kan
- aske
- we
- Correct as is

④ I <u>se</u> a <u>fox</u> by those trees.
- see
- foks
- bi
- Correct as is

⑤ Mom said <u>shee</u> may be <u>late</u>.
- she
- bea
- lat
- Correct as is

⑥ Is <u>he</u> the man <u>you</u> are looking for?
- yu
- mann
- hee
- Correct as is

Standardized Test **27**

 TEKS 1.22A Use phonological knowledge to match sounds to letters to construct known words.
1.22C Spell high-frequency words from a commonly used list. **1.22E** Use resources to find correct spellings.

Planner

Day 1
Day 2

Day 1

Connections to **Thinking**

Student Objectives
- Read, spell, and write words with the **long e** sound in the CVVC pattern.
- Identify the **long e** sound.

Instruction for All Students
- Pretest Dictation Sentences, p. T135B
- Connections to Thinking, p. 135
- Home/School Spelling Practice Master (*Teacher Resource Book*, pp. 111–112)

 TEKS 1.22A, 1.22C

Connections to **Phonics**

Student Objectives
- Identify and write words with **long e** that rhyme with picture names.
- Write words with **long e** spelled **ee** in the CVVC pattern.

Instruction for All Students
- Connections to Phonics, p. 136

Optional Practice
- Extra Pattern Practice Master (*Teacher Resource Book*, p. 113)

TEKS 1.22A, 1.22C

Spelling Words
feel
deep
keep
feed
seed
feet

Challenge Words
weed
sweep
creek
cheek

Day 3
Day 4
Day 5

Day 2
Day 3

Connections to **Reading**

Student Objectives
- Write words with **long e** spelled **ee** to complete sentences in a paragraph.

Instruction for All Students
- Connections to Reading, p. 137

Differentiated Instruction
- Challenge Words, p. 202

TEKS 1.22C

Connections to **Writing**

Student Objectives
- Identify spelling words in a paragraph.
- Identify rhyming words.
- Use spelling words to write sentences to express an opinion.
- Use a dictionary to check spelling.

Instruction for All Students
- Connections to Writing, p. 138

Differentiated Instruction
- Extra Challenge Practice Master (*Teacher Resource Book*, p. 114)

TEKS 1.22A, 1.22C, 1.22E

Assessment

Student Objectives
- Demonstrate mastery of the unit spelling words.

Assessment for All Students
- Posttest Dictation Sentences, p. T138, or
- *Standardized Test Master Book*, p. 28

Differentiated Assessment
- Challenge Dictation Sentences, p. T202

TEKS 1.22C

Unit 24 Materials

Student Edition
pp. I35–I38, 202

Teacher Edition
pp. TI35A–TI38, T202

 Teacher Resource Book
Unit 24 Practice Masters,
pp. III–II4, and
Sound/Symbol Cards

 Standardized Test Master Book
Unit 24 Test Master, p. 28

 Word Sort CD-ROM
Unit 24 Word Sort Cards for Teacher-
Led Sorts and Student Sorts

 **Digital Resources for
Spelling Connections**
Unit 24

Spelling Connections Online
www.spellingconnectionsonline.com

**Spelling Support for
English Language Learners***
Unit 24 Practice Masters and
Audio Conversation

Spelling Center Activities*
Spelling Game Mats
Flip Folder, *TRB*, p. I55

*Spelling Support for English Language
Learners *and* Spelling Center Activities *may
be used at any time during the week.*

Assessment

Pretest Sentences (See procedures on p. Z30.)

1. Can you **feel** the snowflakes on your face?
2. Some animals dig **deep** holes.
3. May we **keep** the kitten?
4. It is time to **feed** the baby.
5. I will plant this **seed**.
6. Your **feet** are muddy.

The Science of Spelling ◄ • •

- In English, the only vowels that are commonly doubled are **e** and **o**, as in **beet** and **boot**. Other double vowels are very rare in English and appear in words from other languages, such as **aardvark**, **radii**, and **vacuum**. **Long e** is spelled **ea**, as in **beat**, and **ee**, as in **beet**, about 9% of the time each. **Long e** is spelled **ie**, as in **field**, only about 3% of the time. This spelling, however, is often confused with the **ei** spelling as in **neither** and **ceiling**, which is used only 1% of the time. Hence the mnemonic: *I before e except after c, or when sounded like a as in* **neighbor** *or* **weigh**.

ELL Support

Choose from the activities below to reinforce English language acquisition.

Beginning

Word Meanings Use gestures, realia, and photos to introduce a few words at a time. For example, point to your feet and say, *These are my feet.* Have students repeat the sentence. Point to a student's feet and ask, *What are these?* The student should say, *feet* or *These are my feet.* Repeat for other words. For multiple-meaning words, teach only the most common meaning.

Completing Sentences Provide spelling word cards. Say a word and have students hold up the corresponding card. Invite students to use each spelling word in an oral sentence. Write each sentence, leaving out the spelling word. Read the sentence, pausing at the blank. Have students hold up the card with the missing word and say the word. Have a volunteer write the word in the blank. Then read the completed sentence. Students can hear the spelling words in context sentences on the audio recording.

Intermediate

Word Meanings Write the spelling words on the board. Say each word and have students repeat it. Ask a volunteer to choose a word and use it in a sentence or tell something about its meaning. If necessary, clarify and expand the definition. Then have students write the word on a piece of paper. Students may look at the word on the board to be sure they have spelled it correctly.

Long e and Short e Help students discriminate **long e** and **short e** sounds. Write /ē/ and /ĕ/ on the board and pronounce each sound. Have students write each symbol on an index card. Tell students to listen carefully for the vowel sound in words you say. After each word, have students hold up the corresponding vowel sound card. Word suggestions: **feel, fed, bed, feet, seed, red, deep, bell, get, keep**.

Words in Context Write the spelling words on the board. Demonstrate how to use more than one word in a sentence. For example, *How do feet feel in deep water? Don't plant the small seed too deep in the dirt. Feed the cat and keep it quiet.* Have students work with a partner to create their own sentences. Tell them the sentences may be silly, but they have to make sense. Have students write and illustrate their sentences. Display students' work for everyone to enjoy.

Support for Spanish Speakers

Comparing Languages All of the spelling words for Unit 24 come to modern English from its Germanic roots. Spanish and English share many cognates from Latin and Greek, and these words may be easier for Spanish speakers to acquire as new vocabulary. However, it is important to keep in mind that many of the most commonly used words in English are Germanic in origin and do not have Spanish cognates. These words include many that are typically learned by children at home before they come to school. Check in with Spanish-speaking students on a regular basis to make sure they are acquiring English vocabulary related to home, family life, and early childhood experiences.

The consonant **d** is pronounced differently in English and Spanish. The /d/ is softer in Spanish and similar to the English unvoiced /**th**/ in **thank** and **thought**. The final /**d**/ in **seed** and **feed** may be difficult for some Spanish speakers to say. Provide opportunities for students to listen closely and watch your mouth and tongue as you pronounce these words.

Students can find Spanish translations of the English spelling words on page 66 of *Spelling Support for English Language Learners.*

Unit 24

Choose from the activities below to reinforce English language acquisition.

Advanced

Word Meanings Make flash cards for the spelling words. Show each card, say the word, and have students repeat it. Provide the following props or similar ones: sandpaper and/or a plush toy; a deep box and/or a picture of a diving pool; a book bag and/or a notebook; a dog bowl and/or a can of pet food; seeds or a picture of seeds; a doll with feet; and a pair of shoes. Invite volunteer to take an item and use the related spelling word in a sentence. To demonstrate, hold up the shoes and say, *I wear shoes on my feet.*

Words and Sentences Provide copies of page 25 of *Spelling Support for English Language Learners*. Have pairs work together to complete the sentences with spelling words. Then have them do the activity at the bottom of the page. Students can hear the spelling words used in context on the audio recording.

Rhyming Words Provide a few words that rhyme with a spelling word. For example, say **feel** and then **peel** and **heel**. Write a spelling word from each word family (**eep, eed, eel, eet**) on a sheet of paper and have students write rhyming words under it. Display the lists in a place where students can add to them at any time.

Advanced High

Word Meanings List the spelling words on the board. Read each word aloud as you point to it. Ask students to identify any words they do not know. Use pantomime and gestures to support explanations of word meaning.

Conversation Practice Provide support for conversational English and listening comprehension by having students listen to and interact with the audio recording. Students can practice the conversations and elaborate on them to improve pronunciations while gaining a better understanding of word meanings. Partners can read the print form of the audio dialogue on page 51 of Spelling *Support for English Language Learners.*

Writing Sentences Have students write cloze sentences from which the spelling words are missing. Tell students to trade papers with a partner and complete each other's sentences by writing the spelling words. As an alternative, students can randomly select one to three spelling words and challenge a partner to write a sentence using all of the words.

Spelling Support for English Language Learners

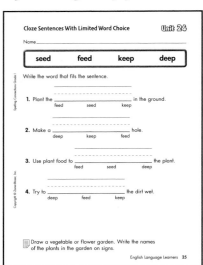

Practice Master, p. 25

Practice Master, p. 51

Audio Conversation
available on CD

English/Spanish
Word List, p. 66

Spelling Connections Online
Interactive online spelling activities provide additional ELL support.
www.spellingconnectionsonline.com

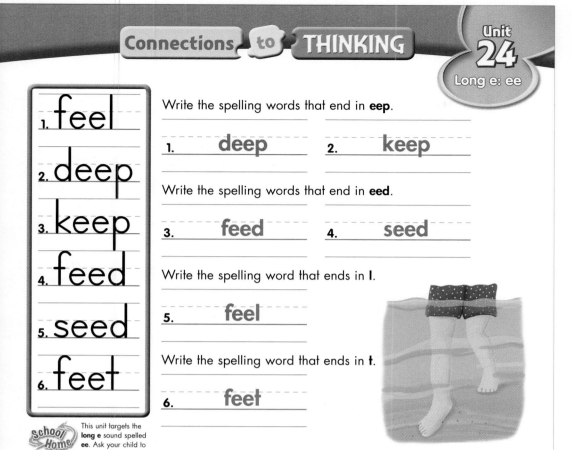

1. feel
2. deep
3. keep
4. feed
5. seed
6. feet

Write the spelling words that end in **eep**.

1. deep
2. keep

Write the spelling words that end in **eed**.

3. feed
4. seed

Write the spelling word that ends in **l**.

5. feel

Write the spelling word that ends in **t**.

6. feet

School Home

This unit targets the **long e** sound spelled **ee**. Ask your child to read each spelling word and circle **ee**.

TEKS **1.22A** Use phonological knowledge to match sounds to letters to construct known words. **1.22C** Spell high-frequency words from a commonly used list.

I35

Day 1

Unit
24

Student Objectives
- Read, spell, and write words with the **long e** sound in the CVVC pattern.
- Identify the **long e** sound.

Unit Pretest
- Administer the pretest on page T135B.

Teaching Tips
- Have students read the spelling words aloud, emphasizing and listening to /ē/.

WORD SORT CD-ROM
- Conduct a **Teacher-Led Sort** (see p. Z31) to introduce or reinforce the spelling pattern.
- Review the **long e** sound by saying the word **feet**. Write **feet** on the board and ask a student to circle the letters that spell the **long e** sound.
- Use the Sound/Symbol Cards for **Jeep, queen,** and **sheep** to further review **long e** spelled **ee**.
- Say the word **fee**. Ask students what two sounds they hear. (/f/ /ē/) Ask what final sound would make this word a spelling word. (/t/, /l/, or /d/)
- Have students complete the page independently or as a class.

Home/School Word Lists TRB
- Have students take home the Home/School Spelling Practice Master.

Home/School Practice

Home/School Spelling
Practice Master, *TRB*, p. III

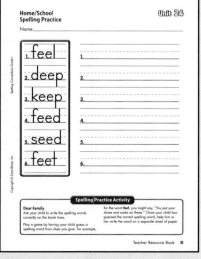

English

Home/School Spelling
Practice Master, *TRB*, p. II2

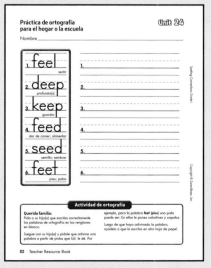

Spanish

TEKS **1.22A** Use phonological knowledge to match sounds to letters to construct known words. **1.22C** Spell high-frequency words from a commonly used list.

TI35

Student Objectives

- Identify and write words with **long e** that rhyme with picture names.
- Write words with **long e** spelled **ee** in the CVVC pattern.

Teaching Tips

- Write **fed** on the board and read it aloud. Ask students what vowel sound they hear. **(short e)** Then write **feed** and read it aloud. Ask students what vowel sound they hear. **(long e)** Review that the **long e** sound in **feed** and the other spelling words is spelled with two **e**'s.
- Remind students that rhyming words have the same ending sounds. Write **feel** on the board. Have students read it aloud. Then erase **f** and write **h**. Have students read the new word and note that **feel** and **heel** have the same ending sounds.
- Have students complete page 136 independently or as a class.

Extra Pattern Practice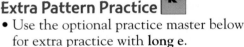

- Use the optional practice master below for extra practice with **long e**.

WORD SORT CD-ROM

- Provide time for students to use a **Buddy Sort** (see p. Z31) to practice their spelling words with a partner.

Connections to PHONICS

Write the spelling word that rhymes with each picture.

feel
deep
keep
feed
seed
feet

1. **feet**

2. **deep**

3. **keep**

4. **feel**

5. **feed**

6. **seed**

TEKS 1.22A Use phonological knowledge to match sounds to letters to construct known words.
1.22C Spell high-frequency words from a commonly used list.

136

Extra Pattern Practice

Extra Pattern Practice Master,
TRB, p. 113

CVVC Practice

Draw two pots on chart paper. In each pot, draw a long stalk with stems. Label one pot **eed** and the other pot **eep**. Cut leaf shapes from card stock. Write **eep** on half of the leaves and **eed** on the other half. Have students select a leaf and write a letter before **eep** or **eed** to make a word. Then have them tape their leaf to the appropriate plant. **(Possible words: deed, feed, heed, need, reed, seed, weed; beep, deep, Jeep, keep, peep, seep, weep)**

TEKS 1.22A Use phonological knowledge to match sounds to letters to construct known words. **1.22C** Spell high-frequency words from a commonly used list.

Connections to READING

Write spelling words to complete the paragraph.

Do you want to grow a pumpkin? Start with a pumpkin __1.__ . Then put dirt in a __2.__ tub. Is the dirt dry? You can __3.__ it to find out. Seeds need water, so __4.__ the dirt wet. You can __5.__ the seed with plant food. Soon the seed will put down roots. The roots are like __6.__ . The plant will stand on them and grow strong.

**feel
deep
keep
feed
seed
feet**

1.	**seed**	2.	**deep**	
3.	**feel**	4.	**keep**	
5.	**feed**	6.	**feet**	

TEKS 1.22C Spell high-frequency words from a commonly used list.

137

Student Objectives
• Write words with **long e** spelled **ee** to complete sentences in a paragraph.

Teaching Tips
• Write the spelling words on the board and have students read them aloud. Review that **ee** makes the **long e** sound.
• Say a sentence omitting the word **feet,** such as *My _____ are tired from walking so far.* Ask students to choose the word on the board that best completes the sentence and read it aloud. Then say the complete sentence. Introduce the remaining spelling words in the same way.
• Have students complete page 137 independently or as a class.

Differentiated Instruction
• Use the **Challenge Words** activity on page 202 with students who are ready to transfer their knowledge of **long e** to new words.
• An Extra Challenge Practice Master is available on page 114 in the *TRB*.
• Dictation sentences for the challenge words are available on page T202.

More Fun With Spelling for Differentiation

Digital Resources for Spelling Connections
Interactive digital resources include word sorts, pattern practice, and proofreading activities for individual and whole-group instruction. (Interactive whiteboard compatible; see p. Z32.)

Spelling Connections Online
Interactive online spelling activities include word sorts, crossword puzzles, sentence completion, proofreading practice, and spelling bees with words from each unit (see p. Z32).
www.spellingconnectionsonline.com

Spelling Center Activities
Spelling Game Mats
Place one of the spelling games in a learning center to provide a fun way for students to practice their spelling words (see p. Z26).

Flip Folder
Students can use a Flip Folder to practice spelling words independently (see p. Z32).

Word Sort CD-ROM
Printable, unit-specific word cards for spelling and challenge words can be used for Teacher-Led, Individual, Buddy, and Speed Sorts (see p. Z31).

TEKS 1.22C Spell high-frequency words from a commonly used list.

T137

Student Objectives
- Identify spelling words in a paragraph.
- Identify rhyming words.
- Use spelling words to write sentences to express an opinion.
- Use a dictionary to check spelling.

Teaching Tips
- Have partners take turns reading the sentences in Part A to each other. The listener should identify any spelling words. Both partners should underline the words.
- Have students complete Part B independently. Have students read the rhyming words aloud.
- Have students complete Part C independently. Remind them to write complete sentences. Tell students to review their work to make sure they have spelled all spelling words correctly. Have students circle at least one word they are not sure about. Have them check the spelling in a dictionary.
- Invite volunteers to read their work aloud. Encourage questions and discussion.

WORD SORT CD-ROM
- Invite students to practice for the weekly test by doing an **Individual Sort** or a **Speed Sort** (see p. Z31).

Day 5

Student Objectives
- Demonstrate mastery of the unit spelling words.

Posttest Assessment Options
Option 1: Administer the unit posttest using the dictation sentences at right.

Option 2: Assess students using the standardized test. See the *Standardized Test Master Book*, p. 28.

Note: Posttest sentences for the on level and challenge lists are available on the audio *Spelling Connections* Posttest CD.

Connections to WRITING

A. Underline the spelling words in the paragraph.

Some people say that a plant has feelings. They dig a <u>deep</u> hole for a <u>seed</u>. They talk to the plant as it grows. They <u>feed</u> the plant. They <u>keep</u> the plant warm. They do not step on the plant with their <u>feet</u>. They want the plant to <u>feel</u> good.

B. Write the spelling words. Draw lines to connect words that rhyme.

1. deep	2. seed
3. feed	4. keep
5. feet	6. feel

feel
deep
keep
feed
seed
feet

C. Do plants have feelings? Use spelling words to write what you think. Check your spelling in a dictionary.

I38

TEKS **1.22C** Spell high-frequency words from a commonly used list. **1.22E** Use resources to find correct spellings.

1-Minute Handwriting Hint

The lowercase **f** begins with a curve back stroke. The letter is crossed at the midline.

CURVE BACK
CROSS

Posttest Sentences
1. You may **keep** this book.
2. My **feet** are tired.
3. How **deep** is that hole?
4. I **feel** happy today.
5. Have you ever eaten a sunflower **seed**?
6. Do not **feed** your dog too much.

Standardized Test Master Book, p. 28

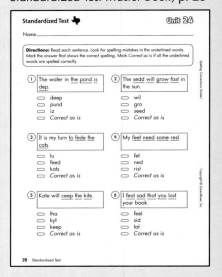

TEKS **1.22A** Use phonological knowledge to match sounds to letters to construct known words. **1.22C** Spell high-frequency words from a commonly used list. **1.22E** Use resources to find correct spellings.

Planner

Day 1 | Day 2

Day 1

Unit 21: Long a: CVCe
Student Objectives
- Review the spelling pattern and words from Unit 21.

Instruction for All Students
- Unit 21 Review, p. 139
- Home/School Spelling Practice Master (*Teacher Resource Book*, pp. 115–116)

Unit 22: Long a: CVCe
Student Objectives
- Review the spelling pattern and words from Unit 22.

Instruction for All Students
- Unit 22 Review, p. 140

Unit 21
Long a: CVCe

came	game
name	gate
same	gave

Unit 22
Long a: CVCe

lake	make
rake	take
bake	made

Unit 23
Long e: e, ee

he	she
me	be
we	see

Unit 24
Long e: ee

feel	feed
deep	seed
keep	feet

Day 3 | Day 4 | Day 5

Day 2 | | Day 3

Unit 23: Long e: e, ee
Student Objectives
- Review the spelling patterns and words from Unit 23.

Instruction for All Students
- Unit 23 Review, p. 141

Unit 24: Long e: ee
Student Objectives
- Review the spelling pattern and words from Unit 24.

Instruction for All Students
- Unit 24 Review, p. 142

Assessment
Student Objectives
- Demonstrate mastery of the review unit spelling words.

Assessment for All Students
- Posttest Assessment Options
  ✦ Posttest Dictation Sentences, p. T142, or
  ✦ *Standardized Test Master Book*, p. 29

Unit 25 Materials

Student Edition
pp. 139–142
Alphabet and Picture Cards
(See pages Z32 for
suggested activities.)

Teacher Edition
pp. T139A–T142

 **Teacher Resource Book
for Differentiated Instruction**
Unit 25 Practice Masters,
pp. 115–116

 Standardized Test Master Book
Unit 25 Test Master, p. 29

 Word Sort CD-ROM
Unit 25 Word Sort Cards for Teacher-
Led Sorts and Student Sorts

 **Digital Resources for
Spelling Connections**
Unit 25

 Spelling Connections Online
www.spellingconnectionsonline.com

Spelling Center Activities*
Spelling Game Mats
Flip Folder, *TRB*, p. 155

*Spelling Center Activities may be used
at any time during the week.*

Developmental Spelling Check

Administer the following **Developmental Spelling Check**
to evaluate spelling growth. Remind students that this is
not a test for a grade; students are not expected to spell
these words conventionally. Author J. Richard Gentry
has provided (in parentheses) typical Phase 4
Transitional Spellings for each word in parentheses.

Tell students you would like them to try writing these bird words. To
administer, say each word aloud, read the sentence, and then say the
word again.

Bird Words and Sample Transitional Spellings

eagle	The **eagle** has big wings.	(EGUL)
blackbird	Where is the **blackbird**?	(BLACKBERD)
red bird	The **red bird** has a yellow beak.	(RED BERD)
bluebird	The **bluebird** flew away.	(BLUBERD)
owl	The wise **owl** said, "Who?"	(AL)
turkey	We will eat **turkey** on Sunday.	(TRKE, CHRKE)
chicken	I love to eat fried **chicken**.	(CHIKEN)

ELL Support

Choose from the activities below to reinforce English language acquisition.

Beginning

Word Meanings Write the spelling words on the board. Review by pointing to a word, saying it aloud and using a real object, picture, or gestures and pantomime to provide context and support meaning. For example, show a picture of a **gate**. Point to the gate and say **gate**. Have students repeat. Students can hear the words for Units 21–24 pronounced singly on the audio recording.

Word Match Have each student make flash cards for the spelling words or provide students with cards. Have students work with a partner. Place the two sets of cards facedown. Have partners take turns drawing one card from each stack. When a student finds a match, he or she reads the word and removes the cards from the table. Cards that do not match are placed back in their original stack.

"Flower Power" Game Have partners play the "Flower Power" guessing game with the spelling words. One partner thinks of a word and draws a line for each letter on a piece of paper. The other partner tries to discover the word by guessing letters. If a letter is in the word, the first partner writes the letter on the line where that letter belongs. If the letter is not in the word, the partner draws a stem. For each incorrect guess, the partner draws more of the flower including three leaves, the center of the flower, and six petals, providing ten guesses. After several rounds of the game, guide students to realize that there are only two vowels in the Unit 25 review words, **a** and **e;** therefore, guessing these letters first is a smart strategy.

Intermediate

Word Meanings Write the spelling words on the board. Say each word and have students repeat it. Ask a volunteer to choose a word and use it in a sentence or tell something about its meaning. If necessary, clarify and expand the definition. Then have students write the word on a piece of paper. Students may look at the word on the board to be sure they have spelled it correctly. Students can hear the words from Units 21–24 in context sentences on the audio recording.

Picture Dictionary Shuffle flash cards for the review words and stack them facedown on a table. Have students fold a sheet of paper vertically and horizontally to create four sections. Have them cut along the folds to make four smaller sheets. Next, have students take turns drawing four cards from the stack. Have students use their small sheets of paper to draw and label a picture for each word. For example, students may draw themselves playing a game, raking leaves, boating on a lake, and planting a seed. Assemble the completed works in alphabetical order as a Class Picture Dictionary. Review words from other units may be added throughout the year.

Support for Spanish Speakers

Comparing Languages The English word **gate** is most often translated into Spanish as *puerta*, which means "door." Spanish speakers may need many experiences with real gates, book illustrations, and photographs to understand that a gate is a special kind of door usually found in a fence.

The English verb **be** translates into Spanish as two verbs, *ser* and *estar*. This difference does not present a problem for Spanish speakers who are learning English. However, for English speakers who are learning Spanish, mastering two words and concepts for the verb **be** is quite challenging!

Unit 25

Choose from the activities below to reinforce English language acquisition.

Advanced

Word Meanings Write the review words on the board. Tell students to use their thumbs to indicate how well they know each word. Thumbs-up means "I know the word," thumbs-down means "I do not know the word," and thumbs-sideways means "I'm not sure about this word." Say each word as you point to it and have students repeat. Use real objects, pictures, and pantomime to provide context and support meaning as needed.

Telephone Relay Organize groups of three or four. Have one student in each group write a sentence using a spelling word. The student pretends to dial a phone and whispers the sentence to another student, who in turn, dials a phone and whispers it to a third student, and so on. The final student writes the sentence. Students then compare the final sentence with the first. If the sentences do not match, impress on students the need to pronounce words clearly, even in a whisper. Repeat the activity. Have students slow down and pronounce each word clearly. The goal is to have the first and last sentences match.

Spell and Write Provide a set of flash cards for the spelling words or have students make their own. Place the cards facedown. Ask a student to select the top card, read the word, segment and blend the word, use it in a sentence, and then put the card facedown and write the word from memory.

Word Sort Explain that some words are naming words, some are action words, and some are telling words. Use **game, bake,** and **deep** as examples. Create a three-column chart on the board with the headings *Naming, Doing,* and *Telling*. Have students take turns writing the review words or taping word cards in the appropriate column. Point out that some words like **rake** and **name** can be used as naming words or doing words.

Advanced High

Word Meanings List the spelling review words on the board. Then ask questions that can be answered using spelling words. For example, *What word do you use to tell that you are happy or sad?* (feel) *What word describes what you do to make a cake?* (bake) *What word do you use to talk about yourself and a friend?* (we) *What word names something you open to go through a fence?* (gate)

Sentence Mix-ups Write simple sentences using the spelling words. Cut each sentence into word cards and place the cards in an envelope. Have students put the sentence back together. Encourage students to write and cut apart their own sentences for a partner to reconstruct.

Illustrated Stories Encourage students to draw a picture that includes illustrations of spelling words. Then have students use the spelling words to tell a partner about the picture. The partner can write the spelling words heard in the story.

Riddles Encourage students to think of riddles using the spelling words. They can share riddles with a partner and see if they can guess the words. For example, *I have two letters. One letter is an* **e**. *I say this word when I talk about myself.* (me)

Spelling Connections Online
Interactive online spelling activities provide additional ELL support.
www.spellingconnectionsonline.com

Unit 21: **Long a: CVCe**

1. came
2. name
3. same
4. game
5. gate
6. gave

A. Fill in each blank to write a different spelling word.

1. _ _ t _   gate

2. _ _ v _   gave

B. Write the words that end with **ame**.

3.   came   4.   name

5.   same   6.   game

139

Student Objectives
- Review the spelling pattern and words from Unit 21.

Reteaching the Skill
- Write **mat** on the board and ask students to read it aloud. Add **e** to the end of **mat** and say the new word. Point out that you can hear the name of the letter **a** in the word **mate**.
- Explain to students that when they hear the name of a vowel in a word, it is a long vowel sound. Point out that the word **mate** has a **long a** sound. Tell students that one way to spell the **long a** sound is with the pattern **a**-consonant-**e**. Remind them that the **e** makes no sound.
- Write **came, name, same, game, gate,** and **gave** on the board. Guide students in reading them aloud. Ask volunteers to circle the **a** and underline the **silent e** in each word.
- Have students complete page 139 independently.

Letters and Sounds Review
- Throughout the unit, use the **Alphabet and Picture Cards** to review letters and sounds. See pages Z32 for activity suggestions.

Review Word List

Home/School Spelling
Practice Master, *TRB*, p. 115

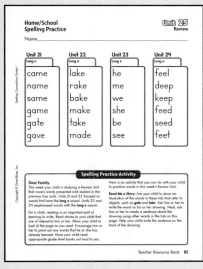

English

Home/School Spelling
Practice Master, *TRB*, p. 116

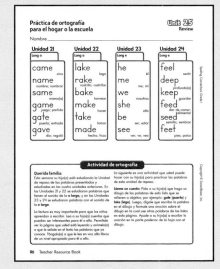

Spanish

Student Objectives
• Review the spelling pattern and words from Unit 22.

Reteaching the Skill
• Write **lake, rake, bake, make, take,** and **made** on the board. Read the words aloud and have students repeat. Ask students what vowel sound they hear in all the spelling words. **(long a)**
• Ask students what spelling pattern is used to spell the **long a** sound in each word. **(a-consonant-e)** Call on volunteers to circle the **a** and **e** in each word on the board. Have students read the words again. Ask which letter is silent or does not make a sound. **(e)**
• Tell students to complete page 140 independently.

Review

1. lake
2. rake
3. bake
4. make
5. take
6. made

Unit 22: Long a: CVCe

Fill in each blank to write a different spelling word.

__a__e

1. lake
2. rake
3. bake
4. make
5. take
6. made

140

Extra Pattern Practice

Make a Sentence
In this Think/Pair/Share activity, have partners write each spelling word on a small piece of paper. Then have them fold the papers in half and mix them up. Ask one student in each pair to pick any two of the words and read them. The second student should then try to say or write a sentence that uses both words. Have students take turns creating as many different sentences as they can from each pair of words.

Review

1. he
2. me
3. we
4. she
5. be
6. see

Unit 23: Long e: e, ee
Change the vowel. Write a spelling word with **long e**.

hi

1. **he**

sea

2. **see**

shy

3. **she**

wa

4. **we**

ma

5. **me**

bo

6. **be**

141

Student Objectives
• Review the spelling patterns and words from Unit 23.

Reteaching the Skill
• Write **he** on the board and read it aloud. Explain that the letter **e** spells the **long e** sound in this word, so **e** says its name. Explain that the **long e** sound can be spelled **e** or **ee**.
• Have students write **h, m, w, sh, b, s, e,** and **ee** on separate index cards. Read each spelling word aloud and have students arrange their letter cards to spell the word.
• Write **b, s, sh, m, h,** and **w** in a column on the board. Say a spelling word aloud. Invite a volunteer to identify the beginning sound on the board and then write **e** or **ee** to complete the word. Repeat for the remaining words.
• Tell students to complete page 141 independently.

More Fun With Spelling for Differentiation

 ### Digital Resources for Spelling Connections

Interactive digital resources include word sorts, pattern practice, and proofreading activities for individual and whole-group instruction. (Interactive whiteboard compatible; see p. Z32.)

 ### Spelling Connections Online

Interactive online spelling activities include word sorts, crossword puzzles, sentence completion, proofreading practice, and spelling bees with words from each unit (see p. Z32). www.spellingconnectionsonline.com

 ### Spelling Center Activities

Spelling Game Mats
Place one of the spelling games in a learning center to provide a fun way for students to practice their spelling words (see p. Z26).

Flip Folder
Students can use a Flip Folder to practice spelling words independently (see p. Z32).

Word Sort CD-ROM
Printable, unit-specific word cards for spelling and challenge words can be used for Teacher-Led, Individual, Buddy, and Speed Sorts (see p. Z31).

Student Objectives
• Review the spelling pattern and words from Unit 24.

Reteaching the Skill
• Write the spelling words on the board and have students read them aloud. Ask what vowel sound students hear in the middle of the words. (long e) Ask how the vowel sound is spelled. (ee)
• Review that rhyming words have the same ending sounds. Ask students which spelling words rhyme. (deep/keep, feed/seed) Ask students to think of another word with **ee** that rhymes with **feel** and one that rhymes with **feet**. (Possible answers: heel, peel, wheel; beet, greet, meet, sweet)
• Have a student write a spelling word on a sheet of paper and pass it to his or her partner. The partner changes one letter to write another spelling word and passes the paper back. Students continue as long as they can. Ask students if they were able to write all of the spelling words.
• Tell students to complete page 142 independently or as a class.
• Explain that they will use the answer to item 1 to answer item 2, item 2 to answer item 3, and answer 3 to answer item 4.

Review

1. feel
2. deep
3. keep
4. feed
5. seed
6. feet

142

Unit 24: Long e: ee

A. Follow the directions to write the spelling words.

1. Write the word that starts like and ends like **reed**.

   feed

2. Change one letter to make .

   seed

3. Change two letters to make a word that means **touch**.

   feel

4. Change one letter to make [feet image] .

   feet

B. Write the words that rhyme with **beep**.

5. **deep**   6. **keep**

Day 5

Assessment
Student Objectives
• Demonstrate mastery of the review unit spelling words.

Posttest Assessment Options
Option 1: Administer the posttest using the dictation sentences at right.
Option 2: Assess students using the standardized test. See the *Standardized Test Master Book*, p. 29.

Note: Posttest sentences for the on level and challenge lists are available on the audio *Spelling Connections* Posttest CD.

Posttest Sentences
1. I **see** a dog in our yard.
2. Jan says that **she** will bring the cups.
3. Kate **came** to my house.
4. The water is **deep**.
5. Mike will open the **gate** for us.
6. What is your **name**?
7. My mom **gave** me this book.
8. When will **we** go to the park?
9. I will **make** lunch for us.
10. Jake and Sam have the **same** shirt.

Standardized Test Master Book, p. 29

Standardized Test		Unit 25
Name		
Directions: Fill in the circle under the word that is spelled **wrong**.		

	Sample	grin	frog	kame
1.	bake		same	se
2.	made		che	feet
3.	take		he	cam
4.	deap		lake	me
5.	goet		make	feed
6.	rake		nane	feil
7.	seed		be	gav
8.	keep		wie	game
9.	mak		deep	made
10.	gate		saem	see

Standardized Test 29

Planner

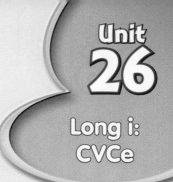

Day 1	Day 2

Day 1

Connections to **Thinking**

Student Objectives
- Identify the **long i** sound.
- Distinguish **short i** from **long i**.
- Read, spell, and write words with the **long i** sound in the CVCe pattern.

Instruction for All Students
- Pretest Dictation Sentences, p. T143B
- Connections to Thinking, p. 143
- Home/School Spelling Practice Masters (*Teacher Resource Book*, pp. 117–118)

 TEKS 1.22A, 1.22Bii, 1.22C

Connections to **Phonics**

Student Objectives
- Distinguish **short i** from **long i**.
- Add an **e** or substitute a vowel to spell **long i** words in the CVCe pattern.

Instruction for All Students
- Connections to Phonics, p. 144

Optional Practice
- Extra Pattern Practice Master (*Teacher Resource Book*, p. 119)

TEKS 1.22A, 1.22Bii, 1.22C

Spelling Words

bite
kite
time
life
line
mine

Challenge Words

vine
pine
hive
tide

Day 3	Day 4	Day 5

Day 2

Day 3

Connections to **Reading**

Student Objectives
- Write words with **long i** spelled with the CVCe pattern.
- Categorize words.

Instruction for All Students
- Connections to Reading, p. 145

Differentiated Instruction
- Challenge Words, p. 203

TEKS 1.22Bii, 1.22C

Connections to **Writing**

Student Objectives
- Identify spelling words in a paragraph.
- Use proofreading marks to revise writing.
- Use spelling words to write a letter.

Instruction for All Students
- Connections to Writing, p. 146

Differentiated Instruction
- Extra Challenge Practice Master (*Teacher Resource Book*, p. 120)

TEKS 1.22A, 1.22C, 1.22E

Assessment

Student Objectives
- Demonstrate mastery of the unit spelling words.

Assessment for All Students
- Posttest Dictation Sentences, p. T146, or
- *Standardized Test Master Book*, p. 30

Differentiated Assessment
- Challenge Dictation Sentences, p. T203

Unit 26 Materials

Student Edition
pp. 143–146, 203

Teacher Edition
pp. T143A–T146, T203

 Teacher Resource Book
Unit 26 Practice Masters,
pp. 117–120, and
Sound/Symbol Cards

Standardized Test Master Book
Unit 26 Test Master, p. 30

 Word Sort CD-ROM
Unit 26 Word Sort Cards for Teacher-
Led Sorts and Student Sorts

 **Digital Resources for
Spelling Connections**
Unit 26

Spelling Connections Online
www.spellingconnectionsonline.com

**Spelling Support for
English Language Learners***
Unit 26 Practice Masters and
Audio Conversation

Spelling Center Activities*
Spelling Game Mats
Flip Folder, *TRB*, p. 155

*Spelling Support for English Language
Learners *and* Spelling Center Activities *may
be used at any time during the week.*

Assessment

Pretest Sentences (See procedures on p. Z30.)

1. Will your dog **bite** me?
2. Please help me fly my **kite**.
3. Is there **time** to finish my picture?
4. This book is about **life** in the city.
5. Try to hop on this **line**.
6. The blue coat is **mine**.

The Science of Spelling ◀ • •

- **Silent e** has many functions in the English language. The most common is in the CVCe pattern, in which the final **e** marks the preceding vowel as a long vowel sound, as in **ripe**. A **silent e** can also mark the preceding vowel as having a long sound in the pattern CVe, as in **die** and **roe**. Other functions of a final **silent e** include marking **c** or **g** as having a soft sound as in **ounce, peace,** and **cage**.

ELL Support

Choose from the activities below to reinforce English language acquisition.

Beginning

Word Meaning Use total physical response to support word meaning. Make a statement and pantomime the action, such as *I can bite an apple.* Have students follow your lead and pantomime the action. Repeat the statement and have students repeat. Then have one student perform the action.

Spelling Pattern List the spelling words on the board. Point to each word, say it aloud, and have students repeat. Ask students what vowel sound is the same in all the words. (/ī/) Then ask students what else is the same in all the words. (They all have four letters; they all have i_e.) Explain that when this spelling pattern is in a word, the vowel sound is usually long. Students can hear the Unit 26 spelling words pronounced on the audio recording.

Flower Power Play a game similar to Hangman, except use a flower with a stem, four petals, and two leaves. Once students understand the idea of the game, have them play as partners to maximize practice time.

Complete Sentences List the spelling words. Say a sentence that includes a spelling word, but pause before you say the word. Have students chorally say the word that completes the sentence. For example, say *I want to fly a _____.* Students say **kite**. Continue with additional sentences and spelling words.

Intermediate

Word Meaning Provide each student with a copy of page 26 of *Spelling Support for English Language Learners.* Have students cut out the cards and make two stacks: picture cards and word cards. Explain the game to students and have partners play. Then have them work together on the remaining activities.

Word Frames Write the word frame _____ i _____ e on the board. Ask a student to write one consonant in each blank space to create a spelling word. Have the student read the word aloud. Then erase the consonants or write another word frame and have another student create a different spelling word.

Categorize Words Draw or show a picture of a foot. Then draw or show pictures of a sock, a shoe, and a mitten. Help students name all the pictures. Ask which pictures go with the first picture. (sock, shoe) Then write **bite** and pantomime biting something. Show or draw pictures of a mouth, teeth, and a hand. Ask students which pictures go with the word **bite**. (mouth, teeth)

Support for Spanish Speakers

Comparing Languages Because the digraphs **ai** and **ay** in Spanish are similar to the **long i** sound in English, Spanish-speaking students may spell the **long i** sound as **ai**. Students may also clip the **long i** sound and pronounce it like **short a** in words such as **glide**. Work with students to help them identify the **long i** sound and differentiate it from the **short i** sound.

Unit 26

Choose from the activities below to reinforce English language acquisition.

Advanced

Word Recognition Compose simple sentences that illustrate each spelling word. When you write the sentences on the board, mix up the spelling words so they are in the wrong sentences. Help students read each sentence and identify the incorrect word. Erase the word and have a student write the correct word. Example sentences: *I will fly my bite. What mine is it? Take a line out of this apple. Draw a time. How long is the kite of a frog? This book is life.*

Rhyming Words Write **ite, ime,** and **ine** on the board. Ask students to call out a consonant to write in front of each word part to make a spelling word. Then invite students to try different beginning consonants to make rhyming words. Possible words include **mite, site, dime, lime, mime, dine, fine, nine,** and **pine**.

Words in Context Have students listen to and interact with the audio recording to support learning the spelling words. Encourage students to practice the conversations and to improve pronunciations while gaining a better understanding of the word meanings. Partners can read the print form of the audio dialogue on page 52 of *Spelling Support for English Language Learners.*

Advanced High

Word Clues Write the spelling words on the board. Then provide clues to help students figure out each word. Examples: clock, minutes, hours (time); eat, teeth, chew (bite). Invite volunteers to give their own clues for other spelling words.

Word Grids Have students fold a sheet of paper into quarters. Have them write a spelling word in one quarter. In the second quarter they write something about the structure of the word. In the third quarter they write something about the meaning of the word. In the fourth quarter they write a sentence using the word. Example: *bite; long i; use your teeth; I will bite the plum.*

Write a Letter Ask students to write a letter to someone. Provide a template for the letter by writing *Dear* at the top of a sheet of writing paper and *Your Friend,* at the bottom with space for a name. Provide the following topics for students to write about: kite flying, a bug bite, a fun time at school. Have students choose a topic and write three sentences for the body of their letter. Remind them to write the recipient's name after *Dear* and then sign their own name at the bottom. Have students circle the spelling words they use.

Spelling Support for English Language Learners

Practice Master, p. 26

Practice Master, p. 52

 Audio Conversation available on CD

	English	Spanish
1.	bite	morder; mordida; picar; picadura
2.	kite	cometa; papalote
3.	time	tiempo; hora
4.	life	vida
5.	line	línea; raya
6.	mine	mío(a); mina; minar

English/Spanish Word List, p. 67

 **Spelling Connections Online**
Interactive online spelling activities provide additional ELL support.
www.spellingconnectionsonline.com

Connections to THINKING

Unit
26
Long i:
CVCe

Day 1

Unit
26

1. bite
2. kite
3. time
4. life
5. line
6. mine

A. Write the spelling words that end in **ine**.

1. line
2. mine

B. Write the spelling words that end in **ite**.

3. bite
4. kite

C. Use the letter clue to write a spelling word.

5. f life
6. m time

School Home

This unit targets the **long i** sound spelled **i-consonant-e.** Ask your child to name the spelling words that rhyme.

TEKS 1.22C Spell high-frequency words from a commonly used list.

143

Student Objectives
• Identify the **long i** sound.
• Distinguish **short i** from **long i**.
• Read, spell, and write words with the **long i** sound in the CVCe pattern.

Unit Pretest
• Administer the pretest on page T143B.

Teaching Tips
• Have students read each spelling word aloud, emphasizing and listening to /ī/.

 WORD SORT CD-ROM
• Conduct a **Teacher-Led Sort** (see p. Z31) to introduce the spelling pattern.
• Write **kit** and have students read it aloud. Ask them to name the vowel sound. (**short i**) Add **e** to spell **kite**. Have students read **kite** with you. Ask them to name the vowel sound. (**long i**) Point out that the **e** changes **i** to a long sound. Add that the **e** is silent.
• Use the Sound/Symbol Cards for **dive, hive, kite, slide, tire,** and **vine** to provide practice with the **long i** sound.
• Say the spelling words and have students repeat, listening for /ī/. Ask volunteers to write the words on the board.
• Have students complete the page independently or as a class.

Home/School Word Lists
• Have students take home the Home/School Spelling Practice Masters.

Home/School Practice

Home/School Spelling
Practice Master, *TRB*, p. 117

Home/School Spelling
Practice Master, *TRB*, p. 118

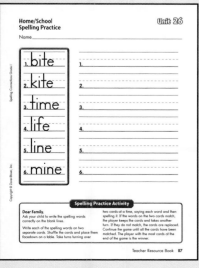

English

Spanish

TEKS 1.22A Use phonological knowledge to match sounds to letters to construct known words. 1.22Bii Use letter-sound patterns to spell: consonant-vowel-consonant-silent e (CVCe) words. 1.22C Spell high-frequency words from a commonly used list.

T143

Student Objectives
- Distinguish **short i** from **long i**.
- Add an **e** or substitute a vowel to spell **long i** words in the CVCe pattern.

Teaching Tips
- Remind students that when a word ends with a vowel-consonant-**e**, the vowel sound is usually long, and the **e** at the end of the word is silent.
- Write **bit** on the board and ask a volunteer to read it aloud. Ask the class, *Is the vowel sound long or short?* (**short**) *What can we do to this word to give it a long i sound?* (**add an e to the end**) Add an **e** to **bit** and ask students to read the new word. Ask, *What vowel sound do you hear now?* (**long i**)
- Write **lone**. Ask how a letter in **lone** could be changed to spell a spelling word. (**o to i**) Call on a volunteer to erase **o** and write **i** to spell **line**.
- Have students complete page 144 independently or as a class.

Extra Pattern Practice
- Use the optional practice master below for extra practice with **long i**.

WORD SORT CD-ROM
- Provide time for students to use a **Buddy Sort** (see p. Z31) to practice their spelling words with a partner.

Connections to PHONICS

A. Rewrite each word so it will have the **long i** sound.

1. bit

    bite

2. mane

    mine

3. kit

    kite

4. tame

    time

bite
kite
time
life
line
mine

B. Write the words that have the same beginning and middle sounds.

5. _____ **life**

6. _____ **line**

TEKS 1.22A Use phonological knowledge to match sounds to letters to construct known words.
1.22Bii Use letter-sound patterns to spell: consonant-vowel-consonant-silent e (CVCe) words.
1.22C Spell high-frequency words from a commonly used list.

144

Extra Pattern Practice

Extra Pattern Practice Master,
TRB, p. 119

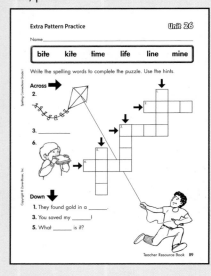

Long i Practice
Cut out a kite shape for each student. Say, *The word **kite** has the **long i** sound. I will read a list of words. When you hear the **long i** sound, make your kite fly. If you don't hear the **long i** sound, keep your kite on your desk.* Read the following words: **kite, me, spin, bite, time, up, life, not, line, mine, tide, pig, it, his, vine, man, pine, hive**.

TEKS 1.22A Use phonological knowledge to match sounds to letters to construct known words. **1.22Bii** Use letter-sound patterns to spell: consonant-vowel-consonant-silent e (CVCe) words. **1.22C** Spell high-frequency words from a commonly used list.

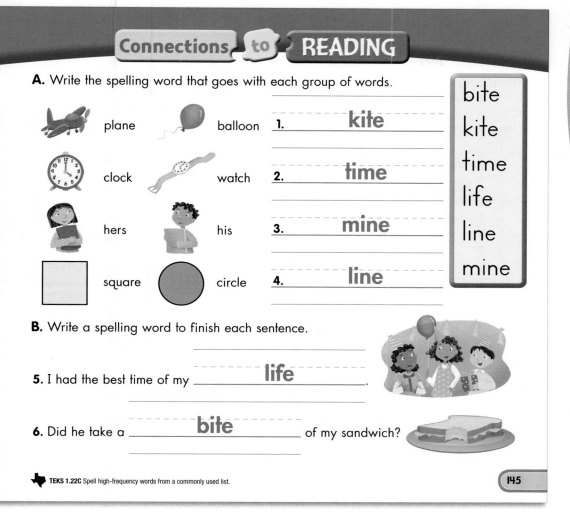

Connections to READING

A. Write the spelling word that goes with each group of words.

plane   balloon   1. **kite**

clock   watch   2. **time**

hers   his   3. **mine**

square   circle   4. **line**

Word Box:
- bite
- kite
- time
- life
- line
- mine

B. Write a spelling word to finish each sentence.

5. I had the best time of my **life**.

6. Did he take a **bite** of my sandwich?

TEKS 1.22C Spell high-frequency words from a commonly used list.

145

Student Objectives
- Write words with **long i** spelled with the CVCe pattern.
- Categorize words.

Teaching Tips
- Remind students that when a word ends with a consonant-vowel-consonant-**e,** the vowel sound is usually long, and the **e** at the end of the word is silent.
- Write the spelling words on the board and read them aloud. Have students repeat the words, emphasizing the **long i** sound.
- Show students a watch, a clock, and a calendar. Ask, *How are all these things alike?* (They tell time.) Point to the spelling words on the board. Ask, *Which word fits in a group with watch, clock, and calendar?* (time)
- Have students complete page 145.

Differentiated Instruction
- Use the **Challenge Words** activity on page 203 with students who are ready to transfer their knowledge of **long i** to new words.
- An Extra Challenge Practice Master is available on page 120 in the *TRB*.
- Dictation sentences for the challenge words are available on page T203.

More Fun With Spelling for Differentiation

Digital Resources for Spelling Connections
Interactive digital resources include word sorts, pattern practice, and proofreading activities for individual and whole-group instruction. (Interactive whiteboard compatible; see p. Z32.)

Spelling Connections Online
Interactive online spelling activities include word sorts, crossword puzzles, sentence completion, proofreading practice, and spelling bees with words from each unit (see p. Z32). www.spellingconnectionsonline.com

Spelling Center Activities

Spelling Game Mats
Place one of the spelling games in a learning center to provide a fun way for students to practice their spelling words (see p. Z26).

Flip Folder
Students can use a Flip Folder to practice spelling words independently (see p. Z32).

Word Sort CD-ROM
Printable, unit-specific word cards for spelling and challenge words can be used for Teacher-Led, Individual, Buddy, and Speed Sorts (see p. Z31).

TEKS 1.22Bii Use letter-sound patterns to spell: consonant-vowel-consonant-silent e (CVCe) words. **1.22C** Spell high-frequency words from a commonly used list.

T145

Unit 26 — Day 4

Student Objectives
- Identify spelling words in a paragraph.
- Use proofreading marks to revise writing.
- Use spelling words to write a letter.

Teaching Tips
- Read the introduction and review the proofreading marks with the class.
- Have students complete Part A independently.
- Read the directions for Part B. Explain to students that they will rewrite the letter on a separate sheet of paper.
- Read the directions for Part C. Tell students they can write about something that really happened or about something from their imagination.
- When students have finished, ask them to review their letters to make sure they have spelled spelling words correctly. Have them circle two words they are not sure about and check the spelling of each in a dictionary.
- Invite volunteers to read their letter aloud. Have the class identify spelling words used in each letter.

WORD SORT CD-ROM
- Invite students to practice for the weekly test by doing an **Individual Sort** or a **Speed Sort** (see p. Z31).

Day 5

Student Objectives
- Demonstrate mastery of the unit spelling words.

Posttest Assessment Options
Option 1: Administer the unit posttest using the dictation sentences at right.

Option 2: Assess students using the standardized test. See the *Standardized Test Master Book*, p. 30.

Note: Posttest sentences for the on level and challenge lists are available on the audio *Spelling Connections* Posttest CD.

Connections to WRITING

Use proofreading marks to fix what you read.
Change a small letter to a capital letter with ≡.
Change a capital letter to a small letter with a ╱.
Use a ⊙ to add a period.

Proofreading Marks	
≡	Capital Letter
╱	Small Letter
⊙	Add a Period

A. Underline the spelling words. Then write them on the lines below.

Dear Mike,
I had a good <u>time</u> today⊙ My <u>kite</u> flew the highest. I let the <u>line</u> out all the way. <u>m</u>y dog tried to <u>bite</u> it. The first ╱Prize was <u>mine</u>. I had never won a prize in my <u>life</u>.

Jake

1. time
2. kite
3. line
4. bite
5. mine
6. life

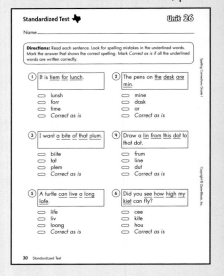

B. Rewrite the letter. Make the changes shown by the proofreading marks.

C. Write a letter about flying a kite. Try to use all the spelling words.

146

Word List: bite, kite, time, life, line, mine

TEKS 1.22A Use phonological knowledge to match sounds to letters to construct known words. 1.22C Spell high-frequency words from a commonly used list.

1-Minute Handwriting Hint

Good paper position is important when making a lowercase **i**.

•← DOT HALFWAY

Posttest Sentences
1. The president has a busy **life**.
2. Is it windy enough to fly my **kite**?
3. Please take just a little **bite**.
4. You will be leader next **time**.
5. Please wait in **line** for your lunch.
6. Your jacket is almost like **mine**.

Standardized Test Master Book, p. 30

Standardized Test — Unit 26

Name _____

Directions: Read each sentence. Look for spelling mistakes in the underlined words. Mark the answer that shows the correct spelling. Mark *Correct as is* if all the underlined words are written correctly.

① It is <u>tiem</u> for lunch.
- ○ lunsh
- ○ forr
- ○ time
- ○ Correct as is

② The pens on the <u>desk are min</u>.
- ○ mine
- ○ dask
- ○ ar
- ○ Correct as is

③ I want <u>a bite of that plum</u>.
- ○ biite
- ○ tot
- ○ plem
- ○ Correct as is

④ Draw a <u>lin from this dot</u> to that dot.
- ○ frum
- ○ line
- ○ dut
- ○ Correct as is

⑤ A turtle <u>can live a long lafe</u>.
- ○ life
- ○ liv
- ○ loong
- ○ Correct as is

⑥ Did you <u>see how high my kiel</u> can fly?
- ○ cee
- ○ kile
- ○ hou
- ○ Correct as is

30 Standardized Test

 TEKS 1.22A Use phonological knowledge to match sounds to letters to construct known words. 1.22C Spell high-frequency words from a commonly used list. 1.22E Use resources to find correct spellings.

Planner

Unit 27
Long i: CVCe

Day 1	Day 2

Day 1

Connections to **Thinking**

Student Objectives
- Identify the **long i** sound.
- Read, spell, and write words with the **long i** sound in the CVCe pattern.

Instruction for All Students
- Pretest Dictation Sentences, p. T147B
- Connections to Thinking, p. 147
- Home/School Spelling Practice Masters (*Teacher Resource Book*, pp. 121–122)

 TEKS 1.22A, 1.22Bii, 1.22C

Connections to **Phonics**

Student Objectives
- Blend onsets and rimes to spell **long i** words with the CVCe pattern.
- Add **-s** to spell plural spelling words.

Instruction for All Students
- Connections to Phonics, p. 148

Optional Practice
- Extra Pattern Practice Master (*Teacher Resource Book*, p. 123)

 TEKS 1.22A, 1.22Bii, 1.22C, 1.22D

Spelling Words
bike
like
hike
hide
ride
side

Challenge Words
wipe
rice
wide
dive

Day 3	Day 4	Day 5

Day 2

Day 3

Connections to **Reading**

Student Objectives
- Write and spell words with the **long i** sound to complete sentences.

Instruction for All Students
- Connections to Reading, p. 149

Differentiated Instruction
- Challenge Words, p. 204

 TEKS 1.22C

Connections to **Writing**

Student Objectives
- Identify spelling words in a poem.
- Use proofreading marks to revise writing.
- Use spelling words to write a poem.

Instruction for All Students
- Connections to Writing, p. 150

Differentiated Instruction
- Extra Challenge Practice Master (*Teacher Resource Book*, p. 124)

 TEKS 1.22A, 1.22Bii, 1.22C

Assessment

Student Objectives
- Demonstrate mastery of the unit spelling words.

Assessment for All Students
- Posttest Dictation Sentences, p. T150, or
- *Standardized Test Master Book*, p. 31

Differentiated Assessment
- Challenge Dictation Sentences, p. T204

Unit 27 Materials

Student Edition
pp. 147–150, 204

Teacher Edition
pp. T147A–T150, T204

 Teacher Resource Book
Unit 27 Practice Masters,
pp. 121–124, and
Sound/Symbol Cards

 Standardized Test Master Book
Unit 27 Test Master, p. 31

 Word Sort CD-ROM
Unit 27 Word Sort Cards for Teacher-
Led Sorts and Student Sorts

 **Digital Resources for
Spelling Connections**
Unit 27

Spelling Connections Online
www.spellingconnectionsonline.com

**Spelling Support for
English Language Learners***
Unit 27 Practice Masters and
Audio Conversation

Spelling Center Activities*
Spelling Game Mats
Flip Folder, *TRB*, p. 155

*Spelling Support for English Language
Learners *and Spelling Center Activities may
be used at any time during the week.*

Assessment

Pretest Sentences (See procedures on p. Z30.)

1. I have a horn on my **bike**.
2. Would you **like** to stay for lunch?
3. We are going to **hike** through the woods.
4. Kip tried to **hide** under the steps!
5. May I **ride** the white horse?
6. One **side** of the paper is blank.

The Science of Spelling ◀ • •

- The **long i** sound can be spelled several different ways. These spelling variations represent differences in pronunciation that have converged into the same sound. Some are more frequent than others. The **long i** sound is spelled **i** (**climb, high**) 79% of the time, **y** (**shy**) 16% of the time, and **ie** (**lie**) 3% of the time. All other spellings (**ei, ai, ey,** and **uy**) are used less than 1% of the time.

ELL Support

Choose from the activities below to reinforce English language acquisition.

Beginning

Word Meaning Introduce the spelling words using gestures, realia, and pictures to provide context and demonstrate word meaning. For example, show a picture of a bike. Say **bike** and have students repeat. Write the word on the board, say it again, and have students repeat. Continue with the remaining words.

Build Words List the spelling words on the board. Provide students with letter cards for **h, d, l, k, r, s, b, i,** and **e.** Have students choose a word on the board and then make the word by selecting and placing letter cards in the correct order. Have students read the word aloud with you. Continue with the remaining words.

Complete Sentences Say, *I will go on a hike.* Have students repeat the sentence. Then write the sentence on the board. Have students read the sentence with you as you point to each word. Point to **hike** and tell students it is one of the spelling words. Then erase **hike.** Read the sentence again, pointing at each word. Then pause and point to the blank space. Have students say **hike.** Invite a volunteer to write the word in the space and read the sentence. Continue with the remaining spelling words.

Intermediate

Word Meaning Make flash cards for the spelling words. Hold up each card and read the word. Have students repeat. Then use gestures, pantomime, and pictures to provide context and support word meaning. Ask questions about the words and have volunteers select and read a card as the answer. For example, *What has two wheels that you can ride?* (**bike**)

Word Chains Give pairs of students several strips of paper and tape or paste. Have the first partner write a spelling word on a strip and tape the ends together. The second partner changes one consonant in the word and writes another spelling word, then threads the strip through the first one and tapes the ends. Partners continue until they have written all of the words and have made a paper chain.

More Than One Display a box. Point to one side and say, *This is one side of the box.* Write **side** on the board, read it aloud, and have students repeat it. Then have students count with you as you point to each side of the box. Ask, *How many sides did we count?* (4) Ask, *What sound did you hear at the end of **sides**?* (/z/) Have a student write an **s** at the end of **side** on the board. Read the word **sides** and have students repeat. Explain that adding an **s** to a word makes the word mean more than one.

Support for Spanish Speakers

Comparing Languages Spanish speakers may have difficulty hearing and pronouncing some English consonants as consonant sounds are quite different in the two languages. For example, the consonant sound /**d**/ is much softer in Spanish and somewhat similar to the unvoiced /**th**/ in English. Give students opportunities to practice listening to and pronouncing spelling words with a native English-speaking adult one-on-one. Brief sessions every day or several times a week can be especially helpful. Praise students' efforts and accept their gradual improvements in English pronunciation.

Unit 27

Choose from the activities below to reinforce English language acquisition.

Advanced

Rhyming Words Remind students that rhyming words have the same ending sounds. Say **rake** and **take** as an example. List the spelling words and read them aloud. Have students repeat. Ask them which words rhyme with **bike** (like, hike) and which words rhyme with **hide** (ride, side). Write the following sentences on the board and ask students to help you complete the poem with words that rhyme.

*Get in the car for a **ride**.*

Or play a game of ____. (hide)

*Maybe we can go on a **hike**.*

But I want to ride my ____. (bike)

I am not sure what I ____. (like)

Complete Sentences Provide each student with a copy of page 27 of *Spelling Support for English Language Learners.* Have students work together to complete the sentences with the spelling words. Then have students discuss the activity at the bottom of the page. Have them take turns reading sentences they write about their hike.

Words in Context Have students listen to the conversation on the audio recording. Partners can read the print form of the audio dialogue on page 52 of *Spelling Support for English Language Learners.* Encourage students to practice the conversation to improve their pronunciation and gain a better understanding of word meanings.

Advanced High

Picture Dictionary Encourage students to add the spelling words to their ongoing picture dictionary. Prompt them to write each word and draw a picture that illustrates it. Also have them write a sentence using the word.

Vowel Sounds Tell students you will say a list of words. If they hear the **long i** sound, they say, *I like that.* Say, **hike, mine, keep, hide, lake, bike, made, feel, line, ride, name, side, gave, feet,** and **kite.** Then write the words on the board. Ask students to circle the words that have the **long i** sound. Ask them how they know the vowel sound is **long i.** (i-consonant-e)

Rhyming Sentences Write the following sentence starter on the board: *I like to ____.* Have students write pairs of sentences beginning with these words and ending with words that rhyme. For example, students may write: *I like to ride. I like to hide.* Ask students to read their sentences.

Storytelling Provide flash cards of the spelling words. Have partners pick two words and work on a story suggested by the words. Tell students that the story can be silly or exciting. Have them write and illustrate their story and read it to another pair of students.

Spelling Support for English Language Learners

Practice Master, p. 27

Practice Master, p. 52

Audio Conversation available on CD

English/Spanish Word List, p. 67

Spelling Connections Online
Interactive online spelling activities provide additional ELL support.
www.spellingconnectionsonline.com

Finish each spelling word.

1. bike
2. like
3. hike
4. hide
5. ride
6. side

1. h__d__

hide

2. r__d__

ride

3. l__k__

like

4. h__k__

hike

5. s__d__

side

6. b__k__

bike

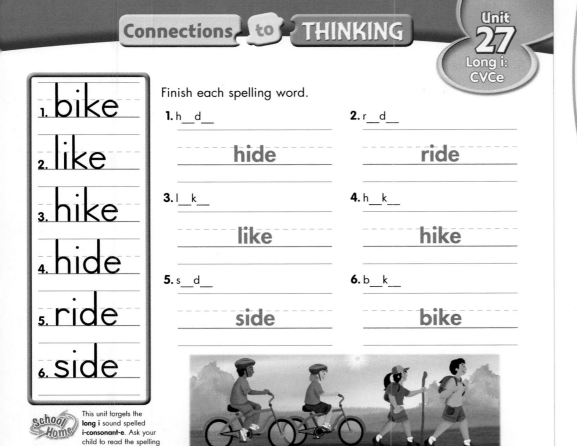

School Home This unit targets the **long i** sound spelled **i-consonant-e**. Ask your child to read the spelling words aloud.

 TEKS 1.22C Spell high-frequency words from a commonly used list.

147

Student Objectives
- Identify the **long i** sound.
- Read, spell, and write words with the **long i** sound in the CVCe pattern.

Unit Pretest
- Administer the pretest on page T147B.

Teaching Tips

WORD SORT CD-ROM

- Conduct a **Teacher-Led Sort** (see p. Z31) to reinforce the spelling pattern.
- Use the Sound/Symbol Cards for **dive, hike, kite, slide,** and **vine** to review the **long i** sound.
- Say the spelling words and have students repeat them, listening for the **long i** sound. Call on volunteers to write the words on the board. Ask students what letter pattern they notice in all the words. **(consonant-i-consonant-e)** Remind students that **i** is a vowel and the **e** is silent.
- Have students complete the page independently or as a class.

Home/School Word Lists TRB
- Have students take home the Home/School Spelling Practice Masters.

Home/School Practice

Home/School Spelling
Practice Master, *TRB*, p. 121

Home/School Spelling
Practice Master, *TRB*, p. 122

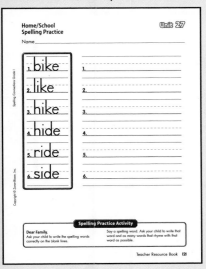

English

Spanish

TEKS 1.22A Use phonological knowledge to match sounds to letters to construct known words. **1.22Bii** Use letter-sound patterns to spell: consonant-vowel-consonant-silent e (CVCe) words. **1.22C** Spell high-frequency words from a commonly used list.

T147

Student Objectives
- Blend onsets and rimes to spell **long i** words with the CVCe pattern.
- Add **-s** to spell plural spelling words.

Teaching Tips
- Write the spelling words on the board and read them aloud with students. Ask, *What vowel sound do you hear in all the words?* **(long i)**
- Write **ike** on the board. Ask, *How would you pronounce this?* **(/ī/ /k/)** *Why?* **(CVCe rule)** *What happens when we add an **l**?* Write **l** in front of **ike**. Blend the sounds to say a spelling word. **(like)** Erase **l**. Ask, *What are some other words we could make by adding a consonant to the beginning of **ike**?* **(Possible responses: bike, dike, hike, mike, pike, tike)** Repeat with **ide**.
- Write **bike**. Ask how to make it mean "more than one **bike**." **(add s)** Have a volunteer add the **s**. Have students read the word aloud.
- Have students complete page 148 independently or as a class.

Extra Pattern Practice **TRB**
- Use the optional practice master below for extra practice with **long i**.

WORD SORT CD-ROM
- Provide time for students to use a **Buddy Sort** (see p. Z31) to practice their spelling words with a partner.

Extra Pattern Practice

Extra Pattern Practice Master,
TRB, p. 123

A. Put the sounds together. Say the words and then write them.

1. l + ike = **like**

2. h + ide = **hide**

3. r + ide = **ride**

Word box:
bike
like
hike
hide
ride
side

B. Add **s** to a spelling word to tell about the pictures.

4. 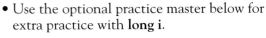 + = **bikes**

5. + = **hikes**

6. + = **sides**

TEKS 1.22A Use phonological knowledge to match sounds to letters to construct known words. **1.22Bii** Use letter-sound patterns to spell: consonant-vowel-consonant-silent e (CVCe) words. **1.22C** Spell high-frequency words from a commonly used list. **1.22D** Spell base words with inflectional endings.

Long i Practice
Cut out large shapes of the letters **b, l, h, r,** and **s.** Write **ike** and **ide** on large cards. Say **bike, like,** and **hike.** Ask, *How are these words alike?* **(they end with /ī/ /k/)** Say, *The sounds /ī/ /k/ together do not make a word.* Then say **bike.** Ask what sound begins the word. **(/b/)** Ask a volunteer to hold the card for **ike.** Then call on another student to hold the letter **b** next to it. Have students read the word. Continue with the other spelling words in the **ike** word family. Repeat the activity with the **ide** word family.

TEKS 1.22A Use phonological knowledge to match sounds to letters to construct known words. **1.22Bii** Use letter-sound patterns to spell: consonant-vowel-consonant-silent e (CVCe) words. **1.22C** Spell high-frequency words from a commonly used list. **1.22D** Spell base words with inflectional endings.

Write the missing spelling words.

In the City

I **1.** living in the city.

I can **2.** on a train.

I can **3.** in the park.

I can **4.** on the street.

I can lean on the **5.** of the building and watch the people go by.

I can ride my **6.** to the store.

1. **like**	2. **ride**
3. **hike**	4. **hide**
5. **side**	6. **bike**

Word box:
bike
like
hike
hide
ride
side

TEKS 1.22C Spell high-frequency words from a commonly used list.

149

Student Objectives
• Write and spell words with the **long i** sound to complete sentences.

Teaching Tips
• Remind students that when a word includes the consonant-vowel-consonant-**e** pattern, the vowel is usually long, and the **e** at the end of the word is silent. Read the spelling words aloud with students.
• Write *I _____ the bus to school* on the board. Read the sentence aloud. Ask, *Which spelling word would make the most sense in this sentence?* (ride) *How do you know?* (The sentence is about a bus, and you can ride a bus.) Point out that the word **bus** is an important clue. Remind students to look for clues in the sentences and in the pictures that will help them complete the sentences.
• Have students complete page 149. Read the completed sentences aloud.

Differentiated Instruction
• Use the **Challenge Words** activity on page 204 with students who are ready to transfer their knowledge of **short i** to new words.
• An Extra Challenge Practice Master is available on page 124 in the *TRB*.
• Dictation sentences for the challenge words are available on page T204.

More Fun With Spelling for Differentiation

▶ Digital Resources for Spelling Connections
Interactive digital resources include word sorts, pattern practice, and proofreading activities for individual and whole-group instruction. (Interactive whiteboard compatible; see p. Z32.)

▶ Spelling Connections Online
Interactive online spelling activities include word sorts, crossword puzzles, sentence completion, proofreading practice, and spelling bees with words from each unit (see p. Z32). www.spellingconnectionsonline.com

🧩 Spelling Center Activities

Spelling Game Mats
Place one of the spelling games in a learning center to provide a fun way for students to practice their spelling words (see p. Z26).

Flip Folder
Students can use a Flip Folder to practice spelling words independently (see p. Z32).

Word Sort CD-ROM
Printable, unit-specific word cards for spelling and challenge words can be used for Teacher-Led, Individual, Buddy, and Speed Sorts (see p. Z31).

TEKS 1.22C Spell high-frequency words from a commonly used list.

T149

Student Objectives
- Identify spelling words in a poem.
- Use proofreading marks to revise writing.
- Use spelling words to write a poem.

Teaching Tips
- Read the introduction and review the proofreading marks with the class.
- Have students complete Part A independently.
- Read the directions for Part B. Explain to students that they will rewrite the poem on a separate sheet of paper.
- Read the directions for Part C. Give students a few minutes to brainstorm ideas. Remind them that poems often use sensory words, or words that tell how things look, feel, sound, and smell. Encourage students to use sensory words in their poems.
- Invite volunteers to read their poems aloud. Discuss any sensory words. Have the class identify the spelling words used.

WORD SORT CD-ROM
- Invite students to practice for the weekly test by doing an **Individual Sort** or a **Speed Sort** (see p. Z31).

Connections to WRITING

A. Underline the spelling words. Then write them on the lines below.

Proofreading Marks
- ☰ Capital Letter
- / Small Letter
- ⊙ Add a Period

bike
like
hike
hide
ride
side

Me

I am six years old,
As happy as can be⊙
I can <u>ride</u> a <u>bike</u>,
And Ǥo on a <u>hike</u>.
I go round the <u>side</u>
In a game of <u>hide</u>.
My name is <u>v</u>ictor
And I <u>like</u> being me.

　　—Victor A. Wheeler

1. ride
2. bike
3. hike
4. side
5. hide
6. like

B. Rewrite the poem. Make the changes shown by the proofreading marks.

C. Write a poem that tells about you. Try to use all the spelling words.

150

TEKS 1.22A Use phonological knowledge to match sounds to letters to construct known words. **1.22C** Spell high-frequency words from a commonly used list.

1-Minute Handwriting Hint

The backward circle in the lowercase **d** begins below the midline. Be sure that the vertical stroke touches the circle.

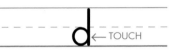

Day 5

Student Objectives
- Demonstrate mastery of the unit spelling words.

Posttest Assessment Options

Option 1: Administer the unit posttest using the dictation sentences at right.

Option 2: Assess students using the standardized test. See the *Standardized Test Master Book*, p. 31.

Note: Posttest sentences for the on level and challenge lists are available on the audio *Spelling Connections* Posttest CD.

Posttest Sentences

1. Does your **bike** have reflectors?
2. The tree's north **side** has moss.
3. Would you **like** to see my picture?
4. Our class is going for a **hike** today.
5. Can you find me if I **hide**?
6. I **like** to **ride** in the back of the bus.

Standardized Test Master Book, p. 31

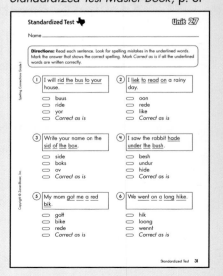

 TEKS 1.22A Use phonological knowledge to match sounds to letters to construct known words. **1.22Bii** Use letter-sound patterns to spell: consonant-vowel-consonant-silent e (CVCe) words. **1.22C** Spell high-frequency words from a commonly used list.

Planner

Day 1 | Day 2

Day 1

Connections to **Thinking**

Student Objectives
- Identify the **long o** sound.
- Read, spell, and write words with the **long o** sound in the CVCe and CV patterns.

Instruction for All Students
- Pretest Dictation Sentences, p. T151B
- Connections to Thinking, p. 151
- Home/School Spelling Practice Masters (*Teacher Resource Book*, pp. 125–126)

 TEKS 1.22Bii, 1.22C

Connections to **Phonics**

Student Objectives
- Read, spell, and write **long o** words in the CVCe and CV patterns.
- List spelling words in alphabetical order.

Instruction for All Students
- Connections to Phonics, p. 152

Optional Practice
- Extra Pattern Practice Master (*Teacher Resource Book*, p. 127)

 TEKS 1.22A, 1.22Bii, 1.22C

Spelling Words
no
go
so
hope
rope
home

Challenge Words
hole
cone
dome
hose

Day 3 | Day 4 | Day 5

Day 2

Connections to **Reading**

Student Objectives
- Write and spell words with the **long o** sound to complete a paragraph.
- Use a dictionary to check and correct misspelled words.

Instruction for All Students
- Connections to Reading, p. 153

Differentiated Instruction
- Challenge Words, p. 205

 TEKS 1.22C, 1.22E

Connections to **Writing**

Student Objectives
- Identify spelling words in a paragraph.
- Use proofreading marks to revise writing.
- Use spelling words to write about a topic.

Instruction for All Students
- Connections to Writing, p. 154

Differentiated Instruction
- Extra Challenge Practice Master (*Teacher Resource Book*, p. 128)

 TEKS 1.22A, 1.22Bii, 1.22C

Day 3

Assessment

Student Objectives
- Demonstrate mastery of the unit spelling words.

Assessment for All Students
- Posttest Dictation Sentences, p. T154, or
- *Standardized Test Master Book*, p. 32

Differentiated Assessment
- Challenge Dictation Sentences, p. T205

Unit 28 Materials

Student Edition
pp. 151–154, 205

Teacher Edition
pp. T151A–T154, T205

 Teacher Resource Book
Unit 28 Practice Masters,
pp. 125–128, and
Sound/Symbol Cards

 Standardized Test Master Book
Unit 28 Test Master, p. 32

 Word Sort CD-ROM
Unit 28 Word Sort Cards for Teacher-
Led Sorts and Student Sorts

 Digital Resources for Spelling Connections
Unit 28

 Spelling Connections Online
www.spellingconnectionsonline.com

Spelling Support for English Language Learners*
Unit 28 Practice Masters and
Audio Conversation

Spelling Center Activities*
Spelling Game Mats
Flip Folder, *TRB*, p. 155

*Spelling Support for English Language
Learners *and Spelling Center Activities may
be used at any time during the week.*

Assessment

Pretest Sentences (See procedures on p. Z30.)

1. There are **no** eggs in the nest.
2. May we **go** fishing?
3. I am **so** excited!
4. I **hope** that we can play outside.
5. Will you jump **rope** with me?
6. This dog followed me **home**.

The Science of Spelling ◄···

- In a closed syllable the vowel is followed by a consonant (**sun, cap**). In an open syllable, nothing follows the vowel (**no, he**). In a closed syllable, the vowel is short. In an open syllable, the vowel is long.

- As students learn to spell words syllable by syllable, their understanding of open and closed syllables will be a big help. For example, a student spelling a word with a double consonant in the middle, such as **button** or **mitten,** will know to write two consonants even though only one is pronounced and at the beginning of the second syllable. Because the first vowel is short, the student will know that it is followed by a consonant.

ELL Support

Choose from the activities below to reinforce English language acquisition.

Beginning

Word Meaning Make flash cards for the spelling words. Hold up each card, spell the word, and then say it. Have students repeat. Choose gestures, pantomime, or pictures along with descriptions or sample sentences as the best method to provide context and illustrate the meaning of each word. For example, shake your head back and forth and say **no**.

Develop Phonemic Awareness List the spelling words on the board. Read the words aloud and ask students what vowel sound they hear in all the words. (long o) Read each word again, segmenting the sounds as in /r/ /ō/ /p/. Ask students how many sounds they hear. Point out that there are four letters in **rope,** but only three sounds. The final **e** in **hope, rope,** and **home** is silent. Students can hear the Unit 28 spelling words pronounced on the audio recording.

Word Sort Explain that the spelling words show the **long o** sound spelled two ways: **o** by itself and **o_e**. Provide flash cards for the words and ask students to sort them according to how the **long o** sound is spelled.

Fix Words List the spelling words on the board. Say, *I will go home.* Write the sentence as *I will goo hom.* Tell students that there are two spelling words in the sentence, but they are not correctly spelled. Have students compare the words in the sentence to the list of spelling words to find the misspelled words. (go, home) Then ask volunteers to come up and correct the words.

Intermediate

Word Meaning Use student-friendly sentences to illustrate the meaning of each spelling word. For example, say, *I will go to the door.* Use pantomime or gestures to provide context and support word meaning as you say each sentence. Invite students to repeat the sentence and the action.

Yes and No Tell students you will say words that have the **long o** sound and words that do not have **long o**. Have them say *no* when the word does not have long **o** and *yes* when it does. Say rope, make, keep, home, so, bike, go, kite, hope, and no. Then write the words on the board. Invite volunteers to point to a word with **long o** and read it aloud.

Spell a Word Provide pairs of students with a list of the spelling words. Have the first partner choose a word and write it incorrectly on a sheet of paper. The second partner writes the word correctly without looking at the list. Then that partner chooses a word. Have students continue until each partner has correctly spelled all of the words.

Support for Spanish Speakers

Comparing Languages In Spanish, each letter stands for one sound, so students may need practice pronouncing and spelling words with the CVC and CVCe patterns. Students will be familiar with the **long o** sound as it is similar in Spanish and English.

Cognates Explain that the word **no** is pronounced the same and has the same meaning in English and in Spanish.

Choose from the activities below to reinforce English language acquisition.

Advanced

Complete Sentences Provide each student with a copy of page 28 of *Spelling Support for English Language Learners*. Invite students to find a partner to work with to complete the sentences on the page. Then have students talk about how they would finish the sentence starting with *I hope* _____. Have them write their sentences and read them to each other.

Spelling Word Dialogue Have partners listen to the conversation on the audio recording. Then have them read the print form on page 53 of *Spelling Support for English Language Learners*. Encourage students to practice the conversation to improve expression and fluency. Invite them to continue the conversation with sentences of their own.

Long O Say **go** and **home**. Ask students what vowel sound they hear in both words. (long o) Point out that the sound is spelled differently in each word. Write the spelling words on the board and have students underline the letters that spell the **long o** sound. Then have partners take turns saying a sentence using a spelling word. The second partner listens and identifies the spelling word. Encourage students to write their sentences and proofread each other's papers.

Advanced High

Words in Context Model how to write a sentence that illustrates the meaning of a spelling word. For example, *My dog tugs on the rope.* Have students find a partner. Have them write a sentence for each spelling word.

Expressive Words Have students choose a spelling word and, with a partner, practice saying the word in different tones of voice to illustrate word meaning. For example, they can say a word in a happy, sad, angry, excited, bored, scared, or questioning voice. Encourage students to create sentences that show why the word was said in that tone.

Illustrate Words Have students illustrate the paragraph on page 154 in their books to show how they interpret the content. Encourage them to label items in the picture that reflect spelling words, such as **go, rope,** and **home**. Encourage students to describe their picture or tell a story about it to a partner.

Tic-Tac-Toe Demonstrate how to play tic-tac-toe. Then prepare grids with spaces large enough to write a spelling word. Have partners play the game. One partner uses the spelling words **no, go, so**. The other partner uses **home, hope, rope**. They take turns writing their words in the spaces horizontally, diagonally, and vertically. The first partner to write three words in a straight line wins the game.

Spelling Support for English Language Learners

Practice Master, p. 28

Practice Master, p. 53

Audio Conversation available on CD

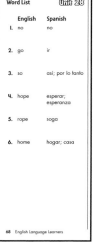

English/Spanish Word List, p. 68

 Spelling Connections Online
Interactive online spelling activities provide additional ELL support.
www.spellingconnectionsonline.com

A. Write the spelling words that have **o** and **e**.

1. hope   2. rope

3. home

B. Write the spelling words that end in **o**.

4. no   5. go

6. so

1. no
2. go
3. so
4. hope
5. rope
6. home

School Home!
This unit targets the **long o** sound spelled **o** and **o-consonant-e**. Ask your child to circle the **o-consonant-e** spelling pattern in the last three spelling words.

TEKS 1.22C Spell high-frequency words from a commonly used list.

151

Student Objectives
• Identify the **long o** sound.
• Read, spell, and write words with the **long o** sound in the CVCe and CV patterns.

Unit Pretest
• Administer the pretest on page T151B.

Teaching Tips
WORD SORT CD-ROM

• Conduct a **Teacher-Led Sort** (see p. Z31) to introduce the spelling patterns.
• Read the spelling words aloud. Ask, *What vowel sound do you hear in these words?* (long o) *What sound does **long o** make?* (/ō/)
• Write **hope, rope,** and **home** on the board. Ask a volunteer to circle the consonants and underline **o** and **e** in each word. Remind students that when a word includes the consonant-vowel-consonant-e pattern, the vowel sound is usually long, and the **e** at the end of the word is silent. Have students read the words aloud.
• Then write **go, no,** and **so.** Point out that **o** by itself can make the sound /ō/. Have a volunteer underline **o** in each word.
• Have students complete the page independently or as a class.

Home/School Word Lists **TRB**
• Have students take home the Home/School Spelling Practice Masters.

Home/School Practice

Home/School Spelling
Practice Master, *TRB,* p. 125

Home/School Spelling
Practice Master, *TRB,* p. 126

Home/School Spelling Practice	Unit 28
Name	
1. no	1.
2. go	2.
3. so	3.
4. hope	4.
5. rope	5.
6. home	6.

Spelling Practice Activity

Dear Family,
Ask your child to write the spelling words correctly on the blank lines.

Ask your child to say to name each of the spelling words on this list. For example, *I have no crayons.* After your child makes a sentence

with one spelling word, challenge him or her to make a sentence using two of the spelling words and then with three of the spelling words. Finally, encourage him or her to make one sentence using as many of the spelling words as possible.

Teacher Resource Book 125

Práctica de ortografía para el hogar o la escuela	Unit 28
Name	
1. no	1.
2. go	2.
3. so	3.
4. hope	4.
5. rope	5.
6. home	6.

Actividad de ortografía

Querida familia,
Pida a su hijo(a) que escriba correctamente las palabras de ortografía en los renglones en blanco.

Pida a su hijo(a) que cree una oración para cada palabra de la lista. Por ejemplo, *I have no crayons.* (No tengo crayones.) Cuando termine,

animelo(a) a crear oraciones que tengan dos palabras de la lista y, luego, anímelo(a) a que haga oraciones que tengan tres palabras de la lista. Por último, anímelo(a) a que trate de hacer una oración que tenga la mayor cantidad de palabras de la lista.

126 Teacher Resource Book

English   Spanish

 TEKS 1.22Bii Use letter-sound patterns to spell: consonant-vowel-consonant-silent e (CVCe) words. **1.22C** Spell high-frequency words from a commonly used list.

T151

Student Objectives
- Read, spell, and write **long o** words in the CVCe and CV patterns.
- List spelling words in alphabetical order.

Teaching Tips
- List the spelling words on the board. Read the words aloud and have students repeat. Ask, *What vowel sound do you hear in all of the words?* (long o)
- Point to **rope**. Ask students how the **long o** sound is spelled. (o_e) Then ask which spelling word rhymes with **rope**. (hope)
- Use an alphabet chart to review alphabetical order. Then point to **no, go,** and **so**. Ask students what letter they would use in each word to help them put the words in **a-b-c** order. (the first letter)
- Have students complete page 152 independently or as a class.

Extra Pattern Practice 📕TRB
- Use the optional practice master below for extra practice with **long o**.

💿WORD SORT CD-ROM
- Provide time for students to use a **Buddy Sort** (see p. Z31) to practice their spelling words with a partner.

Connections to PHONICS

A. Use the clues to find spelling words. Write the words.

This word rhymes with **dome**.

1. **home**

These words rhyme with each other, and they have a **silent e**.

2. **hope**   3. **rope**

B. Write the spelling words that end in **o** in a-b-c order.

4. **go**

5. **no**

6. **so**

| no |
| go |
| so |
| hope |
| rope |
| home |

TEKS **1.22A** Use phonological knowledge to match sounds to letters to construct known words. **1.22Bii** Use letter-sound patterns to spell: consonant-vowel-consonant-silent e (CVCe) words. **1.22C** Spell high-frequency words from a commonly used list.

Extra Pattern Practice

Extra Pattern Practice Master,
TRB, p. 127

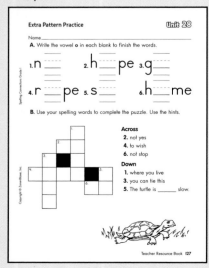

Long o Practice
Say the spelling words **no, go, so, hope, rope,** and **home**, emphasizing the **long o** sound. Have students repeat the words. Ask which words end with the **long o** sound (**no, go, so**) and which have the **long o** sound in the middle. (**hope, rope, home**) Place a long rope on the floor in an open area. Ask students to stand on one side of the rope. Say, *The word **rope** has the **long o** sound. One at a time, name another word with this sound. Then jump over the rope.* Continue until each student has given a word and jumped. Finally, write the spelling words on the board and show students which letters spell the **long o** sound.

TEKS **1.22A** Use phonological knowledge to match sounds to letters to construct known words. **1.22Bii** Use letter-sound patterns to spell: consonant-vowel-consonant-silent e (CVCe) words. **1.22C** Spell high-frequency words from a commonly used list.

Connections to READING

A. Write the spelling words to finish the letter.

Dear Tim,

My __1.__ is in the desert. I __2.__ to a little school. Sometimes there is __3.__ rain for a long <u>tim</u>. It is __4.__ hot and dry. There are <u>noot</u> many plants. I wove this __5.__ for you. I __6.__ you like it.

Love,
Maria

no	
go	
so	
hope	
rope	
home	

1. **home**   2. **go**

3. **no**   4. **so**

5. **rope**   6. **hope**

B. Underline two words that are misspelled in the sentences above. Find the words in your dictionary. Write the correct words.

7. **time**   8. **not**

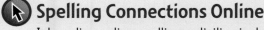

Student Objectives
- Write and spell words with the **long o** sound to complete a paragraph.
- Use a dictionary to check and correct misspelled words.

Teaching Tips
- Write *I tied a knot in the* ____ on the board. Help students read the sentence. Ask which spelling word makes sense in the sentence. **(rope)** Call on a volunteer to write the word in the space.
- Erase **is** and write **iz**. Ask, *Is this right? How can I check this spelling?* Demonstrate looking up **iz** in the dictionary. Say, *Iz isn't in the dictionary because it's not a word. What other letter can make the /z/ sound?* **(s)** *Maybe the correct spelling is **i-s**.* Look up **is** and verify.
- Have students complete page 153.

Differentiated Instruction
- Use the **Challenge Words** activity on page 205 with students who are ready to transfer their knowledge of **long o** to new words.
- An Extra Challenge Practice Master is available on page 128 in the *TRB*.
- Dictation sentences for the challenge words are available on page T205.

More Fun With Spelling for Differentiation

Digital Resources for Spelling Connections
Interactive digital resources include word sorts, pattern practice, and proofreading activities for individual and whole-group instruction. (Interactive whiteboard compatible; see p. Z32.)

Spelling Connections Online
Interactive online spelling activities include word sorts, crossword puzzles, sentence completion, proofreading practice, and spelling bees with words from each unit (see p. Z32). www.spellingconnectionsonline.com

Spelling Center Activities
Spelling Game Mats
Place one of the spelling games in a learning center to provide a fun way for students to practice their spelling words (see p. Z26).

Flip Folder
Students can use a Flip Folder to practice spelling words independently (see p. Z32).

Word Sort CD-ROM
Printable, unit-specific word cards for spelling and challenge words can be used for Teacher-Led, Individual, Buddy, and Speed Sorts (see p. Z31).

Student Objectives
- Identify spelling words in a paragraph.
- Use proofreading marks to revise writing.
- Use spelling words to write about a topic.

Teaching Tips
- Read the introduction and review the proofreading marks with the class.
- Have students complete Part A independently.
- Read the directions for Part B. Explain to students that they will rewrite the sentences on a separate sheet of paper.
- Read the directions for Part C. Remind students to use sensory details.
- Invite students to read their completed stories aloud. Discuss any sensory words. Have the class identify the spelling words used.

WORD SORT CD-ROM
- Invite students to practice for the weekly test by doing an **Individual Sort** or a **Speed Sort** (see p. Z31).

Connections to WRITING

A. Underline the spelling words. Then write them on the lines below.

Long ago winters were bad for people on the plains. the wind blew the snow so hard no one could see. A farmer would tie a rope from his home to the barn. He could get lost in the snow if he let go. The farmer had hope that the snow would stop soon.

Proofreading Marks
≡	Capital Letter
/	Small Letter
⊙	Add a Period

no
go
so
hope
rope
home

1. so   2. no

3. rope   4. home

5. go   6. hope

B. Rewrite the sentences. Make the changes shown by the proofreading marks.

C. Write a story about winter. Try to use all the spelling words.

154

TEKS 1.22A Use phonological knowledge to match sounds to letters to construct known words. **1.22C** Spell high-frequency words from a commonly used list.

1-Minute Handwriting Hint

The lowercase **o** begins below the midline and circles all the way around, touching the midline and the baseline. Be sure that the circle is closed.

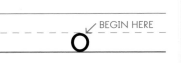

BEGIN HERE

Day 5

Student Objectives
- Demonstrate mastery of the unit spelling words.

Posttest Assessment Options
Option 1: Administer the unit posttest using the dictation sentences at right.

Option 2: Assess students using the standardized test. See the *Standardized Test Master Book*, p. 32.

Note: Posttest sentences for the on level and challenge lists are available on the audio *Spelling Connections* Posttest CD.

Posttest Sentences
1. You are **so** silly today!
2. Can Fran **go** to the store with us?
3. We hang clothes on this **rope**.
4. Will you be **home** on Sunday?
5. I **hope** you can spell the words.
6. There is **no** more milk.

Standardized Test Master Book, p. 32

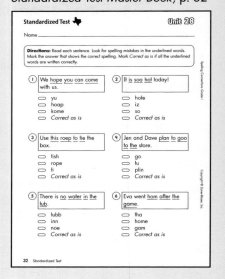

TEKS 1.22A Use phonological knowledge to match sounds to letters to construct known words. **1.22Bii** Use letter-sound patterns to spell: consonant-vowel-consonant-silent e (CVCe) words. **1.22C** Spell high-frequency words from a commonly used list.

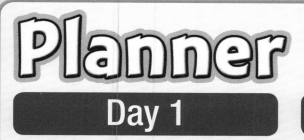

Planner

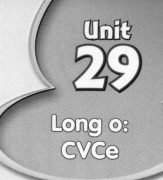

Day 1

Day 2

Day 1

Connections to **Thinking**

Student Objectives
- Identify the **long o** sound.
- Read, spell, and write words with the **long o** sound in the CVCe pattern.

Instruction for All Students
- Pretest Dictation Sentences, p. TI55B
- Connections to Thinking, p. I55
- Home/School Spelling Practice Masters (*Teacher Resource Book*, pp. I29–I30)

 TEKS 1.22A, 1.22Bii, 1.22C

Connections to **Phonics**

Student Objectives
- Read, spell, and write **long o** words in the CVCe pattern.
- Substitute a vowel to write a **long o** word.

Instruction for All Students
- Connections to Phonics, p. I56

Optional Practice
- Extra Pattern Practice Master (*Teacher Resource Book*, p. I3I)

 TEKS 1.22A, 1.22C

Spelling Words
nose
rose
bone
note
pole
rode

Challenge Words
mole
woke
code
stove

Day 3

Day 4

Day 5

Day 2

Day 3

Connections to **Reading**

Student Objectives
- Write and spell words with the **long o** sound to complete sentences.

Instruction for All Students
- Connections to Reading, p. I57

Differentiated Instruction
- Challenge Words, p. 206

 TEKS 1.22C

Connections to **Writing**

Student Objectives
- Identify spelling words in a paragraph.
- Use proofreading marks to revise writing.
- Use spelling words to write about a topic.

Instruction for All Students
- Connections to Writing, p. I58

Differentiated Instruction
- Extra Challenge Practice Master (*Teacher Resource Book*, p. I32)

 TEKS 1.22A, 1.22C, 1.22E

Assessment

Student Objectives
- Demonstrate mastery of the unit spelling words.

Assessment for All Students
- Posttest Dictation Sentences, p. TI58, or
- *Standardized Test Master Book*, p. 33

Differentiated Assessment
- Challenge Dictation Sentences, p. T206

Unit
29

Long o:
CVCe

Unit 29 Materials

Student Edition
pp. 155–158, 206

Teacher Edition
pp. T155A–T158, T206

 Teacher Resource Book
Unit 29 Practice Masters,
pp. 129–132, and
Sound/Symbol Cards

 Standardized Test Master Book
Unit 29 Test Master, p. 33

 Word Sort CD-ROM
Unit 29 Word Sort Cards for Teacher-
Led Sorts and Student Sorts

 **Digital Resources for
Spelling Connections**
Unit 29

 Spelling Connections Online
www.spellingconnectionsonline.com

**Spelling Support for
English Language Learners***
Unit 29 Practice Masters and
Audio Conversation

Spelling Center Activities*
Spelling Game Mats
Flip Folder, *TRB*, p. 155

*Spelling Support for English Language
Learners *and* Spelling Center Activities *may
be used at any time during the week.*

Assessment

Pretest Sentences (See procedures on p. Z30.)

1. Is my **nose** sunburned?
2. I will give this **rose** to my mother.
3. Misty buried her **bone** in the yard.
4. Dad sent a **note** to my teacher.
5. The **pole** needs to be painted.
6. Jessica **rode** in her uncle's boat.

The Science of Spelling ◄ • •

- There are several spellings of /ō/, but in the great majority (85 percent) of words with /ō/, the sound is spelled **o** or **o_e**. The second most frequent spelling of /ō/ is **oa** as in **boat**. In some words, **o** is paired with **e** as in **woe** or with **w** as in **grow**. Many words have /ō/ spelled **o** in the final position, as in **go**. The greatest number of words with final **o** comes from Italian and Spanish; for example, **alto** and **burro**.

ELL Support

Choose from the activities below to reinforce English language acquisition.

Beginning

Word Meaning Introduce the spelling words by listing them on the board, pointing to and reading each word aloud, and having students repeat. Provide context and support word meaning by using gestures, pantomime, and real objects or pictures.

O and Silent E Make letter cards for **n, r, b, p, s, l, d, t, o,** and **e**. List the spelling words. Invite students to select cards to spell a word. Have them place the letters in order, saying each letter name aloud. When they place **e** at the end, have them say **silent e**. Then read the word and have students repeat it. Point out that the final **s** in **rose** and **nose** is pronounced /**z**/. Students can hear the Unit 29 spelling words pronounced on the audio recording.

Substitution Write the following words on the board: **pale, ride, bane,** and **rise**. Tell students that they can change one letter in each word to make a spelling word. Write **o** on several large sticky notes for students to cover the first vowel in each word to make **pole, rode, bone,** and **rose**. Read the spelling word and have students repeat. Then write **dote** and **hose**. Tell students that this time they will change the first letter to write a spelling word. Write **n** on sticky notes for students to cover the letter they want to change to make **note** and **nose**.

Intermediate

Word Meaning Say sentences for students to complete with a spelling word. For example, *Your cheek is on your face, and so is your _____.* (nose) *A _____ is a flower.* (rose) *A kite is on a string, and a flag is on a _____.* (pole) *Your skin is on the outside, and a _____ is on the inside.* (bone) *I walked to school, and Ben _____ on the bus.* (rode)

Switch Letters Write **lope, tone, sore, redo, eons,** and **ebon** on the board. Tell students that the letters in each word can be rearranged to make a spelling word. Have students copy each word and then compare the letters to those in the spelling words. Have them write the spelling word with the same letters next to the first word. As an alternative, write each word on card stock, cut it apart, and have students rearrange the letters to make a spelling word.

Word Hunt Write a simple sentence for each spelling word on the board. For example, *The flag is on the **pole**.* Read each sentence and have students repeat. Ask students to find and underline the spelling word. Then erase all the spelling words. Call on volunteers to write the correct word in each sentence and read the sentence aloud. Encourage students to create their own sentences using spelling words for you to write on the board. Follow the same procedure with these sentences.

Support for Spanish Speakers

Comparing Languages Although Spanish does have an initial silent **h,** as in the words *hambre* (**hunger**) and *honor* (**honor**), Spanish does not have a final **silent e**. Final **e** is always pronounced in Spanish. Have students practice saying words with the CVCe pattern without voicing the final **e**.

Choose from the activities below to reinforce English language acquisition.

Advanced

Words and Pictures Provide each student with a copy of page 29 of *Spelling Support for English Language Learners*. Invite students to cut apart the cards and combine them with a partner's cards in a word stack and a picture stack. Read the directions. Then have partners play the game. Encourage them to work together to complete the sentence and do the activity at the bottom of the page.

Words and Sentences List the spelling words on the board. Then have partners work together to write sentences using each word. Partner 1 writes a sentence with the first word. Partner 2 writes one with the second word, and so on.

Conversation Have partners listen to the conversation using the Unit 29 spelling words on the audio recording. Encourage them to follow along with the print form on page 53 of *Spelling Support for English Language Learners*. Challenge them to continue the conversation.

Advanced High

Write Sentences Write the spelling words on the board. Point to and read each word and have students repeat. Ask students if there are any words they do not know. For these words use pantomime, gestures, pictures, and real objects, along with simple statements, to provide context and support word meaning. Then ask students to write their own sentence for each spelling word.

Word Search Create a word search puzzle with the spelling words. Have students find and circle the words. Explain that the words may be written horizontally, vertically, or diagonally. Provide a tip by telling students to look for the letters **o** and **e** separated by one other letter.

Illustrate Sentences Have partners each choose three spelling words and then write a sentence for each word on a separate sheet of paper. Direct partners to trade papers and underline the spelling words. Then have them draw a picture to illustrate each sentence.

Mystery Words Model how to play a guessing game by giving clues for students to guess a spelling word. For example, *I am thinking of word that describes something on my face. It ends with /z/. It has a **long o** sound.* (nose) Have partners play the game by giving each other clues. Have each partner write the words guessed. Encourage students to include previously learned words.

Spelling Support for English Language Learners

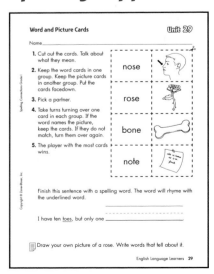

Practice Master, p. 29

Practice Master, p. 53

Audio Conversation
available on CD

English/Spanish
Word List, p. 68

Spelling Connections Online
Interactive online spelling activities provide additional ELL support.
www.spellingconnectionsonline.com

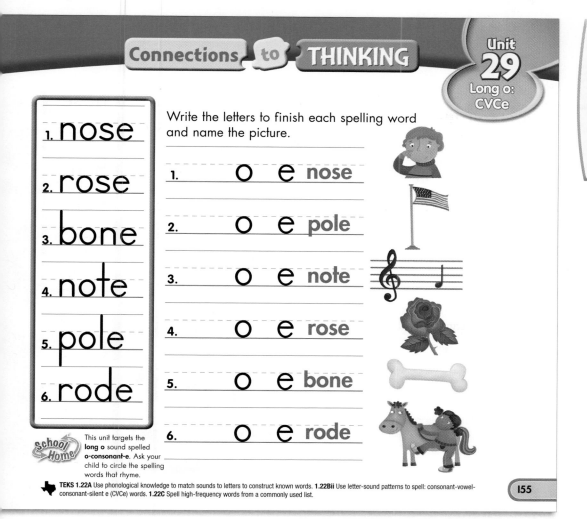

Write the letters to finish each spelling word and name the picture.

1. nose
2. rose
3. bone
4. note
5. pole
6. rode

1. o __ e nose
2. o __ e pole
3. o __ e note
4. o __ e rose
5. o __ e bone
6. o __ e rode

School Home This unit targets the **long o** sound spelled **o-consonant-e**. Ask your child to circle the spelling words that rhyme.

TEKS 1.22A Use phonological knowledge to match sounds to letters to construct known words. **1.22Bii** Use letter-sound patterns to spell: consonant-vowel-consonant-silent e (CVCe) words. **1.22C** Spell high-frequency words from a commonly used list.

155

Day 1

Unit 29

Student Objectives
- Identify the **long o** sound.
- Read, spell, and write words with the **long o** sound in the CVCe pattern.

Unit Pretest
- Administer the pretest on page T155B.

Teaching Tips

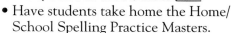 **WORD SORT CD-ROM**

- Conduct a **Teacher-Led Sort** (see p. Z31) to reinforce the spelling pattern.
- Review /ō/ by asking a volunteer to say **rose** and name the vowel sound in the word. Use the Sound/Symbol Cards for **old** and **stove** to give students more practice in listening to and identifying /ō/.
- Write _o_e on the board. Show students the Sound/Symbol Card for **rose**. Ask a volunteer to say the picture name and write the missing letters to spell **rose**. Then have students tell you why the two letters help complete the CVCe spelling pattern. (**Both letters are consonants.**)
- Have students complete the page independently or as a class.

Home/School Word Lists **TRB**
- Have students take home the Home/School Spelling Practice Masters.

Home/School Practice

Home/School Spelling
Practice Master, *TRB*, p. 129

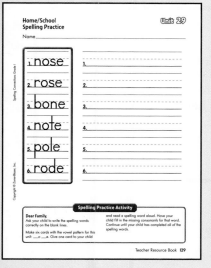

English

Home/School Spelling
Practice Master, *TRB*, p. 130

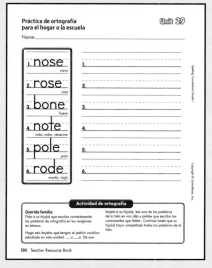

Spanish

TEKS 1.22A Use phonological knowledge to match sounds to letters to construct known words. **1.22Bii** Use letter-sound patterns to spell: consonant-vowel-consonant-silent e (CVCe) words. **1.22C** Spell high-frequency words from a commonly used list.

T155

Student Objectives

- Read, spell, and write **long o** words in the CVCe pattern.
- Substitute a vowel to write a **long o** word.

Teaching Tips

- List the spelling words on the board. Read the words aloud and have students repeat. Ask what vowel sound they hear in all of the word. **(long o)**
- Write **pile** on the board. Read it aloud and have students repeat. Call on a volunteer to erase **i** and write **o**. Ask students to read the new word aloud. **(pole)**
- Show the Sound/Symbol Card for **box**. Ask students to name the picture and identify the first sound. **(box, /b/)** Have students identify the spelling word that begins with the same sound. **(bone)** Repeat with the Sound/Symbol Cards for **nest, pie,** and **rain.**
- Have students complete page 156 independently or as a class.

Extra Pattern Practice

- Use the optional practice master below for extra practice with **long o**.

WORD SORT CD-ROM

- Provide time for students to use a **Buddy Sort** (see p. Z31) to practice their spelling words with a partner.

Connections to PHONICS

A. Change the **a** or the **i** to **o** and write the spelling word.

| nose |
| rose |
| bone |
| note |
| pole |
| rode |

1. pale

    pole

2. ride

    rode

3. rise

    rose

4. bane

    bone

B. Write the words that begin with the same sound as  .

5.   **nose**

6.   **note**

156

TEKS 1.22A Use phonological knowledge to match sounds to letters to construct known words. **1.22C** Spell high-frequency words from a commonly used list.

Extra Pattern Practice

Extra Pattern Practice Master,
TRB, p. 131

Long o Practice

Have students sit in a circle. Say **nose, rose, bone, note, pole,** and **rode,** emphasizing the **long o** sound. Explain that the words have the **long o** sound in the middle. Then show students a rose or a picture of a rose. Say, *I can smell the rose with my nose.* Have students repeat the sentence. Then have them say a new word with the **long o** sound as they pass around the rose. Write the spelling words on the board and show students that each word has the **long o** sound in the middle and a **silent e** at the end.

TEKS 1.22A Use phonological knowledge to match sounds to letters to construct known words.
1.22C Spell high-frequency words from a commonly used list.

Connections to READING

Write the silly sentences.

1. A bee __?__ on her __?__ .

2. A __?__ is on the __?__ .

3. A __?__ is on the __?__ .

> nose
> rose
> bone
> note
> pole
> rode

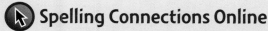

1. ___A bee rode on her nose___ .

2. ___A note is on the bone___ .

3. ___A rose is on the pole___ .

TEKS 1.22C Spell high-frequency words from a commonly used list.

157

Student Objectives
- Write and spell words with the **long o** sound to complete sentences.

Teaching Tips
- Remind students that when a word ends with a vowel-consonant-**e,** the vowel sound is usually long, and the **e** at the end of the word is silent. Read the spelling words aloud with students.
- On the board, draw a fishing pole with a bone on its hook. Write, *I caught a ____ with my fishing ____.* Have students complete the sentence with spelling words. (**bone, pole**) Ask a volunteer to write the words in the blanks. Ask students if they think the sentence is silly.
- Read the directions aloud. Explain to students that they need two words to complete each silly sentence. Point out that there are clues in the illustrations.
- Have students complete page 157. Ask volunteers to read their sentences aloud.

Differentiated Instruction
- Use the **Challenge Words** activity on page 206 with students who are ready to transfer their knowledge of **long o** to new words.
- An Extra Challenge Practice Master is available on page 132 in the *TRB*.
- Dictation sentences for the challenge words are available on page T206.

More Fun With Spelling for Differentiation

Digital Resources for Spelling Connections
Interactive digital resources include word sorts, pattern practice, and proofreading activities for individual and whole-group instruction. (Interactive whiteboard compatible; see p. Z32.)

Spelling Connections Online
Interactive online spelling activities include word sorts, crossword puzzles, sentence completion, proofreading practice, and spelling bees with words from each unit (see p. Z32). www.spellingconnectionsonline.com

Spelling Center Activities
Spelling Game Mats
Place one of the spelling games in a learning center to provide a fun way for students to practice their spelling words (see p. Z26).

Flip Folder
Students can use a Flip Folder to practice spelling words independently (see p. Z32).

Word Sort CD-ROM
Printable, unit-specific word cards for spelling and challenge words can be used for Teacher-Led, Individual, Buddy, and Speed Sorts (see p. Z31).

TEKS 1.22C Spell high-frequency words from a commonly used list.

T157

Student Objectives
- Identify spelling words in a paragraph.
- Use proofreading marks to revise writing.
- Use spelling words to write about a topic.

Teaching Tips
- Read the introduction and review the proofreading marks with the class.
- Have students complete Part A independently.
- Read the directions for Part B. Explain to students that they will rewrite the sentences on a separate sheet of paper.
- Read the directions for Part C. Have students complete this independently.
- When students have finished, ask them to review their work to make sure they have spelled spelling words correctly. Have them circle two words they are not sure about and check the spelling of each in a picture dictionary.
- Invite volunteers to read their work aloud. Have the class identify spelling words used.

WORD SORT CD-ROM
- Invite students to practice for the weekly test by doing an **Individual Sort** or a **Speed Sort** (see p. Z31).

Day 5

Student Objectives
- Demonstrate mastery of the unit spelling words.

Posttest Assessment Options
Option 1: Administer the unit posttest using the dictation sentences at right.

Option 2: Assess students using the standardized test. See the *Standardized Test Master Book,* p. 33.

Note: Posttest sentences for the on level and challenge lists are available on the audio *Spelling Connections* Posttest CD.

Connections to WRITING

A. Underline the spelling words. Then write them on the lines below.

Gifts can be very special. A <u>rose</u> or other flower is nice. It's like a <u>note</u> that says "I love you." It's a treat for you and your <u>nose</u>.Some people would like to get a fishing <u>pole</u>. if you were a dog, a <u>bone</u> would be great. Once I got a Bike as a gift. I <u>rode</u> it every day.

Proofreading Marks
- ≡ Capital Letter
- / Small Letter
- ⊙ Add a Period

nose
rose
bone
note
pole
rode

1.	rose	2.	note
3.	nose	4.	pole
5.	bone	6.	rode

B. Rewrite the sentences. Make the changes shown by the proofreading marks.

C. Write about a gift you would like to give or get. Use as many spelling words as you can.

158

TEKS 1.22A Use phonological knowledge to match sounds to letters to construct known words. **1.22C** Spell high-frequency words from a commonly used list.

1-Minute Handwriting Hint

Tall letters touch the headline, short letters touch the midline, and letters with descenders fill the space below the baseline.

TOUCH HEADLINE
TOUCH MIDLINE
bf en qy
FILL SPACE

Posttest Sentences
1. I **rode** on my grandparents' tractor.
2. Listen to this low **note**.
3. Pinocchio's **nose** grew each time he told a lie.
4. Can I give the dog a **bone**?
5. Mom gave Dad a **rose** today.
6. I can reach the ball with a **pole**.

Standardized Test Master Book, p. 33

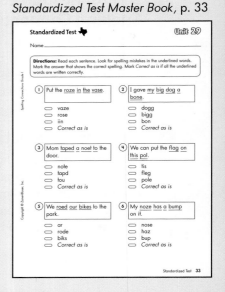

 TEKS 1.22A Use phonological knowledge to match sounds to letters to construct known words. **1.22C** Spell high-frequency words from a commonly used list. **1.22E** Use resources to find correct spellings.

Planner

Day 1

Day 2

Day 1

Unit 26: Long i: CVCe

Student Objectives
- Review the spelling pattern and words from Unit 26.

Instruction for All Students
- Unit 26 Review, p. 159
- Home/School Spelling Practice Masters (*Teacher Resource Book,* pp. 133–134)

Unit 27: Long i: CVCe

Student Objectives
- Review the spelling pattern and words from Unit 27.

Instruction for All Students
- Unit 27 Review, p. 160

Unit 26
Long i: CVCe

bite	life
kite	line
time	mine

Unit 27
Long i: CVCe

bike	hide
like	ride
hike	side

Unit 28
Long o: o, CVCe

no	hope
go	rope
so	home

Unit 29
Long o: CVCe

nose	note
rose	pole
bone	rode

Day 3

Day 4

Day 5

Day 2

Day 3

Unit 28: Long o: o, CVCe

Student Objectives
- Review the spelling patterns and words from Unit 28.

Instruction for All Students
- Unit 28 Review, p. 161

Unit 29: Long o: CVCe

Student Objectives
- Review the spelling pattern and words from Unit 29.

Instruction for All Students
- Unit 29 Review, p. 162

Assessment

Student Objectives
- Demonstrate mastery of the review unit spelling words.

Assessment for All Students
- Posttest Assessment Options
  - ✦ Posttest Dictation Sentences, p. T162, or
  - ✦ *Standardized Test Master Book,* p. 34

Unit 30

Unit 30 Materials

Student Edition
pp. 159–162
Alphabet and Picture Cards
(See page Z32 for
suggested activities.)

Teacher Edition
pp. T159A–T162

 Teacher Resource Book
Unit 30 Practice Masters,
pp. 133–134

 Standardized Test Master Book
Unit 30 Test Master, p. 34

 Word Sort CD-ROM
Unit 30 Word Sort Cards for Teacher-
Led Sorts and Student Sorts

 **Digital Resources for
Spelling Connections**
Unit 30

 Spelling Connections Online
www.spellingconnectionsonline.com

Spelling Center Activities*
Spelling Game Mats
Flip Folder, *TRB*, p. 155

  **Spelling Center Activities may be used at
  any time during the week.*

Developmental Spelling Check

Administer the following **Developmental Spelling Check**
to evaluate spelling growth. Remind students that this is
not a test for a grade; students are not expected to spell
these words conventionally. Author J. Richard Gentry
has provided typical Phase 4 Transitional Spelling(s) for
each word in parentheses.

Tell students you would like them to try writing these
coin words. To administer, say each word aloud, read
the sentence, and then say the word again.

Coin Words and Sample Transitional Spellings

Word	Sentence	Transitional Spelling
penny	Did Mom give you a **penny**?	(PENNE, PENNY)
dime	Ten pennies make one **dime**.	(DYME, DIEM)
nickel	That new **nickel** is very shiny.	(NICKLE)
quarter	One **quarter** equals 25 cents.	(QUARTUR)
silver dollar	A **silver dollar** is large.	(SILVUR DOLLER)

ELL Support

Choose from the activities below to reinforce English language acquisition.

Beginning

Word Meaning Write the review spelling words on the board. Read the words aloud and have students repeat. Ask students if there are any words they don't know. Demonstrate these words using gestures, pantomime, and pictures or real objects along with simple statements to provide context and support meaning. Invite students to follow your lead and act out the words with their own interpretations.

Word Sort Write each review spelling word on an index card. Mix the cards. Have students sort the cards into words with the **long i** sound and words with the **long o** sound. Have students think of additional ways to sort the two piles.

Complete Words Write spelling word frames on the board in which the letter that stands for the long vowel is missing. Have students write either **i** or **o** to complete the word and then read it aloud. Then write word frames in which two letters are missing. Have students write the letters to complete the words.

Identify Long Vowel Words Write the following word pairs on the board: **hid/hide, kit/kite, hop/hope, not/note**. Have students read the words aloud. Ask volunteers to circle the word in each pair that has the long vowel sound. Ask them how the vowel sound is spelled. (i_e or o_e)

Intermediate

Ask Questions Check students' understanding of word meanings by asking student-friendly questions that can be answered with a spelling word. For example, *What is the opposite of "yes"?* (no) *What has two wheels and is something you can ride?* (bike) *What does the clock tell you?* (time)

Making Words Have partners play a game to see how many spelling words they can write. Partner I writes a spelling word. Partner 2 then replaces a letter to make a new word. If a partner cannot make a new word, he or she selects another spelling word and starts over. Have students score one point for each correct word.

Word Families Label four paper bags with the word endings **ime, ike, ope,** and **ole**. Have students write a word, including spelling words, with one of the word endings on an index card or a paper strip. Then have them put the card in the appropriate paper bag. After the activity is completed, take the cards out of each bag and read the words aloud. Have students repeat. Then write the words on the board. (**Possible words: dime, lime, mime, rime, time; bike, dike, hike, like, mike, pike, tike; cope, dope, hope, lope, mope, nope, rope; dole, hole, mole, pole, role, sole**)

Support for Spanish Speakers

Comparing Languages English and Spanish are similar yet different in several ways. Both languages use the same alphabet. However, Spanish uses 18 consonant phonemes while English has 26. Spanish has five vowels as does English. However, English also uses an additional eight vowel sounds. Spanish-speaking students will need practice learning to hear and pronounce unfamiliar vowel sounds, consonants, and blends such as **dg, j, sh, th,** and **z,** which are not part of Spanish.

Unit 30

Choose from the activities below to reinforce English language acquisition.

Advanced

Vowel Sounds Write each of the following words on an index card: **bit, kit, lift, lint, mint, hid, rid, hop, not, rod, got,** and **son.** Have students select a card and think *How can I change this word so it has a long vowel sound?* Tell students to think about changing a letter, deleting a letter, and/or adding **e.** Have students write the words they make.

Words and Pictures Have students select review spelling words to illustrate. Tell students to label their pictures with the spelling words they use. Encourage them to describe or tell a story about their picture to a partner.

Concentration Write each review spelling word on two index cards. Place the cards facedown in a grid. Have partners alternate turning over two cards at a time. If each word has the same long vowel sound, the partner keeps the cards. If the words do not have the same long vowel sound, the cards are turned back over. Partners play until all of the words have been matched.

Advanced High

Word Search Create a large word search puzzle that uses all of the review spelling words. Have partners work together to find and circle the words. Explain that the words can be horizontal, vertical, or diagonal. Encourage students to write each word they find.

Write Stories Write the following story titles on the board: *I Like to Hike, Ride My Bike, Go Home, A Rose for My Nose, Hide the Bone, No Time, The Kite on the Pole.* Encourage students to choose a title and write a paragraph that tells a short story and uses as many of the review spelling words as possible. Have them correct their writing using proofreading marks. Encourage students to illustrate their stories.

Charades Provide partners with a set of flash cards of the review spelling words. Mix the cards and place them facedown. Have each partner choose a card without showing it. Then direct each one to dramatize or act out his or her word in some way. The second partner tries to guess the word. Have partners continue until they have used all of the cards.

 Spelling Connections Online
Interactive online spelling activities
provide additional ELL support.
www.spellingconnectionsonline.com

Review

Unit
30
Review Units 26–29

Day 1

Unit
30

1. bite
2. kite
3. time
4. life
5. line
6. mine

This unit reviews **long i** and **long o**. Ask your child to read the spelling words on each page aloud.

Unit 26: Long i: CVCe

Fill in the blanks to write spelling words.

1. _ _ f _   life

2. m _ n _   mine

3. b _ _ _ _   bite

4. t _ _ e   time

5. k _ _ _ _   kite

6. l _ n _   line

159

Student Objectives

- Review the spelling pattern and words from Unit 26.

Reteaching the Skill

- Write **bit** on the board and ask a volunteer to read it aloud. Add **e** to make **bite**. Circle the letter **e**. Tell students to listen as you say **bite**.
- Point out to students that they hear the name of the letter **i** in **bite** and that, when a letter says its name, it is a long vowel. Remind students that the letter **e** is silent.
- Write **kite, time, life, line,** and **mine** on the board. Have volunteers pronounce each word, circle the **i,** and underline the final **e**.
- Tell students to complete page 159 independently.

Letters and Sounds Review

- Throughout the unit, use the **Alphabet and Picture Cards** to review letters and sounds. See page Z32 for activity suggestions.

Review Word List

Home/School Spelling
Practice Master, *TRB,* p. 133

Home/School Spelling
Practice Master, *TRB,* p. 134

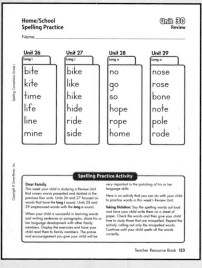

English

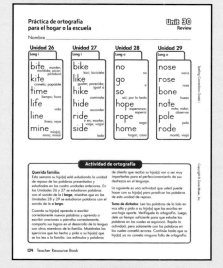

Spanish

Student Objectives
- Review the spelling pattern and words from Unit 27.

Reteaching the Skill
- Write **bike, like, hike, hide, ride,** and **side** on the board. Read the words aloud and have students repeat them. Ask students what vowel sound they hear in all the words. **(long i)**
- Ask students what spelling pattern spells the **long i** sound in each word. **(i-consonant-e)** Call on volunteers to circle the **i** and **e** in each word on the board. Have students read the words again. Ask which letter is silent. **(e)**
- Tell students to complete page 160 independently.

Review

1. bike
2. like
3. hike
4. hide
5. ride
6. side

Unit 27: Long i: CVCe

A. Write the words that end with **ide**.

1. hide   2. ride

3. side

B. Write the words that end with **ike**.

4. bike   5. like

6. hike

160

Extra Pattern Practice

Rhyming Words

Write each spelling word on the board and invite students to erase and replace the first letter. List all the words on the board. Then ask students to write a sentence using each word and a word that rhymes with it. The sentences may be realistic or nonsensical, but the order of the words should be logical and the thought should be clear. Encourage students to illustrate their sentences.

Review

1.	no
2.	go
3.	so
4.	hope
5.	rope
6.	home

Unit 28: Long o: o, CVCe
Circle the **long o** words. Write them.

1. hop
   (hope) ___hope___

2. house
   (home) ___home___

3. (rope)
   romp ___rope___

4. (go)
   got ___go___

5. (so)
   sock ___so___

6. not
   (no) ___no___

161

Student Objectives
- Review the spelling patterns and words from Unit 28.

Reteaching the Skill
- Write **no, go,** and **so** on the board. Ask, *What do you see that is the same in every word?* (**final o**) Read each word aloud and ask students to listen carefully for the **long o** sound at the end.
- Write **hope, rope,** and **home** on the board. Ask, *What do you see that is the same in every word?* Guide students to see the o-consonant-e pattern.
- Ask, *What do you hear in every word?* (**long o sound**) Remind students that when a word ends in o-consonant-e, the o is long and the e is silent. Have volunteers circle the letter **o** in each word and underline the silent **e**.
- Tell students to complete page 161 independently.

More Fun With Spelling for Differentiation

 ## Digital Resources for Spelling Connections
Interactive digital resources include word sorts, pattern practice, and proofreading activities for individual and whole-group instruction. (Interactive whiteboard compatible; see p. Z32.)

 ## Spelling Connections Online
Interactive online spelling activities include word sorts, crossword puzzles, sentence completion, proofreading practice, and spelling bees with words from each unit (see p. Z32). www.spellingconnectionsonline.com

 ## Spelling Center Activities
Spelling Game Mats
Place one of the spelling games in a learning center to provide a fun way for students to practice their spelling words (see p. Z26).

Flip Folder
Students can use a Flip Folder to practice spelling words independently (see p. Z32).

Word Sort CD-ROM
Printable, unit-specific word cards for spelling and challenge words can be used for Teacher-Led, Individual, Buddy, and Speed Sorts (see p. Z31).

Unit 30 — Day 4

Student Objectives
• Review the spelling pattern and words from Unit 29.

Reteaching the Skill
• Write the spelling words on the board. Read each word aloud and have students repeat. Ask what vowel sound students hear in the middle of the words. (long o) Ask how the vowel sound is spelled. (o_e)
• Review that rhyming words have the same ending sounds. Ask students which spelling words rhyme. (nose/rose)
• Have one student in a pair think of a spelling word and write one letter of the word on a sheet of paper. The partner tries to guess the word. If the partner cannot, the first partner gives another letter clue. If the partner guesses the word, he or she writes the word. Partners alternate until they have written all of the spelling words.
• Tell students to complete page 162 independently or as a class.

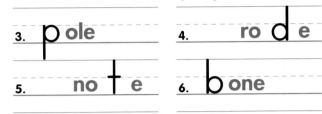

1. nose
2. rose
3. bone
4. note
5. pole
6. rode

Unit 29: Long o: CVCe

A. Write the spelling words that end with **ose**.

1. nose
2. rose

B. Use the letter clue to write a spelling word.

3. p ole
4. ro d e
5. no t e
6. b one

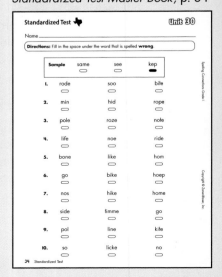

162

Day 5

Assessment
Student Objectives
• Demonstrate mastery of the review unit spelling words.

Posttest Assessment Options
Option 1: Administer the posttest using the dictation sentences at right.
Option 2: Assess students using the standardized test. See the *Standardized Test Master Book*, p. 34.

Note: Posttest sentences for the on level and challenge lists are available on the audio *Spelling Connections* Posttest CD.

Posttest Sentences
1. Please help me fly my **kite**.
2. You will be leader next **time**.
3. I have a horn on my **bike**.
4. I like to **ride** in the back of the bus.
5. I **hope** that we can play outside.
6. You are **so** silly today!
7. Is my **nose** sunburned?
8. Listen to this low **note**.

Standardized Test Master Book, p. 34

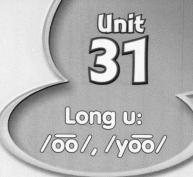

Day 1 | Day 2

Day 1

Connections to **Thinking**

Student Objectives
- Identify words with **long u** and vowel digraph **oo**.
- Identify and write words with /o͞o/ spelled **o, ou,** and **oo** and /yo͞o/ spelled with the VCe pattern.

Instruction for All Students
- Pretest Dictation Sentences, p. T163B
- Connections to Thinking, p. 163
- Home/School Spelling Practice Masters (*Teacher Resource Book*, pp. 135–136)

🔖 **TEKS 1.22A, 1.22C**

Connections to **Phonics**

Student Objectives
- Use letter clues to write words with /o͞o/ and /yo͞o/ sounds.
- Add **-s** to words to form plurals.

Instruction for All Students
- Connections to Phonics, p. 164

Optional Practice
- Extra Pattern Practice Master (*Teacher Resource Book*, p. 137)

🔖 **TEKS 1.22A, 1.22C, 1.22D**

Spelling Words
do
you
zoo
use
room
soon

Challenge Words
moon
spoon
stool
broom

Day 3 | Day 4 | Day 5

Day 2 | Day 3

Connections to **Reading**

Student Objectives
- Write and spell words with /o͞o/ and /yo͞o/ to complete sentences.

Instruction for All Students
- Connections to Reading, p. 165

Differentiated Instruction
- Challenge Words, p. 207

🔖 **TEKS 1.22C**

Connections to **Writing**

Student Objectives
- Identify spelling words in a letter.
- Use proofreading marks to revise writing.
- Use spelling words to write a letter.

Instruction for All Students
- Connections to Writing, p. 166

Differentiated Instruction
- Extra Challenge Practice Master (*Teacher Resource Book*, p. 138)

🔖 **TEKS 1.22A, 1.22C**

Assessment

Student Objectives
- Demonstrate mastery of the unit spelling words.

Assessment for All Students
- Posttest Dictation Sentences, p. T166, or
- *Standardized Test Master Book*, p. 35

Differentiated Assessment
- Challenge Dictation Sentences, p. T207

Unit 31 Materials

Student Edition
pp. 163–166, 207

Teacher Edition
pp. T163A–T166, T207

 Teacher Resource Book
Unit 31 Practice Masters,
pp. 135–138, and
Sound/Symbol Cards

 Standardized Test Master Book
Unit 31 Test Master, p. 35

Word Sort CD-ROM
Unit 31 Word Sort Cards for Teacher-
Led Sorts and Student Sorts

 **Digital Resources for
Spelling Connections**
Unit 31

Spelling Connections Online
www.spellingconnectionsonline.com

**Spelling Support for
English Language Learners***
Unit 31 Practice Masters and
Audio Conversation

Spelling Center Activities*
Spelling Game Mats
Flip Folder, *TRB*, p. 155

*Spelling Support for English Language
Learners *and* Spelling Center Activities *may
be used at any time during the week.*

Assessment

Pretest Sentences (See procedures on p. Z30.)

1. There is a lot to **do** indoors on a rainy day.
2. What are **you** doing with that box?
3. Did you see the bear at the **zoo**?
4. You may **use** my crayons.
5. I share a **room** with my sister.
6. Daddy will be home **soon**.

The Science of Spelling ◀

The /o͞o/ sound is labeled by some linguists as a **long u** sound, while others label it as a vowel digraph in which two vowels together form one sound. The major spellings of /o͞o/ are **oo, u,** and **ue**. Less common spellings are **o, ou, ui, ew, eu,** and **oe**. The /yo͞o/ sound is a **long u** sound because the long sound is the name of the vowel. How **u** is pronounced in words with the CVCe pattern depends on the initial consonant. The /yo͞o/ sound generally follows initial **p, f, m,** and **c** as in **cute**. Two other common spellings of the /yo͞o/ sound are **ew** and **eu,** as in **ewe** and **feud**.

ELL Support

Choose from the activities below to reinforce English language acquisition.

Beginning

Word Meaning Explain to students that the words in this unit are words they will use often in their writing. Introduce the words by listing them on the board. Point to and read each word aloud and have students repeat it. Then demonstrate the meaning of each word using gestures, pantomime, and student-friendly statements to provide context and support meaning, such as spreading your arms to indicate the classroom as you say, *This is our room.*

Mystery Word List the spelling words, read them aloud, and have students repeat them. Tell students you will give clues for them to guess a word. For example, say, *I am thinking of a word that has an /ōō/ sound. The sound is spelled with two o's. There is a letter z in the word. It is a place where animals live.* (zoo)

Spelling /ōō/ and /yōō/ Tell students that the /ōō/ and /yōō/ sounds can be spelled in different ways. Write **room, zoo,** and **soon.** Frame **oo** with your hands in each and explain that when there are two o's together, they make the /ōō/ sound. Ask a volunteer to underline **oo** in each word. Then write **you.** Segment and pronounce the sounds, /y/ /ōō/. Ask students what letters make the /ōō/ sound in **you.** (ou). Write **use** and say it aloud. Ask students what sound they hear. (/yōō/) Point out that this sound is spelled **u_e** in **use.** Remind students that the **e** is silent. Students can hear the Unit 31 spelling words pronounced on the audio recording.

Intermediate

Complete Sentences Give each student a copy of page 30 of *Spelling Support for English Language Learners.* Have them work with a partner to read and complete the sentences with spelling words. Then provide drawing paper and crayons. Have partners discuss and do the activity at the bottom of the page.

Word Frames Write each spelling word on the board, leaving out the vowels: **d __, y __ __, z __ __ __, __ s __, r __ __ m, s __ __ n.** Then write **oo, u_e, o,** and **ou** next to the word frames. Call on students to write the correct vowels to complete each word. Then point to and read the words aloud and have students repeat.

Use Proofreading Marks Help students understand how each proofreading mark is used to correct writing. Write a student's name on the board, using all lowercase letters. Remind students that the first letter of a person's name should be a capital letter. Demonstrate drawing three lines under the first letter to show that it should be a capital letter. Then write the name again, beginning with a capital letter. Have students write their names first with small letters. Then have them underline the first letter three times and write their name correctly. Follow a similar procedure for each proofreading mark.

Support for Spanish Speakers

Comparing Languages English vowels are challenging for many Spanish speakers. Although long vowel sounds in Spanish are similar to those in English, some sounds are spelled with different vowels or vowel combinations. As a result, long vowels and vowel digraphs may be confusing to students. Students also may have difficulty pronouncing the **long u** sound in **use** and **cute.** Spelling words provide an excellent opportunity for Spanish speakers to listen to clear pronunciation of single words, to practice approximating the sounds of English, and to develop English sound-symbol correspondence.

Unit 31

Choose from the activities below to reinforce English language acquisition.

Advanced

Spell and Write Write **o, ou, oo,** and **u_e** on index cards. Have students select a card and write a spelling word that uses the letter or letters to spell the /$\overline{oo}$/ or /y$\overline{oo}$/ sound.

Words in Context Write a sentence for each spelling word on the board, but mix up the words so that they appear in the wrong sentences. For example: *What will we you today? I like my use. There are bears in the room. Will do help me? I can soon this box. We will go home zoo.* Guide students in reading each sentence and finding the incorrect word. Erase the word and have a volunteer write the correct word. Then read the corrected sentences with students.

Write a Sentence/Read a Sentence Have students write a sentence using a spelling word and then trade papers with a partner. The partner reads the sentence aloud and underlines the spelling word. Have students continue until they each have six sentences, one for each spelling word.

Conversation Encourage partners to follow along with the printed text on page 54 of *Spelling Support for English Language Learners* as they listen to the dialogue on the audio recording. Then have partners choose the part of Speaker 1 or Speaker 2 and read the conversation again.

Advanced High

Look for Words List the spelling words on the board. Have students look for these words in classroom materials and books they use during the day. When they find a word, have them copy the sentence in which the word appears. Ask students to read their sentences to you.

Fix Sentences Review the proofreading marks with students. Then have students choose a spelling word and write a sentence that includes an intentional error such as a double word, a misspelling, a missing period, or a missing word. Have them trade papers with a partner and use proofreading marks to correct each other's sentences.

Rhyme Bank Work with students to create a Rhyme Bank for the words **zoo, room,** and **soon** in which the /$\overline{oo}$/ sound is spelled **oo.** (Possible words: moo, boo, coo, goo, too; boom, doom, gloom, loom, zoom; boon, coon, loon, goon, moon, noon, spoon) Then have students play with the words by choosing two or more to use in silly sentences, such as *I hear a* **moo** *in the* **zoo.**

Questions Have partners take turns asking each other, *What do you do?* The answer should include a spelling word, such as *I work at the* **zoo.** Encourage students to also use previously learned spelling words in their replies.

Spelling Support for English Language Learners

Practice Master, p. 30

Practice Master, p. 54

Audio Conversation available on CD

English/Spanish
Word List, p. 69

 Spelling Connections Online
Interactive online spelling activities
provide additional ELL support.
www.spellingconnectionsonline.com

Connections to THINKING

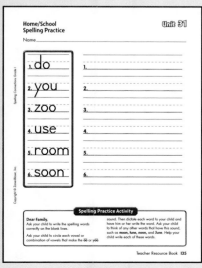

1. do	
2. you	
3. zoo	
4. use	
5. room	
6. soon	

A. Write the spelling words with **oo**.

1.   zoo   2.   room

3.   soon

B. Write the spelling word with the **oo** sound spelled **o**.

4.   do

C. Write the spelling word with the **yoo** sound spelled **ou**.

5.   you

D. Write the spelling word with the **yoo** sound spelled **u_e**.

6.   use

School Home
This unit targets the **oo** and **yoo** sounds. Ask your child to use each spelling word in a sentence.

TEKS 1.22A Use phonological knowledge to match sounds to letters to construct known words. **1.22C** Spell high-frequency words from a commonly used list.

163

Student Objectives
- Identify words with **long u** and vowel digraph **oo**.
- Identify and write words with /oo/ spelled **o, ou,** and **oo** and /yoo/ spelled with the VCe pattern.

Unit Pretest
- Administer the pretest on page T163B.

Teaching Tips

WORD SORT **CD-ROM**

- Conduct a **Teacher-Led Sort** (see p. Z31) to introduce the spelling patterns.
- Introduce /oo/ and /yoo/ by writing **zoo** and **use** on the board. Ask students to listen for the vowel sound as you read each word.
- Use the Sound/Symbol Cards for **food, goose, roof, tooth, unicorn, unicycle,** and **zoo** to reinforce these sounds.
- Write **do** on the board, read it aloud, and have students repeat it. Ask a volunteer to circle the letter that makes the vowel sound. Introduce the rest of the spelling words in a similar way.
- Have students complete the page independently or as a class.

Home/School Word Lists **TRB**
- Have students take home the Home/School Spelling Practice Masters.

Home/School Practice

Home/School Spelling
Practice Master, *TRB*, p. 135

Home/School Spelling
Practice Master, *TRB*, p. 136

Home/School Spelling Practice	Unit 31
Name	

1. do
2. you
3. zoo
4. use
5. room
6. soon

1. _____
2. _____
3. _____
4. _____
5. _____
6. _____

Spelling Practice Activity

Dear Family,
Ask your child to write the spelling words correctly on the blank lines.

Ask your child to circle each vowel or combination of vowels that make the **oo** or **yoo** sound. Then dictate each word to your child and have him or her write the word. Ask your child to think of any other words that have this sound, such as **moon, tune, noon,** and **June**. Help your child write each of these words.

Teacher Resource Book 135

English

Práctica de ortografía para el hogar o la escuela	Unit 31
Name	

1. do (hacer)
2. you (usted; ustedes; tú)
3. zoo (zoológico)
4. use (usa; usar)
5. room (cuarto)
6. soon (pronto)

1. _____
2. _____
3. _____
4. _____
5. _____
6. _____

Actividad de ortografía

Querida familia:
Pida a su hijo(a) que escriba correctamente las palabras de ortografía en los renglones en blanco.

Pida a su hijo(a) que encierre en un círculo cada vocal, o combinación de vocales, que produzca los sonidos: **oo** o **yoo**. Luego, dictele las palabras y pídale que piense en otras palabras que tienen este sonido, como: **moon** (luna), **tune** (tono), **noon** (mediodía) y **June** (junio) y ayúdele(a) a que escriba estas palabras.

136 Teacher Resource Book

Spanish

TEKS 1.22A Use phonological knowledge to match sounds to letters to construct known words. **1.22C** Spell high-frequency words from a commonly used list.

Student Objectives
- Use letter clues to write words with /o͞o/ and /yo͞o/ sounds.
- Add **-s** to words to form plurals.

Teaching Tips
- List the spelling words on the board. Read the words aloud and have students repeat. Ask students which words have the /o͞o/ sound. (do, zoo, room, soon) Have volunteers underline these words. Then ask which words have the /yo͞o/ sound. (you, use) Call on volunteers to circle these words.
- Write **zoo** on the board. Ask students what they could add to **zoo** so that it would tell about more than one. (s) Ask a volunteer to write **s** after **zoo** to make the word plural. Point out that **zoos** begins and ends with different letters that make the same sound.
- Have students complete page 164 independently or as a class.

Extra Pattern Practice 📕TRB
- Use the optional practice master below for extra practice with o͞o and yo͞o.

💿WORD SORT CD-ROM
- Provide time for students to use a **Buddy Sort** (see p. Z31) to practice their spelling words with a partner.

Connections to PHONICS

A. Write the spelling word that sounds like **u** and the word that begins with **u**.

1. **you**   2. **use**

B. Write the spelling word that rhymes with **to** and has two letters. Write the word that rhymes with **moon**.

3. **do**   4. **soon**

C. Write **room** and **zoo** to show more than one.

5. **rooms**   6. **zoos**

do
you
zoo
use
room
soon

164

TEKS 1.22A Use phonological knowledge to match sounds to letters to construct known words. **1.22C** Spell high-frequency words from a commonly used list. **1.22D** Spell base words with inflectional endings.

Extra Pattern Practice

Extra Pattern Practice Master,
TRB, p. 137

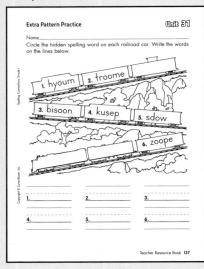

Hearing o͞o and yo͞o
Read the following story aloud. Ask students to make a mark on their paper each time they hear you say /o͞o/ or /yo͞o/.

Do you want to go to the zoo? We will leave soon, but first you need to clean this room. We will use that broom. Stand on the stool to dust the high shelf. Do you know there is a spoon under the bed? Wow! We are finally finished. Put away the broom so we can go to the zoo! **(19 marks)**

Read the story again. This time have students draw an X when they hear the /o͞o/ sound and a check mark when they hear the /yo͞o/ sound. **(15 X's, 4 check marks)**

TEKS 1.22A Use phonological knowledge to match sounds to letters to construct known words.
1.22C Spell high-frequency words from a commonly used list. **1.22D** Spell base words with inflectional endings.

Connections to READING

Write a spelling word to complete each sentence.

do
you
zoo
use
room
soon

1. What can we __?__ ?

2. We will make a __?__ .

3. We can __?__ this box for a pool.

4. It has __?__ for seals.

5. Can __?__ help me find the tape?

6. Our zoo will __?__ be finished.

1.	do	2.	zoo
3.	use	4.	room
5.	you	6.	soon

 TEKS 1.22C Spell high-frequency words from a commonly used list.

165

Day 3 — Unit 31

Student Objectives
• Write and spell words with /o͞o/ and /yo͞o/ to complete sentences.

Teaching Tips
• Write **do, you, zoo,** and **use** on the board. Review that /o͞o/ and /yo͞o/ can be spelled with **o, ou, oo,** and **u**-consonant-**e**. Remind students that the final **e** in **use** is silent.
• Read the directions aloud. Point out that some sentences give a clue about the missing word, but some do not. When there is no clue, students may have to try several words to find the one that makes the most sense in the sentence. Read the first sentence. Ask students if the sentence has a clue. Read the sentence aloud, using a different word in the blank each time. Ask students to tell whether each word makes sense.
• Tell students they will use each word only once.
• Have students complete page 165.

Differentiated Instruction
• Use the **Challenge Words** activity on page 207 with students who are ready to transfer their knowledge of the /o͞o/ and /yo͞o/ sounds to new words.
• An Extra Challenge Practice Master is available on page 138 in the *TRB*.
• Dictation sentences for the challenge words are available on page T207.

More Fun With Spelling for Differentiation

 ## Digital Resources for Spelling Connections

Interactive digital resources include word sorts, pattern practice, and proofreading activities for individual and whole-group instruction. (Interactive whiteboard compatible; see p. Z32.)

Spelling Connections Online

Interactive online spelling activities include word sorts, crossword puzzles, sentence completion, proofreading practice, and spelling bees with words from each unit (see p. Z32). www.spellingconnectionsonline.com

Spelling Center Activities

Spelling Game Mats
Place one of the spelling games in a learning center to provide a fun way for students to practice their spelling words (see p. Z26).

Flip Folder
Students can use a Flip Folder to practice spelling words independently (see p. Z32).

Word Sort CD-ROM
Printable, unit-specific word cards for spelling and challenge words can be used for Teacher-Led, Individual, Buddy, and Speed Sorts (see p. Z31).

 TEKS 1.22C Spell high-frequency words from a commonly used list.

T165

Student Objectives
- Identify spelling words in a letter.
- Use proofreading marks to revise writing.
- Use spelling words to write a letter.

Teaching Tips
- Read the introduction and review the proofreading marks with the class.
- Have students complete Part A independently.
- Read the directions for Part B. Explain to students that they will rewrite the letter on a separate sheet of paper.
- To extend this activity and provide more practice with the spelling words, prompt students to write a story about a zoo. The story can be about something that really happened, or it can be from the student's imagination. Ask volunteers to read their stories aloud. Have the class identify any spelling words used.

WORD SORT CD-ROM
- Invite students to practice for the weekly test by doing an **Individual Sort** or a **Speed Sort** (see p. Z31).

Day 5

Student Objectives
- Demonstrate mastery of the unit spelling words.

Posttest Assessment Options
Option 1: Administer the unit posttest using the dictation sentences at right.

Option 2: Assess students using the standardized test. See the *Standardized Test Master Book*, p. 35.

Note: Posttest sentences for the on level and challenge lists are available on the audio *Spelling Connections* Posttest CD.

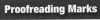

Connections to WRITING

Use proofreading marks to fix what you read. Add a letter or a word with ∧. Take away a letter or a word with ℓ. Start a paragraph with ¶.

Proofreading Marks

≡	Capital Letter
/	Small Letter
∧	Add
ℓ	Delete
⊙	Add a Period
¶	Indent

do
you
zoo
use
room
soon

A. Underline the spelling words. Then write them on the lines below.

Dear Aunt Lil,

¶ I <u>do</u> like the <u>zoo</u>. We went today. We always <u>use</u> a ma̶p map to find new animals. We will ∧ see <u>you</u> <u>soon</u>. I want to show you my new <u>room</u> ⊙

Love,
Jen

1. do
2. zoo
3. use
4. you
5. soon
6. room

B. Rewrite the letter. Make the changes shown by the proofreading marks.

166

TEKS 1.22C Spell high-frequency words from a commonly used list.

1-Minute Handwriting Hint

The descender of the lowercase **y** fills the entire space below the baseline. Be sure that the two slant strokes meet at the baseline.

y → TOUCH
← FILL SPACE

Posttest Sentences
1. When **do** we eat lunch?
2. It will **soon** be time for vacation.
3. Where would **you** like to go?
4. There is a baby lion at the **zoo**.
5. Did you **use** any of the paper?
6. There is **room** for one more chair.

Standardized Test Master Book, p. 35

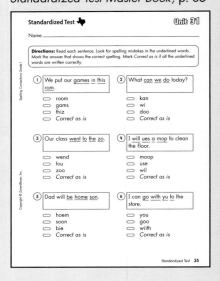

Standardized Test — Unit 31

Name _____

Directions: Read each sentence. Look for spelling mistakes in the underlined words. Mark the answer that shows the correct spelling. Mark Correct as is if all the underlined words are written correctly.

① We put our <u>games</u> in this <u>rom</u>.
- room
- gams
- thiz
- Correct as is

② What <u>can we do</u> today?
- kan
- wi
- doo
- Correct as is

③ Our class <u>went</u> to the <u>zo</u>.
- wend
- tou
- zoo
- Correct as is

④ I will <u>ues</u> a <u>mop</u> to clean the floor.
- moop
- use
- wil
- Correct as is

⑤ Dad will <u>be</u> home <u>son</u>.
- hoem
- soon
- bie
- Correct as is

⑥ I can go with <u>yu</u> to the store.
- you
- goo
- withh
- Correct as is

Standardized Test 35

 TEKS 1.22A Use phonological knowledge to match sounds to letters to construct known words. **1.22C** Spell high-frequency words from a commonly used list.

Planner

Day 1

Day 2

Day 1

Connections to **Thinking**

Student Objectives
- Identify and write words with final consonant digraph **ck**.

Instruction for All Students
- Pretest Dictation Sentences, p. T167B
- Connections to Thinking, p. 167
- Home/School Spelling Practice Masters (*Teacher Resource Book*, pp. 139–140)

TEKS 1.22A, 1.22C

Connections to **Phonics**

Student Objectives
- Use letter clues to write words with final consonant digraph **ck**.
- Add **-s** to words to form plurals.

Instruction for All Students
- Connections to Phonics, p. 168

Optional Practice
- Extra Pattern Practice Master (*Teacher Resource Book*, p. 141)

TEKS 1.22A, 1.22C, 1.22D

Spelling Words
back
pack
neck
pick
sock
duck

Challenge Words
tuck
quack
cluck
crack

Day 3

Day 4

Day 5

Day 2

Day 3

Connections to **Reading**

Student Objectives
- Write and spell words with final consonant digraph **ck** to complete sentences.

Instruction for All Students
- Connections to Reading, p. 169

Differentiated Instruction
- Challenge Words, p. 208

TEKS 1.22A, 1.22C

Connections to **Writing**

Student Objectives
- Identify spelling words in a paragraph.
- Use proofreading marks to revise writing.
- Use spelling words to write a paragraph.

Instruction for All Students
- Connections to Writing, p. 170

Differentiated Instruction
- Extra Challenge Practice Master (*Teacher Resource Book*, p. 142)

TEKS 1.22A, 1.22C, 1.22E

Assessment

Student Objectives
- Demonstrate mastery of the unit spelling words.

Assessment for All Students
- Posttest Dictation Sentences, p. T170, or
- *Standardized Test Master Book*, p. 36

Differentiated Assessment
- Challenge Dictation Sentences, p. T208

Unit 32 Materials

Student Edition
pp. 167–170, 208

Teacher Edition
pp. T167A–T170, T208

 Teacher Resource Book
Unit 32 Practice Masters,
pp. 139–142, and
Sound/Symbol Cards

 Standardized Test Master Book
Unit 32 Test Master, p. 36

 Word Sort CD-ROM
Unit 32 Word Sort Cards for Teacher-
Led Sorts and Student Sorts

 **Digital Resources for
Spelling Connections**
Unit 32

Spelling Connections Online
www.spellingconnectionsonline.com

**Spelling Support for
English Language Learners***
Unit 32 Practice Masters and
Audio Conversation

Spelling Center Activities*
Spelling Game Mats
Flip Folder, *TRB*, p. 155

*Spelling Support for English Language
Learners *and Spelling Center Activities may
be used at any time during the week.*

Assessment

Pretest Sentences (See procedures on p. Z30.)
1. Tracy is at the **back** of the bus.
2. Did you **pack** your bag?
3. The giraffe has a long **neck**.
4. I helped Dad **pick** a tie to wear.
5. Your right **sock** does not match your left one.
6. There is a **duck** on the pond.

The Science of Spelling ◄ • •

Consonant digraphs are two consonants
together that make one sound. In some
digraphs, one consonant is silent while
the other makes the sound, as in **ck**. In
other digraphs, the two consonants
together make a different sound, as in **ch**.
Common initial digraphs include **sh, wh,
ch, th,** and **ph**. Common final digraphs
include **ck, sh, th, gn, mb,** and double
final consonants such as **ll** and **ss**.

ELL Support

Choose from the activities below to reinforce English language acquisition.

Beginning

Word Meaning Write the spelling words on the board, point to each word, say it aloud, and have students repeat it. Then demonstrate the word in some way. For example, hold up a sock and say **sock**. Point to your neck and say **neck**. Invite students to repeat your gestures. Students can hear the Unit 32 spelling words pronounced on the audio recording.

Short Vowel Review List the spelling words on the board. Tell students that every short vowel sound is represented in the list. Say each word and have students repeat it. Ask what vowel sound students hear. Then have a volunteer circle the vowel that makes that sound. Have students say the words with you one more time.

Making Words Plural Write **pack** on the board. Display a school pack or show a picture of one. Say, *This is a pack.* Then show a second pack. Ask students how they would change the word **pack** to name two packs. **(add s)** Ask a volunteer to add an **s** to **pack** and have students read the word. Write the remaining words on the board. Call on volunteers to add an **s** to each word so that it means more than one.

Intermediate

Make a Word Cut a wide strip of card stock and cut two slots, one above the other, about two inches apart in the middle of the strip. Cut a narrow strip of card stock that can be threaded through the two slots in the wide strip. Write a large **ck** on the wide strip to the right of the bottom slot. On the narrow strip write **ba, pa, ne, pi, so,** and **du** widely spaced. Thread the strip through the slots. Have students pull on the strip to bring word parts in front of **ck**. Have them read the words they make. Extend the activity by making additional narrow strips with word parts such as **spe, fli, tru, tri, sla, smo**.

Match Words and Pictures Make a copy of page 31 of *Spelling Support for English Language Learners* for each student. Have students find a partner. Direct them to cut out the word and picture cards and make two stacks. Explain the directions for the game and have students play. Then encourage partners to work together on the other activities on the page.

Support for Spanish Speakers

Comparing Languages Spanish speakers may have difficulty hearing and pronouncing some English consonants. Some consonant sounds are quite different in the two languages. For example, **h** is the only silent letter in Spanish, and the letters **k, w,** and the digraph **wh** are only in words that came into Spanish from other languages. In addition, there are only a limited number of final consonant sounds in Spanish words, so native Spanish speakers may have trouble hearing and pronouncing final consonant digraphs. Provide practice listening for and pronouncing both initial and final digraphs.

Choose from the activities below to reinforce English language acquisition.

Advanced

Make Words Cut card stock into squares. Write **ck** on one square. On other squares, write the letters **b, p, n, s, d, a, e, i, o,** and **u.** Have students use the squares to construct spelling words with final **ck.** Encourage students to write the words they make.

Words and Sentences Have students write a sentence, leaving a blank where a spelling word could be inserted. Direct students to exchange papers with a partner and complete each other's sentences. Then have them read their sentences to each other. Encourage students to continue writing sentences until they each have written a sentence for each spelling word.

Rhyming Words Write the following rhyme on the board and read it aloud: *One sock, two socks, three socks four. I see socks and look for more.* Erase the words **sock/socks.** Invite a volunteer to complete the rhyme by writing another spelling word in place of **sock/socks.** Ask what was added to the spelling word to talk about two, three, four, and more. (the letter s)

Conversation Have students listen to the conversation using spelling words for Unit 32 on the audio recording. Then have them listen a second time, this time following along with the print version on page 54 of *Spelling Support for English Language Learners.* Have partners read the conversation. Challenge them to extend it.

Advanced High

Use Spelling Words List the spelling words and write the following on the board: *I put on my _____ s. I _____ up my _____. I put it on my _____. My pet _____ says quack. I pet his _____.* Tell students that a spelling word can be written on each line to finish the story. Ask students to say the word that makes the most sense in each blank. (sock, pick, pack, back, duck, neck) Call on volunteers to write the words. Then read the story with students. Ask if any changes are needed. Continue until students say the story is correct.

Use Proofreading Marks Ask students to say sentences using the spelling words. Write the sentences on the board. Misspell some of the spelling words, leave out periods at the end of sentences, and make some capitalization mistakes. Tell students you have made some mistakes writing their sentences. Ask them to carefully read the sentences and tell you what the mistakes are. Call on volunteers to mark the mistakes with proofreading marks. Then have students write the sentences correctly.

Write a Story Have partners work together to write a short story about a duck. Suggest they illustrate the story first and then write a sentence or two to tell about each picture. Have partners read their story to each other and correct any errors. Then have them share their story with another pair of students.

Spelling Support for English Language Learners

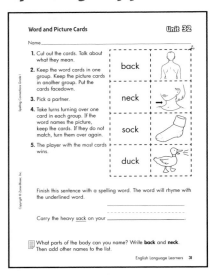

Practice Master, p. 31

Practice Master, p. 54

Audio Conversation available on CD

Word List	Unit 32
English	Spanish
1. back	espalda
2. pack	empaquetar; empacar; paquete
3. neck	cuello
4. pick	escoger
5. sock	calcetín
6. duck	pato(a)

English/Spanish Word List, p. 69

Spelling Connections Online
Interactive online spelling activities provide additional ELL support.
www.spellingconnectionsonline.com

Connections to THINKING

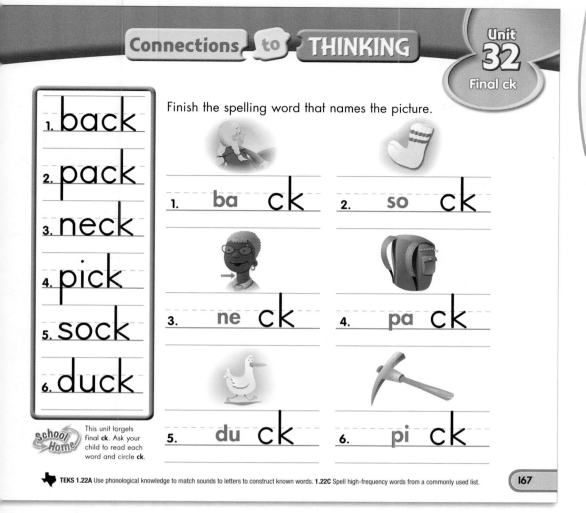

Finish the spelling word that names the picture.

1. back
2. pack
3. neck
4. pick
5. sock
6. duck

1. ba **ck**
2. so **ck**
3. ne **ck**
4. pa **ck**
5. du **ck**
6. pi **ck**

 School Home This unit targets final **ck**. Ask your child to read each word and circle **ck**.

TEKS 1.22A Use phonological knowledge to match sounds to letters to construct known words. 1.22C Spell high-frequency words from a commonly used list.

167

Student Objectives
- Read, spell, and write words with final consonant digraph **ck**.

Unit Pretest
- Administer the pretest on page T167B.

Teaching Tips

WORD SORT CD-ROM

- Conduct a **Teacher-Led Sort** (see p. Z31) to introduce the spelling pattern.
- Have students name the words represented by the Sound/Symbol Cards for **kick, lock, sock, stick,** and **thick.** Ask students what sound they hear at the end of every word. (**/k/**)
- Write the spelling words. Underline **ck** in each word. Point out that **c** and **k** work together to make the **/k/** sound.
- Remind students that when there is only one vowel in a word, the vowel is usually short. Tell them what when **/k/** comes right after a short vowel, it is usually spelled **ck.**
- Guide students in reading each word and using it in a sentence.
- Have students complete the page independently or as a class.

Home/School Word Lists **TRB**
- Have students take home the Home/School Spelling Practice Masters.

Home/School Practice

Home/School Spelling
Practice Master, *TRB*, p. 139

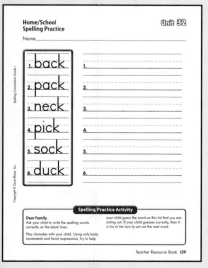

English

Home/School Spelling
Practice Master, *TRB*, p. 140

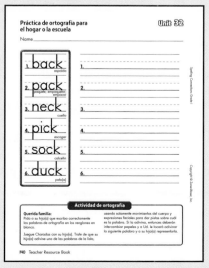

Spanish

TEKS 1.22A Use phonological knowledge to match sounds to letters to construct known words. 1.22C Spell high-frequency words from a commonly used list.

T167

Student Objectives
- Use letter clues to write words with final consonant digraph **ck**.
- Add **-s** to words to form plurals.

Teaching Tips
- List the spelling words on the board. Have students read the words. Ask what sound they hear at the end of each word. (/**k**/) Ask how this sound is spelled. (**ck**)
- Tell students you will give a letter clue for them to guess a spelling word. For example, say, *begins with* **n**. Have a volunteer write **neck**. Say, *short vowel* **i**. Call on a volunteer to write **pick**.
- Write **pack** on the board. Tell students that this word tells about one pack. Ask students what they would add to **pack** so that it would tell about two or more packs. (add **s**) Ask a volunteer to write **s** after **pack** to make the word plural.
- Have students complete page 168 independently or as a class.

Extra Pattern Practice TRB
- Use the optional practice master below for extra practice with final **ck**.

WORD SORT CD-ROM
- Provide time for students to use a **Buddy Sort** (see p. Z31) to practice their spelling words with a partner.

Connections to PHONICS

A. Write letters in the blanks to complete each spelling word.

1. ne__ __
   neck

2. b__ __k
   back

3. p__c__
   pick

4. pa__ __
   pack

back
pack
neck
pick
sock
duck

B. Add and write.

5. 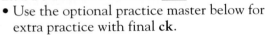 + = 2 **socks**

6. + = 2 **ducks**

168

TEKS **1.22C** Spell high-frequency words from a commonly used list. **1.22D** Spell base words with inflectional endings.

Extra Pattern Practice

Extra Pattern Practice Master,
TRB, p. 141

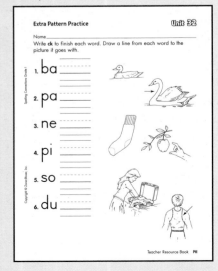

Listen for Final ck
Say **back**, **pack**, **neck**, **pick**, **sock**, and **duck**. Ask students what sound they hear at the end of each word. (/**k**/) Explain that each word ends with two letters—**ck**—but only one sound—/**k**/. Tell students to raise their hand when they hear the word in each group of words below that ends with /**k**/. Call on a volunteer to say the word and write it on the board.

back, pat, has	but, duck, song
car, pick, grab	is, hand, neck
sock, cut, stop	last, tip, pack

TEKS **1.22A** Use phonological knowledge to match sounds to letters to construct known words. **1.22C** Spell high-frequency words from a commonly used list. **1.22D** Spell base words with inflectional endings.

Write the missing spelling words.

Meg's Duck

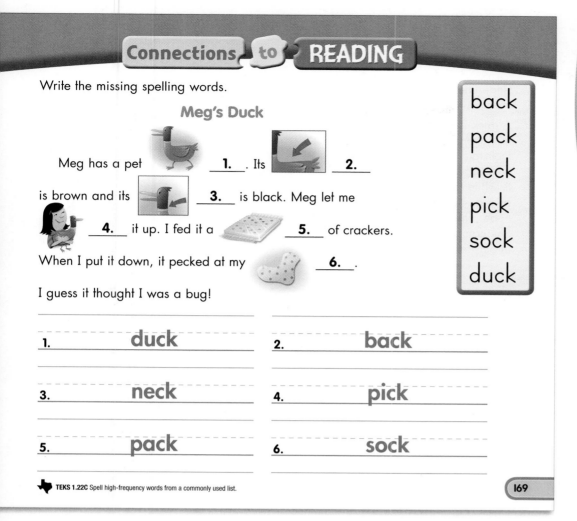

Meg has a pet ___1.___ . Its ___2.___

is brown and its ___3.___ is black. Meg let me

___4.___ it up. I fed it a ___5.___ of crackers.

When I put it down, it pecked at my ___6.___ .

I guess it thought I was a bug!

back	
pack	
neck	
pick	
sock	
duck	

1.	duck	2.	back
3.	neck	4.	pick
5.	pack	6.	sock

 TEKS 1.22C Spell high-frequency words from a commonly used list.

169

Student Objectives
• Write and spell words with final consonant digraph **ck** to complete sentences.

Teaching Tips
• Say **sock**. Ask students what sound they hear at the end of the word. **(/k/)** Ask how this sound is spelled. **(ck)** Have a volunteer write the word on the board.
• List the spelling words on the board. Then write the following sentence: My _____ *has a hole in it.* Help students read the sentence. Talk about which word makes the most sense in the sentence. Explain that **pack** and **sock** would work. Ask a volunteer to write **sock**. Then have students read the sentence together.
• Have students complete page 169.

Differentiated Instruction
• Use the **Challenge Words** activity on page 208 with students who are ready to transfer their knowledge of final **ck** to new words.
• An Extra Challenge Practice Master is available on page 142 in the *TRB*.
• Dictation sentences for the challenge words are available on page T208.

More Fun With Spelling for Differentiation

Digital Resources for Spelling Connections

Interactive digital resources include word sorts, pattern practice, and proofreading activities for individual and whole-group instruction. (Interactive whiteboard compatible; see p. Z32.)

Spelling Connections Online

Interactive online spelling activities include word sorts, crossword puzzles, sentence completion, proofreading practice, and spelling bees with words from each unit (see p. Z32).
www.spellingconnectionsonline.com

Spelling Center Activities

Spelling Game Mats
Place one of the spelling games in a learning center to provide a fun way for students to practice their spelling words (see p. Z26).

Flip Folder
Students can use a Flip Folder to practice spelling words independently (see p. Z32).

Word Sort CD-ROM
Printable, unit-specific word cards for spelling and challenge words can be used for Teacher-Led, Individual, Buddy, and Speed Sorts (see p. Z31).

TEKS 1.22A Use phonological knowledge to match sounds to letters to construct known words. **1.22C** Spell high-frequency words from a commonly used list.

T169

Student Objectives
- Identify spelling words in a paragraph.
- Use proofreading marks to revise writing.
- Use spelling words to write a paragraph.

Teaching Tips
- Read the directions and review the proofreading marks with the class.
- Have students complete Part A independently.
- Read the directions for Part B. Tell students to write on a separate sheet of paper. When they have finished, prompt them to proofread their work.
- Read the directions for Part C. Have students complete this section independently. Provide reference materials.
- When students have finished, ask them to review their work to make sure they have spelled spelling words correctly. Have them circle two words they are not sure about and check the spelling of each in a dictionary.
- Invite volunteers to read their work aloud. Have the class identify spelling words used.

WORD SORT CD-ROM
- Invite students to practice for the weekly test by doing an **Individual Sort** or a **Speed Sort** (see p. Z31).

Day 5

Student Objectives
- Demonstrate mastery of the unit spelling words.

Posttest Assessment Options
Option 1: Administer the unit posttest using the dictation sentences at right.

Option 2: Assess students using the standardized test. See the *Standardized Test Master Book*, p. 36.

Note: Posttest sentences for the on level and challenge lists are available on the audio *Spelling Connections* Posttest CD.

Connections to WRITING

A. Underline the spelling words. Then write them on the lines below.

¶A <u>duck</u> is a bird. Ducks spend a lot of time in water They swim and dive to <u>pick</u> up their fo͜od. Male mallards have a gray <u>back</u> with brown in the middle. the head is green. A white ring around the <u>neck</u> makes it look as if he has a <u>sock</u> on his head. The female is brown. She can <u>pack</u> about 12 eggs in her nest.

Proofreading Marks
≡	Capital Letter
/	Small Letter
∧	Add
ℒ	Delete
⊙	Add a Period
¶	Indent

back
pack
neck
pick
sock
duck

1. duck
2. pick
3. back
4. neck
5. sock
6. pack

B. Rewrite the sentences. Make the changes shown by the proofreading marks.

C. Write more about mallard ducks. Use as many spelling words as you can. Check your spelling in a dictionary.

170

TEKS 1.22A Use phonological knowledge to match sounds to letters to construct known words. **1.22C** Spell high-frequency words from a commonly used list. **1.22E** Use resources to find correct spellings.

1-Minute Handwriting Hint
The lowercase **c** begins just below the midline and ends just above the baseline.

BEGIN
C ← STOP

Posttest Sentences
1. My **sock** is all wet!
2. Did you see the **duck** on the pond?
3. Wrap the scarf around your **neck**.
4. Did you **pack** your suitcase?
5. You may **pick** out clothes.
6. Take your book **back** to the library.

Standardized Test Master Book, p. 36

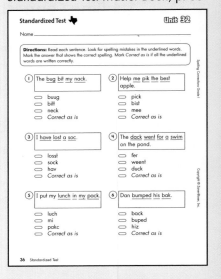

TEKS 1.22A Use phonological knowledge to match sounds to letters to construct known words. **1.22C** Spell high-frequency words from a commonly used list. **1.22E** Use resources to find correct spellings.

Planner

Day 1

Day 2

Day 1

Connections to **Thinking**

Student Objectives
- Read, spell, and write words with initial or final **sh**.
- Match a spelling word with its definition.

Instruction for All Students
- Pretest Dictation Sentences, p. T171B
- Connections to Thinking, p. 171
- Home/School Spelling Practice Masters (*Teacher Resource Book*, pp. 143–144)

🐾 **TEKS 1.22A, 1.22C**

Connections to **Phonics**

Student Objectives
- Identify words that rhyme.
- Match sounds to letters to write words with **sh**.
- Identify opposites.

Instruction for All Students
- Connections to Phonics, p. 172

Optional Practice
- Extra Pattern Practice Master (*Teacher Resource Book*, p. 145)

🐾 **TEKS 1.22A, 1.22C**

Spelling Words
ship
shop
show
dish
wish
push

Challenge Words
shake
hush
shut
crash

Day 3

Day 4

Day 5

Day 2

Day 3

Connections to **Reading**

Student Objectives
- Write and spell words with initial or final **sh** to complete sentences.
- Use a dictionary to check spelling and correct misspelled words.

Instruction for All Students
- Connections to Reading, p. 173

Differentiated Instruction
- Challenge Words, p. 209

🐾 **TEKS 1.22A, 1.22C, 1.22E**

Connections to **Writing**

Student Objectives
- Identify spelling words in a poem.
- Use proofreading marks to revise writing.
- Use spelling words to write a poem.

Instruction for All Students
- Connections to Writing, p. 174

Differentiated Instruction
- Extra Challenge Practice Master (*Teacher Resource Book*, p. 146)

🐾 **TEKS 1.22A, 1.22C**

Assessment

Student Objectives
- Demonstrate mastery of the unit spelling words.

Assessment for All Students
- Posttest Dictation Sentences, p. T174, or
- *Standardized Test Master Book*, p. 37

Differentiated Assessment
- Challenge Dictation Sentences, p. T209

Unit 33 Materials

Student Edition
pp. 171–174, 209

Teacher Edition
pp. T171A–T174, T209

 Teacher Resource Book
Unit 33 Practice Masters,
pp. 143–146, and
Sound/Symbol Cards

 Standardized Test Master Book
Unit 33 Test Master, p. 37

 Word Sort CD-ROM
Unit 33 Word Sort Cards for Teacher-
Led Sorts and Student Sorts

 **Digital Resources for
Spelling Connections**
Unit 33

Spelling Connections Online
www.spellingconnectionsonline.com

**Spelling Support for
English Language Learners***
Unit 33 Practice Masters and
Audio Conversation

Spelling Activities*
Spelling Game Mats
Flip Folder, *TRB*, p. 155

*Spelling Support for English Language
Learners *and Spelling Center Activities may
be used at any time during the week.*

Assessment

Pretest Sentences (See procedures on p. Z30.)
1. I waved to the people sailing on the **ship**.
2. I will help Dad **shop** for groceries.
3. Can you **show** Sissy how to tie her shoes?
4. Please pass me the **dish** of corn.
5. His third **wish** was for a golden egg.
6. Will you **push** me on the swing?

The Science of Spelling ◄ • •

- A consonant digraph is two or more
  consonants together that make one
  sound. The consonant digraph **sh** can
  appear at the beginning (**shout**), in the
  middle (**brushing**), or at the end (**hash**) of
  a word.

- The /**sh**/ sound is spelled **sh**, as in **shoe**,
  31% of the time. It is spelled **t**, as in
  nation, 52% of the time.

ELL Support

Choose from the activities below to reinforce English language acquisition.

Beginning

Word Meaning List the spelling words on the board. Read them aloud and have students repeat. Ask students which words they do not know. Use pantomime, gestures, and pictures along with simple statements to provide context and reinforce word meaning. For words students know, call on volunteers to demonstrate the meaning.

Hearing /sh/ Have each student write **sh** on an index card. Tell students you will say a list of words. Have them raise their card when they hear /sh/ at the beginning or end of a word. Say **dish, chip, push, shut, chop, store, show, shop, crash, wish, spot, chore, slap, hush, best,** and **shell.** Pronounce each word clearly to help students discriminate sounds, especially /ch/ and /sh/.

Check the Word Write **dish** and **shop** on the board. Then write **diish** and **shp** next to the first two words. Ask students to compare the words letter-by-letter and tell what is wrong with the second set of words. (two i's in dish, missing o in shop) Have students turn to the dictionary in the back of their books. Explain that a dictionary is an alphabetical list of spelling words and their meanings. Tell students that this is a good place to check the spelling of a word. Show them how to find **dish** and **shop.** Read the words and have students repeat. Have them compare each spelling to the word on the board. Also read the meaning of each word.

Intermediate

Words and Pictures Write the spelling words on index cards. Find or a draw a picture that illustrates each word. Display a picture. Talk about what is shown. Then ask a volunteer to select the word that names the picture. Place the word card with the picture. Continue until all the words and pictures have been matched.

Write Sentences List the spelling words on the board and ask students to use each one in a sentence. Write each sentence on the board and help students read it. Then erase the spelling word. Read the sentence again and pause at the blank space. Have students say the correct word. Call on a volunteer to write the word in the space. Then read the sentence one more time. Continue with the remaining words.

Alphabetical Order Review the English alphabet using an alphabet chart. Read each letter in order and have students repeat. Then write the letters **w** and **p** on the board. Call on volunteers to find the letters on the alphabet chart. Ask which comes first and which comes next in the alphabet. Then write **wish** and **push.** Have volunteers circle the first letter in each word. Have them use these letters to tell which comes first and which comes next in **a-b-c** order.

Support for Spanish Speakers

Comparing Languages Except for **ch, ll,** and **rr,** digraphs are rare in Spanish. Therefore, Spanish speakers may have difficulty hearing and pronouncing **sh** and may confuse **sh** with **ch.** Provide practice for students in listening to and pronouncing words that will help them discriminate these sounds such as **cheap/sheep, chew/ shoe, chair/share,** and **chip/ship.**

Choose from the activities below to reinforce English language acquisition.

Advanced

Spell and Write Write the following words on the board: **grow, pull, plop, flip, wilt, dips.** Tell students to note where in each word there are two consonants together. Then have them replace these consonants with **sh** and write the spelling words. (show, push, shop, ship, wish, dish)

Word Characters Have students select a spelling word and think of it as the name of a character in a story. Provide card stock for students to make a name tag for their word. Then have them display their name and tell another student or small group what their character is like. For example, **Shop** might always be shopping.

Answer Questions Provide each student with a copy of page 32 of *Spelling Support for English Language Learners.* Have students read and answer the questions independently or with a partner. Encourage them to write their answers to the question at the bottom of the page and then share their list with another student.

Word Wall As students read and work with other classroom materials and books, have them look for words with initial or final **sh**. Provide shapes cut from colored paper. Have students write the words they find on the shapes and tape them to a Word Wall.

Advanced High

Conversation Have students listen to the dialogue on the audio recording. Then have them listen for a second time and follow along with the print version on page 55 of *Spelling Support for English Language Learners.* Finally, have partners read the dialogue. Encourage them to continue the conversation beyond the print version.

Check the Word Have students write a sentence using a spelling word. Tell them to misspell their selected word. Then have them trade sentences with a partner. The partner decides which word is misspelled and then finds and checks the correct spelling in the dictionary in the back of the student book. The partner reports back to the first student to show the selected word and correct spelling.

Word Puzzle Create a crossword puzzle grid to match the following configuration:

```
s  h  i  p
h        u
o     s  h  o  w
p     h        i
      i        s
   d  i  s  h
```

Fill in the bold letters. Then use the definitions on page 171 of the student book as clues. Use these clues for **wish** and **push**: *to want something* and *to shove.* Read each clue aloud and have students complete the puzzle with spelling words.

Spelling Support for English Language Learners

Practice Master, p. 32

Practice Master, p. 55

Audio Conversation available on CD

English/Spanish Word List, p. 70

Spelling Connections Online
Interactive online spelling activities provide additional ELL support.
www.spellingconnectionsonline.com

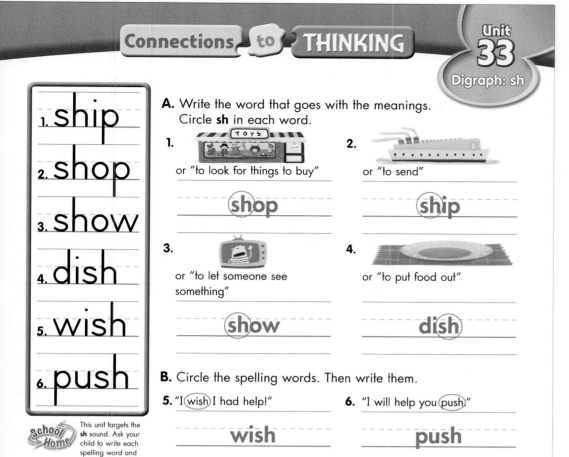

A. Write the word that goes with the meanings. Circle **sh** in each word.

1. or "to look for things to buy"

__shop__

2. or "to send"

__ship__

3. or "to let someone see something"

__show__

4. or "to put food out"

__dish__

B. Circle the spelling words. Then write them.

5. "I (wish) I had help!"

__wish__

6. "I will help you (push)."

__push__

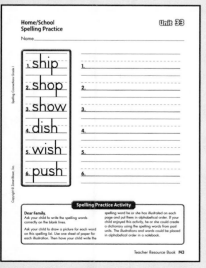

1. ship
2. shop
3. show
4. dish
5. wish
6. push

This unit targets the **sh** sound. Ask your child to write each spelling word and circle **sh**.

TEKS 1.22A Use phonological knowledge to match sounds to letters to construct known words. 1.22C Spell high-frequency words from a commonly used list.

171

Day 1

Unit
33

Student Objectives
• Read, spell, and write words with initial or final **sh**.
• Match a spelling word with its definition.

Unit Pretest
• Administer the pretest on page T171B.

Teaching Tips

WORD SORT **CD-ROM**

• Conduct a **Teacher-Led Sort** (see p. Z31) to introduce the spelling pattern.
• Write **ship** on the board and underline **sh**. Point out that **s** and **h** work together to make one sound. Use the Sound/Symbol Cards for **dish, fish, rash, shave, sheep, shell,** and **shop** to practice identifying and making the /**sh**/ sound.
• Introduce the spelling words with *I am thinking of a word… .* Give clues to the meaning of each word. Have a volunteer write the word on the board and circle the letters that spell the /**sh**/ sound.
• Point to **ow** in **show**. Explain that the **o** makes the **long o** sound and the **w** is silent. Have students say the word.
• Have students complete the page independently or as a class.

Home/School Word Lists
• Have students take home the Home/ School Spelling Practice Masters.

Home/School Practice

Home/School Spelling
Practice Master, *TRB*, p. 143

Home/School Spelling
Practice Master, *TRB*, p. 144

English

Spanish

TEKS 1.22A Use phonological knowledge to match sounds to letters to construct known words. 1.22C Spell high-frequency words from a commonly used list.

T171

Student Objectives

- Identify words that rhyme.
- Match sounds to letters to write words with **sh.**
- Identify opposites.

Teaching Tips

- List the spelling words on the board. Say **ship, shop,** and **show.** Have students repeat. Ask what sound students hear at the beginning of each word. **(/sh/)** Then say **dish, wish,** and **push.** Ask where the /**sh**/ sound is in these words. **(at the end)**
- Read each spelling word aloud. Ask students to identify the vowel sound in each.
- Refer to the list of spelling words. Have students read the words aloud and tell which words rhyme. **(dish, wish)** Prompt students to think of at least one rhyming word for **ship** and **shop.** **(Possible words: chip, dip, hip, lip, rip, sip, tip, whip, zip; chop, hop, mop, pop, top)**
- Have students complete page 172 independently or as a class.

Extra Pattern Practice

- Use the optional practice master below for extra practice with initial and final **sh.**

WORD SORT CD-ROM

- Provide time for students to use a **Buddy Sort** (see p. Z31) to practice their spelling words with a partner.

Connections to PHONICS

1–2. Write the spelling words that rhyme with .

_____ dish _____

_____ wish _____

3. Write the spelling word that rhymes with .

_____ ship _____

4. Write the spelling word that rhymes with .

_____ shop _____

5. Write the spelling word that means the opposite of **pull.**

_____ push _____

6. Write the spelling word with the **long o** sound.

_____ show _____

ship
shop
show
dish
wish
push

TEKS 1.22A Use phonological knowledge to match sounds to letters to construct known words.
1.22C Spell high-frequency words from a commonly used list.

Extra Pattern Practice

Extra Pattern Practice Master,
TRB, p. 145

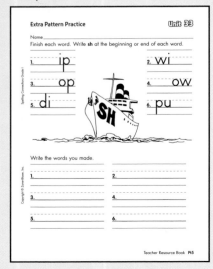

Teacher Resource Book 145

/sh/ and Listen

Put your fingers to your lips and say /**sh**/. Tell students that /**sh**/ is made by the letters **s** and **h** working together. Explain that /**sh**/ may come at the beginning of a word (**ship**) or at the end (**push**). Say, *I will read some words. When you hear the* /**sh**/ *sound at the beginning, shake your hand. When you hear it at the end, put your finger to your lips.*

ship	dish	shop	shell	show	wish	push
shut	crash	bush	hush	shake	she	wash

TEKS 1.22A Use phonological knowledge to match sounds to letters to construct known words. **1.22C** Spell high-frequency words from a commonly used list.

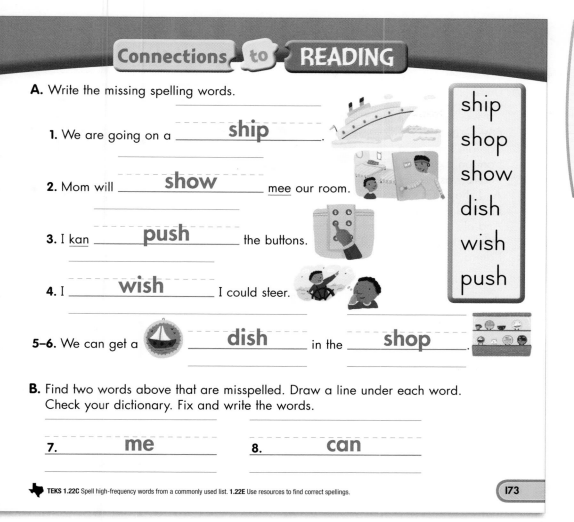

Connections to READING

A. Write the missing spelling words.

ship
shop
show
dish
wish
push

1. We are going on a __ship__.

2. Mom will __show__ mee our room.

3. I kan __push__ the buttons.

4. I __wish__ I could steer.

5–6. We can get a __dish__ in the __shop__.

B. Find two words above that are misspelled. Draw a line under each word. Check your dictionary. Fix and write the words.

7. __me__

8. __can__

TEKS 1.22C Spell high-frequency words from a commonly used list. **1.22E** Use resources to find correct spellings.

173

Student Objectives
- Write and spell words with initial or final **sh** to complete sentences.
- Use a dictionary to check spelling and correct misspelled words.

Teaching Tips
- Write **ship** and **wish** on the board. Ask volunteers to underline **sh** in each word. Review that **s** and **h** work together to make the /**sh**/ sound.
- Write the following sentence: *I ____ to travel on a ____.* Read the sentence and have students tell you which spelling words make the most sense in the blanks. (**wish, ship**) Have volunteers write the words in the spaces.
- Write **pash** and **dissh**. Point out that these spelling words are misspelled. Call on volunteers to locate each word in a dictionary, check the spelling, and write the word correctly. (**push, dish**)
- Have students complete page 173.

Differentiated Instruction
- Use the **Challenge Words** activity on page 209 with students who are ready to transfer their knowledge of **sh** to new words.
- An Extra Challenge Practice Master is available on page 146 in the *TRB*.
- Dictation sentences for the challenge words are available on page T209.

More Fun With Spelling for Differentiation

⌖ Digital Resources for Spelling Connections
Interactive digital resources include word sorts, pattern practice, and proofreading activities for individual and whole-group instruction. (Interactive whiteboard compatible; see p. Z32.)

⌖ Spelling Connections Online
Interactive online spelling activities include word sorts, crossword puzzles, sentence completion, proofreading practice, and spelling bees with words from each unit (see p. Z32). www.spellingconnectionsonline.com

Spelling Center Activities

Spelling Game Mats
Place one of the spelling games in a learning center to provide a fun way for students to practice their spelling words (see p. Z26).

Flip Folder
Students can use a Flip Folder to practice spelling words independently (see p. Z32).

Word Sort CD-ROM
Printable, unit-specific word cards for spelling and challenge words can be used for Teacher-Led, Individual, Buddy, and Speed Sorts (see p. Z31).

TEKS 1.22A Use phonological knowledge to match sounds to letters to construct known words.
1.22C Spell high-frequency words from a commonly used list. **1.22E** Use resources to find correct spellings.

T173

Student Objectives
- Identify spelling words in a poem.
- Use proofreading marks to revise writing.
- Use spelling words to write a poem.

Teaching Tips
- Read the directions and review the proofreading marks with the class.
- Have students complete Part A independently.
- Read the directions for Part B. Explain to students that they will rewrite the poem on a separate sheet of paper.
- Read the directions for Part C. Give students a few minutes to brainstorm ideas. Remind them that poems often use sensory words, or words that tell how things look, feel, sound, and smell. Encourage students to use sensory words in their poems.
- Invite volunteers to read their poems aloud. Discuss any sensory words. Have the class identify the spelling words used.

WORD SORT CD-ROM
- Invite students to practice for the weekly test by doing an **Individual Sort** or a **Speed Sort** (see p. Z31).

Day 5

Student Objectives
- Demonstrate mastery of the unit spelling words.

Posttest Assessment Options
Option 1: Administer the unit posttest using the dictation sentences at right.

Option 2: Assess students using the standardized test. See the *Standardized Test Master Book*, p. 37.

Note: Posttest sentences for the on level and challenge lists are available on the audio *Spelling Connections* Posttest CD.

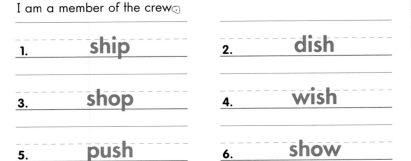

Connections to WRITING

A. Underline the spelling words. Then write them on the lines below.

Proofreading Marks
≡ Capital Letter
/ Small Letter
∧ Add
℘ Delete
⊙ Add a Period
¶ Indent

ship
shop
show
dish
wish
push

My Dream
I dream I am on a trip.
I am on a great big ship.
I have to wash every dish,
And shop to fill every wish.
i push a cart from place to place.
And always show a smiling face.
When I wake up I find it's true.
I am a member of the crew.

1. ship
2. dish
3. shop
4. wish
5. push
6. show

B. Rewrite the poem. Make the changes shown by the proofreading marks.

C. Write a poem about a dream or a wish. Use as many spelling words as you can.

174

🤠 **TEKS 1.22C** Spell high-frequency words from a commonly used list.

1-Minute Handwriting Hint
The two slant right and the two slant up strokes in the lowercase **w** should be parallel. Be sure that the spaces between the strokes are even.

PARALLEL

Posttest Sentences
1. My dad came to this country by **ship**.
2. Will you **show** us how to tie a knot?
3. What does this **shop** sell?
4. This **dish** is from Japan.
5. Will you help me **push** this wagon?
6. I **wish** you were not going away.

Standardized Test Master Book, p. 37

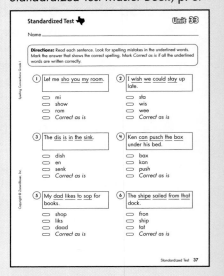

🤠 **TEKS 1.22A** Use phonological knowledge to match sounds to letters to construct known words. **1.22C** Spell high-frequency words from a commonly used list.

Day 1 | **Day 2**

Day 1

Connections to **Thinking**

Student Objectives
- Use letter, rhyme, and definition clues to write words with the digraph **th**.
- Write spelling words to name pictures.

Instruction for All Students
- Pretest Dictation Sentences, p. T175B
- Connections to Thinking, p. 175
- Home/School Spelling Practice Masters (*Teacher Resource Book*, pp. 147–148)

👉 **TEKS 1.22A, 1.22C**

Connections to **Phonics**

Student Objectives
- Blend sounds to say and write words that begin with the digraph **th**.
- Use letter and sound clues to write words that end with the digraph **th**.

Instruction for All Students
- Connections to Phonics, p. 176

Optional Practice
- Extra Pattern Practice Master (*Teacher Resource Book*, p. 149)

👉 **TEKS 1.22A, 1.22C**

Spelling Words
that
then
this
bath
path
with

Challenge Words
thud
thin
booth
thump

Day 3 | **Day 4** | **Day 5**

Day 2 | Day 3

Connections to **Reading**

Student Objectives
- Write and spell words with an initial or final **th** to complete sentences in a story.

Instruction for All Students
- Connections to Reading, p. 177

Differentiated Instruction
- Challenge Words, p. 210

👉 **TEKS 1.22A, 1.22C**

Connections to **Writing**

Student Objectives
- Identify spelling words in a paragraph.
- Use proofreading marks to revise writing.
- Use spelling words to write sentences.

Instruction for All Students
- Connections to Writing, p. 178

Differentiated Instruction
- Extra Challenge Practice Master (*Teacher Resource Book*, p. 150)

👉 **TEKS 1.22A, 1.22C, 1.22E**

Assessment

Student Objectives
- Demonstrate mastery of the unit spelling words.

Assessment for All Students
- Posttest Dictation Sentences, p. T178, or
- *Standardized Test Master Book*, p. 38

Differentiated Assessment
- Challenge Dictation Sentences, p. T210

Unit 34 Materials

Student Edition
pp. 175–178, 210

Teacher Edition
pp. T175A–T178, T210

 Teacher Resource Book
Unit 34 Practice Masters,
pp. 147–150, and
Sound/Symbol Cards

 Standardized Test Master Book
Unit 34 Test Master, p. 38

Word Sort CD-ROM
Unit 34 Word Sort Cards for Teacher-
Led Sorts and Student Sorts

 **Digital Resources for
Spelling Connections**
Unit 34

Spelling Connections Online
www.spellingconnectionsonline.com

**Spelling Support for
English Language Learners***
Unit 34 Practice Masters and
Audio Conversation

Spelling Center Activities*
Spelling Game Mats
Flip Folder, *TRB*, p. 155

*Spelling Support for English Language
Learners *and* Spelling Center Activities *may
be used at any time during the week.*

Assessment

Pretest Sentences (See procedures on p. Z30.)

1. What is **that** book you are reading?
2. I'll read you a story, and **then** you must go
   to sleep.
3. My grandmother gave me **this** hat.
4. I take a **bath** every night.
5. Let's follow the **path** through the park.
6. Can you come out and play **with** me?

The Science of Spelling ◄··

- American English has two sounds for **th**.
  One is a voiceless sound at the
  beginning, middle, and end of words.
  Examples include **thin, mathematics,** and
  bath. The second is a voiced sound
  heard at the beginning of words such as
  this and at the end of words such as
  breathe. The voiceless **th** also occurs in a
  variety of consonant blends, such as in
  the words **warmth, sixth, fifth,** and
  hundredth. The occurrences of the voiced
  th is more limited. In blends, the voiced
  th usually appears with **r**, as in **farther**.

ELL Support

Choose from the activities below to reinforce English language acquisition.

Beginning

Word Meaning Write the spelling words on the board. Explain to students that the words **that, then, this,** and **with** are words they will use often in their writing. Use simple statements and gestures to provide context and illustrate the meaning of each word. For example, point to a book and say, **That** book is your book. Pick up another book and say, **This** book is mine. Use pictures to illustrate the meaning of **bath** and **path**.

Make Words Write the spelling words on the board and print them on card stock. Cut the words apart between the digraph and the rest of the word. Mix the word parts. Have students sort through the word parts and reconstruct the words. Encourage them to say each word they make.

Develop Phonemic Awareness. Many students will have difficulty hearing the difference between the voiced and unvoiced **th**. Have students note the position of their tongue (slightly between their teeth) as they say /th/ in **path**. Then have them note the humming sound they make when saying /th/ in **then**. Note students' ability to distinguish /th/ from other sounds by saying the following word pairs and having students raise their thumbs when they hear /th/ or /th/: **this/dish, bath/bash, this/his.** Have students say the words and listen for the different sounds. Students can hear the Unit 34 words pronounced on the audio recording.

Intermediate

Picture Sentences Display pictures of two children playing together, a picture of a dog being bathed, and a picture of a clock. Say the following sentences: I like to play **with** my friend. My dog gets a **bath**. When the clock says two o'clock, **then** we will go home. Then say the sentences again one at a time. Ask a volunteer to choose the picture each sentence describes.

Scrambled Words List the spelling words on the board. Then write the following sentences with scrambled spelling words: Do you see ahtt car? I am in the htab. We can go on the phta. You can go with me. Is htsi pen mine? I will do my job and nhte go home. Have students read each sentence. When they come to the scrambled word, have them identify the spelling word and write it correctly. Then have students read the words and sentences.

Mark and Fix Write the proofreading marks on the board. Have students copy the marks and practice writing them several times. Then write the following sentence: we can can Go on this pth . Work through the sentence with students to show them each error and how to mark it. (cap w, delete second can, small g in go, insert a in path, period at end) Have each student copy the sentence and have them mark the errors as you did on the board.

Support for Spanish Speakers

Comparing Languages Spanish speakers may have difficulty hearing and pronouncing some English consonants. Some consonant sounds are quite different in the two languages. For example, the consonant sound /d/ is much softer in Spanish and somewhat similar to the unvoiced /th/ in English. Give students opportunities to practice listening to and pronouncing spelling words with a native English-speaking adult one-on-one. Brief sessions every day or several times a week can be especially helpful. It is important to praise the students' efforts and to accept gradual improvements in English pronunciation.

Choose from the activities below to reinforce English language acquisition.

Advanced

Make Words Write **t** and **h** on separate index cards. Write **bat, wit, hat, his, pat,** and **hen** on the board. Tell students that a **t** or an **h** can be added to each word to make a spelling word. Have students study each word and decide if they will add a **t** to the beginning or an **h** to the end. When they think they know, volunteers will hold the correct letter card at the beginning or end of the word. Ask students to write the spelling word as it is constructed.

Round Robin Do a round robin with students to construct sentences. Say a spelling word. Then have a student say the first word in a sentence. The next student says the second word, and so on until the sentence is complete. Make sure the spelling word is included. Write the sentence as students construct it. Then read the complete sentence and have students repeat it. Sentences can be silly. Follow the same process for all the words.

Complete Sentences Give each student a copy of page 33 of *Spelling Support for English Language Learners*. Have partners complete the sentences. Point out the word choices under each blank line. Suggest that they try out each word before deciding on the best one to write in the blank. Encourage partners to read the completed sentence aloud. Students can hear the spelling words in context on the audio recording.

Advanced High

One Letter Clue Tell students you will give them one letter as a clue to a spelling word. Have them guess the word and write it. Provide clues in this order: **w** (with), **n** (then), **b** (bath), **p** (path), **s** (this), **a** (that).

Word Search Create a word search puzzle for the spelling words. Have students find and circle the words. Explain that the words may appear horizontally, vertically, or diagonally. Model circling a word in the puzzle before students start. As a tip, tell students to look for the letters **t** and **h** next to each other to help them find the spelling words.

Conversation Have partners listen to the dialogue on the audio recording while they follow along with the print version on page 55 of *Spelling Support for English Language Learners*. Then have partners decide who will be Speaker 1 and Speaker 2. Have them read the dialogue together and then check their reading by listening to the recording again.

Picture the Story Have students use spelling words in three sentences that tell a story in sequence. Then have them trade sentences with a partner. The partner draws a picture for each sentence to illustrate the story.

Spelling Support for English Language Learners

Practice Master, p. 33

Practice Master, p. 55

 Audio Conversation available on CD

English/Spanish Word List, p. 70

Spelling Connections Online
Interactive online spelling activities provide additional ELL support.
www.spellingconnectionsonline.com

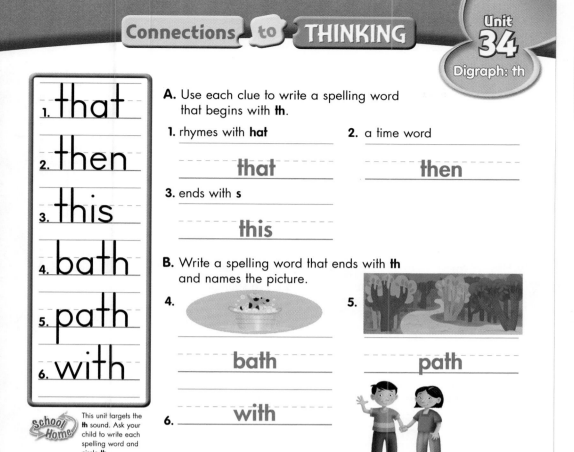

1. that
2. then
3. this
4. bath
5. path
6. with

A. Use each clue to write a spelling word that begins with **th**.

1. rhymes with **hat**

that

2. a time word

then

3. ends with **s**

this

B. Write a spelling word that ends with **th** and names the picture.

4.

5.

bath

path

6.

with

This unit targets the **th** sound. Ask your child to write each spelling word and circle **th**.

TEKS 1.22A Use phonological knowledge to match sounds to letters to construct known words. **1.22C** Spell high-frequency words from a commonly used list.

175

Student Objectives
- Use letter, rhyme, and definition clues to write words with the digraph **th**.
- Write spelling words to name pictures.

Unit Pretest
- Administer the pretest on page T175B.

Teaching Tips

 **CD-ROM**

- Conduct a **Teacher-Led Sort** (see p. Z31) to introduce the spelling pattern.
- Write **that** and **bath**. Read the words aloud and ask students to listen for /th/. Point out that /th/ in **bath** is a softer sound than /th/ in **that**. Have students say the words and note the difference.
- Use the Sound/Symbol Cards for **thumb, path, thick, thin, thimble, thorn, tooth,** and **moth** to reinforce initial and final **th**.
- Write **then**. Help students read the word and use it in a sentence. Ask a volunteer to circle the letters that spell /th/. Have students write **then** and circle the letters that spell /th/. Continue with the rest of the spelling words.
- Have students complete the page independently or as a class.

Home/School Word Lists
- Have students take home the Home/School Spelling Practice Masters.

Home/School Practice

Home/School Spelling
Practice Master, *TRB*, p. 147

English

Home/School Spelling
Practice Master, *TRB*, p. 148

Spanish

TEKS 1.22A Use phonological knowledge to match sounds to letters to construct known words. **1.22C** Spell high-frequency words from a commonly used list.

T175

Student Objectives
- Blend sounds to say and write words that begin with the digraph **th**.
- Use letter and sound clues to write words that end with the digraph **th**.

Teaching Tips
- List the spelling words on the board. Say **that, then,** and **this**. Have students repeat. Ask what sound they hear at the beginning of each word. (/th/) Then say **bath, path,** and **with**. Ask what sound they hear at the end of these words. (/th/)
- Tell students you are thinking of a spelling word. Then give them clues to help them determine which word it is. For example, say, *I am thinking a spelling word. It has three sounds. The sound at the end is spelled with two letters. The sound at the beginning is /b/.* (bath)
- Have students complete page 176 independently or as a class.

Extra Pattern Practice
- Use the optional practice master below for extra practice with initial and final **th**

WORD SORT CD-ROM
- Provide time for students to use a **Buddy Sort** (see p. Z31) to practice their spelling words with a partner.

Connections to PHONICS

A. Blend the sounds to make a spelling word. Write the word.

1. th + is = __this__

2. th + at = __that__

3. th + en = __then__

B. Use the clues to find the spelling word. Write the word.

4. ● four letters ■ three sounds
▲ starts with **b**

__bath__

5. ● three sounds ■ **short i**
▲ starts like **win**

__with__

6. ● four letters ■ three sounds
▲ **short a**

__path__

Spelling word box:
that
then
this
bath
path
with

176

TEKS **1.22A** Use phonological knowledge to match sounds to letters to construct known words. **1.22C** Spell high-frequency words from a commonly used list.

Extra Pattern Practice

Extra Pattern Practice Master,
TRB, p. 149

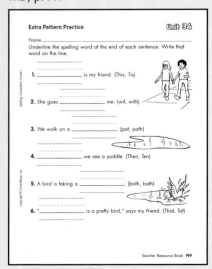

Extra Pattern Practice — Unit 34

Name _____
Underline the spelling word at the end of each sentence. Write that word on the line.

1. _____ is my friend. (This, Tis)

2. She goes _____ me. (wit, with)

3. We walk on a _____ (pat, path)

4. _____ we see a puddle. (Then, Ten)

5. A bird is taking a _____ (both, bath)

6. "_____ is a pretty bird," says my friend. (That, Tat)

Teacher Resource Book P49

Identify /th/
Say the spelling words, emphasizing /th/. Have students repeat the words. Then say the following words and have students put their thumbs up when they hear /th/ or /th/.

pack	path	bath	shop	neck	ship
with	this	that	with	then	thin
show	pick	thump

Write the words with /th/ or /th/ on the board. Call on volunteers to underline **th** in each one.

TEKS **1.22A** Use phonological knowledge to match sounds to letters to construct known words. **1.22C** Spell high-frequency words from a commonly used list.

Write spelling words to finish the story.

1. Jimmy will play __?__ me.

2. Will you hand me __?__ pot?

3. Oh, __?__ it will be your turn to cook.

4. We will take __?__ cake to Mom.

5. "Did you make that __?__?"

6. "It is time for your __?__!"

that
then
this
bath
path
with

1. **with**
2. **that**
3. **then**
4. **this**
5. **path**
6. **bath**

🟥 **TEKS 1.22C** Spell high-frequency words from a commonly used list.

177

Student Objectives
- Write and spell words with an initial or final **th** to complete sentences in a story.

Teaching Tips
- Write **that** and **with** on the board. Ask volunteers to circle **th** in each word. Review that **t** and **h** work together to make the /th/ or /<u>th</u>/ sound.
- List the spelling words. Then write: *I will take a _____, and _____ I will go to bed.* Ask students to suggest spelling words that will complete the sentence and make the most sense. (**bath, then**) Call on volunteers to write the words in the blank spaces.
- Write **this** and **that** on the board. Explain that **this** usually refers to something that is close by. Place a book at either end of a table or desk. Pick up the one nearest you and say, *I am going to read **this** book.* Then point to the book farther away and say, *[Student], will you hand me **that** book?*
- Have students complete page 177. Tell them they will use each word just once.

Differentiated Instruction
- Use the **Challenge Words** activity on page 210 with students who are ready to transfer their knowledge of **th** to new words.
- An Extra Challenge Practice Master is available on page 150 in the *TRB*.
- Dictation sentences for the challenge words are available on page T210.

More Fun With Spelling for Differentiation

▶ Digital Resources for Spelling Connections
Interactive digital resources include word sorts, pattern practice, and proofreading activities for individual and whole-group instruction. (Interactive whiteboard compatible; see p. Z32.)

▶ Spelling Connections Online
Interactive online spelling activities include word sorts, crossword puzzles, sentence completion, proofreading practice, and spelling bees with words from each unit (see p. Z32). www.spellingconnectionsonline.com

🧩 Spelling Center Activities

Spelling Game Mats
Place one of the spelling games in a learning center to provide a fun way for students to practice their spelling words (see p. Z26).

Flip Folder
Students can use a Flip Folder to practice spelling words independently (see p. Z32).

Word Sort CD-ROM
Printable, unit-specific word cards for spelling and challenge words can be used for Teacher-Led, Individual, Buddy, and Speed Sorts (see p. Z31).

🟥 **TEKS 1.22A** Use phonological knowledge to match sounds to letters to construct known words. **1.22C** Spell high-frequency words from a commonly used list.

T177

Unit 34 — Day 4

Student Objectives
- Identify spelling words in a paragraph.
- Use proofreading marks to revise writing.
- Use spelling words to write sentences.

Teaching Tips
- Review the proofreading marks with the class.
- Have students complete Part A independently.
- Read the directions for Part B. Explain to students that they will rewrite the sentences on a separate sheet of paper.
- Read the directions for Part C. Tell students they can write about something real or about something from their imagination.
- When students have finished, ask them to review their work to make sure they have spelled spelling words correctly. Have them circle two words they are not sure about and check the spelling of each in a dictionary.
- Invite volunteers to read their work aloud. Have the class identify spelling words used.

WORD SORT CD-ROM
- Invite students to practice for the weekly test by doing an **Individual Sort** or a **Speed Sort** (see p. Z31).

Day 5

Student Objectives
- Demonstrate mastery of the unit spelling words.

Posttest Assessment Options
Option 1: Administer the unit posttest using the dictation sentences at right.

Option 2: Assess students using the standardized test. See the *Standardized Test Master Book*, p. 38.

Note: Posttest sentences for the on level and challenge lists are available on the audio *Spelling Connections* Posttest CD.

Connections to WRITING

A. Underline the spelling words. Then write them on the lines below.

¶In this forest there is a path. See that bird. It takes a bath in the puddle. Look at the deer. She is with her baby. See this turtle. It is going to its home in in the pond. Then it will be Time for us to go home.

Proofreading Marks
- ☰ Capital Letter
- / Small Letter
- ∧ Add
- ℰ Delete
- ⊙ Add a Period
- ¶ Indent

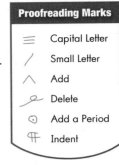
that
then
this
bath
path
with

1. **path**
2. **that**
3. **bath**
4. **with**
5. **this**
6. **Then**

B. Rewrite the sentences. Make the changes shown by the proofreading marks.

C. Write about a path you have walked or would like to walk. Use as many spelling words as you can. Check your spelling in a dictionary.

178

TEKS 1.22A Use phonological knowledge to match sounds to letters to construct known words. **1.22C** Spell high-frequency words from a commonly used list. **1.22E** Use resources to find correct spellings.

1-Minute Handwriting Hint

The lowercase **h** contains two pull-down straight strokes. The curve forward stroke is part of the circle motion.

CURVE FORWARD

Posttest Sentences
1. You may sit **with** your friends.
2. Is **this** the right road?
3. The **path** leads to Ryan's house.
4. Did you see **that** huge bird?
5. I'm going to give my doll a **bath**.
6. Finish your work, and **then** relax.

Standardized Test Master Book, p. 38

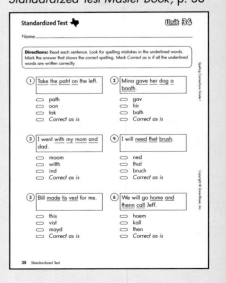

Standardized Test — Unit 34

Name _____

Directions: Read each sentence. Look for spelling mistakes in the underlined words. Mark the answer that shows the correct spelling. Mark Correct as is if all the underlined words are written correctly.

1 Take the paht on the left.
- ○ path
- ○ oon
- ○ tak
- ○ Correct as is

2 Mina gave her dog a boath.
- ○ gav
- ○ hir
- ○ bath
- ○ Correct as is

3 I went with my mom and dad.
- ○ moom
- ○ witth
- ○ ind
- ○ Correct as is

4 I will need thet brush.
- ○ ned
- ○ that
- ○ bruch
- ○ Correct as is

5 Bill made tis vest for me.
- ○ this
- ○ vist
- ○ mayd
- ○ Correct as is

6 We will go home and thenn call Jeff.
- ○ hoem
- ○ kall
- ○ then
- ○ Correct as is

38 Standardized Test

TEKS 1.22A Use phonological knowledge to match sounds to letters to construct known words.
1.22C Spell high-frequency words from a commonly used list. **1.22E** Use resources to find correct spellings.

Planner

Day 1 | Day 2

Day 1

Unit 31: Long u: /oo/, /yoo/

Student Objectives
- Review the spelling patterns and words from Unit 31.

Instruction for All Students
- Unit 31 Review, p. 179
- Home/School Spelling Practice Masters (*Teacher Resource Book*, pp. 151–152)

Unit 32: Final ck

Student Objectives
- Review the spelling pattern and words from Unit 32.

Instruction for All Students
- Unit 32 Review, p. 180

Unit 31
Long u: /oo/, /yoo/

do	use
you	room
zoo	soon

Unit 32
Final ck

back	pick
pack	sock
neck	duck

Unit 33
Digraph: sh

ship	dish
shop	wish
show	push

Unit 34
Digraph: th

that	bath
then	path
this	with

Day 3 | Day 4 | Day 5

Day 2

Unit 33: Digraph: sh

Student Objectives
- Review the spelling pattern and words from Unit 33.

Instruction for All Students
- Unit 33 Review, p. 181

Unit 34: Digraph: th

Student Objectives
- Review the spelling pattern and words from Unit 34.

Instruction for All Students
- Unit 34 Review, p. 182

Day 3

Assessment

Student Objectives
- Demonstrate mastery of the review unit spelling words.

Assessment for All Students
- Posttest Assessment Options
  - ✦ Posttest Dictation Sentences, p. T182, or
  - ✦ *Standardized Test Master Book*, p. 39

Unit 35 Materials

Student Edition
pp. 179–182
Alphabet and Picture Cards
(See page Z32 for
suggested activities.)

Teacher Edition
pp. T179A–T182

 Teacher Resource Book
Unit 35 Practice Masters,
pp. 151–152

 Standardized Test Master Book
Unit 35 Test Master, p. 39

 Word Sort CD-ROM
Unit 35 Word Sort Cards for Teacher-
Led Sorts and Student Sorts

 **Digital Resources for
Spelling Connections**
Unit 35

 Spelling Connections Online
www.spellingconnectionsonline.com

Spelling Center Activities*
Spelling Game Mats
Flip Folder, *TRB*, p. 155

*Spelling Center Activities may be used at
any time during the week.*

Developmental Spelling Check

Administer the following **Developmental Spelling Check** to evaluate spelling growth. Remind students that this is not a test for a grade; students are not expected to spell these words conventionally. Author J. Richard Gentry has provided typical Phase 4 Transitional Spelling(s) for each word in parentheses.

Tell students you would like them to try writing these clothing words. To administer, say each word aloud, read the sentence, and then say the word again.

Clothing Words and Sample Transitional Spellings

hat	Dad bought a new **hat** for winter.	(HATT)
shoes	I like my red **shoes**.	(SHUSE, SHEOS)
socks	You need two **socks** to make a pair.	(SOX)
shirt	My **shirt** lost a button.	(SHERT)
jeans	There is a hole in your **jeans**.	(JENES)
dress	That yellow **dress** is pretty.	(DRES)
jacket	Please button your **jacket**.	(JACKIT)
coat	Where is your **coat**?	(COTE)
belt	The **belt** has a silver buckle.	(BELLT)
tie	That **tie** has a spot on it.	(TY, TYE)
pants	Are those your **pants**?	(PANCE)

ELL Support

Choose from the activities below to reinforce English language acquisition.

Beginning

Word Meaning Check understanding of the review spelling words. List the words on the board. Ask student-friendly questions that can be answered with a spelling word. For example, *Where can you go to see animals?* (zoo) *What floats in water?* (ship) *What animal says 'quack'?* (duck) *What is another name for a place to walk?* (path) Note difficult words and review their meaning using gestures, pantomime, and pictures or realia.

Sound Discrimination Tell students you will say spelling words one at a time. If they hear the /o͞o/ or /yo͞o/ sound, they should say *yoo hoo*. If they hear the final /k/ sound, they should say *quack*. If they hear the /sh/ sound, they should put a finger to their lips and say, *sh*. If they hear a /th/ or /th/ sound, they should raise their thumbs. Practice each response before beginning. Say the spelling words randomly and pause for students to identify what they hear.

Word Match Provide pairs of students with two sets of word cards for the spelling words, one set for each partner. Have Partner 1 choose a card and read the word aloud without showing it to the other student. Partner 2 looks through his or her set of word cards and finds the word, holds it up, and says it aloud. Partner 2 then selects a word. Have pairs continue until they each have used all of their cards.

Intermediate

Word Meaning List the spelling words on the board. Point to each word and have students read it aloud. Ask volunteers to act out the meaning of a word or use it in a sentence. After a word is identified, have students write the word on writing paper.

Missing Letters Write review spelling words on the board, leaving out the spelling pattern and showing a blank line for each letter that is missing. For example: r __ __ m, so __ __, __ __ ow, __ __ en. Allow students to look at the lists of words in their books to identify the words. Then have them write the missing letters in the spaces. Call on volunteers to read the words.

Sound Concentration Arrange word cards for the spelling words facedown on a desk or table. Have partners alternate turning over two cards. Have them determine if the words on the cards share a beginning sound, a vowel sound, or an ending sound. For example, **pick** and **dish** would match because they have the **short i** sound. If the words match, then the cards are removed from the grid. If they don't, the cards are turned facedown again. Have students match as many cards as possible.

Support for Spanish Speakers

Comparing Languages In Spanish there are a limited number of final consonant sounds. As a result, native Spanish speakers learning English have trouble with the consonants **b, g, h, k, m, p, s,** and **v,** and the digraphs **th** (voiced and unvoiced), **sh,** and **ch.** The initial consonant **s** blends may also be difficult for students to distinguish and pronounce. Provide practice time for students to work with an English-speaking adult to hear, pronounce, and read words with these problem elements.

Choose from the activities below to reinforce English language acquisition.

Advanced

Bingo Create modified Bingo cards with four rows of four spaces each. Write review spelling words in the spaces, varying the words and their order for each card. Not every word will be on every card. If students will be making their own cards, make sure the spaces are large enough for students to write in. For student-made cards, list the review spelling words on the board. Have students copy words in the spaces in any order they wish. Provide squares made from card stock or markers to use to cover words. Write the spelling words on index cards, mix them, and place them facedown. Select a card and read the word aloud. If students have the word on their card, they cover it with a marker. The first player to cover four words in a row horizontally, vertically, or diagonally wins the round. Then have students trade cards and play again. Appoint a volunteer to select and read the words.

Picture Sentences List the review spelling words on the board. Have students select one or more words to write in a sentence. Then have students illustrate their sentence. For example, *The duck is on the ship.* Students would draw a picture of a duck on a ship.

Advanced High

Analogies Write the review spelling words on the board. Say the following analogies and have students complete them with a spelling word.

Slow is the opposite of **fast**.
Pull is the opposite of ____. (push)

Some people live in a town.
Some animals live in a ____. (zoo)

A hand goes in a mitten.
A foot goes in a ____. (sock)

First is the opposite of **last**.
Now is the opposite of ____. (then)

Provide additional examples if students want to continue the activity.

Answering Questions Write **wish, shop, show,** and **ship** on the board. Ask students to imagine that they have been granted one wish. To get their wish, they must choose one of the three words: **shop, show,** or **ship**. Explain that if they choose **shop,** they will answer the question *If you owned a shop, what would you sell?* If they choose **show,** they will answer the question *If you were a star of a show, what kind of show would it be?* If they choose **ship,** they will answer the question *If you traveled on a ship, where would you go?* Encourage students to write their answers.

 Spelling Connections Online
Interactive online spelling activities provide additional ELL support.
www.spellingconnectionsonline.com

Review

Unit 31: Long u: o͞o, yo͞o
Fill in the blanks to write each spelling word.

1. do

2. you

3. zoo

4. use

5. room

6. soon

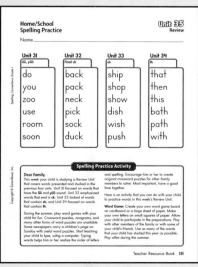

School Home
This unit reviews the o͞o and yo͞o sounds, **ck**, **sh**, and **th**. Ask your child to read the spelling words on each page aloud.

1. z__ __

zoo

2. s__ __n

soon

3. d__

do

4. r__ __m

room

5. __s__

use

6. y __ __

you

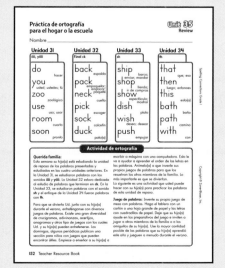

179

Student Objectives
- Review the spelling patterns and words from Unit 31.

Reteaching the Skill
- Write **zoo, room,** and **soon** on the board. Remind students that these words have the /o͞o/ sound. Ask students which letters spell /o͞o/. Pronounce the words as a volunteer circles **oo** in each word.
- Repeat the process using the word **do,** guiding students to see that **o** spells /o͞o/.
- Write **you** and **use** on the board. Pronounce the words and tell students that they have the /yo͞o/ or **long u** sound. Ask, *Which letters spell the **long u** sound?* **(ou, u-consonant-e)** Have a volunteer circle **ou** in **you** and **u** and **e** in **use**.
- Tell students to complete page 179 independently.

Letters and Sounds Review
- Throughout the unit, use the **Alphabet and Picture Cards** to review letters and sounds. See page Z32 for activity suggestions.

Review Word List

Home/School Spelling Practice Master, *TRB,* p. 151

Home/School Spelling Practice Master, *TRB,* p. 152

English

Spanish

Student Objectives

- Review the spelling pattern and words from Unit 32.

Reteaching the Skill

- Write on the board and say **back, pack, neck, pick, sock,** and **duck.** Ask students where they hear /k/ in each word. (**at the end**) Guide students to see that the /k/ sound is spelled **ck.** Explain that the letters work together to make one sound.
- Write the following on the board: **ba____,** **pa____, ne____, pi____, so____, du____.** Have students take turns filling in the letters **ck** to complete each word.
- Erase everything on the board except the letters **ck.** Ask students to add letters to spell the word **back.** Continue the activity until all the words have been completed again.
- Tell students to complete page 180 independently.

Review

1. back
2. pack
3. neck
4. pick
5. sock
6. duck

Unit 32: **Final ck**

Change the last letter in each word to **ck**. Write the spelling word. Then draw a line to match the word with a picture.

1. son   sock
2. pat   pack
3. dug   duck
4. pin   pick
5. bad   back
6. net   neck

180

Extra Pattern Practice

Letter Change

Print **d, l, p, r, bl, ch, cl, sh, st,** and **tr** in large letters on large index cards. Write **ack, eck, ick, ock,** and **uck** on the board. Have a student select a card and hold it in front of a word part on the board. If the student has made a word, say the word aloud and have all students repeat it. List the new words on the board.

Review

1. ship
2. shop
3. show
4. dish
5. wish
6. push

Unit 33: Digraph: sh

A. Write the words that end with **sh** like .

1. dish
2. wish
3. push

B. Write the words that start with **sh** like .

4. ship
5. shop
6. show

181

Student Objectives
• Review the spelling pattern and words from Unit 33.

Reteaching the Skill
• On the board, write and then say **ship, shop,** and **show**. Ask, *How are the words alike?* (They all begin with the same sound and letters.) Pronounce the words again, underlining **sh** as you say the digraph. Ask, *Which letters spell the first sound you hear in* **ship, shop,** *and* **show**? (sh)
• Write and say **dish, wish,** and **push**. Ask students to repeat the words. Ask, *Do you hear /sh/ in these words?* (yes) Ask, *Is it at the beginning or the end of the words?* (end)
• Have volunteers underline **sh** in each word as they pronounce it for the class.
• Tell students to complete page 181 independently.

More Fun With Spelling for Differentiation

 ### Digital Resources for Spelling Connections
Interactive digital resources include word sorts, pattern practice, and proofreading activities for individual and whole-group instruction. (Interactive whiteboard compatible; see p. Z32.)

Spelling Connections Online
Interactive online spelling activities include word sorts, crossword puzzles, sentence completion, proofreading practice, and spelling bees with words from each unit (see p. Z32). www.spellingconnectionsonline.com

Spelling Center Activities
Spelling Game Mats
Place one of the spelling games in a learning center to provide a fun way for students to practice their spelling words (see p. Z26).

Flip Folder
Students can use a Flip Folder to practice spelling words independently (see p. Z32).

Word Sort CD-ROM
Printable, unit-specific word cards for spelling and challenge words can be used for Teacher-Led, Individual, Buddy, and Speed Sorts (see p. Z31).

Student Objectives
- Review the spelling pattern and words from Unit 34.

Reteaching the Skill
- On the board, write **that, then,** and **this**. Say the words aloud. Ask students which letters spell the first sound in each word. **(th)** Have volunteers read each word and underline the letters that spell the first sound.
- Write **bath, path,** and **with** on the board. Say the words. Ask students if they hear /**th**/ in these words. **(yes)** Ask where the sound occurs in these words. **(at the end)**
- Have volunteers read each word and underline the letters that spell /**th**/.
- Tell students to complete page 182 independently or as a class.

Review

1. that
2. then
3. this
4. bath
5. path
6. with

Unit 34: **Digraph: th**

A. Write the spelling words that end with **th**.

1. ____ bath
2. ____ path
3. ____ with

B. Complete each spelling word.

4. __ __ is
   this

5. __ __ en
   then

6. __ __ at
   that

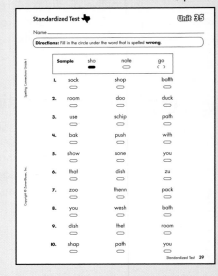

182

Day 5

Assessment

Student Objectives
- Demonstrate mastery of the review unit spelling words.

Posttest Assessment Options
Option 1: Administer the posttest using the dictation sentences at right.
Option 2: Assess students using the standardized test. See the *Standardized Test Master Book*, p. 39.

Note: Posttest sentences for the on level and challenge lists are available on the audio *Spelling Connections* Posttest CD.

Posttest Sentences
1. You may **use** my crayons.
2. There is **room** for one more chair.
3. There is a **duck** on the pond.
4. My **sock** is all wet!
5. I waved to the people sailing on the **ship**.
6. Will you help me **push** this wagon?
7. What is **that** book you are reading?
8. The **path** leads to Ryan's house.

Standardized Test Master Book, p. 39

Standardized Test			Unit 35
Name			

Directions: Fill in the circle under the word that is spelled **wrong**

	Sample	sho	note	go
		●	○	○
1.	sock	shop		bath
	○	○		○
2.	room	doo		duck
	○	○		○
3.	use	schip		path
	○	○		○
4.	bak	push		with
	○	○		○
5.	show	sone		you
	○	○		○
6.	that	dish		zu
	○	○		○
7.	zoo	thenn		pack
	○	○		○
8.	you	wesh		bath
	○	○		○
9.	dish	thet		room
	○	○		○
10.	shap	path		you
	○	○		○

Standardized Test 39

Challenge Words

| ant | lap | tag | pants |

A. Write the word from the box that rhymes with the picture name.

1.  The ants have on
   pants.

2. The cap is on her
   lap.

3. Grant sat on an
   ant.

4. This bag has a
   tag.

B. Complete the sentence.

5–6. The  **ant** is on my **pants**.

TEKS **1.22A** Use phonological knowledge to match sounds to letters to construct known words. **1.22C** Spell high-frequency words from a commonly used list.

183

Student Objectives
- Read, spell, and write new words with **short a** in the initial and medial position.
- Write **short a** words to complete sentences.

Teaching Tips
- Remind students that rhyming words have the same end sounds. For example: **man, ran**. Ask students to suggest additional words that rhyme with **man** and **ran**. (**ban, can, fan, pan, tan**)
- Write the challenge words on the board. Point to each word and read it aloud. Ask students what sound they hear at the beginning of **ant**. (/ă/) Ask what sound they hear in the middle of **lap, tag,** and **pants**. (/ă/)
- Segment the letter sounds at the end of **ant** and **pants**. Read the words again and have students repeat them.
- Read the directions on page 183. Have students complete the page independently or as a class.

Optional Practice and Assessment

Extra Challenge Practice Master,
TRB, p. 30

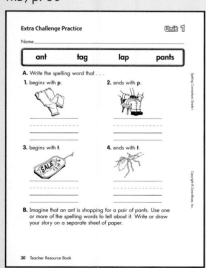

Challenge Dictation Sentences
1. An **ant** is on your leg.
2. What is on the **tag**?
3. The kitten slept on my **lap**.
4. I have a new pair of **pants**.

Note: Posttest sentences for the on level and challenge lists are available on the audio *Spelling Connections* Posttest CD.

TEKS **1.22A** Use phonological knowledge to match sounds to letters to construct known words. **1.22C** Spell high-frequency words from a commonly used list.

T183

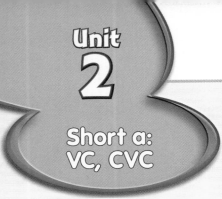

Student Objectives
- Read, spell, and write new words with **short a** in the medial position.
- Write **short a** words to complete categories.

Teaching Tips
- Write the challenge words on the board. Point to each word and read it aloud. Ask students what sound they hear in the middle of **bag, pan, mat,** and **lamp.** (/ă/) Then ask what short vowel spelling pattern is in the words. (**one vowel between two consonants**)
- Segment the letter sounds at the end of **lamp.** Read the word again and have students repeat it.
- Tell students that things that are alike in some way can be put in groups. Say **dog, mouse,** and **horse.** Explain that these words can be put together because they all name animals. Write **cat** and **hat** on the board. Ask students which word belongs with **dog, mouse,** and **horse.** (**cat**)
- Read the directions on page 184. Have students complete the page independently or as a class.

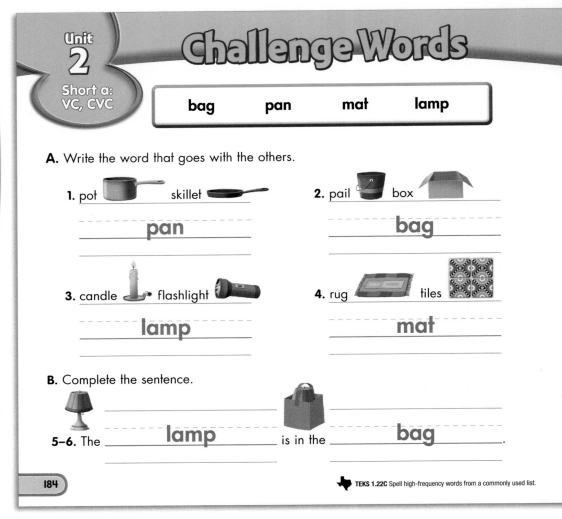

Unit 2 — Short a: VC, CVC — Challenge Words

bag	pan	mat	lamp

A. Write the word that goes with the others.

1. pot   skillet   **pan**

2. pail   box   **bag**

3. candle   flashlight   **lamp**

4. rug   tiles   **mat**

B. Complete the sentence.

5–6. The **lamp** is in the **bag**.

184

TEKS 1.22C Spell high-frequency words from a commonly used list.

Optional Practice and Assessment

Extra Challenge Practice Master, *TRB,* p. 34

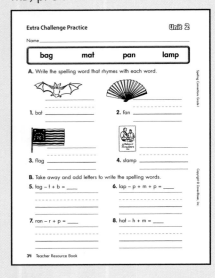

Challenge Dictation Sentences
1. Put your things in this **bag**.
2. Put the dishes on the **mat**.
3. May we use this **pan**?
4. Mom will change the light bulb in the **lamp**.

Note: Posttest sentences for the on level and challenge lists are available on the audio *Spelling Connections* Posttest CD.

TEKS 1.22Bi Use letter-sound patterns to spell: consonant-vowel-consonant (CVC) words. **1.22C** Spell high-frequency words from a commonly used list.

Challenge Words

| hen | den | wet | fed |

A. Complete each word.

Jan __**fed**__ the __**wet**__ __**hen**__ in the __**den**__.

B. Write a sentence using **hen** and **wet**.
Write a sentence using **den** and **fed**.

Sentences will vary.

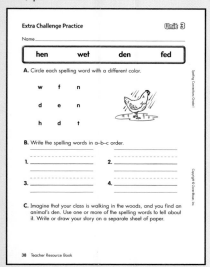

TEKS 1.22C Spell high-frequency words from a commonly used list.

185

Unit 3

Short e: CVC

Student Objectives
- Read, spell, and write new words with **short e** in the medial position.
- Write **short e** words to complete a sentence.
- Write sentences using **short e** words.

Teaching Tips
- Write the challenge words on the board. Point to each word and read it aloud. Ask students what sound they hear in the middle of **hen, den, wet,** and **fed.** (/ĕ/) Then ask what short vowel spelling pattern is in the words. (**one vowel between two consonants**)
- Say, *I am thinking of a word with* **short e**. *The word starts with* **/d/**. Write **d** on the board and call on a volunteer to finish the word. (**den**)
- Talk about what each challenge word means. Then ask students to think of a sentence that uses one of the words. Write students' ideas on the board.
- Read the directions on page 185. Have students complete the page independently or as a class.

Optional Practice and Assessment

Extra Challenge Practice Master,
TRB, p. 38

Extra Challenge Practice   Unit 3

Name _____

| hen | wet | den | fed |

A. Circle each spelling word with a different color.

w   f   n

d   e   n

h   d   t

B. Write the spelling words in a–b–c order.

1. _____   2. _____

3. _____   4. _____

C. Imagine that your class is walking in the woods, and you find an animal's den. Use one or more of the spelling words to tell about it. Write or draw your story on a separate sheet of paper.

38   Teacher Resource Book

Challenge Dictation Sentences
1. The **hen** is sitting on eggs.
2. My shoes and socks are **wet**.
3. The bear is in its **den**.
4. Have you **fed** the animals?

Note: Posttest sentences for the on level and challenge lists are available on the audio *Spelling Connections* Posttest CD.

TEKS 1.22Bi Use letter-sound patterns to spell: consonant-vowel-consonant (CVC) words. 1.22C Spell high-frequency words from a commonly used list.

T185

Unit 4

Short e: CVC

Student Objectives
- Read, spell, and write new words with **short e** in the medial position.
- Write **short e** words to complete a sentence and describe a picture.

Teaching Tips
- Write the challenge words on the board. Point to each word and read it aloud. Have students repeat. Ask what sound they hear in the middle of each word. (/ĕ/) Then ask what short vowel spelling pattern is in the words. (one vowel between two consonants)
- Point to the consonants at the end of **vest, mend,** and **mess**. Segment each word and then say the word to show how the sounds blend together. Point out that even though there are two letters at the end of **mess,** only one /s/ sound is heard.
- Create a small mess of papers on your desk. Ask students how they could use a challenge word in a sentence that tells about your desk. For example, *Your desk is a mess*. Write the sentence on the board.
- Read the directions on page 186. Have students complete the page independently or as a class.

Unit 4

Short e: CVC

Challenge Words

| led | vest | mend | mess |

Write the words to tell about each picture.

1–2. Did the robin ____**mend**____ her old ____**vest**____ ?

3–4. Jan ____**led**____ Tim out of the ____**mess**____ .

186

TEKS 1.22C Spell high-frequency words from a commonly used list.

Optional Practice and Assessment

Extra Challenge Practice Master, *TRB*, p. 42

Challenge Dictation Sentences
1. Mark **led** the pony to the barn.
2. Will you **mend** my skirt?
3. Dad has a nice jacket and **vest**.
4. That room is a **mess**!

Note: Posttest sentences for the on level and challenge lists are available on the audio *Spelling Connections* Posttest CD.

T186

TEKS 1.22Bi Use letter-sound patterns to spell: consonant-vowel-consonant (CVC) words. 1.22C Spell high-frequency words from a commonly used list.

Challenge Words

| sip | lid | tip | wig |

Write a word from the box to complete each sentence.

1. _____ I can __?__ from the glass.

sip

2. _____ The __?__ fits the pan.

lid

3. _____ Nan has a __?__ .

wig

4. _____ The __?__ of the pen is bad.

tip

TEKS 1.22C Spell high-frequency words from a commonly used list.

187

Student Objectives
- Read, spell, and write new words with **short i** in the medial position.
- Write **short i** words to complete sentences.

Teaching Tips
- Write the challenge words on the board. Point to each word and read it aloud. Have students repeat. Ask what sound they hear in the middle of **sip, lid, tip,** and **wig. (short i)**
- Have students point out the CVC pattern in each word. Prompt them to tell you that the vowel in this pattern is short.
- Pantomime using a pan on a stove. Then pantomime putting a lid on the pan. Ask students what you did. **(You put a lid on the pan.)**
- On the board, write *I put a _____ on the pan.* Ask which spelling word completes the sentence. **(lid)** Call on a volunteer to write **lid** in the blank. Then read the sentence aloud with students.
- Read the directions on page 187. Have students complete the page independently or as a class.

Optional Practice and Assessment

Extra Challenge Practice Master,
TRB, p. 48

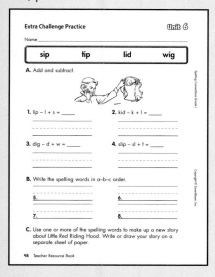

Challenge Dictation Sentences
1. Just take a little **sip.**
2. I broke the **tip** of my pencil.
3. Is there a **lid** for this pot?
4. Robin's doll has a **wig.**

Note: Posttest sentences for the on level and challenge lists are available on the audio *Spelling Connections* Posttest CD.

TEKS 1.22A Use phonological knowledge to match sounds to letters to construct known words.
1.22Bi Use letter-sound patterns to spell: consonant-vowel-consonant (CVC) words.
1.22C Spell high-frequency words from a commonly used list.

Unit 7

Short i: VC, CVC

Student Objectives
- Read, spell, and write new words with **short i** in the medial position.
- Write **short i** words to complete rhymes.

Teaching Tips
- Write the challenge words on the board. Point to each word and read it aloud. Have students repeat. Ask what sound they hear in the middle of **bib, rip, pin,** and **zip**. (short i)
- Have students point out the CVC pattern in each word. Prompt them to tell you that the vowel in this pattern is short.
- Remind students that rhyming words have the same sounds at the end. Provide examples such as **pig–dig** and **did–hid**.
- Write **bit, him,** and **tip** on the board. Ask students to think of words that rhyme with these words. Call on volunteers to write rhyming words under each word. (Possible words: **fit, hit, kit, lit, pit, sit, wit; dim, Jim, Kim, rim, Tim; dip, hip, lip, nip, rip, sip, zip**)
- Read the directions on page 188. Have students complete the page independently or as a class.

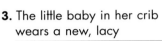

| bib | rip | pin | zip |

Write a word from the box to finish each rhyme.

1. For first place you will win a shiny, purple

_____ pin _____ .

2. My old jacket has a rip and now it will no longer

_____ zip _____ .

3. The little baby in her crib wears a new, lacy

_____ bib _____ .

4. With your scissors you can snip. With your fingers you can

_____ rip _____ .

TEKS 1.22A Use phonological knowledge to match sounds to letters to construct known words. **1.22C** Spell high-frequency words from a commonly used list.

Optional Practice and Assessment

Extra Challenge Practice Master, *TRB,* p. 52

Challenge Dictation Sentences
1. Here is a **bib** for the baby.
2. Would you **pin** this flower on my dress?
3. There is a **rip** in my jeans.
4. You need to **zip** your jacket.

Note: Posttest sentences for the on level and challenge lists are available on the audio *Spelling Connections* Posttest CD.

TEKS 1.22A Use phonological knowledge to match sounds to letters to construct known words.
1.22Bi Use letter-sound patterns to spell: consonant-vowel-consonant (CVC) words.
1.22C Spell high-frequency words from a commonly used list.

Challenge Words

| ox | cod | jog | trot |

Write a word from the box to complete each sentence.
Then circle the word in the same sentence that rhymes with it.

1. An **ox** has horns, but a (fox) does not.

2. A **cod** has fins, and I can catch one with a (rod).

3. Horses **trot** but fish do (not).

4. People **jog** through sun, rain, or (fog).

TEKS 1.22C Spell high-frequency words from a commonly used list.

189

Student Objectives
- Read, spell, and write new words with **short o** in the initial and medial positions.
- Write **short o** words to complete sentences.

Teaching Tips
- Write the challenge words on the board. Point to each word and read it aloud. Have students repeat. Ask what sound is the same in all the words. (short o) Have students point out the spelling pattern (VC or CVC) that signals the short vowel sound in each word.
- Segment and pronounce the phonemes in **trot**. Have students repeat. Slide your hand under **tr** and explain that the sounds of these letters slide together but that each sound is heard.
- Discuss the meaning of each challenge word. Point out that **ox** and **cod** name animals and **jog** and **trot** are action words. Then write *I like to run in the morning.* Ask students which challenge word means almost the same as **run**. (jog) Call on a volunteer to erase **run** and write **jog**.
- Read the directions on page 189. Have students complete the page independently or as a class.

Optional Practice and Assessment

Extra Challenge Practice Master,
TRB, p. 56

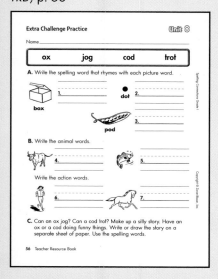

Challenge Dictation Sentences
1. An **ox** can pull heavy loads.
2. Do you like to **jog**?
3. I caught a **cod**!
4. They are teaching the pony to **trot**.

Note: Posttest sentences for the on level and challenge lists are available on the audio *Spelling Connections* Posttest CD.

TEKS 1.22A Use phonological knowledge to match sounds to letters to construct known words.
1.22Bi Use letter-sound patterns to spell: consonant-vowel-consonant (CVC) words.
1.22C Spell high-frequency words from a commonly used list.

Unit 9

Short o: VC, CVC

Student Objectives
- Read, spell, and write new words with **short o** in the medial position.
- Write **short o** words to complete sentences.

Teaching Tips
- Write the challenge words on the board. Point to each word and read it aloud. Have students repeat. Ask what sound is the same in all the words. **(short o)** Have students point out the spelling pattern (CVC) that signals the short vowel sound in each word.
- Point to **body**. Explain that this word has two vowel sounds. Segment and pronounce the phonemes in **body**. Have students identify the first vowel sound as **short o**. Then point to **y** and explain that the **y** in **body** has a **long e** sound.
- Discuss the meaning of each challenge word. Then write *I have a pet pig.* Ask students which challenge word could take the place of *pig*. **(hog)** Call on a volunteer to erase **pig** and write **hog** in its place. Read the new sentence aloud.
- Read the directions on page 190. Have students complete the page independently or as a class.

Unit 9 — Challenge Words

Short o: VC, CVC

| hog | rod | jot | body |

Write a word from the box to solve each riddle.

1. I am a pole used for fishing. My name rhymes with **cod**.

rod

2. I am another name for a pig. My name rhymes with a pet you might have.

hog

3. I go with **any** and **every**.

body

4. I start like **jog** and rhyme with **dot**.

jot

190

TEKS 1.22A Use phonological knowledge to match sounds to letters to construct known words. 1.22C Spell high-frequency words from a commonly used list.

Optional Practice and Assessment

Extra Challenge Practice Master, *TRB*, p. 60

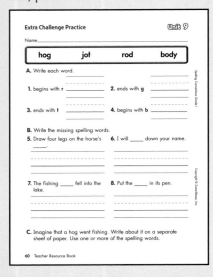

Challenge Dictation Sentences
1. I have a new fishing **rod**.
2. A **hog** got into our garden.
3. Do you have a rash on your **body**?
4. I want to **jot** down your address.

Note: Posttest sentences for the on level and challenge lists are available on the audio *Spelling Connections* Posttest CD.

TEKS 1.22A Use phonological knowledge to match sounds to letters to construct known words.
1.22Bi Use letter-sound patterns to spell: consonant-vowel-consonant (CVC) words.
1.22C Spell high-frequency words from a commonly used list.

Challenge Words

dug	hum	snug	bump

Write a word to complete each sentence.

1. Pip __?__ in the sand.

dug

2. Dad hit a big __?__

bump

3. Cal can __?__ in the tub.

hum

4. I was __?__ in the bag.

snug

TEKS 1.22C Spell high-frequency words from a commonly used list.

191

Unit
11
Short u:
VC, CVC

Student Objectives
- Read, spell, and write new words with **short u** in the medial position.
- Write **short u** words to complete sentences.

Teaching Tips
- Write the challenge words on the board. Point to each word and read it aloud. Have students repeat. Ask students which vowel sound they hear in each word. (short u)
- Point to **snug**. Slide your hand under **sn** and segment the sounds as you say the word. Explain that the sounds slide together, but that each sound can still be heard. Do the same with **mp** at the end of **bump**.
- Discuss the meaning of each challenge word. Then write *I will dig in my garden.* Ask students which challenge word you would use to say that you have finished digging. (dug) Call on a volunteer to erase **will dig** and write **dug** in its place. Read the new sentence.
- Read the directions on page 191. Have students complete the page independently or as a class.

Optional Practice and Assessment

Extra Challenge Practice Master,
TRB, p. 66

Challenge Dictation Sentences
1. I felt **snug** under the blanket.
2. The dog **dug** up a bone.
3. Look out for that **bump**!
4. Can you **hum** a tune?

Note: Posttest sentences for the on level and challenge lists are available on the audio *Spelling Connections* Posttest CD.

TEKS 1.22A Use phonological knowledge to match sounds to letters to construct known words. **1.22C** Spell high-frequency words from a commonly used list.

Unit 12

Short u: CVC

Student Objectives
- Read, spell, and write new words with **short u** in the medial position.
- Write **short u** words to complete sentences.

Teaching Tips
- Write the challenge words on the board. Point to each word and read it aloud. Have students repeat. Ask students which vowel sound they hear in the middle of **cub, bud, pup,** and **hut.** (short u)
- Discuss the meaning of each challenge word. Then write *The ____ barks and runs*. Help students read the sentence. Then ask which spelling word completes the sentence. (**pup**) Encourage students to think about the word that makes the most sense. Call on a volunteer to come up and write **pup** in the blank.
- Read the directions on page 192. Have students complete the page independently or as a class.

Challenge Words

cub	bud	pup	hut

Write a word to finish each sentence.

1. A small [house image] house is a

_____ **hut** _____.

2. A small [dog image] dog is a

_____ **pup** _____.

3. A small closed [flower image] flower is a

_____ **bud** _____.

4. A small [bear image] bear is a

_____ **cub** _____.

192

TEKS 1.22C Spell high-frequency words from a commonly used list.

Optional Practice and Assessment

Extra Challenge Practice Master,
TRB, p. 70

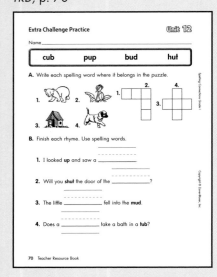

Challenge Dictation Sentences
1. There is a little **hut** by the lake.
2. Is that your **pup**?
3. The **bud** will open soon.
4. The **cub** ran up the tree.

Note: Posttest sentences for the on level and challenge lists are available on the audio *Spelling Connections* Posttest CD.

TEKS 1.22A Use phonological knowledge to match sounds to letters to construct known words. **1.22C** Spell high-frequency words from a commonly used list.

Challenge Words

mix	wag	pop	bend

Write the word that fits each clue.

1. to move from side to side

wag

2. to make a loud, bursting sound

pop

3. to blend together

mix

4. to make something curved

bend

TEKS 1.22C Spell high-frequency words from a commonly used list.

193

Student Objectives
- Read, spell, and write new words with short vowels in the medial position.
- Write CVC words that match definitions.

Teaching Tips
- Review with students that there are five short vowels: **a, e, i, o,** and **u**. Write the challenge words on the board. Point to each word and read it aloud. Have students repeat. Ask which short vowel sound they hear in the middle of each word. (**short i in mix; short a in wag; short o in pop; short e in bend**)
- Point out the letters **nd** at the end of **bend**. Slide your hand under the letters as you segment and pronounce the word. Review with students that the sounds of two consonants can slide together, but that each letter sound can still be heard.
- Read the directions on page 193. Have students complete the page independently or as a class.

Optional Practice and Assessment

Extra Challenge Practice Master, *TRB*, p. 74

Challenge Dictation Sentences
1. Look at the puppy **wag** its tail.
2. Did your balloon **pop**?
3. May I **mix** the batter?
4. Try to **bend** the paper clip.

Note: Posttest sentences for the on level and challenge lists are available on the audio *Spelling Connections* Posttest CD.

 TEKS 1.22A Use phonological knowledge to match sounds to letters to construct known words. **1.22C** Spell high-frequency words from a commonly used list.

T193

Student Objectives
- Read, spell, and write new high-frequency words.
- Write words to complete a paragraph.

Teaching Tips
- Tell students that sometimes letters do not make their usual sound.
- Write the challenge words on the board. Segment and pronounce the phonemes as you say each word. Have students repeat.
- Point out the variations in sounds the letters make. For example, **o** can say its name, as in **only, goes,** and **ago,** or have a short vowel sound, as in **top, box,** and **soft.** Also point out that when two vowels are paired together, the first vowel is usually pronounced and the second is usually silent, as in **easy** and **goes.**
- Read the directions on page 194. Have students complete the page independently or as a class.
- Review how to use a dictionary to find the meaning of unfamiliar words. As students complete the writing activity, have them look up unfamiliar words.

Challenge Words

ago	easy	goes	only

Complete the missing words.

A long time **1.** there were no phones. It was not **2.** to get a message to someone. Now you **3.** have to push a few buttons. Your voice **4.** where you want it to!

1. **a** go

2. **e** asy

3. **o** nly

4. **g** oes

194

TEKS 1.22C Spell high-frequency words from a commonly used list.

Optional Practice and Assessment

Extra Challenge Practice Master, *TRB,* p. 78

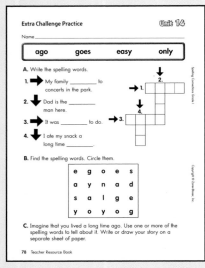

Challenge Dictation Sentences
1. That happened a long time **ago**.
2. My mom **goes** to work on Saturdays.
3. That looks **easy** to do.
4. You **only** need one paper.

Note: Posttest sentences for the on level and challenge lists are available on the audio *Spelling Connections* Posttest CD.

TEKS 1.22C Spell high-frequency words from a commonly used list.

Challenge Words

grab	slip	snap	plug

Complete each word to finish each sentence.

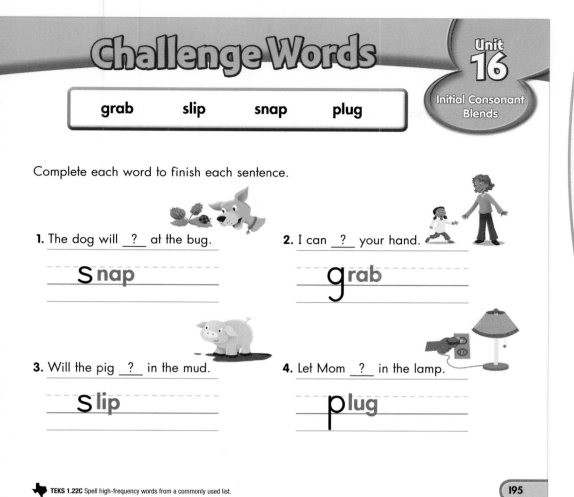

1. The dog will __?__ at the bug.

S nap

2. I can __?__ your hand.

g rab

3. Will the pig __?__ in the mud.

S lip

4. Let Mom __?__ in the lamp.

p lug

TEKS 1.22C Spell high-frequency words from a commonly used list.

195

Student Objectives
- Read, spell, and write new words with initial consonant blends.
- Write words to complete sentences.

Teaching Tips
- Review with students that a consonant blend is two or more consonants together in a word, such as **pl** in **plum**. Note that the sound of each letter can be heard when the word is pronounced.
- Write the challenge words on the board. Point to each word, read it aloud, and have students repeat it.
- Segment the letter sounds at the beginning of **snap**. Ask students what sounds they hear. (**/s/ and /n/**) Call on a volunteer to name the letters that make these sounds and circle them in the word.
- Read the directions on page 195. Have students complete the page independently or as a class.

Optional Practice and Assessment

Extra Challenge Practice Master,
TRB, p. 84

Challenge Dictation Sentences
1. I heard the branch **snap**.
2. The first person to **grab** the beanbag wins.
3. The **plug** to the lamp is broken.
4. Did you **slip** on the wet floor?

Note: Posttest sentences for the on level and challenge lists are available on the audio *Spelling Connections* Posttest CD.

TEKS 1.22Biii Use letter-sound patterns to spell: one-syllable words with consonant blends.
1.22C Spell high-frequency words from a commonly used list.

T195

Student Objectives
- Read, spell, and write new words with initial and final consonant blend **st**.
- Write words to complete sentences.

Teaching Tips
- Review with students that **st** is a consonant blend that can be at the beginning or end of a word.
- Write the challenge words on the board. Point to each word, read it aloud, and have students repeat it. Ask volunteers to underline **st** in each word.
- Talk about the meaning of each word. Ask volunteers to use each word in an oral sentence.
- Read the directions on page 196. Have students complete the page independently or as a class.

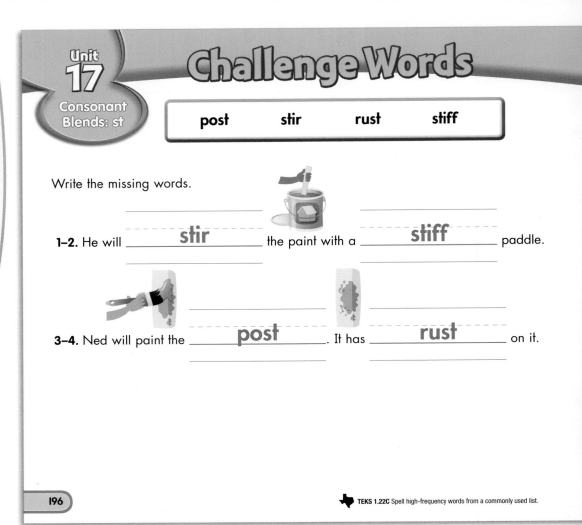

Unit 17 Consonant Blends: st

Challenge Words

| post | stir | rust | stiff |

Write the missing words.

1–2. He will _____ **stir** _____ the paint with a _____ **stiff** _____ paddle.

3–4. Ned will paint the _____ **post** _____. It has _____ **rust** _____ on it.

196

TEKS 1.22C Spell high-frequency words from a commonly used list.

Optional Practice and Assessment

Extra Challenge Practice Master, *TRB,* p. 88

Challenge Dictation Sentences
1. May I **stir** the batter?
2. My arm feels **stiff**.
3. There is **rust** on my bike.
4. Tie the dog's leash to that **post**.

Note: Posttest sentences for the on level and challenge lists are available on the audio *Spelling Connections* Posttest CD.

T196

 TEKS 1.22Biii Use letter-sound patterns to spell: one-syllable words with consonant blends. **1.22C** Spell high-frequency words from a commonly used list.

Challenge Words

cards	chips	pumps	twins

Write the missing words.

1. The two boys are ___?___ .

twins

2. I got lots of ___?___ on my birthday.

cards

3. The cup has two ___?___ in it.

chips

4. Dad ___?___ gas into the car.

pumps

TEKS 1.22C Spell high-frequency words from a commonly used list.

197

Student Objectives
- Read, spell, and write new words with **-s** added to form plurals and present-tense singular verbs.
- Write words to complete sentences.

Teaching Tips
- Review with students that **-s** can be added to naming words to mean more than one and to action words to tell what one person is doing right now.
- On the board, write the challenge words without the final **s**. Point to each word, read it aloud, and have students repeat it. Ask volunteers to come up and write **-s** at the end of each word. Read the new words aloud and have students repeat.
- Talk about the meaning of each word. Ask volunteers to use each word in an oral sentence.
- Read the directions on page 197. Have students complete the page independently or as a class.

Optional Practice and Assessment

Extra Challenge Practice Master,
TRB, p. 92

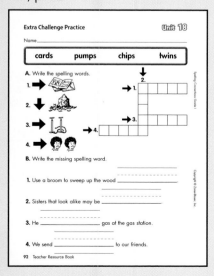

Challenge Dictation Sentences
1. Your heart **pumps** blood through your body.
2. Would you like some ice **chips**?
3. May I see your baseball **cards**?
4. Donald and Jason are **twins**.

Note: Posttest sentences for the on level and challenge lists are available on the audio *Spelling Connections* Posttest CD.

TEKS 1.22C Spell high-frequency words from a commonly used list.
1.22D Spell base words with inflectional endings.

Student Objectives

- Read, spell, and write new words with **-ing** added to form present participles.
- Write words to complete phrases.

Teaching Tips

- Review with students that **-ing** can be added to action words so that they tell what is happening right now.
- On the board, write the challenge words without the final **-ing**. Point to each word, read it aloud, and have students repeat it. Ask volunteers to come up and write **-ing** at the end of each word. Read the new words aloud and have students repeat.
- Talk about how each word can be used to tell about an action that is happening now. Give an example, such as *I am picking plums*.
- Read the directions on page 198. Have students complete the page independently or as a class.

Unit 19 — Inflectional Endings: -ing

Challenge Words

| mowing | packing | bending | picking |

Look at each picture. Write the best word.

1. __?__ down
   bending

2. __?__ plums
   picking

3. __?__ a bag
   packing

4. __?__ grass
   mowing

198

TEKS 1.22C Spell high-frequency words from a commonly used list.

Optional Practice and Assessment

Extra Challenge Practice Master,
TRB, p. 96

Extra Challenge Practice — Unit 19

Name _____

| mowing | bending | packing | picking |

A. Add **ing** to each spelling word to complete the sentence.

1. I must **bend** to pick up the pencil.
   I am _____ down right now.
2. We need to **mow** the grass.
   Dad is _____ the grass.
3. The berries are ready to **pick**.
   We are _____ the berries.

B. Add the missing letters to make spelling words.

1. ___ a ___ i ___
2. ___ e ___ i ___

C. Draw a picture of yourself doing one of the activities suggested by the spelling words. Write a story and tell about your picture. Use a separate sheet of paper.

96   Teacher Resource Book

Challenge Dictation Sentences

1. Jessica is **mowing** the lawn.
2. We are **picking** blueberries in the woods.
3. Mom is **packing** my suitcase.
4. I am tired from **bending** over.

Note: Posttest sentences for the on level and challenge lists are available on the audio *Spelling Connections* Posttest CD.

TEKS 1.22C Spell high-frequency words from a commonly used list.
1.22D Spell base words with inflectional endings.

Challenge Words

| ape | wake | mane | tame |

Write words to complete the sentences.

I had a 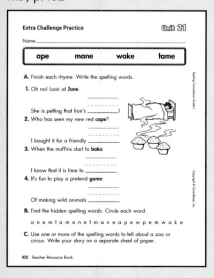 dream about a

🦁 lion and an 🐵 __1.__ .

The 🦁 lion was __2.__ . The ape

was not. The ape pulled on the lion's

🦁🐵 __3.__ . The 🦁 lion

made a loud noise. The noise made me

__4.__ up.

1. ape
2. tame
3. mane
4. wake

TEKS 1.22C Spell high-frequency words from a commonly used list.

199

Unit 21

Long a: CVCe

Student Objectives
- Read, spell, and write new words with **long a**.
- Write words to complete sentences.

Teaching Tips
- Review with students that in words that have **a-consonant-e,** the **a** makes the **long a** sound and the **e** is silent.
- Write the challenge words on the board. Point to each word, read it aloud, and have students repeat it. Ask volunteers to underline **a** and **e** in each word.
- Talk about the meaning of each word. Then write the following sentence: *I set the clock to _____ me up.* Ask students which spelling word they would write to complete the sentence. (wake) Call on a volunteer to write the word in the sentence.
- Read the directions on page 199. Have students complete the page independently or as a class.

Optional Practice and Assessment

Extra Challenge Practice Master,
TRB, p. 102

Extra Challenge Practice — Unit 21

Name

| ape | mane | wake | tame |

A. Finish each rhyme. Write the spelling words.

1. Oh no! Look at **Jane.**

She is petting that lion's _____!

2. Who has seen my new red **cape?**

I bought it for a friendly _____

3. When the muffins start to **bake**

I know that it is time to _____

4. It's fun to play a pretend **game**

Of making wild animals _____

B. Find the hidden spelling words. Circle each word.

a n e m t a m e n e t m a n e a p e w p e m w a k e

C. Use one or more of the spelling words to tell about a zoo or circus. Write your story on a separate sheet of paper.

102 Teacher Resource Book

Challenge Dictation Sentences
1. It is time to **wake** up.
2. Can you swing on a rope like an **ape**?
3. The lion has a **mane**.
4. Most animals in the zoo are not **tame**.

Note: Posttest sentences for the on level and challenge lists are available on the audio *Spelling Connections* Posttest CD.

TEKS 1.22Bii Use letter-sound patterns to spell: consonant-vowel-consonant-silent e (CVCe) words. **1.22C** Spell high-frequency words from a commonly used list.

Student Objectives

- Read, spell, and write new words with **long a**.
- Write words to name pictures.

Teaching Tips

- Review with students that in words that have **a**-consonant-**e,** the **a** makes the **long a** sound and the **e** is silent.
- Write the challenge words on the board. Point to each word, read it aloud, and have students repeat. Ask volunteers to underline **a** and **e** in each word.
- Talk about the meaning of each word. For example, point to the current day on a calendar page. Say, *The date today is (fill in the date).*
- Read the directions on page 200. Have students complete the page independently or as a class.

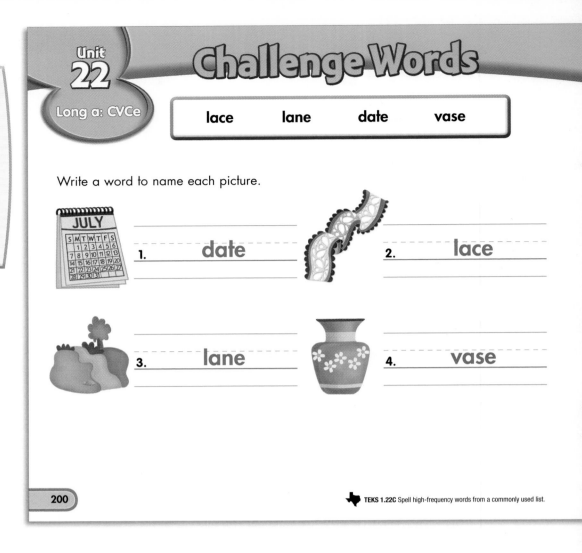

Unit 22 Long a: CVCe

Challenge Words

| lace | lane | date | vase |

Write a word to name each picture.

1. date
2. lace
3. lane
4. vase

200

TEKS **1.22C** Spell high-frequency words from a commonly used list.

Optional Practice and Assessment

Extra Challenge Practice Master, *TRB,* p. 106

Challenge Dictation Sentences

1. The collar of the dress is made of **lace**.
2. Our house is at the end of the **lane**.
3. Put the flowers in a glass **vase**.
4. This fruit is called a **date**.

Note: Posttest sentences for the on level and challenge lists are available on the audio *Spelling Connections* Posttest CD.

TEKS **1.22Bii** Use letter-sound patterns to spell: consonant-vowel-consonant-silent e (CVCe) words. **1.22C** Spell high-frequency words from a commonly used list.

beet   peel   peek   deed

Write a word to finish each sentence.

1. Let me __?__ into the box.

peek

2. Will you __?__ his orange?

peel

3. I ate the big __?__ .

beet

4. When you do something kind for someone, you do a good __?__ .

deed

TEKS 1.22C Spell high-frequency words from a commonly used list.

201

Student Objectives
- Read, spell, and write new words with **long e**.
- Write words to complete sentences.

Teaching Tips
- Review with students that the **long e** sound can be spelled **ee**.
- Point out that two e's can be in the middle or at the end of a word. Write the challenge words on the board. Point to the two e's in the middle of each word. Then read each word aloud and have students repeat it. Ask volunteers to underline **ee** in each word.
- Talk about the meaning of each word. For example, display an orange or a picture of an orange. Pantomime peeling the orange and tell students, *I peel the orange*.
- Read the directions on page 201. Have students complete the page independently or as a class.

Optional Practice and Assessment

Extra Challenge Practice Master, *TRB*, p. 110

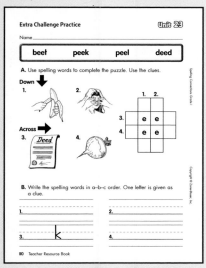

Challenge Dictation Sentences
1. Cover your eyes and do not **peek**.
2. I did a good **deed** for my grandmother.
3. This **beet** came from the garden.
4. Can you **peel** your banana?

Note: Posttest sentences for the on level and challenge lists are available on the audio *Spelling Connections* Posttest CD.

TEKS 1.22C Spell high-frequency words from a commonly used list.

T201

Student Objectives
- Read, spell, and write new words with **long e**.
- Categorize spelling words in groups.

Teaching Tips
- Write the challenge words on the board. Read each word aloud and have students repeat. Ask volunteers to underline **ee** in each word.
- Point to **creek**. Slide your hand under **cr** as you say each phoneme. Point out that the sounds slide together but that each sound can be heard. Do the same for **sweep**.
- Point to **cheek**. Point to **ch**. Explain that these letters together make a sound that is different from either letter sound alone. Say /ch/ and then /ēēk/. Have students repeat.
- Review word meanings. For example, point to your cheek and say **cheek**. Ask students to name other parts of the face. (eyes, nose, chin, eyebrows, forehead, mouth, lips)
- Read the directions on page 202. Have students complete the page independently or as a class.

Unit
24
Long e: ee

Challenge Words

| weed | creek | sweep | cheek |

Write the word that fits each group.

1. dust, ____, mop, ____, _?_

_____ sweep _____

2. nose, ____, chin, ____, _?_

_____ cheek _____

3. river, stream, _?_

_____ creek _____

4. grass, ____, flower, ____, _?_

_____ weed _____

202

TEKS 1.22C Spell high-frequency words from a commonly used list.

Optional Practice and Assessment

Extra Challenge Practice Master, *TRB*, p. 114

Challenge Dictation Sentences
1. Pull that **weed** out of the garden.
2. May I **sweep** the floor?
3. We can wade in the **creek**.
4. The baby patted my **cheek**.

Note: Posttest sentences for the on level and challenge lists are available on the audio *Spelling Connections* Posttest CD.

TEKS 1.22Biii Use letter-sound patterns to spell: one-syllable words with consonant blends. 1.22C Spell high-frequency words from a commonly used list.

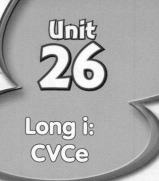
Challenge Words

| tide | vine | pine | hive |

Write a word that rhymes with the word in ( ) to complete the sentences.

1. Did you sit under the ___?___ tree? **(fine)**

pine

2. The jellyfish came in with the ___?___ . **(ride)**

tide

3. The busy bees are in the ___?___ . **(five)**

hive

4. The deer like to eat this ___?___ . **(line)**

vine

TEKS 1.22A Use phonological knowledge to match sounds to letters to construct known words. 1.22C Spell high-frequency words from a commonly used list.

203

Student Objectives
- Read, spell, and write new words with **long i**.
- Complete sentences with words that rhyme.

Teaching Tips
- Write the challenge words on the board. Point to **i**-consonant-**e** in each word. Then read the words aloud and have students repeat. Ask volunteers to underline **i**-consonant-**e** in each word.
- Remind students that words rhyme when they have the same ending sounds. Write **hive** on the board. Say **hide, dive, life**. Ask students which word rhymes with **hive**. (**dive**) Say **dive–hive** and have students note how the words sound the same.
- Talk about the meaning of each challenge word. For example, point to a picture of a pine tree and tell students that a **pine** is a kind of tree.
- Read the directions on page 203. Have students complete the page independently or as a class.

Optional Practice and Assessment

Extra Challenge Practice Master,
TRB, p. 120

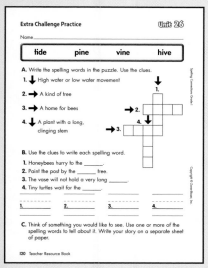

Challenge Dictation Sentences
1. Grapes grow on a **vine**.
2. There is a squirrel in the **pine** tree.
3. Did you see the bee fly into the **hive**?
4. We will look for shells while the **tide** is out.

Note: Posttest sentences for the on level and challenge lists are available on the audio *Spelling Connections* Posttest CD.

TEKS 1.22A Use phonological knowledge to match sounds to letters to construct known words. 1.22C Spell high-frequency words from a commonly used list.

T203

Unit 27

Long i: CVCe

Student Objectives
- Read, spell, and write new words with **long i**.
- Complete alliterative sentences with words that rhyme.

Teaching Tips
- Write the challenge words on the board. Point to **i**-consonant-**e** in each word. Then read the words aloud and have students repeat. Ask volunteers to underline **i**-consonant-**e** in each word.
- Talk about the meaning of each word. For example, wipe your eyes with a tissue and say, *I wipe my eyes.* Use additional pantomime, gestures, and pictures to provide context and illustrate words.
- Say, *Dave did do the dishes.* Ask students what they notice about the words in the sentence. (**Most start with the same sound, /d/.**) Write the sentence on the board and have a volunteer underline the initial **d** in four words.
- Read the directions on page 204. Have students complete the page independently or as a class.

Unit 27 — Challenge Words

Long i: CVCe

| wide | rice | dive | wipe |

Write a word to complete each sentence.

1. Wise Willy opened the window __?__ .

wide

2. Rick's pet rat ate the __?__ !

rice

3. Do ducks __?__ for their dinner?

dive

4. We will __?__ the wagon with wax.

wipe

204   TEKS 1.22A Use phonological knowledge to match sounds to letters to construct known words. 1.22C Spell high-frequency words from a commonly used list.

Optional Practice and Assessment

Extra Challenge Practice Master,
TRB, p. 124

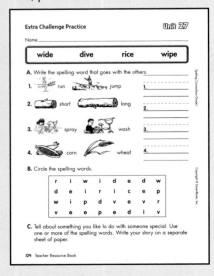

Challenge Dictation Sentences
1. Did you **wipe** your hands?
2. Would you rather have **rice** or potatoes?
3. Some city streets are very **wide**.
4. I watched the swimmers **dive**.

Note: Posttest sentences for the on level and challenge lists are available on the audio *Spelling Connections* Posttest CD.

TEKS 1.22A Use phonological knowledge to match sounds to letters to construct known words. 1.22C Spell high-frequency words from a commonly used list.

Challenge Words

cone	dome	hole	hose

Write the missing words.

1. It lives in a __?__ in the ground.

hole

2. Did you get wet from the __?__ ?

hose

3. Look at the big __?__ on that building!

dome

4. I found this pine __?__ under the tree.

cone

TEKS 1.22C Spell high-frequency words from a commonly used list.

205

Student Objectives
- Read, spell, and write new words with **long o**.
- Complete sentences with spelling words.

Teaching Tips
- Write the challenge words on the board. Point to **o-consonant-e** in each word. Then read the words aloud and have students repeat. Ask volunteers to underline **o-consonant-e** in each word.
- Point to the **s** in **hose**. Explain that the **s** in **hose** is pronounced /z/.
- Talk about the meaning of each word. For example, say, *You can dig a deep **hole** with a shovel.* Ask students what they know about each word. Discuss words they do not know.
- Read the directions on page 205. Have students complete the page independently or as a class.

Optional Practice and Assessment

Extra Challenge Practice Master,
TRB, p. 128

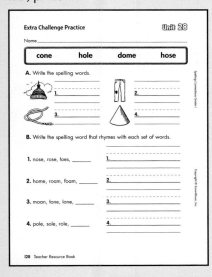

Challenge Dictation Sentences
1. My bag has a **hole** in it.
2. The clown's hat was shaped like a **cone**.
3. The **dome** on that church is shining.
4. Will you please turn on the **hose**?

Note: Posttest sentences for the on level and challenge lists are available on the audio *Spelling Connections* Posttest CD.

TEKS 1.22A Use phonological knowledge to match sounds to letters to construct known words. **1.22C** Spell high-frequency words from a commonly used list.

T205

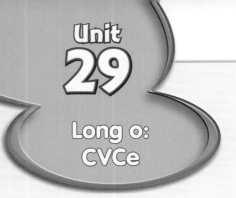

Student Objectives

- Read, spell, and write new words with **long o**.
- Complete sentences with spelling words.

Teaching Tips

- Write the challenge words on the board. Point to **o**-consonant-**e** in each word. Then read the words aloud and have students repeat. Ask volunteers to underline **o**-consonant-**e** in each word.
- Point to **stove**. Move your hand under **st** and tell students that the sounds of **s** and **t** slide together but that each sound can be heard. Ask students what kind of letter-sound pattern these two letters together form. (**a blend**) Say **stove** and have students repeat.
- Talk about the meaning of each word. For example, say, *Use a **code** to write a secret note*. Ask students what they know about each word. Discuss words they do not know.
- Read the directions on page 206. Have students complete the page independently or as a class.

Challenge Words

| code | woke | mole | stove |

Write a word to finish the sentence and tell about the picture.

1. My cat __?__ me up.

woke

2. The __?__ dug a hole.

mole

3. We will make up a secret __?__.

code

4. The pot is on the __?__.

stove

206

TEKS 1.22C Spell high-frequency words from a commonly used list.

Optional Practice and Assessment

Extra Challenge Practice Master,
TRB, p. 132

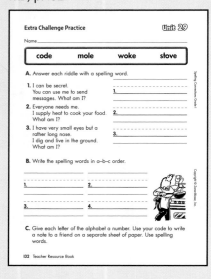

Challenge Dictation Sentences

1. A **mole** lives in the ground.
2. I **woke** up late this morning.
3. These marks look like a secret **code**.
4. Is the **stove** turned on?

Note: Posttest sentences for the on level and challenge lists are available on the audio *Spelling Connections* Posttest CD.

 TEKS 1.22A Use phonological knowledge to match sounds to letters to construct known words. **1.22Biii** Use letter-sound patterns to spell: one-syllable words with consonant blends. **1.22C** Spell high-frequency words from a commonly used list.

Challenge Words

| moon | broom | spoon | stool |

Write the word that names each picture.

1.

moon

2.

stool

3.

spoon

4.

broom

TEKS 1.22A Use phonological knowledge to match sounds to letters to construct known words. 1.22C Spell high-frequency words from a commonly used list.

207

Student Objectives
- Read, spell, and write new words with the /ōo/ sound.
- Identify picture names that have the /ōo/ sound.

Teaching Tips
- Write the challenge words on the board. Ask students what is the same about all the words. (**oo in the middle**) Say each word and have students repeat it. Ask what sound **oo** spells. (/ōo/)
- Point to **broom**. Move your hand under **br** and tell students that the sounds of **b** and **r** slide together but that each sound can be heard. Say **broom** and have students repeat. Do the same with **spoon** and **stool**.
- Ask students what they know about each word. Discuss words they do not know. Talk about the meaning of each word. For example, say, *Use a* **broom** *to sweep the floor.*
- Read the directions on page 207. Have students complete the page independently or as a class.

Optional Practice and Assessment

Extra Challenge Practice Master,
TRB, p. 138

Challenge Dictation Sentences
1. We can see by the light of the **moon**.
2. Does the baby eat with a **spoon**?
3. I can reach the table if I sit on a **stool**.
4. Sweep the floor with this **broom**.

Note: Posttest sentences for the on level and challenge lists are available on the audio *Spelling Connections* Posttest CD.

TEKS 1.22A Use phonological knowledge to match sounds to letters to construct known words. 1.22C Spell high-frequency words from a commonly used list.

T207

Student Objectives
- Read, spell, and write new words with final digraph **ck**.
- Write spelling words that complete sentences.

Teaching Tips
- Write the challenge words on the board. Ask students what is the same about all the words. **(ck at the end)** Say each word and have students repeat it. Ask what sound **ck** spells. **(/k/)**
- Point to **crack**. Move your hand under **cr** as you tell students that the sounds of **c** and **r** slide together but that each sound can be heard. Say **crack** and have students repeat. Have students tell what letter-sound pattern these two letters together form. **(a blend)** Do the same with **cluck**.
- Point to **qu** in **quack**. Tell students that the letters **qu** together spell **/kw/**. Have students say the word.
- Talk about the meaning of each word. Use gestures and pantomime to provide context and support meaning.
- Read the directions on page 208. Have students complete the page independently or as a class.

Challenge Words

| tuck | quack | crack | cluck |

Write the words to finish the sentences.

Mother Hen and Mother Duck carefully __1.__ their eggs under them. They hear a loud __2.__ ! Mother Hen says, " __3.__ !" Mother Duck says, " __4.__ !" See what has happened!

1. **tuck**

2. **crack**

3. **Cluck**

4. **Quack**

TEKS 1.22C Spell high-frequency words from a commonly used list.

Optional Practice and Assessment

Extra Challenge Practice Master, *TRB*, p. 142

Challenge Dictation Sentences
1. Will you **tuck** me in bed?
2. I heard the duck **quack**.
3. Can you **cluck** like a hen?
4. There is a **crack** in the sidewalk.

Note: Posttest sentences for the on level and challenge lists are available on the audio *Spelling Connections* Posttest CD.

 TEKS 1.22A Use phonological knowledge to match sounds to letters to construct known words. **1.22Biii** Use letter-sound patterns to spell: one-syllable words with consonant blends. **1.22C** Spell high-frequency words from a commonly used list.

| shut | crash | hush | shake |

Write a word that goes with the action in the picture.

1. **shut**

2. **hush**

3. **shake**

4. **crash**

TEKS 1.22A Use phonological knowledge to match sounds to letters to construct known words. **1.22C** Spell high-frequency words from a commonly used list.

209

Student Objectives
- Read, spell, and write new words with digraph **sh**.
- Write spelling words to name an action in a picture.

Teaching Tips
- Write the challenge words on the board. Ask students what is the same about all the words. (sh) Say each word and have students repeat it. Ask what sound **sh** spells. (/sh/) Have volunteers underline **sh** in each word.
- Point to **crash**. Move your hand under **cr** as you tell students that the sounds of **c** and **r** slide together but that each sound can be heard. Say **crash** and have students repeat.
- Point to **shake**. Review that the vowel sound in the word is **long a** spelled **a_e**.
- Talk about the meaning of each word. Use gestures and pantomime to provide context and support meaning.
- Read the directions on page 209. Have students complete the page independently or as a class.

Optional Practice and Assessment

Extra Challenge Practice Master,
TRB, p. 146

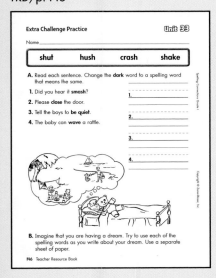

Challenge Dictation Sentences
1. The baby can **shake** his rattle.
2. She tried to **hush** the barking dog.
3. Did you **shut** the door?
4. I heard a **crash** in the closet!

Note: Posttest sentences for the on level and challenge lists are available on the audio *Spelling Connections* Posttest CD.

TEKS 1.22A Use phonological knowledge to match sounds to letters to construct known words. **1.22C** Spell high-frequency words from a commonly used list.

Student Objectives
- Read, spell, and write new words with digraph **th**.
- Write spelling words to replace a word in a sentence.

Teaching Tips
- Write the challenge words on the board. Ask students what is the same about all the words. (**th**) Say each word and have students repeat. Ask what sound **th** spells. (/**th**/ or /**th̲**/) Have volunteers circle **th** in each word.
- Point to **thump**. Move your hand under **mp** as you tell students that the sounds of **m** and **p** slide together but that each sound can be heard. Say **thump** and have students repeat.
- Point to **booth**. Review that **oo** spells /o͞o/.
- Talk about the meaning of each word. Use gestures and pantomime to provide context and support meaning.
- Read the directions on page 210. Have students complete the page independently or as a class.

| thin | thump | thud | booth |

Cross out the wrong word. Write the word that rhymes.

1. First we heard a ~~lump~~!

   thump

2. Then there was a loud ~~mud~~!

   thud

3. I saw a ~~tin~~ shadow on the wall!

   thin

4. This is a scary ~~tooth~~!

   booth

210

TEKS 1.22C Spell high-frequency words from a commonly used list.

Optional Practice and Assessment

Extra Challenge Practice Master,
TRB, p. 150

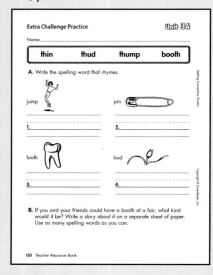

Challenge Dictation Sentences
1. The apple fell to the ground with a **thud**.
2. I like my bread sliced **thin**.
3. Is that Becky in the **booth**?
4. You will make a loud noise if you **thump** on a box with a stick.

Note: Posttest sentences for the on level and challenge lists are available on the audio *Spelling Connections* Posttest CD.

TEKS **1.22A** Use phonological knowledge to match sounds to letters to construct known words. **1.22C** Spell high-frequency words from a commonly used list.

Spelling Study Strategy

Look, Say

1. **Look** at the word.

2. **Say** the letters. Think about how each sound is spelled.

Cover, See

3. **Cover** the word with your hand or close your eyes.

4. **See** the word in your mind. Spell the word to yourself.

Write, Check

5. **Write** the word.

6. **Check** your spelling.

Student Objectives

- Review alphabetical order.
- Practice putting words in alphabetical order.

A-B-C Order

Words in a dictionary are in a-b-c order. Words that start with **a** are first. Words that start with **b** are next. Words that start with **z** are last.

Fill in the blanks to write the **abc**'s in order.

a b ____ d e ____ g ____ i j

____

____ ____ m n ____ p q r s

____

____ u ____ w ____ y ____

Read the words below. Then copy them to show the order you would find them in a dictionary.

zoo	ant	duck
1.	2.	3.

Student Objectives
• Gain information about dictionary guide words.

T213

There are two words at the top of each dictionary page. These words are called **guide words**.

The first guide word is the first word on that page.

The other guide word is the last word on that page.

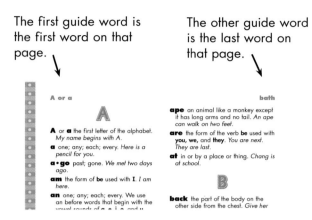

A or a

A

A or **a** the first letter of the alphabet. *My name begins with A.*

a one; any; each; every. *Here is a pencil for you.*

a•go past; gone. *We met two days ago.*

am the form of **be** used with **I**. *I am here.*

an one; any; each; every. We use an before words that begin with the vowel sounds of **a, e, i, o,** and **u**.

bath

ape an animal like a monkey except it has long arms and no tail. *An ape can walk on two feet.*

are the form of the verb **be** used with **you, we,** and **they**. *You are next. They are last.*

at in or by a place or thing. *Chang is at school.*

B

back the part of the body on the other side from the chest. *Give her*

All the words on this page fall between the guide words in a-b-c order.

Circle the words that you would find on the dictionary page above.

ant   dog   milk   fall   are   back

213

Using the  Entries

Here is an entry from your **Spelling Dictionary**.

> **pet** an animal kept with people.
> *A cat may make a good pet.*

A dictionary **entry** is all the information about one word. An entry is the **entry word**, the **definition**, and the **sample sentence**.

1. The entry word is the word you are looking up.

   _____

   Write the entry word here. _____

   _____

2. The definition tells what the entry word means.

   Circle the definition in the entry above.

3. The sample sentence uses the entry word. It helps you understand the word.

   Underline the sample sentence in the entry above.

4. Circle the pair of guide words that could be on the page with **pet**.

   a • back   **soon • sweep**   **path • pop**

214

 **Entries**

Here is an entry from your **Spelling Dictionary**.

> **frog** a small animal with webbed feet that lives near water. *A frog can jump far.*

An **entry word** is the word you are looking up. It is the first word in the entry. The entry word shows you how to spell the word. Entry words are in **bold type**.

1. Circle the entry word in the entry above.

The **definition** is the next part of an entry. The definition tells you what the entry word means.

2. Underline the definition in the entry above.

Here is another entry from your **Spelling Dictionary**.

> **note a.** a very short message or letter. *Let's write Mom a note.* **b.** a sign in music. *This is a quarter note.*

Sometimes an entry word can have more than one meaning. It will have more than one definition in the entry. Find two definitions for the word **note**.

3. Draw one line under the first definition.

4. Draw two lines under the second definition.

215

Using the Dictionary — Sample Sentences

The **sample sentence** in a dictionary entry can be very helpful. The sample sentence uses the entry word in a sentence. The sentence can help you understand the entry word. It can help you know how to use the word. Sample sentences are in *italic type*.

1. Underline the sample sentence in this entry from your **Spelling Dictionary**.

   moon the body that shines in the night sky.
   A full moon looks like a big circle.

An entry also shows different **forms** of words. An entry will show the forms of action words. Forms are in **dark type**.

2. Underline the forms in the entry below.

   hope (hopes, hoped, hop•ing) to wish or expect.
   I hope you will visit us soon.

An entry will show the plurals of naming words. **Plural** means "more than one." Plurals are in **dark type**.

3. Underline the plural form in the entry below.

   bus (bus•es *pl.*) a long car or van that can carry many people.
   We ride a bus to school.

216

Create a separate and personal Spelling Dictionary

1. Help students remove the dictionary pages (pp. 217–240) from the Student Edition.

2. Remove the two pieces of cover stock immediately following student page 247.

Front Cover

Back Cover
"High Frequency Writing Words" and "Manuscript Writing Models"

3. Guide students as they make their personal dictionaries:

- Place the front cover on top of page 217. Make sure the rest of the dictionary pages follow in sequence.
- Add blank pages for students to add other words to make a personal spelling dictionary (optional).
- Place the back cover at the end of the dictionary.
- Staple the pages together at the left edge, or punch holes in the covers and pages and lace them together.

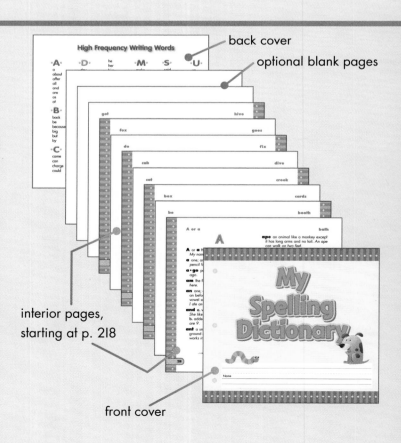

back cover

optional blank pages

interior pages, starting at p. 218

front cover

Using the Dictionary

The **Spelling Dictionary** is the place to learn many helpful things about the spelling words.

The **entry** is the entry word, the definition, and the sample sentence.

The **entry word** is the spelling word you look up. Entry words are listed in a-b-c order.

The **definition** tells you what the word means.

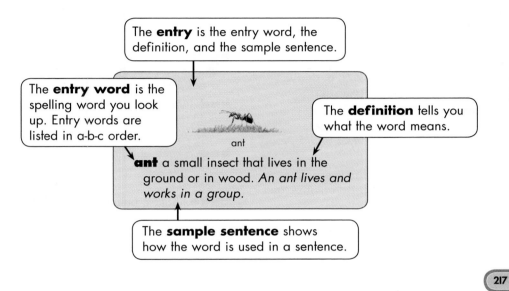

ant

ant a small insect that lives in the ground or in wood. *An ant lives and works in a group.*

The **sample sentence** shows how the word is used in a sentence.

217

Student Objectives
• Learn to use a dictionary to find correct spellings.

T217

4 Ask students to write their name on the cover.

5 Encourage students to take this personal dictionary home at the end of the school year for use during the summer.

A or **a** the first letter of the alphabet. *My name begins with A.*

a one; any; each; every. *Here is a pencil for you.*

a•go past; gone. *We met two days ago.*

am the form of **be** used with **I**. *I am here.*

an one; any; each; every. We use an before words that begin with the vowel sounds of **a, e, i, o,** and **u.** *I ate an apple an hour ago.*

and a. with; together with; besides. *She likes to sing and dance.* b. added to. *In math, 4 and 5 are 9.*

ant a small insect that lives in the ground or in wood. *An ant lives and works in a group.*

ant

ape an animal like a monkey except it has long arms and no tail. *An ape can walk on two feet.*

are the form of the verb **be** used with **you, we,** and **they**. *You are next. They are last.*

at in or by a place or thing. *Chang is at school.*

back the part of the body on the other side from the chest. *Give her a pat on the back.*

bad (worse, worst; bad•ly) not good, right, or healthy. *Eating too much is bad for you.*

bag a sack; a container made of soft material. *Scott will take the bag with food in it.*

bake (bakes, baked, bak•ing) to cook in an oven. *We bake bread.*

bath a washing of the whole body. *We gave our dog a bath.*

218

be (am, are, is, was, were, been, be•ing) **a.** to equal. *Anna answered, "2 and 3 are 5."* **b.** to happen. *What time will the game be?*

bed a thing to sleep or rest on. *Meg can make her bed.*

bed

beet a plant grown for its juicy root. *He ate the red beet.*

bend (bends, bent, bend•ing) **a.** to make something curve. *Help me bend this wire.* **b.** to stoop or lean over. *Can you bend and touch your toes?*

best better than all others. *That was the best lunch I ever had.*

bib a cloth tied under a baby's chin to keep his or her clothing clean. *The baby's bib was full of food.*

big large. *Our school is big.*

bike a bicycle. *Juan rides his bike.*

bit past tense of **bite**. *He bit into the apple.*

bite (bites, bit, bit•ten or bit, bit•ing) to grab, hold, or cut with the teeth. *When I lost my front teeth, it was hard to bite.*

bod•y (bod•ies *pl.*) all the parts that make up a person or an animal. *Take good care of your body.*

bone a hard part inside the body; a part of the skeleton. *Your longest bone is in your leg.*

booth **a.** a stand where something is sold. *Our class ran an art booth at the school fair.* **b.** a closed place. *Use the phone in that booth.*

box (box•es *pl.*) a case to hold things. *I have a toy box.*

box

broom a brush with a long handle, used for sweeping. *You can use the broom to sweep the walk.*

bud the small beginning of a flower or leaf. *That bud will be a rose.*

bug (bugs *pl.*) an insect, usually one that crawls. *Even a small bug can crawl fast.*

bump a. to knock or hit against something. *Try not to bump into the wall.* b. a raised place. *The bump in the road makes the car bounce.*

bus (bus•es *pl.*) a long car or van that can carry many people. *We ride a bus to school.*

but a. yet; however. *I will come, but I want to eat lunch first.* b. except. *We can go any day but Monday.*

came past tense of **come**. *They came to see us last week.*

can (could) a. to know how or to be able to. *He can play the piano.* b. a metal container. *Here is a can of peas.*

cards small pieces of stiff paper. *We wrote the letters on separate cards.*

cat (cats *pl.*) **a.** a small furry animal that can purr. *Our cat loves to sit on my lap.* **b.** any larger animal that is also a part of the cat family. *A lion is a cat.*

cat

cheek the side of the face below the eye. *She had a little smudge on her cheek.*

chips small pieces broken or cut off something. *Glue these chips back onto the cup.*

cluck a sound made by a chicken. *When a hen calls her chicks, it sounds like "cluck, cluck."*

cod a big fish often used for food. *Cod live in cold water.*

code a set of signals for sending messages. *Our club made up a secret code.*

come (comes, came, come, com•ing) **a.** to move closer; arrive. *Come over to my house.* **b.** to happen. *Our birthdays come once a year.*

cone **a.** an object that is round at one end and pointed at the other. *She made a cone of paper.* **b.** the seed pod of an evergreen tree. *That pine cone grew on a white pine tree.*

crack (cracks, cracked, crack•ing) **a.** to break or split without snapping apart. *The glass may crack when I wash it.* **b.** to make a sudden snapping noise. *Did you hear the thunder crack?*

crash the very loud noise of something falling, breaking, or hitting. *The tree fell with a loud crash.*

creek a small stream. *The ducks swim in the creek.*

221

cub a young bear, lion, or wolf. *We saw a bear cub at the zoo.*

cub

cut (cuts, cut, cut•ting) to split with something sharp. *Let's cut this apple in half.*

dad a short word for **father**. *My dad took us for a walk.*

date the time when something happens. *July 4 is an important date.*

deed an act; a thing done. *Helping Jill clean her room was a good deed.*

deep far down or back. *Big fish swim in deep water.*

den **a.** the home of a wild animal. *The lion cubs stay near their den.* **b.** a small room where one can read, relax, or work. *Mother is watching TV in the den.*

did past tense of **do**. *I did my homework last night.*

dig (digs, dug, dig•ging) to make a hole in the ground. *Dogs dig holes with their front paws.*

dish (dish•es *pl.*) **a.** something that holds food. *Put the dish on the table.* **b.** to serve food. *Mom will dish out the green beans.*

dive (dives, dived or dove, div•ing) to jump headfirst into water. *Seals dive to catch fish.*

222

do (does, did, done, do•ing) to act, make, perform, or carry out. *Everyone in the class will do something different.*

dome a round roof or cover. *Dad put the cheese under a glass dome.*

dot **a.** a small round spot. *There was a dot of ink on my new shirt.* **b.** to mark with a small round spot. *Be sure to dot that **i**.*

duck a swimming bird with webbed feet, a short neck, and a flat bill. *The duck swam in the pond.*

duck

dug past tense of **dig**. *Dan dug a deep hole.*

eas•y not hard to get or do. *A toy on wheels is easy to pull.*

fast able to act or move quickly. *We can run fast.*

fed past tense of **feed**. *I fed the dog.*

feed (feeds, fed, feed•ing) to give food to. *We must feed the horses.*

feel (feels, felt, feel•ing) **a.** to touch. *Feel the soft fur of the cat.* **b.** to have the feeling of being. *I feel cold.* **c.** to have an emotion. *I feel sad.*

feet the parts of the body at the end of the legs. *I can stand on two feet.*

fix (fix•es, fixed, fix•ing) to repair or mend. *Grandpa can fix that broken toy.*

223

fox (fox•es *pl.*) a wild animal like a dog but with a bushy tail. *The fox ran into the forest.*

fox

frog a small animal with webbed feet that lives near water. *A frog can jump far.*

fun a good time; happy play. *We had fun at the zoo.*

game a. a way to play that follows rules. *Let's have a game of tag.* **b.** the things needed to play a game. *Where is your game of checkers?*

gate an opening like a door in a fence or wall. *She closed the garden gate.*

gave past tense of **give**. *We gave Mr. Russo a flower.*

get (gets, got, got or got•ten, get•ting) **a.** to come to have; to receive. *Our class will get new desks.* **b.** to bring. *I will get you a glass of milk.*

give (gives, gave, giv•en, giv•ing) to hand over; to let have. *I will give you this ball.*

go (goes, went, gone, go•ing) to move. *Let's go to your house to play.*

goes past tense of **go**. *This car goes fast.*

got past tense of **get**. *She got some carrots for a snack.*

grab (grabs, grabbed, grab•bing) to take hold of suddenly. *The boys grab their coats and run for the bus.*

grin (grins, grinned, grin•ning) to smile broadly. *The teacher may grin at my joke.*

had past tense of **have**. *We had fun at the park.*

has a form of **have**. *She has a sunny smile.*

hat a covering for the head; a cap. *My hat keeps my ears warm.*

hat

have (has, had, hav•ing) to own; to possess. *I have a red cap.*

he that boy or man. *He is a good boy.*

hen a female chicken or other bird. *Your hen can lay eggs.*

hide (hides, hid, hid•den or hid, hid•ing) to put or keep out of sight. *Let's hide the gifts quickly.*

hike a. a long walk. *We took a hike in the woods.* b. (hikes, hiked, hik•ing) to take a long walk. *Let's hike up that hill.*

him that boy or man. *Mike looked hungry, so I gave him an apple.*

his belonging to a boy or a man. *Ted likes to play with his dog.*

hive a box or other place where bees live. *Can you see any honey in the hive?*

hog a full-grown pig. *The hog eats lots of corn.*

hog

hole an opening or empty space. *A nail makes a hole in the wall.*

home the place where a person lives. *My home is an apartment.*

hop (hops, hopped, hop•ping) to move by jumping lightly. *Rabbits hop quickly.*

hope (hopes, hoped, hop•ing) to wish or expect. *I hope you will visit us soon.*

hose a rubber or plastic tube that carries water. *Mom used the hose to water the garden.*

hot very warm; having a high temperature. *The stove is hot.*

hug (hugs, hugged, hug•ging) to put the arms around something. *I hug my brother.*

hum (hums, hummed, hum•ming) to sing with the lips closed. *All day she liked to hum the new song.*

hush (hush•es, hushed, hush•ing) to make still or quiet. *See if you can hush the baby.*

hut a little house or cabin that is plain and simple. *We camped in huts.*

I me; myself; the person talking. *I am learning to spell.*

if **a.** whether. *Do you know if Carmen is coming?* **b.** though. *Even if it rains, we'll still go.*

in **a.** inside. *We live in town.* **b.** during. *It rained in the morning.*

is a form of **be**. *Kevin is tall.*

it that thing. *It is my book.*

J

K

jet a kind of plane with a strong engine. *The big jet took off with a loud roar.*

job the work that one does. *Taking out the trash is my job.*

jog (jogs, jogged, jog•ging) to run at a slow, steady pace. *Mrs. Morgan likes to jog every day to keep fit.*

jot (jots, jot•ted, jot•ting) to write something quickly. *Jot down this name on your list.*

keep (keeps, kept, keep•ing) **a.** to hold on to; to save. *Kim wants to keep all her old schoolwork.* **b.** to let stay; to have. *Todd can keep his socks in the top drawer.*

kite a paper or cloth toy that can fly in the air on the end of a long string. *My kite is red.*

kite

227

L

lace fine threads woven together in an open pattern. *Her dress was trimmed with white lace.*

lake an inland body of water. *We saw a sailboat on the lake.*

lamp an object that gives light. *Turn on the lamp.*

lamp

lane a narrow path or road. *We walked down the lane.*

lap the top part of a person's legs when sitting down. *Dad held the baby on his lap.*

lead (leads, led, lead•ing) to show the way; to take. *Will you please lead the dog back home?*

led past tense of **lead**. *We led the horse to the barn.*

leg the part of the body used for standing and walking. *We put our pants on one leg at a time.*

let (lets, let, let•ting) to allow; to permit. *Please let me go to the park.*

lid a top or cover. *He put the lid back on the pan.*

life being alive. *We study the life of plants.*

like a. the same as; similar to. *Marie is like a sister to me.* **b.** (likes, liked, lik•ing) to enjoy. *I like the new family next door.*

line a. a long thin mark. *Draw a line on the paper.* **b.** a row of persons or things. *We stood in a line.*

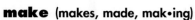

M

make (makes, made, mak•ing)
a. to put together; to build, form, or shape. *Dad can make a great pie.*
b. to cause. *Singing can make me feel happy.*

made past tense of **make**. *We made lunch on Monday.*

man (men *pl.*) an adult male person. *Mr. Green is a nice man.*

mane the long hair that grows on the back of the neck of a lion or horse. *A lion's mane makes him look important.*

mat a piece of fabric or woven straw; a small rug. *Wipe your feet on the mat near the door.*

me I; myself; the person talking. *Eric will go with Ann and me.*

meet (meets, met, meet•ing) to come face to face with; to come together. *I'll meet you down at the corner.*

men more than one man. *We watched the men working.*

men

mend (mends, mend•ed, mend•ing) to repair; to fix. *Can you mend the hole in the roof?*

mess a dirty or sloppy state of things. *My room was a mess before I cleaned it.*

met past tense of meet. *We met the new girl.*

mine belonging to me. *This box is mine.*

mix (mix•es, mixed, mix•ing) to put different things together. *I will mix nuts and raisins to make a snack.*

229

mole a small animal with smooth fur and small eyes that lives underground. *A mole has long claws.*

mom a short word for **mother**. *My mom has a good job.*

moon the body that shines in the night sky. *A full moon looks like a big circle.*

mop a. a long-handled tool used to clean floors. *This mop has a sponge on one end.* **b. (mops, mopped, mop•ping)** to wipe with a mop or cloth. *Please mop up the water.*

mowing form of **mow**. cutting the grass. *She is mowing the lawn this morning.*

must to have to. *You must come home at six.*

N

name a. a word or words to call a person, place, or thing. *His name is Ryan.* **b. (names, named, nam•ing)** to give a name to; to call. *They will name the boy after his grandfather.*

neck the part of the body that joins the head to the shoulders. *A giraffe has a very long neck.*

net a fabric with small holes. *He can catch a fish in his net.*

net

no a. the opposite of **yes**. *I voted "no" in a loud voice.* **b.** not any. *The dog had no food until we got home.*

nose the part of the face just above the mouth. *You smell with your nose.*

not a word that says **no**. *It is not a sunny day.*

note **a.** a very short message or letter. *Let's write Mom a note.* **b.** a sign in music. *That is a quarter note.*

nut a dry fruit or seed with a hard shell. *I ate one nut.*

nut

of **a.** belonging to. *The roof of the house is brown.* **b.** made from. *The birds live in a nest of twigs.*

on **a.** above and held up by. *The lamp is on the table.* **b.** about. *I have a book on kites.* **c.** in use; not off. *She turned the radio on.*

on•ly **a.** single; by itself. *This is my only shirt with stripes.* **b.** no more than; just. *We have only one hour to get ready.*

ox (ox•en *pl.*) a heavy bull used as a work animal. *The ox can pull a cart.*

pack **a.** (packs, packed, pack•ing) to put carefully in a box or trunk. *Help me pack my suitcase.* **b.** a soft bag carried on the back. *My pack is heavy.*

pan a container used for cooking. *Use a small pan to heat the soup.*

pants a piece of clothing that covers each leg separately. *I wear pants.*

path a narrow trail or track. *The path leads up the hill.*

peek (peeks, peeked, peek•ing) to take a quick look. *Close your eyes and don't peek.*

peel (peels, peeled, peel•ing) to take off the skin or outer layer. *We will peel the orange.*

231

pen **a.** a tool used for writing in ink. *My pen has blue ink.* **b.** a closed place to keep animals. *That pig lives in a pen.*

pen

pet an animal kept with people. *A cat may make a good pet.*

pick (picks, picked, pick•ing) **a.** to choose. *Which poem did you pick to read?* **b.** to pull off. *We can pick cherries from the tree.*

pig (pigs *pl.*) a short animal with a thick body and a flat nose. *Our pig likes to dig.*

pin **a.** a thin piece of metal with a sharp point. *A pin can hold things together.* **b.** a small piece of jewelry with a sharp point. *Grandmother wore a pretty pin on her dress.*

pine an evergreen tree with leaves like needles. *We found a lot of cones under the tall pine.*

plug **a.** one end part of an electrical cord. *The lamp will go off if you pull the plug.* **b.** (plugs, plugged, plug•ged) to connect to an electrical outlet. *Please plug in the iron.*

plum a small, soft, juicy fruit. *He picked a wild plum.*

pole a long thin piece of wood or metal. *We hung the flag from a pole.*

pop (pops, popped, pop•ping) to make a short, loud sound. *Did you hear the balloon pop?*

post a wooden or metal pole. *Ted will paint the post.*

pot a deep, round dish or pan. *A pot is used for cooking.*

pumps makes something flow from one place to another. *Mom pumps the gas into our car.*

232

T232

pup a young dog; a puppy. *The happy pup wagged his tail.*

pup

push (push•es, pushed, push•ing) **a.** to press on something to move it. *Push the gate shut.* **b.** to shove. *Try not to push the people in front of you.*

quack the sound made by a duck. *We heard the quack of the wild duck as it flew south.*

rake **a.** a garden tool with a long handle, used to gather leaves. *Put the rake in the shed.* **b.** (rakes, raked, rak•ing) to use this tool. *Will you help me rake the leaves?*

ran past tense of **run**. *We ran fast.*

rest **a.** the other part; what is left over. *I ate ten nuts and Mark ate the rest.* **b.** to stop working; to relax. *Rest a minute before you go on.*

rice a grain that people eat. *We ate chicken and rice.*

ride (rides, rode, rid•den, rid•ing) **a.** to sit on a moving animal or bicycle. *Can you ride a horse?* **b.** to go in a car, bus, or train. *How long does it take to ride to the city?*

rip (rips, ripped, rip•ping) to tear apart. *He may rip his pants on a nail.*

rod a long thin pole of wood, metal, or plastic. *Dad took his fishing rod to the pond.*

233

room **a.** a closed space inside a building. *Jan walked into the front room.* **b.** extra space. *Leave room on your paper for your name.*

rope a strong cord made by twisting smaller cords together. *We used a rope to hang the swing.*

rose a flower that grows on a bush with thorns. *A rose smells sweet.*

rose

rug a covering for a floor; a carpet. *He has a round rug in his room.*

run (runs, ran, run, run•ning) to move quickly; to go faster than walking. *Doug ran to first base.*

rust the coat of red-brown powder that forms on metals when they get damp. *My bike got a spot of rust when I left it outside.*

same just like another; identical. *Do it the same way I do.*

see (sees, saw, seen, see•ing) **a.** to look at; to use the eyes. *I can see a truck on the road.* **b.** to find out. *See if she needs any help.*

seed the part of a plant from which another plant grows. *An acorn is the seed of an oak tree.*

seed

set **a.** a group of things that belong together. *A carpenter needs a set of tools.* **b.** (sets, set, set•ting) to put in a certain place. *Set the dishes on the table.*

234

shake (shakes, shook, shak•en, shak•ing) to move quickly up and down or from side to side. *The label says "Shake well before using."*

she that girl or woman. *She likes to read.*

ship **a.** a large boat. *The ship sailed across the sea.* **b.** (ships, shipped, ship•ping) to send by boat, truck, or plane. *Our aunt will ship us a crate of apples.*

shop **a.** a small store. *We have a good hobby shop on our street.* **b.** (shops, shopped, shop•ping) to go to stores to buy things. *I'm going to shop for food.*

show (shows, showed, shown or showed, show•ing) **a.** to point out. *I will go first to show the way.* **b.** a movie, play, or TV program. *We saw a funny show.*

shut (shuts, shut, shut•ting) to close. *Will you shut the door, please?*

side **a.** a line that makes an edge. *Trace that side of the triangle.* **b.** the part between the top and the bottom or between the back and the front. *Use the door at the side of the house.*

sip (sips, sipped, sip•ping) to drink slowly, a little at a time. *I like to sip juice with a straw.*

sit (sits, sat, sit•ting) to rest on the lower part of the body. *I will sit in this big chair.*

skip (skips, skipped, skip•ping) to move quickly by hopping twice on each foot. *The children want to skip around the yard.*

slam (slams, slammed, slam•ming) to shut hard with a loud noise. *The wind made the door slam.*

slip (slips, slipped, slip•ping) to slide suddenly. *Don't slip on the wet sidewalk.*

snap (snaps, snapped, snap•ping) **a.** to make a quick bite. *Look at that fish snap at the bait!* **b.** to break or crack. *I can snap this twig in two.*

235

snug cozy; comfortable. *Coats keep us snug and warm.*

so **a.** very. *I love you so much.* **b.** in the same way; also. *He is a good helper, and so is his sister.*

sock a short stocking. *A long sock comes up to the knee.*

sock

soon before long. *Dinner will be ready soon.*

spin (spins, spun, spin•ning) to turn around fast. *Can you see the wheel spin?*

spoon a tool for eating or serving that has a small bowl at one end. *Bring a spoon for the soup, please.*

step (steps, stepped, step•ping) **a.** a movement of the foot. *Simon says, "Take a big step."* **b.** a small platform for the foot. *I can stand on the top step.* **c.** to lift the foot and put it down in a new place; to walk. *Step to the front of the line.*

stiff not able to bend easily; hard. *My new toothbrush is stiff.*

still **a.** quiet; silent. *The house is very still at night.* **b.** even; yet. *Do you still have that old ball?*

stir (stirs, stirred, stir•ring) to move around or mix. *Jessica can stir the oatmeal with a spoon.*

stool a seat with no back or arms. *Please push the stool under the table.*

stove something you cook on. *The stove is hot.*

sun the star that gives us light and heat. *The sun sets in the west.*

sun

sweep (sweeps, swept, sweep•ing) to clean by brushing away. *Sweep up this dirt with a broom.*

tag **a.** a small piece of paper, metal, or plastic that contains information. *Can you read the price tag?* **b.** a game of chase. *Let's play freeze tag.*

take (takes, took, tak•en, tak•ing) **a.** to grip; to hold. *Take my hand when we cross the street.* **b.** to carry. *Can you take this box to the office?*

tame not wild; gentle. *You can pet the tame animals in the children's zoo.*

that (those *pl.*) the thing or person over there. *Greg sits at that desk by the window.*

the that one or those. *Did you find the pen or the pencils I lost?*

then **a.** at that time. *They came at 2:00, but I was gone then.* **b.** soon after. *We went to the movies, and then we came home.*

thin (thin•ner, thin•nest) not thick or fat. *A sheet of paper is thin.*

this (these *pl.*) the thing or person nearby. *Is this lunch box yours?*

thud a dull sound made when something big falls. *The suitcase fell with a thud.*

thump a loud bumping noise. *Did you hear that thump in the attic?*

tide the regular rise and fall of the water in the sea. *Let's look for seashells at low tide.*

237

time what a clock shows; the hour and minute. *What time is it?*

time

tip **a.** the end or point. *Can you touch the tip of your nose?* **b. (tips, tipped, tip•ping)** to lean; to push over. *The milk will spill if you tip the glass.*

to as far as; until; toward. *I'll walk to the corner with you.*

top **a.** the highest part. *A bird sat on the top of the tree.* **b.** a cover or lid. *Put the top on the jar, please.*

trot **(trots, trot•ted, trot•ting)** to move at a pace between a walk and a run. *A horse can trot or gallop.*

tub a wide, open container for bathing or washing. *I took a hot bath in the tub.*

tuck **(tucks, tucked, tuck•ing)** to cover or wrap snugly. *I helped tuck the baby in the crib.*

tug **(tugs, tugged, tug•ging)** to pull hard. *My dog likes to tug on his leash.*

twins two persons born to the same mother at the same time. *The twins Don and Ron look alike.*

up in, at, or to a higher place. *The rocket went up into the sky.*

us we; ourselves; the persons talking. *Play with us!*

use **(us•es, used, us•ing)** to put into action; to work with. *Jim will use a hammer to hit the nail.*

238

V

vase a bottle or jar used to hold flowers. *Cindy put the roses in a pretty vase.*

vase

vest a short jacket with no sleeves. *My vest matches my pants.*

vine a plant with a long stem that can twist around things. *Grapes grow on a vine.*

W

wag (wags, wagged, wag•ging) to move from side to side. *My dog likes to wag her tail as she eats.*

wake (wakes, woke or waked, waked or wo•ken, wak•ing) to stop or cause to stop sleeping. *Please wake me at six o'clock.*

was past tense of **is**. *He was sick.*

we us; ourselves; the persons speaking. *We are friends.*

weed an unwanted plant that grows wild. *Weeds grow fast.*

wet not dry. *The paint is still wet.*

wide (wid•er, wid•est) big from side to side. *A street with four lanes is wide.*

239

wig a covering of false hair for the head. *I'm going to wear a wig.*

wig

wipe (wipes, wiped, wip•ing) to clean or dry by rubbing. *Wipe the dust off the table.*

wish a. (wish•es, wished, wish•ing) to want; to hope for. *I wish you could come over.* **b.** something you want or hope for. *Did your wish come true?*

with a. in the company of. *They went with Uncle Charles.* **b.** using. *I washed my hands with soap and water.*

woke past tense of **wake**. *The thunder woke us up.*

Y

yes the opposite of **no**. *Yes, you are right.*

yet a. up to now. *They haven't come yet.* **b.** still. *They may get here yet.*

you the person or persons spoken to. *You may go now.*

Z

zip (zips, zipped, zip•ping) to close with a zipper. *Zip your jacket before you go out.*

zoo a place where live animals are kept for people to see. *In the zoo we saw some polar bears.*

zoo

240

Annual Pretest/Posttest*

Form A

	Word	Dictation Sentences
1.	man	Did that **man** make the toys?
2.	and	Red **and** yellow make orange.
3.	net	Carlos has a fish in his **net**.
4.	leg	Can you hop on one **leg**?
5.	in	Would you like to come **in**?
6.	dig	I helped **dig** that hole.
7.	fox	I saw a **fox** at the zoo.
8.	job	I am done with my **job**.
9.	nut	A **nut** just fell from that tree.
10.	sun	The **sun** is going down.
11.	tub	The water in the **tub** is cold.
12.	of	One **of** those birds sings sweetly.
13.	skip	Can you **skip** down the street?
14.	fast	That train is going **fast**.
15.	gets	The bird **gets** worms for its babies.
16.	same	Your shoes are the **same** as mine.
17.	made	Jason **made** a present for you.
18.	we	May **we** play with you?
19.	feet	Your **feet** are muddy.
20.	time	Is there **time** to finish my picture?
21.	side	One **side** of the paper is blank.
22.	so	I am **so** excited!
23.	rode	Jessica **rode** in her uncle's boat.
24.	zoo	Did you see the bear at the **zoo**?
25.	duck	There is a **duck** on the pond.

*For more information on using these tests, please see page Z30.

Form B

	Word	Dictation Sentences
1.	dad	Your **dad** is tall.
2.	cat	Did your **cat** have kittens?
3.	men	The **men** are singing a song.
4.	met	I **met** a real clown!
5.	sit	May I **sit** by you?
6.	him	I gave **him** a ball.
7.	pot	The **pot** is too big.
8.	mop	Do you have to **mop** the floor?
9.	bus	I rode the **bus** to town.
10.	rug	Jane had a blue **rug**.
11.	fix	Will you **fix** my bike?
12.	are	Those colors **are** bright.
13.	slam	Please do not **slam** the door.
14.	still	Is it **still** raining?
15.	pigs	Did you know that **pigs** eat corn?
16.	gave	My father **gave** Mom a present.
17.	bake	Will you **bake** these potatoes?
18.	see	I **see** a rainbow.
19.	keep	May we **keep** the puppy?
20.	mine	The blue coat is **mine**.
21.	hike	We are going to **hike** through the woods.
22.	home	This dog followed me **home**.
23.	bone	Misty buried her **bone** in the yard.
24.	soon	Daddy will be home **soon**.
25.	neck	The giraffe has a long **neck**.

*For more information on using these tests, please see page Z30.

Scope and Sequence

	Grade 1	Grade 2	Grade 3
Phonics			
Auditory Discrimination	13–42, T47, T51, T52, T55, T63, T67, T71, T75, T83, T87, T91, T103, T107, T111, T115, T123, T127, T131, T135, T143, T147, T151, T155, T156, T163, T167, T171, T175	T123	
Phonemic Awareness	13–16, T44, T48, T52, 64, T68, T76, T84, T88, T92, T96, T104, T108, T112, T116, T124, T128, T132, T136, T144, T148, T152, T156, T164, T168, T172		
Letters and Sounds	17–42, 43–44, 47–48, 51–52, 55–56, 63–64, 67–68, 71–72, 75–76, 83–84, 87–88, 91–92, 95–96	14–19, 20–25, 26–31, 32–37, 38–43, 44, 45, 46, 47, 52–57, 58–63, 64, 65, 68, 70, 71–75, T76, 80–85, 90–95, 96–101, 102–107, 108–113, 114–119, 120–123, 128–133, 134–139, 140–145, 152–157, 158–161, 167, 170, 172–177, 179, 184–189, 190–195, 196–199, 204–209, 210–215, 216–221, 229, 232, 233, 234–237	14–19, 20–25, 26–31, 32–37, 38–43, 44, 45, 46, 47, 52–57, 58–63, 64–69, 70–75, 76–81, 82, 83, 84, 85, 90–95, 96–101, 102–107, 108–113, 115, 118, 120, 121, 122, 128–133, 134–139, 140–145, 146–151, 153, 156, 158, 159, 161, 166–171, 172–177, 178–179, 182, 185, 196, 197, 204, 205, 208, 210–215, 216, 217, 223, 226, 229, 234, 235
Rhyming Words	14, 52, T55, 61, 68, 99, 108, 119, 120, 124, 126, 130, 133, T133, 136, 142, 152, 164, 172, 175, 183, 188, 189, 190, 203, 210	15, 18–19, 24, 26–27, 32, 35, 37, 38, 42, 45, 53, 68, 77, 78, 80, 83, T84, 91, 100, 101, 107, 109, 115, 119, 121, 123, 132, 138, 142, 153, 156, 159, 160, 167, 173, 176, 184–185, 187, 191, 197, 198, 205, 208, 211, 214, 223, 235	15, 17, 21, 23, 24, 30, 33, 36, 39, 46, 47, 53, 59, 61, 71, 77, 80, 83, 84, 97, 122, 149, 153, 156, 157, 160, 173, 191, 197, 223, 229
Blending	44, 64, T44, T56, T64, 76, 108, 148, 176, T186	33, 39, 53, 77, 109, 115	15, T135, T141
Segmentation	T14, T15, 44, 48, 56, 64, 72, 76, 84, 92, 96, 100, 104, 108, 132, T183, T184, T186, T189, T190, T191, T193, T194, T195	T14, T27, T39, T53, 71, 91, 103, T128, 129, 135,	21, 27, 39, 135, 229
Word Building		36, 42, 56, 74, 84, 106, 112, 118, 141, 170, 176, 188, 194, T205, 208, 211, 217, 232	30, 56, 62, 106, 115, 118, 144, 170, 208

Scope and Sequence (continued)

	Grade 1	Grade 2	Grade 3
Phonics (cont.)			
Word Structure	96, 102, 112, 148	15, 18, 21, 24, 27, 33, 36, 37, 39, 42, 46, 47, 53, 56, 59, 62, 65, 68, 71, 74, 77, 80, 84, 91, 94, 97, 100, 103, 106, 109, 112, 115, 118, 121, 122, 129, 135, 140–151, 153, 158, 159, 160, 167, 170, 173, 176, 178–183, 185, 188, 191, 194, 196, 197, 198, 199, 205, 208, 211, 214, 217, 220, 222–227, 235	15, 21, 30, 33, 39, 42, 45, 47, 56, 62, 65, 68, 74, 77, 88, 89, 91, 100, 106, 115, 121, 122, 129, 135, 138, 141, 144, 148, 152–157, 158, 159, 160, 161, 179, 194, 204–209, 210–215, 217, 224, 234, 235
Short Vowels	43–46, 47–50, 51–54, 55–58, 59–62, 63–66, 67–70, 71–74, 75–78, 79–82, 83–86, 87–90, 91–94, 99–101, 176, 183, 184, 185, 186, 187, 188, 189, 190, 191, 192, 193	14–19, 20–25, 26–31, 32–37, 38–43, 44, 45, 46, 47, 70–75, 82, 84, 85, 123, 161, 167, 179, 198, 229, 233, 236	14–19, 20–25, 26–31, 44, 45, 46, 53, 56, 71, 74, 83, 115, 161, 166, 171, 172, 177, 229
Long Vowels	116, 123–126, 127–130, 131–134, 135–138, 139–142, 143–146, 147–150, 151–154, 155–158, 159–162, 163–166, 172, 197, 199, 200, 201, 202, 203, 204, 205, 206, 207	71, 76, 80, 81, 82, 90–95, 96–101, 102–107, 108–113, 115, 120, 121, 122, 132, 160, 161, 179, 191, 194, 198, 211, 217, 223, 226, 229, 232, 233, 236	52, 53, 56, 57, 58–63, 64–69, 70–75, 76–81, 82, 83, 84, 85, 122, 153, 161, 172, 178, 179, 182, 196
Vowel Digraphs and Diphthongs	116, 131–134, 135–138, 163–166, 179, 207	70, 90–95, 97, 98, 108–113, 120, 121, 122, 134–139, 152–157, 158, 159, 172–177, 191, 196, 197, 220, 223, 226, 229, 232	32–37, 38–43, 44, 46, 47, 109, 128–133, 158, 159
r-Controlled Vowels		184–189, 196, 198, 204–209, 234, 235, 236	134–139, 140–145, 146–151, 158, 159, 160
Complex Consonants, Blends, and Digraphs	103–106, 107–110, 119–122, 167–170, 171–174, 175–178, 180–182, 183, 184, 186, 189, 191, 195, 196, 197, 202, 206, 207, 208, 209, 210	21, 24, 25, 27, 30, 31, 36, 37, 52, 53, 58–69, 70, 71, 73, 75–85, 102–107, 114–121, 123, 128–133, 150, 158, 159, 167, 190–195, 196, 199, 210–221, 229, 234–237	15, 24, 27, 33, 36, 39, 42, 68, 90–95, 102–107, 115, 118, 120, 121, 122, 141, 147, 159, 166–171, 172–177, 185, 196, 197, 204, 205, 208, 223, 229
Stressed and Unstressed Syllables			T108, T109, T112, 159, T167, T200
Structural Pattern Skills			
Regular and Irregular Plurals	111–114, 121, 128, 164, 168, 197	140–145, 158	88, 89, 100, 204–209, 210–215, 234, 235
Inflectional Endings	111–114, 115–118, 121, 122, 128, 197, 198	62, 94, 100, 140–145, 146–151, 158, 160, 194	30, 83, 88, 94, 100, 138, 144, 178–183, 184–189, 196, 198, 204–209, 234, 235
Compounds		228–233, 234, 237	56, 94, 106, 118, 150, 228–233, 234, 237

	Grade 1	Grade 2	Grade 3
Structural Pattern Skills (cont.)			
Contractions		178–183, 196, 198	118, 190–195, 196, 199, 202
Prefixes, Roots, and Suffixes/Base Words		94, 100, 140	30, T74, 94, 100, 138, 144, 164, 176, 178–189, 196, 198, 204, 209, 210–227, 234–237
Vocabulary Skills			
High-Frequency Words	43–58, 63–78, 83–98, 102, 103–118, 123–138, 143–158, 163–178	14, 16, 20, 22, 26, 28, 32, 34, 38, 40, 52, 54, 58, 60, 64, 66, 70, 72, 76, 78, 90, 92, 96, 98, 102, 104, 108, 110, 114, 116, 128, 130, 134, 136, 140, 142, 146, 148, 152, 154, 166, 168, 172, 174, 178, 180, 184, 186, 190, 192, 204, 206, 210, 212, 216, 218, 222, 224, 228, 230, 245–248	14, 16, 20, 22, 26, 28, 32, 34, 38, 40, 52, 54, 58, 60, 64, 66, 70, 72, 76, 78, 90, 92, 96, 98, 102, 104, 108, 110, 114, 116, 128, 130, 134, 136, 140, 142, 146, 148, 152, 154, 166, 168, 172, 174, 178, 180, 184, 186, 190, 192, 204, 206, 210, 212, 216, 218, 222, 224, 228, 230, 246–248
Word Meaning	52, 55, 57, 61, 89, 122, 171, 175, 189, 190, 192, 193, 198, 200, 201, 206, 207, 208, 209	18, 22, 24, 28, 30, T36, T39, T42, T56, 60, T68, 72, T74, 78, 80, T94, 100, T112, 118, T132, 138, 144, 148, 150, 156, T176, 182, T194, T208, T214, 220, 226, T230, 232	18, 24, 30, 36, 42, 56, 60, 62, 66, 68, 74, 80, 94, 98, 100, T116, 118, 132, 138, 142, T144, 150, 156, 170, 176, 182, 188, 208, 214, 220, 224, 226
Word Analysis	43, 44, 47, 48, 51, 52, 55, 56, 59, 60, 61, 63, 64, 67, 68, 71, 72, 75, 76, 80, 81, 82, 83, 84, 87, 88, 91, 92, 95, 96, 99, 100, 101, 102, 103, 104, 107, 108, 111, 112, 115, 116, 119, 121, 122, 123, 124, 127, 128, 131, 132, 135, 136, 139, 140, 141, 142, 143, 144, 147, 148, 151, 152, 155, 156, 160, 161, 162, 163, 164, 167, 168, 171, 172, 175, 176, 179, 180, 181, 182	14, 15, 18, 20, 21, 24, 26, 27, 30, 32, 33, 36, 38, 39, 42, 52, 53, 56, 58, 59, 62, 64, 65, 68, 70, 71, 74, 76, 77, 80, 90, 91, 94, 96, 97, 100, 102, 103, 106, 108, 109, 112, 114, 115, 118, 128, 129, 132, 134, 135, 138, 140, 141, 144, 146, 147, 150, 152, 153, 156, 166, 167, 170, 172, 173, 176, 178, 179, 182, 184, 185, 188, 191, 194, 204, 205, 208, 210, 211, 214, 216, 217, 220, 222, 223, 226, 228, 229, 232	14, 15, 18, 20, 21, 24, 26, 27, 30, 32, 33, 36, 38, 39, 42, 52, 53, 56, 58, 59, 62, 64, 65, 68, 70, 71, 74, 76, 77, 80, 90, 91, 94, 96, 97, 100, 102, 103, 106, 108, 109, 112, 114, 115, 118, 128, 129, 132, 134, 135, 138, 140, 141, 144, 146, 147, 150, 152, 153, 156, 166, 167, 170, 172, 173, 176, 178, 179, 182, 184, 185, 188, 191, 194, 204, 205, 208, 210, 211, 214, 216, 217, 220, 222, 223, 226, 228, 229, 232
Antonyms	57, 73, 77, T85, 172	22, 28, 30, 42, 60, T72, T85, 92, 94, 110, 112, 132, 170, 188, 214, 232	T34, 66, 72, 130, 173, 197
Synonyms		22, 30, 40, 62, 66, 104, 174, 192, 205, T208, 211, T213, T219, 223, T225, T231	22, T34, 59, 60, 78, 116, 129, T154, 173, 174, 212, 217, 224
Homographs, Homophones, Multiple-Meaning Words		22, 28, T39, 60, 78, T126, T153, 167, 222–227, 234, T235, 236	T41, 42, 47, 56, 62, 68, 74, T136, 138, 144, 148, T150, 152–157, 158, 160, 161, T193, 194

Scope and Sequence (continued)

	Grade 1	Grade 2	Grade 3
Vocabulary Skills (cont.)			
Idioms			34, 72, 192
Latin and Greek Roots, Word History, Word Origins			T235
Reading Skills			
Classification/Categorization	57, 73, 77, 129, 145, 184, 202	28, 30, 34, 54, 56, 60, 68, 72, 83, 85, 136, 144, 156, 188, 206, 208, 212, 224, 230, 236	22, 66, 77, 136, 142, 148, 154, 168, 182, 186, 206, 212, 218, 232, 235, 236
Context Clues	45, 46, 49, 50, 53, 54, 58, 60, 65, 69, 70, 74, 79, 85, 86, 90, 93, 97, 105, 106, 109, 110, 113, 114, 117, 118, 121, 125, 129, 133, 137, 145, 149, 153, 157, 165, 169, 173, 177, 186, 187, 188, 189, 191, 192, 194, 195, 196, 197, 199, 201, 203, 204, 205, 206, 208	16, 34, 40, 54, 60, 66, 72, 78, 92, 98, 104, 110, 116, 130, 136, 142, 148, 154, 168, 174, 186, 192, 206, 212, 218, 224, 230	16, 28, 34, 40, 54, 72, 92, 104, 110, 116, 130, 136, 142, T148, T152, 154, 168, 174, 180, 186, T194, 206, 218, 230
Analogies		16, 40, 54, 98, 130, 154, 168, 174, 180, 186, 224	16, 22, 28, 34, 40, 54, 92, 104, 110, 130, 180, 230
Inferences			16, 28, 40, 54, 98
Writing Skills			
Descriptive Writing	94, 118, 130, 146, 150, 154	35, 41, 55, 127, 143, 165, 181, 187, 225	61, 93, 105, 127, 149, 175, 181, 193, 213
Expository Writing	86, 110, 118, 126, 130, 138, 158, 170	23, 61, 73, 105, 131, 193, 219, 241	35, 55, 67, 79, 111, 143, 155, 165, 225, 241
Narrative Writing	50, 94, 98, 134, 146, 174	17, 51, 79, 89, 111, 117, 155, 175, 213	23, 29, 41, 51, 61, 73, 89, 117, 137, 187, 231
Persuasive Writing		29, 67, 93, 99, 137, 149, 167, 169, 203, 207, 231	17, 99, 131, 169, 203, 207, 219
The Writing Process		17, 23, 29, 35, 41, 51, 61, 67, 73, 79, 89, 93, 99, 105, 111, 117, 127, 131, 137, 143, 149, 155, 165, 169, 175, 181, 187, 193, 203, 207, 213, 219, 225, 231, 241, 242–243	17, 23, 29, 35, 41, 51, 55, 61, 67, 73, 79, 89, 93, 99, 105, 111, 117, 127, 131, 137, 143, 149, 155, 165, 169, 175, 181, 187, 193, 203, 207, 213, 219, 225, 231, 241, 242–243
Graphic Organizers		T89, T127, T203	T41, T51, T165, T187, T241
Rubrics		T51, T89, T127, T165, T203, T241	T51, T89, T127, T165, T203, T241

	Grade 1	Grade 2	Grade 3
Writing Skills (cont.)			
Proofreading	98, 118, 138, 146, 150, 153, 154, 158, 166, 170, 174, 178	17, 23, 29, 35, 41, 50, 51, 55, 61, 67, 73, 79, 88, 89, 93, 99, 105, 111, 117, 126, 127, 131, 137, 143, 149, 155, 164, 165, 169, 175, 181, 187, 193, 202, 203, 207, 213, 219, 225, 231, 240, 241	17, 23, 29, 35, 41, 51, 55, 61, 67, 73, 79, 89, 93, 99, 105, 111, 117, 127, 131, 137, 143, 149, 155, 165, 169, 175, 181, 187, 193, 203, 207, 213, 219, 225, 231, 241
Grammar, Usage, and Mechanics			
Nouns		51, T83, 89, 127, 164, 165, 202, 203, 240, 241	51, 60, 88, 89, T98, T99, T104, T111, 127, T135, 165, T175, T197, 202, 203, T206, 210, T212, 213, 215, T235, T236, 241
Pronouns			240
Adjectives		T83, T197, 240	T104, T135, T168, T175, T197, 202, 203, T206, T224, T236
Verbs		T62, T72, T83, T100, T106, 146, 147, T148, 158, 202	T56, 60, T92, 94, 126, T135, T136, 164, T175, 179, T186, 188, T198, T224, T236
Adverbs			T135, T224, T226, T236
Conjunctions			T135
Prepositions and Prepositional Phrases			T85, T135
Dictionary and Thesaurus Skills			
How to Use a Dictionary and Dictionary Practice	212–240	15, 17–18, 21–23, 27, T28, 29, 33, 35, 39, 41, 51, 53, 59, 65, 71, 77, 89, 91, 97, 103, T104, T105, 109, T112, 115, T117, 127, 129, 135, 141, 147, 153, 165, 167, 173, 179, 182, 185, 191, T192, 203, 217, 220, T224, T226, 229, T240, 241, 249–288	15, T17, 18, 21, 27, 33, 39, T41, 51, 53, 65, T69, 77, T79, 80, 89, 91, 97, 103, 109, T114, 115, 127, 132, 135, 141, 147, T149, 153, 165, 167, 173, T174, T175, 179, 185, 188, 191, 203, 205, 208, 211, T212, 214, T219, 220, 223, 226, 229, T231, 241, 249–294
Technology (Spell-Check, Word Processor, Online Resources)		T61	89, T105, T117, 127, T137, 165, T181, T193, T207, 241
Alphabetical Order	48, 152, 212	15, 27, 33, 53, 59, 65, 71, 77, 91, 97, 103, 109, 115, 141, 179, 191, 217, 229	15, 33, 91, T93, T115, T225
Phonetic Spellings, Respellings		T129	T25, T31, 53, T69, 109, 111, T129, 141, 153, T159, 191, 205
Thesaurus/Synonyms		205, 211, T213, T214, T219, 223, T225, T231, 289–299	59, 129, 173, 174, 212, 217, 295–309

Scope and Sequence (continued)

	Grade 1	Grade 2	Grade 3
Content Words			
Art		37, 107, 145, 189, 227	37, 75, 113, 151, 189, 227
Math		31, 75, 119, 139, 183, 233	31, 69, 107, 145, 183, 221
Science		19, 37, 63, 101, 151, 177, 221	19, 57, 95, 133, 171, 209
Social Studies		25, 43, 69, 95, 133, 171, 215	25, 63, 101, 139, 177, 215
Technology		81, 113, 157, 195, 209	43, 81, 119, 157, 195, 233
Extend and Transfer			
	T183, T184, T185, T186, T187, T188, T189, T190, T191, T192, T193, T194, T195, T196, T197, T198, T199, T200, T201, T202, T203, T204, T205, T206, T207, T208, T209, T210	118–19, 24–25, 30–31, 36–37, 42–43, 56–57, 62–63, 68–69, 74–75, 80–81, 94–95, 100–101, 106–107, 112–113, 118–119, 132–133, 138–139, 144–145, 150–151, 156–157, 170–171, 176–177, 182–183, 188–189, 194–195, 208–209, 214–215, 220–221, 226–227, 232–233	18–19, 24–25, 30–31, 36–37, 42–43, 56–57, 62–63, 68–69, 74–75, 80–81, 94–95, 100–101, 106–107, 112–113, 118–119, 132–133, 138–139, 144–145, 150–151, 156–157, 170–171, 176–177, 182–183, 188–189, 194–195, 208–209, 214–215, 220–221, 226–227, 232–233
Standardized Test Practice			
	T46, T50, T54, T58, T62, T66, T70, T74, T78, T82, T86, T90, T94, T98, 102, T106, T110, T114, T118, T122, T126, T130, T134, T138, 142, T146, T150, T154, T158, T162, T166, T170, T174, T178, T182	48–49, 86–87, 124–125, 162–163, 200–201, 238–239	48–49, 86–87, 124–125, 162–163, 200–201, 238–239
Handwriting			
1-Minute Handwriting Hints	T46, T50, T54, T58, T66, T70, T74, T78, T86, T90, T94, T98, T106, T110, T114, T118, T126, T130, T134, T138, T146, T150, T154, T158, T166, T170, T174, T178	T16, T22, T28, T34, T40, T54, T60, T66, T72, T78, T92, T98, T104, T110, T116, T130, T136, T142, T148, T154, T168, T174, T180, T186, T192, T206, T212, T218, T224, T230	T16, T22, T28, T34, T40, T54, T60, T66, T72, T78, T92, T98, T104, T110, T116, T130, T136, T142, T148, T154, T168, T174, T180, T186, T192, T206, T212, T218, T224, T230

Note: Each word is identified by grade level, unit number, and list designation. Words may be featured more than once per grade or in more than one grade. Words in the targeted grade level are printed in blue.

A	Assessment
AL	Above Level
BL	Below Level
CH	Challenge
OL	On Level

A

a 1-14-OL
abbreviate 5-19-OL/AL
abbreviation 5-19-OL/AL
ability 5-29-OL/BL
able 4-3-OL/BL; 5-35-BL
abolish 4-31-OL/BL
about 2-26-AL; 3-16-OL/BL; 4-9-BL
above 3-16-OL/AL
absence 6-32-OL/AL
absent 6-10-OL/AL
abstract 6-33-AL
accent 6-1-OL/AL
accept 6-35-OL/BL
acceptable 5-35-OL/AL; 6-19-OL/BL
accident 6-17-OL/BL
accountant 6-36-A
accurate 6-25-OL/BL
accurately 6-11-AL
accuse 6-5-OL/AL
achieve 6-8-OL/AL
achieving 6-8-AL
acorn 2-31-AL
acquire 5-31-AL
acreage 6-21-AL
across 3-19-OL/BL
act 3-1-OL/BL
action 4-36-A; 6-29-OL/BL
active 5-5-OL/AL
actively 6-11-AL
activities 6-2-AL
activity 5-29-OL/BL
actor 5-25-OL/BL
actors' 4-32-AL
acute 6-5-OL/AL
adapt 6-35-OL/AL
addition 4-31-BL
additional 5-8-AL
additionally 6-11-OL/AL
address 5-31-OL/BL
adequate 6-1-AL

admirable 6-19-AL
admiration 5-7-AL
admire 5-7-AL; 6-3-AL
admit 6-1-OL/BL
admittance 6-32-AL
admitted 5-16-AL; 6-15-OL/AL
admitting 6-15-OL/BL
adopt 6-35-OL/AL
adorable 6-19-OL/AL
adore 6-9-OL/AL
advance 6-1-OL/AL
advancement 6-21-OL/AL
advantage 6-21-OL/AL
adventurer 4-30-A; 5-25-AL
adventuresome 6-22-AL
adventurous 5-32-OL/AL
advice 6-35-OL/BL
advise 6-35-OL/BL
affect 5-23-OL/BL
affectionate 6-30-A
affinity 6-13-AL
affirm 6-9-AL
afford 6-17-AL
afraid 3-16-OL/AL
Africa 4-35-OL/BL
after 3-17-OL/AL
afternoon 3-35-OL/BL
afterward 6-11-OL/BL
again 3-16-OL/BL
age 3-14-OL/BL; 4-17-BL
aged 6-33-OL/BL
agent 5-28-AL; 6-31-OL/AL
ago 1-14-CH; 2-16-BL
agree 3-16-AL; 4-4-OL/BL
agreement 4-33-OL/BL; 5-29-BL
ahead 4-14-OL/AL
ahoy 2-20-AL
aid 3-8-OL/AL
ailment 6-24-A
aim 4-3-OL/AL
air 3-22-BL
aircraft 5-12-A
airless 4-28-BL
air mail 4-34-OL/AL
airplane 3-35-OL/AL
aisle 4-24-A; 6-16-OL/BL
alarm 3-16-AL; 4-13-OL/AL
alarm clock 4-34-OL/AL
album 6-1-OL/AL
alert 5-10-OL/AL
alike 2-15-AL
alive 3-7-AL; 4-2-OL/AL; 5-31-BL
all 2-7-OL/BL
alley 5-24-A
alliance 6-3-AL
alligator 4-21-AL

allow 5-14-OL/BL
allowance . . 4-9-AL; 5-14-OL/BL; 6-32-BL
all right 5-31-AL; 6-23-OL/BL
ally 5-24-A
almond 6-16-OL/AL
almost 2-7-AL; 3-11-OL/BL
alone 4-2-OL/BL
aloud 3-4-AL
already 4-14-OL/BL
also 4-7-OL/BL
alternate 5-4-AL; 6-33-BL
although 5-31-OL/BL
altimeter 6-34-AL
always 2-13-AL; 3-8-OL/BL
am 1-2-OL
amateur 6-28-OL/AL
amaze 6-14-OL/BL
amazement 6-21-AL
ambitious 6-27-AL
ambulance 6-32-OL/AL
America 4-35-OL/BL
American 4-35-OL/BL
amiable 6-19-AL
amount 4-9-OL/BL; 5-14-BL
amphibian 6-31-BL
ample 5-12-A
amuse 4-8-AL; 5-3-OL/AL; 6-5-BL
amusement 5-29-OL/BL; 6-21-BL
amusing 6-14-AL
an 1-1-OL
anagram 6-1-AL
analogy 5-35-AL; 6-34-AL
ancestor 6-1-AL
anchor 4-21-AL
and 1-2-OL; 2-10-BL
angel 5-8-OL/AL; 6-10-BL
anger 4-24-A
angle 4-20-AL; 5-8-OL/BL
animal 3-16-OL/BL
animals 3-36-A
ankle 4-19-OL/AL
annex 6-33-AL
anniversary 6-25-AL
announce 6-17-OL/BL
annoy 5-14-OL/AL
annoyance 6-32-AL
annual 5-3-OL/AL
another 3-16-OL/BL
answer 4-15-OL/BL
ant 1-1-CH; 2-34-AL
Antarctica 4-35-OL/AL
antelope 4-2-AL
antibody 6-24-AL
antidote 6-20-AL
antifreeze 6-20-OL/BL
antislavery 6-20-OL/BL

antisocial 6-20-OL/AL
anxious. 6-27-AL
any 2-25-OL/AL; 3-17-BL
anybody 3-35-OL/AL; 4-34-BL
anyone 3-35-AL
anything. 3-35-OL/BL; 4-34-BL
anyway 4-3-OL/AL
anywhere 4-34-OL/BL
apart 4-13-OL/BL
apartment. 4-33-OL/BL
ape 1-21-CH; 2-13-BL
apology 4-17-AL; 5-28-OL/BL
apparent 6-10-AL
appeal. 6-2-AL
appear. 4-11-AL; 5-13-OL/BL
appearance 6-32-OL/BL
applause 6-14-AL
apple. .3-25-BL
apples 2-21-AL; 3-31-OL/AL
applesauce 4-36-A
applicant 6-31-OL/BL
apply. 6-3-OL/AL
appoint 5-14-OL/BL
appointment. 6-21-OL/AL
appreciate 6-28-OL/AL
appreciation 6-30-A
approach. 6-4-OL/BL
approachable 6-19-OL/AL
approve. 5-3-AL; 6-7-OL/AL
approximate 6-25-OL/AL
April. 4-29-OL/BL
aptitude 6-7-OL/AL
aquarium 4-16-AL; 5-11-AL
arch 4-13-AL
archery 6-12-A
arctic 5-32-BL
are. 1-14-OL; 2-28-BL
area. 5-11-OL/BL
aren't 2-27-AL
argue. 4-13-AL; 5-11-OL/AL
argument 4-33-AL; 5-29-OL/BL
arise 6-14-OL/AL
arm. 2-28-OL/AL
armchair. 3-22-AL
armor 5-12-A
army 4-13-OL/BL
around 3-16-OL/BL
arrange 5-28-OL/BL
arrangement. 5-29-OL/BL
arrival. 5-8-AL; 6-17-BL
arrive 4-5-AL; 5-2-OL/BL; 6-3-BL
art. 2-28-OL/AL
article 5-11-OL/BL
artist 5-25-OL/BL
artist's 4-32-AL
as 2-1-OL/BL

Asia 4-35-OL/BL
aside 3-18-A
ask 2-1-OL/BL
asked. 2-22-OL/BL
asleep 3-16-OL/AL
assign 5-2-AL; 6-3-OL/BL
assignment 5-29-AL; 6-21-OL/AL
assist 6-17-OL/AL
assistance 5-35-AL
assistant 6-31-OL/BL
associate 6-4-OL/AL
assume 6-7-OL/AL
assumption 6-17-AL
asteroid. 5-14-AL
astronaut 5-4-OL/AL
at 1-2-OL
ate. 2-13-OL/AL
athlete 5-7-AL; 6-28-OL/BL
athletic 5-7-AL
attachment. 6-24-A
attend. 6-2-OL/BL
attendance 5-35-OL/AL; 6-32-OL/BL
attendant 6-31-OL/AL
attention 4-31-AL; 6-29-OL/BL
attic 6-3-OL/BL
auburn 5-4-AL
auction 4-31-BL
auctioneer 6-31-AL
audible 6-24-A
audience . . .4-10-AL; 5-4-OL/BL; 6-32-BL
audio. 4-10-AL
August 4-29-OL/AL
aunt 2-34-AL
aunt's 4-36-A
Australia. 4-35-OL/AL
Australian 4-35-AL
author. 4-10-AL; 5-4-OL/BL
authority. 5-29-AL; 6-9-OL/AL
autobiographer. . . . 5-25-AL; 6-34-OL/AL
autobiographical 6-34-AL
autobiography 5-34-OL/BL
autograph 5-4-AL; 6-34-OL/AL
automobile 5-4-OL/AL
autopilot. 6-36-A
autumn. 5-4-AL; 6-16-OL/BL
available. 6-19-OL/BL
avenue 5-3-OL/AL
average 4-17-AL; 5-28-OL/BL
aviator 5-25-AL
avoid. 4-9-AL; 5-14-OL/BL
await. 3-18-A
awake 3-16-OL/AL
awaken 5-21-OL/BL
award 3-16-AL
aware 3-24-A; 4-13-AL; 5-11-OL/AL
awareness 6-9-AL

away 2-25-AL; 3-8-OL/BL; 4-3-BL
awful. 4-28-AL; 5-4-OL/BL; 6-22-BL
awhile. 4-2-OL/BL
awkward 5-4-AL

B
babies 3-32-OL/BL; 5-26-BL
baby 3-32-OL/BL
babysitter 4-34-OL/AL
back 1-32-OL; 2-17-BL
background. 5-22-AL; 6-23-OL/BL
backward 5-33-OL/BL; 6-11-BL
bad 1-13-OL
badge 4-17-OL/AL
badges. 5-26-OL/AL
badly. 3-34-OL/AL
baffle. 6-13-OL/AL
bag 1-2-CH
baggage. 4-17-OL/BL
bail 3-12-A
bait 3-12-A
bake 1-22-OL; 2-13-BL
baker. 4-27-OL/AL
baking. 3-27-OL/BL
balance 6-32-OL/BL
ball 2-7-OL/AL
balloon 3-5-OL/BL; 4-8-BL
bamboo. 6-7-AL
banana 3-16-AL
band 3-1-OL/AL
bandage 6-21-OL/AL
banjo 4-7-AL
bank 2-9-OL/BL
banker 4-27-OL/AL
banner 6-17-OL/AL
banquet 6-28-AL
barbecue. 6-5-OL/BL
barber 4-21-AL
bare. 3-22-OL/AL; 4-13-BL
barefoot 2-23-AL; 3-22-OL/AL
barely 6-11-OL/BL
bargain 6-28-OL/AL
bark 2-30-A
barometer. 6-34-OL/AL
barrel 3-25-AL
base. 2-11-OL/BL
baseball. 2-35-OL/AL; 3-35-BL
basic 5-32-OL/AL
basin. 4-6-A
basket 2-1-AL
basketball 3-35-AL; 4-34-OL/BL;
   5-22-BL
bat 2-1-OL/AL; 3-1-BL
bath 1-34-OL
bathroom 3-35-AL
batteries 5-30-A

breeze 4-4-OL/AL
brick 3-1-AL; 4-1-OL/AL; 5-5-BL
bridal 5-23-AL
bridge 3-14-AL; 4-17-OL/BL
bridle 5-23-AL
brief 4-4-OL/AL
briefcase 6-23-AL
briefly 6-8-AL
bright 3-10-OL/BL
brighten 4-20-OL/BL
brightly 3-34-AL
brightness 4-33-OL/AL
bring 2-8-OL/AL; 3-15-BL
British 4-35-OL/AL; 5-32-BL
brittle 4-19-AL
broad 5-4-OL/AL
broaden 5-21-AL
broccoli 5-17-AL
broil 3-4-AL
broke 2-11-AL; 3-7-OL/BL
broken 5-21-OL/BL
bronze 6-4-OL/AL
brook 3-15-OL/AL
broom 1-31-CH; 2-8-BL
broth 5-4-OL/AL
brother's 4-32-OL/BL
brought 4-10-OL/BL
browse 6-14-OL/AL
brush 2-32-AL
brushes 3-31-OL/AL
bubble 3-25-AL; 4-19-OL/AL
bucket 2-17-AL; 3-3-AL
bud 1-12-CH
buddies 3-32-AL
buddy 3-32-AL
budge 6-5-OL/AL
buffalo 6-13-BL
buffet 6-33-OL/AL
bug 1-12-OL
bugle 6-5-OL/AL
bugs 1-18-OL; 2-21-BL
build 4-14-OL/BL
builder 4-27-OL/BL
building 5-5-OL/BL
built 4-14-OL/BL
bulldozer 6-7-AL
bulletin 6-7-OL/BL
bump 1-11-CH; 2-5-BL
bunch 3-3-AL
bundle 6-6-A
bunny 3-26-OL/AL
buoyant 4-9-AL
burden 4-11-AL
bureau 6-28-OL/AL
burglar 5-12-A
burnt 4-11-AL; 5-10-OL/AL

burst 4-11-OL/AL; 5-10-BL
bus 1-11-OL
buses 3-31-OL/BL
bush 2-32-OL/BL
bushel 2-32-AL
bushes 3-31-OL/AL
business 5-5-OL/BL; 6-28-BL
busy 2-25-AL; 3-17-OL/AL
but 1-11-OL
butte 5-3-AL
butter 3-30-A
butterflies 3-32-BL
butterfly 3-32-BL
button 3-3-AL; 4-1-OL/BL
buy 4-5-OL/BL
buzz 3-3-OL/BL
by 2-15-OL/BL
byline 6-3-AL

C

cabbage 4-17-OL/AL
cabin 2-1-AL
cactus 6-6-A
cafeteria 6-28-AL
cage 3-18-A
cake 2-17-OL/BL; 3-7-BL
calendar 4-29-OL/AL
calf 4-25-OL/AL
calf's 4-32-OL/AL
California (CA) 4-35-AL
call 2-7-OL/BL
calm 4-15-OL/BL
calmer 5-16-OL/AL; 6-16-BL
calmest 4-22-AL; 5-16-OL/BL
calves 4-25-OL/AL
calves' 4-32-OL/AL
came 1-21-OL
camera 4-1-AL; 5-31-OL/AL
camper 4-27-OL/AL; 5-25-BL
campfire 5-22-AL; 6-23-OL/BL
campsite 6-23-OL/AL
can 1-1-OL; 2-1-BL
Canadian 4-35-OL/AL
cancel 5-8-AL; 6-1-OL/AL
candle 4-24-A
cannot 2-35-OL/BL; 3-25-BL
can't 2-27-BL
cap 2-1-OL/AL
capable 6-19-OL/AL
capital 4-23-AL; 5-23-OL/AL
capitalism 5-35-OL/BL
capitalization 4-31-OL/AL; 5-21-AL
capitol 4-23-AL; 5-23-OL/AL
captain 6-28-OL/BL
caption 6-1-AL
captive 5-30-A

car 2-28-OL/BL
carat 6-35-AL
carbon 5-9-AL; 6-9-OL/AL
card 2-28-BL; 2-30-A
cards 1-18-CH; 2-28-BL
care 3-22-BL
career 4-11-AL; 5-13-OL/AL; 6-28-BL
careful 4-28-OL/BL
carefully 3-34-AL; 6-11-OL/BL
careless 4-28-OL/BL
carelessly 3-34-AL
caret 6-35-AL
carnival 5-11-AL
carpenter 6-9-OL/BL
carpet 4-13-AL; 5-11-OL/AL; 6-9-BL
carriage 6-21-OL/AL
carrot 3-25-AL
carry 2-17-AL; 3-26-OL/BL
cart 4-13-OL/AL; 5-11-BL
carton 5-11-AL; 6-9-OL/AL
cartoonist 5-25-AL
carve 4-18-A
case 4-2-OL/BL
cash 2-32-OL/AL
cashier 5-5-AL
cast 2-17-AL
castanets 5-26-AL
casual 6-14-OL/AL
cat 1-2-OL; 2-17-BL
catch 3-13-OL/AL
catcher 4-27-OL/AL
categorize 5-21-AL; 6-3-AL
catfish 4-1-AL
cats 1-18-OL; 2-21-BL
cattle 4-19-OL/BL; 5-17-BL
caught 3-19-AL; 4-10-OL/BL
caution 4-31-AL; 5-4-OL/BL
cautious 6-27-OL/BL
cave 2-17-OL/AL
cavities 3-32-AL
cavity 3-32-AL
cease 5-6-A
cedar 3-14-AL
ceiling 5-17-AL; 6-8-OL/BL
celebrate 5-17-OL/BL
celery 2-2-AL
cell 3-23-OL/AL
cellar 3-14-AL; 4-23-OL/AL
censor 6-35-AL
cent 3-23-OL/AL
center 3-14-OL/AL
centimeter 5-34-OL/AL
central 5-17-AL; 6-10-OL/BL
ceramics 5-26-AL
cereal 5-17-OL/AL
certain 4-11-OL/BL; 5-17-BL

complaint 6-1-AL
complement 6-35-OL/AL
complete 4-2-AL; 5-1-OL/BL
completely 6-11-OL/BL
completion 6-29-OL/BL
complex 6-33-AL
compliment 6-35-OL/AL
compose 5-7-AL
composition 5-7-AL; 6-29-BL
compound 6-33-OL/BL
computer 6-5-OL/BL
conceal 5-18-A
conceit 6-8-OL/AL
concern 6-9-OL/BL
concert 6-33-AL
conclude 6-7-OL/AL
conclusion 4-31-AL; 6-14-OL/BL
condemn 6-16-AL
condensation 6-29-AL
condition 6-29-OL/AL
conduct 6-33-OL/BL
cone 1-28-CH
conference 6-36-A
confide 6-3-OL/AL
confidential 6-10-AL
confirm 6-9-OL/AL
confuse 6-5-OL/BL
confusion 4-31-OL/AL; 6-5-AL
Congress 6-4-AL
connect 5-19-AL; 6-17-OL/BL
connection 5-19-AL; 6-29-AL
conscience 6-32-AL
conserve 4-12-A; 5-10-OL/AL
consider 5-5-AL; 6-3-OL/BL
considerable 6-24-A
considerate 6-25-AL
consideration 6-29-OL/AL
console 6-33-OL/AL
constant 6-4-OL/BL
constellation 4-31-OL/AL
constituent 6-31-AL
constitution 4-31-OL/AL
contact 6-4-OL/AL
contact lens 6-24-A
contagious 6-27-AL
contain 4-3-AL; 5-1-OL/BL
container 6-1-AL
contemplate 6-25-AL
content 6-33-OL/BL
contest 4-1-AL; 5-5-OL/AL; 6-33-BL
contestant 6-31-AL
continual 6-5-AL
continue 4-8-AL; 5-3-OL/BL
continued 5-18-A
continuous 6-27-OL/BL
contract 6-33-OL/AL

contribute 5-17-AL; 6-5-OL/BL
contribution 6-29-AL
convert 6-33-OL/AL
convertible 5-35-AL
convict 6-33-OL/AL
convoy 5-18-A
cook 2-17-OL/BL
coop 3-6-A
cooperate 5-15-OL/BL; 6-25-BL
co-owner 5-18-A
copious 6-27-AL
copper 5-9-OL/AL
cordial 6-10-AL
cordless 4-28-AL
corduroy 5-14-AL
corn 2-31-OL/AL; 3-20-BL
corner 3-20-OL/AL
corporal 5-13-AL
correct 5-17-OL/BL
correspondent 6-31-AL
corrode 6-17-AL
corsage 6-14-AL
cosmetician 5-24-A
cosmetics 5-24-A
cost 3-19-OL/AL
costume 5-3-OL/AL
cot 2-4-OL/AL; 3-2-BL
cottage 4-17-OL/AL
cotton 3-25-OL/BL
couch 4-9-AL; 5-14-OL/AL
could 3-17-OL/BL; 6-7-BL
couldn't 2-27-AL
could've 3-29-AL; 6-7-OL/AL
council 5-8-OL/BL
counsel 5-8-OL/AL
counselor 5-30-A
count 2-26-OL/BL; 3-4-BL
counties 3-36-A
countless 6-22-AL
countries 5-26-OL/BL
country 5-23-OL/BL
county 5-23-OL/BL
couple 3-16-OL/AL; 4-19-BL
couples' 4-32-OL/AL
courage 6-21-OL/BL
courageous 6-27-OL/BL
course 5-23-OL/AL
cousin 5-31-OL/BL
cove 2-12-A
cover 3-3-OL/AL
coverage 6-21-AL
cow 2-26-OL/AL
coward 5-14-OL/AL
coworker 5-15-OL/BL
crack 1-32-CH
crackers 5-17-AL; 6-14-BL

cracking 2-22-AL
cranky 2-9-AL
crash 1-33-CH; 2-19-BL
crate 2-11-AL
crawl 2-7-AL; 3-19-OL/AL
crayon 4-3-OL/AL
cream 3-12-A
crease 6-2-OL/AL
create 5-17-OL/BL
creativity 5-29-OL/AL
credit 5-5-OL/AL
creditor 5-25-OL/BL
creek 1-24-CH
creep 3-12-A
crew 3-5-OL/AL
crime 4-6-A; 5-7-OL/AL
criminals 5-7-OL/AL
crisp 2-3-AL
critic 6-6-A
criticism 5-35-AL
criticize 5-21-OL/BL
crooked 6-12-A
crop 3-2-OL/AL; 4-1-BL
croquet 5-31-AL
cross 3-19-OL/AL
cross-country 5-22-AL; 6-23-OL/AL
crossroads 4-30-A
crosswalk 2-7-AL
crouch 3-15-AL
crowd 4-9-OL/BL
crowd's 4-32-AL
cruel 6-10-OL/AL
cruise 5-3-AL; 6-14-OL/AL
crumb 6-16-OL/AL
crush 2-36-A
crust 4-1-OL/AL
cry 2-15-OL/AL
cub 1-12-CH
Cuban 4-36-A
cube 4-2-OL/AL; 5-3-BL
cubic 5-32-OL/AL
cucumber 5-18-A
cue 6-6-A
cuff 3-3-OL/AL
culinary 6-25-AL
culprit 6-5-AL
cup 2-5-OL/BL; 3-3-BL
cupboard 6-16-OL/AL
curfew 6-9-OL/AL
curious 5-32-AL; 6-27-OL/BL
curl 3-21-OL/AL; 4-11-BL
current 5-10-OL/BL
curtain 6-9-OL/BL
curve 3-21-AL
curving 3-27-AL
cushion 6-7-OL/BL

distasteful 6-22-AL
distressed 5-33-AL
distribute 6-7-AL
district 6-3-OL/AL
disturb 5-10-OL/BL
dive 1-27-CH
divide 5-7-BL
divisible 5-35-OL/BL; 6-19-BL
division 4-31-OL/BL; 5-7-BL
dizzy 3-30-A
do 1-31-OL
dock 2-17-AL
document 5-29-AL; 6-21-OL/BL
dodge 4-17-OL/BL
does 2-10-OL/BL; 3-17-BL
doesn't 2-27-OL/AL
dog 2-4-OL/BL; 3-19-BL
doing 1-19-OL; 2-9-BL
doll 2-4-OL/AL
dollar 4-35-AL
dome 1-28-CH
domestic 5-36-A
donate 5-2-AL; 6-4-OL/AL
donation 6-29-AL
done 2-10-OL/AL
don't 2-27-OL/BL
door 2-31-OL/BL
doorstep 2-36-A
dormitory 6-9-AL
dot 1-13-OL
double 4-20-OL/BL
double-header 5-22-OL/AL
doubt 4-15-OL/AL; 5-14-BL
doubtful 6-22-OL/BL
down 2-26-OL/BL
downstairs 4-34-AL; 5-22-OL/BL
downtown 2-35-OL/AL; 3-35-BL
downward 6-11-OL/BL
dozen 5-9-OL/BL
drag 4-1-OL/AL
dragonfly 2-35-AL
drain 3-8-AL
dramatic 5-32-OL/AL
dramatize 5-21-AL; 6-14-BL
draw 3-19-OL/BL
drawer 3-19-AL
drawing 5-4-OL/BL
drawn 5-4-OL/BL
dread 4-18-A
dreadful 5-36-A
dream 3-9-OL/AL
dreamer 4-27-OL/AL
dress 2-8-OL/AL
dresses 3-31-OL/BL
drew 3-5-OL/AL; 4-8-BL
driest 4-24-A

drifted 2-22-AL
drink 2-9-OL/BL
drive 2-19-OL/BL
driven 4-24-A
driver 4-27-BL
driveway 4-34-OL/AL
driving 3-27-BL
drizzle 6-14-AL
drop 3-2-OL/BL
dropped 3-28-OL/BL
drought 5-14-AL
drove 4-2-OL/BL
drown 5-18-A
drugstore 2-19-AL
drum 2-5-OL/AL
drummer 5-30-A
drums 3-31-OL/AL
dry 2-15-OL/AL
duck 1-32-OL
due 4-8-OL/AL
dug 1-11-CH
dull 3-3-OL/AL
dumb 6-18-A
dust 2-5-OL/BL; 3-3-BL
Dutch 4-36-A
duties 4-8-AL
dutiful 6-22-OL/AL
dyed 4-23-OL/AL
dynamite 5-2-AL

E

each 2-29-OL/BL
eager 4-21-OL/AL
eagle 4-20-OL/AL; 5-8-BL
ear 4-11-OL/AL
earlier 5-18-A
early 3-21-OL/BL
earn 3-21-OL/AL
earnest 5-12-A
earrings 4-11-AL
earth 3-21-OL/AL; 4-35-BL
easel 2-14-AL
easier 4-22-OL/BL
easiest 4-22-OL/AL
easily 3-34-AL
east 3-9-OL/BL; 4-35-BL
eastern 5-33-OL/AL
eastward 6-11-OL/AL
easy 1-14-CH; 2-14-BL
eat 2-14-OL/BL
echo 4-15-OL/AL
ecology 5-35-OL/BL
economically 6-11-AL
edge 4-17-OL/BL; 5-5-BL
edible 5-35-AL; 6-19-OL/AL
editor 5-25-OL/BL

eerie 5-13-AL
effect 5-23-OL/BL
effort 5-10-AL; 6-13-OL/BL
eggs 2-21-OL/AL
eighty 5-1-OL/AL
either 3-17-AL; 4-21-OL/BL
eject 5-34-OL/BL
elastic 6-1-AL
elect 5-19-BL
election 4-31-OL/BL; 5-19-BL
electrician 4-31-AL; 6-31-OL/AL
elegance 5-35-OL/BL
elephant 2-2-AL
elevator 5-9-AL
elf 4-25-OL/AL
eligible 6-19-AL
elk 4-25-AL
else 4-1-OL/AL
elves 4-25-OL/AL
embarrass 6-17-AL
emigrate 6-35-OL/AL
eminent 6-35-OL/AL
emotion . . . 4-31-AL; 5-9-AL; 6-4-OL/AL
empire 6-3-OL/AL
employ 4-9-AL; 5-14-OL/AL
employee 6-2-OL/AL
employment 4-33-AL; 5-29-OL/AL;
  6-21-BL
emptiness 4-33-AL
empty 3-2-AL
encouragement 6-21-AL
end 2-2-OL/AL
endless 4-30-A
endorse 6-9-AL
endurance 6-32-AL
energetic 5-32-OL/BL
energy 5-28-OL/BL
enforce 6-13-AL
engage 4-17-AL
engine . . . 3-14-AL; 4-17-OL/BL; 5-28-BL
engineer 6-31-OL/BL
enjoy 4-9-OL/AL; 5-14-BL
enjoyable 5-35-OL/BL
enjoyment 4-33-OL/BL
enormous 4-10-AL; 5-13-OL/BL
enough 4-14-OL/BL; 5-31-BL
enrichment 6-21-AL
enter 4-21-OL/AL
entertain 6-1-AL
entire 5-33-OL/BL
entrance 5-33-OL/BL; 6-32-BL
envelop 6-36-A
envelope 6-36-A
envelopes 5-26-OL/BL
envious 5-36-A
equal 4-16-BL

flash 3-15-OL/AL
flashlight 4-34-OL/AL; 5-22-BL
flat 2-8-OL/AL
flatten. 5-21-OL/AL
flatter 3-33-AL
flattest 3-33-AL
flavor 4-3-OL/AL
flaw. 5-4-OL/AL
flexible 5-36-A; 6-19-OL/BL
flight. 3-15-AL; 4-5-OL/BL
float 3-11-OL/BL
flock 3-2-OL/AL
flood 3-18-A; 4-14-OL/AL
floodlight 4-34-AL
florist 5-13-AL
flounder 4-25-AL
flour 4-9-OL/AL
flow. 3-11-OL/AL
flower 4-9-OL/BL
fluffier 5-16-AL
fluffiest 5-16-AL
fluffy 2-8-AL; 3-26-BL
fluid 6-7-OL/AL
flute 4-8-OL/AL
fly 2-19-OL/AL
foam 2-16-AL; 3-11-OL/AL
focus 6-4-AL
fog. 2-4-OL/BL
foggy 5-1-OL/AL
foghorn 2-35-AL
foil 2-20-AL; 4-9-OL/AL
fold 3-11-AL; 4-7-OL/AL
folio 6-13-AL
follow 2-16-AL; 3-11-BL
followed 2-22-AL
following 4-7-AL
fond 2-6-A
food 2-23-OL/BL
fool 3-5-OL/AL
foolish. 5-32-OL/BL; 6-7-BL
foot 4-25-BL
footage 6-7-AL
football 2-35-OL/AL
for 2-31-OL/BL; 3-23-BL
force 5-13-OL/BL
forceful 6-22-AL
forcible 6-19-OL/AL
foreman 6-9-OL/AL
forest. 3-20-AL; 4-10-OL/BL; 5-13-BL
forester 4-27-AL
forever 4-24-A; 5-13-OL/BL
forget 3-20-OL/BL
forgetful 6-22-OL/AL
forgot 4-10-OL/AL
forgotten. 4-20-AL; 5-21-OL/BL
fork. 2-31-OL/AL

form 3-20-OL/BL; 4-10-BL
formal. 5-13-OL/AL
formally 6-35-OL/AL
formation 6-9-AL
former. 6-13-OL/AL
formerly 6-35-OL/AL
forth 4-10-OL/AL
fortunate. 6-25-OL/BL
fortune 5-13-OL/AL; 6-9-BL
forty 3-20-AL; 4-10-OL/AL
forty-four 5-22-OL/BL
forward 5-33-OL/BL; 6-11-BL
fossil 5-8-OL/BL
fought 4-10-OL/AL
foul 3-23-AL
found 2-26-AL; 3-4-OL/AL; 4-9-BL
foundation 5-14-AL
fountain 5-18-A
four 3-23-BL
Fourth of July 4-29-AL
fowl. 3-23-AL
fox 1-8-OL
foxes 2-21-OL/AL; 3-31-BL
fragrant. 5-32-AL
frame 2-24-A
frantic. 5-17-OL/AL
freckle. 5-8-AL
free 2-19-OL/AL
freedom 4-4-AL; 5-33-OL/BL
freeze 5-1-AL; 6-14-OL/AL
freight. 5-1-OL/AL
French 4-35-OL/BL
frequent 6-10-AL
fresh 2-32-AL; 3-15-OL/BL
freshen 4-20-BL
Friday 4-29-OL/BL
friend 3-17-OL/BL; 4-14-BL
friendliest 5-18-A
friendly 3-36-A
friends. 3-31-AL
friend's 4-36-A
fright. 4-5-OL/AL
frighten. 4-15-AL; 5-21-OL/BL
frightened. 6-18-A
frightening 6-18-A
frisky. 2-8-AL
frog 1-16-OL; 2-8-BL
from 2-25-OL/AL
front 2-8-OL/BL
frontward 6-11-AL
frown 2-26-AL
froze 4-2-AL; 5-2-OL/AL
frozen 5-21-OL/BL
fruit. 4-8-OL/BL; 5-3-BL
fruitless. 6-22-OL/AL
frustrate 6-25-AL

fry 2-15-OL/AL
fudge. 4-18-A
fuel 4-8-AL
fulfill. 6-13-OL/BL
full 2-25-AL
full-time 5-22-OL/AL
fun 1-12-OL
fund 3-6-A
funeral 5-6-A
funnier 4-22-OL/AL
funniest 4-22-OL/BL
funny 3-26-OL/BL
fur 3-21-OL/AL; 4-11-BL
furious. 6-27-OL/AL
furnace 6-9-OL/AL
furnish 5-10-AL
furry 3-26-OL/AL
further 5-10-OL/BL
furthermore 6-9-AL
fuse 4-2-AL
future 5-3-OL/BL
fuzzy 3-26-AL

G

gadget. 3-1-AL; 4-17-AL
galleries 5-26-AL
gallop 3-30-A
game. 1-21-OL; 2-13-BL
garage 6-21-OL/BL
garbage. 5-11-AL; 6-21-OL/BL
gardener 4-27-AL; 5-25-OL/AL
garment 6-9-AL
gasoline 5-1-OL/AL
gate. 1-21-OL
gather. 4-21-OL/AL
gave 1-21-OL
gear. 4-12-A
geese. 4-25-OL/AL
geese's. 4-32-BL
gelatin 4-17-AL
gem 3-18-A; 4-17-OL/BL; 5-28-BL
gender. 5-28-AL
gene 5-7-OL/BL
general 4-17-AL; 5-8-OL/BL
generalize 5-21-OL/AL
generous 5-28-OL/AL; 6-27-BL
genetics 5-7-OL/BL
genius. 5-28-OL/AL
gentle 4-17-OL/AL; 5-28-BL
gentleman 4-30-A; 5-28-OL/AL
gentlemen 4-30-A; 5-26-OL/AL
gentleness. 5-29-OL/AL
gently 5-30-A
geographer 5-25-AL; 6-34-OL/AL
geography 6-34-OL/BL
geologist 5-25-AL; 6-34-OL/BL

heaviest 4-22-AL
heavy 4-14-OL/AL
he'd. 3-29-BL
hedge 4-17-OL/AL; 5-28-BL
heel. 3-23-AL
heir 4-24-A
held 4-1-OL/BL
he'll 3-29-OL/AL
hello 4-7-OL/BL
help 2-2-OL/AL
helpful 4-28-OL/BL; 5-33-BL
helpless 4-28-OL/BL; 5-33-BL
hen 1-3-CH
her 2-25-OL/BL
herb 6-16-AL
herd 4-11-OL/AL; 5-10-BL
herd's 4-32-OL/AL
here 2-34-OL/BL
here's 2-27-OL/AL
hero 4-7-OL/AL
heroes 5-26-OL/BL
heroism. 5-35-BL
herself 3-35-OL/BL; 4-11-BL
he's 2-27-OL/BL
hesitation 6-29-AL
hibernate 5-19-OL/AL; 6-3-AL
hibernation 5-19-OL/AL
hiccup. 3-25-AL
hiccupped. 5-16-AL; 6-17-BL
hiccupping 5-16-AL
hide 1-27-OL; 2-15-BL
hideous. 6-27-AL
high 3-10-OL/BL
higher 4-5-OL/AL
highlight. 3-10-AL
highness 4-33-BL
high school. 4-34-OL/AL
highway 4-5-OL/AL
hike 1-27-OL
hiker 4-27-OL/AL
hilarious 6-30-A
hill 2-3-OL/AL
him 1-7-OL
himself 3-35-OL/AL
hinder. 6-3-AL
hindsight 6-23-AL
hire 4-5-OL/AL
his. 1-6-OL
historian 6-31-AL
historic 5-32-BL
historically 6-11-AL
hit. 2-3-OL/BL
hive 1-26-CH
hoarse. 3-20-AL
hobbies 3-32-OL/AL
hobby 2-4-AL; 3-32-OL/AL

hog. 1-9-CH
hoist 4-9-AL
hold 2-16-OL/AL
hole 1-28-CH
holiday 3-8-AL; 4-3-OL/BL
holly 3-26-AL
home 1-28-OL
homeless. 4-28-AL; 6-22-BL
homemaker 4-27-AL; 5-25-OL/AL
home run 4-36-A; 5-22-OL/BL;
   6-23-BL
homestead 6-2-BL
homeward. 6-11-OL/AL
homework 4-34-AL; 5-22-OL/BL
homograph 6-34-BL
honest. 4-15-OL/BL
honesty. 6-16-AL
honorary. 6-25-OL/AL
hood. 2-24-A
hoof 4-25-AL
hooves 4-25-AL
hop. 1-9-OL
hope 1-28-OL
hopeless 4-28-OL/AL
hoping 3-27-OL/AL
hopped 3-28-OL/AL
hopping 3-30-A
horizon 5-2-AL
horn 2-36-A
hornet. 2-31-AL
horrible. 5-36-A; 6-17-OL/BL
horse. 2-31-OL/BL; 3-20-BL
horseback 5-24-A
horsepower. 5-14-AL
horses 3-24-A
hose 1-28-CH
hospital. 5-7-OL/BL
hospitality 5-7-OL/BL
hot 1-8-OL
hotel. 4-7-OL/AL
hotter 3-33-OL/BL; 4-22-BL
hottest 3-33-OL/BL
hound. 3-6-A
hour 2-34-OL/BL
hourly. 3-34-OL/BL; 4-15-BL
house . . .2-26-OL/AL; 3-4-OL/BL; 4-9-BL
housefly 2-15-AL
how. 2-26-OL/BL
how'd 3-29-AL
however 3-17-AL; 4-9-OL/BL
how's 2-30-A
hug 1-13-OL
huge 4-2-OL/BL
hugged 3-28-AL
hum 1-11-CH
human 4-8-OL/BL; 5-3-BL

humanity 5-29-OL/AL
humble 4-24-A; 5-8-OL/AL
humid. 5-3-OL/AL
humidity. 5-29-OL/AL
humor. 5-3-OL/AL
humorous 5-32-OL/BL; 6-27-BL
hunger 3-15-AL
hunt 2-5-OL/AL
hunter. 3-3-AL
hurdles 5-10-AL
hurry. 3-26-OL/BL
hurt. 3-21-OL/BL
hurtful 4-28-BL
husband 6-14-OL/BL
hush 1-33-CH; 2-32-BL
hustle 6-16-AL
hut 1-12-CH
hydrant. 4-5-AL
hymn 6-16-OL/AL
hysterical 6-10-AL

I

I 1-14-OL
ice. 3-14-OL/BL
icicle. 4-5-OL/AL; 5-17-BL
icy. 4-6-A
idea. 4-5-OL/BL
ideal 6-3-OL/AL
ideally. 6-11-OL/AL
if 1-7-OL
ignite 5-7-AL
ignition. 5-7-AL
ignorance 6-32-AL
ignorant 5-36-A; 6-10-OL/AL
ignore 5-13-AL; 6-9-OL/BL
I'll. 3-29-OL/BL
illegal 6-20-OL/BL
illegible 6-20-OL/AL
illiterate 6-20-OL/BL
illness 4-33-OL/BL
illogical. 6-20-OL/AL
illusion 6-18-A
I'm 2-27-OL/BL
imaginable 6-24-A
imaginary 5-28-AL; 6-25-OL/BL
imagine. 4-17-AL; 5-28-OL/BL
imitation 4-31-OL/AL
immaculate. 6-25-AL
immature 5-20-AL
immediate 6-25-OL/AL
immigrate 6-35-OL/AL
imminent 6-35-OL/AL
impatient 5-20-OL/BL
imperfect 5-20-OL/AL
impolite 5-20-OL/AL
import. 5-34-OL/BL

keeping 1-19-OL
kept 3-2-AL; 4-1-OL/BL
kernel 5-23-OL/AL; 6-35-BL
kettle 4-19-OL/AL
kick 2-17-OL/AL
kicker 4-30-A
kilowatt 6-34-BL
kind 3-10-OL/BL
kinder 4-22-OL/BL; 5-16-BL
kindest 4-22-OL/BL
kindness 4-33-OL/BL
king 2-9-OL/BL
kingdom 2-9-AL
kiss 2-17-OL/BL
kite 1-26-OL
kitten 2-3-AL; 3-25-OL/AL
knack 6-16-OL/AL
knapsack 4-15-AL; 6-16-BL
knead 6-18-A
knee 4-15-OL/BL
kneel 6-16-OL/BL
knelt 6-18-A
knew 3-5-OL/BL; 4-15-BL
knife 4-15-OL/AL
knight 3-10-OL/AL; 4-15-BL
knitting 3-28-AL
knob 6-16-OL/BL
knock 4-15-OL/AL
knoll 6-16-AL
knot 4-15-OL/AL
know 2-16-OL/BL
knowledge 5-28-AL; 6-16-OL/BL
known 4-15-OL/BL
knuckle 4-15-AL
Korean 4-36-A

L

label 5-8-AL; 6-10-OL/BL
labor 6-1-OL/AL
Labor Day 4-29-AL
lace 1-22-CH
ladder 3-25-OL/AL
ladies 3-32-AL
lady 3-32-AL; 4-3-OL/BL; 5-1-BL
laid 3-8-OL/BL; 4-3-BL
lake 1-22-OL
lamb 4-15-OL/AL
lamp 1-2-CH
land 3-1-OL/AL; 4-1-BL
landless 4-28-BL
lane 1-22-CH
language 5-31-OL/BL
lap 1-1-CH
large 3-14-OL/BL; 4-13-BL
larger 3-33-OL/AL; 4-17-BL
largest 3-33-OL/AL; 4-17-BL

last 3-1-OL/AL
lastly 3-34-OL/BL
latches 5-26-OL/AL
late 2-11-OL/BL
lately 3-34-OL/AL
later 3-33-OL/BL; 4-21-BL
latest 3-33-OL/BL
latter 5-9-AL
laugh 4-14-OL/AL
laughable 5-35-AL
laughed 5-16-AL
laughing 5-16-AL
launch 4-10-AL; 5-4-OL/AL
lava 4-25-AL
law 3-19-OL/BL
lawful 4-28-BL
lawn 3-19-OL/AL
lawyer 5-4-OL/AL
lay 3-8-OL/AL
lazy 4-3-OL/AL
lead 4-4-OL/BL
leader 4-27-OL/BL; 5-25-BL
leaf 4-25-OL/BL
league 6-2-AL
learn 3-21-OL/AL
learner 4-27-OL/AL
lease 5-1-AL
least 4-4-AL
leather 4-18-A; 6-2-OL/BL
leave 3-9-OL/AL; 4-4-BL
leaves 4-25-OL/BL
leaving 3-27-OL/BL
led 1-4-CH
ledger 5-28-OL/BL
left 3-2-OL/AL
leg 1-4-OL; 2-10-BL
legal 5-7-OL/AL; 6-10-OL/BL
legality 5-7-OL/AL
legible 5-35-OL/AL; 6-19-OL/AL
legislate 6-25-BL
leisure 6-8-OL/BL
lemon 2-2-AL; 3-2-AL
lend 3-6-A
lengthen 4-20-AL; 5-33-OL/AL
lesson 3-25-OL/BL
let 1-3-OL; 2-2-BL
letter 3-25-OL/BL
letter carrier 4-27-AL
letters 3-2-AL
lettuce 2-2-AL
leverage 6-21-AL
lexicographer 6-34-AL
liberty 5-33-OL/BL
librarian 6-31-OL/BL
libraries 3-10-AL
license 5-17-AL; 6-28-OL/BL

lid 1-6-CH
lieutenant 6-31-OL/BL
life 1-26-OL
lift 3-1-OL/AL
light 3-10-OL/BL
lighten 4-20-OL/BL; 5-9-BL
lightly 4-5-AL
like 1-27-OL
limb 4-15-OL/AL
lime 2-18-A
limit 6-3-OL/BL
line 1-26-OL; 2-15-BL
linen 5-12-A
linguistics 5-26-AL
lion 3-10-BL
list 3-1-OL/BL
listen 4-15-OL/BL
listener 4-27-OL/BL; 5-25-BL
little 2-3-AL; 3-17-OL/BL
live 2-10-OL/AL
living 3-27-BL
load 3-11-OL/AL
loaf 3-11-AL
loan 4-23-OL/AL
loaves 4-7-AL; 5-26-OL/AL; 6-4-BL
lobby 3-26-AL
locate 4-2-AL; 5-2-OL/AL; 6-1-BL
location 6-29-OL/AL
lock 2-17-OL/BL
lodge 5-28-OL/AL
log 2-4-OL/AL
logic 6-3-AL
loiter 5-14-AL
lone 4-23-OL/AL; 5-2-BL
loneliness 5-30-A
lonesome 6-22-OL/BL
long 2-9-OL/BL
longer 3-33-BL
longest 3-33-BL
look 2-17-OL/BL
looked 2-24-A
looking 2-22-OL/BL
loop 3-5-AL
loose 3-5-OL/AL
loosely 6-11-OL/BL
loosen 5-21-OL/BL
lore 5-18-A
lose 4-8-OL/BL; 5-3-BL
loss 5-4-OL/BL
lost 3-19-OL/BL
lot 2-4-OL/BL
lotion 5-2-AL
loud 2-26-OL/AL; 3-4-OL/BL
loudly 3-34-OL/AL
loudness 5-14-AL
lounge 5-14-AL

moisten 4-20-OL/BL
moisture 5-14-OL/AL
mole 1-29-CH
mom 1-9-OL; 2-4-BL
moment 4-7-OL/BL
momentary 6-25-OL/AL
mommy 3-30-A
Monday 4-29-OL/BL
monkeys 5-26-BL
monotone 6-4-AL
monstrous 6-27-AL
month 3-3-OL/AL; 4-29-BL
monthly 3-34-OL/BL; 4-29-BL
monument 6-4-AL
moon 1-31-CH; 2-23-BL
moose 2-23-AL
mop 1-9-OL
morality 6-36-A
more 2-31-OL/AL; 3-20-BL
morning 2-31-AL; 3-20-OL/BL;
  4-10-BL
morsel 5-12-A
mortality 6-36-A
mortar 6-9-OL/AL
moss 2-6-A
mossy 3-19-AL
most 3-11-OL/AL
mostly 3-36-A
motel 4-7-OL/AL
moth 2-33-OL/AL; 3-19-BL
mother 3-13-OL/BL; 4-21-BL
mother's 4-32-OL/BL
motion 4-31-OL/BL
motionless 6-24-A
motor 5-9-OL/BL
mount 4-9-OL/AL
mountain 5-14-OL/BL
mountaineer 6-36-A
mountainous 5-32-AL; 6-27-OL/AL
mouse 4-25-OL/BL
mouth 3-4-AL; 4-9-OL/BL
move 2-25-AL
movement 4-33-OL/BL
movies 4-8-AL; 5-3-OL/BL
mowing 1-19-CH
mown 4-12-A
much 2-29-OL/AL
mud 2-5-OL/AL
muddy 3-26-OL/AL
mug 2-6-A
mule 2-11-OL/AL; 3-7-BL
multiples 5-26-AL
multiplication 4-31-OL/BL
mumble 4-19-OL/AL
murmur 5-10-OL/AL; 6-9-BL
muscle 6-28-OL/BL

museum 5-3-OL/AL
mushroom 3-5-AL
music 4-8-OL/BL
musician 4-31-AL; 6-31-OL/BL
mussel 5-8-AL
must 1-17-OL; 2-5-BL
must've 3-29-OL/BL
mutual 6-5-AL
my 2-15-OL/BL
myself 2-35-OL/AL; 3-17-BL
mysteries 3-32-OL/AL
mysterious 5-32-OL/BL; 6-27-BL
mystery 3-32-OL/AL

N

naive 6-28-AL
name 1-21-OL; 2-25-BL
nap 2-6-A
naphtha 6-16-AL
napkins 2-1-AL
narrow 4-7-AL; 5-33-OL/AL
nation 4-3-OL/BL
nationalize 5-21-AL
natural 6-1-OL/BL
naughty 4-10-AL
naval 5-23-AL
navel 5-23-AL
near 4-11-OL/BL; 5-13-BL
nearby 4-34-OL/BL
nearer 4-22-OL/BL
nearest 4-22-OL/BL
neat 2-14-OL/AL
neatly 3-34-BL
necessary 6-25-OL/BL
neck 1-32-OL
necklace 3-2-AL
need 2-14-OL/BL; 3-9-BL
needed 2-22-OL/BL
needle 4-19-AL; 5-1-OL/AL; 6-2-BL
neighbor 5-1-OL/BL
neighborhood 6-7-OL/BL
neither 4-21-OL/BL
nephew 4-8-AL
nephew's 4-32-AL
nervous 6-27-OL/BL
nest 3-2-OL/BL
net 1-3-OL
neutral 6-10-OL/AL
never 3-16-OL/BL; 4-21-BL
news 3-5-OL/BL; 4-8-BL
newspaper 3-35-AL; 4-34-OL/BL;
  5-22-BL
newsreel 6-2-AL
newsstand 6-23-AL
New York (NY) 4-35-AL
next 2-2-OL/BL

nibble 2-3-AL
nice 2-15-OL/BL; 3-14-BL
nicest 3-36-A
niece 6-8-OL/BL
night 3-10-OL/BL
nightmare 3-10-AL
nineties 3-36-A
no 1-28-OL; 2-16-BL
nobody 3-35-OL/BL; 4-7-BL
nod 2-4-OL/AL; 3-2-BL
nodding 3-28-BL
noise 2-20-AL; 3-4-AL
noisy 5-18-A
nonchalant 6-20-AL
nonconsumable 6-20-AL
nondairy 5-20-AL
nondescript 6-20-AL
none 3-3-OL/BL
nonfat 5-20-AL; 6-20-OL/BL
nonfiction 5-20-OL/BL; 6-20-BL
nonpoisonous 6-30-A
nonproductive 5-20-AL; 6-20-AL
nonprofit 5-20-AL; 6-20-OL/AL
nonreturnable 5-20-AL; 6-20-OL/BL
nonsense 5-20-OL/BL
nonsmoker 5-24-A
nonstop 5-20-OL/AL
nontoxic 6-20-AL
nonverbal 6-24-A
nonviolent 5-20-OL/AL; 6-20-BL
noon 2-23-OL/BL; 3-5-BL
nor 4-10-OL/BL
normal 5-8-OL/BL
north 3-20-OL/AL; 4-10-BL
nose 1-29-OL
not 1-8-OL
notable 6-19-OL/AL
note 1-29-OL
notebook 2-35-AL; 3-35-BL
nothing 2-10-AL; 3-3-OL/BL
notice 6-4-OL/BL
noticeable 6-19-AL
November 4-29-OL/AL
now 2-26-OL/BL
nowhere 3-22-OL/AL
nudge 3-14-AL
nuisance 5-3-AL; 6-32-BL
numb 6-16-OL/BL
nurse 3-21-BL
nursery 6-9-AL
nut 1-11-OL
nutritious 6-27-OL/AL
nylon 2-15-AL

O

oatmeal 6-6-A

pebble. 4-19-OL/AL
pediatrician 6-31-AL
peek 1-23-CH
peel. 1-23-CH
peer. 5-13-OL/BL
pen 1-3-OL; 2-2-BL
penalty 5-12-A
pencil 3-14-OL/AL
pennant 6-12-A
pennies. 5-26-BL
penny 3-26-BL
people. 3-17-OL/BL; 4-19-BL
pepper. 3-25-OL/AL
perceptible 6-19-AL
perfect 4-11-OL/AL
perfectly 6-11-AL
perform. 5-13-OL/BL
performance 6-32-OL/BL
perfume 5-10-OL/AL
perhaps. 4-1-AL
peril 5-12-A
perimeter 5-36-A; 6-34-BL
period. 5-7-OL/BL
periodic 5-7-OL/BL
permission 5-9-AL; 6-29-OL/AL
permit. 6-3-OL/AL
permitted 6-15-OL/BL
permitting 6-15-OL/AL
persecute 6-35-AL
person. 4-11-OL/BL; 5-10-BL
personal 6-35-OL/BL
personnel 6-35-OL/BL
perspire. 6-28-OL/AL
peso 4-35-AL
pessimism 5-33-AL; 6-14-OL/AL
pet 1-3-OL
pharmacy 5-11-AL
phase 6-14-OL/AL
pheasant. 4-14-AL
phobia 5-35-OL/AL; 6-13-AL
phone 6-13-OL/BL
phonics. 6-13-BL
phosphorus 6-13-AL
photo 5-34-BL; 6-13-OL/AL
photocopy 5-34-OL/AL
photo-essay. 5-34-AL
photograph. 5-34-OL/AL
photographer 6-36-A
photography 5-34-AL; 6-34-OL/BL
photojournalism. 5-36-A
photosynthesis 6-36-A
phrase 6-13-OL/BL
physician 6-13-OL/BL
physiology 6-34-AL
pianos. 5-26-OL/BL
pick. 1-32-OL

picked. 2-22-BL
picking 1-19-CH
piece. 3-14-AL; 4-4-OL/BL
pier 5-13-OL/AL
pierce 5-13-OL/AL; 6-8-BL
piercing 6-8-AL
pies 2-21-AL; 3-31-OL/AL
pies' 4-32-BL
pig. 1-7-OL
pigeon. 6-28-OL/BL
pigs 1-18-OL
pike. 2-17-AL
pillow 3-11-AL; 4-7-OL/BL
pin 1-7-CH
pine 1-26-CH
pioneer 5-13-OL/AL
pipe. 2-11-OL/AL
pitch 3-18-A
pitcher 4-27-AL; 5-25-OL/BL
pitiful 6-22-OL/BL
place. 3-14-OL/BL
placement. 4-33-OL/AL
plagiarize 5-21-AL
plaid 4-14-AL
plain 2-13-AL; 3-8-OL/AL
plainly 3-34-OL/AL
plan 3-1-OL/BL
plane. 3-7-OL/BL
planned 3-28-OL/BL
planning 3-28-AL
plant. 2-8-OL/BL
planted 2-22-OL/AL; 3-16-BL
plastic 5-17-OL/AL
plate 2-13-AL
platter. 2-8-AL; 3-25-AL
play. 2-13-OL/BL; 3-8-BL
played 2-22-OL/BL
player 4-27-OL/BL
playful. 4-28-OL/AL
pleasant 4-14-AL; 5-32-OL/BL;
6-10-BL
please 2-19-OL/BL
pleasurable 6-14-AL
pleasure 4-14-AL; 5-33-OL/AL
pleat 2-19-AL
pledge. 5-28-OL/AL
plentiful 6-24-A
plenty 6-6-A
plot. 3-2-OL/BL
plow 4-9-OL/AL
plug. 1-16-CH
plum 1-16-OL; 2-19-BL
plumber 6-16-OL/AL
plummeted 6-17-AL
plunge. 3-14-AL
poach 4-7-AL

pocket. 3-2-AL
pocketbook. 5-24-A
poem. 4-7-OL/BL
poem's 4-32-OL/AL
poet. 4-7-OL/AL
poets' 4-32-OL/AL
poinsettia 5-31-AL
point. 2-20-AL; 3-4-OL/BL
pointed. 4-12-A
poise 5-14-OL/AL
poison. 5-31-OL/AL
poisonous 6-30-A
pole. 1-29-OL
police 5-1-OL/BL
polish 6-6-A
polite 5-2-OL/AL; 6-28-BL
politely 6-11-AL
pollutant. 6-7-AL
pollute 5-3-AL
pond 2-4-OL/BL
pony 4-7-OL/AL
pool 3-5-OL/BL; 4-8-BL
poor 3-17-AL
pop 1-13-CH
popcorn 2-4-AL; 4-25-OL/BL
popular. 6-6-A
populate 5-1-OL/AL; 6-25-BL
population 6-29-OL/BL
porcelain 6-9-AL
porch 2-31-AL
port. 4-10-OL/AL
portable 5-34-AL
Portuguese 4-36-A
pose 6-4-OL/AL
position 6-29-OL/AL
positive. 6-4-OL/AL
positively 6-14-AL
possess 6-17-OL/BL
possession 6-17-AL
possible. 5-8-AL; 6-17-BL
possibly. 6-11-OL/AL
post. 1-17-CH
postage 6-21-OL/AL
postdate 5-15-OL/BL
post meridiem 5-15-AL
post office. 6-23-OL/AL
postscript 5-15-OL/BL
posttest. 5-15-OL/BL
postwar. 5-15-OL/AL
pot 1-8-OL
potato. 3-11-AL
potatoes 6-28-AL
pounce 3-14-AL
powder 4-9-OL/AL; 5-14-BL
power 4-9-OL/BL
powerful 4-28-OL/BL; 5-33-BL

real 2-25-AL; 3-9-OL/BL
realism 5-36-A
realize 5-21-OL/BL
really 3-34-OL/BL
reappear 5-15-OL/BL
rear 4-11-OL/AL
reason 3-9-AL; 4-4-OL/BL
rebel 6-33-OL/AL
rebuild 4-26-OL/AL
recall 5-4-OL/AL
receipt 6-8-OL/AL
receive 5-15-AL; 6-8-OL/BL
recent 5-17-OL/AL
recess 6-17-OL/BL
recession 6-29-AL
recharge 5-15-OL/AL
recheck 4-26-OL/AL
recipe 5-17-AL
recite 5-17-OL/AL
reclaim 4-3-AL; 5-15-OL/AL
recognition 6-29-AL
record 4-10-OL/BL; 5-13-BL
recover 4-26-OL/BL; 5-15-BL
recuperate 5-15-AL
recurring 6-15-AL
redder 3-33-OL/BL; 4-27-BL
reddest 3-33-OL/BL; 4-22-BL
redirect 5-15-AL
reenter 5-15-OL/AL
refer 6-9-AL
reference 5-35-OL/AL
refill 4-26-AL
reflect 5-15-AL
reform 4-26-AL; 5-15-OL/AL
refract 5-15-AL
refrain 4-3-AL
refresh 4-26-AL; 5-15-OL/BL
refreshment 5-29-AL
refrigerator 5-28-AL
refuel 5-18-A
refuse 5-3-AL; 6-33-OL/BL
regain 4-3-AL
regard 5-11-OL/AL
regardless 6-22-AL
region 5-28-OL/AL
register 5-30-A
regroup 4-26-BL
regular 6-2-OL/BL
rehearse 5-10-OL/AL
reheat 4-26-OL/AL; 5-15-BL
reign 6-8-OL/AL
reindeer 4-11-AL
rejoin 5-15-OL/AL
relate 5-12-A
relative 5-12-A; 5-29-OL/BL
relay 4-3-OL/BL

release 6-2-OL/BL
relief 6-8-OL/BL
reluctance 6-32-AL
reluctant 5-32-AL
rely 4-5-AL
remain 3-8-AL; 4-3-OL/AL
remained 6-15-OL/BL
remaining 6-15-OL/BL
remark 5-11-OL/AL
remarkable 6-19-AL
remember 5-9-OL/BL; 6-28-BL
remove 5-3-OL/AL
removed 5-16-OL/BL; 6-15-BL
removing 5-16-OL/BL
rename 4-26-BL
renewal 6-7-AL
reorder 4-26-AL
repair 5-11-OL/BL
repeat 4-4-OL/AL
replace 5-1-AL
replacement 5-29-AL
replay 4-3-AL
reply 4-5-OL/AL
report 3-20-AL; 4-10-OL/BL; 5-34-BL
reporter 4-27-OL/BL
require 6-3-OL/AL
reread 4-26-OL/BL
rescue 5-3-OL/AL
reside 5-12-A
residence 6-32-OL/AL
resident 5-12-A; 6-31-OL/AL
resign 6-3-AL
resistance 6-36-A
respect 5-34-OL/AL
respectable 5-35-OL/BL
respond 6-4-OL/BL
responsible 6-19-OL/BL
rest 1-17-OL
restaurant 6-28-OL/AL
restful 4-28-OL/AL
restfulness 4-33-AL
restless 4-28-OL/AL
result 6-5-OL/BL
resulted 6-15-OL/BL
resulting 5-16-AL; 6-15-OL/AL
retell 4-30-A
rethink 5-18-A
retire 5-2-AL
retreat 6-6-A
return 3-21-AL; 4-11-OL/BL
reverberate 5-15-AL
reversible 6-19-OL/AL
review 4-26-OL/AL
reward 5-13-OL/BL
rewind 3-10-AL
rewrite 4-26-OL/BL; 5-15-BL

rhinoceros 6-16-AL
rhubarb 6-16-AL
rhythm 6-28-OL/AL
ribbon 3-25-OL/AL
rice 1-27-CH
rich 2-30-A
ride 1-27-OL; 2-11-BL
ridge 4-17-OL/AL
right 3-10-OL/BL; 4-5-BL
rightness 4-33-BL
rigid 4-17-OL/AL
rind 3-12-A
ring 2-9-OL/AL
rip 1-7-CH
ripen 3-7-AL
rise 4-2-OL/AL
rising 3-27-AL
rival 6-10-OL/AL
road 2-16-OL/AL; 3-11-BL
roast 2-16-AL
robe 2-11-OL/AL
rock 2-17-OL/AL
rod 1-9-CH
rode 1-29-OL
rodent 6-31-BL
role 3-23-AL; 4-23-OL/BL; 5-2-BL
roll 3-23-AL; 4-23-OL/BL
roof 3-5-OL/BL
roofs 3-31-AL
room 1-31-OL; 2-23-BL
rooster 6-12-A
root 2-23-OL/AL
rope 1-28-OL
rose 1-29-OL
rough 4-14-OL/AL
round 2-30-A; 3-4-OL/AL
roundness 4-33-BL
route 5-31-OL/AL
routine 6-7-OL/BL
row 3-11-OL/BL
rowboat 2-35-AL; 3-36-A
royal 4-9-OL/AL; 5-8-BL
rub 2-5-OL/AL; 3-3-BL
rubbed 3-28-OL/AL
rubber 4-21-AL
rubies 3-32-AL
ruby 3-32-OL/AL
rude 5-6-A
rug 1-12-OL; 2-5-BL
ruin 4-12-A
rule 4-8-OL/BL
rummage 4-17-AL
run 1-12-OL
runners' 4-32-AL
running 3-28-OL/BL
runs 1-18-OL

shipment 4-33-OL/AL
shipwreck 3-13-AL
shirt 3-21-OL/AL
shiver 2-10-AL
shock 3-6-A
shoe 2-32-OL/BL
shoelace 2-35-AL; 3-35-BL
shone 3-7-AL
shook 3-15-OL/BL
shoot. 3-5-OL/AL
shop 1-33-OL; 2-32-BL
shopping 3-28-AL
shore 2-32-OL/BL
short 2-32-OL/BL; 3-20-BL
shorten .4-20-BL
shortly 3-34-OL/BL
should. 3-17-OL/AL
shoulder 4-31-OL/BL
should've 3-29-OL/AL; 6-7-OL/AL
shout. 2-32-OL/AL; 3-4-BL
shovel. 2-10-AL
show 1-33-OL
shower 3-13-AL; 4-21-OL/AL
shown 4-7-OL/BL; 5-2-BL
shriek 6-8-OL/BL
shut. 1-33-CH
shutter 3-25-AL
shy 4-5-OL/BL
sick 2-17-OL/AL
sickness. 4-33-AL; 5-29-OL/BL
side 1-27-OL
siege 6-8-OL/AL
sigh. 3-10-OL/AL
sight 3-10-OL/AL
sign 3-10-OL/BL
signs 6-3-BL
silence 6-32-OL/BL
silent. 4-5-AL; 5-2-OL/BL
silk 2-6-A
silly. 3-26-AL
silver. 4-21-OL/BL
similar. 6-28-OL/BL
simple 4-19-OL/BL
simplify. 6-3-BL
simply. 6-12-A
simultaneous 5-32-AL
since 3-14-OL/BL
sincere 5-13-AL
sincerely 5-31-OL/BL
sing. 2-9-OL/BL
singer 4-27-OL/AL
single 4-19-OL/BL
sink. 2-9-OL/AL
sip. 1-6-CH
sir 3-24-A
siren 3-18-A

sister-in-law 6-23-OL/AL
sisters'. 4-32-OL/BL
sit 1-6-OL
sits 1-18-OL
sitting 3-28-OL/BL
size 2-11-AL; 3-7-OL/BL; 4-2-BL
skate 3-7-OL/AL
skater 4-27-OL/AL
skating 3-27-OL/AL
sketch 2-2-AL
skies .3-32-BL
skiing 5-31-OL/AL
skill. 3-1-AL; 4-1-OL/AL
skillful. 4-28-AL
skip. 1-16-OL
skipped 3-28-AL
skirt 3-21-OL/AL
skirted. 4-11-AL
skis 5-26-OL/BL
skull 4-6-A
sky 2-15-OL/AL; 3-32-BL
skyscraper 6-23-OL/BL
skyward. 6-11-OL/AL
slam 1-16-OL
sled 3-2-OL/AL
sledding 3-28-OL/AL
sledgehammer 5-28-AL
sleep 2-19-OL/AL
sleeping 2-22-AL; 3-9-AL
sleepless 4-28-AL
sleet 6-2-OL/AL
sleeve 2-19-AL
sleigh 5-1-AL; 6-8-OL/AL
slender 5-33-OL/AL
slice 3-14-OL/AL
slide 3-7-OL/AL
sliding 3-27-OL/AL
slight. 3-10-AL; 4-5-OL/AL
slim. 3-1-AL
slimmer. 4-22-AL; 5-16-OL/BL
slimmest 4-22-AL; 5-16-OL/AL
slip 1-16-CH; 2-19-BL
slippers 3-31-AL
slope 4-6-A; 5-2-OL/AL; 6-4-BL
slow 2-19-OL/BL
slowly 2-19-AL; 3-34-OL/BL
sly 2-24-A
small. 2-7-OL/BL
smaller 4-24-A
smart. 4-13-OL/AL
smell 4-1-OL/AL
smile 3-7-OL/BL
smiling 3-27-OL/AL
smock 2-4-AL
smoke 3-7-OL/AL
smooth 2-33-AL; 3-5-OL/AL

smoother 3-33-AL
smoothest 3-33-AL
smoothness. 4-33-AL
smudge 5-28-AL; 6-5-OL/AL
snacks. 3-31-BL
snap 1-16-CH
snare 4-13-AL
sneakers 2-21-AL
sneeze 2-14-AL
snore 3-24-A
snow 3-11-OL/BL
snug 1-11-CH
snuggle 4-19-OL/AL
so 1-28-OL
soak 3-11-OL/AL
soap 3-11-OL/BL; 4-7-BL
soar. 4-23-OL/AL
sock 1-32-OL
socket 3-2-AL
soft 3-19-OL/BL
soften 4-20-OL/AL; 5-21-BL
softly. 3-34-OL/AL
softness 4-33-OL/AL
software 3-22-OL/AL
soil 2-20-AL; 3-4-OL/AL
sold. 3-12-A
soldiers 5-26-OL/BL
solemn 6-16-OL/BL
solitaire. 5-11-AL
solitary 6-25-OL/AL
solo. 3-11-AL
solution 5-9-OL/BL; 6-7-BL
solve 5-5-OL/BL
some 2-10-OL/BL
someone 3-35-OL/BL; 4-34-BL
something. 3-35-OL/AL; 4-34-BL
sometimes. 4-34-OL/BL
somewhere 3-22-AL
son 2-34-BL; 3-6-A
song 3-19-OL/BL
sons' 4-32-OL/BL
soon 1-31-OL; 2-23-BL
sophomore 6-13-OL/BL
sore 4-23-OL/AL
sorrow. 5-2-AL
sorry 3-26-OL/BL
sort 4-10-OL/BL; 5-13-BL
sound 2-26-AL; 3-4-OL/AL
soup 5-6-A
sour. 5-14-OL/AL
south. 3-4-OL/BL; 4-35-BL
sow 6-36-A
soy 2-20-OL/AL
soybean. 2-20-AL
space. 2-13-AL; 3-14-OL/AL
spacious 6-27-AL

suitable 6-19-BL
suitcase 4-8-AL; 5-17-OL/AL
summarize 5-21-OL/AL
summer 3-25-OL/BL; 4-29-BL
summit 3-3-AL
summon 5-5-AL
sun 1-12-OL; 2-34-BL
Sunday 4-29-OL/BL
sung 2-12-A
sunglasses 3-36-A
sunken 4-20-BL
sunlight 3-36-A
sunnier 4-22-AL; 5-16-OL/BL
sunniest 4-24-A; 5-16-OL/AL
sunny 2-5-AL
sunshine 3-35-OL/AL
superficial 6-26-AL
superfluous 6-27-AL
superintendent 6-31-OL/AL
supermarket 6-7-AL
superpower 6-26-AL
supersonic 6-26-OL/AL
superstar 6-26-OL/AL
supervise 6-26-OL/BL
supper 3-25-OL/AL
supplied 5-16-OL/AL
supply 4-5-AL; 5-2-OL/BL
supplying 5-16-OL/BL; 6-15-BL
suppose 5-31-OL/BL
supreme 6-7-AL
sure 3-17-OL/AL
surely 6-28-OL/BL
surprise 4-2-OL/BL; 5-31-BL
surround 6-18-A
surveillance 6-8-AL
survey 5-10-AL; 6-1-OL/AL
suspect 6-33-AL
suspicion 5-9-AL
swallow 3-11-AL
sway 3-12-A
sweater 4-14-OL/AL
sweatshirt 4-14-AL; 5-22-OL/AL;
   6-23-BL
sweep 1-24-CH
sweet 3-9-OL/AL
sweeten 4-20-BL
swerve 5-10-AL
swift 4-1-AL; 5-5-OL/AL
swiftness 4-36-A; 5-29-OL/AL
swim 3-1-OL/AL
swimming 3-28-OL/BL
swing 2-9-AL
swirl 6-12-A
switch 3-15-OL/AL
switches 3-31-AL
sword 4-18-A

sworn 6-12-A
syllable 4-19-AL; 5-8-OL/BL
symbolism 5-35-AL
symptom 6-16-AL
system 6-3-OL/BL

T

table 4-20-OL/BL
tablecloth 4-34-OL/AL
tablespoon 6-7-OL/AL
tackle 2-17-AL
tactics 5-26-AL
tag 1-1-CH
tail 2-34-OL/AL
tailor 3-8-AL
take 1-22-OL
taking 3-27-OL/BL
tale 2-34-OL/AL
talent 6-10-OL/BL
talk 2-7-OL/BL
talking 2-22-OL/BL
tall 2-7-OL/AL
tame 1-21-CH
tangle 4-19-AL
tank 2-12-A
tape 2-11-OL/AL
tardiness 4-33-AL; 5-29-OL/AL
tardy 4-13-AL
tariff 6-13-AL
taught 4-10-OL/AL; 5-4-BL
tea 2-18-A
teach 2-14-AL
teacher 3-9-OL/BL; 4-27-BL
teacher's 4-36-A
teams 5-26-BL
tear 4-11-OL/BL
tease 6-14-OL/BL
teaspoon 6-7-OL/AL
technology 5-35-BL
tedious 6-27-OL/AL
teenagers 5-26-AL
teeth 2-33-OL/AL; 4-25-BL
telecast 5-34-OL/BL; 6-34-BL
teleconference 5-36-A
telegraph 6-34-OL/BL
telemeter 6-36-A
telephone 5-34-AL
telephoto 5-34-OL/BL
telescope 5-34-AL
television 6-14-OL/BL
tell 2-2-OL/BL; 3-2-BL
temple 4-19-OL/AL
temporary 5-11-AL; 6-25-OL/BL
tenant 6-31-OL/AL
tension 6-29-OL/AL
tent 3-2-OL/AL

term 4-11-OL/AL
terrible 6-17-OL/BL
terrific 5-32-AL
territory 6-9-OL/AL
terse 4-11-AL
test 3-2-OL/AL; 4-1-BL
Texas (TX) 4-35-AL
text 6-2-OL/AL
than 2-33-OL/BL
thank 2-33-OL/AL; 3-13-BL
thankful 4-28-OL/AL
thankless 4-28-OL/AL
Thanksgiving 4-29-AL
that 1-34-OL
that'll 3-29-OL/AL
that's 2-27-OL/BL; 3-29-OL
the 1-14-OL; 2-33-BL
their 3-22-OL/BL; 4-23-BL; 6-35-BL
them 2-33-OL/BL
theme 6-2-OL/AL
themselves 5-22-OL/BL
then 1-34-OL; 2-33-BL
there 3-22-OL/BL; 4-23-BL; 6-35-BL
therefore 5-13-AL; 6-9-OL/BL
there's 2-27-OL/AL
thermal 6-34-OL/AL
thermometer . . .5-34-OL/AL; 6-34-OL/BL
thermos 6-34-AL
thermostat 6-34-OL/AL
these 2-33-OL/BL
they 2-33-OL/BL
they'd 3-29-AL
they'll 3-29-OL/BL
they're 4-23-BL; 6-35-BL
they've 3-29-BL
thick 3-13-OL/AL
thicken 4-20-OL/AL; 5-9-BL
thickness 4-33-OL/BL
thief 6-8-OL/BL
thigh 3-12-A
thimble 2-33-AL
thin 1-34-CH
thing 2-36-A; 3-1-OL/BL
things 3-31-OL/BL
think 2-9-AL; 3-15-OL/BL
thinner 3-33-AL; 4-22-OL/AL
thinnest 3-33-AL; 4-22-OL/AL
third base 4-34-AL
thirst 3-21-AL; 4-11-OL/AL; 5-10-BL
this 1-34-OL
thorough 4-15-AL; 5-31-OL/AL
those 2-33-OL/AL
though 3-17-AL; 4-15-OL/BL
thought 4-10-OL/BL; 5-4-BL
thoughtful 4-28-OL/BL
thoughtless 5-4-AL; 6-22-OL/BL

underpass 6-26-OL/AL
understandable 6-19-AL
understanding 6-30-A
understood 6-7-OL/BL
unemployed 4-30-A
unequal 4-16-AL; 5-20-OL/AL
unfair 4-26-OL/BL; 5-11-BL
unfasten 5-24-A
unfortunate 6-25-OL/BL
unfriendly 3-34-AL; 4-26-AL
unhappy 3-26-AL; 4-26-OL/BL;
   5-20-BL
uniform 6-5-OL/AL
union 6-5-OL/AL
unison 6-5-AL
unit 5-3-OL/BL; 6-5-BL
unkind 4-26-BL
unknown 4-26-AL; 5-20-OL/BL;
   6-16-BL
unlikely 5-20-AL
unlisted 5-24-A
unload 4-30-A
unlock 4-26-OL/BL
unlucky 4-26-OL/AL
unpack 4-26-OL/AL; 5-20-BL
unpleasant 6-10-OL/AL
unsafe 4-26-OL/AL
unsure 5-20-OL/BL
untie 4-26-OL/BL; 5-20-BL
until 2-5-AL; 3-3-OL/BL
up 1-11-OL
upon 3-16-OL/AL
uproar 5-36-A
upstairs 4-34-OL/BL
up-to-date 4-29-AL; 5-22-OL/BL
upward 6-11-OL/BL
urge 4-18-A
us 1-11-OL
usage 6-24-A
use 1-31-OL
used 4-8-OL/BL
useful 4-28-OL/BL
usefulness 5-29-AL
useless 4-28-OL/BL
using 3-30-A
usual 6-14-OL/BL
usually 6-11-AL
utensil 5-3-AL

V

vacant 5-32-OL/BL
vacation 6-1-OL/BL
vain 4-23-AL; 5-23-OL/AL
valleys 5-26-OL/BL
valuable 5-33-AL; 6-19-OL/BL
value 4-12-A; 5-3-OL/BL; 6-5-BL

vane 4-23-AL; 5-23-OL/AL
vanish 5-5-AL
vanity 5-29-OL/BL
various 6-27-OL/BL
vary 5-11-OL/AL
vase 1-22-CH
vault 4-12-A
vegetable 2-22-AL
vegetarian 6-31-AL
vein 5-23-OL/AL
velvet 6-2-AL
verb 4-9-LA; 5-10-BL
verses 5-23-AL
version 6-14-AL
versus 5-23-AL
very 3-17-OL/AL
vest 1-4-CH
veterinary 6-30-A
vibrant 5-36-A
vice president 6-31-AL
victory 6-28-OL/AL
video 6-4-OL/BL
videotape 6-23-AL
view 4-8-OL/AL
vigor 5-12-A
vigorous 5-32-OL/AL
vigorously 6-11-AL
village 4-17-OL/BL; 5-28-BL
villain 6-28-OL/AL
vine 1-26-CH
vinegar 4-1-AL
visible 6-19-OL/BL
vision 4-31-AL; 6-14-OL/AL
visitor 5-25-AL; 6-14-OL/BL
visual 6-14-OL/AL
vivacious 6-27-AL
voice 2-20-AL; 3-4-OL/BL
voiced 5-14-AL
void 2-24-A
volleyball 6-23-AL
voluntary 6-25-OL/AL
volunteer 5-13-AL; 6-31-OL/BL
vowel 4-9-OL/BL; 5-8-BL
voyage . . . 4-18-A; 5-14-OL/AL; 6-21-BL

W

wag 1-13-CH
wage 4-18-A
wagon 2-1-AL; 3-16-BL
waist 3-8-AL; 4-23-OL/BL; 5-23-BL
wait 2-13-OL/BL
waive 5-31-AL
wake 1-21-CH
walk 2-7-OL/BL
walked 2-22-OL/AL
wall 2-7-OL/AL

walnut 5-6-A
walruses 3-31-AL
want 2-25-OL/BL
war 3-20-OL/AL
warm 3-20-OL/BL
warmth 5-13-OL/AL
warn 3-20-AL
warning 5-18-A
warp 3-20-AL
wary 5-11-AL
was 1-14-OL; 2-25-BL
wash 2-32-OL/BL
washable 5-35-BL
washcloth 3-35-AL
Washington (WA) 4-35-AL
wasn't 2-27-AL
waste 3-24-A; 4-23-OL/BL; 5-23-BL
wasteful 4-28-OL/AL
watch 3-13-OL/BL
watches' 4-32-OL/BL
water 3-16-AL; 4-21-OL/BL; 5-9-BL
waterproof 5-22-OL/BL; 6-23-BL
wave 2-11-OL/AL
waving 3-27-OL/AL
way 3-23-OL/AL
we 1-23-OL; 2-25-BL
weaken 4-20-OL/AL
weakness 4-33-OL/AL
wealth 4-14-AL
wear 3-22-OL/BL
weary 5-13-OL/AL
weather-beaten 6-23-AL
weather map 5-24-A
weatherproof 6-23-OL/AL
weaving 3-27-AL
we'd 3-29-AL
wedge 5-30-A
Wednesday 4-29-OL/BL
weed 1-24-CH
week 2-14-OL/BL; 4-29-BL
weekend 4-34-OL/AL; 5-22-BL
weekly 4-30-A
weeks 2-24-A
weigh 3-23-OL/BL
weight 5-23-OL/BL; 6-8-BL
weightless 4-28-AL
weird 6-8-OL/AL
welcome 3-2-AL
welfare 5-12-A
well 2-2-OL/BL
we'll 3-29-OL/BL
well-known 6-23-AL
went 2-2-OL/BL
were 3-17-OL/BL
weren't 2-27-AL
west 3-2-OL/AL; 4-35-BL

Bibliography

Word Studies Consulted in Compiling the *Spelling Connections* Word List

The American Heritage Word Frequency Book, Carroll et al. (1971)

"The Barbe, O'Rourke, Nault (BORN) Word List," Barbe et al. (1987)

"A Basic Core for Writing," Fitzgerald (1951)

Basic Elementary Reading Vocabularies, Harris and Jacobson (1972)

A Basic Vocabulary of Elementary School Children, Rinsland (1945)

The Basic Writing Vocabulary, Horn (1927)

Canadian Word Lists and Instructional Techniques, Thomas (1974)

Computational Analysis of Present-Day American English, Kucera and Francis (1967)

"High-Frequency Word List for Grades 3 through 9," Walker (1979)

Instant Words, Fry et al. (1985)

The Living Word Vocabulary, Dale and O'Rourke (1981)

"Nault Content Words" (Grades 1–8), Nault (1988)

The New Iowa Spelling Scale, Green (1954)

"100 Words Most Often Misspelled by Children in the Elementary Grades," Johnson (1950)

Phoneme-Grapheme Correspondence as Cues to Spelling Improvement, Hanna et al. (1966)

The Reading Teacher's Book of Lists, Fry, Kress, and Fountoukidis (2000)

Spelling Difficulties in 3876 Words, Gates (1937)

The Teacher's Word Book of 30,000 Words, Thorndike and Lorge (1944)

3000 Instant Words, 2nd ed., Sakiey and Fry (1984)

"220 Basic Sight Words," Dolch (1939)

"2000 Commonest Words for Spelling," Dolch (1942)*Written Vocabulary of Elementary School Children*, Hillerich (1978)

Written Vocabulary of Elementary School Pupils, Ages 6–14, Smith and Ingersoll (1984)

Complete Bibliography for Grades 1-6

Allal, L. (1997). Learning to spell in the classroom. In C.A. Perfetti, L. Rieben, & M. Fayol (Eds.), *Learning to Spell*. London: Lawrence Erlbaum Associates.

Bean, W., & C. Bouffler. (1987). *Spell by Writing*. Portsmouth, NH: Heinemann.

Bear, D., M. Invernizzi, S. Templeton, & F. Johnston. (2000). *Words Their Way*. Columbus, OH: Merrill/Prentice Hall.

Beers, J.W. (1974). First and second grade children's developing orthographic concept of tense and lax vowels. Doctoral dissertation, University of Virginia. *Dissertation Abstracts International, 35,* 08-A, 4972.

Bloom, B.S. (1956). *Taxonomy of Educational Objectives*. New York: McKay.

Bodrova, E., & D.J. Leong. (1998). Scaffolding emergent writing in the zone of proximal development. *Literacy Teaching and Learning, 3(2),* 1–18.

Brown, J., & D. Morris. (2005). "Meeting the needs of low spellers in a second-grade classroom." *Reading and Writing Quarterly 21,* 165-184.

Chomsky, C. (1970). Reading, writing and phonology. *Harvard Educational Review, 40,* 287–309.

Clay, M.M. (1993). Reading recovery: A guidebook for teachers in training. Portsmouth, NH: Heinemann.

Eeds, M. (1985, January). Bookwords: Using a beginning word list of high frequency words from children's literature K-3. *The Reading Teacher*, pp. 418-423.

Ehri, L.C. (1997). Learning to read and learning to spell are one and the same, almost. In C.A. Perfetti, L. Rieben, & M. Fayol (Eds.), *Learning to Spell*. London: Lawrence Erlbaum Associates.

Ehri, L.C., & S. McCormick. (1998). Phases of word learning: Implications for instruction with delayed and disabled readers. *Reading & Writing Quarterly, 14,* 135–163.

Elkonin, D.B. (1963). The psychology of mastering the elements of reading. In B. Simon & Simon (Eds.), *Educational Psychology in the U.S.S.R.* Stanford, CA: Stanford University Press.

Feldgus, E.G., & I. Cardonic. (1999). Kid writing: A systematic approach to phonics, journals, and writing workshop. Bothell, WA: The Wright Group.

Fitzgerald, J. (1953). The teaching of spelling. *Elementary English, 30,* 79–84.

Galperin, P. (1969). Stages in the development of mental acts. In M. Cole & I. Maltzman (Eds.), *A Handbook of Contemporary Soviet Psychology*. New York: Basic Books.

Ganske, K. (2000). *Word Journeys: Assessment-Guided Phonics, Spelling, and Vocabulary Instruction*. New York: Guilford.

Gentry, J.R. (1977). *A study of the orthographic strategies of beginning readers*. Unpublished doctoral dissertation, University of Virginia, Charlottesville.

Gentry, J.R. (1978). Early spelling strategies. *The Elementary School Journal, 79,* 88–92.

Gentry, J.R. (1982). An analysis of developmental spelling in GNYS at WRK. *The Reading Teacher, 36,* 192–200.

Gentry, J. R. (1985). You can analyze developmental spelling. *Teaching K–8, 15,* 44–45.

Gentry, J.R. (1997). *My Kid Can't Spell*. Portsmouth, NH: Heinemann.

Gentry, J.R. (2000a). A retrospective on invented spelling and a look forward. *The Reading Teacher, 54(3)*, 318–332.

Gentry, J.R. (2000b). *The Literacy Map: Guiding Children to Where They Need to Be (K–3)*. New York: Mondo.

Gentry, J.R. (2002). *The Literacy Map: Guiding Children to Where They Need to Be (4–6)*. New York: Mondo.

Gentry, J.R. (2004). *The Science of Spelling: The Explicit Specifics That Make Great Readers and Writers (and Spellers!)*. Portsmouth, NH: Heinemann.

Gentry, J.R. (2005). "Instructional techniques for emerging writers and special needs students at kindergarten and grade 1 levels." *Reading and Writing Quarterly 21*, 113-34.

Gentry, J.R. (2006). *Breaking the Code: The New Science of Beginning Reading and Writing*. Portsmouth, NH: Heinemann.

Gentry, J.R. (2007a). *Assessing early literacy with Richard Gentry: Five phases, one simple test*. Portsmouth, NH: Heinemann.

Gentry, J.R. (2007b). *Breakthrough in Beginning Reading and Writing*. New York: Scholastic.

Gentry, J.R. (2008). *Step-by-Step Assessment Guide to Code Breaking*. New York: Scholastic.

Graham, S. (1983). Effective spelling instruction. *The Elementary School Journal, 83*, 560–567.

Graves, D.H. (1981). A new look at research on writing. In Shirley Haley- James (Ed.), *Perspectives on Writing Research in Grades 1–8*. Champaign, IL: National Council of Teachers of English.

Hanna, P.R., J.S. Hanna, R.E. Hodges, & E. Rudorf. (1966). *Phoneme-Grapheme Correspondences As Cues to Spelling Improvement*. Washington, DC: U.S. Government Printing Office.

Henderson, E.H. (1981). *Learning to Read and Spell: The Child's Knowledge of Words*. DeKalb, IL: Northern Illinois University Press.

Henderson, E.H. (1985). *Teaching Spelling*. Boston: Houghton Mifflin.

Henderson, E.H., & J. Beers (Eds.). (1980). *Developmental and Cognitive Aspects of Learning to Spell: A Reflection of Word Knowledge*. Newark, DE: International Reading Association.

Henderson, E., & S. Templeton. (1986). A developmental perspective of formal spelling instruction through alphabet, pattern, and meaning. *The Elementary School Journal, 86*, 305–316.

Hollingsworth, P.M. (1965). Spelling lists— outdated? *Elementary English, 42*.

Horn, E. (1919). Principles of methods in teaching spelling as derived from scientific investigations. In G. Whipple (Ed.), *Eighteenth Yearbook, National Society for the Study of Education*. Bloomington, IN: Public School Publishing.

Horn, E. (1954). *Teaching Spelling*. Washington, DC: American Educational Research Association.

Horn, E. (1960). Spelling. *Encyclopedia of Educational Research*. New York: Macmillan.

Horn, T.D. (1969). Spelling. *Encyclopedia of Educational Research, 4th ed*. New York: Macmillan.

International Reading Association. (1998). Learning to read and write: Developmentally appropriate practices for young children. *The Reading Teacher, 52*, 193–214.

International Society for Technology in Education. (2005). National Educational Technology Standards. Retrieved from http://cnets.iste.org.

Juel, C. (1994). *Learning to Read and Write in One Elementary School*. New York: Springer-Verlag.

Laminack, L., R. Laminack, & K. Wood. (1996). *Spelling in Use: Looking Closely at Spelling in Whole Language Classrooms*. Urbana, IL: National Council of Teachers of English.

Marsh, G., M. Friedman, V. Wesch, & P. Desberg. (1980). The development of strategies in spelling. In U. Frith (Ed.), *Cognitive Strategies in Spelling*. New York: Academic.

Morris, D. (1981). Concept of word: A developmental phenomenon in the beginning reading and writing process. *Language Arts, 58*, 659–668.

Paulesu, E., J.F. Demonet, F. Fazio, E. McCrory, V. Chanoine, N. Brunswick, S.F. Cappa, G. Cossu, M. Habib, C.D. Frith, & U. Frith. (2001). Dyslexia: Cultural diversity and biological unity. *Science, 291(5511)*.

Peters, M.L. (1985). *Spelling: Caught or Taught?* London: Routledge & Kegan Paul.

Read, C. (1971). Pre-school children's knowledge of English phonology. *Harvard Educational Review, 41*, 1–34.

Read, C. (1975). *Children's Categorizations of Speech Sounds in English*. Urbana, IL: National Council of Teachers of English.

Read, C. (1986). *Children's Creative Spelling*. London: Routledge and Kegan Paul.

Read, C., & R. Hodges. (1982). Spelling. *Encyclopedia of Educational Research, 5th ed*. New York: Macmillan.

Silva, C., & M. Alvew-Martins. (2002). Phonological skills and writing of presyllabic children. *Reading Research Quarterly, 37*, 466–483.

Smith, C.B., & G.M. Ingersoll. (1984). *Written Vocabulary of Elementary School Pupils, Ages 6–14*. Bloomington, IN: Indiana University.

Smith, F. (1988). *Joining the Literacy Club*. Portsmouth, NH: Heinemann.

Snow, C., M.W. Burns, & P. Griffin. (1998). *Preventing Reading Difficulties in Young Children*. Washington, DC: National Academy Press.

Templeton, S. (1979). Spelling first, sound later: The relationship between orthography and higher order phonological knowledge in older students. *Research in the Teaching of English, 13*, 255–264.

Templeton, S. (1991). Teaching and learning the English spelling system: Reconceptualizing method and purpose. *Elementary School Journal, 92,* 183–199.

Venezky, R.L. (1980). From Webster to Rice to Roosevelt: The formative years for spelling instruction and spelling reform in the U.S.A. In U. Frith (Ed.), *Cognitive Processes in Spelling.* London: Academic Press.

Vygotsky, L.S. (1978). *Mind and Society: The Development of Higher Mental Processes.* Cambridge, MA: Harvard University Press. (Original work published in 1930, 1933, 1935.)

Wood, D., J.C. Bruner, & G. Ross. (1976). The role of tutoring in problem solving. *Journal of Child Psychology and Psychiatry, 17,* 89–100.

Yee, A. (1969). Is the phonetic generalization hypothesis in spelling valid? *Journal of Experimental Education, 37,* 82–89.

Yopp, H.K., & R.H. Yopp. (2000). Supporting phonemic awareness development in the classroom. *The Reading Teacher, 54(2),* 130–143.

Zutell, J. (1979). Spelling strategies of primary school children and their relationship to Piaget's concept of decentration. *Research in the Teaching of English, 3,* 69–80.

Zutell, J. (1992). "An integrated view of word knowledge: Correctional studies of the relationships among spelling, reading, and conceptual development. In S. Templeton & D.R. Bear (Eds.), *Development of Orthographic Knowledge and the Foundations of Literacy: A Memorial Festschrift for Edmund Henderson.* Hillsdale, NJ: Lawrence Erlbaum Associates.

Zutell, J. (1998). Word sorting: A developmental spelling approach to word study for delayed readers. *Reading and Writing Quarterly, 14(2),* 219–238.

Zutell, J. (1999). "Sorting It Out Through Word Sorts." In Irene Fountas & Gay Su Pinnell (Eds.), *Voices on Word Matters.* Portsmouth, NH: Heinemann.

Complete research, word studies consulted for compiling word lists, and bibliography can also be viewed at www.zaner-bloser.com

Index

Index (continued)

Index (continued)

Index (continued)

letters and sounds, (cont.)

u, 42, 83–86, 87–90, 91, 99, 100, 101, 164, 191, 192, 207, T13C, T42, T51B, T83, T83B, T83C, T83D, T84, T85, T87, T87B, T87C, T88, T89, T91, T91B, T91D, T92, T95B, T99, T99D, T163B, T167D, T179

v, 33, 96, 102, T17C, T33, T52, T95B, T123C, T179C

w, 34, T17C, T34, T52, T63C, T64, T99C, T131C, T141, T167C, T171, T171C, T175D, T202

x, 35, T17D, T35

y, 36, T36, T52, T63, T63B, T131B, T147B, T190

z, 37, 102, 112, T13C, T37, T159C

listening comprehension, T13D, T103C, T107C, T111D, T123D, T127D, T135D

making words. See word building
marking pages (how to), T17C
meeting individual needs. See English Language Learners (ELLs)
missing letters. See word building
modes of writing. See writing
More Fun with Spelling. See center activities; Digital Resources for Spelling Connections; Spelling Connections Online; Word Sort CD-ROM

naming words, T112
narrative writing
letter, 94, 146
poem, 50, 98, 174
story, 134
nouns, T55C, T79C, T111B, T111D

1-Minute Handwriting Hint, T46, T50, T54, T58, T66, T70, T74, T78, T86, T90, T94, T98, T106, T110, T114, T118, T126, T130, T134, T138, T146, T150, T154, T158, T166, T170, T174, T178

online resources. See Digital Resources for Spelling Connections; Spelling Connections Online

onsets and rimes, T91C
open syllable, T151B
opposites, 57, 73, 77, 172, T57, T73, T77, T85. See also antonyms
oral and written language. See answer questions; asking questions; dictionary skills; phonics skills; reading skills; writing skills

pacing. See daily planner
past tense, T127C
Pattern Practice Game, T44, T48, T52, T56, T64, T68, T72, T88, T128
patterns
spelling patterns
consonants (see consonants)
vowels (see vowels)
structural patterns
inflectional endings, 115–118, 122, 198, T111B, T115B
plurals, 111–114, 121, 128, 148, 164, 168, 197, T111, T111B, T111C, T111D, T112, T113, T119C, T121, T147C, T148, T164, T167C, T168, T197
suffixes (see suffixes)
penmanship, 17–42, T17B, T17C, T17D
phonemic awareness, T13B, T13C, T151C, T175C. See also phonics skills
phonetic spellings, T59B, T79B, T99B, T119B

phonics skills, 13–16. See also consonants; sounds; vowels
consonant blends, 103–106, 107–110, 119, 120, 195–196, T17B, T17C, T103, T103B, T103C, T104, T107, T107B, T107C, T109, T119, T119C, T120, T131, T159C, T179C, T195, T196
digraphs
consonant digraphs, T17C, T43B, T103B, T167B, T167C, T171B, T171C, T179C, T181
vowel digraphs, 116, 163–166, 179, 207, T51B, T143C, T163B, T163C
discriminating sounds, T63C, T67C, T87C, T135C, T179C
identifying sounds, T47C, T51C
matching sounds, 64, 67, 72, T71C
rhyme (rhyming words) (see rhyme (rhyming words))
segmentation, T13B, T13C, T13D, T14, T15, T43C, T47C, T63C, T67C, T91C, T95C, T100, T103C, T107C, T139D, T151C, T163C, T183, T184, T186, T189, T190, T191, T193, T194, T195
sound blending, 64, 176, T43C, T44, T55C, T56, T61, T63C, T64, T67C, T75C, T91C, T95C, T99C, T103C, T107C, T139D, T148, T186
substituting letters, 67, 88, 99, 112, 141, 142, 156
using pictures (see pictures and words)
word analysis, T103C, T107C
word blending, T47C
word building, T64, T68, T72, T75C, T83C, T87C, T107C, T108, T111C, T119C, T123C, T131C, T147C, T159C, T167C, T167D, T175C, T175D, T179C, T180
word structure, 96, 102, 193 (see also word structure)

R

Index (continued)

Index (continued)

Credits